COERCIVE FAMILY PROCESS

Other volumes in the *Social Learning Approach* series:

VOLUME 1: *Families with Aggressive Children*
VOLUME 2: *Observation in Home Settings*

ISBN for the series: 0-916154-10-6

A Social Learning Approach

VOLUME 3

COERCIVE FAMILY PROCESS

Gerald R. Patterson
Oregon Social Learning Center

Castalia Publishing Company
P.O. Box 1587
Eugene, Oregon 97440

Library of Congress Cataloging in Publication
Data (Revised)
Main entry under title:

A Social learning approach to family intervention.

Vol. 2. edited by J.B. Reid.
Includes bibliographies.
CONTENTS: v.1. Families with aggressive
children.—v.2. Observation in home settings.—
v.3. Coercive family process.
1. Problem children. 2. Juvenile delinquents.
3. Mentally ill children—Family relationships.
4. Family psychotherapy. I. Patterson, Gerald
Roy. II. Reid, John B., 1940-
RJ500.S65   618.92′858206   75-27000
ISBN 0-916154-00-9   AACR1

Copyright © 1982
by Castalia Publishing Company

ISBN: 0-916154-02-5
Printed in the United States of America
Copies of this book may be ordered from the pub-
lisher.

Illustrations by Gerald R. Patterson

Dedication

To Marion S. Forgatch, Richard R. Jones, and John B. Reid, friends and colleagues in a very personal enterprise.

Table of Contents

Preface

This book is about antisocial children and their families. It is based on the study of over 250 families referred for treatment to the Oregon Social Learning Center (OSLC). For comparison purposes, we have also studied several hundred families with normal children. Our efforts to treat the families of social aggressors, stealers, chronic delinquents, and abused children took us into homes, schools, courtrooms, and eventually back into the laboratory. This commitment to treatment provided us with an intensive exposure to the family processes that are associated with violence among family members.

The picture of family structure and process that is presented here is based on multilevel assessment. Our studies included a minimum of six observation sessions in the home. Each observation session provided over 1200 behavioral events describing the interactions among family members. This was further buttressed by extensive assessment batteries including self-report, interviews, achievement tests, laboratory procedures, and telephone interviews. The perspective that has emerged has both a clinical "feel" to it, plus some hard-headed components based on objective data.

There are many reasons for writing a book like this. On the one hand, I wished to communicate our ideas about aggression and family process to young graduate students. I would like to convince them that it is possible to carry out rigorous research on complex clinical and developmental processes. Many features of this volume were designed with this group in mind. I would also like to communicate to them the sense of enjoyment and satisfaction that I have received from a lifetime commitment to clinical research.

The second audience for which the book was designed is comprised of counselors, case workers, and therapists who have devoted themselves to working with antisocial children and their families. Some of these clinicians may find that the chapters on methodology (3) and theory (5, 6, 7, 8, 9) represent areas for which they have only limited training and/or interest. However, the key hypotheses about antisocial behavior come not from theory, but from clinical experience. The practitioner should find his or her clinical experiences reflected in several of the chapters (2, 10, 13). Several other chapters reformulate these ideas into a social-interactional perspective of family process (4, 11, 12). Most clinicians should find this to be a useful way of thinking about these complex families. This perspective does, in fact, serve as the basis for our own treatment procedures for these families.

It may be that one volume cannot serve two such disparate audiences. However, I think it is possible. The central focus upon family members' interactions has a protean quality to it that should interest clinicians and researchers alike. The concepts in this book have very little to do with abstractions such as drives, perceptions, or ego defenses that are typically encountered in books about family aggression. Coercion theory is based on performance (i.e., what people do) as viewed from a bilateral or interactional perspective. The answer to the question of what causes family members to do what they do seems to be found in the behavior of the other person. To understand the aggressive child, you must understand—on a moment-by-moment basis—how other people react to him. Describing such analyses is the central task for this book.

Originally, it was a third audience that prompted me to begin this volume. I had intended to write a single chapter as an introduction to a new book about family therapy. It was to be a brief statement for the OSLC staff and the rather large cadre of consultants who have assisted us during the last several years. The purpose of this single chapter was to pull together the main ideas and findings for a performance theory of family aggression. The "chapter" was neither brief nor simple; it has now taken four years to prepare. The therapy book has not yet been written.

It became apparent that, as a group, we had not carefully thought through the complex issues associated with our attempts to apply concepts such as positive reinforcement, punishment, reciprocity, or negative reinforcement to sequential data. When applied to social interaction, these concepts take on a meaning that is different from the meaning that they had acquired in laboratory settings. Redefining these concepts required an exploration of several different bodies of literature. My studies were enormously facilitated during a year spent at the Center for Advanced Studies in the Behavioral Sciences at Stanford University. After my return, the Oregon Social Learning Center staff systematically protected my time so that I could complete what seemed to them (and to me) to be an endless task. The process of writing this book led to a continuous demand for yet more experiments, and for new analyses of existing data. This, in turn, led to the generation of new hypotheses which required new types of data. This book

is, therefore, not finished; I have simply decided to stop changing it. Analyses completed since that decision have already put some parts of this volume out of date.

There are four major sections in this book. The first section (Chapters 1 & 2) introduces the general research strategy and the topic of the antisocial child. Chapter 2 is essentially a review of the research findings regarding the incidence of aggression in children by age, sex, social class, family size, and birth order. A discussion of the different kinds of antisocial behavior, and a brief introduction to concepts such as arrested socialization, social skills deficits, and deviancy-drift is also presented. The second section (Chapters 3-7) begins with a discussion of field observation procedures, including a review of the research studies relating to observer agreement, observer bias, reactivity, test-retest reliability, and validity. Chapter 4 examines the utility of aversive events in shaping family interaction. This includes a consideration of their effectiveness as punishment for children's behavior. In Chapters 5 and 6 the concepts of positive and negative reinforcement are examined as they apply to interaction sequences. The third section (Chapters 8-10) introduces the reader to both microsocial and macrosocial analyses as they relate to antisocial child behavior. The idea is that disruptions in child-rearing practices can be brought about by crises, marital conflict, and other types of stress impinging on the family. This section discusses our efforts to describe and measure these child-rearing practices. The last section (Chapters 11-13) describes the contribution of the procedures and the concepts to understanding—at an empirical level—families of aggressive children. In Chapter 11, Social Aggressors and Stealers are shown to be the outcome of different familial processes and data differentiating clinical from normal samples are presented. In Chapter 12 the empirical definitions for the role of the mother and father are reexamined. Chapter 13 provides a clinical description of the antisocial child and a speculative typology of the families referred for treatment. Finally, a brief review of the OSLC studies evaluating treatment effectiveness is presented.

Acknowledgments

It became apparent in the mid-1960's that in order to study the problems of treatment and family process that are associated with antisocial children, we needed the full attention of a sizeable staff. These problems required a well-trained professional staff of observers, therapists, and experimenters who could work closely together for long periods of time. These exigencies led me eventually to leave the university setting and design a sanctuary that would be suitable for the long-term study and treatment of aggressive families. We were fortunate in being able to compete successfully for a long series of research grants from the National Institute of Mental Health. Most of them were from the section for Studies of Crime and Delinquency with Saleem Shah as director.

Since the mid-1960's, there have been a number of staff and colleagues who have contributed to the development of a performance theory of coercive family process. I would particularly like to acknowledge the contributions of Gary Birchler, Patti Chamberlain, Joe Cobb, Tom Dishion, Hy Hops, Richard Jones, Marion Forgatch, David Littman, Rolf Loeber, Rudy Lorber, Roberta Ray, David Shaw, Magda Stouthamer-Loeber, John Vincent, Mark Weinrott, Robert Weiss, Tom Wills, and Robert Ziller. There is also a shadow figure whose presence is felt throughout this book, and who should be acknowledged early on—this is John B. Reid, my close collaborator since the in-

ception of the project. In addition to an unusually high threshold for ambiguity, he has an uncanny ability to focus his attention on a problem and then provide a useful (albeit often nonlinear) reaction. Over the years, our discussion of clinical cases and of the data formed a precipitate. I chose to label the result *coercion theory*. It might well have been a joint task, but John is currently occupied with other problem areas such as child abuse and observation methodology. As a result, the task has been undertaken by me.

The demand for expertise in solving a wide range of problems covered by our studies easily exceeded my own personal competencies and those of the staff. For this reason we have relied heavily on consultants from outside the group. In the area of reinforcement theory, this included W. Bricker, F. Kanfer, J. Knutson, R. Littman, W. Sheppard, H. Shoemaker, and J. Straughan; in the area of punishment, R. Parke; in the area of developmental psychology, R. Bell, E.M. Hetherington, and E. Maccoby; in the area of sociology, R. Burgess, D. Elliott, R. Sparks, and M. Wolfgang. We required "hordes" of statisticians and methodologists such as W. Carlson, R. Dawes, R. Freund, D. Hartmann, P. Holleran, G. Sackett, R. Sparks, and E. Thomas. My old friend R. Buehler should see reflected here the outcome of many hours of discussions of social factors as they relate to family life. I am sure that each of these consultants feels privately that we needed many more assistants.

There is another group that has made an important contribution to this volume—the professional observers who not only collected the data but, in part, constructed the code as well: Betty Brummett, Rachel Condon, Peggy Gabrielson, LaVella Garber, Vicki Halper, Jonnie Johnson, Shannon McCarthy, Debbie Toobert, and Irene Troup.

During the last four years, I have been granted special status as a protected species by the OSLC staff. Chief among the protectors has been Will Mayer, guardian of the castle keep, and Gary Morse and Mary Perry, who brought order to administrative chaos. I was also given a series of first-rate research assistants to help follow the leads that were generated during the writing of this book. These people included Marion Forgatch, Sandy Kronsberg, Deborah Toobert, and Katie Whalen. To Trish McNeil, who typed the endless revisions, I owe a very special debt. Finally, there is that rare privilege which attends having a son take his father's words seriously enough to publish them.

In a very real sense, this book is the outcome of a group effort. I consider myself fortunate to have been a participant in such a process.

Editor's Note

During the editing and production of this book I have had the pleasure of working with several very talented people. Their efforts were an integral part of the improvements in this book that have taken place during the past year. I would like to give a special credit to my associate editor, Cheryl Brunette, for her attention to the subtleties of the English language that haunt us all. I would also like to thank John Macioce at the Willamette Valley Observer for his patience in typesetting the text and in constructing the numerous tables and figures. Many people other than myself have been involved in making this book as accurate as possible. In so doing, I am sure that we have disturbed the dust from every book and file at the Oregon Social Learning Center. My thanks to Sandy Kronsberg and Trish McNeil for their assistance in checking the data and the references that were used in the book.

In pushing toward the completion of this book it was my task to hold the author back from feeling the relief that comes with setting the pencil down for the last time. In a book of this size and complexity there were an enormous number of details to be worked out. This was accomplished during regularly scheduled sessions with the author which took place at his home in the early morning hours. At times it seemed as though the book would never be finished. But now, after seeing the page-proofs of the book, there is no question that the project was worthwhile. After all the stress that this book has generated for the Patterson family and our loved ones, it is our hope that the concepts in this book will help others to reduce the stress and aversiveness that is found within many families.

Scot Patterson
Editor

Chapter 1

Changing the Behavior of the Scientists

Although the development of a coercion theory is still in its beginnings, we have developed a way of going about things that differentiates us from others who study aggressive children. Cairns (1979b) noted the similarities in perspective and procedures among investigators such as W. Hartup, J. Gottman, and the Oregon Social Learning Center staff and labeled it "social interactional" (see Appendix 1.1). It is a pleasant surprise to receive such a label, an indication that one has arrived at some station. But such a label also signals that one has moved *from* some other point. This chapter is my retrospective account of the forces that governed this shift in perspective.

Aggressive children are very dramatic in their behavior. This makes the phenomenon easier to study because one can see and measure what the aggressive child does. Furthermore, there is an abundant supply of aggressive children in any community. These children often constitute the bulk of the case load for both child guidance clinics and residential treatment centers. Finally, the linkage between early antisocial problems and later careers in crime is such that it is possible to receive support for programmatic studies. These pragmatic considerations suggest that the aggressive child is a prime candidate for research.

The Best Was Not Good Enough

As a young therapist in training, this writer eagerly applied each new technique to the challenge of helping aggressive children. First nondirective play therapy and then psychodrama were tried as treatment strategies. But each technique, in turn, failed to have an impact. At that time it seemed that I needed advanced training in more sophisticated therapies; from 1953 to 1955 I interned at the Wilder Clinic in St. Paul. It was one of the best psychoanalytic outpatient facilities for the treatment of severely disturbed children. As part of a team effort, the children received intensive individual and group therapy. The parents also received treatment as a means of coping with their contribution to the process. This was the best there was. In our enthusiasm, we wrote a paper about it (Patterson, Schwartz, & Van der Wart, 1956). However, the outcome evaluations for such therapies were in general agreement that the procedures were not effective (Levitt, 1971). The best was not good enough.

By the early 1960's, the writer's clinical experiences suggested that the most highly trained therapists were simply not effective in dealing with the aggressive child. At the time it was not clear whether the problem lay in the theories of aggression or in the treatment technologies. This was particularly puzzling because the therapy experiences provided for the families seemed closely tailored to fit what we thought aggression was all about. Aggression was thought to reflect the in-

1

adequacies of the child's "defenses" against underlying anxiety. Therapy with the child was meant to remedy this problem. The child's anxiety and crumbling ego defenses were thought to be distant reflections of parental neurosis. Intensive therapy for the parents was designed to correct their neuroses. Generally, the senior staff spent their time treating the anxiety reactions, parental neuroses, or childhood schizophrenic reactions. The aggressive child was given to the student or the trainee. We could only go on doing the best we were trained to do and observe our own and our students' treatment failures.

There were, of course, occasional successes in which one could detect real changes in the child. Furthermore, regardless of which treatment was used, the majority of the parents reported that "some improvement" had occurred. The solace brought by these successes was usually short-lived; follow-up reports generally showed that the child was still out of control. The occasional successes and the positive feedback from the parents supported several generations of therapists, despite their failure to effect permanent changes in child behavior.[1]

Reinforcement Concepts

At the same time, there were some powerful forces within psychology that had a bearing upon how we would proceed. Concepts from the reinforcement theories of Thorndike, Hull, and Guthrie found their way into both developmental psychology and personality theory (Miller & Dollard, 1958). These theories translated concepts that were previously nontestable tautologies into an empirical language. This reformulation of clinical concepts led to a series of studies summarized in a book which had an explosive impact on the field, Bandura and Walters' Social Learning and Personality Development (1963). The new area was called "social learning"; it attracted a group of young investigators who produced an enormous number of empirical studies. By applying social reinforcement and modeling concepts to a wide range of theoretical and applied problems in developmental psychology, the studies provided the basis for a new statement of the processes determining social behavior.

There was a parallel revolution in clinical psychology as operant psychologists applied the principles in B.F. Skinner's prestigious Science and Human Behavior (1953) to investigations of clinical problems. Their work was based solely upon reinforcement concepts. The first studies provided data that described observable changes in behaviors such as stuttering, hyperactivity, anorexia,

and bizarre social behaviors. The results presented in Ullmann and Krasner's edited Case Studies in Behavior Modification (1965) did not prove the new techniques worked. Rather, it was a bold statement of what clinical psychology could be like, i.e., it could become scientific. This earlier work also suggested some alternative ways of treating antisocial children. Why not reinforce the child for engaging in nonaggressive behavior? Although this idea did not work, it was so novel and testable that it was an impetus to our work. Rumor had it that Ivar Lovaas had already tested the idea in a laboratory setting and shown it to be feasible (Lovaas, 1961b).

Moving Into the Field

The operant format for social engineering had several characteristics which gave the new work an interesting twist. For one thing, operant psychologists insisted upon collecting data about the observable behaviors of their clients! This led to the birth of a whole new set of dependent variables in clinical psychology. Who had ever heard of daily counts of the number of towels hoarded as being one operational definition for bizarre institutional behavior; or daily counts of "number of bites" as relating to obesity; or "out of seat" as it related to classroom hyperactivity? The ingenuity of investigators such as O. Lindsley, I. Goldiamond, N. Ayllon, M. Wolf, and N. Azrin seemed without limit. Their contributions to clinical assessment may turn out to be even more important than their contributions to the technology of behavior change. As therapists, most of us had been trained to attend to patient self-report. It was not only our vehicle for behavior change, but also our primary means for measuring change. In contrast, the "behavior modifiers" were in the school, on the playground, and in the home counting events. By coincidence, they were learning to do what their revolutionary counterparts in biology had been doing for decades. The ethologists had also been going into the natural environment to observe child behavior (Blurton-Jones, 1966). Unfortunately, this development had been largely ignored by psychologists until the late 1960's.

Parent report had served for decades as the mainstay for constructing theories about child rearing and its impact upon child behavior. But we were looking for data which would give us better purchase on these questions. We began to see field observation as a different scientific enterprise from laboratory and clinical interview techniques. It was not necessarily a better view; it was simply a different one. Fiske's (1974) conclusions were similar. He noted that there seemed to be two approaches to psychological phenomena. One was to judge a person's characteristics, and the other was to observe his actions and the relationship between them. Cairns and Green (1979) were also aware of this distinction. They discussed the work by Radke-Yarrow and Waxler (1979) and others showing little correlation between these two methods; yet they note that this does *not* mean the new method (observation) is good, and the old one (judgment/ratings) is bad. It is, rather, that these methods represent two very *different kinds of information* about a person, and each has a different contribution to make to our understanding of child behavior. For example, rating procedures take into account the ability of human beings to make complex judgments based on heterogeneous sources of information. Such ratings represent an integration of new information with the previously held implicit (or explicit) *theories of the rater* (Wiggins, 1973). However, as Cairns and Green (1979) point out, if the experimenter is concerned with questions relating to stable qualities of the child, then the process of synthesizing these ratings may have some unique properties to which observation systems are not well suited. They go on to suggest that observation systems are well designed for a different set of tasks, such as analyzing those characteristics of the child (a) that are temporary, (b) that vary as a function of the context or setting, and (c) that depend on the quality of social interchange:

". . . *direct observations of behavior can be the key for identifying how actual behaviors are elicited, maintained, and organized.* Such information may be critical for explaining the processes that regulate social patterns, as opposed to describing the social patterns. Both goals—description of individual differences and explanation of how differences arise—are worthy goals, but they are different. Accordingly, observation techniques are useful (or even indispensible) for identifying the dynamic controls that operate during the course of social development.

"Conversely, ratings would not be useful in yielding information about contextual, interpersonal, and developmental processes. Why not? Because these sources of variance are typically eliminated at the first stage of data recording" (Cairns & Green, 1979, pp. 221-222).

However, there were no handbooks detailing how to make this shift to field observation. As a result, our first attempts at field observation were not very successful. For example, in one of our first home visits, we made an appointment with a family and appeared at the door as planned. However, the seven-year-old "out-of-control" child had not been prepared for the sight of two burly men in horn-rimmed glasses appearing in his living room and staring at him. He simply wheeled about, dashed out the back door and climbed a tree. My assistant and I stood nonplussed until the mother gave us a cup of coffee and later sent us home (see Illustration #1).

Another problem with field observation was to learn *how to describe what could be seen.* What form should these descriptions take? P. Schoggen and his colleague, R. Barker, had previously convinced us that observation data should be cast in a sequential form. The relatively high yield from such a strategy was reflected in their publication, *Stream of Behavior* (1963). The importance of the sequential format was also emphasized by the NIMH researchers studying aggressive children (Raush, 1965). However, the most compelling argument for a sequential format was that it fit what the clinician could see in the home. There seemed to be a natural flow to family interaction. The behavior of one family member seemed to follow that of the others in an orderly fashion. Even at this early juncture, it seemed that *some* events were patterned, and that these patterns were repeated again and again. We began to notice that each interaction sequence was *not unique.* Furthermore, the repetitious quality of familial interaction seemed particularly descriptive of unpleasant episodes. It seemed that it should be possible to analyze such patterns.

Simultaneously, a number of investigators, such as R. Wahler at Tennessee, developed a complex observation code system tailored to families of aggressive children. At OSLC the development of a primitive behavioral coding system required three years of pilot work (Patterson, Ray, & Shaw, 1968). It was then used routinely to collect baseline data in the homes of problem and normal children. The fact that the code data described *sequences* of events led eventually to a fundamental shift in our perspective regarding familial aggression. But this happened very gradually. We introduced first one term, then another, into our discussions, e.g., stimulus control, antecedent, probability, structure, process, interactional unit. Eventually journal editors began commenting that our shift was perceptible to them; in many cases it was not clear to them why we were asking certain questions. In retrospect, it is clear that we were continuously *re-examining* traditional assumptions and concepts. The definitions of concepts kept shifting to accommodate this new data. Ideas about observer reliability, the trait of aggression,

3

Illustration #1: A High-Level Beginning

the definition of setting and the temporal and situational stability of aggressive behavior gradually took on very different meanings.

Current Perspective

These transitions were never easy. There were no boundaries showing when a shift began or ended, and no staff meetings to decide when it had become so perceptible that it deserved a label. Looking back, it seems that the times of greatest movement were accompanied by the most humor. For example, our preoccupation with moment by moment shifts in what a child was doing led to a profound interest in the impact of the immediate social environment on the child's behavior. We had been trained to believe that the environment had an effect, but hardly on a second by second basis. We wondered if it was reasonable to break environmental impact into six-second units. With much amusement research seminars were held in the early 1970's to consider the possibility of developing a "six-second personality theory." However, over the next several years the realities of analyzing interaction sequences that were based on these data led us to accept the idea.

The findings from our longitudinal studies completed during the 1970's reiterated the fact that the trait of aggression was stable over long periods of time. But when viewing the same trait at a micro-social level (as sampled by the code categories) the boundaries of that concept were becoming blurred. At that level the definition of aggression had been expanded to include "bilateral" effects. As a result, the definitions now included measures of initiations, and measures of reactions to initiations by both members of the dyad. To understand a child's aggression we now had to measure how others reacted to his aggression.

Later, we became interested in the possibility that forces *outside* the dyad were impinging upon these bilateral interactions (see Chapters 4 and 10). The analyses quickly identified a set of "macrosocial" variables which clearly altered some aspects of the microsocial process. Initiations and reactions reflected, in part, long standing dispositions. But it was becoming clear that they could also reflect, at least on a short-term basis, the impact of such non-trait related variables as illness, loss of income, or other crises.

The concept of a trait had now become a many splendored thing. It retained its traditional component of stability across time. But it now included new concepts and data from interactional psychology which focused upon the process by which traits are changed. These changes in our way of thinking about the trait of aggression were analogous to the changes which took place in many other aspects of our thinking. It was not that the old concepts were discarded, it was that their definitions had been altered.

A New Dependent Variable

Most of us in the mid-1960's were convinced that a simple frequency count was the preferred dependent variable. It was the perfect means for showing that one event occurred more often than another. Given that it was necessary to demonstrate changes in frequency over time, then these data could be transformed to rate measures. It was simple and direct. For most questions these measures served very well. However, rate or frequency concepts are a clumsy way of describing the relation *between* events. The interactional view suggests that most social interactions are structured in the sense that one event is correlated with another. In fact, some methodologists such as D. Hartmann (personal communication) make a persuasive argument for lag and cross-lag correlations as a reasonable statement for what these relations are.

Gradually, we became used to thinking of the structure of social interactions in terms of conditional probabilities. Given that one event occurred, what was the likelihood it was preceded by this or that behavior of the other person? If the child whines and the mother gives him a hug, what is the likelihood that the child will continue? With this flexible language we can place behavioral events in sequence like beads on a string. We are limited only by the quantity and quality of the sequential data itself. Probability theory lends itself beautifully to the problem of functional relations. The reader who plans an investigation of this material would be well advised to provide him- or herself with a solid background in these matters with, for example, the primer by L.D. Phillips, *Bayesian Statistics for Social Scientists* (1973). Many interactional concepts are based on probability theory but require some additional effort, e.g., Markov chains, signal detection, Guttman Scalogram, and information theory. Because these concepts are such useful tools for the new questions being raised, I find myself reaching more frequently for Coombs, Dawes, and Tversky's *Mathematical Psychology* (1970) than for the more familiar texts on parametric statistics.

Probability theory and mathematical psychology are not new to the social sciences. They are "new" to persons such as myself. Currently, there are a number of individuals who are exploring the interface between these mathematical concepts and the concepts emerging in interactional psychology. Individuals such as John Gottman, University of Illinois, Gene Sackett, University of Washington, Ewart Thomas, Stanford University, Roger Bakeman, University of Georgia, and Don Hartmann at the University of Utah are the "methodologists" for this new area. Its "theorists" include many of the above and Ross Parke, University of Illinois, Willard Hartup, University of Minnesota, and Robert Cairns, University of North Carolina.

Performance Theory

Since its inception as a field of study, psychology has been preoccupied with the general problem of human learning. Most of the early theorists, such as Skinner, Hull, and Guthrie carefully differentiated between learning and performance. In that context, what is learned is not necessarily performed. With the exception of Hull, the bulk of their writings deal with the analysis of variables thought to determine "learning." As a result, most of the variables concerning "laws" of human behavior relate to learning; few, if any, are concerned with changes in performance per se.

Questions about the structure of social interaction led us away from traditional concerns about human learning. Our major preoccupation was *not* with the question of how children *learned* aggression. Instead, the question became, "Why do they *perform* aggression at different rates?"

If one accepts the persuasive arguments of modeling theorists, such as Bandura (1977) and Kanfer and Phillips (1970), much of what is learned about social interaction is that which is *modeled* by *other persons*. The intricacies of what the child must learn about complex social behaviors and language are presumably acquired in this manner. If one accepts this position, and the present writer does, then by the age of *five* most *children* in this society have *learned* most of the garden-variety *aggressive behaviors* employed by children. With this in mind, the following questions arise: Why does one child perform aggressive behaviors at rates ten times higher than another child? Why does one child perform aggressively at a higher rate in one setting than another? Why does he use a particular aggressive response more than another? The answers to these three questions constitute a performance theory. The variables which relate to these questions outline what is meant by a coercion theory. It is a set of statements about pain-control techniques employed by one or both members of a dyad. Each variable impacts either the performance of the other person or the performance of the target subject.

Generating Hypotheses

What variables determine shifts in social interactions? Social psychology had only indirectly concerned itself with such questions. For this reason, we proceeded with the study of interaction unencumbered by very much theory. There were, in addition, few "facts" to keep in mind—a comfortable or uncomfortable state of affairs depending upon one's taste for uncertainty. The goal in constructing a performance theory was to express the relative contributions of the variables controlling ongoing behavior by the amount of variance accounted for. Within this framework, some variables would account for variance relating to differences between subjects in the performance of aggressive events. It is possible that the variables accounting for differences across settings would be different.

The investigator begins by selecting a pet hunch about variables determining social interaction. Ultimately, the score for a favored variable must be tallied. The crucial test for any variable is the amount of variance on any of the three dimensions (among subjects, among responses, and across time) accounted for. If it does not contribute in this sense, then the variable must be dropped from the performance theory.

In constructing a performance theory we did not examine any particular set of hypotheses or variables. Because we were more familiar with reinforcement theory, that literature served as a starting point for hypotheses conceptualizing aggression in families. However, it soon became apparent that conventional terminology such as stimulus, response, and reinforcement provided an awkward fit to many aspects of social interaction. As a result it was necessary to generate a supplementary set of terms that described antecedents, target events, and consequences in a language that was as neutral as possible.

Clinical contacts with families of antisocial children provided another important source of hypotheses. As therapists we were committed to the task of helping these people. This exposed us to some aspects of aggression in family interactions that were not sampled by our observation code. These omissions from our assessment device led us to search for new methods for measuring what the therapist could "see." As a result we began to include measures of parent monitoring, setting consequences, crises, insularity, and sidetracking, which fit the clinical phenomena but were not derived from any particular "theory." Ultimately, the constraint operating in selecting a specific variable revolved around the question of how well it could be measured. In most instances we had to innovate our own means of assessment.

An Applied Mission

In this section, I argue for the need to carry out mission-oriented programmatic work on *applied* social problems. At present, much of the work in developmental and child clinical psychology is a piecemeal affair. The majority of the studies are carried out by investigators who publish a single paper on a topic and then move on to a new problem. Quite properly, these investigators select problems which are amenable to current procedures. They also tend to select problems which fit within some favored paradigm. For example, cognitive and reinforcement theories are currently possible candidates in psychology for status as paradigms. If one is trained to work within either of these frameworks, the strategy becomes that of searching for phenomena *fitting the explanation.* The phenomena that do not fit the explanation are set aside in favor of those that will. *One is not committed to a problem, rather, to a single explanation of behavior.* As a result, one can find studies using reinforcement or modeling concepts to study aggression, but as a whole the findings lack coherence. It is as if one were looking through a kaleidoscope with lovely p values and F values floating within ANOVA's that are whirling across the screen. They do not fit together in any satisfying pattern. Each group of investigators has its own language and its own set of publication sources. It is noteworthy that they rarely cite another group's publications.

As an alternative, the OSLC group first selected a problem and employed those models that seemed necessary and most useful to study the problem. It makes little difference which paradigm one initially selects. Each investigator begins with the paradigm of choice and discovers its inadequacies. The present author was better trained in reinforcement than in the research areas relating to human memory, perception, and cognition. For this reason, I began the study of aggression with reinforcement concepts and applied them first to studies of child and peer interactions (Patterson, Littman, & Bricker, 1967), and later to parent-child interactions as well (Patterson & Cobb, 1971, 1973). There was, however, never any doubt that other models inevitably had to be introduced to solve some aspects of a problem. At OSLC the addition of new variables goes on continuously. The process begins when one or more people become convinced of the necessity for introducing a new variable to explain a particular resistant wrinkle in the data. The goal is always to *solve* the problem, "Why are children aggressive?" If the new variable can account for a significant amount of variance in the child's performance, then it is added to the "theory." The overall effect is an accumulation of information and a gradual shift in one's perception of what the phenomenon is all about.

In the final analysis, sequential data can be used only to generate functional relations. As noted by Parke (1979), functional relations are not proof of causality. For that reason, the development of social interaction theories requires the employment of *both* observation data and experimental manipulations. In other words, the analysis of sequential data from field observations generates hypotheses, but the analyses themselves provide only a weak test of the hypotheses. Ultimately, the concepts generated by our observations require *experimental* and *longitudinal* designs to establish causal connections. In the work described in this volume, considerable effort has been made to develop experimental procedures designed to test hypotheses on coercion processes. Whenever possible, the manipulations are carried out *in* the natural setting.

The recent publications by Petrinovitch (1979) and Fiske (1974) alerted me to the fact that we have not drifted so far. Both emphasize the need for sampling behavior in natural settings. Petrinovitch (1979) also talks about the utility of a concept in terms of variance accounted for. From his Brunswickian viewpoint, relationships between variables are described in probabilistic terms. So the wheel comes full turn; the emerging perspective that we thought was so unique was anticipated several decades ago in the writings of Brunswick.

Conclusion

The focus of our research is to understand why children are aggressive. Because we were most familiar with reinforcement theory, that literature served as a starting point for hypotheses conceptualizing aggression in families. Our clinical contacts with families of antisocial children provided another important source of hypotheses. As therapists, we were committed to the task of helping these people.

Early in our efforts to treat families, we found it necessary to measure change in families. To measure change, we decided we should observe in the home itself prior to and following treatment. Later, we added many more assessment devices, but the important decision was to *observe.* The sequential form in which these data were cast led to analyses of family interaction which altered the questions we had about the nature of aggression.

Gradually, we became used to thinking of the structure of social interaction in terms of the conditional probabilities that described the *performance* of aggressive behavior. In constructing a performance theory, variables were selected on the basis of the amount of variance accounted for. These variables described the use of pain-control techniques in families with aggressive children. The label that we have given to the resulting social interactional perspective is coercion theory.

Acknowledgments

The writer wishes to thank the members of the OSLC writing seminar, who carefully critiqued an earlier draft of this manuscript: P. Chamberlain, M. Forgatch, R. Lorber, D. Littman, D. Moore, J. Reid, and D. Toobert. Sandra Kronsberg fulfilled a similar role for a later version.

Footnotes

1. As it is ordinarily used, parent global report of treatment outcome constitutes a trap for the unwary therapist. There have been a series of studies reviewed in Chapter 3 of this volume analyzing parent global report data. The studies consistently showed that parents of deviant children were significantly biased to report improvement even when more objective data showed no changes occurred. As a rough figure, 60% to 70% of the parents will give such biased reports. The studies do not prove that parents lie to therapists. They simply assert that parents are human and wish to retain their hopes for the child's eventual adjustment. However, the findings mean that, regardless of one's treatment technique, the feedback to the therapist will be that he or she is helping the *majority* of the clients! This, in turn, is a powerful reinforcer for continuing what one has always done in the past; therein lies the trap.

Chapter 2
Abstract

The research literature is reviewed regarding the incidence of aggression in children by age, sex, social class, family size, and birth order. Support is presented for the stability of measures of aggression across time and settings.

Traditional factor-analytic studies of children's conduct-problem behaviors suggest the feasibility of considering two major patterns for antisocial behavior, *Social Aggressive* and *Stealer*. Most children referred for treatment for antisocial problems can be classified into one or the other of these patterns. It is assumed that these patterns may require separate explanations as to the kind of family processes which produce them. They may also require different forms of treatment.

It is hypothesized that extremely antisocial children represent a form of arrested socialization. Their development is retarded in two different respects. First, the rate and form of the problem child's deviant behavior represent that which is acceptable for 3- and 4-year-olds. It is assumed that problem children have been *allowed* to continue this behavior. Second, the problem child is often deficient in social skills, e.g., work, self-management, and relation to peers.

A deviancy-drift hypothesis is also presented. It relates the child's relative deficiencies in social skills and his ranking on antisocial behaviors to his later adjustment problems. The child who is both extremely aggressive *and* extremely retarded in the development of social skills is thought to be at risk for later problems as an adult; i.e., extremely antisocial children do not outgrow their problems.

Chapter 2

Antisocial Children

The purpose of this chapter is to draw together the research literature regarding antisocial children. However, these materials are not being held up to view in an altogether dispassionate manner. Instead, the literature is examined for themes and trends which would be of particular relevance to coercion theory. This brief introduction is intended to forewarn the reader as to the kind of filter being applied.

Aggressiveness, such as hitting, is viewed as a subset of the coercive techniques employed by family members to alter each other's behavior. Extremely aggressive children who are referred for treatment employ these techniques at very high rates in a variety of settings. There is a strong case to be made for thinking about child aggression as a *trait,* a disposition to react aversively which is stable across time and settings. This trait can be measured, and the performance score can be expressed in terms of the frequency or probability of an aggressive response. However, the determinants for this score reflect the dispositions of the child *and* the persons who are targets for this aggression. In effect, the trait score reflects the interactions which occur in that setting. An extremely aggressive child has a supply of "victims" who react to him in a predictable manner. Each of these victims contributes to the performance level of the aggressive child.

√Parents of aggressive children are generally un-skilled, but they are particularly unskilled in their use of punishment for deviant behavior. Their punishment doesn't work. Many of them are also inept at providing modeling and reinforcement for their child's prosocial behaviors. As a result, *some* of these problem children are not only extremely aggressive, but they also lack basic social survival skills; e.g., they cannot engage their peers, they cannot work, and they tend to have poor academic skills. Family management skills can be taught; in fact, at OSLC training in these skills is the central focus for the treatment of families with antisocial children. When these skills are not practiced, the level of aggression for all family members tends to rise. The net result is that the system begins to drift toward a kind of psychological anarchy. As this happens, the key figure, such as the caretaker, becomes increasingly dysphoric. Family members also become increasingly dissatisfied with the family. As a result, they tend to avoid each other and engage in fewer shared activities. Thus, the entire family is caught up in a *process* which produces changes in mood and self-esteem. In families of antisocial children some parental "neuroses" can be thought of as the *outcome* of a process rather than its cause.

Children who drift into extreme deviancy *and* retardation of social skills are thought to be most at risk for adult maladjustment. Generally, the extremely aggressive child does *not* outgrow his problems. While the nature of the problem may change over time, his status as deviant does not. These children constitute a major social problem. It is from their ranks that the chronic delinquent is drawn. As Garmezy (1976) points out, the antisocial child is at even greater risk for major adjustment problems as an adult than is the child of a schizophrenic parent. Thus it is important that we understand who these people are and where they come from.

What Is Aggression?

The generally accepted definition for the term aggression involves one person inflicting pain upon another. Some writers stipulate that the act must have the *goal* of injuring the other, i.e., the aggressor *intended* to hurt his victim (Berkowitz, 1973a; Feshbach, 1970). Others, such as Buss (1961), Bandura (1973), and the present author, do not include intention in the definition of aggression.

Regardless of which stance one adopts, there are difficulties. There are many aversive events that impinge upon us during our lives: for example, a dentist drills your teeth; you are awakened by loud noises from a jackhammer being operated on the street beneath your hotel room early in the morning; or your children have turned the TV up very loud. In all of these instances someone is doing something which, to you, is aversive. Are all to be classed as instances of aggression? Writers such as Berkowitz and Feshbach would be quick to point out that the dentist, jackhammer operator, and the children did not necessarily intend to inflict injury. Therefore, none would be labeled as aggressive acts. At this point some psychoanalytic writers might also raise the issue that dentists select their occupation because of an unconscious intent to inflict injury. The difficulty in using this concept lies in the complex issues involved in measuring intentions. The idea itself has great appeal. It is the focal point for much of our great literature, and it is an integral part of our legal structure. However, we have no ready means for measuring intention. Even those writers who include it as a variable in their definition of aggression seldom introduce it as a variable in their empirical studies.

√ There is, then, the problem of distinguishing aversive events that are aggressive from others that are not. There is no definitive resolution of this issue. However, we have adopted two strategies which we think facilitate empirical research on aggression. The first is to focus upon only a small subset of the total spectrum of human behaviors which could potentially be classed as aggressive.

Textbooks on aggression typically cover an enormous range of phenomena such as homicides in families, hijacking airplanes, schoolyard bullies, marital conflict, muggings, riots, and wars. Some ethologists (Eibl-Eibesfeldt, 1974) even include Eskimo song competitions as instances of aggression! All of these phenomena might satisfy that part of the definition which includes inflicting pain upon victims. However, this writer assumes that each of these phenomena should be studied separately. It seems unlikely that, in the near future, there will be any *general theory* of aggression which covers all of these events. It is more useful to establish an empirical foundation for a small subset of aggressive phenomena, e.g., those events which occur in family interaction. Understanding the variables relating to family aggression may or may not contribute to an understanding of interpersonal aggression in other settings, such as those found in football "games," ghetto riots, or barroom brawls. Each of these phenomena will probably require its own techniques of study and data analysis; each probably involves very different determining variables.

Within the family those events will be labeled as aggressive which can be shown to be *both aversive and contingent*. Assessment of either characteristic is a complex process. Field studies in the homes of aggressive children produced 14 categories of events which seemed aversive and could be coded reliably (Reid, 1978). A priori ratings by parents showed surprising consensus about which events were perceived as aversive and which were not (Jones, Reid, & Patterson, 1975). They agreed that if these events were experienced by a victim, they would be perceived as painful. A functional analysis showed that these aversive events effectively suppressed ongoing prosocial behaviors; i.e., these aversive events functioned like punishment when contingent upon ongoing prosocial interactions (Patterson & Cobb, 1971). The details of these analyses will be presented in later sections (Chapter 6). For the moment, it is sufficient to say that there was a modest convergence between the a priori ratings by parents and the functional analyses of the suppression effect.

√ Once an event is classified as aversive, how can we determine if it is being used contingently? To be classed as contingent, it would have to be shown that an aversive event reliably *follows* some behaviors and not others. In natural settings this can be done by first collecting data which accurately describe interactional sequences. If Sister-Tease is followed by Brother-Hit in a repeated pattern, then it seems likely that the two events are contingent. To determine whether the sequence is random or contingent, one can compare the base-rate value of Brother-Hit to the likelihood that he will hit when he is teased. Given a significant difference between the two values, then one can assume a contingent relation; i.e., Brother-Hit is more likely to occur given a specific behavior of the sister. Aggression in families does not consist of fortuitous events. This is a key assumption in coercion theory.

The dentist does not apply the drill contingent upon any particular behavior of the client. Similarly, the aversive events provided by the jackhammer operator and the children watching TV are not contingent upon a specific behavior. They would, therefore, be categorized as aversive but not necessarily aggressive.

One might object that an increased understanding of microsocial events, such as teasing, scolding, and whining is an unwarranted concern with trivia; usually aggression refers to high-amplitude behaviors, such as hitting, stabbing, or shooting. However, a second key assumption in coercion theory is that the innocuous, garden-variety aversive events, such as teasing and scolding, can, under certain conditions, escalate to high-intensity aggression. One of the goals of the present formulation is to understand how this process operates within families. Under what conditions will escalations in intensity come about?

Buss (1966a), Bandura (1973), and Berkowitz (1978) distinguish between instrumental aggression which produces an external reinforcer, and hostility for which the reinforcer is a pain reaction by the victim. The cross-cultural observation study by Lambert (1974) showed that 80% of the time children's aggression was instrumental, and 5% of the time it was hostile. Hartup (1974) showed that while object-oriented aggression characterized a large proportion of the aggression of the preschool-age child, it decreased from ages 4 through 7 years. He also speculated that threats to self-esteem produced hostile attempts to injure others, i.e., person-oriented aggression. Other writers, such as Rule and Nesdale (1976) have pointed out that anger is more likely related to person-oriented aggression and therefore a better differentiation might be between anger and non-anger.

John Knutson has made a differentiation which neatly summarizes our findings from analyzing family interaction (Knutson & Hyman, 1973; Follick & Knutson, 1977). He distinguishes between irritable aggression and instrumental aggression. Instrumental aggression is controlled by its positive consequences. Irritable aggression, on the other hand, is elicited by its aversive antecedent; that is,

the termination or withdrawal of the antecedent constitutes a reinforcement for the response. In family interaction about two-thirds of the child's coercive interchanges can be classified as instrumental aggression. The antecedents for the behaviors are neutral or positive, and the most likely outcome is a continuation of attention or some other prosocial behavior by other family members (see Chapter 5). The remainder of the child's aggression is in reaction to attacks by other family members. This is analogous to Knutson's irritable aggression.

A wide spectrum of aversive events are employed in a contingent fashion by family members. It is assumed that all of these events reflect a *common process*. From this perspective the code categories Whine, Tease, Disapproval, Yell, Humiliate, Noncomply, and Hit all differ in topography yet are members of the same set. Members of this set share several characteristics: (1) they are aversive; (2) they are used contingently; (3) they produce a reliable impact upon the victim; and (4) the reaction of the victim has both a short-term and a long-term effect upon the aggressor. The rates at which these events occur differentiate normal families from families of antisocial children. The functional relations between these events and the reactions they provoke also differentiate these samples.

Throughout this volume I will sometimes refer to this process as "pain control" and at other times as "coercion." The term coercion, however, has a somewhat broader coverage. It includes hypotheses which relate family management disruptions to the performance of aggressive behaviors. In addition, there are functional relations between microsocial structures and mood changes. There is also a relation between macrosocial stressors which impinge from outside the family and their assumed impact upon both family management skills and microsocial processes. Finally, coercion includes the escalation hypothesis, which describes the process by which a dyad moves from the exchange of rather innocuous aversive events to the higher amplitude aggressive behaviors which characterize child and spouse abuse.

The term coercion also includes the child problem behaviors usually labeled "aggressive." We will examine the literature to see what is, in fact, normally included in the definition of that term. However, coercion includes some behaviors that, while aversive, would ordinarily *not* be included in the definition of aggression, e.g., Noncomply, High Rate, Cry, Ignore, Whine, and Yell.

In early drafts of this volume I used terms such as conduct-problem and out-of-control to label the identified problem child. M. Rutter (personal communication) pointed out that the latter term includes in its history implicit assumptions about a breakdown in inner controls, with the symptoms representing uncontrolled motivational forces. To avoid that kind of confusion, I deleted the phrase from this volume and substituted in its place the term "antisocial." However, D. Olweus (personal communication) has pointed out to me that this term also has a history which gives it a meaning that does not altogether fit my present purpose. He notes that the term has been traditionally applied to older delinquent youths. I agree with his point but believe that the term antisocial can serve equally well when applied to younger children. From the perspective of coercion theory, behaviors such as Whine, Yell, Hit, and Steal, all involve other persons as targets. In a sense, all coercive behaviors involve a victim and the term *antisocial* would seem to be appropriate.

As we pursue these studies, I believe it will be shown that there are a number of different *patterns* of coercive behaviors. When a child displays one member of such a subset, he is very likely to perform the others as well. Furthermore, there is enough consistency in these interrelations among the symptoms that the patterns recur regularly in referrals for treatment (e.g, Achenbach & Edelbrock, 1978; Patterson, 1964). These patterns are important because they reflect different familial processes. In the present volume we explore only two of the most salient subsets, *Social Aggressors* and *Stealers*. However, we are convinced that there are other more subtle forms of coercion, e.g., Immature and Hyperactive patterns, where the victim is less clearly identified but contributes nevertheless to the coercive process.

Throughout this volume the term antisocial child will be used as a synonym for the coercive child. In this context, it will ordinarily refer to the two typologies which we have studied, *Social Aggressors* and *Stealers*. By implication, if later analyses were to show immature and hyperactive children to be coercive, then the meaning of the term antisocial would be expanded to include them as well.

The Assessment of Coercive Events

The interview and the questionnaire are the traditional techniques for gathering data on aggression in families. While such data have a place in the present volume, they have only limited value for the study of interaction. As R. Cairns (1979a) pointed out, *the study of process requires sequential data.* Data from interviews and ratings are ill-suited to such a task. There is good reason to believe that parental interviews provide serious dis-

tortions even for such simple tasks as estimating event frequencies. These studies will be reviewed in detail in Chapter 3; suffice it to say here that interview data lack the precision necessary for the study of functional relations between one event and another.

These considerations led us to seek a new kind of data for the study of familial aggression. The sample to be studied were families referred for treatment because one or more of their members had been labeled as aggressive.[1] After conducting an interview and administering the usual self-report questionnaires, the writers took notebooks in hand and went into the homes of these families. The code system described in Chapter 3 was designed while sitting in their kitchens and living rooms. Three years of trial and error led to the construction of a 29-category code system which could reliably document some of what could be seen in these families. Fourteen of the categories sampled aversive behaviors occurring in family interactions. The methodological studies on reliability, stability, observer bias, observer presence effects, and validity are summarized in Chapter 3.

It is literally impossible to devise a code that describes *all* aversive events found in *all* families. It is also true that most families employ some aversives which are so subtle that they can only be detected by other family members. It seems reasonable, however, to begin by designing a behavioral coding system which samples the most obvious events. Such a system would accurately reflect what is going on in most families most of the time. The 14 aversive events, their definitions, and base rates of occurrence are shown in Table 2.1. The data were based on a sample of distressed families referred for treatment to the Oregon Social Learning Center (OSLC). Six to ten home observations were conducted in which each of the family members was sampled for a minimum of 60 minutes (Reid, 1978).

It may be that our culture assigns children and parents different types of aversive events as part of their roles. Disapproval by mother occurred, on the average, once every three minutes; mothers used Destructive and Physical Negative less often. Some categories, such as Cry, Whine, Yell, Noncomply, and Destructive (of property) were used primarily by children. Others, such as Command Negative and Ignore were used primarily by parents. Some aversive events were used often by all family members.

For many purposes the data from the 14 categories can be summed to form a single score, Total Aversive Behavior (TAB). The score serves as a general measure of level of coerciveness. Its test-

Table 2.1
The Definitions and Mean Base Rates (per minute) of
Aversive Behavior for Members of Distressed Families

(adapted from Reid, 1978)

Code Categories	Definitions	Problem Boys N = 27	Mothers N = 27	Fathers N = 18	Siblings N = 54
Command Negative	Command in which immediate compliance is demanded, aversive consequences threatened, sarcasm or humiliation directed toward receiver.	.008	0.046	0.023	.008
Cry	Whining or sobbing sounds.	.019	0.000	0.000	.024
Disapproval	Verbal or gestural criticism of another person's behavior or characteristics.	.134	0.314	0.182	.120
Dependency	Request for assistance when person is obviously capable of doing task himself.	.007	0.003	0.000	.008
Destructive	When a person damages, soils, or breaks something.	.031	0.000	0.000	.011
High Rate	Physically active repetitive behavior which is likely to be annoying.	.044	0.000	0.000	.042
Humiliate	Embarrassing, shaming, or making fun of another person.	.020	0.011	0.015	.015
Ignore	Intentional and deliberate nonresponse to an initiated behavior.	.005	0.023	0.019	.010
Noncomply	A person does not do what is requested of him in response to a command, command negative, or a dependency within 12 seconds of the request being made.	.092	0.011	0.009	.064
Negativism	A neutral verbal message delivered in a tone of voice which conveys an *attitude* of "Don't bug me." Also included are defeatist statements.	.115	0.019	0.012	.059
Physical Negative	Physical attack or attempt to attack another person.	.042	0.019	0.003	.021
Tease	Act of annoying, pestering, mocking, or making fun of another person.	.050	0.001	0.014	.028
Whine	A slurring, nasal, or high-pitched voice. The content of the statement is irrelevant.	.036	0.001	0.000	.052
Yell	Shouts, yells, or loud talk.	.057	0.009	0.000	.036
	SUM OF MEANS FOR ALL FOURTEEN AVERSIVE BEHAVIORS	.660	.457	.277	.498
	MEAN TOTAL AVERSIVE*	.047	.033	.020	.036

*This mean is obtained from the sum of the fourteen means. Typically, this score is obtained by summing up fourteen scores for each subject and calculating the mean of that distribution.

retest correlation for a 12-month period was .74 ($df = 7$, $p < .05$).

These codes catalog the aversive events used by family members to control each other's behavior. Their employment constitutes an operational definition of the components in the pain-control process. It is one thing to construct a system which can be used to code aversive family interactions; however, to prove its worth as a measure of family aggression, it is necessary to demonstrate the validity of these categories in at least three different ways. First, the aversive categories must significantly differentiate between identified aggressive boys and matched nonproblem boys. Antisocial boys were shown to perform these behaviors at significantly higher rates than normals by Patterson (1976) and by others using comparable coding systems (Bernal et al., 1976; Lobitz et al., 1976; Snyder, 1977). Other analyses have shown that mothers and siblings of aggressive boys differed significantly from comparable members of nonproblem families (Patterson, 1980b; and Chapter 10). Second, it must be shown that these 14 code categories which assess aversive events covary with measures of what parents mean by the term "antisocial." To test this, the parents of families referred for treatment were asked to give daily reports on whether or not certain problem behaviors of concern to them had occurred. The mean daily reports for a two-week baseline were then correlated with the mean TAB score based upon the observation data. In three different samples the two measures of general deviancy correlated .69 ($df = 14$, $p < .01$), .46 ($df = 21$, $p < .02$), and .59 ($df = 31$, $p < .001$). Other studies relating to the validity of the coding system are reviewed in Chapter 3. In the final analysis, the validity of the coding system as a measure of familial aggression relates to the extent to which these data facilitate our understanding of the process. This cannot be summarized in a single index. It is, in fact, the function of this volume to demonstrate that analyses of interactions involving these 14 aversive events provide a proper empirical base for understanding aggression in families.

Demographic Data Relating to Child Aggression

Age

It is assumed that infants instinctively employ aversives such as crying. This may have survival value in that an infant can use the techniques of punishment and negative reinforcement to train the mother in more effective parenting behaviors. To date the writer has been unable to find studies which give data on the likelihood of crying by age level of infant. Given an awake condition, the probability of such an aversive behavior seems very high during the first few weeks and then gradually diminishes. Presumably, there are important individual differences among infants in both the base-rate values and variability of this behavior. It would be of interest to know if fluctuations in crying covaried with changes in the mother's mood. In addition, longitudinal studies are needed to determine if mothers who quickly learn to meet the child's needs are also more adept at child management when the child is 2 or 3 years old.

In his review of preschool aggression, Cairns (1979b, p. 206) makes the interesting observation that half of the interchanges among 1- and 2-year-olds could be thought of as "aggressive." He cites the Holmberg (1977) study, which showed that this amounted to little more than taking a toy from another child. However, even at this early age, they had learned not to deal with adults in this manner; only 5% of their interactions with adults were aggressive. By the time the children were 2½ years of age, only 20% of their interactions with peers were aggressive. This trend is in keeping with our assumption that the socializing process increases the child's prosocial interaction and steadily decreases that which is coercive. As we shall see, parents seem to accept 3% to 5% of the preadolescent child's coercive behavior as being within normal limits. Lambert (1974) found in summing data from six cultures that children playing outside the home, primarily with peers, averaged about 10% coercive interaction.

With the exception of the investigation by Henry and Sharpe (1947), studies in nursery school settings generally indicate a decrease in children's coercive behavior as a function of age (Green, 1933; Dawe, 1934; Hartup, 1974; Ricketts, 1931).[2] For example, Dawe (1934) studied children in a free-play situation. The average quarrel was a brief 23.6 seconds; it tended to last longer if the setting was outdoors (35.1 seconds) rather than indoors (17.4 seconds). For younger children, 78% of the quarrels were possession related; this dropped to 38% for the 4- and 5-year-olds. Attempts on the part of the teacher to intervene had relatively little impact upon duration. The "attacks" were usually directed at children of the same sex, and were usually centered around conflicts over possession of an object. The coercive behavior usually consisted of pushing, pulling, and physical negatives (pinch, hit, kick). The correlation between age and frequency of quarrels was −.41.

Hartup's (1974) review of his and others' find-

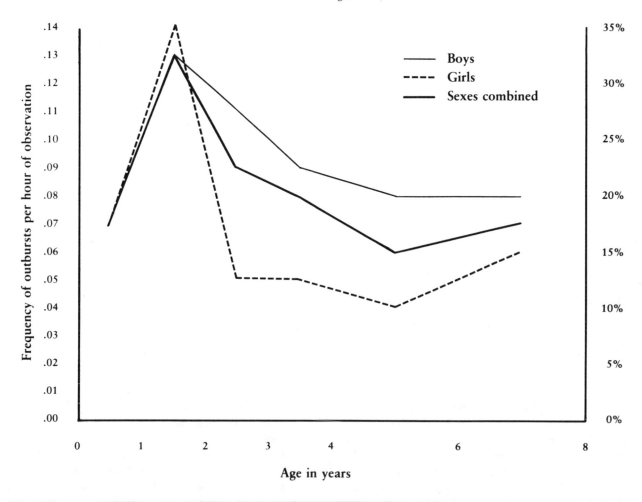

Figure 2.1
Age and Sex Differences in Frequency of Outbursts
(from Goodenough, 1931)

ings suggests that the kind of aggression employed also changes as a function of age. His data showed proportional decreases in conflicts concerning object possession or blocking (instrumental aggression) but only slight changes in person-directed, retaliatory, and hostile outbursts. In Lambert's (1974) six culture study, the mean figure for the range of age groups was 80% instrumental aggression and 5% hostile.

Studies of preschool children in the home showed a comparable decrease in aversive interactions as a function of age. In the classic study by Goodenough (1931) 45 mothers kept daily diaries for children ranging in ages from 7 months to 7 years 10 months. The diaries were kept for a minimum of seven days and a maximum of 133 days. The data for the frequency of the children's anger outbursts are summarized in Figure 2.1. As shown

there, the 18-month-old child performed at the highest level, averaging an outburst about every seven or eight hours. Holmberg (1977, cited in Cairns, 1979b) found the peak frequency of child aggression toward adults in the nursery school to occur at 24 months. Goodenough found a steady decrease in conflicts through age 6. These findings are in keeping with the observation study by Fawl (1963), who studied less intense conflicts. He showed an average of 5.4 disturbances per hour for children aged 2 to 11 observed in the home. In his study, the correlation between age and conflict frequency was −.76, demonstrating that younger children performed aggressive behavior at higher rates. Again, a majority (80%) of the outbursts lasted less than one minute.

The OSLC code was used to collect observation data in the homes of 44 children from normal fam-

Table 2.2
Changes in Total Aversive Behavior Scores by Age

OSLC Samples	Mean TAB Score by Age						F Values	df
	2-4	5-6	7-8	9-10	11-12	13-15		
Social Aggressive							3.28*	4:135
N	41	22	29	37	11			
Mean	1.23	1.18	.99	.82	.68			
S.D.	.79	.86	.53	.35	.18			
Stealer							7.47***	5:72
N	4	7	21	22	19	5		
Mean	1.83	.80	.40	.39	.60	.56		
S.D.	.93	.66	.27	.27	.60	.44		
Normal							3.29*	3:48
N	12	15	10	15	6	4		
Mean	.56	.32	.21	.13	.22	.11		
S.D.	.50	.46	.22	.13	.13	.06		
Mean TAB Score at 90th percentile	.92	.53	.35	.21	—	—		

*$p < .05$
***$p < .001$
— indicates insufficient N for calculation.

ilies. This was essentially a working-class sample (see Chapter 3 for details). As summarized in Table 2.2, the findings from six to ten observation sessions showed a significant decrease in TAB scores as a function of age.[3] The children aged 2 to 4 performed at an average rate of .56 responses per minute. By the time the child was of school age his rate was down to .32 responses per minute, and then further decreased to about one aversive every eight minutes. The results for the analysis of variance showed these changes with age to be reliable.

The level of coerciveness for normal 2- to 4-year-olds is comparable to the mean baseline TAB score of .75 reported for the first sample of antisocial children referred for treatment at OSLC (Patterson, 1974a). This finding is reiterated in Figure 2.2. It can be seen there that the average 10- to 11-year-old antisocial child referred for treatment is performing at the level of coercion which our culture finds acceptable in 2-, 3-, and 4-year-olds.

The children from distressed families were generally referred to OSLC for treatment because the parent or a community agency had perceived several behavior problems. If this included "stealing," and the baseline Parent Daily Report (PDR) data indicated that these behaviors occurred, then the family was categorized as a member of the Stealer sample. The details for the classification procedures and sample characteristics are summarized in Chapter 3. If the baseline observation data in the home provided a TAB score of .45 and none of the referral symptoms included stealing, then the family was placed in the Social Aggressor sample. The data in Figure 2.2 suggest a significant decrease in the level of aversiveness as a function of age for both of the clinical samples. Younger referred children were significantly more coercive than the older children. Children who were Stealers were intermediate in their level of coerciveness, performing more coercively than Normals but less so than the Social Aggressors.

These findings for age differences relate to the general hypothesis that antisocial children represent a form of arrested socialization. It is assumed that a longitudinal study would show that the to-be-labeled deviant preschool boy may perform at only slightly higher rates than nonproblem boys prior to age 3. However, as he matures he *continues to perform* at about that same level. If he continues at this level long enough, someone in the community will finally label him as "deviant." Pre-

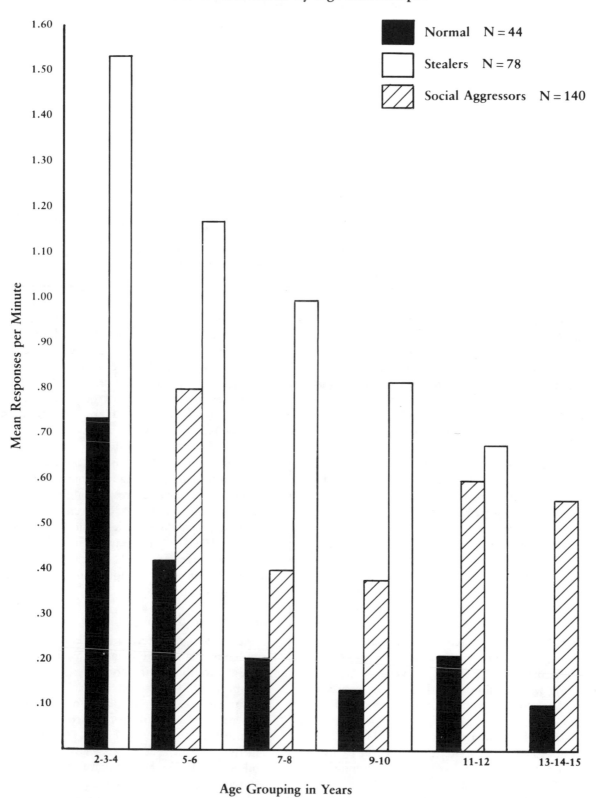

Figure 2.2
Mean Aversiveness by Age and Sample

Note: The data for Stealers and Social Aggressors have been combined for the 2-3-4 age group.

Table 2.3
Percentage of Out-of-Control Behaviors by Age
(from Rutter, Tizard, & Whitmore, 1970)

Behavior	Age		
	10 years N = (1018)	11 years N = (996)	12 years N = (1050)
Parents' Data			
Often fights	12.2	11.0	8.0
Temper loss at least once a week	4.7	3.1	2.6
Wet bed at least once a month	4.1	2.6	1.8
Restless and overactive	34.6	30.2	21.8
Teachers' Data			
Wets pants	1.0	0.5	0.1
Fidgety	18.9	14.7	18.1
Steals	3.0	3.1	1.2

sumably his parents are unable and/or unwilling to impose the sanctions which parents of normal children impose for these same behaviors.

Survey data for preschool- and school-aged children show a general trend toward reduced levels of antisocial behaviors as a function of age. Griffith (1952) studied children ages 6 through 14. Parent ratings of child aggression showed a decrease with age for such behaviors as impudent, noisy, and anger outbursts. (It is interesting to note that the child's self-perception data showed a curvilinear relation between age and aggression.) Similar decreases were reported in the longitudinal study of maternal reports of quarrelsomeness and temper tantrums by MacFarlane, Allen and Honzik (1962). Their small, highly selective sample was followed from age 21 months through age 14 years. Some problems, such as negativism and irritability, showed large fluctuations but no regular trends as a function of age. Observations in six cultures showed a decrease in frequency of assaults when comparing ages 3 to 5 with ages 6 to 8 (Whiting & Whiting, 1975). However, when this measure was combined with measurements of horseplay and insults, the combined score did not covary significantly with age.

The Isle of Wight study by Rutter, Tizard, and Whitmore (1970) is perhaps a classic in its own right. The total population of 2,199 ten- and eleven-year-olds was assessed by a multiple-screening procedure. First, parent and teacher questionnaires were used to identify a subgroup of 268 children who might be at risk for psychiatric disorders. This subgroup was asked to participate in more intensive assessment procedures. Those questionnaire items which described out-of-control behaviors and which showed significant changes with age are summarized in Table 2.3. Of particular interest were not only the age-related changes but the relatively high base rate for some of these behaviors. According to the parents' perception, about one in eight of the 10-year-old children *fights* often. The base rate for temper tantrums and stealing were about one in 30. It would be useful to have correspondingly high-quality data for a U.S. sample of children of all ages.

In sum, the data indicate a general trend toward reduced levels of antisocial child behaviors as a function of age (2 through 12 years). These trends are fairly consistent in home and school settings and across cultures.

Sex of Child
Reviews of the literature on childhood aggression consistently note higher rates of physical aggression for boys than for girls (Mischel, 1966; Feshbach, 1970; Maccoby & Jacklin, 1974). For example, observation studies in preschool settings showed boys generally performed at higher rates than girls (Dawe, 1934; Henry & Sharpe, 1947; Hartup, 1973). The large-scale study by Smith and Green (1975) showed that in 13 of 15 nursery schools, boys tended to be more aggressive than girls. Dawe (1934) found a mean of 13.5 quarrels for boys and 9.5 for girls. While the differences found in other studies were generally of this order,

they were not always significant (Henry & Sharpe, 1947).

These overall performance trends are of interest. There is reason to believe that even at the preschool level, boys and girls may differ in the *kind* of aggression which they display (Maccoby & Jacklin, 1974). While the findings are not always consistent, many of the studies point to a greater use by girls of verbal attacks. Furthermore, the two sexes may be differentially responsive to setting constraints within the nursery school. For example, D.S. Patterson (1976) found the overall trend was for boys to be more assertive than girls. However, when only boys were placed in the Art Center of the room, they quickly *escalated* to high-intensity aggression, whereas girls did not. For boys, art defined a setting which related to escalation in aggression; for girls, this same setting was apparently defined very differently. Studies which systematically sample settings, kinds of aggression, age, and sex of the child could tell us important things about how our culture programs aggression for children.

These fragments of data suggest that sex differences in some kinds of aggression appear very early in the nursery school. The data from Goodenough (1931) showed that in the home the mean rate of outbursts per hour for boys was consistently higher for all age groups (2 through 7 years 11 months). Incidentally, at ages 12 through 23 months it appears that girls have slightly *more* anger outbursts than boys. However, the Holmberg (1977) study found no difference by sex for children 24 months and younger.

Maccoby and Jacklin (1974) review the evidence for biological variables which may account for some of the variance in these early sex differences. The evidence is sufficient to give pause to any who might wish to take a strictly environmental stance on the issue of early sex differences. Hopefully, the next generation of studies will take these variables into account as they systematically explore the process by which these differences occur. The question is, at a molecular level, how does a culture arrange for 5-year-old boys to learn *how* and *where* to be physically aggressive? How do we teach 5-year-old girls *not* to use physical force?

Sex differences among older children. Typically, teachers and parents refer more boys than girls to child guidance agencies for treatment of conduct problems. This tendency was noted in the classic study of several thousand referrals during the 1920's by Ackerson (1931). Studies carried out three decades later in a different country showed a similar pattern. British boys were significantly more likely than girls to be referred for treatment of conduct-problem behaviors such as stealing, lying, and fighting (Wolff, 1967).

It is not only adults who perceive more boys than girls to be extremely aggressive; the children themselves perceive these sex differences. The cross-cultural studies of adolescents' self-report data showed that girls described themselves as more conforming to adult values (Devereaux, 1970). The careful review by Hood and Sparks (1970) showed consistent sex differences in self reported crime for high school students in both America and Scandinavia. The self-report frequency of delinquent behavior for boys was two to four times higher than that for girls. Comparable sex differences characterize the self-report data for adult men and women: e.g., the rates of assault were 49% and 5% respectively; for car theft, 26% and 8%; for burglary, 17% and 4%; and for robbery, 11% and 1%.

The findings from the Isle of Wight survey detailed parent and teacher concerns for preadolescent children (Rutter et al., 1970). All of the findings shown in Table 2.4 portray significant differences between boys and girls. The categories denoting high rates of activity indicated that boys were significantly more involved than girls. In the home, these differences were modest in magnitude; however, in the classroom, they were exacerbated. Teachers perceived that almost twice as many boys as girls presented problems which involved restlessness and fidgeting. Parents and teachers agreed that two or three times more boys than girls were involved in stealing, truancy, fighting, lying, bullying, and destructiveness. These findings reiterate the theme that boys are perceived as more out of control; but they also suggest that there is a complex interaction between setting, sex of child, and kind of out-of-control behaviors.

Reid (1978) provided data for base rates of various responses by age and sex for an extremely small sample of 27 normal families observed in their homes. The data are summarized in Table 2.5 separately by age groups. Note that the same family may have contributed to more than one age group. Of the 30 comparisons, ten were significant. With certain interesting exceptions, the general drift of the findings re-emphasized that boys are more out of control than girls. Again, it was the younger boys who were more likely to hit, push and shove. This theme was noted earlier in the studies of nursery school aggression. In the home, young boys were also significantly more likely to Disapprove and Yell. Young girls were significantly more likely than boys to be Negative,

Table 2.4
Percentage of Out-of-Control Behaviors by Sex
(from Rutter, Tizard, & Whitmore, 1970)

Problem Behaviors	Parents' Report		Teachers' Report	
	Boys N = (1564)	Girls N = (1500)	Boys N = (1743)	Girls N = (1683)
Poor concentration	25.1	18.2	39.1	25.0
Restless/overactive	32.0	25.5	16.8	8.1
Fidgety/squirmy	14.4	9.8	23.3	10.9
Steals	5.7	2.6	3.4	1.6
Truant	1.8	0.2	2.1	0.7
Fights	15.2	5.3	13.6	4.4
Lies	16.1	9.7	9.4	2.9
Bullies	6.7	4.0	7.4	2.1
Destructive	7.1	1.4	3.0	0.7
Temper tantrum (at least once a week)	4.4	2.5	—	—
Irritable	34.5	27.9	11.7	6.5

Tease, and Cry.

The mean TAB scores for the older children showed a general decrease in rate for both sexes. Older normal girls were significantly more likely than their male siblings to Cry and Whine. These behaviors hardly seem like *attack* behaviors; they are more likely to be a victim's technique for dealing with attacks by other family members. Older male siblings were, on the other hand, significantly more likely to Noncomply, Tease, and High Rate.

Socioeconomic Status

In the research literature there is no consistent relation between socioeconomic status and aggressive behavior in children. While the early work on delinquency suggested that the working class contributed a disproportionate amount to official delinquency rates, the review by Hood and Sparks (1970) showed that a significant confound existed in these analyses. Using official delinquency rates (offenses known to the police), the early studies showed an average ratio of about 5:1 when comparing low to high socioeconomic status groups. If, however, the estimate was based upon the adolescent's self-report, then the ratio would have to be revised to about 1.5:1.0.

If one moves away from delinquency rates as a measure of antisocial behavior, then the difference among social classes diminishes further. The review by Feshbach (1970) showed no consistent relation between child aggression and social status when teacher and parent reports served as criteria.

The longitudinal study by Eron et al. (1971) actually showed higher rates for the high-status boy. The dependent variable was a peer sociometric measure of aggressiveness. The Isle of Wight study showed few parent-reported deviant-child behaviors related to status differences for boys or girls. However, in that study the teacher data indicated that low-status boys and girls had a significantly higher incidence of poor concentration and absence from school for trivial reasons. Fighting for boys, and stealing and truancy for girls, showed similar correlations.

Olweus' (1978) study of bullies in schools also failed to find a correlation between social status and bullying or peer ratings on aggressiveness. The distribution by status for the OSLC sample suggests a disproportionate sampling of working-class families. It is likely that these differences reflect the dynamics of local referring agencies more than an estimate of the incidence of aggressiveness in Eugene's general population. Presumably, middle- and upper-class aggressive children are referred for treatment to local physicians rather than to OSLC.

Family Variables: Size, Father Absence, Birth Order

Family Size. It seems reasonable to suppose that as the number of children in the family increases, there would be a proportionate decrease in the amount of time parents spend with any given child. The number of crises and parental responsibilities would also be likely to increase to the point

Table 2.5
Sex Differences in Normal Sample

(from Reid, 1978)

Behavior	6 years and under				7 years or over			
	Boys N = (15)		Girls N = (7)		Boys N = (37)		Girls N = (22)	
	Mean	S.D.	Mean	S.D.	Mean	S.D.	Mean	S.D.
Total Aversive Behavior	.581	(.543)	.514	(.256)	.221	(.149)	.215	(.214)
Command	.043	(.036)	.022	(.021)	.040	(.036)	.043	(.028)
Command Negative	.005	(.007)	.000	(.000)	.003	(.006)	.002	(.005)
Cry	.016	(.024)	.114*	(.125)	.000	(.000)	.018*	(.037)
Disapproval	.111*	(.088)	.054	(.045)	.083	(.054)	.083	(.054)
Dependency	.006	(.009)	.008	(.016)	.003	(.008)	.001	(.002)
Destructive	.009	(.013)	.007	(.008)	.003	(.008)	.001	(.002)
High Rate	.042	(.063)	.020	(.024)	.012*	(.027)	.001	(.003)
Humiliate	.004	(.007)	.000	(.000)	.002	(.005)	.004	(.009)
Noncompliance	.088	(.070)	.078	(.048)	.044*	(.051)	.021	(.033)
Negativism	.013	(.030)	.031*	(.032)	.024	(.024)	.032	(.050)
Physical Negative	.029*	(.027)	.013	(.013)	.009	(.016)	.008	(.017)
Tease	.020	(.040)	.040*	(.038)	.023*	(.039)	.005	(.011)
Whine	.124	(.176)	.137	(.169)	.009	(.013)	.026*	(.055)
Yell	.108*	(.198)	.013	(.015)	.005	(.010)	.008	(.019)

* p value for "t" was < .05. However, in that the same family may have contributed a child to each age group, the assumptions underlying the "t" statistic may have been violated. For this reason, the reader should interpret these findings with caution.

where many tasks ordinarily carried out by the mother might be delegated to an older sibling. From a social learning viewpoint, this would imply an increasing contribution of siblings to the socialization process.

The analysis by Patterson (1980b), and those presented in later sections of this volume, indict the siblings as major determinants for aggressive behavior. In large families the parents are less able to track and punish their children's out-of-control behavior. These hypotheses are in keeping with the findings from the study by Zajonc (1976). Zajonc found an inverse relationship between family size and intelligence. The assumption was that in larger families members spent increasing amounts of time interacting with children rather than with adults. Presumably this results in less stimulation and enrichment, which in turn is related to lower IQ scores.

A number of writers, such as Douglas (1966), have commented that delinquent youths tend to come from larger families. The Isle of Wight study provided additional support for the relationship between antisocial behavior and family size (Rutter et al., 1970). For boys there were significant covariations between family size and the following: destructiveness, fighting, disobedience, lying, bullying, stealing, and temper. Girls showed comparable relations for destructiveness, fighting, lying, and bullying. Rutter goes on to point out that there were significant correlations between IQ and these same variables; furthermore, IQ correlated inversely with family size. Although the data were not shown, he claimed that partial correlations which took IQ into account showed greatly reduced relations between family size and out-of-control behaviors reported by parents and teachers.[4]

The observation study by Burgess, Kimball, and Burgess (1978) provided a direct test of the hypothesis. They observed interaction in the homes of normal and abused children. The data showed a significant correlation (.43) between family size and physical aggression. Furthermore, with increasing family size, the relative amount of interaction with siblings increased while the relative amount of interaction with parents decreased.

The general tenor of the findings suggests that family size and rates of deviant behavior covary. It would seem appropriate to begin investigating the

Table 2.6
Mean TAB Scores for Intact and Father-Absent Homes

(from Horne, 1980)

Family Member	Distressed Sample				Nondistressed Sample			
	Father Absent		Intact		Father Absent		Intact	
	Mean	N	Mean	N	Mean	N	Mean	N
Target Child	.981	(9)	.412	(15)	.223	(9)	.277	(16)
Mother	.681	(9)	.362	(15)	.329	(9)	.233	(16)
Older Sister	.988	(4)	.129	(8)	.148	(5)	.132	(6)
Younger Sister	.754	(6)	.513	(7)	—		.414	(7)
Older Brother	.544	(6)	.165	(6)	.134	(5)	.128	(4)
Younger Brother	—		—		.420	(5)	.627	(7)

—indicates that there were insufficient data for analyses.

determinants for the covariations. For example, the interesting study by Circirelli (1976) showed that mothers' reactions to their children in a laboratory setting varied as a function of whether the children had older siblings at home. In large families, the mothers delegated part of their maternal role to an older sibling. The differential reactions presumably reflected this shared role.

Broken homes. Traditionally, this variable has been thought to be associated with antisocial children. In our culture the likelihood of living in a broken home is now rather high. As shown in the studies reviewed by Hetherington, Cox, and Cox (1976), approximately 10% of the children in our culture are being reared in single-parent families.

Most of the early studies on the effect of broken homes did not control for the contribution of social class. The carefully designed survey of Rutter et al. (1970) did provide such controls. Their findings showed a general relation between child psychiatric disorders and broken homes. However, within these disorders the incidence of broken homes for the antisocial child (25%) was not significantly greater than the incidence reported for the other psychiatric subgroups. A *broken home,* then, seems to relate to an *increased likelihood* for a *disturbed child* (neurotic or antisocial).

A study of divorced families by Hetherington et al. (1976) showed that following the absence of the father, there were significant increases in out-of-control behavior, especially for boys. The study also demonstrated the causal relation between broken homes and antisocial behavior. For example, one could assume that having an antisocial

child caused the divorce. However, the Hetherington et al. (1976) and the Wallerstein and Kelly (1976) studies showed that the increase in antisocial child behavior *followed* the divorce. These studies do not tell us why the break-up of the home produces child aggression. The hypotheses detailed in Chapter 10 would have it that crises such as divorce or illness can disrupt the practices of family management skills. It is suggested that even a temporary abeyance in monitoring and setting consequences for violating house rules is likely to be accompanied by increases in antisocial child behavior.

There is another aspect of the broken home which is not clearly identified in the existing literature. Our clinical experience suggested that father-absent homes were associated with the more extreme forms of antisocial behaviors. Two analyses by Horne (1980) demonstrated that a case could be made for this hypothesis. First, he compared the TAB scores for each of six members from distressed and nondistressed families that were either intact or father-absent. The findings are summarized in Table 2.6. Only the ANOVA values for the intact and father-absent comparisons were included. In the clinical sample, the effect of father absence was to produce TAB scores twice as high as for members from intact families. In the nondistressed sample, father absence was not related to significant changes in TAB scores. This suggests that it is not father absence, per se, which determines the increase in coercive performance. I think it is the interaction between father absence and the disruption of family management practices. In families where these management skills are marginal, the father's leaving may tip an already precarious balance. This assumption is supported by the next step in Horne's analysis. The fathers from intact families were asked to absent themselves from their homes on alternate evenings. A comparison between the three sessions in which he was present and the three sessions in which he was absent showed no consistent effects for the 16 nondistressed (intact) families. Some family members showed nonsignificant increases in TAB scores during absent nights (*mother* and older brother), while others showed decreases. Similar comparisons for the distressed sample showed that, with the exception of the problem child, *all family members were more coercive on father-absent nights.*

The findings from the Horne (1980), Hetherington et al. (1976), and Wallerstein and Kelly (1976, 1980) studies lead us to assume that the presence of the father contributes to the effective practice of family management skills. A broken home places the family at risk for a disruption in these practices. If such a disruption occurs, then the likelihood of the broken home producing an antisocial child appears to be very high.

Ordinal Position. Coercion theory implicates siblings and peers as important agents for teaching social aggression (Patterson, 1980b; Patterson, Littman, & Bricker, 1967). The ideal training situation has a supply of vulnerable victims, such as younger siblings, and some effective models, such as an antisocial older sibling or parent. This would be compounded if the parent is inept in managing coercive interchanges. If this scenario is correct, then the antisocial child would most likely be a middle child, the second most likely being either the youngest or oldest. Only-children should be the least likely. These *post hoc* speculations are consistent with the findings from reviews of the literature. The highly aggressive child tends to be the middle child (Rutter et al., 1970; Anderson, 1969). Rutter's data showed that 48.6% of antisocial children were in the middle ordinal rank; a comparable figure for that position for the control group was 22.2%. As compared to the control group, youngest and only-children were underrepresented in the antisocial group.

Aggression as a Trait

As used here, the term "trait" refers to a disposition to respond which is somewhat stable across time and settings. The studies reviewed in this section represent a substantial body of literature which supports this contention. This is somewhat contradictory to the well known findings presented in Mischel's (1968) early formulation. The studies he reviewed at that time demonstrated little consistency across time and no consistency across settings for traits such as aggression. Developments since then have caused Mischel (1979) to modify his earlier extreme position; but his dramatic (1968) statement served a useful function as a goad for research in this area.

The samples upon which Mischel based his (1968) formulation were essentially normal. The present writer would argue that children at the extremes (95th percentile or greater) on traits such as withdrawal or antisocial do *not* outgrow these behaviors. I also believe that these children are consistent across settings in their practice. Their style of coping with social situations is such that people react to them in a highly predictable manner. These reactions, in turn, "maintain" the withdrawn or antisocial behavior across time and settings. The traits constitute a kind of "life style," or at least a consistent orientation towards social interaction. It appears that the pattern of the "difficult child" is discernible at a very early age. For example, the MacFarlane et al. (1962) longitudinal study showed a correlation of .73 ($df = 32$, $p < .001$) between the total number of problems at age 6 and at age 14.

The issues raised by Mischel (1968, 1979) require answers. The sections which follow review the studies related to the stability of the trait of aggression across time and settings.

Stability of Coercive Behaviors Across Time

It is assumed that the coercive child becomes highly skilled in the use of aversive events to alter his immediate social environment. In this fashion, he alters the ongoing social behaviors of other persons with whom he interacts.[5] With maturation, the *mode* of coercion might change; but his commitment to using these techniques at high rates (above 95th percentile) remains relatively constant.[6] As he acquires verbal skill he might, for example, replace whining, crying, and yelling with sarcasm and argumentativeness. A later section will present data which shows that the antisocial child is retarded in the development of many social skills. This further locks him into the necessity of using coercive means to impact his environment. Gradually, an increasing number of people report experiencing him as unpleasant. At this point he is finally labeled "deviant."

It is assumed that extremely coercive children will persist in using coercive techniques over time. Presumably these techniques maximize short-term

Figure 2.3
Stability Correlations as a Function of Age at First Test and Follow-up Interval
(from Olweus, 1979)

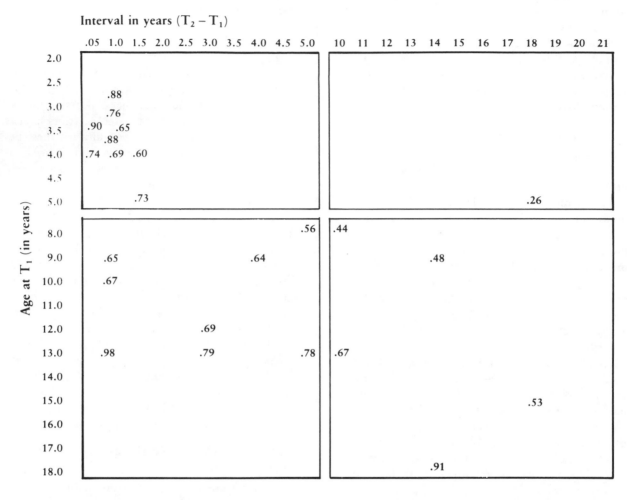

payoffs and are unlikely to be given up unless the child is trained in delay of gratification *and* in pro-social techniques for bringing about changes in other persons. After the age of 9 or 10, special training by the family and/or community is very unlikely. The extremely coercive child, therefore, is very likely to become an extremely coercive adult.

D. Olweus (1976, 1979) has performed the useful service of pulling together 16 studies of children's aggression which employed a longitudinal design. His review covered samples ranging in age from kindergarten to high-school-aged students. The follow-up periods ranged from 6 months to 10 years. The measurement procedures varied from observation, peer sociometric, to parent and teacher ratings. The findings consistently demonstrated the stability of children's aggression across these time intervals. The mean stability correlation across these studies was .63; the mean interval for the retesting was 5.7 years. Figure 2.3 summarizes the data from these studies. Some studies employed measures of aggression at several different intervals. All of these findings are included. As Olweus points out, the evidence for test-retest stability for measures of aggression is on a par with comparable measures for children's intelligence. As a general case, I think an argument can be made for the long-term stability of measures of aggression after the ages of 5 or 6. For example, the early study by Kagan and Moss (1962) showed a correlation of .61 ($df = 87$, $p < .001$) between assessments at age 6 and at age 14 of child aggression toward mother. The comparable correlation for behavioral disorganization (cry, temper, destruction, rages) was .52 for boys and $-.03$ for

Table 2.7
Stability of Extremely Aggressive Subjects

Given a peer sociometric aggressive score at Grade 3, at or above the:	Then at ten year follow up the proportion of subjects at or above:	
	the same percentile for Grade 13	the *median* for Grade 13
95th percentile	38.5%	100%
90th percentile	32.0%	88%
85th percentile	32.3%	79%

girls. A study by Gersten et al. (1976) also supports this hypothesis. In their study, 732 children ranging in age from 6 to 18 years were followed for five years. Data were obtained from interviews with their mothers. The findings again showed impressive stability for cluster scores on aggression (correlation .50) and for delinquency (correlation .44). Of even greater interest was the finding that there is greater stability for these conduct-problem clusters than for the neurotic clusters. In fact, the authors suggested that neurotic disabilities were best left untreated, letting spontaneous remission receive due credit as the treatment agent.

We would expect to find that the more extreme the child's aggression score, the more extreme the child's aggression at follow-up. This hypothesis is contrary to the idea that extreme scores tend to regress toward the mean. The reason for believing this hypothesis lies in the assumption that extremely deviant persons, whether antisocial, depressed, or schizophrenic, *reprogram* their social environments. There are two lines of support for this idea.

The first set of findings are from the ten year follow-up study of Eron et al. (1971, 1974). They obtained peer sociometric ratings at Grade 3 and again at Grade 13. The stability correlation for aggression was a modest .38 ($p < .001$). I assume that the extremely antisocial children were the main contributors to this covariation. I reanalyzed their data to test the hypothesis that the upper 5% or 10% of the coercive boys would be highly stable across time. The alternative hypothesis would be that children with the most extreme scores would be the most likely to demonstrate the phenomenon of regression toward the mean. As shown in Table 2.7, boys at the 95th percentile at Grade 3 had a .38 chance of being at, or above, the same percentile ten years later! Ten years later, *all* of the children rated at the 95th percentile in Grade 3 were perceived as being above the sample mean on the trait aggressive.

These studies assert that extremely coercive

children do not "outgrow" their problems. The extremely deviant child may train others to react to him in such a way as to maintain his deviant status; but I think there are also several other factors which contribute to this continuity. First, there are the previously noted social skill deficits thought to characterize some antisocial children. These deficits have implications for one's ability to form lasting relations, and for one's ability to make a living. Given extreme deviance plus social skill deficits, then the extremely antisocial child would be likely to grow up to be an adult who, at *best*, makes a marginal adjustment. The findings from the large-scale, 14-year, follow-up study by West and Farrington (1973) were in keeping with these speculations. A boy rated by teachers as extremely aggressive at age 9 had a .14 chance of being a *violent* adolescent delinquent! In fact, 70% of the violent adolescent delinquents had been rated as aggressive at age 13; 48% had received this rating at age 9. The findings are being replicated and extended by the programmatic studies of children at risk at UCLA (Rodnick & Goldstein) and at Minnesota (Garmezy). M. Shea (1972) described a large-scale follow-up study by A.J. Hafner and W. Quast of clients referred to the psychiatry section of the University of Minnesota Medical School. A sample of 284 adolescents referred for general medical conditions were also followed up. Ninety-two percent were located and interviewed. The follow-up interview as adults (mean age 38 years) covered areas of family life, social, educational, sexual, marital, and occupational experience. In addition, records were obtained from the schools, military, court, prison, FBI, Veterans Administration, and hospitals. The data available from their initial hospital contacts were categorized by the system described by Achenbach (1966) into Externalizers (antisocial) and Internalizers (excessive inhibition, anxiety, psychosomatic). The externalizing male adolescents tended, as adults, to have behavior or personality disorders. They were also more likely to be committed to correctional hospitals, have a lower social status, and lower occupational level.

The first follow-up study at OSLC was reported by Moore, Chamberlain, and Mukai (1979). They studied over 200 families referred to OSLC since 1968, in which the problem child was age 14 at follow-up. These families were followed each year after termination of treatment to determine whether a police contact occurred. The data showed that referred boys (mean age 9.8 years) who engaged in high-rate stealing tended to be greatly at risk for being picked up by the police by the age of 14; the likelihood was .84. In fact, 67% of these young Stealers became *chronic offenders*.

Early in the 1960's, there was a series of retrospective studies which related childhood antisocial patterns, especially those leading to poor peer relations, to later adult problems such as dishonorable discharge from the military (Roff, 1972, 1961; Roff, Robins, & Pollack, 1972). Retrospective studies of adults in psychiatric hospitals, with prior admission to child guidance clinics, focused the findings more clearly. Pritchard and Graham (1966) showed that conduct problems in childhood were associated with adult problems ranging from depression and antisocial character disorders to inadequate personality. The antisocial child was most likely to be identified as an antisocial adult. The classic study by Robins (1966) compared 524 children studied at a child guidance clinic with a matched sample of nonreferred children from the same area. As adults, 71% of the antisocial group had been arrested, 11% had been diagnosed as psychotic, 22% were sociopathic, and 70% were divorced. Only 20% of the antisocial group showed adequate adjustment as adults. In passing, it should be noted that if the father was antisocial, there was a considerable increase in the likelihood of the child exhibiting antisocial behavior as an adult. Furthermore, when these antisocial children later had families there was an increased likelihood that their offspring would, in turn, display high rates of antisocial behavior.

Stability Across Settings[7]

It wasn't until the 1960's that systematic observation data were collected in settings other than nursery schools. The classic field studies by R. Barker and his colleagues left little doubt that children behaved differently in different settings (Barker, 1963; Barker et al., 1962). In the late 1960's Mischel's challenging statement called attention to the fact that most contemporary personality theorists had not properly addressed questions concerning the impact of settings upon behavior:

"Although behavior patterns often may be stable, they usually are not highly generalized across situations." (Mischel, 1968, p. 281)

Somehow the effect of this stance has been translated into an adversarial *either* situational *or* personality disposition. The writer's own perspective on the "debate" which ensued is stated by Lazarus and Lanier (1978) as follows:

"In response to Mischel's (1968) challenge that situational rather than personality factors by and large determine behavior, there has been much current debate (cf. Endler & Magnusson, 1976) about what seems to us to be a pseudo-issue that, one might have thought, had already been disposed of long ago. Aside from mobilizing analytic thought and serving as a refresher course on the complexities of human behavior, the debate merely capitulates extreme ideological positions long ago referred to by Murphy (1947) as the 'organism error' and the 'situational error.' We would have supposed that most personality and social psychologists, regardless of their own particular interests, had by now implicitly or explicitly accepted a multifactorial and interactional view of the determinants of human action and reaction (see also Pervin's discussion of the centralists and peripheralists) . . ." (p. 287)

The author feels that the early researchers were misled by investigating a pseudo-issue. The question of stability should be cast in interactional terms. From that position a child's coercive performance score is a joint function of what the child brings to a setting and the manner in which the setting is programmed by adults.

From the social interaction perspective, it is the adult who determines what *level* of child aggression is allowable, e.g., usually very little in the classroom but more of it on the playground. Adults control the aggression level for a setting by effectively imposing negative sanctions for *prototypes* of deviant behavior.[8] For the eleven classrooms observed in the Patterson et al. (1972) study, the mean likelihood of inappropriate behavior for *normal* peers ranged from .41 to .11! (The mean was .25). These considerable differences suggest that there are very different levels of control being exerted by teachers. Mothers also vary in the limits that they set for aggressive behavior in their homes. As a result, if one observed 50 antisocial boys in each of their classrooms and homes and then calculated the across-settings correlations, it would almost certainly be close to zero. Fifty mothers set the performance limits in the home and 50 teachers set the limits for their classrooms. There is no reason to expect that a given mother/teacher pair will set similar levels. From a social interaction point of view, performance level is primarily "in the setting" and only secondarily "in the child." Observation data collected in the homes and classrooms for problem children demonstrated low-positive to zero-order correlation in *rates* of deviant behviors across settings (Patterson, Cobb, & Ray, 1972; Bernal et al., 1976; Johnson, Bolstad, & Lobitz, 1976).

Correlating *performance* scores from classrooms and homes generates little or no evidence for stability across settings. These findings are in keeping with Mischel's (1968) position. However, if coercive performance level is primarily determined by the adults present, then how is one to test the claim that extremely aggressive children are "stable" across settings? The interactional viewpoint suggests two hypotheses: 1) the antisocial child's *rank among his peers* with respect to his performance of aggressive behavior is stable across settings; and 2) there is stability *among responses* across settings.

To test the first hypothesis one can calculate the child's relative ranking among his peers for aggressive behavior in each of two settings. It would be expected that the extremely aggressive child would rank high in both settings. Adults in both settings should label the child as deviant because of his high status within his own group. Most epidemiological studies find that about 10% of a sample of school-aged children are "disturbed." By chance, a child would be labeled as deviant in two settings about 1% of the time. In point of fact, the data show that a child *labeled* as deviant in the home has a good chance of receiving the same label in the school. The converse is also true. For example, of 27 boys actually shown to have conduct behavior problems in the home, 52% were also claimed to have social and/or academic problems in the classroom (Patterson, 1976). Johnson et al. (1976) observed the classroom behavior of a small sample of children identified as having conduct problems at home. The observation data indicated that 50% of these children were deviant in the classroom as well. Forty-five percent of the children referred for conduct problems in the classroom were also shown to be deviant in their interactions with members of their families. This overlap is considerably more than would be expected by chance. An even higher percentage was found in a comparable study by Moore (1975). However, in another study, only one in five disruptive children in the classroom were observed to be deviant in the home (Walker, Hops, & Johnson, 1975).

The second hypothesis is concerned with intra-individual consistency across settings *among responses*. Coercive response hierarchies exist because they produce predictable reactions from other people. Given that these reactions are consistent, then the ordinal rankings among coercive responses should be stable across settings. A simple means for testing this hypothesis would require that the same child be observed in both home and school settings; a ranking of the coercive responses actually used in the two settings should demonstrate significant correlations. Thus, if a given child whines at very high rates at home, this should also be his "favorite" technique even in a well-run nursery school. While he may whine very little in the nursery school, it should nevertheless be his most favored coercive ploy.

In the first study, two deviant boys from the OSLC sample were observed at home and at school. For one child the rho for the rankings of 20 coercive responses across the two settings was .73 ($df = 19, p < .01$) and for the other .87 ($df = 19, p < .01$). These data suggest that the coercive response that was most preferred in one setting tended to be the one most frequently employed in the other. However, findings from two subjects hardly constitute a confirmation of the hypothesis. It is, therefore, heartening to report that A. Harris and J. Reid (in preparation) have replicated the effect for a sample of 53 normal children observed in the classroom and on the playground. The mean correlation was .68 (range from .042 to .96).

While the performance scores for the aggressive child may vary, he receives the same ranking among his peers and is consistent in his use of particular coercive responses in setting after setting. The data relating to these two hypotheses lend support to the idea that aggressiveness is a trait that is relatively stable across settings.

The more general hypothesis that extremely aggressive children show consistency *across settings and time* received indirect support from the analysis of OSLC data files by Kirkpatrick (1978). Her analysis of the community follow-up data showed that children who committed police offenses by age 14 had, at age 9, been labeled as deviant in *both* the home and school settings. M. Rutter (personal communication) also reported that children who were identified as antisocial in both home and school settings had the poorest prognosis for later adjustment.

Some Dimensions of Antisocial Behavior[9]

Ordinarily, a wide spectrum of behaviors are subsumed under the terms "antisocial" or "conduct problem." For example, teasing, firesetting,

Table 2.8
Results from Correlational Analyses of Referral Symptoms for Two Samples

Studies	Unsocialized Aggressive		(Socialized) Delinquent	
Jenkins & Hewitt, 1944		Mean Correlation		Mean Correlation
	Destructive at school	.41	Stealing	.53
	Violence	.37	Truant from home	.51
	Fighting	.35	Truant from school	.48
	Quarrels	.34	Police arrest	.48
	Destructive	.33	Stays out at night	.44
	Incorrigible	.32	Bad companions	.42
	Boastfulness	.32	Gang running	.39
	Teasing	.32	Loitering	.37
	Expulsion from school	.31	Lying	.36
	Unpopularity	.31		

	Aggressive		Delinquent	
Achenbach, 1978		Mean factor loading		Mean factor loading
	Argues	.71	Steals outside home	.70
	Disobedient at home	.66	Steals at home	.67
	Temper tantrums	.64	Destroys things belonging to others	.57
	Fighting	.61	Vandalism	.54
	Cruel to others	.60	Sets fires	.50
	Teases	.56	Truant	.48
	Shows off	.55	Runs away	.48
	Loud	.51	Bad friends	.44
	Disobedient at school	.51	Lies, cheats	.44
	Screams	.49	Swears	.37
	Swears	.46	Disobedient at school	.31
	Poor peer relations	.45		
	Brags	.45		
	Lies, cheats	.43		
	Moody	.43		
	Demands attention	.41		
	Unliked	.40		

disobedience, stealing, fighting, truancy, and temper tantrums would all fit into these categories. The parents of the children referred for treatment at OSLC reported an average of three to four of these "symptoms." The pattern seemed to vary widely from one child to another. From the beginning, it became apparent that children labeled as antisocial really constituted a very heterogeneous group. This was of immediate concern because it seemed likely that different subgroups would require not only different "explanations" but different treatments.

The traditional literature was examined for insight into these issues. In the classic studies by Jenkins and Hewitt (1944) and Jenkins and Glickman (1946), the data consisted of the referral problems abstracted from case files for 500 referrals to a Michigan child guidance clinic. There were a number of clusters of problem behaviors identified by correlation analysis. Two were of particular interest. One, *Unsocialized Aggressive,* described 10.4% of the cases and was comprised of abrasive events found in social interaction. The other described rule-breaking behaviors; it was labeled *Socialized Delinquent.* Table 2.8 gives the mean correlation of each symptom with other members of the cluster for the Jenkins and Hewitt study. The referral problems are ordered by the magnitude of the correlations.

The behaviors defining the *Social Aggressive Cluster* have two very important characteristics in common. Almost all of them would be experienced by others as aversive. Furthermore, they have both a direct social impact and a victim. Secondly, they occur at sufficiently high rates so that they could be observed in the home, e.g., quarrels, teasing, and boastfulness. However, the behaviors listed under the *Delinquent Cluster* were not necessarily events one could observe as the child's immediate *reaction to* another person. In addition, stealing, truancy, staying out late at night, and loitering are all low base-rate events. They may occur once a week, or at most, a few times each day. Certainly they did not lend themselves to the usual observation formats.

In their replication study, Jenkins and Glickman (1946) used behavior ratings from 300 institutionalized delinquents. The findings extended and essentially replicated the original work. The work stimulated many other investigators to become committed to the problem and to search for convergence across age groups, settings, and various modes of data collection. This literature has been carefully reviewed by Quay (1965), who was also one of the most prolific contributors to this field. His review underscored the general consistency of the findings in this area. The two factors (Social Aggressive and Delinquent) appeared in study after study.

Achenbach's programmatic work began in 1966. It constitutes the most rigorous and large-scale effort to date. He carried out a careful analysis of case study material for 300 male and 300 female patients from a child psychiatry department. Seventy-four symptoms were intercorrelated and the data subjected to a principle-factor method of analysis. The analyses produced a bipolar principle factor, *Internalizing-Externalizing,* and a unipolar second-principle factor labeled *Severe* and *Diffuse Psychopathology.* This pilot study led, in turn, to the development of a parent checklist which samples social competence, school performance, social activities, and problem behaviors (Achenbach, 1966, 1978). Systematic work has been carried out for different age groups and separately by sex; further studies are in progress.

For the 1978 study, data were available for 450 problem boys. Of the nine factors derived, two were more germane to the present discussion. The factor loadings for these two are summarized in Table 2.8. Not only were these current findings related to the narrow-band factors in his earlier work, they also look surprisingly consistent with the work carried out 30 years earlier by Jenkins and Hewitt (1944). The systematic work by Achenbach and his colleagues lends itself nicely to the identification of "types" of antisocial children. The distribution of scores for each factor has been normalized and converted to *T*-scores. Thus, one can construct typologies based upon profiles that

are defined by the available factor scores. Of particular interest are the children high on Achenbach's Aggression and Delinquent factors. They seem to describe two very different kinds of cases referred for treatment at OSLC. In fact, the many antisocial children referred to OSLC could be ordered along these dimensions.

When the family comes to OSLC for the intake interview, the parents are asked to select from a checklist those problem behaviors which are of most concern to them, i.e., those which they wish to change during treatment. The checklist is provided in the book by Patterson, Reid, Jones, and Conger (1975). It was modified somewhat and standardized by Chamberlain (1980). In her extensive study, 65 parents of normal children identified problems each day for a 12-day baseline from a 34-item checklist. For the ten families where the mothers and fathers gave independent reports on problems of concern to them (targeted), the correlation between parents was .89 ($df = 8$, $p < .001$). The hierarchical-cluster analyses of the reported frequencies produced four clusters. The first three clusters are presented in Table 2.9. They are consistent with the earlier findings which employed clinical samples. Her two clusters, Aggressive and Immature, intercorrelate .50 ($df = 63$, $p < .001$) and define what I mean by *Social Aggression.* Her third cluster, Unsocialized, defines what I mean by *Stealer.* The children studied at OSLC are, on the average, 8 to 9 years of age, a bit young to be called (Unsocialized) Delinquent. For this reason, the term Stealer[10] is used throughout this volume.

These rather consistent differentiations into *types* of antisocial behavior are in keeping with our clinical experience. There, too, the treatment of Stealers proved to be a very different matter than did the treatment of Social Aggressors (Reid & Patterson, 1976). The first look at family interaction data also convinced us that families which produce Stealers may be quantitatively different from both Normals and from Social Aggressors. The analysis by Reid and Hendricks (1973) showed them to be more coercive than Normals but less than Social Aggressors in their interactions with family members. The mothers of Stealers were shown to be less friendly than mothers of either normal or socially aggressive boys. This pilot study was replicated and extended by the findings summarized in Chapter 11.

It appears that the Stealer and Social Aggressor patterns share a common base. In fact, the base occurs so often for *all* of these children that it may not show up consistently in correlational analyses. The base is that the parents allow all of the antisocial children to disobey, that is, to be *noncompliant*. For example, .89 of the 142 antisocial children were described by their parents as being disobedient (from Table 11.1). In their observation study of problem children, Griest et al. (1979) found a correlation of .50 ($p < .05$) between the likelihood of Noncomply and the number of problem behaviors.

Given that the child is disobedient, most families insist that he specialize in one antisocial pattern.

Table 2.9
Symptom Clusters
and Reliability Coefficients

(from Chamberlain, 1980)

Chamberlain's Items			Loadings
Aggression	Alpha = .88	Beta = .79	
Yell			.759
Run around			.743
Talk back			.721
Aggressive			.687
Noisy			.677
Argue			.674
Defiance			.621
Noncompliance			.618
Immature	Alpha = .80	Beta = .71	
Complain			.748
Whine			.696
Irritable			.670
Pout			.568
Temper tantrum			.567
Negative			.523
Unsocialized	Alpha = .65	Beta = .46	
Hyperactive			.765
Parent hits			.580
Stealing			.537
Lying			.428
Bedwetting			.345
School contact			.294

---

tern or another. Parents of problem children will *vehemently* reject some kinds of antisocial behavior, e.g., "No kid of mine would get away with stealing." However, the same father may accept hitting and temper tantrums with equanimity. Very few parents allow *all* of the symptoms to occur. In that regard, J. Tuppin, University of California at Davis (personal communication) mentioned that in his retrospective studies of multiple murderers, he found that as children they showed a combination of firesetting, bed wetting, and hyperactivity!

However, the assumption is that regardless of which antisocial pattern(s) the parents allow, all antisocial children will be described as basically *disobedient*, i.e., *out of control.* For example, in one study of referrals to the OSLC clinic, the likelihood of Steal as a complaint given the occurrence of Disobedient was a conditional p of .56. Better than half of the children who disobeyed were *also* viewed as Stealers. Given Disobey as a complaint, the likelihood of Whine was .62; the likelihood of Hit was .64; and the likelihood of Temper Tantrums was .61. The apprenticeship for becoming an antisocial child seems to be a process of learning disobedience.

The Drift Toward
Marginal Adjustment as Adults

As noted earlier, children with severe conduct-problem disorders can be described by their position on two different dimensions. One is a deviancy dimension; and the other dimension refers to the acquisition of social skills. I assume that these variables are negatively correlated; for purposes of discussion, I would think of the magnitude of the covariation as being around $-.4$ to $-.5$.

The deviancy dimension describes the child's position on some measure of antisocial behavior relative to peers of the same age. In the present context, the measure would be parents' reports of persistent stealing or the TAB score based upon observation data. The greater the deviation from the mean, the more likely the child is to be labeled as deviant. However, even if his rates of coercive behavior exceed the 95th percentile, there is little chance that he will be labeled as deviant before the age of 4 or 5. I suspect that the majority of these coercive preschoolers at the 95th percentile are not thought of as deviant by their parents. However, as the problem child penetrates community agencies such as the nursery school, the pediatrician's office, and finally the elementary school, the parents are increasingly likely to be given negative feedback about the behavior of the child. Eventually the school, the court, or neighbors may force the parents to contact community professionals. The OSLC referral data suggest that by the age of 9 or 10 many of these extremely coercive children have been so labeled.

Being labeled deviant is just one stage in the drift towards marginal adjustment as an adult. Labeling, per se, does not *determine* the drift; it is simply an indication that it has occurred. Elliott's

(1979) elegant study showed that for delinquent youths, contact with police or the court (which constitutes being labeled) did not alter their self-perception, nor did it alter other people's evaluation of them. However, being involved in counselling *did* produce negative changes in evaluation.

As the child develops, there are certain social survival skills which parents must teach. In the preschool years these are self-help skills, such as feeding and dressing, toilet training, and solitary play. If the child is delayed in the acquisition of these skills, it is probably of little significance. It means that either the parents are not very effective socializing agents, or the child is, by temperament, difficult to train. These skill deficits are not likely, by themselves, to be highly correlated with the likelihood of later deviancy labeling. If, however, the child is *also* extremely coercive, then the writer assumes that the child has begun a perceptible drift toward marginal adjustment as an adult.

There are two reasons for this assumption. First, as the child becomes increasingly out of control, both peers and adults will reduce the amount of contact with him. They avoid and escape his presence whenever possible because he is thoroughly unpleasant to be around. As a result, the extremely coercive child becomes a "loner." He is, therefore, spending less time in his peer group learning the subtle social skills necessary for adequate survival in the forthcoming adjustment phases. His explosive response to negative feedback is a further block to learning both social and academic skills. Reduced interaction together with his abrasive style makes it increasingly difficult for him to acquire the survival skills he will need later on. The large-scale survey by Achenbach (1978) indicated that parents of deviant children perceived their children to be significantly less competent than did parents of normals. The parents reported less participation in sports, hobbies, jobs and chores; these children had fewer friends and failed more often in school.

Limited exposure to peer socializing influences may be one determinant for deficits in social competencies. Another determinant has to do with reduced responsiveness to positive and negative sanctions. The studies reviewed in Chapters 6 and 11 suggest that aggressive boys were less responsive than nonaggressive boys to both social reinforcers and to punishment provided by *adults*. This would suggest that even when parents do try to use reinforcers to shape prosocial skills, they may be relatively ineffective. The coercive child fails to learn simple work skills at home (chores), then fails to learn academic skills. Later, he fails to learn skills which are necessary to form intimate relationships as an adolescent and adult. These omissions create more situations in which coercive skills may be employed to maximize short-term gains.

It should be noted that not all socially unskilled children become antisocial. Programmatic studies by H. Hops (in preparation) have shown that many unskilled children are withdrawn. Incidentally, some of the studies by Walker and Hops (in preparation) showed that effectively increasing social skill behaviors *did not* reduce the level of deviant behavior for extremely antisocial children. There seem to be two systems, each with its own set of determinants.

Not *all* extremely coercive children are socially unskilled; conversely, not *all* children labeled as unskilled are antisocial. For example, young Stealers or Social Aggressors from some middle-class families might attain academic proficiency. The writer believes that it is the drift toward extreme positions on *both* the deviancy dimension *and* the skill deficit dimension which predicate poor adult adjustment. It is the socially unskilled young Stealer who will most likely continue his offenses against property and may eventually be represented in official police records. The socially skilled Stealer or Coercer is *less likely* to be *labeled as deviant*; his social competencies presumably function as a moderating variable. At present, there are no data available which could test these hypotheses about the interactive nature of coercion level and social skill deficits. There is, however, extensive literature demonstrating that antisocial children are less skilled.

The Early Deficits

The general position taken here fits well with the author's recollection of the stance presented by John E. Anderson just before his retirement as the esteemed Chairman at the University of Minnesota Child Welfare Station. He repeatedly pointed out that children diagnosed as "emotionally disturbed" were really "just socially unskilled people." It was not then, and is not now, a popular position. However, that kind of thinking has recently been applied to a number of problems in "psychopathology," e.g., depressed adults, and withdrawn children. Anderson's common-sense position was supported by the Achenbach (1978) study reported earlier and by a questionnaire study (Ferguson, Partzka, & Lester, 1974). In the latter, an item analysis of questionnaires filled out by a sample of parents of disturbed children and parents of nonreferred families showed that the former perceived their children as lacking social competencies.

Table 2.10
Studies Relating Social Skill Deficits to Antisocial Behavior

Early Management Phase

Investigators	Findings
1. Douglas (1966); Robins (1966); Schlesinger (1978); West and Farrington (1973); Fagan et al. (1977)	1. Antisocial child reported to have had difficulty in training for bowel/bladder control.
2. Kaffman and Elizur (1977)	2. Enuretics more likely than non-enuretics to be rated as deviant, including more aggressive.
3. Wahler and Moore (1975)	3. Inverse correlation between observed nonsocial toy play and occurrence of problem behavior in home.
4. Saxe and Stollak (1971)	4. No correlation solitary play and aggression, mother-child interaction in laboratory.
5. Werner and Smith (1977)	5. Social immaturity on the Vineland during preschool correlated with later delinquency during adolescence. Infant activity at year one and later hyperactivity also correlated with later delinquency.

Peer Relationships

Investigators	Findings
1. Moore (1967)	1. Nursery school children tended to reject aggressive child.
2. Jennings (1950); Olweus (1974); Roff (1972); Rutter et al. (1970)	2. Aggressive children have low acceptance by peers in elementary school.
3. Roff (1961) (1972); Eron et al. (1971); Hirschi (1969); Jenkins and Hewitt (1944); Cureton (1970); West and Farrington (1974)	3. Delinquents have or had poor relations with peers and/or socially immature.
NOTE: McCord (1977); Elliott (1979); Elliott and Voss (1974) did *not* find this relation.	

Work Skills

Investigators	Findings
1. Minton, Kagan, and Levine (1971)	1. Very few antisocial children complete chores at home.
2. Cobb and Hops (1973); Hops and Cobb (1977); Cobb (1970); Hops and Cobb (1974)	2. Aggressive children tend to be low in classroom survival skills, such as attend, volunteer, stay in seat, work at desk.
3. Hirschi (1969); McCord (1977) [trend but not significant] Conger and Miller (1966); Wadsworth (1979)	3. Delinquent children spent less time doing homework or generally have poor work habits.
4. Rutter et al. (1970); Maccoby (1966); Werner and Smith (1977); Benning, Feldhusen, and Thurston (1968); Glairn and Annesly (1971); Graubard (1971); Camp, Zimet, Doomineck, and Dahlm (1977); Wadsworth (1976); Roff (1972); Shea (1972); Cobb (1970); Eron et al. (1971); Scarpitti (1964)	4. Antisocial boys read less well, also perform less well on IQ tests and achievement tests, grades.
5. McCord (1977); Glueck and Glueck (1968); Scarpitti (1964)	5. Antisocial children lower than normals only for nonverbal IQ test. Delinquent children more likely to have dropped out of school and/or be truant.
NOTE: Hirschi (1969) found no relationship.	

It seems that the skill deficits may be apparent at a very early stage in development. As shown in Table 2.10, children diagnosed as antisocial are frequently described as having difficulty with bladder and bowel control training. Does this identify them as constitutionally different and, in some sense, more difficult to train? Many parents who bring their children to OSLC would have us believe so. Or, does this lag in training underscore the effects of rather inept parenting practices?

None of these studies provides a base for choosing one or the other of these two alternatives. At this point, it can only be said that children who are slower in achieving self-control over bowel and bladder may have a greater likelihood of being labeled as antisocial. The large-scale follow-up study by Werner and Smith (1977) also showed that extremely active and socially immature behavior during the preschool years correlated significantly with adolescent delinquency. These children were at risk only if the mother was poorly educated and living under rather chaotic conditions. Active and immature children from intact middle-class families were not at risk for later delinquency.

Later Deficits

Peer relations. There is a general relation between the child's status as deviant and the likelihood of his being rejected by peers (Gottman, Gonso, & Rasmussen, 1975). The sociometric study by Sells and Roff (1967) showed that low peer acceptance was associated with parental reports of disruptive coercive behaviors at home. This general relation has been noted by several writers (Gottman et al., 1975; Lott & Lott, 1965; Taguiri, 1952). Peer rejection was shown by Gottman (1977) to be unrelated to the amount of interaction with peers; rejection was, however, significantly related to *negative* interactions with peers. Hartup (1969) also identified the child's use of aversives as being related to peer acceptance. The child who was accepted also gave more positive reinforcement. As a consequence, the extremely coercive child is very likely to be rejected. In a study of classroom interaction, H. Hops (personal communication) found that children who were disruptive of classroom routines were accepted. The child who was extremely aggressive on the playground was *likely* to be rejected. It seems, then, that rejection implies that the peers *experience* the behavior as being aversive. The study of school bullies by Olweus (1975) showed that it was not aggression per se which related to rejection. The bully directed most of his aggression to preselected targets. His popularity was only slightly diminished by his role as bully.

The study by Gottman et al. (1975) further demonstrates that the nature of the skills involved in producing peer acceptance may vary as a function of social class. His elegant multiple regression analyses of observed interactions showed that skill as a reinforcer accounted for most of the variance in peer acceptance for both middle- and lower-class children. However, for the former it was skill in *verbal* reinforcement that mattered; for lower class children it was skill in nonverbal reinforcement. Incidentally, other variables related to peer acceptance included the amount of off-task behavior and the amount of punishment given.

There is another more subtle sense in which these children do not fit in. The observation of nursery children by Strayer (1977) showed that aggressive children tend to ignore the metastructure in groups. They behaved as if the dominance hierarchy which influences their peers did not exist. This, in turn, would be a constant source of discomfort and annoyance to others.

Until he enters nursery school, the child has minimal contact with his peer group. Then he must learn how to *initiate* interactions and how to respond to those of others. He learns to share, to follow rules in playing games, and to lead without being bossy. With increasing age, these social skills become increasingly subtle, e.g., how to form friendships, how to be a leader, how to become intimate, how to give and receive affection, and how to give and receive criticism. This is the time when he must defend himself against attack by others. Without being devastated, he must learn to deal with another child grabbing his toy.

Apparently a certain amount of skill in aggression is necessary to survive in the nursery school environment. In our culture, the normal preschool child who has developed skills in sharing, cooperation, and leadership will also have learned to be mildly aggressive. However, I think that his rates of aggression are well within normal limits, i.e., less than the 95th percentile. For example, Murphy (1937; cited by Radke-Yarrow & Waxler, 1976) found a consistent positive correlation between nursery school children's aggression and their ability to express sympathy. Henry and Sharpe (1947), Feshbach and Feshbach (1969), Friedrich and Stein (1973), and Barrett and Radke-Yarrow (1977) all found *positive* correlations between observed aggression and prosocial behaviors such as comfort, sharing, and sympathy. The observation study by Radke-Yarrow and Waxler (1976) clarified the problem by demonstrating that these positive correlations were obtained only for nursery school children who performed at *low levels of aggression*. In their study, for boys below the mean in aggression, the correlation between aggression and sharing-comforting was .50 ($p <$ .05) in one setting and .48 ($p < .05$) in another. However, for boys *above* the mean on aggression, the comparable correlations were $-.45$ (n.s.) and $-.19$ (n.s.). One might label lower rates of aggression as "assertiveness" and reserve the term "aggression" for extremely high rates, i.e., the upper 5%. Presumably it was the latter who were identified in the peer sociometric study by Moore (1967). That study showed that the aggressive child tended to be rejected by nursery school peers.

Clinical experience with the several hundred cases referred to OSLC underscores the theme that these are *not* highly skilled children who are effective competitors. They are not the "occasional aggressors" popular among children. On the contrary, the problem child is usually *unskilled* at fist fighting or wrestling; he tends to be an inept competitor. He is usually isolated and rejected by his peer group. The studies cited in Table 2.10 attest to the consistency of this finding in the research literature. Roff (1961, 1972) found that poor peer relations characterized adults who were given dishonorable discharges from the armed forces. Incidentally, Roff and his group also found poor peer relations as a consistent precursor to a wide spectrum of adult psychopathologies.

A number of recent major studies on delinquency have also found that youths officially labeled as delinquents were characterized by poor relations with their peers (Hirschi, 1969). This theme was noted previously in juvenile delinquency research (Jenkins and Hewitt, 1944). The covariation is so reliable that it is now a regular feature in longitudinal studies designed to predict later delinquency. West and Farrington (1973) found that less popular 8- and 9-year-old boys were significantly at risk for *later* delinquency. Roff (1972) found that low peer acceptance was associated with later adolescent delinquency for middle-class but *not* for lower-class boys. In the same study, low peer status was correlated with later status as a school dropout.

Work skills. Two skills required prior to adolescence are critical to adult adjustment. We must learn to relate, and we must learn to work. There is no single source for acquiring either of these skills. The way in which we relate to casual acquaintances and to intimates must be some *joint* function of earlier relations among family members and later peer relations. However, the details of this most important process are only beginning to receive the attention of empirically oriented investigators.

The world of work is not much better understood. In emphasizing this as a crucial skill, the writer is perhaps falling into our cultural stereotype about which values are central; but if one does not solve the problem of income/work, then as individuals our degrees of freedom as decision makers are extraordinarily constrained. Poverty seldom offers freedom of movement or thought. On the other hand, one can be trapped by work it-self to the point where one throws away degrees of freedom, e.g., the type of businessman (or scholar) who becomes so immersed in the work process that he shortens his life.

A priori, there would seem to be a sequence through which most children in middle-class families move. First, there are childhood experiences which provide on-the-job training for work related skills. These fortuitous and/or planned components of the socialization process generally reflect the middle-class commitment to the Protestant work ethic. First the child is taught to pick up his own personal effects and put them away. Later he is expected to keep his room clean and orderly, then to assist in minor household chores. Later still, he may accept responsibility for major tasks. By elementary school age, this might include part-time jobs for pay. In adolescence it might include summer employment. The coercive child meets all of these requests by learning how to escape and avoid them.

The classroom functions as another setting for training in work skills. The very earliest clinical classroom observations of families referred to OSLC showed that these children lacked the skills to adjust to academic demands. Cobb (1970) observed a sample of normal first-grade children in the classroom. He found significant correlations between achievement test scores and "survival skill" scores for boys. These correlations were .71 for reading and .63 for arithmetic. The comparable correlations for girls were lower. The child who was disruptive, nonattending, and noncompliant did less well on the achievement tests. In the next study, Cobb and Hops (1973) trained the teachers to shape survival skills for first-grade children who were deficient in these areas. The training effectively increased both survival skills and achievement test scores for this subgroup of children. They then replicated the effect for an entire first-grade classroom (Hops & Cobb, 1974). In their final study, Hops and Cobb (1977) compared training in survival skills, direct instruction, and a no-treatment control. Both experimental groups showed significantly greater gains on reading achievement tests than did the control group. As might be expected, the gains for direct instruction were greater than those for training in survival skills. This important series of studies emphasized the need to consider *noncognitive survival skills* as they relate to academic achievement. It seems very likely that the conduct-disordered child lacks the skills necessary for adequate performance at even the first-grade level.

There is another thread running through these studies which would be interesting to examine more carefully. The survey study by Rutter et al. (1970) showed a relation between reading difficulties and antisocial behavior. The follow-up study by Werner and Smith (1977) showed a correlation of .24 between a need for remedial education at age 10 and later delinquency.

The remainder of Table 2.10 reads like a litany for failure. As the aggressive child moves through school, the studies reiterate a theme of lower grades and lower scores on achievement tests and IQ tests. As might be expected, there are related findings of early truancy and tardiness and finally dropping out of school.

Self-Perception

Coopersmith (1967) and others affirm that as the child matures, he becomes increasingly capable of differentiating himself from others. The antisocial child receives more aversive input than the other members of his family. He is very likely to be rejected by his peers and to fail in his academic subjects as well. Given such an accumulation of negatives, one would expect that midway through the elementary grades the aggressive child would conclude that he is clearly different from other children. This differentiation should become clearer with age. At some point, the antisocial child would presumably develop a negative image of both self and others.

The research literature is far from complete in its quality or quantity. However, the literature that does exist suggests that the extremely coercive child does *not* assign blame to himself, nor does he see himself as less worthy than others. What he *does* develop is an extremely *negative view of others,* his family, his peers, and eventually the police and the social system itself. His *attitudes* towards others are antisocial; his self-esteem is unimpaired.

Two studies (Magee, 1964; Silverman, 1964; both cited by Feshbach, 1970) showed that aggressive boys had lower self-esteem than did nonaggressive boys. However, in three studies of *normal* children, there was no correlation between aggressiveness and children's self-esteem (Coopersmith, 1967; Eron et al., 1971; Olweus, 1975). Olweus (1975) studied two samples of normal boys ages 13 to 14. They filled out a self-report questionnaire which included a scale, *Positive Self-Report.* The scores on this scale correlated .06 with peer sociometric data scored for *Starts Fights* and −.07 with the score on *Verbal Protest.* The corresponding correlations for the second sample were −.05 and .14 respectively. These findings from this large-scale study showed the tendency to view oneself in a positive light did not covary with

aggressive behavior. Several follow-up studies have also shown very little relation between the child's self-concept and his later delinquency, e.g., Benning et al. (1968). In her intensive follow-up of the Cambridge-Somerville sample, McCord (1977) found that low self-esteem in children did *not* predict later criminal careers. These findings should not surprise us. Questionnaires and interviews given to adult criminals showed that rapists, embezzlers, and auto thieves do not see themselves as criminals (Elliott, Ageton, & Canter, 1979)!

West and Farrington (1973) reviewed four studies which showed that delinquents have more negative self-images than nondelinquents. In one study, delinquents were more prone to endorse such adjectives as bad, dirty, cruel, dangerous, dishonest, and worthless. Several of these studies found a significantly greater loading for delinquents on the bad-evaluation dimension for the Osgood semantic differential. However, in the extensive survey study by West and Farrington (1973), while delinquent-prone youths described themselves as more aggressive, even these findings were not greater than one would expect by chance. These aggressive self-concepts did not predict later delinquency.

It seems that in focusing upon self-esteem, we may have been asking the wrong question. There are two alternatives that seem promising. Garmezy and his colleagues at the University of Minnesota have been studying children who are at risk for psychopathology (Garmezy & Streitman, 1974; Garmezy & Nuechterlein, 1972). Their analyses repeatedly underscore the importance of the child's *feelings of efficacy* in arranging his own life. For the ghetto child, this sense of being in control correlated more highly with achievement test scores than did that venerable variable, socioeconomic status! One wonders if rephrasing the question in this manner wouldn't also differentiate the normal child from the child with a conduct disorder. In clinical situations many antisocial children convey a sense of events moving outside of their control as if they were almost "forced" to strike that other child or take that purse.

In a similar vein, the longitudinal study by West and Farrington (1973) strongly implicates the essentially antisocial *attitude* toward others, particularly toward the police, as being an important concomitant of early antisocial patterns. This misanthropic view is reiterated in the large-scale survey by Olweus (1975). A factor analysis of a large pool of self-report items generated three which related to aggression. There is a self-righteous quality to these answers, a commitment to violence as a solution to problems. In some ways the antisocial child is a caricature of the cultural emphasis upon the rugged individualist. There is no sense of uncertainty or doubt. He stands against the tide, resisting all onslaughts upon his individualism. His victims deserve what they get. For him there is no existential anxiety. He is a hero. Failure in school is not his doing: "It is a lousy school." Being rejected by peers is not his fault: "Those kids are snobs; they don't know anything." There are conflicts at home: "They pick on me all the time." It is not *him*; it is *their fault*. He has no control over what teachers do or over what victims do. These victims are the objects of his contempt, but they are not a matter for his concern.

Conclusion

Children's antisocial behaviors were shown to be a heterogeneous set of symptoms. For convenience in studying these problems, the focus in the present volume is upon two patterns thought to be "homogeneous." These groups are labeled as Stealers and Social Aggressors. These patterns describe children who maximize immediate payoffs at another's expense. In either case, it is assumed that a labeled deviant child is an example of "arrested socialization"; e.g., his abrasive and/or thieving behavior is simply something which his family accepted and allowed to persist. The children at the extremes do *not* outgrow these problems. These are personality traits which are relatively stable across time and across settings.

For many antisocial children there is an accompanying deficit of social skills. The relative social incompetency increases with age. Deviancy and social skills are thought to interact in defining marginal adjustment as an adult. This interactive process is labeled "deviancy drift."

The family processes relating to stealing are thought to be different from those which determine socially aggressive behaviors. The remainder of this book will focus upon how family processes relate to social aggression and to a lesser extent, stealing.

Acknowledgments

The writer wishes to acknowledge the contribution of the writing seminars in which earlier versions of this chapter were critiqued. My colleague, Rolf Loeber, made numerous suggestions for improving later drafts. I particularly wish to thank Professor D. Olweus whose detailed comments produced many changes in the manuscript.

Footnotes

1. The label deviant or aggressive is not, of course, *always* earned. Analyses of the first sample of 27 families referred to OSLC for treatment showed that 11% were false-positive errors (Patterson, 1974a). Referral sources cited problems occurring either at home and/or school. However, neither observation or Parent Daily Report data in the home, nor observation in the classroom demonstrated above normal rates for problem behaviors.

2. Hartup (1973) and others have noted that while overall measures of aversive behaviors may decrease, what this really reflects is a reduction in the frequency of physical aggression. The same data showed *increases* in frequency of verbal aggression with age. Green (1933) reported a similar increase in verbal aggression for preschool children.

3. For the present analysis, only one child in each family contributed a TAB score. Wherever possible, the score was selected which described the youngest child in the normal family. This allowed a somewhat better description of normal preschool children than we would otherwise have obtained.

4. Rutter and others also noted that neurotic reactions in children were associated with smaller families. There was a tendency for these children to be an only child. The latter finding was also noted by Anderson (1969).

5. It is hypothesized that when a child coerces, the prosocial behavior of the other person becomes more predictable. The findings relating to this issue are reviewed in Chapters 6 and 7. Presumably the prosocial reactions of family members are more uncertain, or at least their sustained positive reactions are less likely. If this is true, then the function of a child's coercive behavior is to reduce this particular uncertainty. Ironically, his efforts to make others more predictable in the long run insure the *stability of his own traits to be coercive!*

6. The question is, how should one determine which 6-year-olds are above the 95th percentile? McCaffrey and Cummings (1967) introduced a refinement in the assessment that bears upon this issue. They interviewed 164 teachers to identify in each classroom those considered to be problems. Twelve percent were identified as having problems of some kind. Thirty percent of these were again identified as problem children when teachers in the next classroom were interviewed in the ensuing two years. A sequence of two probes separated by a year might be a more powerful way of identi-

fying children at risk for later adjustment problems as adolescents.

7. Many of the ideas here are the outcome of extended discussions with the contumacious Alice Harris. Her persistent refusal to understand my perfectly lucid position led to extensive revisions of earlier hypotheses.

8. Martens and Russ (1932) showed that parents of normal and problem children report the *same kinds* of concerns. In fact, the rho between rankings of frequencies for various child behaviors was .90. The samples, however, differed in the overall rates with which problems occurred: a mean of 3.63 for problem and 1.3 for nonproblem children. Incidentally, Shepherd, Oppenheim, and Mitchell (1966) *excluded severe acting out cases* and showed *no* difference between frequencies in listings of parental concerns for normal and problem children.

Survey studies showed surprising consistency even across cultures in the incidence of certain conduct problem behaviors among normal families. For example, stealing in 10- to 11-year-old boys was 5.7% for Rutter's sample in the Isle of Wight study (1970) and 4% in the MacFarlane et al. (1968) California sample. The rates of parents reporting concerns about lying were 15% and 16% respectively; disobedience was 31.5% and 22%. Such consistency may be coincidental but seems worthy of note.

9. Roach (1958) reported that antisocial problems constituted the largest single basis for referral to child guidance clinics. Similarly, cases referred by teachers for treatment consisted of assaultive (30.9%) and delinquent (30.6%) (Rogers, Lilienfeld, & Pasamancek, 1954). The extensive survey by Rutter et al. (1970) showed that for the disturbed 9- and 10-year-old group, 41% were diagnosed as conduct problems; another 27% consisted of a mixed pattern of neurotics *plus* acting out. Thus the majority (68%) of psychiatric problems involved conduct problems as a major, or at least secondary, consideration.

10. The covariation between hyperactive and Steal, Lie, Bed Wet, and School Contact was a surprise. The children in Chamberlain's sample were, on the average, 7 years of age. Is hyperactivity in the very young 4- or 5-year-old a precursor for later problems relating to Steal? I've not encountered this relation before. However, I notice that in Achenbach (1978) the item Hyperactive loads upon a variable of the same name.

Chapter 3

Observations of Family Process[1]

The observation devices currently used at OSLC represent almost two decades of evolution. These data collection systems were developed in response to a need for an assessment methodology which could accurately measure changes in family interaction. In the 1960's we began with exhaustive narrative accounts of family interaction, but this data collection technique was extremely cumbersome. The next step was to develop an item pool for a standard coding system that sampled discrete units of deviant and coercive behavior. To accomplish this, we spent time in the homes of both normal families and families with antisocial children. In terms of clinical impressions, these two groups were sharply delineated; being an observer in one home was a very different experience from observing in another. The function of the code that emerged was to reflect these differences in family interaction. Eventually, there was a consensus among staff members that the code categories adequately described *aversive* behaviors in family interaction. However, we knew at the time that our coverage of prosocial interactions was far from complete.

After three years and six revisions, the Family Interaction Coding System (FICS) was ready for application as an assessment device (January, 1968). By that time, the preliminary psychometric evaluations had been completed and the results were promising (Reid, 1967). Since then, the FICS

has been used to measure family interactions in over 200 families with aggressive children and 60 families of matched normals.

As we began to use the new code it quickly became apparent that it was necessary to assess family interaction at many different *levels*. The FICS seemed uniquely adapted to the description of the molecular structure of interaction sequences; but it was a clumsy and inefficient method for sampling low base-rate events. Given that the key referral problem for half of our sample was stealing and/or fire-setting this quickly generated a crisis. This exigency led to the introduction of the Parent Daily Report (PDR); data was collected by contacting the parents daily for a report on specific problem behaviors that had occurred during the previous 16 hours.

The purpose of this chapter is to review the development of the FICS and PDR as assessment devices. Particular emphasis has been given to the methodological problems which are inherent in these data collection systems. The psychometric properties of both devices are also discussed.

Prior Observation Approaches

Reviews of early applications of observation methodologies with children (e.g., Wright, 1960) reflect a narrow conception of the scope and scientific usefulness of observation procedures. Not only were early observational studies limited primarily to preschool subjects, but the settings sampled were, for the most part, restricted to nursery schools. In addition, the data consisted of simple frequency counts. As Wright (1960) pointed out, such gross descriptive data simply did not allow for precise hypothesis testing. In fact, these early studies generated few hypotheses about children's social behaviors. The main contributions of these early observational investigations were their sophisticated studies of the psychometric problems involved in the collection of observation data. Analyses by Thomas, Loomis, and Arrington (1933) of observer reliability, stability of event sampling, and observer error were models in this regard. Although crude by today's standards, the data collected in these early studies merit closer review than they have received. Some of the findings relate to current issues and theories. For example, an incidental finding reported in the classic study by Goodenough (1930) showed that situational changes produced differential effects on behavior.

Early work in the development of observation techniques, except in the area of child psychology, was astonishingly unsophisticated regarding the measurement problems inherent in the collection of observation data. This is reflected in a review by Heyns and Lippitt (1954), which points out that the problems of event sampling, observer presence, observer bias, observer drift, sequential dependencies, and validity had *hardly been considered,* much less investigated. Certainly, the generation of investigators trained in the 50's and 60's in the complex problems of response bias, social desirability, test-retest reliability, internal reliability, itemetrics, and construct validity could hardly be expected to take seriously a branch of science that ignored these realities. Recent reviews of observation techniques by Wiggins (1973), Johnson and Bolstad (1973), and Jones, Reid, and Patterson (1975) take the position that *all* of the traditional psychometric puzzles are found within the observation methodologies. Jones (1973) suggests that there are, in fact, additional problems raised by observation methodologies for which traditional assessment literature has no answers.

In the early 1950's, Roger Barker and his colleagues devised a methodology that included descriptions of the environment *as it interacted with the child* (e.g., Barker, 1951, 1968; Barker & Wright, 1954; Willems & Raush, 1969). This was a significant development in that Barker was one of the first to adopt an interactive position. In the two and a half decades following the publication of Barker's *One Boy's Day* (1951), data were collected over a broad range of settings in both the USA and England. The range of subjects and behaviors was expanded far beyond the limits of the nursery school classroom. Barker and his group emphasized the necessity of collecting data relating to such macro-units as Behavior Episodes, Behavioral Settings, and Environmental Force Units. Observation data were collected in narrative form. It was assumed that discrete units of "behavior" occurred in nature and could be identified by examining these narrative accounts. The hypotheses generated by these data were of sufficient quality that by the mid-1960's, reviews of the literature were optimistic about the utility of this approach. Furthermore, the large number of hypotheses tested by these data seemed to attest to the power of this approach.

Recent observational studies (e.g., Bobbitt et al., 1969; Caldwell, 1971) differ from the pioneering efforts of Barker and his colleagues. Rather than stressing exhaustive narrative reports of interaction, the emphasis is upon tailoring the code systems to test hypotheses about limited aspects of behavior. Rather than simply analyzing event frequencies, behavior is examined for interdependencies with environmental events. The theories which emerge are interaction theories. Our experience in developing the FICS suggests that a coding system must be tailor-made for each setting and perhaps for each purpose. As a result, it appears unlikely that it will ever be possible to develop an omnibus coding system that could sensitively measure all child behaviors in all settings. The FICS primarily samples coercive behaviors that are used among family members. The data that are generated lend themselves to the analyses of changes in rates of specific behaviors that are of clinical interest. They also lend themselves to analyses of more complex units such as the frequency with which a parent responds punitively to a specific kind of child behavior (e.g., Taplin & Reid, 1977). Of even greater interest are the data showing changes in the behavior of dyad members as a function of extended interaction chains (e.g., Patterson, 1974c).

Parent Report as an Assessment Device

Our approach to family therapy stresses the need for *change* in intervention procedures (Patterson, Reid, Jones, & Conger, 1975). The reason for this emphasis lies in the fact that the best existing procedures meet only the minimal requirements for effective treatment of problem children. Although outcome studies have shown that many severely aggressive children can be helped by the present procedures (Patterson, 1974a, 1974b, 1975b; Reid & Patterson, 1976), a significant minority realize no measurable benefits. In addition, two follow-up studies suggest that some parents slip back or retain many of their earlier modes of interacting with their children (Patterson, 1976; Taplin & Reid, 1977). Although a perfectly effective treatment for aggressive children is unlikely, the odds for therapeutic success can always be improved if treatment procedures are continuously modified on the basis of outcome effectiveness.

The possibility of improving therapy practices comes not from the therapist's good intentions, but from the therapist's use of frequent inputs of relatively high quality data. This contingency arrangement requires that the therapist receive at least weekly assessments of the behavior of the child, and perhaps of his own therapeutic behavior as well. Given feedback of reasonably reliable and valid data, then the therapist is in a position to continuously *change his own behavior* to achieve optimal effectiveness. Over time, favored techniques which are not supported by the data must be discarded. The void created by discarded techniques must be filled by innovations which in turn will be evaluated. Over time, one would expect the treatment procedures not only to look different, but also to become increasingly useful.

Therapists in traditional treatment settings have almost always received verbal feedback from parents and sometimes from teachers. However, the reviews of child therapy studies by Levitt (1957, 1971) suggest that over a period of two decades, there have been *no* increases in the efficiency of traditional therapies being applied by well-trained personnel. The present writer assumes that this impasse occurs because the feedback data given to therapists have been consistently biased. The bias is a relatively consistent tendency on the part of parents of disturbed children to report improvement in the behavior of the child when in fact no real changes have occurred. Data reviewed in the section which follows suggest that roughly two-thirds of such parents will report improvements when asked for global judgments. This means that even if the therapy *isn't working,* the therapist will receive supportive comments from the *majority* of the families with which he works. Given such reinforcement, there is, of course, little reason for the therapist to change his behavior.

Reliability and Validity of Parent Global Report Data

The following is a review of the research pertaining to three different types of parents' *global* judgments: (a) parents' descriptions of child-rearing practices, (b) parents' descriptions of their child's behavior, and (c) parents' reports of changes in deviant behavior. In this context, the term global refers to attempts by parents to synthesize information from extended time periods (e.g., more than 24 hours) and/or covering a range of broad-spectrum variables which are defined only by conventional usage (e.g., such terms as "warmth," or "destructive"). Such global judgments have typically been made in the *absence of prior systematic observations* by the parent.

Child-rearing. One commonly used method for obtaining data from the parent is the clinical interview. In some instances, the parent uses rating scales to make judgments of the child's adjustment. In other cases, the interviewer summarizes the information provided by parents. Regardless of format, there are studies which suggest that different interviewers obtain very different information from parents, and that the same interviewers receive different information from parents from one interview to the next (e.g., MacFarlane, Allen, & Honzik, 1962).

Much research on socialization has been based upon parents' recollection of childrearing patterns. The reliability of such recall, however, has repeatedly been called into question (e.g., Robins, 1963; Radke-Yarrow et al., 1964, 1970). These data which show that parents are not always accurate in reporting information about their children raise doubt about the utility of intensive efforts to get developmental histories using traditional child guidance interview procedures.

The validity of parent global ratings has also been checked by comparing such ratings with reports from the child, school records, and systematic observations. In one study (Burton, 1970), mothers' judgments and school records showed low correlations. A study by Schelle (1974) showed *no* correlation between *changes* in school attendance reported in school files and parent reports. Burton (1970) reported little convergence between parent and child judgments about trait measures describing the child. This finding is consistent with the low level of agreement (40%-60%) between parent and child for even relatively well-specified symptoms such as fears, overactivity, and temper tantrums found by Lapouse and Monk (1958).

This lack of support for the validity of parents' global judgments is also found in studies using observation procedures as a criterion measure. These studies show only low level correlations between ratings based upon interviews with the mother and observations of mother/child interaction (e.g., Antonovsky, 1959). Many of our "facts" concerning the functional relationships between mothers and children may be determined primarily by the method of data collection, e.g., interview versus observation (Bing, 1963). Although some studies show modest agreement for molar variables across methods (e.g., Smith, 1958), the majority of studies show discontinuities (e.g., Baumrind & Black, 1967; Burton, 1970; Honig, Tannenbaum, & Caldwell, 1968; Sears, 1965).

In examining the problem further, it seems that persons living within the same system do not necessarily agree in their global perceptions of child behavior. Mothers' and fathers' trait ratings of their children show only modest positive correlations (Becker, 1960). Similarly, Novick, Rosenfeld, and Block (1965) showed only 36% agreement between parents in identifying problem behaviors in their own child. The conclusion to be drawn from these studies is that parents are unable to provide reliable or valid global reports of their children's behavior.

Therapy change. Several studies suggest that parents have a bias to report improvement in the behavior of problem children when no observable changes have occurred. This is of some importance because of Levitt's (1957, 1971) claim that better than two-thirds of *non*-treated emotionally disturbed children improve over time. His reviews were based upon studies which used parent report as the primary outcome criterion. Given the presence of parental bias his estimates for base rates of spontaneous change would seem considerably inflated.

In a study by Collins (1966), the treatment of children with problems had been delayed and it was therefore necessary to re-establish a baseline measure of adjustment. The parents did not know of this situation. When asked for new ratings of their children, they assumed the children had been receiving treatment. Their ratings showed significant improvement, even though treatment had *not* yet begun. A similar finding was obtained for a no-treatment control condition in a study by Clement and Milne (1967). It is possible that the children's behavior improved simply as a function of the passage of time. However, the findings also support the hypothesis that parents perceived change when none, in fact, occurred.

A study reported by Walter and Gilmore (1973) showed that parents' global ratings of changes were unrelated to the actual behavior of the child. In that study, families were randomly assigned to experimental and placebo groups. Multiple criterion data were collected during baseline and again five weeks later to assess changes in child behavior. Observation data were collected in the homes. In addition, each parent, during baseline and intervention, made daily reports on the occurrence/ nonoccurrence of a list of behaviors for which they had come for assistance. Both sets of criterion data showed significant decreases in observed rates of targeted deviant behaviors for families in the experimental group. There was a nonsignificant *increase* in rates for the families in the placebo group. However, parents' global descriptions of improvement in their children revealed that all of the parents in the experimental group and two-thirds of the parents in the placebo group believed that the child was "improved." The performance of the placebo group is of interest because it exactly matches Levitt's (1971) estimate of the proportion of disturbed children who will improve without treatment.

The tendency of parents to overestimate treatment efficacy was also shown in two other studies. Patterson and Reid (1973) reported that observation and parent *daily* report data agreed in assigning 63% of a sample of treated families to an "improved" status. However, parents' *global* judgment data suggested 100% improvement. The authors would obviously like to accept the latter figure, but our clinical judgment suggests that we were really helping about two out of three families. Johnson and Christensen (1975) carried out a similar treatment study, using comparable criteria. Their observation data showed that 38% of the treated children showed significant improvement in their behavior, while parents' global judgments suggested that 93% had improved! A study by Schelle (1974) evaluated the validity of parental estimates of improvement on an extremely specific behavioral dimension: school attendance. He reported that for the group in which parental questionnaire data showed the greatest improvement, the actual school attendance data showed that the children were worse! While much more work must be done on this problem, it is the author's opinion that pre- and post-test measures of parental global estimates of change in problem child behavior will tend to overestimate treatment effects.

Improvements in Parent Report Data. In retrospect, it seems likely that the *wrong questions* have been asked of parents. Global judgments have been elicited which require memory of events over long time spans. For example, some investigators have obtained information from mothers about child behaviors occurring over a twenty-four hour time period. In addition, parents have been required to use complex and/or poorly defined variables. A study by Douglas et al. (1968) showed rather substantial correlations for parent and observers' data when the child behaviors were well defined. It would seem more reasonable to make more modest demands upon the parents and in the process perhaps obtain higher quality data. A laboratory study of three mother/child pairs by Peine (1970) showed promising results. Each mother/child pair participated in a series of five laboratory sessions in which the mother was asked to count well defined behavioral events as they occurred (e.g., such behaviors as "touch toys," "follows directions," and "aggressive"). Many of the intra-subject correlations between observers and mothers were in the .80's and .90's. However, the mothers consistently underestimated the *level* of deviant behavior by as much as 600%! This finding is consistent with a study reported by Herbert (1970) in which low absolute agreement was found between observers and parents. It seems that under the best of conditions, parent data may provide an accurate estimate for the ordinal rankings of subjects but may underestimate actual mean level.

In our treatment research, *parent report* data are consistently collected at three different levels (Patterson, Reid, Jones, & Conger, 1975). The levels vary in the specificity of the behaviors and the time intervals involved. First, parents are asked at termination to fill out rating scales which require global estimates of improvement such as those employed by Patterson and Reid (1973). In accord with our own findings and those of Johnson and Christensen (1975), it is expected that better than 90% of the parents will perceive some areas of improvement. At this level, parent global judgment is viewed as a necessary, but not sufficient, criterion for status as a success.[2]

Second, a method is used for obtaining more differentiated data from parents, which systematically samples centroid factors describing child personality. A significant change between pre- and post-ratings would be viewed as a necessary, but not sufficient, criterion for success status. The scales and scoring keys are to be found in Patterson, Reid, Jones, and Conger (1975).

Third, the Parent Daily Report (PDR) criterion has been developed to provide a more powerful criterion measure based upon parent data (Patterson, Cobb, & Ray, 1973). As part of the intake interview, the parents are asked whether each of the list of 31 "symptoms" are of sufficient concern to warrant changing. The list is published in Patterson, Reid, Jones, and Conger (1975). Parents are asked to collect data on the occurrence of these symptom behaviors during two weeks of baseline and at the end of treatment. These data are collected each day; the number of problems picked by each family usually ranges from three to nine. The parents indicate the occurrence or nonoccurrence of each of those events during a given day. It is as-

sumed that asking parents to make binary decisions (occur/nonoccur), covering only the preceding eight to ten hours, will minimize distortions in memory and judgment. The current practice is to express this score as mean frequency of symptoms per day. The reliability, stability, and validity of PDR data will be discussed in the psychometric properties section of this chapter.

The PDR criteria may well turn out to be the first choice as an evaluation measure. Assuming that it survives further psychometric analyses, it has some definite advantages. First of all, it is a means for obtaining data describing low base-rate events which are often foci for treatment but seldom seen by observers (e.g., fire-setting, truancy, stealing). Second, PDR is much less expensive to obtain than the observation data.

In current clinical practice, the PDR score constitutes one of our two major criteria for evaluating treatment. Its long range utility will be further defined by its correlation with police offense rates as the child moves through adolescence. In lieu of these data, which are now being collected, it might be noted that the PDR score at termination is the Oregon Social Leaning Center's best predictor of status during follow-up. Using six months' follow-up data, the termination PDR score was in 83% agreement with the follow-up PDR score and in 58% agreement with the Total Deviant follow-up score. Again, success was arbitrarily defined as ≥ 30% decline from baseline levels.

Development of the Family Interaction Coding System (FICS)

In the mid-1960's a social learning group was formed at the University of Oregon (G. Patterson, D. Anderson, W. Bricker, M. Ebner, A. Harris, R. Littman, J. Reid, and J. Straughan). Their concern with disturbed children led them into classrooms, homes, and institutions. Several methods were tried as a means of collecting data in these settings. At first, narrative accounts were written in longhand describing the target subject's behavior and the environmental consequences supplied for it (Buehler, Patterson, & Furniss, 1966). To speed up this process, aggressive events were described on magnetic tape using the face-mask microphones and portable tape recorders developed by the Barker group (Schoggen, 1964). These tapes could then be transcribed and coded (Patterson, McNeal, Hawkins, & Phelps, 1967); but the cost was very high. In addition, the data analysis required endless tabulations. As a result, it was decided to construct a coding system that could be used in a field setting. Furthermore, the coding system was designed so that the data could easily be punched

Table 3.1
Behavioral Code Definition

AP	Approval	HU*	Humiliate	PP	Physical Positive
AT	Attention	IG*	Ignore	RC	Receive
CM	Command	IN	Indulgence	SS	Self-stimulation
CN*	Command Negative	LA	Laugh	TA	Talk
CO	Compliance	NC*	Noncompliance	TE*	Tease
CR*	Cry	NE*	Negativism	TH	Touch
DI*	Disapproval	NO	Normative	WH*	Whine
DP*	Dependency	NR	No Response	WK	Work
DS*	Destructiveness	PL	Play	YE*	Yell
HR*	High Rate	PN*	Physical Negative		

*indicates categories that are included in the Total Aversive Behavior (TAB) score.

onto cards and stored for computer analyses.

As an opening strategy, it was decided that progress could be maximized by focusing upon the assessment of a single type of problem, the severe conduct problem child. This meant giving up investments of clinical time already made to the assessment and treatment of autistic, phobic and withdrawn children. From the late 1960's on, most of the time and energy of the reconstituted social learning group (G.R. Patterson, J. Reid, R. Ray, D. Shaw, J. Cobb, H. Hops, and K. Skindrud) was invested in three complex problems: (a) how to conceptualize the process of aggression in families; (b) how to treat the families in which it occurred; and (c) how to measure changes in aggressive family interactions.

The first task in developing this observation system was to come up with an item pool or set of categories which could constitute an observation system. The "items" in this case were specific behaviors thought to be relevant to either the clinical or theoretical purposes of the assessment task. Clinical experience and discussions with parents of socially aggressive children suggested some relevant behaviors. These clinical impressions provided a general perspective from which to view family interaction. The investigators ventured into the homes of families with antisocial children. It was this experience which led to the development of the specific code categories which define the FICS (Reid, 1967). Three years of study were required for the development of a workable field observation coding system. After six revisions, the data showed that the observation procedures provided a reasonably complete description of family interaction (Patterson, Ray, Shaw, & Cobb, 1969; Reid, 1967). In addition, it seemed that the field observation data collected in continuous sequen-

tial form were effective in generating many hypotheses about aggressive behaviors occurring within families. The preliminary psychometric evaluations were promising (Patterson, Cobb, & Ray, 1973; Reid, 1967).

The FICS was designed to describe aggressive behaviors and the antecedents and consequences associated with them. About half of the code categories in the FICS describe aversive behaviors. The other half of the categories include various prosocial behaviors. Currently, the FICS is composed of the 29 code categories listed in Table 3.1. A definition is provided for each behavioral code in Appendix 3.1.

Family interactions were categorized into discrete units as they occurred. The observer alternately coded, in sequence, the behavior of the subject and then the person(s) with whom the subject interacted. Each event was described by code letters referring to the category to which it was assigned, together with the number identifying the family member with whom the target subject was interacting. If required, several subject numbers and code categories were used to describe a single interaction. For example, a child could be crying and hitting at the same time.

The data were recorded continuously, and provided a relatively complete, sequential account of the interaction of a target subject with all other family members. The observer received an auditory signal every 30 seconds from a device built into the clipboard. At the beginning of each 30-second interval the observer shifted to the next line of the protocol sheet. On the average, observers were able to record five interaction units (both members of a dyad) every 30 seconds. For each observation, the order in which family members were selected as target subjects was randomly determined. Each

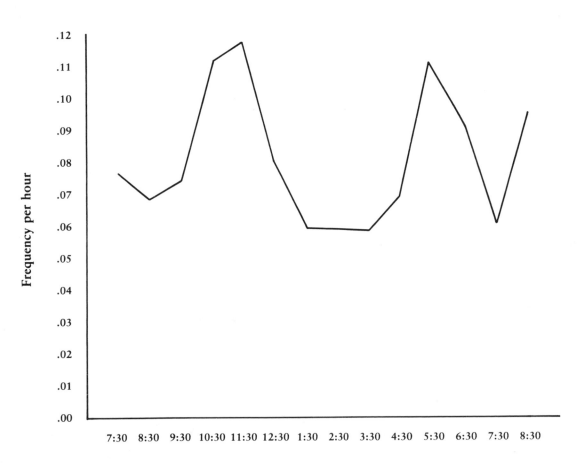

Figure 3.1
Diurnal Variations in Frequency of Outbursts
(from Goodenough, 1931, p. 107)

Hour of day

family member served as target subject for five minutes; then the whole series was replicated. The observers keypunched the data shortly after returning from the field.

In the chapters which follow, many of the variables will be expressed as "rate per minute." Within the present context, the upper limit of the rate per minute is approximately ten six-second responses per minute for any given subject. In addition, because the coding system "chunks" the behavior of the target person into six-second intervals, what may have been "continuous" events become discrete occurrences, e.g., a child crying for 18 seconds would be coded as a sequence of three "Cry." For this reason, it is not possible to differentiate recurrence from duration.

Some Practical Problems

During these first several years we had very little information regarding the procedures for observing family interactions in the home setting. As a result, many of our early decisions concerning how these observations were to take place were made on a trial and error basis. We wondered, for example, if we should schedule our observations for some standard time of day. If so, what time of day was best suited for observing aggressive family interactions? The best data that we could find relating to that question were collected a half-century ago by Florence Goodenough in her classic, *Anger in Young Children* (1931). As shown in figure 3.1, the diaries kept by mothers of preschool-aged children indicated that there were two prime

Illustration #2: Family Interaction in the Age of Technology

times for "conflict." The witching hours for these young children seemed to be just prior to lunch and just prior to dinner. The data were in agreement with our own hunches, so for the next decade most of the families were observed just prior to, or during, dinner.

In the beginning our goal was to observe families in "natural" settings. But, as noted earlier, our very first contact with families demonstrated that this was going to be difficult to achieve. The first "subject" of these attempts at observation chose to climb an apple tree instead. The next few families that were observed brought other aspects of the problem to our attention. For example, as the observer walked in the front door, the family simply melted away. Somebody had to go to the grocery store, another person disappeared into the bathroom. The remaining two turned on the television and remained transfixed for an hour (see illustration #2). The staff discussed this problem at length, and finally decided that the data would have to be collected in *semi-structured* home settings. This structuring of the home environment was represented by a set of formal rules for observation sessions as set forth in Table 3.2.

As we proceeded, it became clear that in some

real sense we were not viewing the family in their ordinary environment. Many of the families that we were seeing for treatment told us that all of the family members were rarely in the same room at the same time. As a consequence, the rules that were being implemented for observation *produced an unnatural situation.* The wheel had come full turn, for this was the very reason we had left the laboratory in the first place. However, the trade-

---

Table 3.2
Rules for Observation Sessions

(from Reid, 1978, p. 8)

1. Everyone in the family must be present.
2. No guests.
3. The family is limited to two rooms.
4. The observers will wait only 10 minutes for all to be present in the two rooms.
5. Telephone: No calls out; *briefly* answer incoming calls.
6. No TV.
7. No talking to observers while they are coding.
8. Do not discuss *anything* with observers that relates to your problems or the procedures you are using to deal with them.

---

off for bringing the family together in a semi-structured environment was that it maximized the occurrence of the events we wished to study. Studies are now being designed for the new interaction code that will tell us if imposing this type of structure was, indeed, the best way of achieving this maximization.

Another immediate concern was whether or not observers should talk or otherwise interact with the families that they were observing. Most of the observations were of families referred for treatment. The OSLC staff devoted an enormous amount of time and energy to helping these families. As a result, the observers quickly became enmeshed in the treatment process taking place in the families they observed. These developments led to rule number seven (Table 3.2). Families were told before the study began that the observers were forbidden to talk with them. The routine for observers was to enter the home at the appointed time, greet the family, seat themselves, and begin their observation procedures. For a number of years, the observers also called the families at regular times every other day to obtain Parent Daily Report data.

Over the next decade, several spinoffs occurred that were not anticipated. These were primarily new assessment devices which may well turn out to be as useful as the coding system itself. We be-

gan to measure, for example, a variable that we called family noncooperation. It appeared that those families who missed appointments, were not at home, or arrived late tended to be the ones that the therapists later had the most difficulty in treating. An empirical study is now being carried out to determine just how useful this variable might be in predicting successful treatment outcomes for individual families.

Observer Effects on the Data

Structuring the home environment was our guarantee that the observers would see the events that we wished to study. But we had to account for several other variables before we could assume that the data collected by observers represented a true picture of what was really going on in these homes. It occurred to us that the use of observers to record behavioral events in the home may generate other sources of distortion in the data. As a result, a series of studies were designed to measure effects of observer agreement (reliability), observer drift, observer bias, and observer presence on the data. The results of these investigations are summarized in the sections which follow.

Observer Agreement

Reliability is a basic requirement for any measurement system. Observer reliability in coding is defined as the degree to which observers code behaviors in accordance to some predefined criteria (e.g., a comparison of one observer's protocol [coding sheet] to that of another; a comparison of one observer's protocol to a precoded videotape of a family session). In our system, every third home observation session during baseline, and every fourth session thereafter is attended by two observers. The percentage agreement level is then calculated separately for each 30-second line on the protocol:

$$\frac{\text{number of frames of agreement}}{\begin{array}{c}\text{number of frames of agreement plus number}\\\text{of frames of disagreement}\end{array}}$$

A frame is defined as a six-second time sample of behavior, and is subdivided into two parts: the subject number and antecedent behavior (part one) and the respondent's number and consequation (part two). Agreement involves all four components. An instance of double-coding (two behaviors per subject or respondent) would be considered an additional interaction segment, and would add to the denominator. Therefore, while one line on a rating sheet contains five six-second time samples the total number of agreement points may exceed ten points if either the subject or other

49

family members emitted more than one behavioral response during any six-second time sample (or frame) on that line.

Calculating observer agreement on a line-by-line basis provides a general estimate of the quality of the data. Typically, these data on interobserver reliability are obtained on a regular basis for project cases and posted on a bulletin board. It is expected that the values will *not* fall below a mean of 70% for a given observer pair on any given session. The average is around 75%. As pointed out by Cohen (1960) and others, the interpretation of this agreement score must take into account the level of chance agreement. Cohen's Kappa is such a means of expressing agreement, and at the same time correcting for chance level; it is, in fact, a preferred method for analyzing observer agreement.

As Johnson and Bolstad (1973) point out, there are a large number of methods one *could* use in calculating observer agreement. Each has its assets and liabilities. For some purposes, the technique outlined above might constitute an underestimate of agreement. For example, the stress upon correct notation of events *and* sequence could very well be irrelevant to tasks requiring only an estimate of mean rate of occurrence. For these analyses, a more appropriate dependent variable could be the mean frequency of a given code category obtained from the *entire* protocol.

Table 3.3 summarizes the available data relating to observer reliability on 28 of the code categories. As shown there, the agreement between observers present during the same sessions was reasonably good. The median correlation of .92 (across categories) was as high as that found for some of the better assessment devices. Note, however, that these important findings were based upon only 11 pairs of observer protocols. This is hardly a sufficient sample upon which to base important decisions about the precision of a measuring instrument.

It should be noted that structural analyses of the type described in Chapters 8 and 9 are based upon statements such as $p(A|B)$ and so forth. As pointed out by Hartmann (1977), global measures of reliability hardly apply to such variables. What is needed are estimates of the reliability for these functional indices. To the writer's knowledge, such an analysis has been made in only one study (Patterson & Moore, 1979). The data from a single case study showed the conditional p values calculated from protocols of two observers were in good agreement.

J.B. Reid has noted that observer agreement is largely a function of the complexity of the interaction. By selecting *simple* interaction segments, one

---

Table 3.3
Observer Reliability
(from Reid, 1978, p. 77)

Code	R_{xy}[1]	Percent agreement[2]
AP	.76	54
AT	.96	90
CM	.93	86
CN	.66	65
CR	.96	72
DI	.92	72
DP	.88	91
DS	.92	75
HR	.65	59
HU	.92	74
LG	.93	68
IN	.86	61
LA	.96	74
NC	.67	61
NE	.59	38
NO	.99	95
NR	.95	96
PL	1.00	75
PN	.94	57
PP	.73	59
PX	Not observed	—
RC	.89	59
SS	.67	30
TA	.99	94
TE	.86	56
TH	.88	91
WH	.71	49
WK	.94	92
YE	.80	56
Median	.92	72

1. Based upon entry-by-entry agreement.
2. Based on analysis of 11 protocols.

---

may obtain *very* high observer agreement. Reid has worked with several methods for calculating complexity. For example, if complexity was defined as N different entries divided by the total entries for five minutes, then the correlation between percent agreement and complexity was $-.52$ ($p < .001$). Those same measures were then applied to another set of OSLC data; the correlation was $-.75$ ($p < .01$). These results indicate that reliability was lower for the more complex protocols.

Skindrud (1972) defined complexity as the percent of unreplicated interactions within each segment. This measure correlated $-.53$ with observer agreement for one sample, and $-.65$ for anoth-

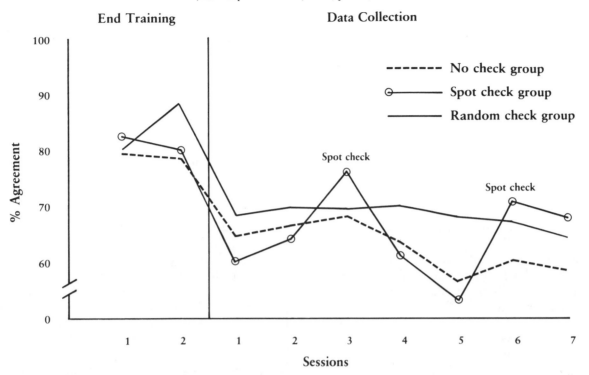

Figure 3.2
Decay in Observer Reliability

(from Taplin and Reid, 1973, p. 551)

Reprinted with permission from "Effects of instructional set and experimenter influence on observer reliability," *Child Development*, 1973, *44*, 547-554. Copyright 1973 by The Society for Research in Child Development.

er. Reid extended these analyses in the report by Jones et al. (1975). He found, for example, that the protocols for child subjects were consistently less reliable than those for adults. They were also significantly more complex.

Future presentations of this kind will probably be centered around a different theory of measurement. The theory of generalizability by Cronbach, Gleser, Nanda, and Rajaratnam (1972) provides a very different conceptual base for considering problems such as agreement, stability, and validity. So far, we have only begun to apply this model to OSLC data; this was done by Jones et al. (1975). The model will be used to analyze our new observation coding systems.

Skindrud (1972) found that he could train observers to be reliable in the use of the FICS in about 20 hours. This figure seems fairly representative of our experience since that time. However, Reid (1970) was convinced that observers became highly variable *after* they had been trained. He used a variant of the FICS, and trained his observers until they reached the usual criterion of accuracy in coding videotapes of mother-child interaction. Following this training, the observers were

covertly assessed as to their accuracy. On the first day of covert assessment, there was a mean drop in accuracy of 25%! Romanczyk et al. (1971) found that their observers performed at 76% accuracy during overt checks, and 39% when checked covertly.

Taplin and Reid (1973) then began to analyze those variables that might explicate this phenomenon. It was now obvious that being a "reliable observer" was not a static disposition and therefore the entire enterprise was in jeopardy. In this first study, they compared the performance of three different groups. The first group was told that their data would not be checked; the second was told that their protocols would be compared to the criterion observer on a random basis. The third group was told they would be spot-checked at regular intervals. There were six observers in each group. The results are shown in Figure 3.2. The gradual decay from the training level of 80% was significant for all three groups. The no-check group showed the largest decrement; and, although the difference is not statistically significant, the random-check group performed the best.

The next study examined the possibility that the

observer group itself could be used as a feedback and support device to maintain reliability. DeMaster, Reid, and Twentyman (1976) trained and randomly assigned 28 observers to one of three groups. Group 1 received daily feedback as to accuracy, and discussed the prior protocols with the group. Group 2 also held daily discussions about the finer points in coding decisions, but was not given feedback as to accuracy. Group 3 was given no feedback and did not participate in group discussion. Group 1 did significantly better than either of the other groups; in fact, their accuracy improved over time. Group 2 observers tended to drift away from their original decision rules.

This important series of studies by Reid and his students led to permanent changes in the data collection procedures employed at OSLC. Observer training sessions are now held every other week. All four observers view a tape, code it, and then discuss any decision problems that they have encountered. At regular intervals, pairs of observers accompany each other into the field. After their protocols have been tabulated, their agreement scores are posted.

Observer Bias

Rosenthal (1966) has defined experimental bias as the extent to which experimenter effect or error is asymmetrically distributed about the "correct" or "true" value. In the present context, such distortions could take the form of a constant bias on the part of the observer. Conceivably, some of these errors could arise because observers *intentionally* distort their data. While intentional errors in recording and computation have been reported in the literature (Azrin, Holtz, Ulrich, & Goldiamond, 1961; Rosenthal, 1966; Rosenthal & Fode, 1963; Rosenthal & Lawson, 1964), those reports have primarily related to students serving as data collectors for their instructors. The possibility of observer error, whether intentional or not, must, however, be guarded against. The most likely mechanism for creating observer bias would seem to be the situation in which the experimenter communicates his expectations to the observers, thereby exerting a subtle influence on the moment-by-moment coding decisions they make. Although few studies have systematically assessed the effects of observer bias in the natural setting with human subjects, many researchers have taken measures to minimize its potential effects (O'Connor, 1969; Thomas, Becker, & Armstrong, 1968). A preliminary study by Kass and O'Leary (1970) showed that experimenter expectations produced a small but significant effect on the data coded by one group of observers, but not for another. However,

additional studies from both the Stony Brook and the Oregon laboratories using well-trained observers have not supported that finding.

Skindrud (1973) described one of the first well-controlled field studies testing for the effect of bias upon well-trained observers. These observers had several years' field experience and regular (re)training sessions in applying an earlier version of the FICS. Over a period of several years, two different "calibrating observers" had offices separated from the rest of the project. They were kept uninformed of the status of the families being treated. The regular cadre, on the other hand, knew which families were in the clinical and which were in the matched normal samples. They also knew for the clinical sample whether the family was in baseline, treatment, or follow-up. A comparison of the rates of deviant behavior obtained from the informed versus the uninformed observers showed no significant effects for either family status (clinical or normal) or for treatment status (baseline or termination). However, the small sample involved in this field study led to the decision to carry out a large-scale laboratory study.

In this study, Skindrud (1972) enrolled 28 observers (women from the local community) in an intensive three-week training program. They learned to use the present code by viewing videotapes of parent/child interaction. The minimal level of accuracy required to participate in the remainder of the study was 70%. The trainees were then divided into three groups. One group was given a bias to expect the next series of 12 sessions to reflect a 30% increase in deviant child behavior. A second group was given a bias to expect a decrease of the same magnitude. A third group was not instructed as to the experimenter's expectations. The data indicated that there was no significant effect of bias upon the *data coded* by the observers. Even the trends were not in accord with the expectations the experimenter had given to the groups. Thinking that perhaps the less reliable observers might reflect the bias, a separate analysis was run for this subgroup. Again, there were no significant effects. When tested to determine their understanding and acceptance of the experimenter's expectations, the observers showed that they did understand. A power analysis showed that groups of the size used in the second study were sufficient to detect a bias greater than 15%. Taken together, the studies suggested that if well-trained observers are biased, the magnitude of the effect is not very large.

Kent, O'Leary, Diament, and Dietz (1974) replicated Skindrud's findings. Ten well-trained observers were assigned to one of two groups. One group was told the next series of videotapes would show a child getting better, and the other group was told that they would show a child getting worse. Again, there was no significant effect of experimenter expectations upon the *data actually coded* by the observers. In this analysis, they even searched for the effect by analyzing each code category separately. Experimenter expectations were, however, dramatically reflected in the observers' *global* judgments! Ninety percent of the observers in the first group thought they detected a decrease in the child's rate of deviant behavior. Seventy percent in the second group thought they detected an increase.

In his 1972 investigation, Skindrud reported a pilot study in which he *reinforced* the observers for collecting data congruent with experimenter expectancies. Even with an N of six he obtained changes in coded data of borderline significance. O'Leary, Kent, and Karpowitz (1975) carried out a study along the same lines that closely paralleled field situations. Four observers viewed videotapes, and were told to expect changes in two code categories. The observers were reinforced when their coded data were congruent with the experimenter's expectancies, and punished when they did not. The changes in the data for the two target categories were in accord with the reinforcement contingencies, while code categories not involved did not reflect these changes. These findings strongly emphasize the necessity for therapists *not* to provide observers with this type of feedback on their observations.

As things now stand, it does not seem that experimenter or therapist expectancies *ipso facto* bias the data collected by *well*-trained observers. However, expectancies *can* affect observers' global judgments about what they are seeing. Experimenters could perhaps bias their coded data by using reinforcement contingencies, but this is not likely to happen in most well-run field studies.

Observer Presence Effects

Each of us has experienced being observed, and we know that in some settings such an intrusion sets constraints upon some of our behaviors. The problem is that it is difficult to delineate these effects empirically. An unpublished study by Paul (1963) showed that mothers being observed in their homes "felt constrained." In that study, ten mothers and their preschool children were observed over a ten-week period. The mothers reported feeling very much aware of the observers' presence throughout the study. However, when the mothers' ratings of their children's behavior were compared for intervals when observers were present versus intervals when the observers were absent, the data indicated that there was no effect on the mothers' ratings. These data supported none of the various hypotheses being tested relating to the impact of observer presence on mother/child interaction.

One can conceptualize the problem of observer presence in a variety of ways. However, the studies completed thus far seem to arrange themselves in terms of the following sequence of questions: (a) do subjects being observed notice the observer?; (b) does being observed produce increases in socially acceptable behaviors?; (c) does observation elicit a set to suppress socially undesirable behaviors?; and (d) can families "fake" good and "fake" bad?

Questions concerning the effect of the observer's presence upon the behavior of the target subject represent a central issue in evaluating the utility of observation techniques. Earlier studies in this area posed the question as an either/or proposition. At this time, it seems more reasonable to assume that the presence of an observer produces *some* alteration in ongoing behavior, e.g., at the very least, the target subject *notices* the observer. The more productive stance is to assume some effect and to identify its magnitude and quality. It is suggested that the *kind* of effect and its magnitude must vary as a function of setting and target subject. This seems reasonable enough, but how does one proceed to measure such effects?

The task of constructing an adequate design to test this question has occupied investigators for the last decade. Three general approaches have been followed; none have proven entirely satisfactory. One approach suggests that the target subjects are aware of the observers, and that they behave accordingly by presenting the most socially desirable facade possible. Therefore, "aware" subjects would be expected to demonstrate lower rates of deviant behavior and higher rates of socially desirable behavior throughout the sessions. As an alternative, one might expect that over repeated sessions the subject would habituate to the sensitizing effect of the observer's presence, and gradually approximate baseline rates of deviant and socially desirable behaviors. The second and perhaps most powerful approach has involved the use of experimental manipulations in which subjects are requested to fake "good" and fake "bad." The third approach involves using unobtrusive technology (hidden recording devices).

Reactivity to Observer Presence. Pollack, Vincent, and Williams (1977) proposed a two dimensional model describing the demand characteristics involving observers. The first factor, *nonspe-*

cific reactivity, describes orienting behaviors that indicate the subject is aware of the observer. This may include behaviors signifying discomfort, self-conscious "fiddling" behavior, and perhaps a general increase in variability. These behaviors are thought to habituate over time. The second factor, *impression management,* does not habituate; it implies a general attempt to present a socially desirable demeanor to the observer.

There is ample evidence attesting to the viability of the Pollack et al. (1977) nonspecific reactivity factor. For example, Barker's (1951) data describes attempts by children to interact with the observers. Observation data collected in nursery schools by Connolly and Smith (1972), showed high rates of orienting behavior among the children, particularly during the first few observation sessions. It should be noted that even though habituation effects were reported over the eight sessions, the orienting behaviors did *not* fall to zero. Grimm, Parsons, and Bijou (1972) also noted in a classroom setting that high rates of orienting behaviors persisted over a six-month period in which the children were regularly observed. Studies of family interaction also showed that parents remained very much aware of the observers. An unpublished study by Paul (1963) showed that during a ten-week series of observations, mothers' global ratings indicated a continuing awareness throughout the sessions.

Bechtel (1967) devised some fascinating measures of nonspecific reactivity for visitors to an art gallery. He assigned visitors to one of four groups. One group was asked to rank their preferences for the pictures while an observer was present. A second group was also asked to rank their preferences, but remained unaware of being observed. A third group was asked to wait, and the fourth group consisted of visitors following the usual procedure. The effect of the overt observers was to reduce the number of seconds spent in that area; their movement within the area was also more restricted.

In the series of studies concerning impression management, consistent changes in social behaviors were demonstrated, but the effects did not always fall neatly along a dimension of social desirability. The complex effects varied as a function of the kind of subjects and the setting. Nelson, Lipenski, and Black (1976) collected data on college students' baseline rate of face touching. The mean rate was 12.3 responses per session when the students were unaware that they had been observed. An observer was introduced and the students were informed that face touches would be recorded. The resulting decrease in rate to 8.4 responses per

session was significant. In a study of adults, Moos (1968) compared the effects of psychiatric patients carrying a microphone transmitter to the effects of being observed. When psychiatric patients were in a day room setting, the effect of the observers was to elicit significantly higher rates of socially appropriate behaviors such as smiling, talking with hands, looking at the speaker, playing with an object, and arm and foot movements. Zegiob, Arnold, and Forehand (1975) studied 12 mother/child pairs as they sat in a waiting room. On two successive visits, they were either informed or uninformed of the fact that they were being observed. Under the informed conditions, there was a significant increase in the amount of play interaction and in the mothers' use of positive verbal comments and attempts to structure the interaction. Randall (1975) showed a significant effect for ten of the 27 mother/infant behaviors that were examined. During observer present conditions, the mothers talked less to their infants and gave fewer directions and prohibitions. As might be expected, the infants' behavior also showed significant changes.

With children as subjects in a classroom setting, there seemed to be no consistent effect of observer presence upon child behavior. For example, a study by Surrott, Ulrich, and Hawkins (1969) involved observation of four target subjects in an intervention study. Comparisons of observer-present to videocamera-only conditions showed greater time working for all four subjects under the observer-present condition. Mercatoris and Craighead (1973) extended the design to include all subjects in the classroom, and an ABAB reversal. The study lasted for 30 sessions, with the observer alternately present during consecutive five- to ten-day blocks, then absent during the B condition for an equivalent amount of time. The videocamera was present during the entire study. There were no differences between conditions for rates of inappropriate or appropriate behaviors. Weinrott, Garrett, and Todd (in preparation) studied six children in a special class. After manipulating observer presence and absence conditions, they concluded that virtually none of the variance in the data could be attributed to observer presence effects.

Neither the habituation nor the variability hypotheses are supported by research findings. The Mercatoris and Craighead (1973) study failed to find any changes in mean level for either appropriate or inappropriate behavior. As noted earlier, Patterson and Cobb (1973) and Johnson and Bolstad (1973) found no significant changes in the mean level over six to ten sessions in the home. A corollary of this hypothesis would be that the subjects would display increased variability during the first few sessions, and then stabilize as they became accustomed to being observed, i.e., the estimate from the first block of sessions would tend not to correlate well with estimates from later sessions. Neither the correlational analysis of classroom sessions nor comparable analyses of family sessions supported the variability hypothesis.

In summary, the studies carried out to date provide consistent support for the Pollack et al. (1977) nonspecific reactivity factor. As shown by their orienting responses, subjects definitely seem to be aware of being observed. There is also some evidence for adults that support the impression management factor. However, the sparse findings do not support a simplistic model of deviancy suppression. Rather, it seems that adult social behaviors that are altered by the presence of an observer vary as a function of both setting and sample. Classroom studies of children offer little support for the impression management factor. There is essentially no support for either the habituation or variability hypotheses.

Manipulation of sets to "fake." If one assumes family members *could* distort their interactions when the observer was present, then it should also be possible to directly manipulate such a set. This, in fact, was the format adopted in a series of classic studies by Steve Johnson and his colleagues. In the first study (Johnson & Lobitz, 1974a), 12 parents of normal families were instructed to make their preschool children "look bad or deviant" for three observation sessions, and to "look good" on three alternate sessions. On "bad" days, the rates of deviant child behavior and rates of negative and parent commands were significantly higher than they were during "look good" days. The design made it possible to demonstrate that parents of normal children could definitely alter the behavior of their children. However, it was not clear that parents of distressed families would be equally skilled in controlling child behavior.

A second study by Lobitz and Johnson (1975) involved volunteer parents of younger children. One sample of 12 families had "problem children" as labeled by one or both parents. The children in the other sample of 12 families were presumably problem-free. On two consecutive days, the parents in both groups were instructed to make their children "look good"; then on two consecutive days to make them "look bad"; finally, on two consecutive days they were to "look normal." Families were randomly assigned to one of the six possible orderings of these conditions. As shown in Figure 3.3., parents in both samples produced significant increases in deviant child behaviors

when comparing "look normal" to "look bad" conditions. Ten of the 12 deviant families and nine of the 12 nonproblem families seemed effective in producing this shift. These shifts were accompanied by significant increases in parental commands and punishment, and a significant decrease in parental positive consequences. The data from the combined sample showed no significant shift in child behavior from the normal to the good conditions. Seven of the 12 normal families were effective in producing this shift, whereas only four of 12 in the problem sample were successful. Questionnaires given to the parents showed they generally perceived themselves as more effective in accelerating good behavior than in accelerating bad behavior. However, parent perceptions of behavior change were not in accord with observations of the same behavioral events.

Weinrott and Jones (1977) followed a similar format, but this time in the classroom setting. Forty pupil-teacher pairs from grades one through three participated in the study. Half of these teachers had identified a socially withdrawn child, the other half a disruptive child. Baseline observations were collected in all classrooms during all phases of the study. After two baseline sessions, the teachers were instructed to make their target child look as socially desirable as possible. If the target child was withdrawn, the teacher was to help the child appear to be as outgoing as possible. If the child was disruptive, the teacher was to help him look as cooperative and as quiet as possible. During the demand conditions, the behavior of the teachers changed significantly in the expected directions. The withdrawn children showed *significant* changes from baseline toward a more outgoing pattern of interacting; but the changes in the disruptive children were nonsignificant. These results were in keeping with the results from the Lobitz and Johnson (1975) study. The author believes that these results demonstrate the *control* exerted by the *antisocial child over his environment*. It is apparent that both normal and withdrawn children can be helped to "look good" (at least to a limited degree); but it also seems that antisocial children are not so readily manipulable.

A more recent study involved distressed and nondistressed married couples (Vincent et al., 1979). The results again emphasize the constraints that coercive interactions have upon those who are involved in this process. In the laboratory analogue situation, after a baseline period, the couples were instructed to fake good or fake bad. The adults in both samples were able to significantly alter their *verbal* behavior in accord with the instructions. For example, during fake good, the

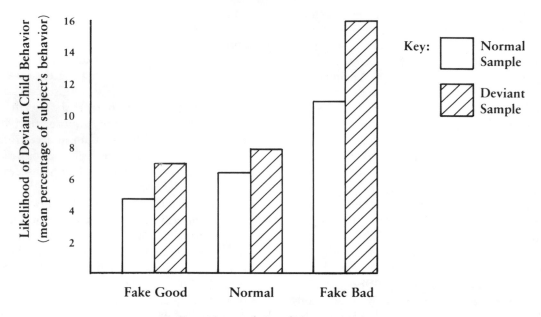

Figure 3.3
Fake Good, Fake Bad, and Normal Conditions for Two Samples
(adapted from Lobitz & Johnson, 1975, p. 72)

Parent Behavior:	Fake Good		Normal		Fake Bad	
	Normal	Deviant	Normal	Deviant	Normal	Deviant
Negative	2.6	5.1	6.4	5.9	12.6	13.0
Command	7.9	11.0	11.7	11.4	13.4	16.4

distressed couples were able to reduce their negative statements and increase their positive statements relative to their baseline levels. During fake bad, both groups increased their verbal negative responses. It seems that distressed couples are more effective as impression managers than are antisocial children, i.e., they *can* alter the quality of their verbal behavior if they choose to do so. It is, however, fascinating to note that *neither* sample of couples was able to manipulate their *nonverbal* behaviors in accordance with the instructions. Under the fake good and fake bad conditions, the groups remained discriminable. In addition, neither sample shifted significantly from their own baseline levels.

Pending further research in this area, it seems reasonable to assume that both parents and children from out-of-control families find it difficult to "fake good." Habitual modes of interacting provide powerful constraints for familial interaction patterns. Presumably, these constraints are more effective in controlling behavior than is the desire to look good. It also seems that the present investigators just happened to select a clinical phenomenon that best lends itself to observation *in situ*. We remain convinced that the observers do set constraints upon the rate and intensity of familial violence. We are also convinced that the families of antisocial children are sufficiently disrupted so that many elements of the basic process are clearly visible: for example, Reid, Taplin and Lorber (1981) found that mothers of abused children were observed to *hit* their children at ten times the rates of normal mothers even though the mothers *knew* that they were being observed *because* they were abusive!

Unobtrusive measures and deception studies. One would hope to have some unobtrusive measure that provides an absolute base for comparing the effect of observers being present to their not being present. While there are no studies that have successfully accomplished this, several investigators have made innovative approximations.

Purcell and Brady (1966) equipped 13 boys in a residential treatment center with radio transmitting devices. Raters coded the transcripts of their interactions according to a set of personality trait dimensions. Another set of data was collected by observers using Barker's technique for obtaining specimen records. The mean correlation between the two modes of data collection was .79. Cottage parents rated the boys before and during the study. There was no significant change in their behavior as a function of the observers and radio transmitter. This latter finding was in accord with the data from mothers' ratings of preschool child behaviors emitted prior to and during the observation session (Paul, 1963).

Bernal et al. (1971) experimented with the placement of an audiotape recorder in the home of a mother and her three children. Over a six-week period, the observer was present for one session per week; recordings were made for seven-minute intervals four times each day throughout the period. Family members knew when the two sets of data were being collected. For the response "mother command," the correlation between the two modes of data collection was $+.89$ ($p < .02$). It was interesting to note that the deviancy rates were *lower* for the audiotape data than for data from observers in the home. Johnson and Bolstad (1975) replicated and extended this basic design to include 12 families of younger children (ages 4 to 8). One hour prior to dinnertime, an audio recorder was turned on; all family members were aware of the arrangement. On alternate days over the six-day period, observers were present while the recorder was on. The data from the audiotapes showed no significant effect for the observers' presence or absence on the occurrence of deviant child behaviors. Correlational analyses also showed observer presence or absence was not related to children's or parents' rates of coercive behaviors.

The three studies employing unobtrusive measures were consistent in demonstrating that observer presence did not produce significant changes in deviancy as compared to results from audio recordings. The possibility remains, of course, that the mechanical recording devices themselves produced distortions if they could be compared to normal baseline levels. The problem here is to estimate the "real" or absolute level that would exist if the subjects were unaware of the presence of a recording process.

Deception studies. Two deception studies have been carried out to get at the problem of estimating an absolute level for deviant behavior.

Harris (1969) trained 15 mothers as observers to a reliability level of 80%. The mothers were then randomly assigned to one of three groups. For the outside observer (OO) group, mothers from other families served as observers, and they collected data for six sessions. For the mother-observer (MO) group, the mothers collected data for three sessions in their own homes. During the last three sessions, an outside observer collected the data. When the mother collected the data in her own family, she wore dark glasses. The family members were told she was participating in a psychology experiment to determine the impact of social interaction on encoding perceptual symbols. In the third group, the mothers (MM) coded the entire six sessions for their own families. In all three groups, the subjects consisted of fathers interacting with their children. The mean proportion of social interaction for the groups in the various conditions was recorded. It was predicted that the impact of the outside observer would be to increase socially desirable behaviors, i.e., social interaction. However, a 3x2 ANOVA for repeated measures showed that none of the main effects nor any of the interaction terms were significant. In fact, the trends for two of the three relevant comparisons were in the opposite direction from that which was predicted. A comparable analysis for rates of total deviant child behavior also produced nonsignificant results.

However, it is possible that mother observers might have dropped markedly in their reliability following their training program. Because Harris did not carry out any reliability checks *during* her experiment, the lack of findings could have been due to a decrease in the reliability of the data. In addition, there were enormous differences among families in their rates of deviant behavior, and in their rates of social interaction. Finally, the Harris study used such a small N that it might not have had the power necessary to test for subtle effects. With these qualifications in mind, White (1972) used professional observers, a larger N (25 families, 50 children), and shifted the setting from the home to the laboratory. He also used an $A_1B_1A_2B_2$ repeated measures design involving four 30-minute sessions. During the observer absent periods, A_1 and A_2, the mothers and their children were told they were "waiting" for the observers. During B_1 and B_2 an observer appeared and coded their interactions while sitting in the same room with them. Actually, the family was observed by concealed observers who coded their interactions during all four trials.

The data from White's experiment can be interpreted in several ways, depending on one's pre-

Table 3.4
Mean Total Deviant Behaviors for Four Conditions
(from White, 1972)

Family member	Experimental conditions				
	Observers were:				
	Absent	Present	Absent	Present	F value
Mother	.072	.068	.120	.148	2.17**
Older child	.072	.044	.240	.158	3.80*
Younger child	.180	.170	.180	.305	2.27**

*$p < .05$
**$p < .01$

dilection. The data for the family as a whole showed nonsignificant variations across the conditions. In that sense, one could say the study replicates the Harris (1969) study. However, an examination of the data in Table 3.4 points to an inadequacy in the design. The data clearly showed effects for trials; note that baseline two is higher than baseline one for two of the three family members. A pilot study showed no order effects, but it seems evident in comparing baselines one and two that White did have a significant order effect (not tested). The order effect serves as a confound, making these data noninterpretable. The study should be redone, using a design controlling for the likelihood of an order effect.

Psychometric Properties of the FICS and PDR

As a data collection device, a coding system reflects the outcome of a number of arbitrary decisions, e.g., the content of what one observes, the number and size of the behavioral units, and the use of frequency or duration measures. However, once these decisions have been made, the resulting system is "just" an assessment device. As Jones (1973) points out, an observational system, like any assessment device, should be evaluated in terms of the various psychometric properties subsumed under the traditional notions of reliability, stability, and validity. Modern systems of coding parent/child interaction demonstrate varying degrees of psychometric sophistication (e.g., Bales, 1950; Bobbitt et al., 1969; Caldwell, 1968; Moustakas, Sigel & Schalock, 1956; Radke-Yarrow et al., 1976). Contemporary reviewers of this literature reflect the increasing demand for careful psychometric analyses of these instruments (Johnson & Bolstad, 1973; Jones, Reid & Patterson, 1975; Lytton, 1971; Mash, 1976; Wahler, in

preparation; Weick, 1968; Wiggins, 1973).

High-quality data is critical to the research and clinical activities at OSLC. As a consequence, we have carried out extensive evaluations of the psychometric properties of both the FICS and the PDR. The evaluations began when these assessment devices were first constructed and continue into the present. This section summarizes the relevant findings.

Test-Retest Reliability (and related questions)

In the context of observational coding systems, the traditional notion of test-retest reliability becomes a rather complex affair. One can begin by asking whether scores obtained during one week's observation correlate significantly with scores obtained a week later, or with scores obtained a year later. Such data will be presented here. But within the context of six to ten repeated observations in the home there is the possibility that the family members change as a function of being observed. This is a variant of the observer reactivity hypothesis. In the present context it refers to the possibility that there may be systematic changes in mean level as a function of repeated testing. Do family members display high rates of prosocial behaviors during early sessions and increasing rates of deviant behavior during later sessions? The habituation hypothesis would suggest that this may happen. If this were a significant phenomena, and families were differentially affected, it would contribute to lowering the correlation between scores collected early and those collected later in a series of observation sessions. Data relevant to the habituation hypothesis will also be considered in this section.

There is one further query to be considered; it is analogous to questions about the internal consistency of scores from personality questionnaires.

58

How many items, with what kind of psychometric properties, are required to establish an internally consistent measure of a trait such as anxiety or aggression? In the context of observational coding systems the question is altered somewhat. The home is *not* constant as a setting. Even within the constraints set by our procedures, there are tremendous differences from one evening to another in terms of *setting variables*. To obtain a stable estimate of a trait measured by a coding system both the test and retest scores must be based upon representative samplings of *settings*. Settings (and sessions) are somewhat analogous to items on a questionnaire. How many sessions are sufficient to insure an adequate sampling of settings? Incidentally, this implies that if one could construct a taxonomy of settings then setting complexity would covary with measures of test-retest reliability. However, these are questions which have yet to be explored systematically. For the present, we will focus on the simpler form of the event sampling question—how many minutes of sampling are required to reliably predict what a child's rate will be over the next six or seven sessions? In the sections which follow, we will first consider the findings which relate to the habituation hypothesis, then those which relate to event sampling, and finally those which relate to test-retest reliability.

Habituation Hypothesis. If the habituation hypothesis is correct, we would expect the mean frequency of deviant behaviors to increase over time, while socially desirable behaviors should show a concomitant decrease. Our first attempts to assess habituation effects were based on small samples in which session changes were compared separately for mothers, fathers, and problem children (Patterson & Cobb, 1971). The results indicated that there were no significant changes in mean level across sessions for any of the code categories, for any of the family members. The next study combined the data collected on 14 boys from normal families and 17 boys from distressed families (Patterson & Cobb, 1973). Again the ANOVA for repeated measures showed no significant changes for any of the categories. Similarly, Johnson and Bolstad (1973) found no evidence for changes in mean level of family interaction over sessions. Mercatoris and Craighead (1973) observed children in a classroom setting for 20 sessions and found no significant changes in mean level over trials. None of these studies offer support for the habituation hypothesis. As a result, low test-retest reliability scores could not be attributed to this source.

Even if there are no changes in mean level for deviant and/or prosocial behaviors there may be habituation effects that can be identified by using correlational analyses. As mentioned earlier, Harris (1969) suggested that observer presence may produce increased variability in family interaction in the first few sessions. As family members become habituated to observer presence, this variability presumably decreases. However, the correlational analyses of classroom behaviors by Masling and Stern (1969) did not support the variability hypothesis. Similarly, the home observation study by Paul (1963) failed to support it. A home observation study by Harris (1969) showed a trend for the data from observer-present trials to correlate at low levels with data from observer-absent trials. However, a comparable study by White (1972) failed to replicate the trend.

Event Sampling. Given that the setting varies somewhat from session to session, then how many samplings are necessary to establish a stable estimate for a particular code category? In the report by Jones et al. (1975) the data base consisted of 60 to 100 minutes of observation data per subject from sessions in the first week of baseline. The scores were correlated with comparable estimates from the second week. Roughly two-thirds of these correlations were significant at $p < .01$ (see Table 3.5). For the 14 code categories describing coercive behavior for boys, the median correlation was .58. These findings suggest that estimates based upon 60 to 100 minutes of observation data provide a reasonably accurate score. This much data, collected in three to five sessions, serves as an absolute minimum for assessing performance. It should be noted that this does not apply to estimates of low base-rate events. We simply cannot gauge the accuracy of estimates of events which occur less than once during a 50-minute interval.

Thomas et al. (1933) found that 120 minutes of data in five-minute segments distributed over a period of months gave stable estimates. They also noted that some social behaviors required greater sampling than others. In one analysis, the data for 20 boys were collected in a series of 12 five-minute samples. The correlation based upon odd/even samples from this set was .69 for Talking and .56 for Physical Contact. Increasing the amount of time in sampling increased the stability correlations to .94.

Smith (1931) also examined these questions in detail. He reviewed studies by other writers who were concerned with estimating the amount of data required for obtaining a stable estimate of the rate or likelihood for any given variable. Most of these studies showed that 70 minutes, sampled in five-minute blocks, gave minimally stable results. Currently, this serves as a rough rule of thumb in

Table 3.5
Stability Correlations for First and Second Half of Baseline[1]
(from Jones et al., 1975, p. 72)

Code categories	Family members		
	Target boys (N = 54)	Mothers (N = 54)	Fathers (N = 41)
Approval	.02	.48	.15
Attention	.36	.38	.43
Command	.23	.73	.44
Command Negative	.68	.80	.54
Compliance	.67	.37	.38
Cry	.90	—	—
Disapproval	.66	.62	.48
Dependency	.24	—	—
Destructiveness	.46	—	—
High Rate	.16	—	—
Humiliate	.73	.54	.33
Ignore	.27	.63	—
Laugh	.23	.46	.35
Noncomply	.63	.34	.45
Negativism	.54	.68	.39
Normative	.44	.49	.15
No Response	.21	.20	.12
Play	.51	.59	.48
Physical Negative	.38	.63	.63
Physical Positive	—	.69	.19
Receive	.32	.21	.16
Self-Stimulation	.29	.05	.06
Talk	.26	.53	.38
Tease	.35	.85	.43
Touch	.31	.68	.38
Whine	.63	—	—
Work	.59	.50	.16
Yell	.74	.45	—

[1]The sample consisted of 27 normal plus 27 problem families.

—: Insufficient data for calculations.

designing studies at OSLC. It should, however, be replaced as quickly as possible with rules based upon more extensive empirical studies.

Thus far there is little information available regarding the amount of event sampling required to obtain accurate assessments of functional relations. Taplin (1974) calculated the conditional probability that a positive parental consequence would follow a particular coercive child response. The means based upon the first three sessions correlated .56 with the means for the three sessions that were obtained during the following week. At OSLC, R. Loeber is currently preparing a more systematic study of this problem.

Notice that all of these studies sample behavior and settings *across time*. The assumption is that within a physical setting (such as the home or nursery school) the same general interactional settings will repeat themselves. Given enough sampling of sessions, it should be possible to obtain an accurate estimate at least for high-rate events. However, these event sampling correlations are, by definition, somewhat confounded. A significant correlation implies two things. First, it suggests that enough behavioral events were sampled to provide an estimate whose accuracy is specified by the magnitude of the correlation. However, the same correlation implies that the behavior of the individual is stable across time. In this manner the problem of event sampling combines elements from two problems in traditional psychometric analysis. Our studies were somewhat similar to studies of internal consistency; they are also similar to short-term test-retest reliability. In that the studies of event sampling were based upon a series of sessions over a two-week period, the correlation of the first three with the last seven also gives information about short-term reliability. Future studies might be better served by using an odd (three sessions) versus even (three sessions) format when studying event sampling.

Test-Retest Reliability. Given that we now have an estimate based upon at least 60 minutes of observation data per subject then how reliably can we predict a score for the following month or year? We have carried out only a limited analysis of this problem. We were mainly concerned with the long-term stability of the TAB score because it is the score most often used in studies at OSLC. In the first study, the TAB score was calculated for each of 27 boys based on three or more sessions during the first week of baseline and again for the second week (Patterson, 1974a). The reliability score of .78 ($df = 25$, $p < .01$) showed that the instrument provided a relatively stable estimate of deviancy based upon three or more sessions. In the next study, a small sample of nine normal children were studied for six baseline sessions and then observed again twelve months later for two sessions. The TAB scores correlated .74 ($df = 7$, $p < .05$). This small-scale study showed that the test-retest reliability for an extended time interval was in the same range as that found for other instruments used to measure children such as the Stanford-Binet.

The psychometric studies of PDR have just begun (Chamberlain, 1980). Recent studies suggest that mothers' reports on PDR may reflect transient mood states (Chamberlain, in preparation). As yet there has been no event sampling analysis for this instrument. However, there have been several studies of the test-retest reliability of composite scores for limited time intervals.

For a clinical sample, over a two-week interval, the test-retest reliability of the PDR score was .60 ($df = 16$, $p < .01$) (Patterson, 1974b). Chamberlain (1980) obtained a test-retest correlation of .82 ($df = 60$, $p < .001$) for a sample of normal families. She also found a correlation of .89 between mothers and fathers for their estimates of targeted deviant behaviors. Christensen (1976) obtained independent data from mothers and fathers for weekends. The correlations for reports from mothers and fathers ranged from $-.47$ to 1.00 with a mean of .51.

These studies demonstrate that PDR is a reliable procedure for collecting data. In many ways it is an inexpensive method for obtaining a general measure of child deviancy level. The problem which is of most concern to us lies in the reactivity of the measure. There is good reason to believe that it is *highly reactive* as a measure of treatment outcome. The review of studies by Patterson (1980b) showed that mothers were likely to perceive improvement as measured by the PDR score even though little or no change was shown in TAB scores.

Validity

When expressed as a single index, validity specifies the degree to which an instrument measures what it was designed to measure. The FICS was designed to describe coercive interchanges among family members—how well does it do this? There is no single test which will provide the answer to this question. There are, however, a series of tasks which a valid measure of coercion should fulfill. First, one would expect a valid code to significantly differentiate families of normal children from families with identified antisocial children. Second, the observation scores should correlate with reports of aggressiveness provided by parents, teachers, or peers. Finally, there is the matter of the construct validity of the coercion variables that make up the coding system. To the extent that these variables contribute to our understanding of familial aggression they also contribute to the validity of the coding system.

Does the FICS consistently differentiate families of normal children from families of children identified as antisocial? There are a number of investigators who have employed the FICS, or a revision of it, to make such a comparison. In all such studies, the problem child and members of his family have been shown to be more coercive than comparable members of normal families (Patterson, 1976; 1981b, Reid et al., 1981; Snyder, 1977; Conger & Burgess, 1978).

Differentiating normal from clinical samples is a first step in demonstrating the validity of the FICS. However, it is conceivable that the differentiation between samples relates to some dimension other than the one which we put forward. For this reason, it is necessary to demonstrate that scores based upon the FICS correlate with some other measure(s) of antisocial child behavior. The Parent Daily Report (PDR) criterion was developed to provide another measure of child deviancy. As noted earlier, PDR is a reliable procedure for collecting data. The prediction would be that some composite measure of deviancy based upon observation data should covary with PDR deviancy

61

scores. In the FICS, the most frequently used composite score is Total Aversive Behavior (TAB). It sums across the frequency of occurrence for each of 14 code categories measuring coercive behaviors. This score also provides a reliable estimate for general coerciveness.

The two methods vary not only with respect to data source (parents versus observers) and format (informal versus systematic data), but also in terms of the time intervals sampled (one hour versus an entire day). One might expect, therefore, to find low intercorrelations between TAB and PDR scores. Nevertheless, the mean frequency for PDR scores collected during baseline correlated .69 ($df = 14, p < .01$) with the mean TAB scores derived from the observers' data collected during the same baseline period (Patterson, 1976). The comparable correlation for a sample of children who steal was .58 ($df = 31, p < .001$). Chamberlain (1980), in her study of normal families, found a correlation of .48 ($p < .05$).

It seems that the two modes of data collection do, in fact, covary in their assessment of the general level of antisocial behavior. This sets the stage for a more definitive evaluation of the two procedures. Each instrument shared in common measures of Cry, Destructive, Negativism, Non-Comply, Whine, and Yell. Each instrument also measured deviant traits that were not shared. First, do the two modes agree in identifying the occurrence of the traits that are shared in common? Is a child identified by observers as high rate on Yell also reported by the mother to be high rate on the same trait? Secondly, there is the question of how precisely the two instruments measure individual traits. Can each procedure differentiate *among* deviant traits? The study by Waksman (1977) used OSLC baseline data from 47 boys for an analysis of convergent and discriminant validity using the multi-trait/multi-method procedure. Of the six traits measured in common by the two methods, significant convergent correlations were obtained for Whine (.47), Cry (.37) and Destructive (.33). However, only Whine met the criteria for discriminant validity. The across-method correlation for Whine was greater than any of the within-method correlations for Whine with the other five traits.

The two modes of assessment show consistent agreement in identifying general deviancy levels for child behavior. There is even modest convergence in measures of three deviant traits. When taken together, the findings strongly support the claim of validity for the coding system as a measure of antisocial behavior.

In the context of discussions about validity one might also examine the agreement between the two methods in measuring treatment outcome. In a treatment outcome study, Patterson (1974b) reported that 67% of a treated sample of children showed a reduction of at least 30% on both the PDR and the TAB scores from baseline to treatment termination. Weinrott et al. (1979) also carried out an elegant time series analysis of PDR measures for single subjects. The findings from this study suggested that the PDR scores showed substantial agreement with the observation data for the measurement of treatment impact for a replication sample. More recent studies (Chamberlain, in preparation) indicate that the PDR score may be somewhat reactive. About ten percent of the mothers in the clinical sample report that their children are much more deviant than is reflected in their TAB scores. These "distortions" seem to relate to the mother's depression and anger as measured by the MMPI. We are particularly interested in this phenomenon because it may relate to the fact that the PDR score also seems somewhat reactive as a measure of therapy outcome.

In the final analysis, the validity of the code will be determined by its contribution to our understanding of coercive family processes. Are the variables measured by the code relevant to that process? One might think of this question as being the focal point for this book. As noted earlier, the purpose for a performance theory was to identify variables from the code which account for the variance related to individual differences among children in the level at which they perform coercive behaviors. The multivariate analyses in Chapters 11 and 12 directly address the issue of the validity of the key constructs that are measured by the code.

Sample Characteristics

Since January 1968, the FICS has been used routinely to collect data on the clinical cases that have been referred to OSLC for treatment. The majority of these clinical cases were preadolescents that were referred for antisocial behavior. As noted earlier, the clinical population at OSLC is composed primarily of children who steal and children that are socially aggressive. About one-fourth of these antisocial children were also physically abused (Reid et al., 1981). Carlson (1979) re-examined the case files for OSLC referrals and found that about one-fifth had been previously diagnosed as hyperactive and were medicated prior to referral to OSLC. None of the chronic delinquent children treated at OSLC since 1977 are included in the sample described in this section, nor are any of their observation data included in the

Table 3.6
Parent Occupation for Two Samples

	Percentage for	
Occupational level*	Nonproblem families (N = 40)	Problem families (N = 170)
I. Major professional or large business	5	1.8
II. Lesser professional or business	15	5.3
III. Administrative or small business	12.5	10.6
IV. Clerical	15	18.8
V. Skilled laborers	17.5	10.6
VI. Semi-skilled laborers	10	19.4
VII. Unskilled laborers or welfare recipients	22.5	31.8
Not classifiable	2.5	1.8

*from Hollingshead & Redlich (1958)

analyses in this volume.

Local newspaper advertisements were placed at intervals offering payment to nonproblem families for participating in an OSLC study of family interaction. During the first ten years of the study normal families were selected only if they provided a close match to a clinical family on SES, family size, age of the target child, and father presence. The demographic data for these samples are described in this section (the data were tabulated in 1979).

The occupation of the parent was classified according to the procedure used by Hollingshead and Redlich (1958). As can be seen in Table 3.6, about 80% of both samples were working-class families. It also seems that the matching for the two samples was not as carefully done at the lower occupational levels. Forty percent of the distressed families were from father absent homes; the comparable figure for nonproblem families was 21.1%. The lack of fit is apparently due to the fact that following the careful matching of normal and clinical cases there have been changes in the kinds of cases referred to OSLC. The new referrals increasingly involved welfare and lower-class families. These families were participating in studies concerned with children who steal, and more recently, child abuse.

The age distribution data show that the majority of the cases ranged in age from 5 to 12 years, with a median age of 7 to 8 years. These data are presented in Table 3.7.

During the first few years, referrals of families with only two members were not accepted because we were interested in sibling interaction as well as in parent/child interchanges. Also, because of observer fatigue, families with more than seven or eight members were seldom accepted. By the early 1970's, both sets of restrictions were lifted. As the data stand in Table 3.8, they cannot really be thought of as representative of the total population of antisocial cases that *might* have been re-

Table 3.7
Age Distributions for Both Target and Problem Children

	Percentage for	
Age grouping	Nonproblem target children (N = 40)	Problem children (N = 170)
2-4	10.6	5
5-6	17	15
7-8	31.2	42.5
9-10	23.5	12.5
11-12	19.4	17.5
13-15	5.3	7.5

Table 3.8
Family Size for Two Samples

Number of people in family	Percentages for	
	Nonproblem families (N = 40)	Problem families (N = 170)
2		8.2
3	7.5	20.6
4	30	27.6
5	35	21.2
6	20	11.2
7	5	5.3
8		4.7
9		.5
10		
11		
12		.5
over 12	2.5	

ferred. The epidemiological study by Rutter et al. (1970) found that 34% of his control group of families had four or more children, as compared to 44.4% for his antisocial group. Because of the manner in which the OSLC data were tabulated, it is not possible to make an exact comparison. Even as it stands, however, the OSLC sample does seem in keeping with the idea that antisocial children come from large families.

Normative Data. Normative data for an earlier sample are provided in the book by Reid (1978). The data were collected from 27 distressed and 27 nondistressed families referred to OSLC. The rate and standard deviations are given separately for each code category for mother, father, deviant child, and siblings. In addition, the sibling data are subdivided into younger and older, male and female.

Epilogue

Science is only as good as its instruments. It is, therefore, necessary to move on and develop instruments of greater fidelity and precision than the relatively primitive FICS. Undoubtedly, the use of six-second units distorts some aspects of family interaction. It was convenient to construct the first coding system in this manner; it even provided a rough estimate (within a six-second error) of the duration of events. It would, of course, be better to use real time in describing behavior. As noted by Hartup (1979) and others, this would permit the use of density and duration as dependent variables; either of these would be preferable to the use of rate or frequency.

The second and more serious problem with the FICS is that it was not designed to explore the intricacies of *prosocial* interactions. It was tailored to measure *aversive interchanges* in families. But in most family interactions, these categories describe only 5% to 10% of what is going on. Categories such as Work and Talk constitute the *majority* of the prosocial behaviors that are coded. But these categories are really wastebasket categories that obfuscate the subtleties of prosocial interchanges. We were aware of this limitation when we designed the FICS, but we did not have the time or the funds to develop a code which would provide a more complete picture of prosocial interactions. In 1976, a group comprised of Marion Forgatch, Dennis Moore, Leona Mukai, Mark Weinrott, and the author began work on a new code that would correct some of these inadequacies. The revised code was field-tested for several years and, in fact, provided a basis for carrying out most of the *in situ* experiments described in Chapters 5, 7, 8 and 9. In 1979, D. Toobert, D. Moore, and the author spent a summer studying normal and "super" normal families. This led to the development of new categories which described the socialization processes in these families. The interactional events were recorded in real time.

This new code (the MOSAIC) is now being field-tested (Toobert et al., in preparation). These trials will address one further deficit in the FICS which we had to overlook in our earlier work because of time constraints. We are now evaluating the generalizability of the data from one "standard" time of sampling (the dinner hour) to other times of the day. A related concern is the generalizability of the data collected in a semi-structured format to unstructured home settings.

Like its predecessor, the MOSAIC is expensive to use. It costs an average of about 3.5 hours of observer time for each session; appointments are missed, the journey to the home takes time, and the data must be proofed and stored. The cost for six observation sessions in the home is about the same as the cost for the standard write-up for the intellectual assessment of a child.

Wright (1960) reviewed the 1,409 empirical studies in child psychology for the period 1890-1960. He noted that 8% of these studies employed observation techniques. Bronfenbrenner (1977) carried out a comparable survey for the period 1972-1974; again, only 8% employed observation procedures. It is apparent that this technology is one whose time has not yet come. Perhaps the problem with its adoption lies in the complexity of the task.

Footnotes

1. This chapter is an update of material presented in *A Social Learning Approach to Family Intervention,* Volume 2: *Observation in Home Settings,* by John B. Reid (Ed.), 1978. Readers who are familiar with that publication may want to skip this chapter.

2. The Walter and Gilmore (1973) and Wiltz and Patterson (1974) studies showed that four weeks of treatment were sufficient to produce significant changes in behavior. For this reason, *any* case receiving this much treatment was tallied as treated in evaluating success. This is in contrast to many of the traditional therapy studies which do not include data from these dropouts in evaluating treatment success rates. For example, two studies reviewed by Graziano and Fink (1973) showed uncounted dropouts of 40% and 60%!

Chapter 4
Abstract

Aversive events in family life arise both from conflicts among family members and from sources external to the family. These events serve the dual function of altering mood and shaping behavior.

This chapter reviews the literature describing the relation of aversive events to autonomic reactions, anger, and mood changes. Conditions of arousal in which negative attributions are made are most likely to be followed by attacks. The literature suggests that antisocial children may be more likely to attribute hostile intentions than normals.

Child-rearing years are generally associated with reduced happiness. It is hypothesized that aversive events from conflicts with children and crises external to the family produce lowered self-esteem and depressed mood for the caretaker. Data are presented that test for the covariation of mother's daily fluctuations in mood with frequency of crises, community contacts, and aversive child behavior. The Multiple R values ranged from .55 to .78, with mothers' Lubin scores as criterion measures.

Chapter 4

Aversive Events: The Innocuous Determinants

Coercion theory gives central status to the low-key aversive events that are commonly found in social interactions. These events are part of everyone's experience, and are therefore thought to be of little importance. While day-to-day variations in the density of these events may be noted, little weight is given to their passage. Extremes in density might be labeled a "bad day," something to be expected, somewhat analogous to a case of psychological smog. They are accepted as just another facet of everyday life.

In contrast, the present stance is that the rate and intensity with which these "innocuous" events occur defines a process which, under certain conditions, can lead to dramatic outcomes. For example, the replicated studies of G.W. Brown and his colleagues showed that the relapse rate for schizophrenic patients correlated with the *suspected rate of low-key aversive interchanges* with their family members (Brown & Rutter, 1966). The measure upon which this prediction was based consisted of a scoring of hostile and critical remarks made by relatives about the patient prior to admission for treatment. The relapse rate for patients that were returned to highly aversive families was 58%, as compared to 16% for low-aversive families. The study was replicated by Brown, Birley, and Wing (1972).

Chapter 7 of this volume describes a general model for conceptualizing the escalation in inten-

sity from the innocuous exchanges that are commonly found in all families to the high-intensity violence that is found in only a few. Based on their observation studies of child abusive families, Reid, Taplin, and Lorber (1981) formulated the steps by which the parents' interchanges with the child may escalate in intensity to include hitting. A prime function of coercion theory is to provide an empirical base for understanding the determinants of this process.

In the context of family interaction, aversive events are thought to play a dual role. On one hand, these events are the key components in a behavior shaping or changing process. Given time, this process can produce dramatic changes in behavior for families of socially aggressive children. The second role relates to the short-term effects these innocuous events have upon the autonomic system and the alteration in mood or affect that is associated with their continued presentation.

Taken individually, most of these aversive events are trivial, a psychological mote as it were. The fact that they are part of a slowly unfolding process means that their contribution to dramatic outcomes goes largely undetected. This is in stark contrast to the colorful explanations for the same phenomena that are offered by traditional psychology. The metaphors of the latter have become themes for drama and literature, e.g., the love of Oedipus for his mother; the hydraulic forces of instinctual aggression lurking beneath the surface in Golding's *Lord of the Flies;* the relation between a sexual love of the father and obesity in Lindner's classic *Jet Propelled Couch.* Whatever their eventual status as explanations, the reading public has come to expect psychologists to provide formulations at least as dramatic as the phenomena they purport to explain. What is offered here will be a divergence from these dramatic explanations. Rather than cataclysmic episodes, flood tides of rage, or crumbling defense structures, we are concerned with coercive family processes that change with glacial slowness, a process that is comprised of events that are inherently banal.

This chapter details the stressors that are generated by aversive interchanges among family members and from sources external to the family itself. The impact of these events as elicitors of changes in affect and mood is emphasized particularly as they relate to the caretaker role within the family. When the density of these aversives, or stressors, exceeds some threshold value held by the caretaker, it is hypothesized that he or she will report feeling "down," "depressed," "anxious," or "tired." The related hypothesis is that an individual's general feelings of life satisfaction will be associated with some ratio of aversive to positive events. Finally, it is suggested that the impact these aversive events have on behavior is related to the processes of arousal, attribution, and anger.

Arousal, Attribution, and Anger

Our initial attempts to build a performance theory made little use of the concepts of arousal, attribution, and anger. Our primary focus was upon the analysis of structure in family interactions. But even then, these other processes were obviously present. During our first contacts with antisocial children and their families, anger was a salient feature of the behavior of both the parent and the child. A considerable percentage of the parents, especially the mothers, were very angry in their dealings with problem children. In many cases, they seemed angry with the world in general. In fact, even after successful treatment some parents continued to make negative attributions about the child, e.g., "he is really bad," or "you can't trust him." Their attributions turned out to be a self-fulfilling prophecy; a follow-up of treated families often showed these cases to be failures.

Observers often described angry interchanges as being a part of sequences in which someone would be physically assaulted. It was about that time we began appreciating the fact that a sizable proportion of the OSLC sample was made up of child-abusive parents (Reid et al., 1981). The observers often saw these parents hit. The parents also seemed to attribute malevolent intentions to the child. The combination of negative attribution and anger seemed to be an important part of the process leading to physical abuse.

Our clinical contacts with chronic delinquents began in 1977. The majority of these families seemed to be involved in very intense, long-standing "struggles." The family members were palpably angry with each other. They held one another in complex webs of attribution. In case after case, the impact of this was to seriously impair the treatment process. While we had rarely encountered these problems before, it now seemed as though angry struggles characterized every other case.

Finally, there was a growing awareness that the treatment process itself was inundated by flood tides of crises. The parents came in with perfectly good "excuses" for not being able to carry out their planned programs. They had been caught up in a crisis that would have disrupted the plans of even the most organized middle-class family. However, as treatment progressed, it became apparent there was not just *one* crisis, but a series of them. Each family seemed to be caught up in its own sequence of disasters. These crises were macrosocial events that clearly had an impact upon family interaction patterns; they disrupted the ability of the parents to practice effective family management skills. These macrosocial events also covaried with the negativity of parental reactions to their children.

A General Formulation

Bandura (1973) viewed the determinants listed in Figure 4.1 as potentiating pre-existing dispositions to aggression. The external event, by itself, might increase the likelihood of an attack. Arousal would further increase this likelihood. In addition, if the individual attributed a hostile intent to the intruder, this may further increase the general level of arousal and add to it the label "anger." This, in turn, would be accompanied by further increases in the likelihood of initiating an attack.

The writer is in accord with this view, but would suggest that the arousal-attribution process is associated with *longer* coercive sequences. These, in turn, correlate with increased likelihoods for high-intensity aggression at each juncture in the chain (Loeber, 1980). In this sense the arousal-attribution process is thought to be an important determinant of high-amplitude initiations of aggression characterizing violent children and adults.

It would be expected that persons who engage in violent assaultive behavior would be more likely to describe themselves as angry than would nonas-

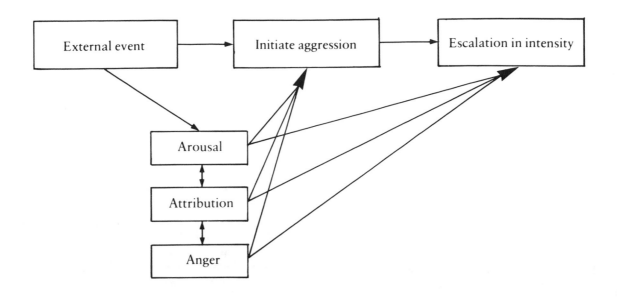

Figure 4.1. Processes Relating to Likelihood of Aggression

saultive individuals. They would also be more likely to attribute a hostile intention to their victims. For example, child-abusive mothers might view their children as trying to upset them or get their goat. If frequent extensive sequences are related to the arousal-attribution process, then it follows that the more violent individual would engage in longer sequences of coercive behavior.

It is thought that most coercive interchanges among normal family members involve low-level arousal-attribution processes. They are what John B. Reid has labeled "nattering." This is also analogous to what John Knutson calls "irritable aggression." A natterer is a coercive dilettante. Although John B. Reid has never formally defined this term, his usage of it implies that it is a haphazard aversive reaction. The parent could ignore the situation and remain uninvolved, but instead becomes a thoughtless participant in an aversive exchange. As will be shown later, the parents' involvement in no way clarifies or alleviates the situation. Rather, it serves to extend these low-intensity interchanges. In the present context, it is interesting to note that periodically these sequences escalate in intensity. Thus it appears that nattering can become the prelude to events that are much more painful. High rates of background nattering are thought to be related to increased likelihoods for becoming involved in high-amplitude aggression.

Arousal

The social learning position has considerably

expanded the list of aggression-related determinants for autonomic arousal. For example, the studies reviewed by Bandura (1973) demonstrate the arousing function of shock, frustration and insults. In addition, he holds that viewing the behavior of an aggressive model or an aggressive film serves as a potentiator for aggressive behavior; it also serves an arousing function. He cites four studies that show that viewing violent films is emotionally arousing. As shown in figure 4.1, under some conditions arousal is thought to be facilitative for aggression. Anger-related arousal resulting from goal blocking or insult has also been shown repeatedly to facilitate aggressive interactions (Bandura, 1973; Berkowitz, 1973b; Rule & Nesdale, 1976). However, the latter point out that the state of arousal produced by temperature changes is not related to aggression. Similarly, Holleran's (1977) review found that, in and of itself, high-decibel noise did not produce aggression; it was associated with aggression only when the subjects were angered. His own laboratory study replicated the findings of Rule and Nesdale (1976).

One feature of Bandura's (1973) work received a good deal of attention in the last decade because it had major implications for social policy. He demonstrated the possibility that viewing aggressive films was not only arousing, but also facilitated aggressive attacks in later social interactions. Berkowitz (1974) also believes that viewing such films enhances a "readiness to aggress"; i.e., given an appropriate external stimulus, then the likelihood of attack is increased. The issue is still being debated, but a substantial number of well-designed studies now provide support for the Bandura-Berkowitz position. As things now stand, the laboratory studies provide a consensus for the idea that aggressive films significantly facilitate the likelihood of attack behaviors for subjects who are already angry. This probably has some bearing on children watching television at home. If further research lends support to this position then the American people may have to decide if it is necessary to censor media presentations for violence.

There are a number of studies reviewed in Bandura (1973), and in Chapter 7 of this volume, demonstrating the not very surprising finding that a range of aversive events—shock, heat, insults, noise, and humiliations—all elicit autonomic reactions. It might be noted, however, that there is little consensus as to *which* physiological measures are best suited to measure this activation. Lacey (1967) proposes that one should consider patterns of these measures; it is possible that each individual may have an idiosyncratic pattern. Lang (1971), in his classic review of these and related matters, put the problem into perspective as follows:

"Investigators originally hoped that single measures of autonomic functioning would have a simple indicant relationship to the psychological constructs in vogue. However, it became apparent very soon that skin conductance increase, for example, did not equal "anxiety" or "drive," nor was its relationship to these constructs simple or fixed. In point of fact, a great variety of situations and events will evoke skin conductance changes, ranging from the closing of a door or the sound of a friendly voice, through a whole gamut of emotional and physiological stressors. Nearly all physiological responses can be generated by a great variety of internal and external stimuli, and it seems unlikely that any physiological event could be used in an exact substitutive way, as an index of psychological state. Thus, by observing the physiology of an organism, we are not able to go backwards and reconstruct the stimulus input or the psychological state that contributed to its generation. To assume this kind of reciprocal relationship is the classic *indicant fallacy*." (p. 99)

In the context of Lang's position, a judgment about an event as being aversive or nonaversive is based on information about the stimulus context, plus interoceptive cues denoting autonomic arousal. Each subject may have his or her own idiosyncratic rules for combining this information. As

some of Lang's later studies showed, there was little covariation among measures of autonomic arousal, self-ratings of anxiety, and approach behaviors.

We would like to begin working at OSLC with autonomic measures. In that regard, some of the recent literature suggests that measures of nonspecific skin conductance might be most useful. The review of Miller and Grant (1979) found that nonspecific skin conductance responses were closely linked to emotional arousal, while tonic skin conductance level and heart rate more sensitively reflected cognitive and attentional factors. Szpiler and Epstein (1976) also found that nonspecific skin conductance was a highly sensitive measure of threat, and alone among arousal measures reflected successful avoidance of threat. As noted earlier, the tendency of family members to make critical, aversive comments about schizophrenic patients was related to the patients' later tendency to relapse (Brown & Rutter, 1966; Brown et al., 1972). In the study by Tarrier et al. (1979), after a baseline period, critical and noncritical relatives were introduced into a situation in which schizophrenic patients were being interviewed. The presence of noncritical relatives was associated with declining scores for nonspecific skin conductance measures. The presence of relatives who were critical was associated with the maintenance of the high arousal levels found in baseline. Normal subjects showed lower baseline levels, and a steady decline throughout the session.

More directly relevant is the study which showed a covariation of arousal with aversive events found in social interaction. In working with small groups, Kaplan, Burch and Bloom (1964) used sociometric measures to form dyads with a negative, neutral, or positive affinity for each other. During a 20-minute discussion, the number and amplitude of the GSR reactions were recorded each minute; then correlations were calculated for each dyad. The number of positive correlations above .29 was 75% for the negative affinity groups, 37% for the positive groups, and 26% for the neutral groups. In the replication study, the comparable figures were 55%, 15%, and 18% respectively. The groups did not differ in the number of negative acts or in the amount of participation. The authors suggested that the greater magnitude of covariation in the negative affinity group was due to a greater sensitivity or tracking of each other's aversive behavior. It appears that this might be true for family members as well. Recent studies indicate that families of antisocial children are more likely to engage in unprovoked attacks upon each other (Littman & Patterson, 1980). This, in turn, could relate to increased arousal and tracking for aversive events.

Control of Aversives and Arousal

The lay person and professional would agree that personal control over a forthcoming aversive event would be related to reduced arousal. Miller and Grant (1979) expand on this idea by pointing out that during conditions in which aversives are predictable the subject can identify a "safety time," and let down a bit. The authors also identify various techniques—such as self-relaxation, denial, distraction, and reinterpretation—that might reduce the impact of aversives, whether controlled or uncontrolled. Lefcourt (1973) reviews studies demonstrating that subjects who were able to control high-decibel white noise suffered less disruption in their work performance than subjects experiencing the same amount of noise outside their control. Other studies indicated that self-reports of the perceived intensity of aversive stimuli showed decreases in the intensity reported when the subjects were able to exercise control over the stimuli. Lefcourt also cited studies by Corah and Boffa (1970), and Haggard (1943) showing that physiological measures of stress were reduced if the subject could control the aversive stimulus. In the same vein, he describes the study by Weiss (1971), involving pairs of rats in which one member could work to terminate a shock. The yoked control received the same number of shocks, but the shocks were outside of control. Weiss concluded:

"The present experiment showed that regardless of whether electric shock was preceded by a warning signal, by a series of warning signals forming, so to speak, an external clock, or by no signal at all, rats that could perform coping responses to postpone, avoid, or escape shock developed less severe gastric ulceration than matched subjects which received the same shocks but could not affect shock by their behavior . . . the present results, in combination with earlier experiments, serve to establish that the beneficial effect of coping behavior in stressful situations is of considerable generality." (p. 8)

Many writers, such as Seligman (1975) have emphasized the same points. The lack of control over aversive events, or the absence of an effective coping response, seems to be an operational definition of what is meant by "stress." As Seligman emphasizes, this may, in turn, produce a state of conditioned helplessness accompanied by feelings of depression and anxiety. He describes a series of laboratory studies expanding upon the earlier work of Maier (1961) and others who had demon-

strated the dramatic effects of exposure to inescapable shock. Seligman extended the earlier findings by demonstrating that both *noncontingent reward* and *noncontingent aversive* events produced a state in which the individual was characterized by a reduced ability to escape and avoid future stress situations. In the case of noncontingent reward (e.g., the welfare state), the effect, as he labeled it, was "learned laziness." In the case of noncontingent shock, the effect was labeled "learned helplessness."

The Seligman metaphor seems to provide a very close fit to experiences characterizing members of out-of-control families. To an outside observer, many of the attacks by family members upon each other seemed "unprovoked." Our data indicate that over two-thirds of the coercive chains for the deviant child were apparently "unprovoked" (see Chapter 11). In the remaining one-third of the attacks, the deviant child is responding to attacks by other family members. It is assumed that this kind of uncertainty characterizes the majority of the interactions within these disrupted families. It is worthwhile to point out that the caretaker role is a focal point for such uncertainty. This is particularly true if the mother is inept at terminating the attacks that are launched against her. The implication is that the caretaker role, as a result, is accompanied by an increase in stress, and by concomitant increases in self-reports of anxiety, depression, and psychosomatic reactions (Seligman, 1975).

The control or lack of control over aversive events seems to relate consistently to disruption in performance on future escape and avoidance tasks. There is some evidence for somatic reactions (duodenal ulcers) being more likely and more severe for uncontrollable shock (Brady et al., 1958; Weiss, 1971). However, Weiss (1971) also found that the group that was given the opportunity for a coping response *also* showed the somatic reactions. This emphasizes the importance of the stress characteristics of aversive events per se, regardless of whether or not they are controllable. It should be noted that a review of the burgeoning literature in this area by Averill (1973) leaves in doubt the issue of whether control or perceived control is associated with greater reduction in physiological measures of stress.

Many of the parents with aggressive children that are referred for treatment report that they feel helpless, anxious, and depressed. Many also indicate that they have a variety of somatic complaints (Patterson, 1980a). As Maier (1961), Seligman (1975) and others have noted, direct guidance and manipulation is usually required before conditioned animals can re-engage in effective problem-solving behavior. In the case of parents, specific training in child and family management were shown to produce reductions in these self-reported stress reactions (Patterson, 1980a). Additional training in self-control procedures may further reduce the stress reactions. For example, the laboratory studies by Kanfer et al. (1974), and Kanfer and Seidner (1973) demonstrated increased tolerance of extremely aversive stimuli given simple training in thought (attentional) control and in the manipulation of internal standards. Training parents in relaxation, meditation skills, or giving them tranquilizers might serve a similar function. All of these coping devices would be perceived by the mother as resulting in a reduced stress reaction to aversive family interactions.

The other necessary component of treatment would include a means by which the family could reduce the overall level of aversive interchanges. It is not only how one *perceives* the aversive events in the environment, but their actual density and intensity that determines stress. Mothers with antisocial children are constantly coping with family crises. One might, in fact, characterize these women as being subjected to *chronic* stress. Even if medication or changes in attribution are provided, it would be less than humane to leave these mothers in a world in which aversives impinge upon them at very high rates.

Attribution and Anger

Berkowitz (1973b), Bandura (1973), and others have noted that the attributions made by the victim about the intention of the attacker are significant determinants for anger and aggression. The general formulation is based on Schachter's two-factor theory of emotion (Schachter & Singer, 1962). Emotional reactions are characterized by two necessary components: the first is the arousal state and the second is the cognitive label. Taken together they define the emotional response. As explained by Schachter (1964):

"Given a state of physiological arousal for which an individual has no immediate explanation, he will 'label' this state and describe his feelings in terms of the cognitions available to him. To the extent that cognitive factors are potent determiners of emotional states, it could be anticipated that precisely the same state of physiological arousal could be labeled 'joy' or 'fury' or any of the great diversity of emotional labels, depending on the cognitive aspects of the situation." (p. 53)

Two mothers might experience the same high density of quarrels among children, telephone cri-

ses from unpaid bills, or other similar situations, but label their emotional reactions in very different ways. One mother could see all this unpleasantness as being an expected "slice of life, as it really is," and experience only profound fatigue and vague depression. The other might attribute the sibling conflicts to a malevolent intent on the part of the children "to get her goat." Such an attribution might, in turn, lead her to believe that the arousal she is experiencing is anger. This attribution-labeling process, in turn, might increase the likelihood of a high-amplitude physical reaction by her. This dual attribution-anger reaction seems to characterize many of the mothers of families seeking treatment at OSLC. Because of its obvious relevance to escalations in physical violence, it is important that we learn to measure and investigate both the affective and the attributional behaviors. In the clinical studies by Toch (1969) and Berkowitz (1978), assaultive males often described themselves as having a "short fuse," i.e., quick to anger. It seems very likely that these shorter latencies and higher amplitudes were accompanied by increased likelihoods for attributing hostile intentions to their opponents.

Dodge (1980) hypothesized that aggressive children might engage in faulty attribution, particularly in inherently ambiguous situations. A peer sociometric identified 15 aggressive and nonaggressive boys in each of three grades. In the laboratory situation, the puzzle on which boys had been working was rearranged, presumably by the other child. Three different attributions were made for this episode: hostile, benign, and neutral. In the last phase, the subject was given an opportunity to aggress against the other boy. The hostile attribution condition produced significantly more aggression for both aggressive and nonaggressive subjects. As expected, there was a significant main effect for samples with the aggressive subjects showing more aggression. Much of this difference was attributable to the ambiguous attribution condition; here, the aggressive child was *significantly more likely to attack*.

The findings suggest that aggressive boys may be significantly more likely to attribute hostile intent to peers in ambiguous situations. Thus, what may seem to be an unprovoked attack may relate to cue distortions.[1] This is extremely interesting considering the extensive literature (see Chapter 11) showing that antisocial children are characterized in study after study as having "attentional deficits." Those studies show that these children generally do not track carefully, nor do they usually make careful discriminations. The complex interactional flow of the family or the playground would offer a rich field of possibilities for cue distortions or misattributions. Both the home and the playground are environments in which many brief, unpleasant experiences occur. They are likely to be accidental, but can easily be misconstrued as affronts or attacks.

To provide a more direct test of this possibility, Dodge (1980) carried out a second experiment. The subjects who served in the earlier study also participated in this second one. They were told a story in which a peer was involved in a negative outcome (from the viewpoint of the subject). The intention of the peer was left ambiguous. The subject was instructed to describe how it might have happened, that is, to reconstruct the intentions of the peer. Aggressive subjects attributed a hostile intention to the peer 50% more often than did the nonaggressive subjects. The aggressive subjects also said they would retaliate when they perceived the peer's intentions as hostile. Only 26% of the subjects who made a benign attribution said they would retaliate. There was one further outcome of interest: if the *peer* was known to be an aggressor, then the likelihood of a hostile attribution was five times greater. In the context of family interaction, the antisocial child has already learned that his siblings and/or parents are aggressive, and in situations where an affront was unintended or the intent was unclear the antisocial child might be more likely to attribute a hostile intent and attack. The formulation may relate to the finding by Littman and Patterson (1980) that antisocial boys were eight times more likely than normal boys to launch "unprovoked" attacks upon other family members. These findings are parallel to the findings of Raush (1965) in his study of the interactions of antisocial boys.

It seems the two concepts of attribution and intention potentially have much to offer a coercion theory. The problem now is to find a means of measuring them as they occur in ongoing interactional process.

Anger and Aggression

According to writers such as Berkowitz (1973b), the purpose of instrumental aggression is to produce a reinforcement (e.g. money or social approval), contingent on the response. Hostility was thought by these writers to relate to anger and an intention to hurt the other person. In that conjunction, Rule and Nesdale (1976) write:

". . . the observation that the goal of injuring another person can be construed as serving an instrumental function (Bandura, 1973; Hartup, 1974) indicates that a more appropriate differenti-

ation of aggression might be entertained. Thus, rather than distinguishing between hostile and instrumental aggression, it might be more appropriate to draw a distinction between angry and nonangry aggression, the latter encompassing those responses that are directed toward obtaining a nonaggressive goal. Although Buss (1971) has previously drawn the angry versus nonangry distinction. . . ." (p. 861)

Berkowitz (1973b) emphasized the position of anger as a motivational state intervening between frustration and aggression. The presence of anger potentiates existing cues which, in turn, elicit aggressive responses. The experimental studies reviewed by Rule and Nesdale (1976) are generally supportive of this position. When subjects were angered, there was an increased likelihood of aggressive attacks. Typically, the anger condition consisted of an aversive stimulus (shock or insult) plus a clear communication to the effect that the other person *intended* to inflict pain upon the subject.

Aversive Events in Family Life

Some of the aversive events altering mood and satisfaction are generated by interactions within the family. Others impinge on the family from sources external to it. Regardless of the source, the mothers of antisocial children must deal with more aversive events than mothers of normal children. The rate of conflicts among children is higher for families of antisocial children than for families of normal children. Similarly, there are probably higher rates of conflicts between spouses. As detailed in Chapters 10 and 12, these families are thought to be deficient in the problem-solving skills which would lead to the resolution of these conflicts. This same deficit is thought to relate to the higher frequency for crises external to the family. The unpaid bills, and altercations with neighbors, schools and community agencies contribute to a crescendo of pressures. In their aggregate, these crises are a prelude to the frequent moves, the disconnected telephone, and the isolation characterizing the families of antisocial children. As shown in Figure 4.2, these rising tides of adversity are thought to be determined partly by a breakdown in the performance of problem-solving skills. In some cases the disruption may be only temporary, as in the case of divorce (Hetherington, Cox, & Cox, 1976). In other instances, the parents have simply never learned how to solve familial conflicts; for them life crises seem to be due to the machinations of fate.

The next hypothesis was that these accumulated

Figure 4.2. The Relation Between Familial Stress and Changes in Mood

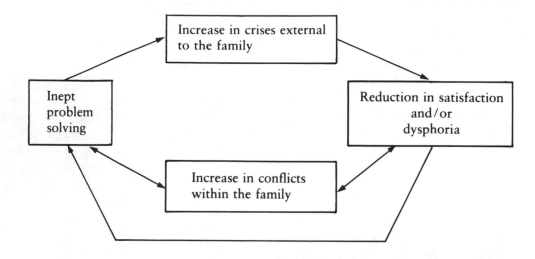

aversive events are major determinants for satisfaction with one's role, family, and with life itself. It was also thought to relate to changes in affective states such as mood, depression, and happiness. As documented by Holmes and Masuda (1974), there is a relation between physical and psychiatric illness on the one hand, and a high density of life stress events on the other. Marriage, divorce, change in employment, death, and similar factors each take their toll. Some investigators have shown a higher incidence of such life events for members of lower social classes, and relate this finding to a higher incidence of psychiatric disorder among that group (Myers, Lindenthal, & Pepper, 1974). Paykel (1974) demonstrated that the amount and intensity of these events varied across psychiatric disorders. Suicidal patients declared the greatest density of stress just prior to onset. The next greatest density of stress was declared by depressed patients and the schizophrenics. Most of these studies were *retrospective* in format, so their findings must be accepted with some caution. However, the findings from the predictive studies of Rae and Holmes, reviewed in Dohrenwend and Dohrenwend (1974), suggest that 79% of major life events were *followed* by illness. However, in that appropriate base-rate data were not provided, it is difficult to know just how to interpret these findings.

The life event studies represent a major contribution to our understanding of illness and stress. However, many of the family conflicts to be reviewed in this section would not even appear among Holmes' items, e.g., sibling fighting. Similarly, telephone calls regarding unpaid bills, extended illness among family members, or minor traffic accidents would not be noted. The present writer assumes these "minor" events have a *cumulative effect* directly determining satisfaction and/or mood. Any given event is, by itself, trivial, but the cumulative effect can be debilitating. Other things being equal, the happy, satisfied person is one who has developed a high order of skills in coping with normal life stress; a lack of skill results in a steady accumulation of crises and conflict.

The Attrition of Satisfaction and Happiness

Happiness and satisfaction are related variables, but they do not measure exactly the same thing. As used here, satisfaction involves a comparison between what is expected and what is obtained, while happiness ratings reflect current mood. It is assumed that the cumulative effect of aversive events from within family interactions, plus crises from external sources, produce both an erosion in satisfaction and a general dysphoria. A lack of skill in managing these events and/or a series of unaccountable misfortunes will covary with reductions in satisfaction and happiness. If the condition becomes chronic, then one might expect somatic repercussions and the development of somatic symptoms.

There is a considerable body of literature on the variables relating to the determinants of "happiness" among normal adults, e.g., Bradburn and Caplovitz (1965). It is not surprising to find that education, income, good health, and adequate leisure time were among the variables significantly associated with increased happiness (Wilson, 1967). Individual variations in happiness have also been related to the number of close friends contacted, the frequency of pleasant events, and those that are anticipated for the future (Shelly, 1970). Other studies have shown that for women these variations covary with the quality of interactions with friends, and for men with the quality of work experiences (Wessman & Ricks, 1966). Unhappiness has been related to difficulty at work, unemployment, marital tension (Wilson, 1967), poor peer relations, conflict with siblings (Wessman & Ricks, 1966), and general tension (Shelly, 1970; Wilson, 1967).

Several writers suggest that happiness with one's lot is best described by the *ratio* of positive to negative experiences (Bradburn & Caplovitz, 1965; Shelly, 1970). From this perspective, a person may have many positive experiences but may still feel unhappy because the density of negative events is much higher and produces a ratio which is out of balance. Conversely, some persons with a great many crises may still perceive themselves as happy because the situation is more than balanced by positive experiences from friends, work, and family. For example, Dawes (1978) summarized the data from a series of his own studies by writing, "If we love more than we hate, we are happy. If we hate more than we love, we are miserable." In his studies he simply subtracted the frequency of arguments from the frequency of intercourse. In one sample of 30 happily married couples, only two couples argued more than they had intercourse. In contrast, all 12 of the unhappily married couples argued more often than they had intercourse. In his studies he finds a consistent covariation between ratings of marital satisfaction and the frequency of lovemaking minus the frequency of arguing. The correlations for various samples ranged from .40 to .81.

Survey studies of married people usually identify men as being happier than women (Bradburn & Caplovitz, 1965; Gurin et al., 1960; Wilson, 1967). To the writer, this suggests an imbalance for women in the amount of aversives they receive while fulfilling the requirements of the *caretaker* role. It is very likely that husbands and wives differ on both the numerator and denominator in a happiness ratio; wives receive fewer positives and more aversives. In a study by Wills, Weiss, and Patterson (1974), wives reported that they received 6.4 Instrumental Pleases from their spouses per day; the number of Instrumental Displeases received was 2.1 per day. Similarly, the wives reported receiving about three times as many Affectional Pleases as Affectional Displeases. The means were 1.8 and .7 per hour respectively. Husbands reported that they received 5.4 Instrumental Pleases and 1.5 Instrumental Displeases from their spouses per day. For husbands, the means for Affectional Pleases and Affectional Displeases were 1.7 and .6 respectively. These data suggest that husbands and wives exchange pleasant and unpleasant events in an equitable fashion. However, wives receive far higher rates of aversive events from children than do husbands. When taken together, these two sources of aversive events result in a decrease in happiness and an increase in stress for mothers in the caretaker role.

A further modification of the Please and Displease list (which combined Affectional and Instrumental events) was then used for a sample of 12 distressed and 12 nondistressed couples. The ratio of Pleases to Displeases was 29.7:1 for nondistressed couples, and 4.3:1 for distressed couples. These results suggest that for nondistressed couples, the ratio of pleasant to unpleasant events was on the order of 30:1. When this ratio falls to 4:1 the couples reported feeling distressed. It should be kept in mind that the spouses were describing events from *their* relationship. If exchanges from children were included, then mothers of normal children would probably report almost equal daily *totals* of Pleases and Displeases, while mothers in antisocial families would likely report a heavy imbalance in favor of Displeases.

Wills et al. (1974) calculated the across-subject multiple *R* using the mean ratings of marital satisfaction as the dependent variable. The analysis for this tiny sample showed that Instrumental Displeases accounted for 44% of the variance and Affectional Displeases for 21%; the data for Pleases accounted for 27%. These findings were in keeping with the general findings in the literature on marital relations, which indicated that aversive events contribute more heavily to marital satisfaction than do positive events. The Wills study was replicated by Barnett and Nietzel (1979). In their study, 11 distressed and 11 nondistressed couples filled out the daily measure of pleasant and unpleasant experiences. The distressed couples described significantly more unpleasant (Instrumental) events than did the nondistressed couples. Again, Instrumental Displeases accounted for most of the variance in couples' ratings of satisfaction with their marriage.

The findings for the covariation of aversive

events with measures of mood and satisfaction are highly suggestive. Studies are needed now that systematically delineate the contribution of aversive events from different sources such as conflicts with spouse, coercive interactions with children or relatives, and crises from outside the family. These, in turn, should be systematically related to measures of the mother's mood and/or satisfaction with her role as caretaker. If the studies could be carried out over extended periods of time we might also obtain measures on the relation of these events to physical and psychiatric impairments. These studies are badly needed; they are the means by which we can understand this little-known side of the "caretaker role" in our society. What are the stressors accruing in the caretaker's role; what is the cumulative impact of "innocuous" stressors; is it the same at different phases in the development of the family? Weiss (1978) provides some insight into this last question. His findings suggest that the contribution of aversive events from the spouse becomes even more important for marriages lasting ten or more years. Ultimately, our success in producing nondistressed families may depend upon our ability to teach young people crisis and conflict management skills that will reduce the amount of stress that is associated with the caretaker role.

Children as Stressors

For the caretaker, children are prime generators of aversive events. This is generally experienced more intensely by mothers of *younger* children. It is also the case that some young children are more difficult to manage than others. These differences in ease of socialization may be constitutional. There is some evidence, for example, that activity level is inheritable. Willerman (1973) found a correlation of .93 for monozygotic twins in examining a measure of activity level. The comparable correlation for dizygotic twins was .52. There are, however, well-known problems with confounding due to identical twins shaping each other to a greater extent than fraternal twins; but even so, these findings are suggestive. Willerman (1973) also reported significant correlations between ratings by parents of the activity level of their children and recollections of their own activity level during childhood. The present writer assumes that there are differences in activity level and irritability at birth. If such differences persist, it seems reasonable to suppose that extremely active children present more difficult child management problems. This results in an increase in stress for the caretaker.

Differences in ease of socialization may also be due to abnormalities in the birth process. The Harvard follow-up studies of premature births compared them to children who experienced a normal birth (Shirley, 1939). In preschool, children that were born prematurely were characterized by a higher frequency of ratings as distractable during testing sessions (45% versus 13%). During the play session observed at the center, the prematures showed a higher incidence of crying (80% versus 57%), rapid shifts in toys played with (43% versus 23%), help-seeking (43% versus 17%), and nervousness (83% versus 27%). A similar study was reported by Parmillee (1962). The two- to five-year follow-up indicated that infants with abnormal signs at birth were more likely to be rated as having a short attention span (35% versus 6%) and hyperactive (46% versus 12%). Children described as irritable, crying, restless, hyperactive, and having a short attention span directly stress their caretakers.

Even normal children may provide a formidable source of stress for parents. This is especially true for younger children. Clarke-Stewart (1973) observed normal infants (ages 9 to 18 months) in their homes. The infants spent 8% of their waking hours crying (range 1.6% to 16.3%). The more fretful child was associated with mothers who were viewed as less skilled. It is difficult to separate out cause and effect here, however, the cross-lag analyses showed that the extent to which the mothers were rejecting at t_1 correlated .51 with negative infant behaviors at t_3. These results suggest that the mother's reaction to aversive infant behaviors may exacerbate the situation, i.e., caretaking skills probably interact with infant characteristics in determining the degree of stress.

It is part of the conventional wisdom to perceive 2-year-old children as "negativistic." The findings from a study by Reynolds (1928) are in keeping with this. Children of ages 2 through 5 years were given a number of requests to solve problems. Two-year-old children gave an average of eight refusals out of a possible 13. The comparable score for 3-year-old children was 4.61 refusals, 3.26 for 4-year-old children, and 2.42 for 5-year-old children. In that study, the correlation between age and negativism was −.53.

Observations made in the homes of normal preschool children showed an average of 3.4 disturbances per hour in the interaction of mother and child (Fawl, 1963). The preschool child was characterized by higher frequencies of conflict than were older children. For the range of children 2 to 11 years old, the frequency of conflicts correlated −.73 ($p < .01$) with their age. The general tenor of these findings is in keeping with that presented

Table 4.1
Status as Aversive Events

| | Mean ratings by mothers of: | | |
| | Stealers | Normals | |
Child Behavior	OSLC (N = 15)	Jones et al. (1975) (N = 20)	Johnson & Bolstad (1973) (N = 31)
Command Negative	7.5	7.2	1.83
Hit	8.2	7.7	1.07
Dependency	4.9	7.2	—
High Rate	7.1	7.5	1.31
Noncomply	8.1	8.1	1.28
Tease	6.9	7.9	1.20
Yell	7.1	7.9	1.54
Disapproval	5.3	5.8	1.87
Ignore	7.3	8.3	1.37
No Response	—	6.2	—
Whine	6.3	7.8	1.06
Negativism	6.8	7.2	1.69
Cry	7.1	5.8	1.96
Humiliate	6.4	8.0	—
Destructive	8.2	8.5	1.20
Command	3.2	5.6	2.30

in Table 2.2. As shown there, the observed rate of coercive behavior for normal 2- to 4-year-old children was comparable to the rate of 9-year-old antisocial children referred for treatment.

The presence of a young child provides several kinds of stress for the caretaker. The child tends to spend only brief interludes in solitary play, then returns to his mother's side. In fact, the observation study by Schoggen (1963) showed that one of the most frequent goals of young mothers was simply to terminate the demands that were being made upon them by their preschool children. This is compounded by the fact that in the home there are many things that can injure or be disrupted by the child. As a consequence, a day with a 2-year-old child is a study in vigilance. In her role of monitor, the mother finds herself issuing frequent stop commands. In a laboratory setting, mothers interacting with 2- and 3-year-old children issue these commands at the rate of about one every three minutes (Minton, Kagan & Levine, 1971). Even higher rates were reported by Forehand et al. (1975). It is not surprising to find that mothers report feeling maximally stressed when their children are 6 years old or under (Campbell, 1975).

However, these general findings are only indirectly related to the hypothesis that aversive interactions with children result in a dysphoric mood for the caretaker. The data that have been presented thus far do not demonstrate that mothers giving commands every few minutes actually experience these interactions as *aversive*. In addition, evidence has not been presented for the idea that these child behaviors *covary* with the mother's dysphoric mood or with her dissatisfaction with the caretaker role. The data that is relevant to these considerations is provided in the sections which follow.

It occurred to us that if family members could not agree as to what is and what is not perceived as aversive, then there would be little hope of proceeding with the study of coercive processes. Therefore, one of our first studies investigated the agreement among parents of normal preschool children in rating the 29 code categories on a nine point scale of "aversiveness-pleasantness" (Jones et al., 1975). The main ratings are summarized in Table 4.1. It can be seen that the categories classified by the experimenters a priori as aversive were also perceived as such by mothers. Mothers rated Destructive child behaviors as the most aversive with a mean rating of 8.5, and Command with a mean of 5.6 as the least. The ordering of the coercive behaviors correlated .86 with comparable rat-

Table 4.2
Covariation of Mother's Mood and Aversive Events

	PPM Correlations of Lubin Score* with:		
Subjects	Child TAB score	Mother TAB score	Mean Lubin scores
Pumpkin	−.19	−.15	1.55
Pluto	.25	.43	0.25
Spring	.19	.09	4.30
Tofu	.42	.26	2.15
Eclipse	.34	.67	3.15
Median	.25	.26	

*The "Lubin Score" consisted of the frequency of negative adjectives checked.

ings by a sample of mothers of older normal children from Johnson and Bolstad (1973). These findings suggest a general consensus among psychologists and three samples of parents as to the rank ordering for aversive child behaviors.[2] It can also be seen that the mothers of stealers ranked these events in a very similar manner; however, with four exceptions (CN, HT, NC, CR), they tended to provide ratings that were slightly lower than ratings by mothers of normals. Their ordering of the events by aversiveness correlated .60 with the ratings by mothers of normals in the OSLC sample, and .69 with the mothers of normals in the Johnson and Bolstad (1973) study.

The next question concerned the covariation between coercive child behavior and the mother's mood. To provide a data base, five mother-child dyads participated in extended baseline studies lasting 20 days. On each day the observation data collected in the home was used to calculate a Total Aversive Behavior (TAB) score for the mother and a comparable score for the child. During each session, the mother also filled out three self-report measures. She completed one of the three Lubin Mood Scales and the number of negative adjectives checked provided an estimate of her dysphoric state for that day. In keeping with the study by Wessman and Ricks (1966), it was expected there would be sizable shifts in the mood scores from one day to the next. It can be seen from Table 4.2 that in four of the five cases there was a covariation between mother's mood and coercive child behavior. On days when the mother described herself as being dysphoric, the child was more likely to perform coercive behaviors at high rates. Note, too, the high covariation between mothers' moods and their own aversive behaviors for Pluto and Eclipse. It was assumed that each of the variates

was serially dependent; therefore, no attempt was made to estimate the significance of these correlations.[3] In future studies of this kind, it would be useful to include coercion rates for all family members, as well as a report on Instrumental Displeases received from the spouse.

Crises as Stressors

The amount of external stress coming to bear upon a family is to some extent fortuitous, e.g., epidemics, social upheavals, natural disasters, and recessions. The frequency of crises also correlates with the status of the family in the economic hierarchy. For example, writers in the ecological tradition emphasize the destructive impact of poverty upon the family and upon individuals. Lewis' *La Vida* (1968) documents the steady attrition of spirit and gradual sense of helplessness accompanying prolonged enmeshment in extreme poverty. Systematic interviews by Tonge, James and Hillam (1975) documented the overwhelming frequency and intensity of the crises encountered by multi-problem families seeking assistance from community agencies. In the survey study of a borough in London, Brown, Bhrolchain and Harris (1976) found that stressful events were more likely to occur in the lives of working-class women than middle-class women. Interestingly enough, the impact of these crises was decreased if the woman had a close friend, husband, or relative with whom crises could be shared.

While suggestive, none of these studies provide a direct test of the impact of crises upon the mood of the mother. To provide data to test such a hypothesis, a family crises checklist was constructed at OSLC. The crisis checklist is provided in Appendix 4.1. The data were collected daily, and sampled events from general categories such as

Table 4.3
Covariations of Mothers' Mood, Crises and Community Contacts

Subject	Mean Insularity Scores				Correlations of Independent Variables with Lubin Scores				
	Crises per day	Contacts per day	Minutes	Positive Contacts	Crises per day	Contacts	Minutes	Frequency Positive Contacts	Multiple R†
Pumpkin	4.35	4.35	429.8	2.70	.55	.02	.21	−.11	.771‡
Pluto	1.60	3.15	41.75	1.35	.42	.09	−.04	−.30	.675
Spring	5.50	5.70	343.5	4.05	−.02	−.26	.31	.02	.546
Tofu	2.20	3.15	122.2	2.05	.34	.16	−.23	−.32	.686
Eclipse	5.55	3.70	287.0	2.90	.12	−.30	−.11	−.05	.780

†The Multiple R was calculated with Lubin score as criterion. The value includes the contribution of mother and child TAB scores as independent variables in addition to the four listed in this table.

‡The value also includes the contribution of sibling TAB score.

Household, Economic, Health, Employment, School, Social Interchange, Legal, Drugs, and Recreation.

Since its recent inception, the checklist has been used with eight normal families. They showed a range of two to nine relatively minor crises or "hassles" per week, e.g., bills to pay, arguments with spouse, an illness in the family, the car breaking down, or a dinner that was ruined. The mean for this sample was 4.75 crises per week. The checklist was also filled out daily by five mothers who participated in an extended baseline study of 20 sessions. As can be seen in Table 4.3, the five mothers reported a considerably greater incidence of crises than did the mothers in the (minuscule) sample of normals. The correlational data showed that mood shifts for two of the mothers (Pumpkin and Pluto) covaried more with crises than with aversive child behavior. The writer would believe the crises caused the shift in mood; however, the alternative hypotheses are equally reasonable. The mothers filled out the checklists for mood and crises at the same time, therefore the correlations may only describe their efforts to be internally consistent; or perhaps a bad mood in some way generated the increase in crises. However, it can be seen that for most of the mothers their moods covaried with some pattern of crises, insularity, and coercive interactions with their children. The multiple R values were high enough to suggest that mothers' daily fluctuations in mood may be a sensitive indication of what is going on in the family.

Of the five families who participated in the extended baseline study, some thought of their children as being problems and were later treated; others did not. The combination of mixed sample and minuscule sample size means we are in no position to make *simple generalizations* about what covaries with what. Crises *do* occur in both normal and distressed families. Some mothers reported that the crises covaried with their moods. However, the covariation could reflect the simple fact that both variables were based upon mothers' self-report. We will see in Chapter 12 that mood and crises covaried with how coercive the mothers were when interacting with their children. But there is no single pattern of covariation that characterizes all families.

Kohn (1973) and others have noted it is not *just* the amount of stress or the number of crises that must be considered. It is the individual's *resources* for *coping* with crises that determine the long-term impact. In his review, he makes the fascinating observation that, at any given level of stress/crisis, persons from lower social classes are more likely to manifest breakdown symptoms than are middle- or upper-class individuals in similar straits. He goes on to make the point that, with the same amount of stress, the lower-class person has fewer community, financial, and inner coping resources. The Brown et al. (1976) study also implicated the contribution of the spouse, friends, and relatives as support systems for coping. Several investigators give us reason to believe that families of antisocial children may have reduced community support networks (Tonge et al., 1975; Wahler, 1979).

For some time, multiple-problem families have been seen by caseworkers as being relatively isolated from the community. The clinical data provided by Tonge et al. (1975) portray in graphic detail the feelings of alienation and mistrust that members of these families have toward school, government, police, and welfare agencies. These families tend to have few contacts with friends, neighbors, or family. The contacts from the community that do occur are largely aversive in nature. These findings for multiple-problem families are certainly in accord with our own clinical experience. When we attempted to treat families of stealers, socially aggressive, and multiple-offending adolescents, we were confronted with their relative lack of support networks. In our experience, these families do not seem to cope with crises. As a result, they accumulate problems, and eventually become the concern for a committee of caseworkers from a half-dozen agencies. These families seem to be more mobile than other families, a finding also noted in the longitudinal study of aggressive children by Eron et al. (1974). Perhaps this increased mobility is a convulsive effort to escape from the mounting crises and largely abrasive communications received from neighbors and community agencies.

Robert Wahler at the University of Tennessee and his colleagues have provided an ingenious (and simple) means of obtaining data describing the "insularity" of these families (Wahler, 1979; Wahler, Leske, & Rogers, 1977). Daily reports of contacts with the community are obtained from the mothers. Wahler's first sample of eight high-risk families had an average of 2.6 community contacts per day; 30% involved friends. This was in contrast to an average of 9.5 per day for low-risk families; 58% of these contacts were with friends.

The OSLC data in Table 4.3 showed three to four daily contacts with persons from outside the family. This could be either a telephone call or personal contact; it seems that the majority were positive. There was a surprising range in the amount of time involved in these contacts; from less than an hour per day to more than five hours. The intraindividual correlation (across days) with the Lubin scores showed that the fewer the positive contacts, the lower the mother's mood. However, these correlations were obtained for only three of the five mothers; they were also of very low magnitude. In any case, the Wahler approach to measuring the important variables is seen as a promising beginning.

Contribution of the Composite to Mood

It is perhaps commonplace to document the difficulties encountered in raising young children. In the centuries prior to the advent of research studies in child psychology, these "facts" had probably not gone unnoticed. However, it is assumed by the writer that recent cultural changes that have broken up the extended family have reduced some of the primary support systems designed to buttress the role of caretaker. These cultural shifts bring aversive events into greater prominence, particularly as they disrupt the mood and self-esteem of those engaged in this role. Given the loss of support from relatives, friends, and community, then crises could play a more central role in an arena in which they were once balanced by positive support systems such as the extended family. The aversive events experienced by contemporary mothers may not necessarily be of greater frequency or intensity. They are, however, part of a process in which their presence is felt more keenly.

The pilot data from the five mother-child pairs suggest that future studies will find many combinations of variables, such as coercive child behavior, crises, and community contacts that are "determinants" for shifts in mothers' mood. For the present, only an overweening curiosity could lead an investigator to ask how much of the variance in mothers' daily mood shifts can be accounted for by these variables. This task is confounded by faulty constructs that read like a litany for a failed doctoral dissertation: six variables and an N of only 20, serial dependencies unknown, only five cases studied, degree of freedom unknown, and true magnitude of correlations unknown. However, curiosity prevails. The multiple-regression coefficient in Table 4.3 employed the Lubin score as the criterion. Thirty to 60% of the variance in the mood scores covaried with measures of aversive events and support systems.

If these correlations are replicated, the writer would assert that these variables are causally connected. It appears that high densities of aversive events and the lack of a support system *produces* mild and perhaps chronic depression in mothers. This should be particularly true for young, isolated mothers who lack effective problem-solving skills (see Chapter 10). In lieu of such studies, there are findings from treatment studies relevant to this issue. The test for causal connection will require experimental manipulations. It would be expected, for example, that if a sample of mothers was trained to use family management procedures to reduce coercive child behavior, these mothers should report that they feel less depressed. There are two studies relating to this issue that did not include the necessary control group. However, in both studies the mothers were trained to use social learning procedures to significantly reduce aversive child behaviors. Both studies showed decreases in mothers' self-reported depression (Patterson, 1980a; Griest et al., 1979).

The Effect of Stress upon Caretakers

Even in a normal family, the caretaker role is analogous to a storm center. It is the pivot point for external and internal stress. If there are many children at the preschool level, then the degree of stress may be considerable. In addition, if there is a disruption in family management skills (see Chapter 10), then external crises may accumulate. If this stress persists for long periods of time, it may be thought of as chronic. Selye (1976) summarized several decades of programmatic work, making a strong case for a nonspecific physiological reaction to chronic stress. Prolonged stress, with its accompanying adrenocortical reaction, may lead to eventual exhaustion of one or more physiological systems. However, it remains to be shown that there is a relation between stress accruing to the caretaker role and some manifestations of Selye's General Adaptation Syndrome (GAS).

Theorell (1974) did report a set of findings relating life stress events to physiological changes analogous to the GAS. Twenty-one males were interviewed each week for one to three months. In addition to having their life change events measured (Holmes), they also gave a urine sample. The life change and catecholamine scores were correlated for each subject. The median correlation was .40. These data indicate that a week with more life changes was characterized by an increase in the indicators of physiological stress.

Russell (1974) obtained data from crises relating to young couples experiencing their first child. As might be expected, many of the young mothers perceived the birth process, with its aftermath of fatigue, altered physical appearance, and change in mood, as constituting a crisis. Those experiencing an irritable or colicky infant perceived the crisis to be more severe. The 12 studies reviewed by Rollins and Feldman (1970) consistently underscored a sharp decline in happiness and/or marital satisfaction concurrent with the advent of the first child. The reduction in happiness persisted until the children left home, at which time there was an increase in reported happiness. More recent results from national surveys are in accord with these findings. For example, Glenn (1975) found that 45.6% of fathers in their 40's reported being

happy, in contrast to the figure of 60.6% for fathers of that age whose children had already left home. There were only modest increases related to child absence in happiness for mothers in that age group; however, for mothers in their 50's, the comparable percentages were 29.4% (children present) and 41.9% for post parenting. Parents seem to agree that they are happier *after* the children have left home, and least happy during early child-rearing years.

Prolonged exposure to aversive events over which one has little control might eventually lead to the evaluation of oneself in negative terms. Seligman (1975) labels this conditioned helplessness, which he suggests is accompanied by anxiety and depression. Even in normal families the person occupying the caretaker role must cope with an onslaught of crises, conflicts with spouse, and aversive child interactions. With a lack of skill and/or an overwhelming density of external stressors, the person occupying the caretaker role may be conditioned into a state of helplessness. The self-report data reviewed in Chapter 12 present a picture of a depressed, angry woman.

Traditionally, our culture has taken the position that one should ignore these aversive inputs. The mother is encouraged to: "Turn the other cheek," "Ignore it and the child will grow out of it," "Accept it, everybody gets a little depressed." At the same time, there is the tacit acceptance of the idea that mothers have the right to be bitchy. Xanthippe, while an historical figure, always has her modern counterparts. Her real-life counterpart's presence in a household is accepted as one accepts a visitation of influenza or any other "natural" phenomenon.

Conclusion

The studies reviewed thus far suggest that aversive events *are* a ubiquitous feature of family life. However, these events are *not* innocuous, and they should not be ignored. The data presented here suggest that aversive events may covary with marital satisfaction and with general happiness. At a more molecular level they covary with day-by-day changes in mood. These events elicit autonomic reactions that, depending on the setting, may also serve as an important source for negative attributions to the intentions of others. These changes, in turn, correlate with an increased likelihood of aggressive attack. The writer believes that these events are major determinants for the depression and unhappiness many mothers describe as their lot.

The aversive events found in family interaction have a further function: they serve as units in a process, the outcome of which may be even more insidious than a change in mood or decrement in self-esteem. Aversive events are the tools-in-trade for the coercive person who seeks to mold and shape the behavior of others. Garden-variety aversive events are the basic building blocks for a process that may eventually escalate to physical assault among family members. The means by which this process occurs in families will occupy the bulk of the next six chapters.

Footnotes

1. Berkowitz (1970) has suggested that low self-esteem plays an important role in determining the attack behaviors of violent adults. This variable may also play a role in the misattributions made by aggressive children in the Dodge study, i.e., children with low self-esteem may be more likely to distort cues in otherwise ambiguous situations. The problem with this formulation is that current measures of self-esteem do not differentiate aggressive children from normals (see Chapter 2).

2. In a study by Lorber (1978), nine of the aversive codes were also rated by 23 male and 23 female college students. Their ratings correlated only .26 (*n.s.*) with the ratings from the mothers of preschool children. This suggests that the set to perceive certain child behaviors as more aversive than others may reflect a "cultural norm" to only a very limited degree.

3. It is likely that the data for consecutive days would demonstrate significant serial correlations. If this is the case, then one is in the position of not knowing what the degrees of freedom really are for these correlations (Hoffman, 1967). In addition, a positive autocorrelation would mean that the estimates of magnitude are inflated (Hibbs, 1974).

Perspective on Chapter 4
by Dr. Robert G. Wahler

The beauty of Patterson's formulation in this chapter centers on his confirmation that most aversive events in family life *are* "innocuous" and ubiquitous—yet they are critically important determinants of psychopathology. A paradox? Yes, if one were to follow an early Watsonian view of behaviorism in which stimulus-response associations are the fundamental units of analysis. However, Patterson is clearly one of those Gestalten Behaviorists who seem to be saying that it is the patterning or relationship among these *S-R* events that should be seen as basic units. Thus, "innocuous" events become pathology inducing events when they appear in certain patterns (e.g., a marital relationship "feels" o.k. if the ratio of positives to aversives is approximately 30 to 1—when the ratio drops to 4:1 it feels bad; it seems to be the duration of each mother-child coercive exchange that may lead to the child's classification as deviant).

This chapter provides one of the rare hard data looks at the family system and the operating or functional levels within such a system. Certainly the system concept is not a novel notion by any means. But, to present a nuts and bolts schema for the concept offers not only a set of guidelines for system researchers—it also offers potential improvements in the clinical skills of applied workers. Let me now touch on this behavioristic systems concept from my perspective.

When a family therapist examines the basis of a clinical referral, the initial "problem" is almost always seen in the context of a coercive dyadic relationship. Two people in the family, usually the mother and one child, are entrapped in a reciprocally aversive pattern of interchange. The clinical solution, as parent trainers have documented, involves some specific means of changing the patterns—a means that is teachable in a didactic sense to both of the entrapped parties. But, there are also related coercive processes operating simultaneously at other functional levels within this family. At the individual level each party can be viewed as a system of covarying responses, some of them directly instrumental in social relationships and others indirectly related as attentional (or possibly attributional) responses. The latter, while not obviously connected to each party's coercive input to the dyad, has been shown to exert stimulus control over such input. Now, the complexity of this attentional or tracking control unit is that its function may be affected not only by the dyadic coercion problem; coercive relations beyond the troubled dyad can also add variance to the attentional processes. Thus, aversive events provided by a third family member or by members of the community might strongly influence the ways in which each member of the troubled dyad attend to one another. For example, a mother's ability to see clearly her coercive entrapment with her son will be affected not only by that dyadic problem—coercive problems with her husband, her own mother or a helping agency representative will also add a certain degree of "cloud cover" to her attentional processes.

To find coercive processes operating at different levels within the family system is of paramount importance in a diagnostic sense. The severity of psychopathology is usually viewed in terms of the likelihood of change: the more unlikely the change possibilities, the more serious the clinical problem. Suppose, for example, that an assessment of coercive interchange reveals the presence of such entrapment at three levels of the system: mother-child, mother-father, and mother-kinfolk. I believe that a "hierarchical levels" rule of thumb will become evident in judging problem severity. The greater the number of different dyads entrapped within a particular system, the more difficult it will be to produce therapeutic change. Since these different dyads do demonstrate a functional interdependence, there is probably some sort of additive impact on the coercive stability of each dyadic operation. Thus, while a parent training intervention ought to be successful in changing the parent-child problem, its therapeutic effects might be attenuated if the parent is also entrapped with other people in the family-community system. I think the treatment issue message is clear. We will develop treatment strategies based on our understanding of how coercive processes operate within the system. Our current strategies are largely geared to particular dyadic problems (e.g., parent training, marital contracting). It is reasonable to anticipate the development of new strategies based on triadic and even quadratic units.

Chapter 5
Abstract

Coercion theory is focused upon the probabilistic relation between the antecedent behavior of one family member (A_i) and the reaction (R_j) of some other members of the family. It is proposed that positive reinforcement increases $p(R_j|A_i)$ and that this probability value is the proper dependent variable for the measurement of reinforcement effects. Recent studies are reviewed which demonstrate that reinforcement can have an automatic effect in strengthening the connection between the A_i and the R_j; i.e., the effect occurs without the subject's "awareness."

In the homes of normal and distressed families, members provide positive consequences for coercive child behaviors 55% to 72% of the time. There are no significant differences in consequation by family agents or by sample. Procedures are reviewed which test for the status of positive consequences that serve as reinforcers for coercive behaviors. In addition, some speculations are outlined as to why children differ in their responsiveness to positive reinforcers.

Glossary of Symbols

A_i	antecedent event
$\overline{A}_i$	aversive antecedent
$C+$	positive consequence
$C-$	negative consequence (punishment)
NR	negative reinforcement arrangement
PR	positive reinforcement arrangement
$S+$	positive reinforcer (this is a $C+$ that has been shown to strengthen $A_i \rightarrow R_j$ connections)
R_j	response
$\overline{R}_j$	coercive response
$p(R_j)$	probability of occurrence for a specific response
$p(R_j|A_i)$	conditional probability for the occurrence of a specific response given the occurrence of a specific antecedent behavior
$p(R_1|A_1)$	conditional probability that R_1 will occur given the occurrence of A_1 at time-one (t_1)
$p(R_2|A_2)$	conditional probability that R_j will recur at a later point in time (t_2) given a presentation of the same A_i

Chapter 5

Positive Reinforcement for Aggression

There are certain behaviors of family members which reliably produce aggressive reactions from antisocial children. The connection between the aggressive response of the child and the stimulus which controls its occurrence is maintained by both positive and negative reinforcement. In this chapter we will examine only the contribution of positive reinforcement to this process. The distinctive feature of positive reinforcement in the context of familial aggression is that the victim's reaction increases the likelihood of *future* attacks. The victim is responsible for a dual contribution to this process. First, the victim provides a cue which sets the occasion for an aggressive reaction; and second, the victim's reaction functions as a positive reinforcement for the aggressive attack.

As a general case it is assumed that both the family and the culture provide rich schedules of positive reinforcement for aggressive behavior. It is further assumed that most of the stimuli which control familial aggression are *external;* i.e., they are the observable behaviors of other family members. A prerequisite for understanding aggression in families is that we understand how some stimuli control aggressive reactions while others do not. It is suggested that the mechanisms of positive reinforcement play a crucial role in determining which specific behaviors of family members will act as controlling stimuli for the performance of aggressive behavior. A functional analysis of familial interactions identifies certain persons and certain behaviors as weak elicitors for coercive reactions by other members. As used here, the term "elicitor" refers to the probabilistic relation between the behavior of one family member and the reaction of another. It implies neither an invariant nor reflexive connection. In fact, the relation is so subtle that it would be difficult for the untrained observer to detect its presence; they are subtle counterpoints usually obscured by the dramatic ebb and flow of the *content* of family interaction. Who notices a momentary shift in the likelihood of Brother-Yell given Sister-Tease when one is trying to understand content problems such as: "Why did she tease just then?" or "Why did he yell?" These perfectly reasonable questions are the traditional concerns for many of us, but they draw our attention away from the fact that structural changes are also occurring in these interchanges.

What is changing from one interaction to another is the probability (p) value describing the relation between the antecedent or prior behavior of one family member (A_i) and the reaction which follows it (R_j). The functional relation can be expressed as $p(R_j|A_i)$. As detailed in Chapter 8, it is thought that these conditional p values are constantly shifting about some mean value. Increases in the p value reflect the impact of positive and negative reinforcement; decreases result from punishment or extinction arrangements.

One could identify the stimuli controlling the behaviors of family members, and use them to make predictions for a future set of interactions. That would satisfy the requirements of a performance theory. However, an understanding of *why* these stimuli control behavior requires the introduction of concepts from reinforcement theory. This question, in turn, is necessary if one is concerned with matters of intervention and behavior change. To treat an antisocial child will require that the functional relations be disrupted between the controlling stimuli and the child's aggressive behavior. This problem in social engineering will require family members to learn how to manipulate their exchanges of reinforcement and punishment.

About Reinforcement

The Nature of Reinforcement and Reinforcing Stimuli

There seems to be a polarization within psychology with regard to reinforcement theory. On the one hand, there is a diminishing number of radical behaviorists who embrace reinforcement theory as a necessary and sufficient concept for the explanation of most behaviors. This group explicitly rejects all other explanations of human behavior. On the other hand, there is an expanding number of psychologists fervently embracing "everything else" (cognitions, perception, motives and genes); they reject reinforcement concepts with equal passion. The writer would suggest that it is not necessary to be a radical behaviorist in order to employ reinforcement concepts. They are extremely useful as a starting point for studying social behavior. However, there are some problems associated with the use of reinforcement as an explanation of behavior.

This section is focused upon three questions which tend to enter into most discussions about reinforcement theory: (1) What is reinforcement?; (2) Which stimuli are reinforcers and/or how do they become reinforcers?; and (3) Are all reinforcers mediated directly? Some investigators claim that they cannot use the concept of reinforcement until they have satisfactory answers to these questions. At present, the empirical base is not sufficient to provide definitive answers to these questions. As pointed out by Estes (1971), the majority of empirical studies testing reinforcement hypotheses lack coherence. In their aggregate, the findings do not define a theory. There is, however, a reasonable perspective that has been adopted by many of us who wish to use the ideas from reinforcement theory. It is this perspective that will be presented here.

The first question is: What is reinforcement? A related question is: What do reinforcers have in common? Schoenfeld (1978) has most recently posed these questions and reviewed the literature relating to them. As he notes, it was Hull (1943) who made the major effort to answer these questions. From this position, all reinforcers are drive reducing. Unfortunately, this position quickly encountered difficulties. For example, certain *drive-activating* events were shown to function as reinforcers (Berlyne, 1967). While there are other more recent explanations, such as the Premack Principle, each has its own particular flaw. "Simply put, it is that *any* stimulus can act as a 'reinforcer.' There is no special class or group of characteristics of 'reinforcement' which sets it apart from other stimuli, but rather that all stimuli can act so depending upon their intensity, static, and dynamic patterning." (Schoenfeld, 1978, p. 142)

Given the state of the art, one can identify a reinforcer only by its effect on behavior. This, of course, is also Skinner's position (Skinner, 1948, 1953, 1969).

When considering the question of how a previously neutral event could come to serve as a reinforcer for aggression, we are again led back to a simplistic position. As Schoenfeld notes in his review, theorizing in the 1940's and 1950's differentiated between primary and secondary reinforcers. Presumably, some contingent pairing of the neutral event with a primary reinforcer could alter the stimulus such that it would become a "conditioned" or "secondary" reinforcer.

"The upshot of all this thought and effort regarding possible distinctions between 'primary' and 'secondary' reinforcement was a disillusion with the problem. Where once the literature was crowded with studies and discussions of the topic, there is now a disappointed and exhausted silence. It seems safe to say that the two cannot be distinguished. When an experimental animal is chosen, he is taken as he is. A stimulus is a stimulus, and a 'reinforcer' is as a 'reinforcer' does." (Schoenfeld, 1978, p. 139)

Some investigators may be put off by the stark reality of the statement—*a reinforcer is as a reinforcer does.* Worse yet, it makes the tautological nature of the reinforcement concept evident. What is a reinforcer? It is that which strengthens behavior; but how does one determine whether or not the contingent arrangement "strengthened" a particular response?

In effect, any stimulus can, under certain conditions, serve as a reinforcer. However, there exists no means for classifying events, in advance, as reinforcing or nonreinforcing. This appears to be an insurmountable barrier—can we apply the concept if we do not really understand how some events become reinforcers while others remain neutral? The answer to this question is an emphatic yes! Concepts relating to genetics, magnetism, and synapses served very useful functions in scientific enterprise long before they could be explained. The concept of reinforcement will probably occupy a similar niche for some time to come; but, in the meantime, it will continue to serve a useful function.

For present purposes we do not need to know why or how something becomes a reinforcer, but we do need to know how to identify an event as a reinforcer (this problem will be considered in due course). We can understand the impact of reinforcers on behavior. That information is available to us; it forms the basis of reinforcement theory as it stands today.

Learning or Performance?

Does reward modify *learning,* or does reward modify the *performance* of the R_j given the A_i? Again, the present writer draws heavily from Estes' (1971) perspective, "The *learning* of stimulus-response and stimulus-outcome relationships is assumed to proceed simply according to association by contiguity" (p. 25). Bandura (1973) documents the possibility that much of what a child learns about the connection between social events and his or her behavior is based upon observation of the social environment; i.e., the child sees, and stores, many of the contiguous relations among A_i and R_j events. As Bandura notes, the child also stores in memory observations about the relation between specific behaviors and likely outcomes. This kind of learning by contiguity can be based on observing social interaction, films, role-play, pictures, or stories. The programmatic work of Bandura (1973) and his colleagues beautifully documents the power of this concept as it applies to a wide range of children's social behaviors. As noted by Estes (1971) and others, it is not altogether clear as to what, if any, contribution reinforcing contingencies make to this stage of learning. Reinforcement could augment the saliency of the A_i and/or R_j events. Contingent reward could increase the likelihood that a particular event will be stored in memory. Learning associations may also be more rapid under conditions of reward; however, modern theory gives reinforcement per se only a secondary role to play in the learning process.

The next question concerns the relation between reinforcement and what is *performed.* Again, Estes (1971) states the current perspective in a very succinct manner (italics by the present author):

"For the lower animals, for the very young children, and to some extent for humans of all ages who are mentally retarded or subject to severe neurological or behavior disorders, behavior from *moment to moment* is largely *describable* and *predictable* in terms of response to particular stimuli and the rewarding or punishing outcome of previous stimulus-response sequences." (p. 23)

Estes then went on to state that he does *not* believe this will hold for mature adults! The behavior of the latter is, rather, governed by cognitive strategies and anticipated consequences for future actions. In the same vein, he suggested that manipulation of reinforcing contingencies would prove to be of little practical value for persons other than those in institutional settings.

The present writer agrees with the notion that the power of reinforcing contingencies is most manifest when considering matters relating to performance. However, I disagree with Estes in my belief that reinforcing contingencies serve as a major determinant for many social behaviors of *both children and adults.* The recent successful applications of reinforcement concepts to studies of adults in marital conflict (Jacobson & Margolin, 1979), smoking (Lichtenstein, 1971), and obesity (Stunkard & Rush, 1974) would lead one to believe that this issue has not been completely resolved.

In keeping with the general position taken by Estes (1971) and Bandura (1973), reinforcement during trial and error learning is not the most efficient way for a child to learn about driving a car or about social interaction. Rather, it is more efficient to arrange for the child to observe the process. The child should also observe the outcomes for various reactions to the same or similar stimuli. Now, let us assume that the child has observed his parent driving the car; in effect, he has learned something about the process. The next stage in acquiring skill as a driver requires that the child be supervised while *performing* these skills. This second stage in skill acquisition is a polishing and smoothing process. It has been described in detail in B.F. Skinner's *Contingencies of Reinforcement* (1969). As Skinner points out, driving the car requires that one repeatedly expose oneself to the natural contingencies produced by this or that response and then be allowed to correct the *S-R* connection accordingly. This takes time; it also takes a sympathetic audience and a safe place. This kind of polishing is so demanding that it most typically occurs in our early years and in specially designed environments, such as the home or school. If this training does not occur, the deficits may be extremely difficult to make up later. There are literally no social agencies that have the staff available for such large investments of time.

This book describes our effort to analyze family interaction as an example of *performance*. All of the family members have learned a variety of coercive behaviors, but their performance of these behaviors changes from day to day and month to month. Why is this? Some families perform coercive behaviors at higher rates than others; and within families, some members perform these behaviors at higher rates than others. Why is this? In the context of a performance theory, reinforcement concepts are not *the main* explanation for these questions. However, reinforcement concepts *are* a necessary part of the picture.

$A_i \rightarrow R_j$ connections

The term reinforcement has been used by association-based learning theorists, such as Pavlov, Thorndike, and Hull, to convey the idea of *strengthening* (Schoenfeld, 1978). As Schoenfeld points out, Pavlov's use of the term referred to the pairing of the *UCS* with the *CS*. What was strengthened by these pairings was the increased likelihood of the conditioned response being elicited by the *CS*. In instrumental conditioning, as used by Hull and Guthrie, a reward was thought of as strengthening the connection between a stimulus (S) and a response (R). This relationship can be expressed as $p(R|S)$.

As used here, the functional relationship will be expressed as the likelihood of a particular response (R_j) given the occurrence of a specific antecedent (A_i) or $p(R_j|A_i)$. The term antecedent (A_i) is more precise than the more traditional term stimulus (S). To be identified as an antecedent (A_i), the event must occur *immediately prior* to the response (R_j). Throughout the discussion, the term R_j refers to a specific target event serving as the focus in calculating the conditional p value.

To understand reinforcement effects we need to have *three* events in sequence. This sequence can be represented symbolically as $A_i \rightarrow R_j \rightarrow S+$. The effect of the third event, which is a reinforcer, will be to increase the probability that a particular R_j will follow a specific A_i. In other words, it will increase the $p(R_j|A_i)$. The calculation of this p value is relatively straightforward. For example, let's assume that a baseline study shows that there is a connection between Sister-Whine and Brother-Tease. In this example we have Sister-Whine as A_i and Brother-Tease as R_j. The functional relation

that is of concern to us is $p(\text{Tease}|\text{Whine})$. When observed over a two-day period, several thousand behavioral events (interactions between brother and sister) were recorded. Let's say that among the matrix of these interactions, we find that 100 of the sister's behavioral events were Whine and that 12 of these were followed by Brother-Tease. So our baseline conditional value for $p(\text{Tease}|\text{Whine})$ at time-one is .12. In our example we are going to assume that Sister-Cry is a reinforcer for the sequence Sister-Whine followed by Brother-Tease. Thus, the three events that we are looking at are Sister-Whine (A_i) → Brother-Tease (R_j) → Sister-Cry ($S+$). Let's say that during our baseline study at time-one that Sister-Whine → Brother-Tease was followed by occasional outbursts of Sister-Cry. However, now on day three (time-two), it happens that *every* time Brother-Tease occurs, it is followed by Sister-Cry. During day three several hundred interactions between brother and sister were recorded. Within the matrix of these interactions, Sister-Whine occurred 50 times and was followed by Brother-Tease 20 times. The value of $p(\text{Tease}|\text{Whine})$ at time-two is .40. A comparison of this p value with the baseline value of .12 indicates more than a threefold increase in the strength of the connection between Sister-Whine and Brother-Tease. This suggests that Sister-Cry is a reinforcer for the sequence Sister-Whine → Brother-Tease.[1] It should be noted in the context of this example that Sister-Cry may also serve as a reinforcer for other sequences of events. Furthermore, there are probably reinforcers other than Sister-Cry which strengthen the connection between Tease and Whine.

This emphasis on the connection between A_i and R_j is not in keeping with the current Skinnerian perspective which stresses the operant as *the* important functional unit. In that paradigm, the strength of the response is defined by a measure of the rate of occurrence or $p(R_j)$. Skinner rejected the idea that reinforcement strengthed the connection between a stimulus and a response.[2]

The problem with the Skinnerian stance is generated in part by the fact that in natural settings the complexity of social interactions is greater than that found in most laboratory situations. In social interaction *most changes in $p(R_j)$ have little to do with changes in reinforcement and punishment*. Rather, it is the case that in social interaction R_j is evoked by the immediately prior behavior of the subject or the other person. The presentation of these controlling events is changing all of the time and the $p(R_j)$ changes accordingly.

If the frequency of R_j reflects the impact of controlling stimuli then how is one to test for the impact of a reinforcer? The answer is to use $p(R_j|A_i)$ as the dependent variable. This will sensitively reflect the impact of punishment and reinforcement. When a reinforcing event $(S+)$ follows an $A_i \rightarrow R_j$ sequence, the probability that R_j will follow a presentation of the *same* A_i should increase. Here, even massive changes in the density of controlling stimuli do not mask the contribution of reinforcement to the connection between the A_i and the R_j. Given that a Whine-Tease sequence is followed by Cry is there an increase in $p(\text{Whine}|\text{Tease})$ *on the next trial?* The next trial could be in two minutes, two hours, or two days; this should make very little difference. In addition, what happens in the sequences that follow the $A_i \rightarrow R_j \rightarrow S+$ arrangement has little bearing on our analysis of reinforcement effects per se unless the sequence involves our fundamental unit of A_i and R_j.

Before leaving this topic it should be noted that understanding and predicting $p(R_j)$ is the task for a performance theory. The determinants for these variables are considered in detail in Chapters 8 and 9. Suffice it to say that reinforcement and punishment account for only trivial amounts of variance in measures of $p(R_j)$ when analyzed in the context of social interaction.

As noted by methodologists such as Parton (1967), measures of rate change used in laboratory studies with human subjects proved to be both unreliable and heavily correlated with baseline level. There were, in addition, many variables other than changes in reinforcement schedule which affected the rate measures. The present writer believes that $p(R_j|A_i)$ will prove to be a more sensitive measure of response strength.

When applied to family interaction, measures of rate change can often underestimate reinforcement effects. For example, the sequence of child-open-door, followed by mother-thank you, then both walk to the car, would be tabulated as *no reinforcement* effect. The behavior did not persist into the adjacent time interval, therefore, no reinforcement effect! That, of course, makes no sense at all. Child-Whine followed by mother-Talk, then child-Talk, would be another case in point. Actually, observations of family or nursery school aggression contain many sequences like this. Again, the measure $p(R_j|A_i)$ seems better suited as a dependent variable. If "thank you" or "mother-Talk" are indeed reinforcers, then the p value describing future interactions will show a slight increase.

What is needed is some means for untangling the obvious *thematic* control exerted by ongoing stimulus events from the effects that we wish to attribute to reinforcement effects. For example, if a child is playing at t_1 there is a good chance that the child will be playing at t_2. Responses tend to exert their own thematic control over the responses which follow. The fact that a particular behavior continues into the next time interval usually has little to do with the immediate changes in reinforcement. Moment-by-moment changes in ongoing behavior are typically reactions to shifts in immediately impinging stimuli. This is *stimulus control* which has its own logic, means of analysis, and utility (see Chapters 8 and 9). *Reinforcement control* must be tested by other means which require control for thematic components.

In retrospect, our first efforts to use sequential data to identify reinforcement effects for aggression were misguided. With unerring skill we committed all of the errors delineated above. In the Patterson, Littman, and Bricker (1967) study of nursery school aggression, the immediate recurrence of an attack by the aggressor served as a measure of reinforcement effects. Presumably, a positive reinforcer provided by the victim increased the likelihood of a recurrence. By combining the data for immediate recurrence with data from trials that were separated by minutes and/or hours, the measurement of reinforcement effects was inextricably confounded.

This difficulty with rate as a dependent variable should have been obvious. But, in the mid-1960's, the problem was not apparent. Literally months and years of data analysis slipped by before the perspective we now have finally emerged. This is a small problem, but dozens like it had to be worked through. Most of them will not be detailed in this fashion. This particular problem is described in depth because it continues to be a difficulty for many who wish to study interactional data.

Before leaving the concept of $A_i \rightarrow R_j$ connections, it would be wise to reiterate a point that has been only alluded to. One of the key assumptions regarding coercive family processes is that there are *two reinforcement* mechanisms involved—one is positive reinforcement and the other is negative reinforcement. In negative reinforcement, the antecedent would be an aversive event $(\bar{A}_i)$ supplied by a family member; the child's coercive counter-attack followed by a termination of the intrusion would be an example of negative reinforcement (see Chapter 7). The termination could be either a neutral or a positive reaction by the initiator. In this instance, what would be strengthened would be the connection between the aversive antecedent $(\bar{A}_i)$ and the counterattack. For example, mother-Scold $\rightarrow$ child-Whine $\rightarrow$ mother-Talk would be a negative reinforcement arrangement that strengthens the connection between mother-Scold and child-Whine. The child's behavior (Whine) may be controlled by *both positive* and *negative* reinforcement. For this reason, it becomes particularly important to classify A_i into positive, aversive and neutral categories. These, in turn, differentially relate to attack and counterattack response categories, as well as to positive and negative reinforcement mechanisms. These matters will be discussed in detail in Chapter 7.

Awareness

Coercion is a social skill that takes practice. Some people are more skilled at it than others. An extremely coercive 10-year-old child, a well-practiced master sergeant, and the authoritative professor are all masters of pain control. Their level of skill comes from thousands of trials and years of exposure to natural contingencies (most of which involved "winning"). In the course of this chapter we will show that coercive behaviors that are performed at high rates are maintained by rich schedules of reinforcement.

How aware are the aggressor and/or the victim of the slow shifts in $p\,(R_j|A_i)$ that are taking place? Do these shifts take place without the individuals being aware of them? During social interaction, the individual can focus only on a limited subset of the complex matrix of behavioral events. Of that subset to which the individual does attend, only a small proportion of the events find their way into long-term memory. The question, then, concerns what it is that the individual attends to, and what it is that goes into short- or long-term memory. If the individual did not know that a given event was a reinforcer he or she might attend to a more salient feature of the interaction. Furthermore, if the individual is not trained in reinforcement theory, he or she might miss the fact that these events occurred contingently, and were followed by changes in $p\,(R_j|A_i)$ or in $p(R_j)$.

If one accepts the reality imposed by the OSLC coding system, then in one hour of interaction a child would be required to sort through 600 of his or her own behavioral events! In addition, the child would view at least 600 events generated by the reactions of other family members. The question arises as to just how aware the individual can be of these processes. How accurately might he or she describe the contingencies that are found within these interactions? The writer assumes that most of the "explanations" we give for our own behavior are not isomorphic with the molecular processes which determine them. Modern developments in cognitive theory suggest that what we do is far more reasonable. To store and actively search for the functional relations between 1200 events would take up a great deal of the individu-

al's information processing time and would quickly surpass his or her processing ability. Instead, the individual relies on his or her own a priori causal theories to acount for the relation between the stimuli to which he or she does attend (Nisbett & Wilson, 1977). In Nisbett and Wilson's review, they cite a number of studies in which subjects were unaware of even dramatic changes in their behavior. In other studies, when asked to explain certain decisions they made, their explanations had little to do with the variables actually manipulated by the experimenter to control their decisions. In their attempt to explain their behavior, the subjects employed the kind of representative heuristic described by Kahneman and Tversky (1973). Here, the subject first examines the behavior and the context. The subject then searches within his or her representative theory for possible "causes" for that behavior. If the new experience seems to fit the subject's causal theory then the event may be identified as causal when, in fact, it had no impact upon the subject's behavior.

The general tenor of these findings is further buttressed by the findings reviewed by Slovic, Fischhoff, and Lichtenstein (1977). Their programmatic research indicated that subjects had little awareness of the weights they attached to cues that were being used to make decisions. Slovic et al.'s studies showed serious discrepancies between subjective estimates and the objectively determined weights for these cues. In some studies the subjects tended to overestimate the importance they attached to minor cues and underestimate the weighting given major cues. In another series of studies they showed there was little relation between a subject's confidence in his or her rating and accuracy.

The idea that we have little or no accurate awareness of higher order cognitive processes seems well-established, at least as it applies to fairly complex situations. However, given an extremely "simple" situation, there may be a correspondence between the functional relations actually occurring and the subject's theory about them (Wilson & Nisbett, 1978). An excellent example of such a simplistic situation can be found in the verbal conditioning studies that were popular in the early 1960's. In these studies, the subject was brought into a room with the experimenter, and asked to say whatever words came to mind, or perhaps to make up sentences employing particular words. During the baseline period, the experimenter interacted *very little* with the subject. Following this, the experimenter began to interact by saying, "Hmmm," "Good," or "Uh-huh" contingent on a particular response of the subject. Nisbett et al. (1977) reviewed these early studies and concluded:

"The present analysis makes it clear that there is every reason to expect that subjects in these experiments *should* be able to accurately report about cause and effect. (a) The response possibilities allowed the subject are extremely constrained. He is permitted very little latitude in the sorts of behavior he may emit. (b) The stimulus situation is even more fixed and static. In fact, virtually the only stimulus that occurs is the experimenter's 'uhhuh' or 'good.' (c) Finally, the causal connection between this critical stimulus or reinforcement and the increased frequency of a particular response class should be a highly plausible one. . . . Devotees of learning-without-awareness could scarcely have designed a paradigm more likely to result in accurate verbal report if they had set out deliberately to do so. There is some evidence, in fact, that when even relatively minor steps are taken to disguise the connection between stimulus and response, subjects will fail to report such a connection." (pp. 253-254)

It is a pleasant state of affairs for the iconoclast when a group considers any variable or arrangement as a *necessary* and *sufficient* condition for determining human behavior. If one were to hold the position that reinforcers must always be present in any learning situation, then it is only necessary to find *one* exception and the entire logical construct is in jeopardy. It requires but one demonstration of a young chimpanzee learning the use of a new tool by observing a peer successfully employing it to produce an intellectual scramble to extend the logic so that it explains the exception. Certainly the work of the modeling theorists such as Kanfer (1970) and Bandura and Walters (1963) in the mid-1960's set limits on the expansive horizons claimed by the reinforcement theorists of that time. However, in that most investigators did not take seriously the claim that reinforcement was *necessary* for behavior change, the findings from modeling studies did not require a drastic readjustment.

The assumption at the core of the enterprise concerned the automatic strengthening of the *S-R* bond as a function of reinforcement. The early studies of verbal conditioning were held up as centerpieces demonstrating this effect in study after study. Then the careful laboratory controls introduced by Spielberger (1962) and others demolished that premise. His work and that of other investigators published in Eriksen (1962) showed that if the subject could verbalize his or her awareness of the connection (between the response and the rein-

forcer), then "conditioning" occurred. If the subject was not aware, there was no conditioning.

These demolition studies were well done; there was no real argument about either their design or interpretation. It had been assumed that reinforcement produced an automatic strengthening between the *S* and *R* without awareness. This assumption was no longer tenable. As a result, many investigators left the area of social reinforcement to work on other problems.

During the next decade, studies concerning automatic strengthening were few in number and went largely unnoticed. Reinforcement principles did become part of the social learning theory that was developed in the mid-1960's. Reinforcement remained a crucial variable in the 1970's, but the form in which it was expressed was radically altered.

"Although the empirical issue is not yet completely resolved, there is little evidence that rewards function as automatic strengtheners of human conduct. . . . Behavior is not much affected by its consequences without awareness of what is being reinforced . . . reinforcement—its image has changed from a 'mechanical strengthener' of conduct to an 'informative and motivating influence.'" (Bandura, 1974, p. 12)

Bandura's statement accurately reflects the current status of reinforcement within social learning theory with its emphasis on cognitive variables. His statement stands as a "strong law of cognition." Subject awareness (as expressed by a verbalized statement of contingencies) is thought to be necessary for reinforcement effects to occur. However, the present writer believes that there are now a number of studies which show that reinforcement effects can be demonstrated under conditions in which the subject is not able to verbalize the contingencies. If an awareness of the informational characteristics of reinforcers is assumed to be a necessary condition, then all that is required to refute this is one demonstration that behavior changed via reinforcement without the subject being able to report awareness. The format for these studies is simple—provide the subject with salient stimuli to which he or she attends, while arranging for contingencies which produce behavioral changes that are not noticed.

Some of the work demonstrating automatic strengthening was done *prior* to the demolition by Spielberger (1962), but these studies had gone unnoticed by him (e.g., Hefferline, Keenan, & Harford, 1959). In a later study by Hefferline, Keenan, and Birch (cited in Hefferline, 1963), 12 adults participated in an experiment consisting of three phases. During the baseline period, they listened to music while an apparatus recorded very small muscle twitches. During the conditioning trial, white noise was introduced—its termination was made contingent on the occurence of these minor muscle movements. An interview revealed that the subjects had no awareness of the contingent arrangement and yet all of the subjects showed a conditioning effect. They were then told that some aspect of their behavior was related to turning off the white noise. In the next phase, the conditioning trials continued while the subjects searched for the arrangement. While they were unsuccessful in stating the correct hypothesis, all of the subjects showed increases in muscle twitches while the white noise was present.

This early study has many overtones that are reminiscent of modern biofeedback studies. Even though the format was of historical interest, the results could not necessarily be generalized to social situations in which the R_j event could, at least in principle, be observed. For this reason, the double-agent studies by Rosenfeld and Baer (1969) and by Gewirtz and Boyd (1977) are more directly relevant to the present discussion. In the first study by Rosenfeld and Baer (1969), a college student was cast in the role of subject; he also served as "double agent." The experimenter (a graduate student) planned to reinforce the subject for "chin-rubs." However, the student (in collusion with Rosenfeld) had a prior agreement to make a chin-rub response contingent on the "experimenter" saying "yeah." This well-designed single-subject experiment began with a baseline measure of the experimenter's frequency for saying "yeah." The assumption was that the target behavior for the experimenter's experiment would function as a reinforcer if made contingent upon his behavior. During the next phase, chin-rub was made contingent upon the experimenter's "yeah." The data reflected a marked increase in rate; during the next baseline the rate fell again. Reinforcing an alternative response of the experimenter's had no effect on his rate of saying "yeah." This was demonstrated in an ABAB reversal design, in which "hmmm" was reinforced during the A conditions and "yeah" during the B conditions. A carefully designed interview probe at the end of the study failed to reveal an awareness on the part of the experimenter that his behavior had been repeatedly changed during the experiment.

There are, however, several considerations that give one pause in wholeheartedly accepting these findings. First, the experiments were carried out in a setting (University of Kansas) that could not be thought of as neutral with regard to the awareness hypothesis. Second, complete data were reported for only one subject. Clearly, the work needed to be replicated. This was provided by Gewirtz and Boyd (1977) working in a different laboratory setting and using mothers as subjects. In this double-agent design, the mothers had been instructed to use verbal reinforcers to shape their infants' verbal behavior. The infants were in an adjoining room. The mother was told that whenever a light came on it meant that her infant had turned its head. While the mother focused on infant sounds, the experimenter made the information about infant head turns contingent on mother smiles. The rate of mothers' smiling increased without their being aware of the change in their behavior or the contingencies that produced it. In the next study, the mother was to reinforce head turning. This time infant sounds were fed back to the mother; the sounds were made contingent (by the experimenter) on the mother smiling. Again, the reinforcement arrangement had a significant effect on the smiling behavior of the mother. No evidence of awareness could be obtained from the interviews.

It may be the case that more skillful interviewers could demonstrate that the subjects in such arrangements *really* are aware. Indeed, this is a compelling reason for carrying out double-agent studies in other settings. However, as things now stand, these findings cast serious doubt on the assumption that an awareness of the reinforcing contingencies is a *necessary* condition for changes in performance.

The findings from recent developments in cognitive psychology strongly suggest that behavior changes occur in complex social interactions without the participants being aware of them. The writer believes that most changes in behavior have this quality. The changes occur in very small increments and are embedded in a rich matrix of ongoing stimulation. The shifts are seldom constant and are not necessarily unidirectional. The contingencies producing these changes tend to go unnoticed. If there is a systematic arrangement for these contingencies, then over a period of time these changes will be directional. Such large changes would lead to labeling or explanations which reflect the conventional wisdom about such matters. For most people, the causes and nature of behavior changes are a profound mystery. In fact, most parents of antisocial children are convinced that the behavior of their children cannot be changed. It seems likely that at the microsocial level many changes in behavior do occur, and that most of us are not aware of these changes nor do we have accurate explanations as to their cause. In this sense we are in agreement with Freud who also believed that most persons were unable to give an accurate account for behavioral determinants. At the very least, the data call for a wait-and-see attitude regarding the necessity of cognitive mediation in reinforcement. There is obviously much to be learned about cognitive processes. It is no longer believed that there is a simple relation between cognition and behavior. For example, recent studies demonstrate that changes in behavior are more likely to determine changes in attitude rather than the more traditional belief that attitudes determine behavior (Bem, 1967).

In sum, the relationships between cognition, reinforcement, and behavior define a set of complex relations that are not yet well understood. For example, it would be fascinating to study when it is that a victim will reinforce an attack. What attributions are given to the victim's behavior and the behavior of the attacker? Our own structural questioning concerning this kind of relationship suggests the participants are poor trackers of what they do and what is being done to them. They are being altered by minutiae that, as isolated events, seem innocuous enough. However, when they are repeated a dozen times, they do have an effect on performance. Because these events are not considered to be important, they pass unnoticed. If brought into awareness, would such knowledge facilitate or inhibit changes in behavior?

The Learning of Aggression

It is reasonable to believe that some coercive behaviors are present at birth, and, in that sense, do not need to be learned. The infant's crying is aversive. It is elicited by various discomforts experienced by the infant, e.g., extremes of temperature, or hunger. The ethologist would point out that it also has survival value; crying is used to alert the caretaker as to when to change diapers and when to feed. As time goes on, the infant learns other means for coping with hunger or discomfort. It should be noted that while these particular S-R connections are probably innate, they are also definitely modifiable.

There are probably other coercive behaviors for which the connection between eliciting stimuli and responses is innate. In his ethological studies of primates and children, Eibl-Eibesfeldt (1974) identified temper tantrums as having such a status. He found this reaction in a deaf and blind girl. The pattern of facial grimace and posture was very similar to that observed for sighted children and young primates.

Modeling theorists such as Kanfer and Phillips (1970) and Bandura (1973) put forth the persuasive argument that much of what a child learns is modeled by other people. The intricacies of complex social behaviors, as well as language, aggression, and other social skills are first observed and, together with the likelihoods of various outcomes, stored in memory.

"In the present context, it was assumed that the average three-year-old, in our society, has *learned* all of the 14 noxious behaviors identified by our code system. This early acquisition is facilitated by the ubiquitous presence of coercive models in the home, nursery school, and on television. For example, observations (Jones et al., 1975), in the homes of *normal families* showed coercive behaviors occurred from a range of .02 to .50 responses per minute! Because the code sampled only dyads, these figures represent *minimal* estimates of the rates with which such aversive stimuli occurred. Presumably these events provide rich opportunities for vicarious learning for young children. Extensive observations from two nursery schools showed a range of 11 to 40 verbal or nonverbal attacks per session. . . . In the review of studies evaluating the content of children's TV programs, Friedrich and Stein (1974) cited a study that showed an average of 25.1 aggressive episodes per hour for children's cartoons. For 'adult' shows, there was a mean of five *violent* episodes per hour for shows presented on prime TV time. Most children surveyed were found to watch three to four hours of TV per day. . . ." (Patterson, 1976, p. 280)

While all children in our culture may have "learned" a variety of coercive behaviors, they differ profoundly in the rate and skill with which they perform them. But, as noted earlier in the discussion, in order to become a complex social skill, what is learned must be subjected to the polishing touch of natural contingencies. One might master the art of using a spoon at the table by viewing a film. A brief period of practice with its concomitant set of contingencies would probably be sufficient. However, no amount of viewing and modeling would directly produce a concert violinist or a race car driver. Similarly, many of the subtle coercive skills seen on video tapes of clients in therapy require years of extensive practice and shaping.

Over a period of time, the to-be-aggressive child must learn which set of coercive responses will be successful with which family member. For example, observation data showed both normal and deviant boys learn that they may not hit their mothers, but they can hit siblings (Patterson, 1980a). The young boy learns that whining, noncompliance, and yelling are appropriate when mothers are the targets; teasing, humiliation, and negative commands are useful coercive modes for siblings.

The coercive child must also learn about settings. The reinforcing/punishing contingencies provided during practice sessions will teach the coercive child where and when coercive behaviors are likely to be successful. For example, most families do not permit coercive interactions in churches, hospitals and restaurants. Some will permit its occurrence when company is present, others will not. Some parents control its occurrence in public places such as supermarkets and parks; others do not.

By the age of 6 years, most normal children have these lessons well in hand. Their rate is about one aversive event every two to three minutes; most of these are relatively low-intensity events such as disapproval, noncompliance, and teasing. The patterns of these behaviors are relatively stable over time with regard to overall rate. By this age the child carefully discriminates between victims, settings, and responses. In the home, behavior patterns have been shaped by the family members. People in other settings will teach the child to make comparable discriminations in those settings. The normal child's coerciveness is acceptable; it *looks* normal in that things are seldom carried too far. It is the victims' reactions (which function as reinforcement and/or punishment) that polish these skills. In effect, the victims teach the child what is acceptable and what is not.

Cultural Programming

At a time when it is popular to consider aggression as an instinct (Lorenz, 1966), it is perhaps not fashionable to consider the possibility that *our culture is programmed to reward many kinds of aggression.* However, the present writer believes our particular culture has a history in which certain kinds of aggression are highly prized. Our folk heroes have been the cowboy and the pioneer; both are individualists. In our mythology about them, we emphasize their combativeness. Sports such as football, boxing and hockey glorify aggressiveness. Shaw's (1972) illuminating *Meat on the Hoof* describes the payoffs for professional football players who are extremely aggressive. The reinforcers range from money, cars, and sex to membership in a supportive group. Winning is the primary goal. Shaw's account leaves little doubt that the dual process of enduring pain and inflicting pain on the opponent is a means to achieve that end.

At a more macrolevel, war is the ultimate expression of aggression. In his statistical analysis, Wright (1972) noted the correlation between the status or strength of a nation and the frequency of its wars and battles. The great powers, including the United States, have been the most frequent fighters. Wars seem to accompany a country's march to power; until recent times, wars were rewarding to the winner.

Prior to the nineteenth century and the advent of the modern conscript armies, 30% to 50% of those engaged in a battle were likely to be casualties. One wonders what the reinforcer could possibly have been for those combat troops. Even a cursory examination of history suggests that the rewards were well understood and carefully spelled out in advance for all participants from kings, generals, and lieutenants to foot soldiers. For example, Grant's (1974) analysis of the structure of the armies of the Caesars read:

"The imperator called the soldiers *my* soldiers; and they were prepared to follow him loyally if he rewarded them sufficiently well. Rewards meant not only their pay and the occasional bonus, but above all a suitable provision for their retirement. Without that all the pay in the world would not have satisfied them.

"Ex-soldiers enjoyed many privileges, and exemptions. On a papyrus of 31 B.C., the victor of Actium listed some of them. 'I have decided to decree that all veterans be granted exemption from tribute . . . to grant to them, their parents and children, and the wives they have or shall have, exemption of all their property from taxation; and to the end that they may be Roman citizens with fullest legal right, they shall be exempt from the performance of compulsory public services.'" (Pp. 79-80).

In Tuchman's (1978) account, this model was the rule rather than the exception for 14th century English, French, and German armies. For many of the participants the incessant wars represented an escape from the crushing poverty and taxes of that time. For foot soldiers, knights, and lords alike, it was the possibility of dramatic material gain that determined whether an army functioned well or melted away (as many of them did). What was impressive was the meticulous care with which these reinforcers were spelled out *in advance.* For example, when Cortes invaded the Aztec kingdom, land, slaves and gold were the primary reinforcers.

"The gold dollar or sterling value of the total gold and silver put together, counting Motecucuma's treasure and the gold received from the provinces, has been calculated at six million three hundred thousand dollars. . . . But the distribution could not possibly be so simple. The deep loyal feelings of the army to the Crown may be seen in the promptness with which the royal fifth is set aside. Then Cortes claimed the fifth which had been promised him in Veracruz. Then, Bernal Diaz grumbles, Cortes set aside sums for the expenditures he had made towards the expedition, and for Diego Valazquez' expenditures, and for the procurators sent to Castille, and for the men left behind in Veracruz, and a double share for the horsemen; and in the end the common soldier found his share so small that many shouted they would not receive it." (de Madariaga, 1967, pp. 282-283).

The countries that were most involved in programs of military expansion also emphasized early training of their youth in organizations espousing duty, obedience, competition, and endurance of pain. The external reinforcers for these activities were carefully planned. For many ancient wars the reinforcers were agreed upon prior to the engagement. These facts do not prove that the presence of reinforcers was a contributing *cause* for wars. However, they do suggest that the presence (then and now) of these and other contingencies should be considered as playing a role in maintaining socially condoned aggression such as that found in football, boxing, and war. War is *the* exemplar of aggression. It is unfortunate that there are no historical studies analyzing the reinforcing contingencies supplied for mass killings.

The topic of cultural programming for aggression was introduced to illustrate the *feasibility* of viewing this and other macro-problems within the framework of behaviors perhaps partially determined by reinforcers. A culture, like a family, may have some unspoken assumptions about the relative utility of aggression as it relates to survival. Whether or not it is a stated assumption, one could test for its presence by examining the extent to which competition, aggression, and violence are presented to its youth as models for the solution of problems. It is assumed that those cultures most frequently engaging in war would model these "solutions" at the highest rates in their stories, drama, and films. Their sports activities would probably also emphasize body contact and the skillful employment of pain control techniques. In the values they place upon antisocial behavior, some families are like those cultures. However, they differ in one fundamental respect; the family permits coercion to occur among its own members. If a society were to behave in a similar way, anarchy would be the immediate outcome.

The Reinforcement of Aggression

One can identify the external reinforcers claimed by the victors of ancient wars. It takes no inferential leap to view the small infantry squad as providing the day-by-day reinforcement necessary to maintain each other's effective combat performance. But these contingencies are only distantly related to the processes maintaining aggression in the home. While reinforcement is thought to be a key mechanism, this time it is dispensed by the victim; the victim's reaction maintains the behavior of the attacker. If the adults in those settings give their tacit permission, then the more skilled coercers will seek out the more compliant victims and the coercion process will begin.

There are two general questions to consider. The first has to do with the likelihood of positive consequences for aggression in the classroom and the home. It seems contrary to common sense to believe that victims provide positive outcomes that are sufficient to maintain the attacking behavior. At a simple descriptive level, what *is* the likelihood of a positive outcome for a particularly coercive response? Is the likelihood of a positive outcome stable from one week to another? To understand the antisocial child it is imperative that we obtain answers to these questions. A related question concerns the impact of these consequences in strenthening the $A_i \rightarrow R_j$ connections. Do these consequences function as reinforcers? How is this to be demonstrated? This second set of questions will be discussed in a later section of this chapter.

Richard Walters suggested several decades ago that the contingencies are likely to be very different for high- and low-amplitude aggression. I am not convinced that this is true, but I do believe that they differ in the *processes* producing them. Within family interactions the main function of high-amplitude aggression is to produce compliance and/or submission. For the purpose of the present discussion, suffice it to say that if a sudden increase in intensity is followed by victim compliance then there is an increase in the likelihood that the next trial will begin at or above the same intensity. The details of this process are presented in Chapter 7. High-amplitude responses have their beginnings in rather low-amplitude interchanges. In that context, it becomes imperative to understand the processes that maintain relatively innocuous interchanges. These microsocial processes are thought to be necessary as antecedents for more violent forms of abuse among family members.

What are the positive outcomes for familial coercion? For that matter, what are the positive outcomes for family interaction in general? Descriptive data generated by such questions emphasize the banality of much of familial interaction. At any particular time there does not seem to be very much going on. As we shall see in later discussions, even in very distressed families only around 12% of the interactions are coercive. It is also the case that there is a general lack of high-grade positive consequences such as Approving, Touching, or Kissing. The normative data in Reid (1978, p. 72) showed Approval was given by parents to family members only about once every ten minutes. Hugs, Touches, and Kisses were forthcoming only about once every 200 minutes! The ratio of positive consequences (Talk, Attend, Physical Positive, and Approve) to aversive consequences for normal families was 13.9:1. The findings for home settings are reminiscent of the conclusions reached by White (1975), who reviewed 16 observation studies conducted in classroom settings. She found that, prior to grade two, teachers' use of Disapproval more or less balanced their use of Approval. However, from that point on they used punishment much more often than positive consequences! White points out that this is also about the same time that most persons report a loss of the sense of joy in being in school. These findings suggest that, as a culture, we are *not* committed to the idea of providing what might be considered high-incentive positive reinforcers for child behavior.

Why Coerce?

The schedules for Touches, Hugs, and Approvals are very lean. I think that most family interactions are, instead, maintained by a variety of less interesting consequences which are in greater supply. The consequences would include Attend, Talk, and Play. The observation data from the homes of 33 normal children by Johnson, Wahl, Martin, and Johansson (1973) showed 17% positive consequences for prosocial child behavior (for example, the child Talks and the mother Attends; the child Plays and a sibling Plays with him). In most families, there is an abundance of garden-variety positive consequences. In disrupted families, coercive child behaviors are a fairly reliable *means for producing these positive outcomes.*

In a sense, modern social learning theory is in agreement with the clinical impressions reported by Alfred Adler one-half century ago (Adler, 1929). He believed that most of the so-called *disturbed child behavior* was exemplary of "attention getting." To this we, in turn, add one interesting bilateral twist. When the family member responds by Attending or Talking, then the child terminates the coercive behavior. In so doing, the child *reinforces* the victims for supplying the reinforcer. If one grants a high likelihood of Talk or Attend given prosocial child behavior, then why does the

child, or any family member, employ coercive means to achieve this same end? It should be said at the outset that there is not, as yet, an adequate answer to this question. However, the author believes that when the answer is in hand, it will include a reference to some peculiarities in adult-child interaction patterns. The essence of it seems to be that adults quickly tire of interactions with young children. Technically speaking, adults seem to satiate rather quickly to the reinforcers found in ongoing interaction with children. The first clue to this was to be found in the classic study by the Barker group for American and English children (Barker et al., 1962). They showed that, for Midwestern children, 89% of all interaction episodes lasted less than one minute! The comparable figure for English children was 84%. The term *episode* was used to describe a unit of social interaction in which some action was completed.

The theme of the brief encounter is reiterated in a study of 30 socially aggressive and 20 normal children from the OSLC files. The details of the sample and procedures are described in Appendix 5.1. For each child the likelihood was calculated that the mother would continue interacting with the child in a prosical manner, given that the child had been prosocial in the immediately preceding interaction. The analysis was carried out to the eighth interchange in the sequence. The ANOVA for repeated measures controlled for age (young/old) and normal or clinical status of the child. The analyses showed a significant main effect for trials, but nonsignificant main effects for groups or age. For this reason the data for all four groups were combined and summarized in Figure 5.1. Given a prior prosocial child response, then the likelihood was .65 that the mother would continue interacting with the child into the adjacent six-second interval. If she continued through two interchanges, then the conditional p was .35 that she would continue interacting in the third interval. For both normal and distressed children it is unlikely that interactions with their mothers will extend beyond 18 seconds. I think that it is at intervals four, five, etc. that the child becomes increasingly likely to initiate a coercive response. Here the function is to reinstate parental attention.

Context

Thus far the formulation about consequences for coercive behavior has twice introduced assumptions emphasizing the critical role of the antecedent in defining the meaning of the coercive event itself. In one instance events having aversive antecedents were set aside as being examples of

Figure 5.1
Mothers' Responsiveness

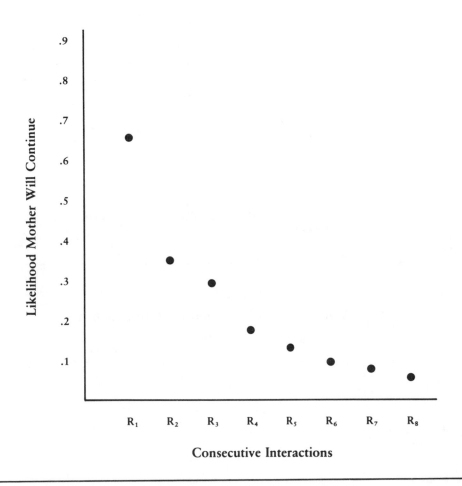

negative reinforcement. The preceding section emphasized intervals during which people stopped attending as setting the occasion for coercive behavior. Are neutral events an important source of the antecedents for attacks? If so, then coercive events in such a context might be thought of as attention *getting*. Attacks that follow positive antecedents might be thought of as attention *maintaining*. Presumably, these functions would be served whether the participants were parents or children (e.g., some wives may nag just to get their husbands' attention).

To provide the necessary descriptive data, samples were drawn from a population of problem and non-problem families studied at OSLC since 1968. (The samples are described in Appendix 5.1). Cases were selected that fell into the age group of 3.0 to 8.5 years old or 8.6 through 13.5 years old. For the clinical sample ($N = 30$), only those cases were included that met the dual re-

quirements for both age and the diagnostic label of *socially aggressive*. It consisted of children referred by parents and/or community agents because of high rates of coercive behaviors directed toward other people (e.g., Fight, Not Mind, Tease, Temper Tantrums, Whine, Yell). Of those referred for such problems, cases were selected for the sample when the observation data collected in the home showed their rates of coercive behavior to exceed .45 responses per minute. The normal sample ($N = 20$) was obtained by advertising in the newspaper for families with nonproblem children to be observed. The two samples were matched for father absence, number of siblings, age of the target child, and occupational level. As indicated in Table 5.1, the findings showed the samples to be comparable on all variables.

Context was defined in terms of the behavior of the other people which occurred as an immediate antecedent (A_i) to the coercive target event. The

Table 5.1
Antecedent Contexts for Coercive Child Behavior

	p(Coercive|Antecedent Context)								
	Nondistressed			Socially Aggressive			F values for		
Contexts	Younger (N = 10)	Older (N = 10)	Mean	Younger (N = 15)	Older (N = 15)	Mean	Sample	Age	Interaction
Aversive	.33	.19 (9)[b]	.26	.35	.33	.34	2.22[a]	1.94	1.18
Neutral	.17	.24 (9)	.21	.26	.29	.28	2.12	.134	0.17
Positive	.50	.57	.54	.40	.38	.39	5.70*	.14	0.43

[a]$p < .10$

*$p < .05$

[b]The numbers in parentheses refer to the size of the sample. The information is given only when the sample differs from the expected values of 10 for normal subsamples and 15 for deviant subsamples.

Table 5.2
Positive Consequences for Coercive Child Behaviors

			Percent of positive outcomes:	
Settings	Age	Provided by	Normal samples	Deviant samples
1. Institutions for delinquents (Buehler, Patterson, & Furniss, 1966)	Adolescents	Peers & Staff		70%
2. Nursery school (Patterson, Littman, & Bricker, 1967) N = 36	3-4	Peers	80%	
3. Home (Wahl, 1971) N = 33		Parents	47%	
	4-6	Siblings	28%	
(Snyder, 1977) N = 20	5-10	Family	64.7%	69.5%

comparisons were based on the proportion of coercive episodes involving neutral, positive, and aversive antecedents or p (Coercive\|A_i). As shown in Table 5.1, the trends for the clinical sample showed higher proportions of aversive and neutral contexts than was the case for the normal samples. These trends were, however, of borderline significance. The finding with real surprise value involved the significantly higher likelihood of attention maintaining episodes for the normal sample. On the average, 54% of the normal child's attacks occurred in a positive setting, as compared to 39% for problem children. In fact, across all groups, attacks were *most likely* to occur in a *positive context,* i.e., the other family member was engaged in some prosocial behavior such as talking or playing with the target child.

Empirical Findings

The data collected in the home and school have consistently shown very high rates of positive consequences provided by adults and peers contingent upon coercive child behaviors. For example, in the study by Walker and Buckley (1973) deviant children received 77% of one teacher's attention! A similar situation was found for one teacher but not for another in the study by Madsen, Becker, and Thomas (1968).[3] The earlier studies also pointed out that in institutions designed to treat antisocial children there were surprisingly rich schedules of positive consequences for deviant behavior (Buehler, Furniss, & Patterson, 1966). The supporting reactions were typically provided by peers (but on occasion by the staff as well) for verbal statements

Table 5.3
Positive Payoffs for Coercive Child Behaviors: Normal Sample

(from Johnson, Wahl, Martin, & Johanssen, 1973, pp. 44-45)

Coercive behavior[1]	Rate per minute	Percent positive consequences[2]	Percent negative consequences	Number children emitting behavior
1. Destructiveness	.0013	17.6%	35.2%	6
2. Physical negative	.0167	34.5	53.0	21
3. Command negative	.0126	38.2	57.8	16
4. Smart talk	.0080	51.5	39.0	13
5. Command	.1204	61.1	35.8	32
6. High rate behavior	.0644	21.6	6.5	25
7. Negativism	.0061	43.1	39.2	13
8. Tease	.0110	41.7	38.2	13
9. Yell	.0410	55.8	21.8	24

[1]Only behaviors evidenced by four or more subjects were included, e.g., only two showed Temper Tantrums.

[2]These percentages will not total 100% because neutral reactions were not analyzed here.

Reprinted with permission from "How deviant is the normal child: A behavioral analysis of the preschool child and his family." In R.D. Rubin, J.P. Brady, & J.D. Henderson, editors, *Advances in Behavior Therapy.* Copyright 1973 by Academic Press, Inc.

with antisocial connotations. Gelfand, Gelfand, and Dobson (1967) found essentially the same pattern for patients in a mental hospital; i.e., staff and patients tended to react supportively to deviant behavior. Table 5.2 summarizes the findings from several studies. In the nursery school setting coercive responses were reacted to by the victims withdrawing from the area, crying, or giving up an object or play setting. As can be seen, peer victims reacted supportively 80% of the time.

For normal families, the findings represent a range in likelihoods from .47 to .65. Though these are indeed rich schedules, their existence does not directly support the hypothesis that the schedules for positive consequences $(C+)$ are functionally related to the target behaviors. The implication is that the probability of a positive consequence given an attack response or $p\ (C+|R_j)$ is significantly higher than the base-rate $p\ (C+)$. For example, it could be that no matter what the child does, he or she will receive positive payoffs that are of this magnitude. In further studies, the base-rate values should be included so that results such as those in Table 5.2 can be interpreted. However, at a simple descriptive level these findings are extremely interesting. The social environment does provide a rich supply of positive consequences for coercive child behavior. It is not known if they are functionally related, or if they function as rein-

forcers. If these consequences *are* reinforcers then their density is certainly sufficient to maintain behavior.

It would be of some interest to know if some coercive responses receive more positive consequences than others. The study of preschool children by Johnson, Wahl, Martin, and Johansson (1973) provides data that are relevant to this question. They used a home observation code that was a modification of the FICS. They analyzed for each of nine coercive responses both the rate of occurrence and the proportion of aversive and positive consequences for that response.[4] As described in Table 5.3, child-Command was the most frequently occurring coercive behavior. About 62% of these behaviors received a positive consequence from family members. There was no covariation between response rates and likelihoods of positive consequences. The correlation between base rates of occurrence and likelihood of positive outcome was only .13 (n.s.). The covariation question will be considered in more detail in a later section. But the Johnson data emphasize the differences among coercive responses. Some are more likely to be punished, others are more likely to receive positive consequences.

The next question involves potential differences in the reactions of the various family members. Are mothers more or less likely to respond in a

Table 5.4
Likelihood Child Coercion Followed by Positive Consequence: $p(C + | \bar{R}_j)$

Family agent	Dependent variable	Samples: Normal	Social Aggressive	Abused
	All deviant			
Father	(TAB score)	.72	.65	.66
Mother		.71	.73	.70
Brothers		.63	.60	.71
Sisters		.67	.63	.66
	Hostile			
Father		.63	.61	.64
Mother		.69	.72	.74
Brothers		.73	.67	.67
Sisters		.67	.70	.67
	Social Aggressive			
Father		.34	.24	.57
Mother		.34	.40	.34
Brothers		.39	.51	.76
Sisters		.40	.46	.52

In this analysis, a positive consequence included neutral plus positive behaviors (i.e., approve, attend, command, comply, indulgence, laugh, normative, no response, play, physical positive, receive, self-stimulate, talk, touch, work).

positive manner than fathers? Are siblings more likely to be supportive than parents? As suggested by Johnson's work, family members will respond differently depending on which coercive behaviors are presented to them. To facilitate these comparisons three different response classes were used as dependent variables. The first combined the reactions to all 14 coercive responses. The other two variables consisted of functionally defined classes (Patterson, 1977a; Patterson & Cobb, 1973). Each class was comprised of responses controlled by the same network of antecedent events (see Chapter 8 for details). The comparisons were made for three samples drawn from the OSLC data files: 36 Normals, 44 Social Aggressors, and 19 Abused Children. The age range was from 4 through 12 years.

Table 5.4 indicates few differences among family members or between samples. The findings for the Total Aversive Behavior (TAB) category are directly comparable to those obtained by Snyder (1977). Comparisons for the Hostile class also showed no significant difference.

In Table 5.4 the fewest positive consequences were provided for events in the Social Aggressor class. In both clinical samples siblings were more likely than parents to respond positively to socially aggressive behavior (e.g., Teasing or Physical

Negative) directed toward them. This finding reiterates the fine discriminations involved in the performance of coercive skills. The skilled antisocial child must learn which people, what coercive behavior, where (the setting), and when to practice his trade successfully. It also seems certain that a child can make discriminations of a finer order than shown here. For example, the antisocial child probably knows just when to Tease a brother in order to produce a conditional p value for positive payoffs which is considerably above the .51 shown in Table 5.4.

There is a problem relating to these descriptive data which must be considered. The difficulty lies in the fact that 30% to 40% of coercive child behavior comes in *bursts*. While these matters will be considered in greater detail both in this chapter and in Chapter 8, suffice it to say here that, for problem children, one deviant behavior is likely to be followed by another. Antisocial children are characterized not only by more of these sequences, but the chains are of longer duration as well (Patterson, 1976). If the deviant chains are lengthy, it is quite likely that family members are reacting to the child *while* the chain is occurring. As will be discussed in Chapter 8, these *concomitant events* are the critical factor determining the eventual length of the chain and the overall rate of aggres-

Table 5.5
Likelihood of Positive Final Outcome

| Context | Normal | | Socially Aggressive | | F values for | | |
	Younger N = 10	Older N = 10	Younger N = 15	Older N = 15	Sample	Age	Interaction
Positive	.69	.47	.55	.40	1.95	5.94**	0.16
	(9)†	(9)					
Neutral	.20	.68	.45	.21	1.74	2.02	18.20**
	(8)	(9)	(14)				

**p < .01

†The numbers in parentheses refer to the size of the subsample. These figures are included only when they differ from the expected values.

sion. In analyzing discrete six-second events, the writer (1976), Johnson, Wahl, Martin, and Johansson (1973), and Snyder (1977) combined the positive events found in mid-chain with those occurring as the outcome. The writer now has reason to believe that they serve very different functions. If this formulation is correct, then the earlier analyses may not provide an accurate description of the incidence of positive consequences for coercive events (the likelihood of a positive consequence might be very different at mid-chain than the likelihood as a final outcome).

To investigate this possibility, the same samples were used as the samples employed for Table 5.1. In the present analysis only those events that followed an isolated coercive behavior or those found at the end of a coercive sequence were tabulated. Comparisons were made between normal and clinical samples as well as between younger and older target children. As expected, the findings for final outcomes in Table 5.5 were somewhat lower than those obtained for concomitants plus outcomes. For the normal sample, the mean for the combined data (concomitants plus outcomes) was .68. This is in contrast to the mean of .51 for final outcomes shown in Table 5.5. The comparable data for the Social Aggression sample were .65 and .40 respectively. One number is no more real or accurate than the other. Rather, they represent two different ways of describing the supportive reactions of family members. It could turn out that they mean different things, but that is yet to be established.

What stands out among the findings represented in Table 5.5 is the intricate relation between final outcome, age of the target child, context, and clinical or nonclinical status. Young normals received only a 20% payoff in the neutral context, but a whopping 69% in the positive context. There was a significant tendency for younger children in both samples to receive higher payoffs for attention maintaining behaviors (i.e., positive contexts). In the neutral context it was the older normal children and the younger deviant children who received significantly higher payoffs than other age groups.

Relation of Consequences to Inter- and Intraindividual Variance

One of the primary goals claimed for a coercion performance theory is that it will account for significant portions of the variance in behavior. In what sense does knowledge of positive consequences for behavior contribute to this particular enterprise?

The traditional literature from reinforcement theory would lead one to conclude that there will be no correlation between the likelihood of positive consequences and individual differences in rates of aggression. As Herrnstein (1961, 1974) and others have pointed out, there is *not* a linear monotonic relation between response strength and reinforcement density. The correlation data from field studies are in accord with that position.

Taplin (1974) carried out the first study of the relation between coercive child behavior and positive consequences provided by parents for these behaviors. He first examined the test-retest stability of p (C + |DevBeh). The likelihoods were based on the mean for three sessions from the first week of baseline and the comparable mean for the second week of baseline. The PPM correlations (uncorrected) for mothers was .48 ($df = 23$; $p < .001$), and for fathers .11 (n.s.). For both parents combined, the correlation was .82 ($df = 23$; $p < .02$). During baseline, the correlations between mother's $p(C+|Dev)$ and child's rate of coercive behavior were .10 for week one, and .08 for week two. The comparable data for fathers were .15 and .15.

The Taplin analysis did not support the idea of a linear monotonic relation between the *strength* of a child's coercive behavior and the likelihood of the child being reinforced for it. As noted earlier, this is in keeping with the traditional findings from learning theory. There is a possibility that Taplin's finding was obtained because of the double confounding due to combining data across contexts, and combining data for concomitants and outcomes. As a check, the data for final outcomes were analyzed for the combined reactions of all family members to the problem child. The correlation between the problem child's baseline TAB score and the $p(C+|Dev)$ was .25 (n.s.) for positive contexts and .11 (n.s.) for neutral contexts. Incidentally, the families most likely to pay off in one context were also most likely to do so in the other. The correlation between the two likelihoods was .47 ($df = 22$; $p < .02$). The disposition to react positively seems moderately stable across time and settings.

The prime function assigned to positive consequences has been that of strengthening the S-R bond. From this perspective, reinforcers make an *indirect* contribution to performance. Reinforcement alters the status of the controlling stimuli which, in turn, account for one type of performance variance. It is thought that day-by-day fluctuations in coercive behaviors are determined primarily by changes in the density of the stimuli controlling their occurrence.

Some Functional Relations

At the crux of the interactional stance is the idea that each member of a dyad changes the ongoing behavior of the other (Bandura, 1974; Bell, 1968; Bell & Harper, 1977; Gottman, 1979). This has some interesting implications for reinforcement theory which have been largely ignored.

There are three functional relations of interest. The first is the familiar $p(\overline{R}_j|A_i)$. The A_i is the prior behavior of the victim that elicited the attack. The conditional p value describes how efficacious that A_i is in producing the $\overline{R}_j$. Here, the victim *trains* the attacker by providing positive reinforcement for the attack.

The second relation describes the likelihood of a positive consequence ($C+$) given an attack ($\overline{R}_j$) or $p(C+|\overline{R}_j)$. One might think of this as a statement about the richness of the reinforcement schedule

for aversive responses. How efficiently does the response produce the positive consequence? The presence of this structure implies that something is being done to control the behavior of the victim as a *reinforcer*. In effect, the attacker trains the victim to reinforce her or him for the attack. Chapter 7 considers this matter in detail as one component of the reinforcement trap. For the present, it is sufficient to note that when the victim complies, the aggressor terminates the attack.

J.S. Watson (1979) and E. Thomas (personal communication) make the extremely important point that in the real world matters do not stop here. There is a third function that is very important. In the laboratory the two p values $p(R_j|A_i)$ and $p(C+|R_j)$ tell the greater part of the story. However, in social interaction we need a measure of how often the reinforcer occurs when it is *not* contingent upon that particular R_j. In the laboratory, the reinforcer occurs *only* when the response occurs. That is, p (prior $R_j|C+$) is always 100% (if a positive consequence occurs it is always preceded by R_j). But in family interaction, Talk, Approve, and Comply may follow many child behaviors other than coercive acts. In social interaction this important variable is left free to vary and the p (prior $R_j|C+$) is considerably less than 100%. One might think of this value as a measure of the *sufficiency* with which the response produces the reinforcer. As Watson points out, in social interaction the values p (prior $R_j|C+$) and $p(C+|R_j)$ vary independently. In his laboratory studies of infants, Watson has investigated the relative contribution of each in determining the shaping of the infants' behavior. The largest reinforcement effects were obtained under conditions of matched indices of contingency. However one may interpret these specific findings, these seminal studies make a major point that must be considered in the present context. The impact of a reinforcer on the $A_i \rightarrow R_j$ connection may be relative to the general availability of the reinforcer as expressed in Watson's sufficiency index. This point will be considered in more detail in a later section. What a reinforcer means, as expressed by its impact on the $A_i \rightarrow R_j$ connection, is partly a function of the matrix in which it occurs.

Some Further Considerations

To understand the structure of social interaction it is useful to think of reinforcement as one determinant for many of the functional relations. The review of the empirical findings emphasized that the social environment is characterized by a rich supply of positive consequences for coercive child behaviors. However, is it the case that these positive consequences are *reinforcers?* What is the evidence that the $C+$'s identified in field studies function as reinforcers? These issues are discussed in the section which follows. In addition, some brief speculations are presented concerning the question of why people respond to social reinforcers, and why there are individual differences in this responsiveness.

Tests for Status as a Reinforcer

How is one to determine that a $C+$ identified in a field setting functions as a reinforcer? This section examines three approaches found in the current literature. They are ordered from the least to the most powerful as tests.

Changes in $A_i \rightarrow R_j$ Connections. The first attempt to employ an $A_i \rightarrow R_j$ format was a rather crude affair because we did not fully appreciate the complexity of the problems involved. For this analysis, the nine most aggressive nursery school children were selected as targets (Patterson, Littman & Bricker, 1967). At a minimum, each produced two or more aggressive responses per session. The positive consequences provided by the victim included: gives up toy, withdraws, does not respond, cries, and defensive posture (e.g., covers up head). If these outcomes functioned as reinforcers, they should have been associated with the increased likelihoods that for his or her next attack the aggressor would select the *same* victim (A_i) and employ the same category of attack (R_j). Attacks included the following: physical with object, verbal, invades territory. Punishment would be associated with a change in the A_i and/or a change in R_j. Either the attack would shift its form, or a new victim would be selected. Punishment included: tell the teacher, hit back, and recover object. As found in Table 5.6, the shifts were in accord with these predictions. The chi square analysis showed a significant effect for six of the nine children.

The analysis was clumsy in several important respects. First, the behavior change reflected the effects of both rewards *and* punishment. However, in that the study was designed to demonstrate that these two variables controlled aggressive behavior, that was not a serious problem. To provide a fit to the $A_i \rightarrow R_j$ format, it would have required that $p(R_j|A_i)$ be calculated separately for each of the aggressor's victims. That simple recalculation could easily be carried out. The reason this was not done is that there was a more serious confound. In fact, it is of such magnitude as to call into question any conclusion about whether these data reflected reinforcement effects at all.

Thematic Effects. The problem lies in parceling

out the thematic effect of the subject's own ongoing behavior. Chapter 8 documents the fact that one of a subject's aggressive events will tend to follow another, i.e., aggression comes in "chunks." When analyzing for shifts in the attacker's behav-

---

Table 5.6
Shifts in Attack and/or Victim as a Function of Victim Reaction
(from Patterson, Littman, & Bricker, 1967, p. 22)

Subject	Frequency assertive events	Chi square
5C	106	13.59***
8C	86	2.73
11C	56	10.36**
14C	401	6.97**
11P	335	14.68***
12P	56	2.37
13P	212	10.79**
14P	340	71.80***
15P	49	0.04

**$p < .01$
***$p < .001$

---

ior, the 1967 study combined immediately following events with those occurring several days later. We know now that only the latter could be thought of as being a test of reinforcement effects, i.e., changes in the p of R_2 given A_2.[5]

One-half decade later the problem had become clearer. A proper test of reinforcement effects using sequential data requires *that the thematic effects found in ongoing behavior be parceled out.* This requires that one identify an A_i and R_j followed by a $C+$ that is suspected to be a reinforcer. Then, at some later time, when the same agent performs the same A_i, what is the likelihood that it will be followed by the same R_j? If the consequence functioned as a reinforcer, then the $A_i \rightarrow R_j$ connection should be strengthened. There are many problems associated with doing such an analysis, e.g., what is the appropriate time interval? Is the stimulus the presence of the agent, the behavior of the agent, or both?

Thus far, we have carried out only one pilot analysis of this problem (Patterson & Cobb, 1971). Those data were from the first 24 families referred to OSLC. We were searching for an $A_i \rightarrow R_j$ connection at t_1 that was followed during the same five minutes by another presentation of the same A_i. Given that constraint, then the question of how to control for thematic effect becomes very difficult. How long must one wait to control for "chunking?" We do not know the answer to that question. It is, however, the kind of question for which G. Sackett's sequential lag analyses seem ideally suited to provide an answer (Sackett, 1977). Patterson and Cobb arbitrarily imposed an interruption period consisting of at least three six-second units following interchanges in which a former attacker who had hit a victim interacted with some family member other than the former victim.

There were 69 episodes in which the same agent reappeared, but emitted a behavior other than the A_1 associated with the reinforced hit. The $p(\text{Hit}_2|\text{Same Agent})$ at t_2 was .061. Similarly, if the same A_1 behavior reappeared, but was performed by a different agent, the $p(\text{Hit}_2|\text{Same Behavior})$ at t_2 was .064. One could think of each of the p values as a kind of base rate.

In addition, those episodes were analyzed in which the former victim who had been hit reappeared or the same behavior appeared, but with a new agent. The likelihood for Hit was .002. The data showed only ten instances in which the same agent and agent behavior recurred in the same five-minute segment; the $p(R_2|A_2)$ was .200.

These meager findings *suggest* that agent presence and agent behavior may combine in a unique way to form the A_1. The data available suggest that the positive consequences provided by the victims served as positive reinforcers for hitting. Because of the limitations in the number of reinforced events, the analysis can only be thought of as illustrative. However, the results provide such a close fit to expectations that they emphasize the potential of this mode of testing for status as a reinforcer. Large amounts of data are required underlining, in turn, the need to collect the data in larger time blocks than the five-minute segments used in the 1971 study. It would also be imperative to carry out empirical studies demonstrating the relation of time following the episode and the calculation of $p(R_2|R_1)$. How long does it take to overcome the thematic effect of R_1 as an elicitor for R_2; is it six seconds, 60 seconds, or five minutes? This is crucial because it determines how one forms the base-rate values against which the $p(R_2|A_2)$ is compared.

One would also be considerably reassured if the investigator went on to submit $C+$ events surviving such analyses to experimental manipulation. A number of such demonstrations would be needed to convince a reasonable critic that the conditional p format did not contain some unsuspected confounds. There could be variables embedded in social interaction, which could contribute to a reinforcement-like effect, but have nothing to do per se with the phenomenon. Ultimately the test of causal connections must include an experimental manipulation.

Experimental Manipulations. Motivational theories served as the primary focus for much of the early work on aggression, e.g., the frustration-aggression hypothesis by Dollard, Doob, Miller, Mowrer and Sears (1939). The emphasis on motivational variables was so overwhelming that only a few studies were carried out testing the effect of positive reinforcers on aggressive behavior. For this reason, the classic study by Miller (1948) was of particular importance. He showed that withdrawal of shock could serve as a negative reinforcer for aggression, and demonstrated the potential importance of reinforcement as a determinant. It took more than a decade to return to this line of thought. Then, the study by Reynolds, Catania, and Skinner (1963) showed that pigeon attacks could be shaped by food as a reinforcer. Ulrich, Johnston, Richardson, and Wolff (1963, cited by Ulrich et al., 1973) used water to shape fighting behavior in water-deprived rats.

In the early 1960's, a generation of young children participated in studies in which they were reinforced and/or punished for striking rubber Bobo dolls. These studies (reviewed in Patterson & Cobb, 1971) established the fact that social and nonsocial reinforcers increased the rate of hitting Bobo dolls. Programmatic studies at Stanford provided a careful analysis of the variables such as sex, age of children, and sex of reinforcing agent. These studies were summarized in Bandura (1973).

There were some methodological problems inherent in these early studies but they did not seem overwhelming. For example, an extended baseline study by R. Jones at the University of Oregon found that a laboratory measure of the *rate* of hitting was an unstable measure. In his study the rate increased in the *absence* of reinforcement! This led to our decision to use amplitude as well as frequency as dependent variables. It also led to the construction of a high-tech Bobo doll (amplitude and frequency were automatically recorded) who squatted in automated splendor in his own throne room. The studies which followed demonstrated satisfactory reliability and validity for the new dependent variables. In the last study in the series, positive social reinforcement from adults significantly increased the amplitude of the child's blows to the Bobo doll. The magnitude of the increase in amplitude correlated .66 with peer sociometric

Table 5.7
Mother as Reinforcer for Child Coercion

Day	Baseline$_1$		Experimental		Baseline$_2$	
Phases:	p(attack)	p(reinforced)	p(attack)	p(reinforced)	p(attack)	p(reinforced)
First	.25	.50	.81	.88	.70	.70
Second	.00	—	.49	.58	.74	.71

ratings of aggressiveness in school. A second study replicated this general relation between laboratory conditioning for aggression and school behavior. Similar generalizability from laboratory measures had been demonstrated by Walters and Brown (1963) and Lovaas (1961b).

At that time, it seemed we had some leverage on the problem. Aggression-like behaviors could be shaped in the laboratory. Antisocial children were generally more "conditionable" than were nonaggressive children. We began thinking about how this rather consistent set of laboratory findings might apply to children's aggression in the real world. The general idea was that other persons (e.g., spectators or parents) might give positive reinforcers for successful aggression. In that vein, the parent interview study by Bandura and Walters (1959) reported that parents of aggressive boys *supported* the child's aggression toward persons outside the family. It seemed reasonable that in certain machismo-oriented subcultures the parents, as well as peers, might provide explicit approval for aggressive behavior directed toward outsiders. Peer-dispensed social reinforcers for aggression seemed like another possibility as a source for the reinforcement of aggressive behavior.

At about this time, a university colleague (K. Polk) called the author and offered to provide a small amount of funding to support a project related to antisocial children. The actual amount was too small to finance an experiment (which at that time was our preferred approach). However, it was just enough to pay two observers to go to one nursery school for two or three weeks. The results from that pilot study revealed to us what, in retrospect, was probably intuitively obvious to everyone but a Ph.D. psychologist. Positive consequences were seldom delivered by onlookers, whether peers or adults. The reinforcers were supplied by the victim! As shown by the results from the NIMH supported study that followed (Patter-son, Littman, & Bricker, 1967), the rates at which victim-dispensed reinforcers were supplied seemed astonishingly high.

It took another ten years to learn how to design experimental tests for the hypothesis that victims dispensed the primary reinforcers for children's aggression. The studies that have been designed to test for the effect of negative reinforcement will be summarized in Chapter 7. The general format for all these studies has been a single-subject ABA reversal design. All of the sessions take place in the home; the reinforcing agents have been the mothers. Training mothers to use reinforcement has proven to be a valuable prelude to training them to manage their contumacious preschool children. In these studies the mother participates in prior role-playing sessions in order to facilitate her delivering the right reinforcers at the right time. During the more recent studies, the mothers not only received several pretrial training sessions, but in addition, cuing devices were used during the experiments. Typically, the design also included a replication of the ABA procedures on a second and third day.

For example, in the case of the preschool child, Eclipse, the mother was observed in the home to provide positive consequences for coercive behaviors. A younger sibling also provided a rich schedule. As can be seen in Table 5.7, on the first day the mother reinforced (Talk, Attend) half of the target child's coercive interactions with her. At that time about 25% of the child's interactions with her were coercive. During the experimental phase the mother was cued to respond positively when a coercive behavior occurred. On the first day she was able to reinforce 88%, and on the second day 58%. The likelihood of the child's attacks (given interaction with her) increased on both days. Note that during the second baseline, even though the mother was no longer cued, she continued to reinforce the child's coercive attacks.

The case for parent and/or sibling attention as a

reinforcer for some coercive behaviors is not proven by a single case study. The case for sibling attention and/or compliance as a reinforcer for coercion has not been tested. The study of Eclipse and his mother is an example of how such studies might be done. The thought is that they should be done in the home, and with as little disruption of the natural setting as possible.

Pain as the Reinforcer

The majority of the outcomes for coercive child behavior consists of positive behaviors such as Talk or Attend. A study of the impact of these outcomes upon low-amplitude aversive events will presumably contribute to our understanding of why antisocial children are rejected by peers and family alike. As noted earlier, understanding how this process develops may also clarify the antecedents for some high-amplitude familial violence. However, it is difficult to believe that Talk and Attend will prove to be the *primary* reinforcers for high-amplitude attacks. More likely, the reinforcer will prove to be compliance and/or submission. In that context, it may also be the case that the pain reaction of the victim may function as a positive reinforcer for both high- and low-amplitude coercion. Unfortunately, the limitations of the current OSLC code systems were such that measures of pain reactions (other than Cry) were not feasible. The new code (MOSAIC) should remedy this situation. In the meantime, a discussion of the positive reinforcers for aggression would seem to be incomplete if it did not take into account the possibility of pain cues functioning as a powerful reinforcer for some aggression in some settings.

Buss (1961) differentiated outcomes for aggressive behavior into extrinsic reinforcers and those reinforcers supplied by the victim. The latter included pain reactions by the victim as well as submission and compliance reactions. Observers of children's play in six cultures coded five percent of their aggression as designed to hurt the victim (Lambert, 1974). Toch (1969), in his classic *Violent Men,* emphasized the fact that both violent prison inmates and violent police officers reported that they *enjoyed* inflicting pain on their victims. B. F. Skinner (1969) also emphasized that a reaction by the victim that indicated damage had occurred was a likely reinforcer for aggression. Incidentally, in the same volume he makes a general case for genetic determinants of differential responsiveness to certain reinforcers. When applied to aggression, the argument could be generalized to suggest a genetically determined differential responsiveness to the victim's pain reaction.

Most of the tests for victim pain as a variable have been made in laboratory analogue situations in which the Buss type shock machine was employed. The study by Hartmann (1969) was a prototype for much of the later work. Antisocial adolescents served as subjects in an experiment in which they were to deliver shocks to another subject engaged in learning a task. In this situation those subjects with longer histories of antisocial behavior tended to be more punitive. Hearing a reaction from the victim that signified pain was correlated with an increased likelihood of aggression. That finding is in keeping with Berkowitz's (1973a, 1973b) speculations about victim pain reactions as a reinforcer. However, it is not clear in such a procedure whether pain reactions served to *elicit* attacks or *reinforce* them.

In reviewing the extensive literature on this subject, Rule and Nesdale (1976) cited a number of studies showing that pain cues from a victim were associated with a reduction in anger. The study by Baron (1971a, 1971b) demonstrated that pain cues reduced delivery of shocks by nonangered people, but increased the delivery of shocks by angered people. These findings support the general distinction between angry and nonangry aggression made by Bandura (1973) and by Hartup (1974). It seems reasonable to suppose that the reinforcer for angry aggression would be a pain reaction from the victim.

Swart and Berkowitz (1976) provided a powerful test for the effect of pain cues as a reinforcer. They reasoned that if pain cues functioned as a reinforcer, then pairing a neutral stimulus with the pain cue should produce a conditional reinforcer. In subsequent trials, this should function as a reinforcer. In their study, a light was paired with the victim's pain reaction. In later trials with another victim, the conditioned stimulus was associated with more intense attacks. In that there was no group controlling for noncontingent employment of the pain cue or for the conditioned stimulus itself, one may well ask whether the conditioned stimulus served to arouse or reinforce. In either case, it seems clear that pain cues were a powerful determinant for attacks.

There are a number of studies demonstrating that the impact of pain cues on attacks is a joint function of several other variables. Baron (1971a, 1971b) and Buss (1966a), cited by Perry & Perry, 1974) found victims' pain reactions produced an *inhibition* of aggressive attacks (shorter duration and less intensity) rather than an escalation. John Knutson (personal communication) described a study carried out at his laboratory that also failed to find the relation. Perry and Perry (1974) take the position that the pain reinforcement effect would occur *only* if the subject were *angry,* and then perhaps only if the subject were also *antisocial.* They tested for these possibilities in a well-controlled large-scale study. First, a peer sociometric was used to identify 128 aggressive and nonaggressive elementary-school-aged boys. The 2X2X2 factorial design also controlled for angry and nonangry, and high-and low-pain victim feedback conditions. The main effects were significant for both the aggressive and the anger arousal conditions. The antisocial and the angry (borderline significance) conditions were associated with higher scores on the Buss aggression machine procedure. However, the effects of feedback about victim pain *inhibited* the reactions of aggressors and nonaggressors alike. It should be kept in mind that in this study the children labeled as aggressive were *normal* children in the public schools. They were not, as in the case of Hartmann's (1969) sample, institutionalized delinquents. In this writer's opinion, this is a crucial variable. As noted earlier for the Radke-Yarrow and Waxler (1979) study, the covariations of measures of aggression were reversed in sign depending on whether the children were in the normal or extreme ranges for aggression.

Perry and Bussey (1977) repeated this general design with a second sample of normal children. Again, feedback from the victim *inhibited* attack behaviors in both aggressive and nonaggressive children. The inhibition effect was, however, significant only for the nonaggressive sample. In this study, they added a new component which involved the question of the relation between the victim's pain reaction and the self-evaluation of the attacker. For the nonaggressive sample the correlation between the average pain-cue feedback received and the amount of self-reward at the end of the test was $-.65$ ($p < .001$). For the more aggressive sample, the comparable correlation was $-.10$ (n.s.).

As things stand, the notion of victim pain reaction as a *reinforcer* for aggression remains plausible but unproven. Adequate controls for arousal effects have not been used. The literature would suggest that anger, arousal and prior status as (extremely) antisocial may also be necessary conditions. These hypotheses should be tested for family interactions. For example, does victim Cry serve as a reinforcer, i.e., strengthen the p $(R_2|A_2)$?[6] Is Cry most likely to follow high-amplitude attacks? Is Cry a reinforcer that contributes to the escalating cycles of high-amplitude interchanges in wife- and child-abusive families?

Changes in Responsiveness

Prosocial behaviors such as Talk and Attend are considered to be primary reinforcers for a wide range of prosocial *and* coercive behaviors. However, from early on, our clinical experience with families of antisocial children suggested that these children were not particularly responsive to positive reinforcers. The empirical studies reviewed in Chapter 11 support this assumption. It was also the case that following treatment many of these antisocial children seemed to become more responsive to social reinforcers. When taken together, these findings and our clinical impressions point to the fact that at some level, responsiveness to social reinforcers is not a static trait. There are not only individual differences, but intraindividual shifts over time. This last section is a highly speculative account of how this might come about.

There is an interesting sense in which the perspective of the ethologists such as Hinde (1974) melds with that of operant psychology (Skinner, 1969). Both emphasize the function of evolutionary selection in producing species that are differentially responsive to certain reinforcers. In that context, it is reasonable to speculate that, among other things, humans may be uniquely responsive to reinforcers found in the behavior of other persons. For example, even very young infants can be conditioned by the contingent presentation of a face. It is also the case that even at that age there is a marked variability in responsiveness.

The seminal work of J.S. Watson (1979) extends this formulation. He introduced a concept which may explain why responsiveness to positive reinforcers varies over time. He proposed that even infants *directly* perceive the contingent relation between their behavior and its impact on the environment. His study of eight-week-old infants demonstrated that they were sensitive to very small changes in contingencies. The behaviors controlled by contingent presentations were accompanied by smiling, while noncontingent presentations were not. Watson posits a relation between attraction on the one hand and contingent reactions on the other. We are attracted to a partner *because* he or she responds *contingently* (and nonaversively) to our behavior. Presumably the same could apply to pinball machines, trout fishing and to our affection for our mothers as well.

Watson adds one further postulate of fundamental importance. If the event is presented noncontingently, it does not shape behavior, but noncontingent presentations do alter the *responsiveness* of the *individual* to those *presentations* made *contingently.* To understand responsiveness, two conditional values are required. It is, in fact, their ratio that determines behavior control. The first is the by now familiar $p(C+|R_j)$, and the second is some estimate of how likely $C+$ is to occur in situations not involving R_j. If the likelihood is very high that $C+$ will occur in the absense of R_j, then $p(C+|R_j)$ will have less effect. Watson's own work is concerned with the problem of estimating the ratio that gives maximum control. Those issues have yet to be resolved, but the general concept has important implications for many areas of socialization research.

From this viewpoint, the impact of a contingency is a relative matter. This, of course, is a general concept having a long history in experimental psychology. For example, the Crespi-type studies of negative contrast effects still find consistent empirical support (Black, 1968). Similarly, the finding from Rotter-type studies emphasize the general importance of the past history of reinforcement in assessing the impact of current contingencies (Baron, 1966). The Watson formulation takes this relativity stance, and puts it into the immediate present. In a given setting, it is some ratio of the contingent to noncontingent characteristic of a reinforcer which determines its impact. This is reminiscent of Estes' (1971) focus on the informational values of reinforcers as differentiated from their hedonic value.

The position is directly related to the systematic studies by R. Cairns' students reviewed in Chapter 11. Those studies demonstrated that noncontingent presentations of social reinforcers were followed by reduced responsiveness when the same events were later presented contingently. Cairns emphasized that the noncontingent presentations reduced the informational value of the events.

Is it true that parents of antisocial children are about as likely to reinforce one response as another? It is our impression that this is the case, but as yet there are no analyses that are appropriate for this question. As a hunch, I believe that it is this noncontingent aspect of the parents' behavior which produces the relatively nonresponsive child. I also think that one of the key features of the OSLC treatment is training parents to be contingent (to reinforce contingently and to punish contingently). The conventional wisdom gives the adage "be consistent." To this we would add *be contingent*. A well-intentioned parent who is often noncontingently warm and affectionate may create a situation in which she or he will *produce* a problem.

Acknowledgments

The writer gratefully acknowledges the efforts of L. Lippsitt and R. Loeber in correcting some of the misconceptions in earlier drafts of this manuscript. I am also grateful to Beverly Fagot for her careful editing of the final draft of the chapter. Her efforts resulted in several major changes in the organization of the material which did much to enhance its readability.

Footnotes

1. It should be noted that the binomial Z has found some favor as a statistic for making such comparisons (Sackett, 1977). However, as noted by Gottman (1979), the Z statistic approximates a normal distribution only when N is larger than 25. If the base-rate value is close to zero or one, then even larger values are required. This point constitutes a major difficulty in that many social behaviors of interest occur at a base rate so low as to violate the assumptions underlying the use of the Z statistic.

2. As discussed by Schoenfeld (1978), this rejection more clearly delineated the differences between the theories of Skinner and Pavlov.

3. It would be important to have a series of studies to determine just how widespread the phenomenon really is. The writer is aware of two other studies with similar findings: Hall, Lund, and Jackson (1968), and Hotchkiss (1966). In their aggregate, these studies sample only a very small number of teachers. However, it cannot be true that coercive behaviors work that effectively in *all* classrooms.

4. Each investigator tends to define categories of positive consequences in a slightly different way. For example, Johnson, Wahl, Martin and Johansson (1973) included Approve, Attend, Comply, Indulge, Laugh, Physical Positive, Receive, Talk, Touch, and Nonverbal.

5. As shown in Patterson (1977b, 1980b), for family interactions, the effect of an aversive consequence is to *increase* the likelihood of an immediate continuation of the attack. In the nursery school data this would have been counted as a "miss," i.e., the effect of a negative consequence did not lead to a change in victim or attack response, but rather a continuation. Thus, the 1967 study *underestimated* the effect of punishment. $C+$ reactions are associated with the termination of ongoing attacks. As a result, in the 1967 study, the inclusion of the short-term effects for $C+$ also led to an underestimate of the true relationship

(the analysis was too conservative). The problem is that we do not know if these assumptions apply to school interactions. Therefore, the most sensible position is to be extremely cautious in accepting the 1967 findings as offering direct support for the hypothesis.

6. Two field studies included Cry as a consequence for aggressive behavior. In both studies, however, the analyses were partially confounded at least as they relate to the issue of Cry as a reinforcer for attacks. In the first study, Patterson, Littman, and Bricker (1967) studied nursery school attacks. Cry was one of three outcomes grouped a priori as an example of a positive consequence. The analyses suggested that this class of outcomes was associated with an increase in the probability of the same type of attack being directed to the same victim. Such an increase was demonstrated, but the specific contribution of Cry was lost in this analysis. Unfortunately, the results for even the general class of consequences cannot be viewed as demonstrating their status as a reinforcer. The 1967 analysis was based to a rather large extent on bursts or chains in which one child attacked the other, sometimes in a sequence lasting for several moments. Thus, some predictions were based on the adjacent attack in the chain, and some were based on an attack during the next day. The latter may reflect reinforcement effects, but the former more likely reflect thematic arousal and/or suppression effects. Because the 1967 study summed across both kinds of predictions, the data are simply not interpretable. At that time the writer simply did not understand the differences between accelerators and reinforcers.

The next analysis by Patterson and Cobb (1971) of Cry as a consequence for Hit was based on family interaction data. The focus for the analysis was only on its function as an accelerator or decelerator, and not as a reinforcer. The base rate for a second Hit given the first Hit for family members was .24. If Cry occurred as a consequence for the first Hit, then the conditional p was .22. It seems Cry did not function as an accelerator for ongoing hitting. No test was made for Cry as a reinforcing event.

Chapter 6
Abstract

Effective parental punishment is thought to weaken the connection between a stimulus and the child's coercive response. Most parental punishment consists of threats to punish, scolding, and so on. To be effective, these threats must occasionally be paired with back-up punishment. Parental threats which are not backed up are categorized as "nattering." The effect of parental nattering is to increase the likelihood that the child's aversive behavior will continue.

This chapter reviews survey studies on the incidence of various kinds of parental punishment. Observation data are presented comparing normal and deviant samples for the likelihood of various parental punishments for various coercive responses. The samples are also compared for the effectiveness of parental punishment in suppressing coercive behavior. Generally, the impact is to increase the likelihood of the immediate recurrence of the deviant behavior. This "facilitation effect" relates differentially to context, age, agent, and kind of coercive behavior. Various explanations for this phenomenon are presented: mixed schedules of reward and punishment, timing of the punishment, inadequate pairings of *CS* and *UCS*, lack of clearly stated rules, and heritability for hyporesponsiveness to aversive events.

Chapter 6

Punishment for Aggression

If I were allowed to select only one concept to use in training parents of antisocial children, I would teach them how to punish more effectively. It is the key to understanding familial aggression. The study of punishment is very complex; we now know that we have only begun to understand this aspect of the coercion process. This is peculiar because it was the study of punishment that led to the development of much of what we now call coercion theory.

The same aversive consequences that effectively altered family members' prosocial behavior were relatively ineffective in suppressing Hit (Patterson & Cobb, 1971).[1] How could an event serve as a punishment for one response but not for another? It was this question that eventually led us to the study of family structure and the irritability cycle (Chapter 8). This question, however, still stands as a kind of Gordian knot. After a decade of work, we understand this question much better. We also continue to find new ways of studying it. This dedicated effort was engendered by a second surprise that we encountered very early in our investigation. We found that when parents tried to punish the coercive behavior of problem children, the immediate effect was to make things worse (Patterson, 1976, 1977a)! Again a surprise, and, again, the question of how can this be? This chapter addresses these two questions.

We have come to view parental punishment as serving two very different functions. In some contexts aversive consequences indicate parental irritation. It is a kind of irritable aggression, a reaction to the child's annoying behavior. Sometimes these reactions indiciate that more intense punishment is forthcoming. They function as conditioned stimuli (*CS*) for threats or warnings of more intensive punishment (*UCS*). The threats must periodically be "backed up" or they lose their power to control behavior. Typically the back-up events would be loss of privilege, time out from reinforcement, work, or, for the unskilled parent, physical assault (spanking). If threats and scolding are seldom followed through, then in their role as *CS* they will have only weak control over antisocial aggression.

For each family there are some aversive consequences which all members understand to have special status. They do *not* indicate that a more intensive punishment (*UCS*) is forthcoming. Their function is to make the other person feel bad but they do not necessarily mean that he or she must "stop." Our culture defines the meanings of certain aversive words, gestures, and facial expressions. Events such as insults or humiliations are experienced as aversive for this reason rather than because of their prior association with more powerful punishment. When these aversives are used as consequences, they elicit a counterattack rather than suppressing coercive behaviors. I assume that in distressed families there are many more categories of aversive consequences that function in this way than there are those which signal, "Stop or else!"

As a general case, the writer assumes that parents of antisocial children seldom follow through on their threats or scolding (Patterson, 1976). The child is aware of this and responds to most aversive consequences with counterattacks. From his standpoint, insults, humiliations, and scolding are *all* aversives; few of them signal that punishment will follow. They are responded to not as signals for him to "stop" but rather as irritants and elicitors of counterattack.

My longstanding colleague, John Reid, has coined the word "nattering" to describe this process (he claims the term was created by Mavis E. Hetherington). The parent experiences some aspect of the child's behavior as unpleasant and wishes it to stop. Nattering is an expression of parental displeasure. It signifies irritation with no intention of following through. We believe that parents of antisocial children employ nattering at higher rates than parents of normal children. In this way they avoid the major conflict which would accompany their efforts to confront the child and try to make him stop what he is doing. They do not really try to stop coercive behavior; they only ineptly meddle in it. The effect of their nattering is to produce extensions of the behaviors which elicit their displeasure.

In most families the parents use certain cues that are well understood. They indicate that the parent will now back up his or her threats (e.g., they glare, or use key words with accompanying voice inflections). In the heat of the moment, the antisocial child often misses these cues and may be badly beaten as a result. One-third of our antisocial children were abused (Reid, Taplin, & Lorber, 1981). By definition, a beaten child means that the parents are unskilled; but it could also mean that the child is unskilled. He should track his parents more carefully. I think that even child-abusive parents send these signals, but they are missed by the child. At this point, our problem as investigators is that we have no ready means of differentiating nattering from a punishment confrontation. We need some new assessment device for this task.

Beatings and spankings *work*. They effectively stop annoying child behavior for a short time. For several hours or even days following this, scolding and threats may have an increased effect. Even though the parents may express extreme guilt about the assault, this one back-up punishment is all that they have. They have neither the skills nor the discipline required to effectively use the back-up punishments used by most parents. Deprivation of privileges often results in an extended verbal confrontation which is aversive to all parties. It also requires the parents to give up their own pleasures in order to monitor the child for several days. Physical assault, in contrast, is brief and satisfying. After all the effort involved in deprivation of privileges, the child will eventually *do it again*. To the parent of the antisocial child, this means the *punishment did not really work*. They do not understand the concept of "training" which requires the parents to react consistently during many trials using punishment repeatedly.

They are left, then, with nattering as their only means of suppressing unwanted behavior. In a sense they punish, or at least are aversive, more often than most parents. They also beat the child more often; but they are less likely to confront him. In contrast, normal parents are more likely either to ignore an event or to confront it and effectively stop the behavior. They are less likely to natter and less likely to beat the child. From this viewpoint, we would have to assume that nattering and beating covary.

Some Background Considerations

When viewed historically within experimental psychology, the concept of punishment is characterized by strange twists and turns. First of all, punishment describes an arrangement which includes a *painful* stimulus. However, very little is understood about the perception of pain. There is, as yet, no physiological basis for believing that a pain center exists in the brain (Barber, 1959). The second peculiar characteristic of punishment lies in the efficiency with which it controls human behavior. Arrangements involving positive reinforcers often require hundreds of trials to produce minor changes in behavior. In contrast, there are studies which demonstrate that the use of punishment arrangements results in the *total suppression* of certain human and animal behaviors in a *single* trial (Church, 1963)! The classic avoidance conditioning studies by Solomon and Wynne (1954) showed a failure of extinction for avoidance responses. After two or three pairings of the *CS* and *UCS*, the presentation of the *CS* elicited up to 650 avoidance responses! This "irreversibility" had also been noted in earlier studies by Pavlovian investigators.

At a cultural level, punishment has always played a central role in the control of human behavior. The more important the goal, the shorter the amount of time available, then the more likely it is that punishment will play a central role. When faced with a national emergency requiring the training of millions of young men for a wide range of new roles, the armed forces resorted to established punishment procedures. The trainees were isolated from the usual distractions and were subjected to massive amounts of information and modeling for the new skills. The performance of these skills was maintained largely by punishment. If one did not follow time schedules, did not dress in the appropriate uniform, did not follow military protocol when addressing an officer, or gave a perfunctory performance on the drill field, then punishment was almost certain to follow. The punishments employed were often highly innovative and multidimensional, including components of physical pain, fatigue, boredom, shame, and on occasion, were extended to include one's peer group as well. There was no question about the relationship between threats and back-up punishments.

Punishment is an ancient idea that has been well understood and deftly used by most persons responsible for administrating large social units. It is an integral part of our public school system with its focus on producing a few winners. As a by-product, it also produces an enormous number of "losers."[2] In the classroom the ratio of critical to supportive comments is overwhelmingly in favor of the former. The process of training graduate students to "do" a dissertation is so punishing that 90% of Ph.D.'s never repeat the process of doing research.

It seems that a heavy reliance on punishment characterizes many families as well. While as a culture we extol the family as a concept synonymous with love, survey studies suggest that this is not the experience of many. Straus and his co-workers have found that for many people, marriage can be characterized as a "license to hit." They found that in the family, hate is more likely than love (Steinmetz & Straus, 1974). As a society, we emphasize parental warmth and laissez-faire attitudes as crucial in child rearing; but at the same time we condone physical assault as a necessary mechanism for socializing the child (Stark & McEvoy, 1970).

Making an aversive event contingent upon an undesirable behavior is our culture's most efficient means for altering performance. Punishment works. Its effectiveness is experienced by one and all. In fact, most members of our culture are unaware of any other mechanism for bringing about behavior change. Most parents dismiss the recent emphasis on positive reinforcement as being relatively *unimportant*. "It's okay for pigeons and rats; but it won't work on people." Most parents are unaware of the fact that some of their own be-

havior functions as a positive reinforcement for other family members. When this is pointed out to them, they are not inclined to believe it. The changes in behavior brought about by reinforcement are simply too slow for them to understand the relevance of the concept. When they do attempt to use positive social reinforcement, they find it a difficult and embarrassing task to make their reactions contingent on certain child behaviors and not others. In the majority of cases, questions to parents concerning how to get effective performance result in discussions about punishment. However, at the same time, the general question of why a child does what he or she does remains a profound mystery. The most frightening child of all is one who is cunning enough to convince his or her parents that he or she does not respond to parental punishment.

Most parents rely heavily upon information-giving to control behavior. In practice, this means giving a "lecture": the assumption is that *knowing is doing*. For some parents the lecture is a primary mechanism for behavior change; nagging, threats, and punishment serve as occasional back-up contingencies. Studies carried out in the classroom showed rule-giving without back-up contingencies does not change behavior (Becker, Madsen, Arnold, & Thomas, 1967; Greenwood, Hops, Delquardri, & Guild, 1974). This same finding would probably also hold true in the home. It comes down to the fact that most parents must use some kind of punishment. The question is which punishments work and which do not?

The Practice of Punishment

The Stark and McEvoy (1970) survey found that even middle-class parents found it necessary to use physical force in dealing with recalcitrant children. They found that 84% of American parents had spanked their children. The earlier study by Sears, Maccoby, and Levin (1957) found a comparable figure of 98%. All of these parents were presumably advocates of the cultural adage, spare the rod and spoil the child.

Gelles (1972) intensively interviewed a small sample of families identified as violent, together with a sample from the community at large. In this study, he found a general attitude toward physical punishment which he characterized as "normal violence," i.e., it is normal and thought to be necessary to achieve goals that are valued by parents and society (italics added by the present author):

"Parents use the slap, the spanking, and the strap to teach their children not to do things, to

113

pay attention, and to control behavior. Force often is used as a resource when the parent cannot think of anything else that would be as effective.

"Mrs. (56): 'Well, if I put him on the toilet and he won't do it and then I leave him there for an hour and then I take him off, and then ten minutes later he's done it in his pants, I mean that upsets me. What do I do? I spank him and let him know it's wrong then the time after that for a couple days he's all right. And then he'll do it again. I think he avenges me. I don't know what it is. I think it's psychological—he's out to get me.'

"There is one pattern that emerges from the discussion of violence used to teach and control. *Each parent who employs violence in this manner believes that force is necessary and cannot be avoided.* Another important rationale is simply that striking a child in these situations is not considered violent: *it is normative.* . . .

"Mrs. (75): 'If he spits his food at me I slap his leg. No time to learn like the present—if he is old enough to do it, he's old enough to learn not to do it.' Mrs. (75) was speaking about her six-month-old baby." (Gelles, 1972, pp. 65-67)

In the Gelles (1972) study, 23% of the families suspected to be violent reported hitting their children at least daily. One of the 38 families not known to be violent also reported punishing their child at this rate. A surprising number of families also reported hitting their children at least once a week or once a month; the figures were 21% and 42.5% respectively. The review of studies by Blumberg (1974) showed this phenomenon is not restricted to the American culture. In one study of 700 average English families, 62% of the babies had been "smacked" by the time they were one year old.

Physical punishment is a ubiquitous facet of parenting in our culture. This is, perhaps, not so surprising when one evaluates the general attitude of males in our culture toward violence. The extensive survey of 1,374 males by Blumenthal, Kohn, Andrews, and Head (1972) reported that violence was viewed by the majority as a useful tool to *produce* changes that were desirable or to *control* changes that were undesirable. Fifty percent thought that shooting was almost always a good way of handling campus disturbances. In keeping with this attitude, the survey by Stark and McEvoy (1970) found that about one-fifth of adults approved of slapping one's spouse. It seems, too, that physical punishment of children is a part of our historical heritage. Stone (1977) documents the ubiquitous use of the ferula in the homes and schools of sixteenth century Europe.

The ferula was a whip ingeniously designed to raise blisters as well as inflict pain. The blisters served as a reminder. Stone describes these early practices as follows:

"This disciplinary practice can be followed in great detail in that of the young heir and King Louis IV of France. . . . The child was first whipped at the age of two, and the punishment continued after he became King at the age of nine. He was whipped on the buttocks with a birch or switch, administered first by his nurse, the time being immediately after he woke up. . . . The whippings increased in frequency when he was three . . . as he grew older, his nurse could not control him, and the child was held down by soldiers while she beat him. At the age of ten he still had nightmares of being whipped. . . . The threats to whip him only stopped at the age of thirteen, not long before his marriage." (Stone, 1977, p. 169)

In our culture, what is shocking is the frequency with which punishment practices escalate to high-intensity interchanges. For example, Gelles (1972) found that 20% of the wives and 32% of the husbands in a combined sample actually engaged in slapping, hitting (with an open hand), scratching,

Table 6.1
Percent of Mothers and Fathers Who Practiced Violence on their Children
(from Gelles, 1972, p. 57)

Violent Act	Father (N = 78)	Mother (N = 78)
Spank on bottom	60	92
Spank using object	19	28
Slap on body	13	21
Slap in face	5	14
Slam or push into wall	0	3
Punch	3	1
Hit with hard object	1	1
Choke	0	1

Reprinted with permission from *The Violent Home*, by R.J. Gelles, ©1972 (revised, 1974) by Sage Publications, Beverly Hills/London.

or grabbing behavior with each other. Table 6.1 summarizes the dolorous findings from the same study regarding the intensity of child punishment employed by parents. One child in seven was slapped in the face, one in five was slapped on the body, and one in four was spanked using an object. Mothers were more likely than fathers to be involved in these high-amplitude attacks.

Survey studies are important in that they underscore the attitudes held by parents toward the physical punishment of children. However, the parents' verbal reports may not provide accurate estimates for some of these events. The classic study by Goodenough (1931) provides data germane to this point. In that study, mothers recorded in their daily diaries the punitive measures that they employed in dealing with their preschool children. Before the study began, they had also filled out a questionnaire asking for information regarding the punishments that they typically employed. The daily report data did not correspond with the information they had given on the questionnaire. However, it may not matter too much that our estimates of incidence are somewhat unreliable. It is, perhaps, sufficient to know that there are a great number of children subjected to the daily or weekly indignity of being beaten by an enraged parent. There are, perhaps, an equal number of parents feeling both guilty and frightened by their participation in these rituals.

The writer believes that, in our culture, there are shared norms about the kinds of parental punishment that should be practiced most and least; e.g., it is acceptable to scold frequently, if necessary, but hitting should be used sparingly. This assumption is based on the fact that when families are observed in their homes, their punishment practices are surprisingly consistent across samples. Table 6.2 summarizes the likelihoods of various kinds of punishment employed by parents for coercive child behaviors. In both the clinical and the normal samples, Command and Disapproval were the most likely and Humiliate the least likely to occur. The rho between the rankings from the two samples for parental punishment was .83 ($df = 9$; $p < .01$).

There is probably also a consensus as to which coercive child behaviors *should* be punished and which should not. The observation study by Johnson and Bolstad (1973) employed a derivative of the FICS to collect data in the homes for a sample of 33 families of normal 3- and 4-year-old children. The likelihood of parental punishment was calculated for each of 16 coercive child behaviors. The findings are summarized in Table 6.3. As can

Table 6.2
Likelihood of Various Kinds of Parental Punishment for Coercive Child Behaviors

Consequence	Distressed	Nondistressed
Command	.30	.38
Command Negative	.14	.10
Disapproval	.35	.31
Humiliate	.01	.01
Ignore	.05	.05
Noncomply	.05	.02
Negativism	.02	.03
Physical Negative	.06	.05
Tease	.00	.03
Yell	.02	.02
	100%	100%

Table 6.3
Proportion of Negative Consequences for Coercive Child Behavior: A Normal Sample

(from Johnson & Bolstad, 1973, p. 53)

Child Behavior	Likelihood of Parental Punishment
Command Negative	.57
Physical Negative	.53
Aversive Command	.43
Smart Talk	.39
Tease	.38
Negativism	.38
Command	.36
Destructive	.35
Disapproval	.24
Yell	.22
Ignore	.21
Noncompliance	.18
Whine	.13
Cry	.10
Demand Attention	.08
High Rate	.06

be seen there, if a child engaged in Smart Talk, there was a likelihood of .39 that the parents would punish. If the child Hit a family member, then the likelihood was .53. These mores about what is to be punished probably also take into account the sex and age of the child. For example, Goodenough (1931) found a decrease in mothers' use of physical punishment for older children.

Bronfenbrenner (1958) noted the trend for the middle class, and later the working class, to use more permissive or laissez-faire methods of child rearing. The later review of survey studies by Erlanger (1974) suggested cultural changes in this century in the attitude toward parental punishment. He suggests a curvilinear relation in which less parental punishment occurred both early and late in this century.

Formulations about Punishment

More than six decades of experimental psychology have produced findings from laboratory studies which make the cultural predilection for the use of punishment more understandable (Campbell & Church, 1969). I assume that punishment is frequently employed in child training because it works so well. There have been a number of attempts to explain why punishment is so efficient as a behavior control mechanism. The earlier reviews by Church (1963), Solomon and Wynne (1954), and Solomon (1964) support this position. They also capture the variety of perspectives taken in viewing some of the paradoxical effects associated with this phenomenon. Some theorists emphasize the role of emotional states, such as fear, which are elicited by the aversive event. This state can also be elicited by previously neutral stimuli which have been contiguously associated with the aversive event itself. From this stance, the connection between a stimulus and the escape/avoidance behaviors which it elicits is reinforced by the reduction of the elicited fear. Other theorists, such as Guthrie (1978), denied the relevance of elicited emotional states and focused instead upon the competing skeletal responses elicited by the aversive event or by its conditioned stimulus. In effect, punishment suppresses ongoing behavior because it elicits incompatible reactions (i.e., the competing response changes the situation).

These and related theoretical issues have yet to be resolved. There was, however, a second set of issues raised in the earlier reviews by Church (1963) and Solomon (1964) that has been partially clarified. Estes (1944) and Thorndike (1932), as cited by Rachlin and Herrnstein (1969), took the position that punishment did not really alter behavior but only temporarily suppressed it. This would mean that punishment would not change the probability for R_1 when, on future occasions, the same antecedent (A_i) was presented (i.e., $p(R_1|A_i)$ does not change. From that position, punishment temporarily suppressed R_1 by increasing the likelihood of R_2. It did not, however, alter the basic connection between A_i and R_j. Skinner also adopted the position that the effect of punishment was only temporary (italics added by the present author):

"*It is true that there is a temporary suppression of responses, but all responses originally in the reserve eventually emerge without further positive reinforcement.* Such an effect is, by definition, emotional. It is an effect upon the relation between the reserve and the rate, not upon the reserve itself. In this experiment there is no evidence whatsoever for a process of negative conditioning directly the opposite of positive conditioning. The behavior of the rat, on the other hand, is quite in accord with the assumption that the slap establishes an emotional state of such a sort that any behavior associated with feeding is temporarily suppressed and that eventually the lever itself and incipient movements of pressing the lever become conditioned stimuli capable of evoking the same state." (Skinner, 1978, p. 107)

Skinner further developed the implication of this position in his *Walden Two* (1948). Here he emphasized the long-term effects of positive reinforcement and the high cost of employing punishment. Punishment was presented as an impractical means for producing behavior change. In addition, it was claimed that punishment produced side effects, such as neurosis, fear, and shame. While Solomon (1964) and Church (1963) pointed out at that time that the research findings were inconclusive, their statements were ignored. Skinner's position coalesced into what Solomon labeled *The Legend,* that punishment is ineffective (italics added by the present author):

"Later on, avoidance-training experiments in the 1940's and 1950's added impressive data on the *long-lasting behavioral control exerted by noxious stimuli* (Solomon & Brush, 1956). In spite of this empirical development, many writers of books in the field of learning now devote but a few lines to the problems of punishment. . . . Most contemporary introductory psychology texts devote but a paragraph or two to punishment as a scientific problem. . . . Perhaps one reason for the usual textbook relegation of the topic of punishment to the fringe of experimental psychology is the widespread belief that punishment is unimportant because it does not really weaken habits; that it pragmatically is a poor controller of behavior; that it is extremely cruel and unnecessary; and that it is a technique leading to neurosis and worse." (Solomon, 1964, pp. 248-249)

The studies by Church (1969) and by Rachlin and Herrnstein (1969) address several aspects of this issue. Both showed that the effect of contin-

Figure 6.1
Short-Term and Long-Term Effects of Punishment

	Short-term effects	Long-term effects
Antecedent event $(A_i) \longrightarrow R_1 \longrightarrow C_1 -$	Increase $p(R_2)$ (Escape)	Increase $p(A_i \rightarrow \text{other than } R_1)$ (Avoidance)
$\searrow$ R_2		Decrease $p(A_i \rightarrow R_1)$

gent shock was significantly greater than noncontingent shock. This would suggest that the suppression of ongoing behavior could not be accounted for by mere distractions due to emotional states or the disrupting effect of competing responses elicited by the aversive stimulus. Studies from both laboratories showed that the effect of contingent aversive stimuli was more than could be accounted for by a pseudo-instrumental conditioning (noncontingent). Rachlin and Herrnstein (1969) go on to argue for Thorndike's original formulation. They present a case for the idea that positive reinforcement and punishment lead to opposite effects on behavior. The former strengthens the S-R connection, and the latter weakens it.

This writer would suggest that pending a wide acceptance for a negative law of effect, it is a convenient metaphor for examining several aspects of social interactions. Figure 6.1 illustrates that punishment of one family member by another can be thought of as having *two* simultaneous effects. There is the immediate effect in that the aversive event suppresses the response upon which it was made contingent. In social interaction terms, this means there is a reduced likelihood that the response will continue as the next event in the sequence. Under these circumstances, some response other than R_1 is likely to occur. As noted in the previous chapters, it is assumed that aversive events often elicit autonomic reactions; but in the present context, this state does not necessarily play a part. The reduction in p value for the immediate recurrence of the punished response does not require arousal as an explanation. The child has previously learned a variety of alternative responses which he can make to a stimulus. In Figure 6.1 these alternatives are symbolized by R_2. They represent coping responses of a kind. In the laboratory studies they are the *escape* responses. The immediate effect of punishment is to increase the likelihood of one of these alternatives. Their occurrence marks a deflection of an ongoing behavior. Of course, this could also be called response suppression.

The other effect is a more long-range reduction in the connection between the S and R. This long-range effect was what Rachlin and Herrnstein (1969) referred to as the negative law of effect. In the context of social interactions, punishment is assumed to alter the connection between a social behavior and its antecedent. In Figure 6.1, the phrase *long-term effect* refers to the p value which describes the connection between the A_i and R_j at some future time. At the time when A_i is presented again, the impact of the punishment will be reflected in the reduced p value describing the likelihood of R_1. The long-term effect of punishment is a reduction in the connection between the response and its controlling stimulus.

As noted by Church (1969) and others, one does not have to assume that punishment wipes out a connection to believe that the connection can be weakened by punishment. Extinction (nonreinforcement) *also* weakens these connections. Perhaps only extinction reduces these p values to zero. The net effect is that these p values are constantly shifting as a result of punishment, reinforcement, and extinction contingencies. These p values define a dynamic interactional structure.

Praise and Disapproval in Discrimination Training

One of the lines of research which undermined what Solomon called *The Legend* of punishment ineffectiveness were the studies on discrimination learning. In these studies, the individual was required to learn to respond in one way to Stimulus X and in some other way to Stimulus Y. The studies of particular interest are those in which the individual was rewarded for the correct response and punished for the incorrect response. The study by Warden and Aylesworth (1927) employed such a design and found that rewarded rats learned twice as fast as did a punishment-only group. However, reward for a correct response and punishment for incorrect responses produced learning to criteria nine times as quickly as a reward-only condition. Meyer and Seidman (1961) obtained similar results using two age groups of children as subjects. Both preschool- and elementary-school-aged children were more responsive to "wrong" than to "right." However, one suspects that the outcome of such comparisons must depend upon the kind of reward or the kind of punishment employed. For example, Terrell and Kennedy (1957) found learning to be equal under conditions for praise and disapproval; but candy was more effective than either of the social consequences.

There are two studies which compare the effects of social consequences provided by parents in a discrimination-like procedure. A mobile laboratory was taken to the home and provided a means for making parent reinforcement contingent upon the child's making a correct discrimination. In one study, parents were cued to use a variety of positive social reinforcers, resulting in an average of a 7% shift in preference (Patterson, Littman, & Hinsey, 1964). In a second study using the same apparatus, a second sample of parents were cued to use such terms as "no," and "wrong." During reinforcement the mean shift in preference from the baseline condition was .155; the punishment condition was about twice as effective as the positive reinforcement. These findings were supported by Casey (1967), who used the same apparatus but male adults served as reinforcing agents. One group of children was reinforced and the other was punished. Punishment changed children's preferences significantly more than did positive reinforcement. Kelly and Stephens (1964) found a comparable effect, using the marble-drop procedure with preschool boys. It should be noted in passing that punishment was not always found to be more effective. Brackbill and O'Hara (1958) found that withdrawal of a reinforcer (candy) was less effective than giving the candy contingent on the correct response.

These findings suggest that one reason our culture condones the use of parental punishment is that it tends to be a very effective means for changing behavior. If the parent is maximizing short-term gains, a technique producing an immediate impact is likely to be employed. In a situation involving a contumacious child and an impatient parent, punishment is likely to occur. If that punishment suppresses the noxious child behavior, then the parent is likely to use it again. Negative reinforcement strengthens the connection between child noxious behavior and parental punitiveness. Just as there are reinforcers supplied by the victims for attack behaviors, there are also reinforcers which strengthen the use of punishment by parents.

Some Parametric Studies of Punishment

Laboratory studies have shown that the effectiveness of a CS for controlling behavior was determined by: (a) the frequency of the CS-UCS pairings, (b) the intensity of the UCS, and (c) the latency between the CS and the UCS (Church, 1963; Solomon, 1964). From this perspective, the mother who threatens (CS) but seldom follows through (UCS) will be less effective in using her threats and warnings to control deviant child behavior. This arrangement produces the parent who natters. They express their annoyance by threats and scolding, which serve only to elicit counterattacks. It may be that these natterers simply do not know what to use as a nonviolent back-up (USC). They periodically respond with physical assault; but the favorite back-up for parents of antisocial children seems to be "grounding the child," e.g., for a month. When this occurs, the parent and the child know that the parent does not really mean it. Within two days of being grounded (staying at home) the child can slip away; and when he or she does, the parents simply natter. The infrequent assaults and groundings produce some brief respite, but things quickly return to "normal." As a result, the parents report that, in the long run, nothing works.

Whether they confront their children or natter at them, the parents of out-of-control children also seem to wait too long before intervening. Coercive interchanges often occur over long periods of time. In that context, a parent saying "Don't do that" means very little. If, instead, the parents had intervened when the conflict first began, they might have had some chance of success.

The treatment procedure for parents of antisocial children involves, among other things, teaching the parents to consistently pair their stop-commands with a five-minute time out (TO) (Patterson, Reid, Jones, & Conger, 1975). Toobert's (1980) extensive review of the research literature on time out showed that a simple statement of the house rule, followed by four minutes of time out was effective for most (nonautistic) children ages 3 through 12 years. As she points out, this nonphysical form of punishment is replete with complexities such that parents of problem children should receive instruction and supervision. For older children, work chores and loss of privileges serve an analogous function as a back-up UCS. In either case, the parent is given back-up consequences which substitute for the role served by physical violence and grounding as UCS.

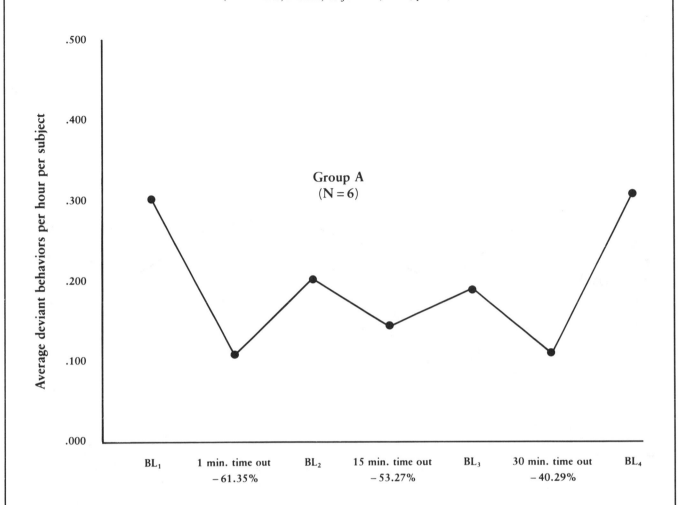

Figure 6.2

Mean Rates of Deviant Behavior for the Sequence 1, 15, and 30 minutes of Time Out

(from White, Nielsen, & Johnson, 1972, p. 116)

Reprinted with permission from "Time out duration and the suppression of deviant behavior in children," *Journal of Applied Behavior Analysis, 5,* 111-120. Copyright 1972 by the Society for the Experimental Analysis of Behavior, Inc.

Time Out

Most time out studies have used control groups or reversal designs to provide a clear demonstration of the control of behavior. Some of the studies have been carried out in natural settings. The study by White, Nielsen, and Johnson (1972) is a good example. Three groups of retarded, institutionalized subjects were randomly assigned to three different sequences of time out intervals. In these sequences, time intervals of one, 15, and 30 minutes were counterbalanced. The dependent variable consisted of a measure of deviant behavior such as aggression, self-destruction, tantrums,

and running away. The ABABABA design permitted a test for the effect of varying time intervals and for order effects as well. It was, in fact, their analyses of the order effects that provided the most intriguing outcome of the study.

The data for Group A are presented in Figure 6.2. Following an extended baseline, the subjects received one minute of time out contingent upon any of the deviant responses listed above. After three weeks of this phase, the contingencies were removed for a two-week baseline period. Each of the remaining experimental periods lasted for three weeks and were followed by baseline periods of two weeks. The numbers at the base of the

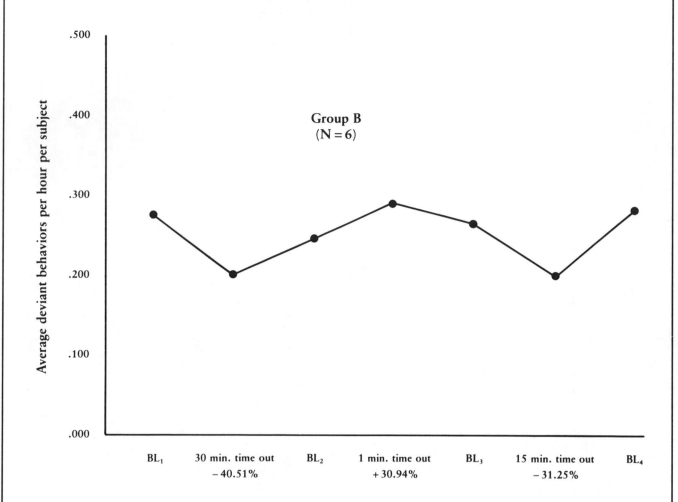

Figure 6.3

Mean Rates of Deviant Behavior for the Sequence 30, 1, and 15 minutes of Time Out

(from White, Nielsen, & Johnson, 1972, p. 116)

graph refer to the drop in deviancy rate compared to the preceding baseline. It can be seen there that the introduction of even a one-minute time out punishment was dramatically effective for most of the children. In fact, there was no increase in control when longer intervals were added in later manipulations. It should be noted at Baseline$_4$, when time out was no longer in use, the behavior again came under reinforcement control and quickly returned to its former level.

It should be noted that if one began with 30 minutes of time out, and then later attempted to reduce the interval to one minute, there was an immediate loss of control. Figure 6.3 summarizes the outcome for this manipulation. As reported there, the first time out interval of 30 minutes produced a dramatic reduction in rates of deviant behavior. During the next two weeks (Baseline$_2$) there was a gradual increase in deviancy. When a time out period of one minute was introduced, it had little impact; in fact, the acceleration in deviancy continued at the same rate as before. Introducing a time out period of 15 minutes reinstated control.

The effective use of nonviolent punishment, such as TO, has an additional important effect. Its use can have a vicarious modeling effect for the other children in that setting. For example, in a study of classroom intervention, various reinforc-

120

ing and punishing contingencies were employed to bring the problem children under control (Patterson, Cobb, & Ray, 1972). Pre- and post-observation data for *peers* in the classroom indicated that there were dramatic reductions in deviancy levels in four of the five classrooms. Wilson, Robertson, Herlong, and Haynes (1979) cite four additional studies which also demonstrated vicarious effects in untreated peers. In their own study, Wilson et al. (1979) collected observation data in a nursery school setting for an aggressive child and his 13 peers. The data demonstrated the expected impact of time out in reducing the aggressive behavior of the target child. During Baseline₁, on the average, the peers were observed to be aggressive in about 4% of the intervals. When the target child received time out, the average for peers fell to 1.27%, then rose to 3.17% during Baseline₂. The mean for peers during the second time out phase was 1.97%. The findings suggest that, in some respects, the peers were being affected by the manipulations designed for the target child. It was hypothesized that the changes in peer aggression might reflect the fact that the target child initiated fewer attacks during the experimental phase than in the baseline phase. A second hypothesis concerned differential changes in the teachers' reactions to peer aggression during the three phases. However, their analyses of attacks by the target child and teacher reactions offered no support for either assumption. The authors concluded that the use of time out in the classroom can have a vicarious impact on the peer group; when it is being used, peers can see that aggression is likely to be punished. This conclusion is in keeping with the studies by Bandura (1973) which indicated that children's aggressive behavior was significantly altered by vicarious reinforcement and punishment.

One of the tenets of coercion theory is that it is the adult who determines how much aggression will occur in a setting. The performance level is related to the willingness of the adult to use an effective punishment. For example, in the home, if siblings see that one of their peers "gets away with it," this serves as further incentive for their own coercive behavior. Similarly, if they observe that a fellow sibling is now being punished with alarming consistency and effectiveness, it may lead to an inhibition of their own deviant behavior. Indirect support for this hypothesis is to be found in the correlation of .74 ($df = 26$; $p < .001$) between baseline TAB scores for siblings and problem children (Arnold, Levine, & Patterson, 1975). The pre- and post-treatment comparison also showed significant reductions in sibling coerciveness following treatment. However, no attempt was made

in that study to control for the fact that much of the sibling aversive behavior was elicited by behaviors of the target child. In addition, there was no control for the fact that many of the parents applied the same programs directly to the siblings. The reactive and vicarious effects cannot be separated from this treatment study; but it seems plausible to assume that family members were influenced by watching punishment being used effectively on one of the members. Similarly, if a mother loses control of one child, she may very well lose control of the others.

A careful analysis of the treatment procedures for institutionalized, chronic schizophrenic adults revealed that assaultive behavior was one of the most difficult episodes to handle for all treatment strategies employed (Paul & Lentz, 1978). The only effective treatment for this behavior was time out. It effectively controlled the aggressive behavior and helped make it possible to eventually return these people to the community.

Parental Warmth

The traditional child development literature has strongly emphasized the nature of the relationship between parent and child as a primary determinant for the effectiveness of parental punishment (Bandura & Walters, 1963; Sears, Maccoby, & Levin, 1957). Control theorists, such as Hirschi (1969), represent a modern variation of this position; it is suggested that the attachment or bond of the child to the parent determines the impact of parental efforts to control the child.

The influential paper by Sears, Whiting, Nowlis, and Sears (1953) provided one of the first data bases for these speculations. Their interview data suggested the nurturant parent was more effective in using punishment. Presumably, punishment by such a parent would be associated implicitly or explicitly with the loss of love. In his review of the punishment literature, Parke (1970) notes that this position assumes that parental punishment has two components: (a) the aversive event itself (e.g., a spanking, or threat of loss of privileges), and (b) an aversive state analogous to anxiety relating to a possible loss of love.

"In fact, a certain degree of positive interaction and affection between a parent and a child is necessary if social punishment is to be an effective means of producing response inhibition. This argument rests on the assumption that withdrawal of affection is an effective component of all forms of social punishment. . . . On this basis, it is assumed that a nurturant punishing agent arouses a greater degree of anxiety than a neutral agent and that consequently the former agent is more effective in producing response inhibition in the child." (Parke, 1970, p. 88)

Casey (1967) tested the effect of a brief period of warm versus distant interaction in the control of adult-dispensed punishment. Neither condition had a significant effect on the children's responsiveness to punishment or reward. The primary data in support of this position came from the large-scale survey by Sears, Maccoby, and Levin (1957). Mothers who were rated as warm and who claimed to use frequent physical punishment said that spankings were effective. Those mothers described as cold or hostile, who also used frequent physical punishment, said that spankings were not effective. Schuck (1974) carried out a path analysis of the data for both the Sears, Maccoby, & Levin (1957) sample and the replication study by Radke-Yarrow et al. (1968). The latter sample consisted of highly educated and/or professional families. His analysis showed that for the Sears study, mothers' warmth did play a significant role in child aggression. The effect was, however, indirect, being mediated by both the physical punishment and punishment of aggression variables. Mothers lacking in warmth tended to use more physical punishment and to punish aggression more often. However, his path analyses for the replication study reported the reverse relation. Mothers lacking in warmth tended to use less physical punishment and to punish aggression less often. However, neither of these path coefficients for warmth were significant. Incidentally, Schuck (1974) found two variables directly relating to child aggression for both of these middle-class samples. In both instances, parental permissiveness *caused* child aggression. Secondly, those parents permitting aggressiveness tended to not punish it as severely.

One of the problems with using parent-report data to describe both the child and the parent is that the correlations obtained may reflect the implicit theory of the parent as much as the true state of affairs. This potential confound was controlled in the large-scale study by Eron, Walder, Huesmann, and Lefkowitz (1974). Ratings from parent interviews on parental nurturance for boys in both the third and thirteenth grades correlated −.16 and −.15 with peer nominations for aggressiveness. Parental punishment correlated .18 and .13 respectively.[3]

Parke and Walters (1967) experimentally manipulated the warmth of the relationship to determine its impact on punishment effectiveness. The manipulation involved two 10-minute sessions in a free-play situation. In the warmth situa-

tions, the room was stocked with attractive toys, and the adult provided encouragement, support, and approval. The other group had two sessions with a relatively distant adult and unattractive toys. The children experiencing the positive interactions later showed significantly greater responsiveness in a punishment situation. This general effect was then replicated in the study by Parke (1970). He used a 2x2x2x2 factorial design controlling for timing and intensity of the punishment and levels of nurturance and cognitive structure. The nurturance manipulation was similar to that for the Parke and Walters (1967) study. There were two levels of cognitive structuring. At one phase of the experiment, children in all groups were told that they should not touch or play with some of the toys; and if they picked an incorrect toy, the buzzer would sound. The low-cognitive-structure group heard only the buzzer. Those in the high-cognitive-structure group received an elaborate explanation as to why the restrictions were placed on their behavior. In addition, each time the buzzer sounded, the experimenter said, "No, that one might get broken." Following this phase, all subjects were left alone with the toys that they had been punished for choosing.

The number of deviations served as dependent variables. The findings summarized in Figure 6.4 report high-nurturance subjects deviated significantly less than did low-nurturance subjects; but this held only under conditions of low-cognitive structure; i.e., the condition obtained in the earlier study. Under conditions of high-cognitive structure, there was no significant difference between the nurturance conditions. The reader should note, however, that under the high-cognitive-structure condition the trend was the reverse of what might be suggested by the warmth-attachment theorists: high-nurturance was associated with more deviations.

When viewed from the perspective of a traditional development theorist, there is a *thread* of consistency here. Across the studies there were low-level negative correlations between parental warmth and aggressive child behavior. Low nurturance and high deviations in child behavior were also found to correlate in two experimental studies. The findings from the correlational studies also showed the expected (low-order) positive correlations between the amount of parental punishment and aggressive behavior. The attachment theorist might well claim that these results support his or her position: low-nurturance parents were less effective as punishing agents; and they, therefore, punished more although their child continued to be more aggressive. There is,

Figure 6.4
The Relationship of Cognitive Structure and Agent-Nurturance to Punishment Effectiveness

(from Parke, 1970, p. 96)

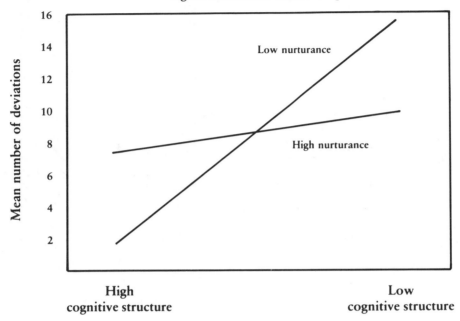

**Cognitive structure
Agent-nurturance relationship**

Low nurturance

High nurturance

(y-axis: Mean number of deviations, marked 2, 4, 6, 8, 10, 12, 14, 16)

**High
cognitive structure**　　　　**Low
cognitive structure**

however, an equally plausible alternative explanation which fits these same data. The parents of antisocial children tended to be less attached to their children; they were also less skilled in family management (see Chapter 10). They tended to natter rather than to stop the deviant child behavior. The effect of nattering was to increase the performance of coercive child behavior. Less skillful parents punished more often but with less effect. It is not that one thing causes the other; it is, rather, that the effect is interactive. The traditional finding of antisocial children receiving more punishment is caused by this interplay of effects. These same unskilled parents tend to be less attached to their children. It is not a lack of warmth, per se, lowering the impact of parental punishment; it is that unskilled and unattached parents do not back up their threats.

Mixed Schedules, Timing, Rules, and Contingencies

All parents effectively punish *some* child behaviors (e.g., the toddler ambling toward the busy street). Even parents of antisocial children do not permit *all* forms of out-of-control behavior. Most of them are quite selective. They effectively punish some deviant behaviors and *stop their occurence;* while for other kinds of deviant behavior they simply express displeasure by nattering. Selectivity implies that the parent must cue the child as to when he or she means *stop* and when he or she simply means, "I don't like that." These cues may be idiosyncratic to each parent. For some it is a glare, for others it is a facial grimace or a rising voice inflection. Our current inability to differentiate one cue from the other represents a major im-

Figure 6.5

Mean Number of Punches in the Post-Training Period as Related to the Type of Training

(from Deur & Parke, 1970, p. 407)

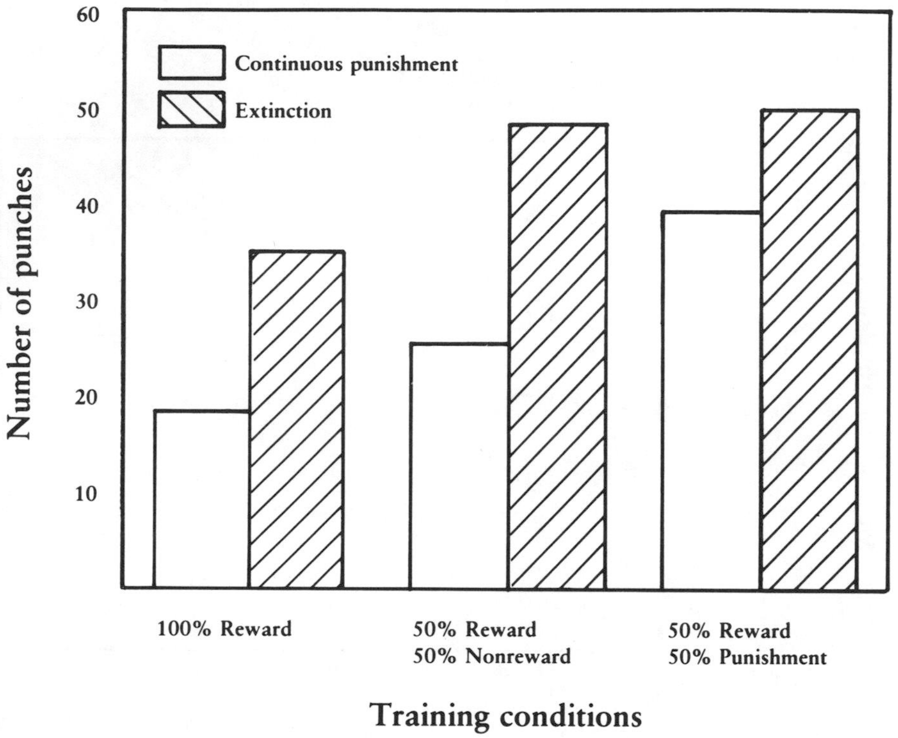

passe in the development of a coercion theory.

Parents use mixed schedules of reinforcement and punishment. The actual schedule varies from one coercive response to another, reflecting parental sensitivity to certain types of coercive child behaviors. The formulation by Solomon (1964) suggests that behaviors maintained by mixed schedules might be particularly resistant to punishment control. Ordinarily, the resistance of a response to extinction can be decreased if punishment is introduced. However, there is an arrangement in which the effect of punishment may be reversed.

"If the subject is habituated to receiving shock together with positive reinforcement during reward training, the relationship can be reversed, and punishment during extinction can actually increase resistance to extinction (Holz & Azrin, 1961). Evidently, punishment, so employed, can functionally operate as a *secondary reinforcer*, or as a cue for reward, or as an arouser." (Solomon, 1964, p. 241)

In his review, Martin (1963) pointed out that as a general case, mixed schedules of reward and punishment produced greater resistance to extinction. Deur and Parke (1970) tested this hypothesis for its relevance to aggression using children as subjects. Subjects were assigned to three training experiences: continuous reinforcement (marbles), partial reward and nonreward, partial reward and punishment (loud noise). After they received training, the groups were then further divided into either punishment or extinction conditions. The results are summarized in Figure 6.5. While punishment slowed down the acquisition of aggression, it was associated with significantly greater resistance to extinction. The mixed schedule condition was also the most resistant to continuous punishment.

Figure 6.6
The Relationship of Punishment Intensity and Timing

(from Parke, 1970, p. 93)

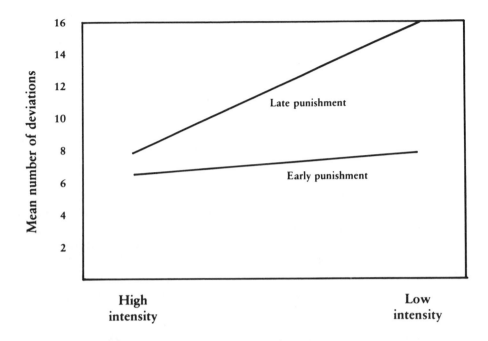

Ross Parke has intensively analyzed the parameters relating to punishment effectiveness for children (Parke, 1970; Parke & Levy, 1972; Parke, Deur, & Sawin, 1970; Parke & Walters, 1967). His work on timing is most germane to the question of parental effectiveness. Parke (1970) assumes that punishment for events that occur earlier in a sequence more effectively suppresses behavior than punishment for those events that occur later in a sequence of deviant acts. He cites several studies in support of this hypothesis. Figure 6.6 summarizes the outcome for one of his own studies in which he manipulated the intensity of the punishment (90 db versus 65 db tone) and early versus late timing. The response being punished was the child's deviations from the adult's request to not touch certain toys. As shown there, late punishment became particularly ineffective under conditions of low intensity. While this interaction of timing and intensity is not always found, the significantly greater impact of high-intensity punishment seems to be a consistent finding.

In a series of studies, Parke also manipulated the child's cognitions about the punishment. He assumed, along with Aronfreed, that giving the child a rule would enhance the inhibiting effect of punishment. He first tested the possibility that restating the rule would overcome some of the liabilities thought to accrue to delays in punishment; e.g., "I told you at the store that if you whined there you would have to go to time out when we got home. Go to time out now." The study cited by Parke and Walters (1967) directly addressed this issue. In that study, punishment following either a video-tape replay of the deviation or a verbal restatement of the rule was as effective as punishing the original deviation itself. This effect was replicated in a single-subject design for a 10-year-old child (Verna, 1977). The rule statement at the time of delayed punishment (four hours) was equally as effective as immediate punishment. Parke (1970) went on to demonstrate that rule statements interacted significantly with almost all of the other parameters he manipulated (nurturance, timing, and intensity).

Parke's (1975) update of his earlier reviews fur-

Table 6.4
Aversive Reactions by Family Members to Target Child's Coercive Behavior

Sample	Mother			Father			Male Sibling			Female Sibling			Grand Means
	Mean	N	SD	Mean	N	SD	Mean	N	SD	Mean	N	SD	
Normal	.18	36	.22	.18	25	.24	.34	23	.26	.29	27	.32	.25
Social Aggressor	.25	44	.18	.31	24	.23	.40	23	.23	.38	31	.18	.34
Abused	.30	19	.19	.33	13	.17	—[a]	—	—	.34	15	.18	.32

[a]There were fewer than 10 subjects.

ther substantiated the significant contribution of intensity and timing; and again, rule statements were shown to increase the effectiveness of punishment. In fact, conditions of rule statements were so powerful that they overcame the usual effects of both timing (early and late equally effective) and intensity (high and low equal). Peer endorsements further enhanced the impact of rule statements. If the child was allowed to choose the means of rule enforcement, there was significantly greater resistance to deviation from the rules.

These studies are of particular interest because they relate directly to our clinical experience in working with families of antisocial children. In these homes there are not only fewer house rules but those that do exist are not clearly stated. For example, ambiguities as to who should clear the table after supper may result in endless bickering. Because the rule about when to return in the evening is not clearly stated the child can talk his way out of being punished. Parental commands are given more often in these families, but they also tend to be vaguely stated. Many of these commands seem to be more an affirmation of parental displeasure than a statement of what they want the child to do. Given these kinds of ambiguities it is perhaps not surprising to find that their punishment is less effective.

Field Studies of Parental Punishment

The first problem in carrying out field studies of punishment was to identify the aversive events. Which aspects of social interaction could weaken $A_i \rightarrow R_j$ connections in a fashion analogous to electric shock or loud buzzer sounds? Although never clearly stated, our implicit assumption was that the aversive events found in social interaction would have a similar effect. This would mean that even the low-intensity aversive events found in social interaction would weaken the $A_i \rightarrow R_j$ con-

nection. Presumably the more intense the aversive event, the more it would weaken the connection.

The studies reviewed in Chapter 4 showed that parents of normal children and parents of antisocial children agreed in their perceptions about what is and what is not aversive about children's social behavior. The next question is whether there is a correlation between what the parents perceive as aversive and how they react in the home. The Johnson and Bolstad (1973) study found a correlation of .73 between parent ratings of deviancy for code categories and the likelihood that the parents would be observed to react aversively to these behaviors. Also, the more deviant the child behavior was perceived to be, the more likely the parent was to react in a punitive manner.

Do family members differ in the likelihood of providing aversive consequences for deviant child behavior? Do these reactions vary as a function of membership in a clinical or nonclinical sample? Data relating to these questions were analyzed from three different samples. The samples consisted of 36 Normals, 43 Social Aggressors, and 19 Abused children. For each subject the reactions of parents to coercive child behaviors were combined across events occurring in initial, middle, and final sections of coercive chains. Combining data across agents, the mean likelihood of parental aversive consequences for deviant behavior was .250 for the normal sample.[4] The differences in likelihood between mothers and fathers or between male and female siblings were relatively small. However, the siblings were significantly more likely than their parents to react aversively to coercive behaviors presented by the problem child. Johnson and Lobitz (1974a) also found this to be the case in their study of normal preschoolers and their families. Siblings from the Social Aggressor sample were more likely than parents to respond punitively. The trends were consistent for all comparisons. While a one-way ANOVA for repeated measures would be the analysis of choice, there were only nine families for which data were available for all four family agents. For this reason, agent-by-agent comparisons were made; two of the six possible comparisons were significant. Male siblings were more punitive than mothers ($t = 2.63$; $p < .01$ two-tailed). Female siblings were also more punitive than were mothers ($t = 2.67$; $p < .01$ two-tailed).

Family members of socially aggressive children were generally more likely than their normal counterparts to be punitive. The differences between fathers from the normal and the clinical samples were of borderline significance ($t = 1.62$; $p < .06$ one-tailed), as were the differences between mothers ($t = 2.23$; $p < .05$ one-tailed). These findings plus the comparable nonsignificant trends for the siblings were in keeping with the findings reported in the traditional child development literature (Feshbach, 1970). Most of those studies have shown that antisocial children receive more punishment than Normals (Eron et al., 1971; Sears, Maccoby, & Levin, 1957). Typically, these findings were based on parents' reports of how frequently they punished their children. The findings presented in Table 6.4 are in agreement in that parents of antisocial boys reacted aversively to deviant behavior more frequently than parents of normal boys. The present data add one component to the traditional findings by demonstrating that parents of antisocial boys were also *more likely* to react aversively given that the child was being coercive.

The pattern of findings for the Abused-Child sample was quite different. Here, parents and siblings were *equally* punitive in their reactions to the problem child. In fact, these parents were more punitive than were parents from any other sample. Mothers of abused children were significantly more punitive than mothers of Normals ($t = 3.79$; $p < .001$ one-tailed). Also, fathers of abused children were significantly more likely than fathers of normal children to be punitive ($t = 2.22$; $p < .05$ one-tailed). The differences between parents of abused and socially aggressive children were not significant.

Goodenough's (1931) analysis of parental diaries showed that mothers of preschool children often cope with conflicts by resorting to bribery, reasoning, surrendering to child demands, coaxing, or diversionary tactics. As illustrated in Table 6.5, mothers were generally more likely to punish boys' conflict behavior (.42) than girls' (.18). In addition, they were more likely to use spanking and physical force for boys (.16) than for girls

Table 6.5
Parental Reactions to Out-of-Control Child Behavior ("Outbursts")

(adapted from Goodenough, 1931, pp. 197-201)

Parental Reaction	Boys	Girls
Ridicule	0.5%	1.2%
Deprivation privileges	2.3%	0.3%
Ignore	29.6%	38.9%
Deprivation food	1.0%	0.5%
Put child chair, bed, room	10.7%	3.4%
Scold	8.8%	4.5%
Threat	6.4%	3.1%
Spank, slap	7.7%	3.4%
Physical force	8.7%	2.4%

(.06). Note that the punishments emphasized by social learning approaches (deprivation of privileges, time out) were used in less than 10% of the conflicts involving boys.

The data already presented in Table 6.2 summarize the comparable data from OSLC samples. As noted earlier, parental reactions to coercive child behavior for distressed and non-distressed samples were very similar. Parents in both samples were most likely to use (CM) Command, e.g., "Stop teasing your sister." They were also very likely to use (DI) Disapproval or (CN) Command Negative. Presumably, parents in the two samples differ in that parents in distressed families were less likely to follow through on their threats. Unfortunately, this most crucial assumption has yet to be tested.[5]

The cross-cultural observation study by Lambert (1974) showed an interesting shift in punitive reactions to aggression by peers as a function of age. When children aggressed against 3- and 4-year-olds, they were punished by their peers only 36% of the time. By age four, the likelihood of being punished for aggression exceeded the likelihood of a positive outcome. Aggression directed toward adolescents was punished 67% of the time.

The Impact(s) of Aversive Consequences

Do these aversive reactions function as punishment? For an event to function as punishment it must first be identified as aversive and then be presented contingent upon the occurrence of a target response. If these contingent arrangements are followed by decreases in the likelihood of the target behavior R_j given the occurrence of its controlling antecedent A_i, then an event may be said to be "punishment." The weakening of the $A_i \rightarrow R_j$ connection describes the long-term effect of a punishing event. That same punishing event also has an immediate short-term effect. In fact, in the context of social interaction in a natural setting, these aversive consequences have such a profound impact upon ongoing interaction that our efforts to understand punishment have been limited almost entirely to the study of these short-term effects.

We satisfied ourselves that an effective punishment (time out) significantly reduced the likelihood of a child's Noncomply given mother-Command; i.e., the $A_i \rightarrow R_j$ connection was reduced. The data for these two single case studies are described in Chapter 8. However, the long-term impact of the 14 aversive consequences has yet to be determined. The study would require both a correlational and an experimental format analogous to what was described in Chapter 5 for positive reinforcement. Each of the 14 consequences would be considered separately. Given that it was made contingent upon a specific A_i and target response R_j, was this accompanied by a reduced likelihood for the R_j when the A_i was next presented?

As an alternative, a single-subject ABA reversal design would seem to be the experimental manipulation of choice. Here, the mother could be cued during the B phase to use one of the 14 aversive events contingent upon a specific A_i and target R_j. The punishment should be accompanied by a reduced likelihood of R_j given A_i *during* the experimental phase. This effect should persist during the second baseline. When a parent plans to confront and stop a deviant child behavior, which punishment does he or she use? How effective is it? In that we have not carried out these studies, our understanding of parental punishment is very limited.

An aversive consequence is very likely to elicit an aversive reaction from the other person. If the other person is doing something *pro*social, such as Talk, and you provide an aversive reaction, such as Humiliate, then its eliciting function will very likely suppress ongoing Talk behavior. When we first encountered this phenomenon, we thought it was an example of punishment functioning as a temporary suppressor of behavior (Patterson & Cobb, 1971). This was the view of punishment in vogue in the late 1960's. Imagine our surprise when we discovered in the same analysis that these aversive consequences had an accelerating effect when made contingent upon coercive behavior! How could the same aversive event *suppress* (i.e. punish) prosocial behavior and *accelerate* ongoing

coercive behavior? This paradox confronted us in the early 1970's. It was eventually resolved by removing the short-term impact of coercive events from the punishment concept and considering it, instead, as an example of the eliciting effect of coercive events upon ongoing behavior. Given that aversive events elicit aversive reactions, then, when used as a consequence, the effect will be to "decelerate" ongoing prosocial behaviors and "accelerate" ongoing coercive behaviors.

Aversive Events as Accelerating Consequences

In the first study of the eliciting effect of aversive consequences, Patterson and Cobb (1971) analyzed 56,632 interactions involving Talk from members of 24 families. If a family member was talking, the likelihood was .519 that she or he would continue talking into the next six-second time frame. The data indicated that each of the 14 noxious behaviors was effective in deflecting (suppressing) this ongoing prosocial behavior. Some aversive events, such as Command or Hit, were very effective; the conditional p of $Talk_2$ given $Talk_1$ followed by Command or Hit was .014 and .059 respectively. More recently, Snyder (1977) replicated this decelerating effect for a sample of normal and distressed families.

The data from the Patterson and Cobb (1971) study of 24 disturbed families generated a total of 615 Hits, Pushes, and Shoves. These target behaviors were performed by parents, siblings, and problem children alike. In these clinical families, the 14 aversive consequences *did not suppress* Hit. Quite the reverse, aversive consequences were associated with increased likelihoods for continuance of the attack. The more aversive the consequence, the greater its effect as an accelerator for Hit. A comparable sequential analysis of problem children in an institutional setting by Kopfstein (1972) replicated the finding and extended it to the full range of coercive target responses. Garden-variety punishments facilitated the recurrence of coercive child behaviors. More recently, this effect was also replicated for families of normal and antisocial children by Snyder (1977). Snyder obtained ratings of aversiveness for each of the code categories separately for mothers, fathers, and the children. For the normal families, the correlations between a family member's *perception* of the aversiveness of an event correlated very highly with the event's observed impact in accelerating the individual's ongoing coercive behavior.

Table 6.6
The Impact of Aversive Consequences Provided by Parents for Coercive Child Behaviors
(from Patterson, 1976)

| Parental Consequences | The likelihood of immediate recurrence for: | | | | | |
| | Hostile[1] | | Social Aggression[2] | | Total Aversive Behavior | |
	Normal Sample	Problem Sample	Normal Sample	Problem Sample	Normal Sample	Problem Sample
Aversive	.23	.41	.12	.29	.36	.50
All Nonaversive Consequences[3]	.32	.26	.30	.29	.32	.34

[1]Hostile is comprised of DI, NE, HU, WH, and IG.

[2]Social Aggression is defined by PN and TE.

[3]This includes nonaversive reactions by parents and siblings. Nonaversive would include events classified as neutral *and* prosocial.

Furman and Masters (1978) were also concerned with the validity of a priori classifications of events as aversive or positive. They assumed that positive events should produce more positive reactions (e.g., Laugh, Talk) from the recipient. Similarly, events identified a priori as aversive should be followed by more negative reactions (e.g., Disapprove, Yell) and fewer neutral and positive reactions. Preschool children's interactions in classroom and gym settings served as the data base. These events were negatively correlated with the likelihood for both neutral and positive reactions. Their analysis showed a convergent correlation of .58 between the data for a priori categorizing for aversive consequences and the data for the recipient's negative reactions. In other words, the investigators' a priori notions about aversive consequences were in agreement with the data from the children's actual reactions to these events. The investigators also carried out a discriminant analysis showing the heterotrait-monomethod correlations to be less than the convergent, monotrait-heteromethod correlation. These data demonstrated the convergent and discriminant validities for their measures of aversive consequences.

Once this accelerating effect was identified, we began to study differences between age groups, and normal and clinical samples concerning interactions between various family agents. It was also at this time that we identified two response classes, each of which was controlled by a common network of antecedent events (Patterson & Cobb, 1973). When we studied these classes (Social Aggressive and Hostile) further, we found that responses which formed each class also shared a common set of aversive consequences which functioned as "accelerators" (Patterson, 1977a). These data will be discussed in detail in Chapter 8.

The first comparison study for differential reactivity to aversive consequences examined the differential effect of parent and sibling punishments for coercive behavior of the problem child (Patterson, 1976). The comparison included samples from nonproblem families and from families referred to OSLC for treatment. The dependent variables were three classes of coercive child behavior: Hostile, Social Aggressive, and a composite score (TAB) comprised of all 14 coercive responses. For both samples, the findings consistently showed that punishment by siblings was ineffective in suppressing coercive behavior. The results for parental punishments are summarized in Table 6.6. In that table, the corrected base rates described the residual effect when the impact of aversive consequences was removed from the calculation of the base rate. If one looks only at these corrected values, then about two out of three times, boys in both samples tend to perform a single six-second coercive act and then stop (given no parental punishment). In families of normal children, the impact of parental aversive consequences (C−) varies as a function of the class of coercive responses. For the total composite score, (TAB), there is a slight increase in recurrence (.36) as a function of Parental C−. When similar consequences are applied to the child's socially aggressive behavior, the effect is to *suppress* the ongoing behavior. The conditional p of .12 for the recurrence of socially aggressive behavior showed a re-

129

duction when compared to the corrected base-rate value of .30. This is of particular interest in that the responses which comprise this class were controlled by antecedents and consequences provided largely by siblings (Patterson, 1977a). Parents of normal children seem to be effective in suppressing sibling conflicts. However, note that they were only moderately successful in suppressing the coercive events in the Hostile class. Interestingly, this class was controlled by antecedents and consequences that were mainly provided by mothers and older sisters.

The aversive reactions by parents of antisocial children did not effectively suppress ongoing behaviors for any of the response classes. For overall coercive child behavior there was roughly a 50% increase in the likelihood of occurrence as compared to the corrected base-rate value of .34. In effect, their attempts to punish coercive child behavior made things worse. The same study also showed that these parents punished *more often* but less effectively. No wonder some of these parents described their children as being possessed by an evil spirit which required the expertise of an exorcist rather than a psychologist to remedy the situation. The problem child was out of control both in his referral symptoms and in his failure to respond to this basic mechanism of socialization.

Our confidence in these findings was considerably enhanced by the comparison study of problem and nonproblem families by Snyder (1977). Using a derivative of the OSLC code, he first replicated the finding from our 1971 study that parental aversives decelerated prosocial behaviors. He then examined the impact of these parental aversive consequences for overall child coercive behaviors. He found a corrected base-rate value of .28 for immediate recurrence of coercive child behaviors in his normal sample. This is very close to the comparable value of .32 found in Table 6.6. In Snyder's study, given parental punishment, the conditional p for recurrence was .32. The results for his clinical sample were in keeping with those presented in Table 6.6, but the acceleration effect was not as dramatic. In his clinical sample, the base rate for recurrence was .27. When punished, the deviant child was significantly more likely to continue, as shown by the conditional p value of .36. Note, however, that the acceleration effect is only minimally greater for the clinical sample than for the normal sample.

A simple index of the child's reaction to aversive consequences which are made contingent upon his coercive behavior has some interesting implications. For example, it seems like a good operational definition of "deviancy" in general. As suggested by John Reid, the real deviant is a person whose behavior cannot be controlled by the reactions of other people. If such a person cannot be controlled *even* by punishment, then there is cause for alarm. These considerations led to the decision to carry out yet further methodological studies on the index, $p(R_2|R_1 \rightarrow C-)$. This index represents the probability that a coercive response will recur given that the first presentation of the aversive response was followed by a negative consequence.

Up to this point, estimates of the effect had been based upon samples of events rather than subjects. Secondly, it would be of some interest to *compare* various *clinical* samples and to differentiate among the reactions of various agents. For this purpose, OSLC files were used to form samples comprised of 36 Normals, 43 Social Aggressors, and 19 Abused children. The differential effectiveness of aversive consequences for the ongoing coercive behavior of the problem child was examined for mothers, fathers, and siblings. The data summed across the effects of punishment at all junctures in the target child's coercive chains. In Appendix 6.1 the corrected base rates specified the likelihood of the target child's Stop given that the target child was interacting with various family members, and given that they reacted to his coercive behavior in a neutral and/or positive manner. It can be seen there that socially aggressive boys were generally more likely to continue their coercive behavior than were boys in normal families. They were also more likely to continue their coercive behavior when interacting with their mothers than with their sisters.

The data from the samples are summarized in Table 6.7. The mean likelihood of the child's Stop given an aversive reaction to the prior coercive behavior was calculated separately for each of four family agents and for the normal and two clinical samples. The mean, standard deviations, and N's are presented for each of the cells. The t-tests for correlated means compared the conditional p values to the corrected base-rate values (Appendix 6.1) for that cell. A negative value indicated that the conditional p value was *smaller* than the corrected base-rate value; i.e., the child was less likely to Stop when he was "punished."

The effect of aversive consequences upon coercive child behavior varied as a function of sample and the family member with whom the child interacted. In keeping with the earlier findings (Table 6.6), the acceleration effect was more likely to be significant for socially aggressive boys than for boys from normal families. As shown by the negative "t" values, for normal boys the effect of nattering by family members was generally to reduce

Table 6.7
The Likelihood of Problem Child Stop Given Family Members' Aversive Consequences

p(Stop|Prior Response Punished)

Sample	Mother Mean	N	SD	Father Mean	N	SD	Male Sibling Mean	N	SD	Female Sibling Mean	N	SD
Normal	.66	29	.41	.52	19	.49	.50	22	.37	.60	21	.40
"t"[a]	−1.14			−1.57			−4.31***			−1.25		
Social Aggressor	.63	44	.30	.55	24	.38	.51	22	.30	.60	31	.24
"t"	−0.55			−1.80*			−2.39**			−4.52***		
Abused	.47	18	.33	.73	13	.30				.66	14	.29
"t"	−3.06**			−0.09						−1.64		

*$p < .05$

**$p < .01$

***$p < .001$

[a] All comparisons are two-tailed tests.

the likelihood that he would Stop. Nattering produced a small increase in the likelihood of an immediate recurrence of a coercive behavior. This effect was significant only when the target child was interacting with male siblings. This suggests the necessity for studying *sibling* interaction in particular when trying to understand coercion in families.

This sibling theme is reiterated and even more strongly emphasized in the Social Aggressor sample. Here, interactions with both male and female siblings are implicated. In both cases their aversive consequences produced significant increases in the likelihood of an immediate continuance of the problem child's deviant behavior. Note, too, the fact that it was the nattering of the father, *not the mother*, which significantly accelerated ongoing coerciveness for this sample.

The two clinical samples (Social Aggressors and Child Abusive) seem fundamentally different, a fact also noted by Reid, Taplin, and Lorber (1981). Notice first that in the Abused-Child sample aversive consequences by fathers *did not* produce an acceleration effect! Only nattering by the mother had a significant impact. The situation for the Abused-Child sample seems analogous to the Sadomasochistic Arabesque families described in Chapter 13. In such families one parent has very tight punitive control over the child and the other has no control at all. This seems exactly the state of affairs here—the father has control, but no one else does.

There are more parameters which need to be considered. What is the effect of age of the target child given that the parent tries to control his coercive behavior? Second, what is the effect of context upon the likelihood of acceleration? These questions are considered for mothers as agents in Chapter 12. The analyses showed that the nonsignificant acceleration produced by mothers in Table 6.7 most likely involved younger Social Aggressors, where the mothers "started" the process with an aversive antecedent. For mothers of Normals, the borderline acceleration effect in Table 6.6 was most likely produced by mothers interacting with older normal siblings. Further comparative studies are badly needed, particularly those which involve siblings. As shown in Table 6.7, it is siblings who play *the* central role for producing acceleration effects for Social Aggressors and for Normals.

We are beginning to see measures of this effect as central to evaluating treatment effectiveness. The central concern of parents who bring their children to OSLC is *not* that they are out of control; it is that *they cannot control their children*. The measures of punishment acceleration ($p[R_2|R_1 \rightarrow C-]$) indicate the magnitude of this disruption in control. As a single index, the p combines *two* kinds of information that relate to the loss of control. Its magnitude reflects, in part, the child's general disposition to extend coercive chains *and* his disposition to extend these chains when punished. Given that the OSLC treatment program empha-

131

Table 6.8
Likelihood of Punishment Acceleration by Dyads and Samples
p(Go|Prior Deviant Behavior Punished)

| Dyads | Mean Likelihood for Samples of | | | F Values | Correlation with Child TAB score | |
	Normals	Social Aggressors	Stealers		PPM	N
p(Child Accelerate|Mother Punish)	.15	.42	.34	11.64***	.47***	111
p(Mother Accelerate|Child Punish)	.29	.41	.30	2.45	.17	111
p(Child Accelerate|Father Punish	.04	.41	.24	13.59***	.46***	68
p(Father Accelerate|Child Punish)	.25	.50	.31	3.11	.22	68
p(Child Accelerate|Sibling Punish)	.24	.41	.38	3.99*	.31***	103
p(Sibling Accelerate|Child Punish)	.32	.43	.44	1.74	.16	103

*$p < .05$
**$p < .01$
***$p < .001$

sizes the use of nonviolent back-up punishments, this should lead to a situation where parent Stop-Commands are more effective in controlling deviant child behavior. A comparison of pre- and post-treatment measures showed significant decreases in the p values for the acceleration index (Patterson, 1976). At termination of treatment, parental attempts to control coercive child behavior were as effective as they were for Normals. This effect was also replicated by Szykula (1979), who used the same coding system and treatment procedures at another site.

The results from the intervention studies are in keeping with our general formulations about parental nattering. An increase in the pairing of threats or Stop-Commands with back-up punishment should give the parents better control. Support for the hypothesis would be even more convincing if experimental data could be brought forward. Does noncontingent use of punishment (nattering without back-up) produce an increment in the p value for chain extension? Until these studies are done, we cannot be sure of exactly what this index means.

The parameters which account for variance in individual differences in coercion performance level will be developed in Chapters 8, 11, and 12. The acceleration index is thought to be an important covariate, particularly in accounting for variance in the lower ranges of performance. For a heterogeneous sample of antisocial children, the index shows a modest correlation with performance level. In an earlier study the baseline TAB scores for 33 referrals were correlated .34 ($df = 31$; $p < .06$) with the acceleration index (Patterson, 1979c). This sample was comprised of both high-rate Social Aggressors and lower rate problem children (Stealers). As a replication, three samples from OSLC files were examined for 38 Normals, 37 Social Aggressors, and 38 Stealers (see Appendix 6.2 for details of study). The punishment acceleration index was calculated separately for each dyad involving the target child. As shown in Table 6.8, the children in the clinical samples were significantly more likely than Normals to accelerate when punished.

The correlational data in Table 6.8 show that the child's disposition to accelerate when punished correlates significantly with his TAB score. The likelihood of accelerating when parents punished accounted for twice as much variance as the comparable likelihood for siblings. The reader should keep in mind the fact that this acceleration index is a composite which partially reflects the child's general disposition to persist in his coerciveness. This would tend to insure a correlation with his overall performance.

Summary

Field studies indicate that parents of antisocial children are *more likely* than parents of Normals to provide aversive consequences for coercive child behaviors. These consequences have a short-term effect upon ongoing social interaction that is produced by the aversive events which elicit aversive interactions. These same consequences are also thought to produce long-term changes in $A_i \to R_j$ connections; but, as yet, there are no field studies which have investigated this crucial aspect of punishment. Our assumption is that for the antisocial child, there are *fewer* consequences that would weaken these connections, and that the *magnitude* of the reduction would be *less*. In that there are no systematic studies of this phenomenon, it remains a purely clinical impression.

All of the studies to date have focused upon the short-term impact of aversive consequences as they accelerate ongoing coercive behavior. The antisocial child is about twice as likely as a normal child to extend his coercive behavior. The analyses showed that aversive consequences significantly accelerated these chains when the socially aggressive child was "punished" by female or male siblings and by fathers. For Child Abusive samples, a significant acceleration effect was produced by maternal punishment. For Normals, only aversive consequences provided by male siblings produced a significant effect.

In families of Social Aggressors and, to a lesser degree, families of Normals, acceleration following punishment seems related to *sibling* interactions. It seems likely that in these families they play a crucial role in determining performance levels for the target child. Perhaps one can consider a high acceleration index as a kind of dominance measure. The problem child is more likely to respond to threats, scolding, and warnings with a continuation of his antisocial behavior. In effect, he is about as powerful as his siblings or his parents. I think that very high indices for chain extension and for acceleration when punished means that the child *is* in control most of the time.

A proper understanding of the role of punishment in coercion processes requires a new generation of studies such as those by Ross Parke. These studies should compare antisocial and normal children for their responsiveness to such nonsocial punishment as time out, point loss, and deprivation of privileges. We also need to compare these samples for their reactions to low key aversive events (e.g., statements such as "wrong," and "no"). The question here is how generalizable is this nonresponsiveness? Do any of the 14 aversive consequences produce long-term reductions in the $A_i \to R_j$ connections? Is the reduction the *same* for antisocial and for normal children?

The nattering hypothesis has yet to be directly tested. *Does* pairing of parental Stop-Commands with time out increase the decelerating impact of future commands? Finally, there is an intriguing idea based upon J. Watson's (1979) formulation that merits investigation. To what extent are par-

ents of antisocial children *noncontingent* in their use of aversives? From the Watson point of view, it could be the ratio of contingent to noncontingent punishment that is at issue here. How often does the parent "punish" a prosocial behavior? The data in Chapters 8 and 12 show that this happens more often than you might think, even in normal families. The unprovoked aversive event was significantly more likely to be provided by mothers of antisocial children than by mothers of Normals.

Differences in Responsiveness to Punishment

The focus of the OSLC treatment program is upon training parents to use nonviolent punishment in a consistent manner. If parents can learn to do this, they will be successful in changing their problem child; if they can't, the child is likely to remain a problem child. This position has two implications for the etiology of antisocial behavior; both are equally tenable. One is that antisocial behavior occurs because the parents can't (or won't) confront the child in a consistent manner when he is deviant. Personally, I favor this hypothesis. The alternate hypothesis is not necessarily antithetical. The assumption is that antisocial children are by temperament *less* responsive to punishment than normal children. There are laboratory studies which suggest that this indeed may be the case.

There is *some* evidence for the hypothesis that antisocial children may be less responsive than Normals to *mild* (social) punishment on *neutral* laboratory analogue tasks (Kuenstler, 1970; Johnston, 1976; Orzech, 1962, cited by Hedlund, 1971). However, the design for many of these studies is similar to the design employed by the verbal conditioning studies in the 1960's. The difficulties with these procedures were detailed in Chapter 5. The modern counterparts of these laboratory studies are found in the attentional deficit studies reviewed in Chapter 11. These studies showed that the attentional deficits of antisocial children were quickly remedied when money was used as a reinforcer for accurate performance. What at first seemed to be an attentional problem turned out to be a motivational problem. I wonder if the studies which showed a lack of responsiveness to punishment might demonstrate little more than a lack of involvement in the task.

It is possible that antisocial children are less responsive to aversive events. However, before that conclusion is tenable we need a series of more convincing studies than those published to date.

Variables Relating to Dispositions within the Child

The child's responsiveness to social reinforcers and to punishment is not a static disposition. Responsiveness to these consequences is thought to be related to states that are, themselves, readily manipulable (Patterson, 1969). For example, the studies reviewed by Gewirtz (1967) and Stevenson (1965) suggested that responsiveness to social reinforcers was altered by prior conditions of satiation and deprivation. Other variables relating to responsiveness to positive reinforcers were reviewed in Chapter 5. Similar considerations are thought to apply to responsiveness to punishment.

It may be that involvement in a coercive system produces, as a side effect, members that are relatively less responsive to each other's coercive behaviors. Quinsey (1970) suggests that being in a coercive system alters one's general adaptation level so that the threshold for what is perceived as extremely aversive is altered. This would suggest that siblings and parents from antisocial families would be less responsive than normal siblings and parents to garden-variety aversive consequences. This may be in keeping with the findings discussed in this chapter, which indicated that Social Aggressors reacted significantly more than Normals to aversive consequences as elicitors rather than as suppressors of antisocial behavior.

Heritability and Responsiveness to Aversive Events

The literature suggests that species differ in the (innate) disposition to learn aggression. For the animal lacking social experience, aggressive behavior may be expressed in an incomplete form. Skill in aggression requires additional learning. The form in which aggressive behavior is expressed may also change as a function of age. For example, its earliest manifestation in primates may be temper tantrums, which do not have to be learned. D. Hebb (1972, cited by Hamburg & vanLawick-Goodall, 1974) writes:

"Neither a human nor a chimpanzee baby needs to learn how to have a temper tantrum . . . the baby does not have to practice it (nor to see how others do it) in order to produce, on first try, a first-class sample. It is therefore 'unlearned.' But it is not independent of learning." (p. 63)

Eibl-Eibesfeldt (1974) reported that a deaf child's pattern of temper tantrum was indistinguishable from those of normal children or young primates. Experience will teach the young child when to use the temper tantrum, where, with whom, and at what intensity. The vehicles for the training are the familiar tools of modeling, reinforcement, and punishment.

As viewed by Hamburg and vanLawick-Goodall (1974) and Hinde (1974), the development of aggressive behavior would involve movement through a progression of such experiences. The unskilled individual may be particularly responsive to certain stimuli eliciting, in turn, partially formed aggressive responses. These skills are shaped by experience. There is no single path to aggression; each individual finds his or her own way. The learning process may be facilitated, however, by the individual's genetic history, by selective responsiveness to certain kinds of eliciting stimuli and to certain kinds of reinforcers, as well as by the presence of some partially formed but unlearned aggressive responses (such as temper tantrums). Regarding both animals and humans, this general formulation is still tentative. The recent text by R. Cairns (1979b) gives a first-rate overview of this body of literature. Hamburg (1974) goes on to say, "We certainly do not believe that there is anything like definitive evidence on these matters at the present time. Rather, we are trying to construct plausible models that would stimulate and guide inquiry . . ." (p. 62).

For animal species, including primates, the research findings clearly support a genetic differentiation for aggressiveness. As developed by Hinde (1974) and by Cairns (1979b), the model is clearly an interactional one, i.e., genetic dispositions modified by experience. As we shall see, the findings for genetic and/or constitutional variables which are related to individual differences among humans are not so clear-cut. Nevertheless, the data for humans are sufficient to be taken seriously. The current attitude seems to be "wait and see," with some cautious speculation about which variables might *possibly* be involved. For example, variables, such as hyporesponsiveness to aversive stimuli, differences in activity level, testosterone, or irritability could all covary with coercive performance. All of them could also have genetic and/or constitutional components.

One cannot properly evaluate the importance of genetic contributions to the performance of aggressive behavior without considering the matrix of social interactions within which it occurs. This is also the position of behavioral geneticists such as McClearn and DeFries (1973). They have extensively reviewed the literature demonstrating the well known fact that some strains of mice and dogs are more aggressive than others. An example of these studies is provided by the programmatic work of Lagerspetz (1964). In this study she measured aggression in male mice in successive generations selectively bred for high and low aggressiveness. The findings provide compelling evidence for some type of genetic determinants for aggressiveness in mice. The precise mechanisms involved are not clear; but the search for them constitutes the focus for Lagerspetz's current work. This programmatic work is also very much in the interactional mode. Among other things, she has found that being defeated reduced aggressiveness for both aggressive and nonaggressive strains (Lagerspetz, 1980).

In the same vein, the fostering studies reviewed by Denenberg (1973) demonstrated the interaction between genetic endowment and environment. Kuo (1930, 1938, cited by Denenberg, 1973) reared kittens and rats together and found that this experience inhibited later rat-killing behavior. Denenberg's (1973) own elegant cross-fostering studies demonstrated that rearing mice with rat mothers reduced the rats' later aggression toward mice. Thus, while other studies demonstrate that rats' mice-killing behavior was unlearned, these studies demonstrated that the same behavior was alterable. For these species, then, aggressive behavior was the outcome of the interaction between genetic contributions and social experience.

How generalizable are these findings to primates and/or humans? Studies of monozygotic (MZ) and dizygotic (DZ) twins are relevant to this question. Presumably, MZ and DZ twins have the same social environment but vary in their genetic similarities. In the Scarr (1966) studies of parents' ratings of their children, she found an intraclass correlation of .35 for MZ twins on aggression. The comparable correlation for DZ twins was −.08. In their review of the literature on studies of twins, Mednick and Hutchings (1977) note concordance rates for criminality of 60% for MZ twins and 30% for DZ twins. As the authors pointed out, there were probably serious sampling errors that characterized most of these early studies. For example, in many studies the proportion of MZ twins was higher than expected, suggesting biased samples. However, the recent study by Christiansen (1974) overcame many of these difficulties. He sampled all twins born in Copenhagen between 1884 and 1910. Of 3,586 twin pairs, the concordance rates for crimes were 36% for MZ and 13% for DZ twins. While these findings suggest a genetic component for criminality, Christiansen (1974) and Mednick and Hutchings (1977) note that the key assumption underlying these studies may be open to question. As they point out, there is some reason to expect that the shared social experience for MZ twins may be more homogeneous than for DZ twins.

Mednick and Hutchings (1977) proposed a cross-fostering design to obviate these difficulties. As part of their studies in Denmark, they obtained the files for 1,145 male adoptions, including information about criminal behavior of the adoptee, the biological father, and the foster father. There were 143 adoptees with criminal records for whom complete data were available for both biological and foster fathers. This sample was matched for age and social class of the father with a sample of noncriminal adoptees. In both samples there was little or no contact between the adoptee and the biological father. Given that neither father was criminal, then 10.5% of the adoptees were criminal; given a noncriminal biological father and a criminal adoptive father, the figure for the adoptee was 11.5%; if the foster father was not criminal and the biological father was, then the rate was 21.4%; if both fathers were criminal, the rate was 36.2%. These findings suggest a genetic base for criminality. Mednick's programmatic work continues and has been expanded to include speculations as to how fathers transmit such proclivities to their sons.

There are several variables identified in the research literature which may be genetically (or constitutionally) determined that also relate to the learning of aggressive behavior. For example, Lagerspetz (1980) and McClearn and DeFries (1973) reported that aggressive strains of mice were more active. The next question is, in what sense might activity level determine aggressive behavior? Vigorous activity was the dependent variable identified by Cairns (1972) in his studies of the aggressiveness of mice reared in isolation. When placed together isolated mice tended to respond in a hyperstimulated fashion to overtures from other mice. This, in turn, often produced a vigorous counterreaction from the isolated subject. These reciprocal interchanges quickly escalated to fighting.

Willerman (1973) presented data for twins showing an intraclass correlation of .71 for hyperactivity in MZ twins. He also cited several other studies supporting these findings. Bell's (1968) careful review also provides a number of studies supporting the notion of heritability of impulsiveness and assertiveness in children. What is missing here are data which demonstrate that more active children are also more likely to learn aggressive behavior. The observation study of nursery school aggression by Patterson, Littman, and Bricker (1967) gave partial support to this hypothesis; but the interpretation varied depending on how one defined *activity level*. Children interacting at high rates tended to be more aggressive. The correlations of activity level with aggression were positive (but nonsignificant) for measures of distance traveled and for ratings by observers of intensity of motor behavior. However, observer ratings for *vocalization rate and intensity* correlated .66 ($p <$ .05) with observed aggression.

There is yet another plausible set of variables stemming from Lykken's (1957) well known studies demonstrating that psychopaths were less effective in learning escape responses to aversive events. The variable implicated was the psychopaths' *hypo*responsiveness to the aversive stimuli. The position has been reaffirmed by Hare (1968). He showed that psychopaths had lower resting levels for skin conductance and less responsivity to mildly aversive auditory tones. They also reacted slower than Normals on two measures of autonomic activity: cardiac deceleration and digital vasoconstriction.

Mednick and Christiansen's (1977) edited volume brings into focus the literature investigating the *hypo*reactivity of adult and juvenile criminals to aversive stimuli. They present two key hypotheses. One suggests that hyporesponsiveness to punishment impedes avoidance learning. The second hypothesis is that a slow autonomic recovery contributes to this impedance. The studies relating to these hypotheses were reviewed by Siddle (1977). Most of these studies involved selected subgroups of adult criminals, primary and secondary psychopaths. His review suggests that these out-of-control adults cannot be considered to be generally underaroused because, at best, the findings from at-rest conditions were ambiguous. However, during aversive stimulation or the threat of aversive stimulation most of the studies cited by Siddle supported the hypothesis of hypoarousal. The psychopaths showed both smaller skin conductance response to the signal and the shock, as well as a slower recovery. Presumably, a lowered responsiveness and slower recovery from punishment would lead to slower learning of avoidance responses. Siddle cites the well known studies by Lykken (1957) and Schmauk (1970) in support of this hypothesis.

Mednick and Hutchings (1977) reviewed a series of studies demonstrating that electrodermal recovery rates were significantly slower for criminal and delinquent samples than for noncriminal populations. One of the studies cited involved a sample of twins for which these measures were available. The heritability coefficient for that sample was .83. The authors make the point that a slow electrodermal recovery rate is a physiological mechanism that might be transmitted from father to son. They also speculate as to how this could relate to the faulty development of self-control mechanisms. Their current studies include a longitudinal design providing for electrodermal recovery rates for parents and children. The long-term follow-up data will demonstrate if this measure predicts later criminality.

It seems reasonable to suppose that small individual differences in activity rates and/or responsiveness to aversive stimuli might interact with inept child management techniques to produce an antisocial child. The empirical basis for specifying these relationships is far from satisfactory and, at best, is only suggestive. However, the data which are available indicate that a simplistic environmentalist position is probably inadequate. One cannot conclude which of these variables is more important based on present data. However, my own subjective bias is that inept parenting will be the key variable and that the problem child's hyporesponsiveness can be altered by improvements in the parents' child management skills.

Some Implications

Punishment is Treatment

The findings from studies analyzing punishment have direct relevance to the treatment of families with antisocial children. Parents of normal children tend to ignore most coercive child behavior; as a result, the episodes tend to be of short duration. When they want to, these parents are able to use punishment to stop or suppress these behaviors. Parents of antisocial children *ignore less* and *natter more*. However, unless they use extreme measures, they cannot stop coercive behaviors. Furthermore, their nattering contributes directly to extended coercive episodes. During the last five years of treating samples of extremely difficult chronic delinquent and abused children, we have become convinced that training parents to use a *nonviolent* form of punishment is a *necessary component* of *successful intervention*. That position is certainly not in keeping with our original stance (Patterson, 1965a; Patterson, Littman, & Bricker, 1967). At that time, it was thought that positive reinforcement of prosocial responses that competed with the deviant responses would serve as *the* treatment base. However, clinical experience quickly underscored the fact that this was not to be the case. The studies reviewed here and in Chapter 11 showed that extinction, per se, was not successful even when combined with reinforcement of competing responses. As one of the original "true believers," I found it extremely difficult to accept the idea that extinction would not work. If it were possible to stop all positive and negative reinforcement for coercive behaviors then it seems that these responses would eventually be extinguished. In principle, extinction *should* work. But I think that it is simply not possible for parents to control all of their own reactions plus the reactions of siblings to the skillful intrusions of the problem child. At a practical level, in social situations the reinforcement schedules can be altered but never reduced to zero. Therefore, the pragmatics of family interactions are such that punishment is a necessary, but not sufficient, component for effective child management (Patterson, Reid, Jones, & Conger, 1975).

A beautifully controlled study by Walker, Hops, and Greenwood (in preparation) addresses this issue. They applied a multiple baseline ABABAB design to a small token-culture classroom. After a baseline period and a prior manipulation, the disruptive children were placed on a schedule in which they received tokens for positive, achievement-oriented responses. The observation data showed the expected steady increase in rate for task-oriented behaviors. After a slight reduction, the disruptive behaviors returned to their baseline level. Following another baseline phase, the teacher punished disruptive behavior by taking away points or, occasionally, by using time out procedures. Task-oriented behaviors were again reinforced by giving points. Over sessions, the disruptive behaviors were dramatically reduced, and the prosocial behaviors remained at a high level. The study demonstrated that for extremely antisocial children *achievement and disruptive behaviors are functionally independent of each other.* Second, the findings indicated that in order to control deviant behavior, it was necessary to employ an effective punishment.

Punishment Causes Aggression?

The position taken in this volume is that the control of antisocial behavior requires the contingent use of some kind of punishment. This position is contrary to a well-established finding in developmental psychology. Studies that investigated parental reports about their punitive practices consistently showed a positive relation with antisocial child behavior (Feshbach, 1970). Parents of problem children report that they use punishment *more frequently* than parents of normal children. Their punitive practices are also more likely to be extreme. These covariations also stand up in some of the more recent studies which control for the possible confounds inherent in using parent reports for both the dependent and the independent variables (Eron et al., 1971, 1974).

As shown in this chapter, the parents of socially aggressive children did punish more often; at least they were more likely to provide an aversive consequence in *reaction to* sibling and problem child aggressive behavior. Others have noted this correlation and have put forth several interpretations of what it means. The most widely accepted position is the modeling-frustration hypothesis, which suggests that parental punishment *produces* an emotional reaction and provides a model of aggressive behavior for the child. This theme was succinctly stated by Bandura (1973):

"In exercising punitive control, prohibitive agents model aggressive styles of behavior not unlike those they wish to discourage in others. Recipients may, on later occasions, adopt similar aggressive solutions in coping with the problems confronting them. . . . Although the direction of causal relationships cannot be unequivocally established from correlational data, it is clear from controlled studies that aggressive modeling breeds aggression." (p. 226)

Other writers sweep aside Bandura's cautions regarding the correlational nature of the findings. For example, Welsh (1976) leaps to the inference of causality: "A number of field studies indicate that severe parental punishment is definitely a precursor of aggression in humans" (p. 17). He goes on to document the frequency with which extreme physical punishment (using a belt, a board, an extension cord, or a fist) are reported by samples of male delinquents. He labels this causal relation his *belt theory of juvenile delinquency.* In effect, he states that parental punishment *causes* aggressive behavior, and that extreme punishment causes extreme acting out.

Other writers, such as Berkowitz (1973a), take a more moderate stance in interpreting these correlational findings. He first examines the possibility that other variables may mediate parental effectiveness as punishing agents, e.g., nurturance, consistency, and rule statements. While accepting the importance of these variables, he emphasizes the possibility that the kind of punishment used by parents of aggressive children may be ineffective. He goes on to provide a case for the necessity of punishing aggressive child behaviors, but in the context of a warm, loving parent, who uses reasoning or explanations in conjunction with nonviolent punishment, such as time out.

The present writer is in total accord with Berkowitz's position. His statement perfectly reflects our conclusions from the last decade's intervention studies with families of aggressive children. Time out and analogous consequences (such as work details or loss of privileges) are certainly aversive. Relatively speaking, they are very effective; however, *they are not violent*. When point loss, time out, and loss of privileges are effectively applied, the correlation found in traditional development studies will be reversed. After a few weeks the likelihood of p (Time Out|Coercive) should correlate negatively with observed TAB score; i.e., the frequently punished child is less aggressive. It is assumed the traditional finding of a positive correlation between parent punishment and child aggression is a process *outcome, not the cause,* as suggested by Welsh (1976).

Again, more studies are needed. What do the parents of the antisocial child *do* when they want to stop coercive behavior? How do they signal to the child that they really mean it this time? When they natter, do they want to stop the behavior, or do they only want to "bitch" a lot? Our present assessment devices cannot differentiate effective punishment from nattering, so these concepts are, for the moment, not directly testable. Obviously some new measures are needed. Perhaps some variant of the Parent Daily Report (Chapter 3) would give us daily records of parents' back-up punishment. Is it true that parents of normal children are more likely to ignore and to use back-up punishment, and less likely to natter?

Given that the child coerces and the father natters, there is no change in the likelihood of future problems. Nattering is analogous to a whine or a whimper, an indication that things are getting out of control. It seems to be a danger signal of some kind. It is a declaration that the parent has taken a *non*training stance. I think that the normal parent intervenes to reduce long-term misery and to teach the child. The parent of the antisocial child does not seem to make this commitment.

There is another facet of this process that would be fascinating to study. It has to do with the apparent skill with which some parents (and children) employ guilt induction as punishment. On one occasion, for example, I was present when an adolescent brought home three D's as term grades. In the following discussion he skillfully turned it around so that his mother was to blame for his bad grades! He first pointed out that she worked full time and this meant *she* could not supervise *him* enough. He then skillfully punished her for even bringing up the topic of his poor grades. One has the feeling this technique is used often, especially in some subcultures. It also seems to be terribly effective in the hands of the skilled practitioner; but its subtlety defies our existing code system.

Conclusion

What then has been learned? For one thing, the concept of punishment seems to be at the core of antisocial child behavior. The parents of these children cannot or will not stop these behaviors from occurring. To understand more, we must now shift our focus somewhat. We need to know more about signal cues, about back-up punishment, and about hyporesponsiveness to aversive stimuli.

It also seems the case that we may have to train parents and teachers in our culture to accept the idea that punishment *is not a bad thing* for a child. In moving away from the excesses of physical violence previously directed against children, we have created a dilemma for those who must devote their lives to training children. The old adage, "It takes two to fight," is *not true*. One well-trained coercer can disrupt an entire classroom, an office, or a home. In dealing with a problem child it helps to have rules clearly stated and rational discussion, but sooner or later someone has to *confront* him and teach him that coercion does *not work*. If the teacher or the parent has been taught that all punishment is bad then they will not employ the one mechanism that we have found necessary for the control of antisocial behavior.

Footnotes

1. It should be noted that the study cited here measured only the short-term suppressing impact of aversive consequences. It remains necessary to use these events in a comparison of their long-term effects in altering $p(R_j|A_i)$ when applied to prosocial and to coercive family behaviors.

2. The attribution studies by Lepper (1980) demonstrate in a convincing manner that even those children who *successfully compete* in that system experience it as aversive. Prizes won in competition are not experienced as rewards. These effects have been replicated in a number of laboratories. They serve as a major indictment of modern educational practice, with its emphasis on competition and grades, which compare the child to all other children. The alternative to the competition model is, of course, to provide meaningful positive external reinforcement contingent on the child's moving from his or her own baseline level. Why not design schools where feedback is tailored to the individual? Why not use external reinforcers, such as praise, instead of relying upon the fear of not competing successfully?

3. Unfortunately, there is a confound here. Given that parents of normal and antisocial chil-

dren were equally *likely* to punish deviant behavior, then it would follow that the latter *should* report more frequent attempts to punish. These children are performing deviant behaviors at nearly twice the rate so their parents should report almost twice as much punishment. As seen in Table 6.4, the parents of Social Aggressors not only *punish more often,* they are also *more likely* to punish. If one uses this likelihood index and correlates it with the child's level of aggression (TAB score), the relation is just the reverse of the traditional finding. The correlation between p (Parental Command Negative|Child Deviant) and the child's TAB score was $-.10$. This was based upon a sample of 30 OSLC cases. In either case, the parent frequency and/or likelihood of punishment account for very little of the variance.

4. An earlier analysis by Patterson (1976) used a heterogeneous sample of out-of-control boys and a normal sample similar to that employed in Table 6.4. In the earlier analysis, the population was events rather than subjects; some high-rate boys contributed many events to the analysis, others contributed only a few. For the 1976 study, the mean likelihood of parental punishment for the distressed sample was .62, and for the nondistressed .40. A comparison to the findings in Table 6.4, based on samples of subjects, shows marked discrepancies. Evidently, some individuals in the 1976 sample did contribute extreme scores. I think the analysis of events rather than subjects gives an overestimate of the likelihood of parental punishment.

5. The OSLC code makes no provision for recording critical information on the use of time out, withdrawal of privileges, and so on. After the code was developed, John B. Reid added the Observer Impression Checklist. The three pages of ratings contain items relating to such events. The checklist is filled out after each session. These data are presently available but have not yet been analyzed.

Chapter 7
Abstract

Negative reinforcement (NR) is an arrangement in which an aversive event is followed by a response which, in turn, has a neutral or positive outcome. Such arrangements apply to about one-fourth of the problem child's coercive behavior. These NR arrangements serve in several different roles. First, it is a means by which one may cope with the aversive intrusions of other family members. NR arrangements are also involved in the process by which the aggressor trains *his victim* to *reinforce him*. The third contribution is its key role in escalating interchanges to high-amplitude violence.

Data are presented for normal and clinical samples, describing the likelihood of aversive antecedents and the proportion of episodes in which the counterattack effectively terminates the aversive antecedent.

Experiments are described which show that the termination of an aversive event is followed by a strengthening of the $A_i \rightarrow R_j$ connection. Victim compliance is also shown to reliably produce a cessation of the counterattack.

The literature describing physical violence in families is reviewed. It is assumed that this is the end product of an escalation process. Increases in amplitude are more likely to occur during extended coercive chains. If an increase in amplitude produces victim compliance, it increases the likelihood of higher amplitude interchanges during future trials. Given both members of a dyad have relatively equal power, escalation on the part of one member will lead to synchronous increases by the other. This process continues until one person submits.

Negative Reinforcement and Escalation

Coercive behaviors are maintained by both positive and negative reinforcement. Data to be reviewed in a later section show that about one-fourth of the time the child's coercive response is followed by the removal of an aversive intrusion by another family member. If the counterattack is successful, the intruder withdraws and the connection between the antecedent (intrusion) and the response (counter) is strengthened. This arrangement is negative reinforcement (NR).[1] One of the striking features of negative reinforcement is that it can produce massive changes in antecedent-response connections with very few trials.

NR plays a crucial role in coercive interchanges. NR is not only responsible for the maintenance of many coercive events, it is also the means by which the aggressor trains a victim to comply or submit. In this context, the person initiating a coercive event is the attacker. The person who ends a coercive exchange with a positive or neutral reaction is the victim. Within coercion theory it is the victim who trains the aggressor when, how, and where to attack; the aggressor also trains the victim how and when to *reinforce* the attack. This Machiavellian twist is achieved by a NR arrangement. If the victim complies, then the aggressor *immediately terminates his attack*. In this manner submission is reinforced by the withdrawal of the aversive antecedent. This (hypothesized) sudden termination of hostilities on the part of the aggres-

sor may seem counterintuitive. If the mother gives in, does the whining child *really* stop within seconds? Data relating to the victim-training hypothesis will be presented in a later section of this chapter. Suffice it to say here that the data support these ideas.

Let's assume that a young sibling has observed and thus learned about coercive responses. On occasion he serves as a victim for these attacks. Given that the attacks are not overwhelming, then he or she will sometimes counterattack. If the counterattack meets with some success, then the lamb may become a lion. The child may also increase the likelihood that he or she will perform these same attack behaviors. Again, NR is thought to play the crucial role. The formulation was based on the results of the study of nursery school conflicts (Patterson, Littman, & Bricker, 1967). In that study, 21 children were identified, each of whom had displayed two or less coercive behaviors during the first five nursery school sessions. During the following sessions, 12 children in this group were observed to interact at high rates with their peers and were victimized an average of 70 times. When they counterattacked, they were reinforced, on the average, 69% of the time by a termination of the attack. These NR arrangements seemed, in turn, to be accompanied by an increase in the rate at which the children initiated their own attacks. Children who were seldom victimized, or who were not successful in their counterattacks, showed little or no change in the rate at which they later initiated coercive interchanges. Presumably, a similar process takes place in the home as well.

A further contribution of NR concerns the key assumption that physical violence among family members is the outcome of a process whose components consist of low-amplitude aversive events. The mechanism serving this process is negative reinforcement.

In each context the NR arrangement makes an important contribution to our understanding of social interaction. The arrangement is a variation on a theme of pain control. In the matrix of ongoing social interaction, it has some things in common with punishment. There are a substantial number of experimental findings which relate to NR arrangements. The laboratory studies of this phenomenon are straightforward. Typically, an aversive stimulus is presented and is terminated only when the animal performs the desired response. Contingent termination of pain has been shown to be a powerful method for teaching a variety of responses. In these experimental designs, learning varies as a function of the intensity of the painful stimulus and the number of training trials (Hineline, 1977). The precursor for studies of this kind was clearly the escape and avoidance learning paradigm, with its long tradition in the history of learning theories. The recent extensions of this work within the operant paradigm have explored the function of schedules of negative reinforcement and their contribution to concurrent and multiple-chain components (Hineline, 1977). This new work has established a solid empirical base for the concept.

Some Peculiar Properties of NR Arrangements

There are a number of ways in which NR differs from positive reinforcement (PR) in its impact upon behavior. For example, NR is associated with stimulus *reduction* (withdrawal of A_i), while positive reinforcement can be thought of as stimulus *producing*. While NR arrangements are associated with significant *reductions* in physiological arousal, the studies reviewed by Fowles (1980) showed that positive incentives were related to *increases* in arousal.

Both PR and NR arrangements have a long-term impact. The contingent arrangement strengthens the connection between the antecedent and response; i.e., $p(R_j|A_i)$ increases. However, in addition to this long-term impact upon future oc-

currences of A_i, the NR arrangement also produces *immediate* changes in behavior that are not related to the probabilistic connection between A_i and R_j. Not only does NR produce a duality of effects (long-term and short-term), NR also produces greater changes in the $A_i \rightarrow R_j$ connection with fewer trials. Given the presentation of highly aversive stimuli, a few training trials may produce escape or avoidance responses which are extremely resistant to change (Maier, 1961; Solomon & Wynne, 1954). Taken together, these characteristics make NR a powerful mechanism for behavior change. In view of the potential it has for contributing to our understanding of family interaction, it is unfortunate that it has been ignored for so long.

Before addressing these issues, there is one further problem that must be discussed. When the format is applied to ongoing social interaction, there are some subtle changes in NR arrangements. Because the aversive events are embedded *within a sequence*, the interpretation becomes more complex than for NR analogues found in the laboratory. This increase in complexity occurs at several different points. In laboratory studies, the typical NR sequence begins by presenting an aversive event *continuously* until the animal makes the escape response which has been preselected by the experimenter. In another type of design, the aversive event is programmed to occur, but the animal can avoid this possibility by pressing a lever, delaying the occurrence of the aversive event for a certain period of time. Social interaction, of course, typically does not have such an urgent quality to it, but there are some examples which come close. One can think of a mother continuing to glare until the child closes the door, a harried spouse continuing to nag until her husband fixes the faucet, a sibling crying until the mother comes in and forces the older sibling to return a toy, or the mother using guilt induction until her son gets straight "A's." The most analogous situation in our data would be one in which a person presented a series of two or three aversive events until compliance was obtained.

There is, however, a fundamental difference between the NR arrangements found within the matrix of social interaction and the NR arrangements found in the laboratory. In social interaction, all the components in the NR arrangement are connected only in a probabilistic sense. The mother does *not* always issue commands until the child complies; when she issues a command ($\overline{A}_i$), there is a certain likelihood that the child will comply. If the child complies, there is a certain likelihood that the mother's next response will be neutral or positive. How does this collection of fluctuating

Figure 7.1
The Negative Reinforcement and Punishment Family

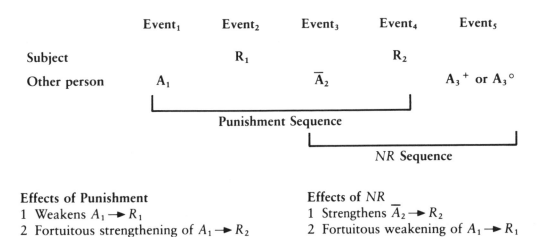

	Event_1	Event_2	Event_3	Event_4	Event_5
Subject		R_1		R_2	
Other person	A_1		$\overline{A}_2$		$A_3{}^+$ or $A_3{}^\circ$

Punishment Sequence

NR Sequence

Effects of Punishment
1 Weakens $A_1 \rightarrow R_1$
2 Fortuitous strengthening of $A_1 \rightarrow R_2$

Effects of NR
1 Strengthens $\overline{A}_2 \rightarrow R_2$
2 Fortuitous weakening of $A_1 \rightarrow R_1$

---

conditional p values constitute a NR arrangement? I think that when the social-interaction sequence is: aversive → response → nonaversive, then it is appropriate to think of it as a NR arrangement. The utility of this convention lies in the prediction that the $A_i \rightarrow R_j$ connection was strengthened.

There is another sense in which NR arrangements become more dynamic when embedded within the context of social interaction. In the relatively fixed laboratory environment, the aversive stimulus is either present or absent. This binary condition is in contrast to the situation found in social interaction. Here the escape response usually changes *only part* of the stimulus. For example, following a successful counterattack, the family member may still be present, even though he or she has stopped behaving in an aversive manner. The subject does not leave the situation; he *changes* it. His behavior has altered the social-interactional setting; the matrix of events now mean something different than they did prior to his response.

When NR is embedded within social interactions, it becomes obvious that some of the segments which define it are also related to punishment arrangements. Figure 7.1 describes an interchange between two people. The subject reacts with a sequence of two responses (R_j's) to what the other person is doing (A_i). The other person changes the valence of his or her behavior from neutral A_1 to aversive $\overline{A}_2$ and then to either a positive or a neutral A_3. As is shown in Figure 7.1, punishment and NR arrangements share *overlap-

ping segments (A_2 through R_2) of the same sequences*. Those who investigate punishments are generally interested in the effect of $\overline{A}_2$ in weakening the probabilistic connection between A_1 and R_1. However, if the analysis of the punishment episode were continued, it would include the NR segment. In most punishment studies there is little interest in what happens next. When an animal subject is shocked for R_1, it does something else (for example, crouch down on the opposite side of the cage); this is R_2. Note this response, R_2, is followed by a termination of the shock. Some theorists, such as Guthrie, have explained punishment effects in this way. The competing response, R_2, replaces the original response. As Church and Getty (1972) point out, an aversive event must always terminate at some point. The immediately prior response will then be reinforced. Given the occurrence of an aversive event then, by definition, NR will occur for *some* response.

When studying NR, the focus shifts from strengthening A_1 and R_1 to strengthening the probabilistic connection between $\overline{A}_2$ and R_2. Notice, however, that punishment and NR have an effect on events *beyond* the segment which is typically at the center of the experimenter's attention. What seems to be a simple NR process that strengthens $\overline{A}_2 \rightarrow R_2$ also weakens the $A_1 \rightarrow R_1$ connection. What seems to be a simple punishment arrangement that weakens $A_1 \rightarrow R_1$ *also* strengthens $A_1 \rightarrow R_2$. This *mutuality* of effects defines punishment and NR arrangements as *members of the same family*.

Table 7.1
Changes in Latency and Duration Following Reinforcement
(from Devine, 1971)

Group Reinforced for:	Mean Duration (seconds)			Mean Latency (seconds)		
	Pre	Post	F	Pre	Post	F
Prosocial Behaviors	29.9	64.2	6.12*	46.0	15.4	5.81*
Coercive Behaviors	12.9	40.0	21.79**	60.3	16.6	9.75*

*p < .05
**p < .01

The Efficiency of NR

The first attempts to produce an experimental test of *NR* revealed one particularly surprising finding. *NR* arrangements produced very rapid changes in behavior. Devine (1971) created a laboratory situation in which the mother initiated an aversive behavior; the aversive behavior was then terminated contingent upon specific child behaviors. The arrangement produced significant changes in the behavior of the child in only *four* trials. This effect is in stark contrast to earlier OSLC studies of aggression in which up to 120 social reinforcers were required to produce even minimally reliable increases in aggressive behaviors directed toward Bobo dolls (Patterson & Cobb, 1971). In our treatment programs, positive social reinforcers plus nonsocial reinforcers (such as points and money) produced changes only in prosocial behavior and these changes were produced over a period of weeks or months.

In Devine's (1971) study, 22 mother-child pairs participated in a laboratory task. After a baseline period, the mother was instructed to work on a task and ignore the child. Previous studies had shown this to be highly aversive for preschool children (Atkinson, 1971). For one group, the mother's attention was made contingent upon the child's prosocial behavior; e.g., if the child played, the mother immediately attended to the child. For the second group, the mother's attention was made contingent upon the child's performance of a coercive response. Each trial was followed, in turn, by baseline and free-play periods. There were a series of four training trials alternated with baseline phases. Table 7.1 summarizes the data. The two groups were compared on their baseline and post-test trials with respect to two measures of response strength. Devine assumed that reinforcement would increase the duration of a response and decrease the latency of its occurence given the presentation of the antecedent stimulus. These data indicated that as few as four trials were sufficient to produce significant changes in the reinforced responses. Negative reinforcement seemed equally effective in changing prosocial and coercive responses.

In discussing these results, Devine made the very important observation that when *NR* was embedded within the matrix of social interaction, it may have a *double payoff*. A response may be associated *both* with the removal of the aversive antecedent *and* with the positive consequence which follows (such as Attend, Talk, or Laugh). His point is well taken. Laboratory studies are needed that test the impact of neutral and positive outcomes upon *NR* arrangements. Is *NR* more efficient than positive reinforcement in changing behavior? It seems to be, but as yet there have been no systematic comparisons. Nevertheless, if this is the case, it may relate to the rapid shifts in performance level which describe some children.

The Reinforcement Trap

This section is concerned with the multiplicity of effects that can be brought about by introducing a single aversive event into an interaction sequence. One of the most fascinating features of social interaction is the possibility of simultaneous short- and long-term outcomes for a single event. From the situation in Figure 7.2, one may obtain five different outcomes from a single exchange at time-one (t_1). In the example, the mother and child both behave in such a way as to maximize short-term gains. The child behaves in such a way as to maximize the likelihood that Mother will termin-

144

Figure 7.2
The Reinforcement Trap

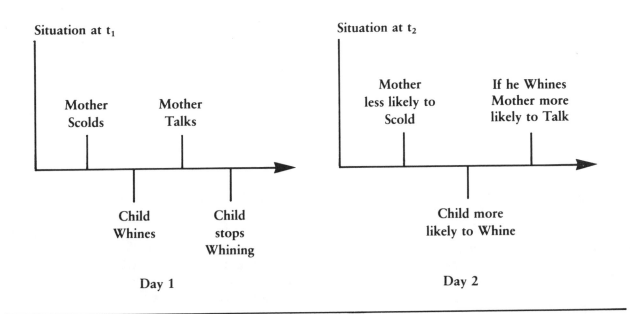

ate her scolding. The mother behaves in such a way as to maximize the likelihood that the child will terminate his whining. What makes this interesting is the fact that the short-term effects seem, to the participants at least, to be unrelated to the long-term effects. For example, in the short run, the mother got "rid of" child-Whine but in doing so, *increased* the likelihood that child-Whine will occur in the future! This lack of agreement between short-term and long-term effects makes it extremely difficult for the participants to understand what has happened. It is, in other words, an ideal situation for behavior change without awareness (see Chapter 5). It is this characteristic that leads the writer to describe this arrangement as a "reinforcement trap."

The situation depicted in Figure 7.2 has a history. There have been many previous trials in which the mother nagged the child about his messy room. At t_1, the scene opens with mother-Scold; as previously rehearsed, the child begins to whine. Normally this would induce the mother to continue scolding (Patterson, 1977a), but for the sake of illustration, let's assume that child-Whine effectively terminates mother-Scold. She now talks to the child in a soothing manner. The first outcome of interest is that child-Whine produced mother-Talk. The second outcome is that mother-

Talk produced a termination of child-Whine. This is in keeping with findings from the laboratory analogue study by Dengerink, Schnedler, and Covey (1977). In a Buss-type shock situation, when the other member terminated attacks, subjects quickly reduced their level of aggression. Within family interaction does the coercer terminate the attack within seconds of victim compliance? In a study of three mother-child pairs, Woo (1978) found that during baseline the mean duration of child-Whine was 28 seconds. Given an aversive stimulus followed by child-Whine and mother-Comply, the child stopped whining in an average of 4.6 seconds!

In the example above, the child reinforced (*NR*) the mother's shift from nagging to talking by terminating his whining. In the short term, both members reduced the number of aversive events impinging upon them. It should be noted, however, that the child's room remained a mess. Because the mother gave in, the child won the battle. The mother (who is the victim) lost because she opted for an immediate reduction in pain, not knowing, of course, it was at the expense of an increased likelihood that messy rooms will occur in the future.

I believe that this general scenario is repeated many times for parents of the Social Aggressor.

While the parents may repeat their demands several times, they eventually give in. At time-two (t_2) the situation is repeated. However, there is technically a slight reduction in the likelihood of the mother nagging. This third outcome is the result of the child punishing the mother for nagging on the previous trial. Incidentally, most antisocial children have trained their parents in this manner. As a group, these children are given very few chores to do. Fourth, the child is more likely to whine because it worked so well earlier. Fifth, the mother is more likely to give in if the child whines because of the conditioning she received on the preceding trial; i.e., he terminated his whining as soon as she submitted. The mother attends only to the short-term impact of her behavior upon the child. In so doing she contributes to her own misery. On future occasions, the child is even more likely to behave in a coercive fashion.

Arousal Reduction and Rigidity

This section reviews two additional characteristics of NR that may or may not be interrelated. First, it seems that when a response is reinforced by the withdrawal of an aversive event, it may also be accompanied by a reduction in arousal. This relation has some very interesting implications for the clinical processes associated with aggression. The second characteristic is that some escape-avoidance responses become particularly resistant to extinction. This may relate, in turn, to some problems frequently encountered in the treatment of antisocial children.

The studies reviewed in Chapter 4 showed that a wide range of aversive stimuli produced autonomic arousal. These studies investigated the effect of shock and frustration on highly generalized measures of arousal such as blood pressure and skin conductance. Interestingly, one study showed that antisocial people showed greater arousal (Hokanson, 1961). It should be noted that recent advances in psychophysiology are suggesting the possibility of three activating systems, one of which reflects reactions to aversive stimulation, and another of which reflects active coping responses to aversive stimuli (Fowles, 1980). According to this new formulation, electrodermal activation may be a more sensitive measure of the arousal that is produced by an aversive stimulus.

It is hypothesized that responses which produce a termination of an aversive stimulus will be associated with arousal reduction. The case for this arousal-reduction hypothesis is only marginally convincing, but sufficient to merit our attention. The study by Hokanson and Edelman (1966) found the expected elevation in blood pressure fol-

lowing frustration by a colleague. Those male subjects who were permitted to aggress against their frustrator showed a more rapid decline in systolic blood pressure than a control group that was not given an opportunity to counteraggress. Bandura (1973) cites three additional studies demonstrating a similar effect. However, as he notes, this arousal-reduction effect is not invariant. For example, it was not found for female aggressors in the Hokanson and Edelman study, nor was the effect always reflected in measures of heart rate or dystolic blood pressure.

A variety of responses may terminate an attack. For example, a friendly overture in response to a hostile initiation may serve this function. Such a response, if successful, would also be accompanied by reduction in autonomic level. The Hokanson et al. (1968) study demonstrated that both friendliness and counterattacks were accompanied by rapid reductions in arousal if they were followed by termination of the attacks. In this regard, the methodological study by Szpiler and Epstein (1976) used shock as the aversive stimulus and several measures of heart rate and electrodermal response were the dependent variables. All of the arousal measures consistently reflected the impact of shock. However, only the measure of nonspecific skin-conductance responses reflect the arousal-reduction effect for the group of subjects who were provided with a nonaggressive means of avoiding the shock.

What is needed is a study that tests for a reduction in arousal following successful counteraggression and demonstrates the strengthening effect of NR as it relates to future attacks. The study by Green, Stonner, and Shope (1975) found a connection between arousal reduction and the strengthening of aggression. In that study, 90 males were either attacked or treated in a neutral manner by a confederate. Then in the maze-learning trials which followed, one group shocked the confederate (counteraggressed), a second group waited, and a third group observed the experimenter attack the confederate. The counteraggressive group showed the greatest reduction in dystolic blood pressure during these second trials. Vicarious counteraggression, or not responding, resulted in less arousal reduction. All three groups then participated in a third set of trials in which all of the subjects could shock a confederate who was working on coding problems. The group that had been the counteraggressors during the previous trials employed shocks of greater intensity on this new task. Interestingly, they also expressed a greater dislike for the confederates in their ratings of them. A greater reduction in arousal was associated with an increased likelihood for high-intensity future attacks.

Incidentally, this finding is contrary to some of the prevailing interpretations of catharsis theory which suggest that draining off anger is associated with a reduced likelihood for future aggression. One should accept the concept of arousal reduction with some caution. However, these studies have important implications for the concept of catharsis. They should give pause to anyone entertaining the notion that catharsis is a necessary and/or sufficient condition for the treatment of antisocial children. The arousal-reduction data support the idea that letting the child have a temper tantrum *will* make him *feel* better. However, the side effects are just the *opposite* of what one wants. If the child "won" by using a temper tantrum, then he will not only feel better but he will be more likely to do it again. The catharsis theorists accurately portray the fact that the child feels better after the tantrum, but these theorists ignore the reinforcement trap.

In passing, there is another aspect of the arousal-reduction studies which is relevant to the catharsis concept. Catharsis theory suggests that substitute activities, such as viewing aggression that is directed against others, "drains off anger," thereby reducing aggression. In his review, Bandura (1973) noted that arousal reduction was not likely to occur if the counter-response was displaced toward a target other than the tormentor; nor did it occur if the counterattack was expressed as a fantasy. His review suggests that arousal reduction is maximized when the counterattack is immediate and directed toward the tormentor.

In Chapter 11, studies are reviewed which demonstrate that extinction is an ineffective method for altering coercive child behaviors. In these uncontrolled treatment studies, it is difficult to determine why nonreinforcement of aggressive behavior by parents is not accompanied by a reduction in rates of aggression. One reasonable hypothesis is that a behavior that is maintained by mixed schedules of NR and positive reinforcement may be more resistant to extinction. As pointed out by J. Knutson, there is an extensive literature which suggests that nonreinforcement is itself aversive. Parent nonreinforcement may, therefore, induce further coercive child behaviors. Extinction for NR would be equally complex. The parent would have to present an aversive such as scolding and *continue* scolding *until* the child complied. Few parents could be so persistent in their presentation of an aversive. What this would really mean is that the child's noncompliance is being *punished*. In a social context, extinction for NR is simply not a

reasonable arrangement. Given that a substantial share of coercive behavior maintenance is due to NR arrangements, then only punishment would alter the connection between the aversive antecedent and the response. For child management purposes, extinction of coercive behavior is not a useful concept.

In the traditional studies of escape and avoidance learning, a number of writers have noted the extreme rigidity of behaviors acquired under these arrangements (Maier, 1961; Seligman, 1975; Solomon & Wynne, 1954). In those studies, the animals continued to display stereotypic escape responses long after the original conditioning trials (Solomon & Wynne, 1954). Hineline (1977) reviewed the extinction literature relating to shock-delay studies of NR. Leaving the animal in the setting with the shock turned off eventually produced extinction for the lever presses which previously delayed shock onset. However, extinction effects were not obtained for those subjects for whom shock was made noncontingent. These groups continued lever pressing for thousands of responses when the response no longer delayed shock onset. Animals trained in situations where they could not avoid the pain also displayed stereotypic responses persisting for many trials (Maier, 1961). These studies reiterate the theme that NR arrangements may result in a rapid acquisition of coercive behaviors that are *highly resistant to extinction*. For treatment purposes, there are two options. One is to reduce the number of aversive events presented by family members. The other is to effectively punish each counterattack. The OSLC treatment program emphasizes both components (Patterson, Reid, Jones & Conger, 1975).

In extending these earlier studies, Seligman (1975) noted that when the animals (from the escape and avoidance studies) were later placed in solvable escape situations, they showed themselves to be slow learners. The series of studies by Nelson and Knutson (1978), as well as their review of the literature, showed that the metaphor, "learned helplessness," has only limited generalizability when applied to aggression. They found that reduced responsiveness was specific to the sex and strain of the animal and whether or not the animal had been housed in isolation or in a community cage. While the status of learned helplessness as a scientific concept may be in doubt, it is an appealing metaphor. Clinical experience brings to mind the picture of some parents of aggressive children who long ago learned that nothing they could do would work in their attempts to deal with the problem child. Their expressed feelings of helplessness and stereotypical responses to the prob-

Table 7.2
Aversive Antecedents Given that the Subject Performed a Coercive Response

Category	Clinical Sample ($N = 33$)		Nonproblem Sample ($N = 27$)	
	N^*	$p(\overline{A}_i \mid \overline{R}_j)$	N^*	$p(\overline{A}_i \mid \overline{R}_j)$
Command Negative	17	.37	8	.44
Cry	8	.34	—	—
Dependency	7	.12	5	.20
Destructiveness	12	.22	—	—
Disapprove	33	.33	26	.23
High Rate	15	.34	9	.12
Humiliate	19	.27	7	.00
Ignore	17	.63	8	.45
Negativeness	25	.23	17	.16
Noncomply	32	.29	25	.16
Physical Negative	24	.39	14	.40
Tease	27	.31	17	.37
Whine	23	.31	12	.23
Yell	19	.36	8	.22
Mean		.32		.25

* refers to the number of subjects performing the response. It was this N that was used to calculate $p(\overline{A}_i \rightarrow \overline{R}_j)$.

lem child seem to fit the Seligman model.

It is a fact that children's aggressive behaviors are extremely difficult to change. The studies detailed in Chapter 5 suggest the difficulty of applying extinction procedures to alter coercive behaviors. It is an open question as to why this is the case. However, I believe that part of the difficulty lies in the fact that *NR* arrangements are an important source of maintenance for coercive behavior. Given an aversive antecedent, you can comply with it, punish it, or try to pretend it doesn't exist. The field studies which demonstrated the failure of extinction arrangements manipulated only positive reinforcers. Would the outcomes have been different if they had focused only upon the child coercive response previously shown to be maintained only by positive reinforcement? I don't think so; as noted earlier, extinction arrangements may evoke further coercion. What are the characteristics of responses maintained by mixed schedules of *PR* and *NR*? These are key questions for the next round of studies.

Descriptive Data

The Likelihood of an Aversive Antecedent

First, what proportion of coercive child behaviors have aversive antecedents? Data collected for two different samples provided the data base. One sample consisted of 33 boys referred to OSLC as out of control; the other was a group of 27 nonproblem boys matched for age, occupation of father, family size, and father presence. Whether the coercive behavior occurred within a chain or in isolation, the computer identified the antecedent event that was supplied by other family members. These A_i were classified as aversive or nonaversive. This calculation for the likelihood of an aversive $\overline{A}_i$ antecedent was carried out separately for each coercive response. The data are summarized in Table 7.2. The two samples differed in several important respects. There were proportionately more children in the clinical sample who used Destructive, Yell, Whine, Humiliate, Command Negative, and Cry. Given that there was a coercive response, there was a slightly higher likelihood of an aversive antecedent for the clinical sample (.32) than for the normal sample (.25). In effect, a sizable proportion of coercive child behaviors could be thought of as *counterattacks,* i.e., they were *reactions* to noxious intrusions. In effect, for both normal and clinical samples the stage is frequently set for the *possibility* of a NR arrangement. Clearly, then, much of children's aggression is not attack but *counter*attack behavior.

There were also dramatic differences among the responses. For both samples the coercive re-

Table 7.3
Likelihood of Aversive Antecedents for Isolated or Initial Coercive Events

| Sample | $p(A_i\|$Coercive Sequence) for | | | F Values for | | |
	Younger	Older	Mean	Sample	Age	Interaction
Normals	.33	.19	.26			
	(10)	(9)†		2.22	1.94	1.18
Social Aggressors	.35	.33	.34			
	(15)	(15)				

†Numbers in parentheses refer to sample size.

Table 7.4
Likelihood of "Start-Up" by Family Agents

| Dyads | Mean likelihood of $p(-\|+)$ by sample | | | F Values |
	Social Aggressors	Stealers	Normals	
$p(\overset{-}{\text{Mother}}\|\overset{+}{\text{Child}})$	.05	.04	.02	11.00***
$p(\overset{-}{\text{Child}}\|\overset{+}{\text{Mother}})$	.04	.03	.01	8.35***
N	37	36	37	
$p(\overset{-}{\text{Father}}\|\overset{+}{\text{Child}})$	.04	.02	.01	6.91**
$p(\overset{-}{\text{Child}}\|\overset{+}{\text{Father}})$	.02	.02	.00	1.58
N	17	26	26	
$p(\overset{-}{\text{Sibling}}\|\overset{+}{\text{Child}})$	.03	.03	.01	5.97**
$p(\overset{-}{\text{Child}}\|\overset{+}{\text{Sibling}})$	.02	.02	.01	1.67
N	36	35	33	

*$p < .05$
**$p < .01$
***$p < .001$

sponses of Physical Negative, Ignore, Command Negative, and Tease were most likely to have aversive antecedents.

It is conceivable that the OSLC figures for aversive antecedents were distorted by the six-second chunking procedure built into the code.[2] For this reason, a second analysis was conducted employing a "natural" unit. Here the entire uninterrupted sequence of coercive behaviors was tabulated as a chain. Only the antecedents for the chain were analyzed (see Appendix 5.1 for details). Table 7.3 summarizes the likelihood for aversive antecedents for these chains—$p(\bar{A}_i\|$Coercive Sequence). The comparisons were based upon data from 30 families of 30 socially aggressive boys and 20 families of 20 normal boys. In the former, the chains from younger (3.1 to 8.5 years old) and older (8.5 to 13.5 years old) coercive boys provided the data base. The data are very similar to the findings based on six-second units. Note that the differences between samples were of only borderline significance.

Now the question should be turned around. We know that roughly one-third of the child's coercive behavior was evoked by an aversive antecedent. However, what is the likelihood that an $\bar{A}_i$ will be

149

Table 7.5
Aversive Antecedents for Counterattacks in Distressed Families

Aversive Antecedent	$p(\overline{A}_i)$	p(Child initiate $\overline{R}_j \mid \overline{A}_i$)			
		Hit	Tease	Disapproval	Whine
		(.010)†	(.011)	(.061)	(.011)
Command	.085	.000	.000	.028	.011
Disapprove	.055	.000	—	.200*	.032*
Hit	.007	.296*	—	.141	—
Humiliate	.003	—	—	.270*	—
Tease	.006	.060*	.149*	.209	—
Whine	.002	—	.160*	.160*	—
Yell	.004	—	.077*	—	—
Talk‡	.367	.060	.007	.074	.019

†The figures in parentheses are base-rate values for $p(\overline{R}_j)$.

*In the Patterson and Cobb (1973) report, where conditional p values are listed, these $\overline{A}_i$ were identified as controlling stimuli for that target response. The term, controlling, means that the $\overline{A}_i$ was accompanied by a significant increase in the likelihood of the target response.

‡Although Talk is not considered an aversive antecedent, it has been included for comparison purposes.

presented to him? To answer this question, data were examined for samples of Normals, Stealers, and Social Aggressors (see Appendix 6.2 for a description). The data in Table 7.4 were tabulated separately for each dyad. Given that the target child's antecedent had been prosocial (+), what was the likelihood that a family member would crossover and launch an "unprovoked attack?" The figure in row one column one showed that in the Social Aggressor sample 5% of the mother's interaction with the problem child fit into this category.

The data for the clinical sample showed that each family agent was significantly more likely than their normal counterparts to launch such attacks. Mothers were more likely than fathers or siblings to engage in crossover attacks. Note, too, that the problem children were invariably *less likely* than the *parents* to initiate a conflict. When compared to Normals, problem children were two to three times more likely to cross over. This is in keeping with the earlier findings of Raush (1965), who showed that this variable differentiated hyperaggressive from normal boys observed in a residential setting. He found that crossover was five times more likely to occur in the interactions of the clinical sample than in the normal sample.

It seems, then, that a child from clinical samples must learn to cope with noxious intrusions by other family members. If his coping behaviors successfully terminate these intrusions, this would mean that *NR* mechanisms play an important role in *maintaining* coercive child behavior.

The Likelihood of Counterattack

As Bandura (1973) noted, the optimum condition for eliciting an aggressive reaction is simply to do something aversive to the other person. For example, interactions in a residential treatment setting showed very high likelihoods of counterattack (Raush, 1965). His study of disturbed and nondisturbed boys showed that for both samples the likelihood of an unfriendly act following an unfriendly initiation by the other person was about .80. Aversive behaviors elicit aversive reactions.

The likelihood of attack and counterattack is determined by a complex set of variables, including setting, age, and sex of the other person. For example, in their review, Maccoby and Jacklin (1974) noted boys were more likely than girls to retaliate (counterattack).

Several investigators have found an interesting interaction between the type of provocation and the type of counterattack. In a nursery school setting, Hartup (1974) found that if the target child was insulting or derogatory, a large proportion of the younger child's counterattacks were likely to be Hit. With the same provocation, only 22% of the older child's counterattacks were Hit; 78% were reactions in kind.

To study this among family members, Patterson

Table 7.6
Likelihood of Counterattack by Sample and Agents

Dyads	Mean likelihood of counterattack			F Values
	Normals	Social Aggressors	Stealers	
p(Mother|Child)	.15	.23	.16	4.12*
p(Child|Mother)	.09	.27	.16	20.82***
p(Father|Child)	.08	.14	.10	2.33
p(Child|Father)	.08	.18	.13	4.67*
p(Sibling|Child)	.19	.21	.28	2.84
p(Child|Sibling)	.10	.19	.19	5.89**

*$p < .05$
**$p < .01$
***$p < .001$

and Cobb (1973) analyzed the antecedents for the *initiations* of a coercive response. Events were classed as initiations if the child had previously been engaged in 18 seconds or more of prosocial behaviors. For example, given all prosocial and deviant initiations, the base rate for the initiation of Hit was .010 and for Disapproval was .061. The first column of figures in Table 7.5, headed by $p(\overline{A}_i)$, lists the base-rate values for the antecedents for the four most frequent target responses.[3] For example, for all initiations the most likely A_i would be Talk. Only the functional relations thought to be significant were listed in Table 7.5.

Each coercive response was controlled by slightly different networks of aversive antecedents. Given that a family member Disapproved, the problem child's most likely counterattack was to reciprocate in kind. The conditional probability for Disapprove, given Disapprove, was .200. If a family member Teased, the most likely aversive response was to Disapprove (.209) or Tease (.149). Hitting functioned as a means of coping with family members' Tease and Hit. If a family member Hits, the most likely counter was for the problem child to respond in kind (.296). In the 1973 analysis of Normals, the comparable value was .200. In distressed and nondistressed samples alike, Hit evokes Hit.

The likelihood of counterattack was calculated separately for each dyad involving a target child for samples of Normals, Stealers, and Social Aggressors (see Appendix 6.2 for details). The events

were taken from all points within coercive chains. Given that the other person was coercive, what was the likelihood that the target family member would counterattack? As shown in Table 7.6, the likelihood of counterattack varied as a function of sample and dyad. In normal families the figure ranged from .08 to .19, the range in the clinical samples was .10 to .28. In all comparisons the problem children in clinical samples were significantly more likely to counterattack than were normal children.

Utility of NR

The key assumption is that coercive child behavior may serve the important function of terminating aversive intrusions by other family members. Buss (1966a) states that the major reinforcer for attack-instigated aggression is termination of the attack. Do counterattacks by problem children serve this function? Just how effective are these behaviors?

The first analysis of this problem was based on six-second units of data from clinical and nonclinical samples. In what proportion of these sequences was the counterattack followed by a favorable outcome (i.e., the interchange was terminated by a positive and/or neutral outcome)? The findings are summarized in Table 7.7. The first column identifies the number of subjects in each sample who actually engaged in one or more counterattacks. The second column gives the mean proportion of successful outcomes for each response. On

Table 7.7
Favorable Outcomes (Utility) for Counterattacks in Two Samples

Child's Counterattacks	Distressed Sample		Nondistressed Sample	
	Number of subjects with $\bar{A}_i \rightarrow \bar{R}_j$ episodes	Mean $p(C^+|\bar{A}_i \rightarrow \bar{R}_j)$†	Number of subjects with $\bar{A}_i \rightarrow \bar{R}_j$ episodes	Mean $p(C^+|\bar{A}_i \rightarrow \bar{R}_j)$
Command Negative	17	.30	8	.38
Cry	8	.30	—	—
Dependency	7	.36	5	.00
Destructiveness	12	.29	0	.00
Disapprove	33	.57	26	.48
High Rate	15	.19	9	.00
Humiliate	19	.16	7	.00
Ignore	17	.68	8	.43
Negativeness	25	.35	17	.28
Noncomply	32	.43	25	.31
Physical Negative	24	.43	14	.25
Tease	27	.35	17	.41
Whine	23	.41	12	.32
Yell	19	.37	8	.36

†The likelihood of a positive and/or neutral outcome for a counterattack.

Table 7.8
Successful Final Outcomes for Counterattacks

Agent(s)	Normals		Social Aggressors		F values for:		
	Younger	Older	Younger	Older	Group	Age	Interaction
	Likelihood Successful						
All family members							
% C^+	.40	.62	.42	.37	1.71	0.95	2.48*
% $C°$	.23	.22	.22	.31	0.31	0.28	0.59
Total $(C^+ + C°)$	.63	.84	.64	.68			
	Likelihood Negative Reinforcement						
All family members	.16	.13	.21	.22	7.17**	0.08	0.30

*$p < .05$
**$p < .001$

the average, the counterattacks were about 30% effective in producing successful outcomes. The general trend was for a slightly greater likelihood of success for counterattacks when employed in distressed families.

As shown in Table 7.7, the major differences in utility were *among* the coercive responses. Disapproval functioned effectively about half the time, while Humiliate was relatively ineffective. Why is

this? Why do we allow some kinds of counterattacks to work but not others? Do these utilities vary as a function of age and sex of persons in the dyad? These are questions for the next round of studies.

Again, there was a possibility that the six-second chunking used in the code distorted the findings. The utility score could have been confounded because each score summed across outcomes for the different components of a chain such that outcomes early in the sequence are added to those at midpoint, and so on. The next analysis focused only on the final outcomes for chains. The data were based on an analysis of 30 socially aggressive children and target boys from 20 normal families (see Appendix 5.1). The analysis also compared the likelihoods for younger and older subjects as they interacted with other family members. The findings are summarized in Table 7.8. The *final* outcomes for counterattack chains were successful about 40% of the time. This figure did not vary significantly as a function of sample or age.

The next question required that two different pieces of information be combined into a single index. One piece describes the proportion of coercive responses having an aversive antecedent. The second describes the proportion of this subset which had a successful outcome. The index, Negative Reinforcement, combines these two variables. As shown in Table 7.8, there was a significantly larger proportion of coercive behavior maintained by *NR* arrangements in the distressed samples than in the nondistressed samples. For normal children, about 15% of their coercive responses could be said to be maintained by *NR* schedules. For the clinical sample, the comparable figure was about 21%.

The descriptive data support the assumption that *NR* arrangements *do* occur in family interaction. They are particularly likely to occur in a clinical sample. As a general rule, they are surprisingly effective in terminating the noxious intrusions of other family members. As a result, it seems plausible that *NR* may, indeed, play an important role in maintaining coercive behavior. The next question is, do these *NR* arrangements strengthen antecedent $\rightarrow$ response connections?

Experimental Manipulation of NR *in Situ*

The fact that aversive events and *NR* arrangements occur in family interactions does not mean that they actually control behavior. Only experimental manipulations can demonstrate that an event or an arrangement actually exerts significant control. This section reviews the evidence for the contention that altering *NR* contingencies will alter the probabilistic connection between the aversive antecedent ($\overline{A}_i$) and the coercive response ($\overline{R}_j$) or $p(\overline{R}_j|\overline{A}_i)$. It is assumed that *NR* arrangements will increase this likelihood (this is analogous to the earlier discussion of positive reinforcement).

The results from the study by Devine (1971) summarized in Table 7.1 showed that as few as four *NR* pairings significantly strengthened the behavior on which it was made contingent. The effects were significant for both prosocial and deviant behaviors. But to provide a closer fit to this discussion of *NR* it would be necessary to introduce two refinements in the experimental design used by Devine (1971). First, it was an analogue study carried out in an artificial setting; can these results be generalized to the home? The second problem involves the means by which response strength was measured. While the latency and duration measures were germane to the general issue, they are not directly relevant to this discussion. As stated here, a test of the *NR* hypothesis requires a direct measure of the change in the probability of $\overline{R}_j$ given $\overline{A}_i$. For the present, nothing is known about the relation between duration, latency, and $p(\overline{R}_j|\overline{A}_i)$ as measures of response strength.

John Knutson and his colleagues at the University of Iowa have studied pain-elicited aggression with animal subjects. The dependent variable that they employed met the present requirements, and their design provided a powerful test of the relation of *NR* to aggression. The victim was restrained. If the experimental subject was shocked, but the victim was not, there was a very low likelihood of an attack. Typically, the attacks were most likely to occur when both the experimental subject and the victim received inescapable shocks. During five consecutive trials, both animals received a shock; if an attack on the restrained victim occurred, then the shock was terminated; i.e., *NR* occurred. Then, in a subsequent trial, a new victim was introduced; this victim was allowed to move freely about the cage. Given a shock, the probability of attack was significantly higher for the *NR*-trained group. In a second study, the training sessions involved a freely moving victim, and the test condition involved a restrained victim. The effects were replicated. Negative reinforcement arrangements strengthened attack behavior.

The next question is whether such *NR* arrangements serve a similar function in family interaction. Woo (1978) carried out the first such study. After several days of baseline observation data were collected in the home, the mother and child participated in two days of experimental manipulations. During these sessions the mother received telephone calls (from an experimenter). When a call came, she told the child: "I'm going to be busy on the phone now; please don't bother me, okay?" She then talked on the phone while an observer collected data on the likelihood and duration of the child's whining.[4] On each day the pair participated in an ABA reversal design. During the first

Table 7.9
Experimental Tests of NR for Mother-Child Interactions

Subjects	Arrangement	BL$_1$	$p(\overline{R}_j|\overline{A}_i)$ Manipulation	BL$_2$
Woo (1978, p. 19)				
Chris	p(Child Whine|Mother on Telephone)	.05	.33	.48
Marty	p(Child Whine|Mother on Telephone)	.08	.25	.28
Poy	p(Child Whine|Mother on Telephone)	.22	.39	.25
Mean		.12	.32	.34
OSLC Replication				
Autumn	p(Child Complain|Mother Restrain)	.33	.67	.57
Pumpkin	p(Child Provoke|Mother Command)	.13	.30	.04

baseline the mother received two calls, during which time she talked for up to 15 minutes. If the child whined during this time, she waited until the child had stopped whining for 12 seconds and then hung up the phone. If calls that were received during the experimental phase led to whining, then the mother was to hang up the telephone immediately. Over the two days, each child received about 12 NR pairings during the experimental phase. In the Woo study, each of the three subjects showed a dramatic increase over baseline levels in the probability of Whine given the telephone call (see Table 7.9). Note also that the conditional p value for the post-test did *not* return to Baseline$_1$ levels.

The Woo study provided data that was relevant to the study of NR arrangements in family interaction. However, the experimental procedure introduced an aversive event that was atypical for parent-child interaction. The next studies were designed to use events that are commonly found in mother-child interaction. They also studied coercive child behaviors other than whining. Note, however, that all of these studies share in common the "confound" noted by Devine (1971). Within the matrix of social interaction, a NR arrangement is very likely to be accompanied by a positive reinforcer.

Autumn was a 5-year-old boy from a middle-class family (see Appendix 5.1)[5] The baseline data showed that when Autumn was restrained by his mother, he was likely to complain. The conditional probability of Complain, given Restraint, was .33. The corrected base rate for Autumn-Complain was .15. The binomial Z testing for the dif-

ference was 3.72, significant at $p < .01$; $(df = 16)$. The mean duration for his Complain was 6.98 seconds. On each of two days an ABA design was followed; each condition lasted 20 minutes. Following condition A, a period of normal interaction, the mother was instructed to use the procedures she had previously practiced with the experimenter. She was cued to restrain Autumn; when he complained, she was to behave in a prosocial manner. There were approximately 10 of these pairings each day. The data in Table 7.9 summarize the findings. As shown there, the predicted reinforcement effect was obtained (on both days). During the experimental condition, given that the mother restrained, Autumn was increasingly more likely to complain. The mean p value of .67 for the two days during which the manipulations took place was larger than the mean baseline value of .33. The binomial Z comparing these values was 4.24 $(df = 35; p < .001)$. The hypothesis that (negative) reinforcement arrangements may have an immediate effect on functional relationships between responses and controlling events was supported by these findings. As was the case in the Woo (1978) study, the effects persisted into the (20-minute) second baseline period. This difference between the first and second baseline periods was also significant, as shown by the binomial Z value of 1.89 $(df = 13; p < .10)$.

The data for Pumpkin describe a similar experiment for a second mother-child pair. The ABA design was again followed on each of two consecutive days. When Mother gave a Command, and Pumpkin behaved provocatively, the mother either reacted positively or ignored it. The experimental phase was associated with increases in p (Pumpkin-Provoke|Mother-Command).

This brief series of studies showed that *NR* arrangements did increase the likelihood of coercive child behavior. Even though positive reinforcement components may also have been involved, I think that *NR* arrangements were responsible for the bulk of the experimental effect. This assumption requires further testing. The observations made in homes showed that these arrangements occur with sufficient frequency to warrant being taken seriously as a major mechanism relating to deviant child behavior.

Variance Accounted for by NR

It was not expected that *NR* components would contribute *directly* to the problem of accounting for the variance associated with individual differences among subjects. For reasons discussed in Chapter 5, it was not expected that there would be a linear relation between $p(NR)$ and the strength of the coercive response. The analysis in Patterson (1979b) showed that, indeed, there was no correlation between $p(NR)$ and TAB scores. While *NR* increases $p(\overline{R}_j|\overline{A}_i)$, this has little to do directly with overall performance level. As shown in Chapters 8 and 11, the performance level for deviant behavior is determined primarily by the disposition of other family members to provide stimuli which start up conflict *and* stimuli which accelerate conflict once it starts. In effect, individual differences in performance are determined by variations in the *density of the stimuli which control that behavior.* Day-by-day fluctuations in performance are also thought to covary with shifts in the density of controlling stimuli. It is *NR* (and *PR*) arrangements which give these controlling stimuli their power; however, *NR* contributes only indirectly to individual differences in performance.

In social interaction the main direct contribution of *NR* arrangements is to account for the variance associated with differences *among aggressive responses.* The reader might well ask why *NR* should account for variance relating to differences among responses but not for variance relating to differences among subjects or sessions. The general formulation is in keeping with the earlier statement of this matter (see Chapter 5). To understand what implications the probability of reinforcement has for a given response, it is necessary to compare it to the schedules provided for *competing responses.* The base-rate values for responses sum across subjects, thus surmounting the individual differences problem. In the case of a set of responses, the information for the probability of reinforcement for each relative to the other is known and enters directly into the correlation. Does Disapproval get more reinforcement than does Hit? The assumption is that if this is so, it will occur more often. If *NR* is, in fact, the arrangement determining the strength of the response, then there should be a significant correlation between $p(R_j)$ and $p(NR)$ among the coercive responses being compared.

To study the variance associated with differences in response rates, it would be useful to have some prior knowledge about which aggressive responses are primarily controlled by *NR* and which are not. For example, if all 14 coercive responses are controlled by *mixed* schedules of *NR* and *PR* arrangements, then neither arrangement by itself would correlate with $p(\overline{R}_j)$. The analysis by Patterson and Dawes (1975) employed a replicated Guttman Scalogram analysis for observation code variables to identify a transitive progression for the following coercive categories: Disapproval, Noncomply, Negativism, Tease, Physical Negative, Command Negative, and Humiliate. The writers suggested that the underlying dimension shared in common by these seven variables might be that all were controlled primarily by *NR* arrangements. A. Harris and J. Reid (in preparation) replicated this progression for the classroom. Patterson (1979b) then showed that the response hierarchies for these seven coercion variables covaried with the richness of their *NR* schedules. The correlation for one sample was .59 (n.s.) and for the second, .93 ($df = 5$; $p < .05$). Differences in rates among these seven coercive responses varied as a function of their usefulness in terminating aversive intrusions. Those working most effectively (e.g., Disapproval) tended to occur most often.

Escalation

One of the key assumptions in coercion theory is that the analyses of processes comprised of innocuous, garden-variety aversive events will lead to an understanding of physical violence among family members. Wife and child beatings are thought to be the *outcome* of processes that have been set in motion for some time. The progression is thought to move in a transitive fashion from low-amplitude to high-amplitude aggression (e.g., from threaten, yell, throw objects, push, hit, hit with fist, to hit with an object). Each increment in intensity has been reinforced by the submissive reaction of the victim to the prior increase in amplitude. These increases in amplitude were thought to be most likely to occur during extended coercive interchanges. A recent analysis by Loeber (1980) showed that hitting was, indeed, significantly more likely to occur in coercive chains of longer duration. Surrender or compliance by the victim constitutes a *NR*, increasing the likelihood of future high-amplitude attacks. One further assumption is that escalation in families is most likely to occur when the participating members are equally likely to employ pain-control techniques, i.e., they are of equal power. Escalation is extremely difficult to study in field settings. The problem lies in the difficulty of defining the dimension of *intensity* as it relates to social behavior.[6]

One could take a static-trait position and assume that angry people marry angry people, and angry mothers produce aggressive children; i.e., these traits existed prior to the formation of the family. From this position, beatings are simply the logical outcome of a Markov process describing interactions among people with a prior disposition to be aggressive. This might well be true. However, there are published findings describing physical aggression as a concomitant for divorce proceedings among otherwise nonaggressive people. For example, Wallerstein and Kelly (1980) found that in the process of separating during divorce, about one-half of the middle-class couples studied engaged in physical aggression. These people tended *not* to be aggressive either before or following the separation. I believe that this may be an example of a *process* in which relatively nonaggressive people can become physically aggressive. The increases in rates of coercive behavior and in extended coercive chains would place them at increasing risk for escalation. Given that both spouses have a disposition to be aggressive, then the escalation process would undoubtedly be accelerated.

What is novel about this formulation is that people who were initially *non*aggressive can find themselves trapped by the escalation process. For example, I have worked with several teachers who were overwhelmed with guilt because they had lost their tempers and struck children in the classroom. Many of the parents referring their antisocial children to OSLC are gentle, nonaggressive people. They perceive both themselves and their child as being under the influence of forces beyond their control. Some parents express extreme guilt because of the beatings they have given their children. A study of children referred to OSLC showed that about one-third of the parents of antisocial boys have physically abused their children (Reid et al., 1979). Was this the outcome of a gradual progression in which discipline was increasingly supplemented by physical assault? By definition, mothers who beat their children are aggressive, but many of them will tell you that they have never physically assaulted another person.

How is it they end up attacking their own children? How do middle-class, nonaggressive couples come to use physical violence? These and related questions serve as the focus for the following discussion.

Violence in the Home

In our culture violence has been given a central role as a problem-solving technique. However, it is generally thought that violence is not a technique that is used in the home except by a few extremely aggressive persons (Forster, 1966). The age of innocence concerning conditions in the American home is rapidly coming to an end. The extensive survey studies carried out by M. Straus and his colleagues suggest that violence in the home is as likely to occur as love (Steinmetz & Straus, 1974; Straus, Gelles, & Steinmetz, 1979). As pointed out by Steinmetz and Straus (1974), "Most parents feel not only that it is okay to hit. In the case of children, it is more than just okay. Most American parents see it as an obligation . . . and this carries over to the relationship between husbands and wives" (p. 3). They also cite a study by Stark and McEvoy (1970) which showed that about one parent in four takes the explicit view that there are circumstances in which it is acceptable for one spouse to hit another. Straus goes on to review other studies which lend support to his claim that *a marriage license is a hitting license*. According to his studies, one couple in ten claim that hitting is a common experience. For example, he cites the in-depth interview study of 80 families by Gelles (1973). About 60% of the families described at least one instance in which physical force was used between spouses. Margolin (1979) cites studies asserting that 16% of American couples engage in physical violence at least once a year; for 10% of the couples the interchanges were extremely violent. It is, therefore, not surprising to find that among lower class applicants for divorce 40% mention physical abuse (Levinger, 1966). The comparable figure among middle-class participants was 22%. Marital violence is not selective; it occurs in all classes.

It is a commonly shared assumption among investigators in this area that fighting between spouses often gets out of control. Occasionally beatings escalate to homicides. In keeping with this assumption, there are a dramatic number of homicides among family members. Field and Field (1973) showed that during 1965, killings within the family represented 31% of all murders. In one-half of these instances one spouse was the victim and the other spouse was the murderer. The violent character of spouse fighting is well known to the police, whose task it is to intervene in these domestic quarrels. Twenty-two percent of police deaths and 40% of their wounds result from attempts to intercede (Singer, 1971).

Familial violence is, of course, not limited to altercations between spouses. Helfer and Kempe (1968) brought the battered child to national attention. In the national survey involving 1,000 families by Gelles (1977), 58% of parents reported slapping or spanking their child during the past year. Thirteen percent reported hitting the child with an object; 3% attacked the child by kicking, biting, or pushing. It might be interjected here that many of these battered children are themselves extremely coercive. Several observation studies of abused children revealed them to have significantly higher rates of coercive behaviors than normal children (Burgess, 1978; Reid, Taplin, & Lorber, 1981). These findings suggest the possibility that the child may *contribute* to family processes in which he or she is beaten.

Straus et al. (1979) makes the point that violence is an *accepted* part of family life in this culture. Eighty to ninety percent of parents said that sometimes physical violence involving the child may be necessary. Most parents do not allow siblings to fight it out and interfere regularly in sibling quarrels. However, some of the parents referred to OSLC report that they sometimes allow a good fight to run its course so that the children can "get it out of their systems." In one survey study, modern practitioners of the catharsis theory found that 62% of high school seniors had struck a sibling during the past year (Straus et al., 1979). Thirty-five percent had also hit someone outside the family. It is interesting to note that the official records indicate that most violent crimes against persons are committed by older teenagers. The follow-up study by Wolfgang (1977) showed that violent delinquents were those with a prior history of many police offenses. The analyses in Chapter 11 suggest that these delinquents are likely to have been children who received little parental monitoring and ineffective punishment for antisocial behavior. I think that much of society's problem with violence is due to disruptions in the processes of family management.

Escalation Process

As used here, the term escalation refers to changes in intensity over time. When the coercive interchanges between members of a dyad move from lower to greater intensity, the increments are likely to be small. First, one person increases the intensity of his or her attack, and the other eventually reciprocates by responding at an equally high

intensity. These synchronous increases in intensity have been well documented in the laboratory studies reviewed by Dengerink (1976). Over a period of weeks or months, the level at which coercive interchanges begin increases in intensity, and/or it very quickly moves to a higher level during ensuing interchanges. In a given episode resulting in hitting, the dyad may move quickly through several increases. If one member is a well-trained aggressor, he may move so quickly through a sequence that the victim is hardly aware that the confrontation has begun.

Probably the best source of descriptive material for such interchanges is to be found in the clinical study by H. Toch, *Violent Men* (1969). He interviewed policemen who had a history of frequent violent assaults and prison inmates who were incarcerated because of their violent behavior. The policemen described a process that began when the police officer perceived the suspect as having a "negative attitude." The policeman then reacted to this with a blunt demand for immediate compliance. From the perspective of the suspect, the officer's tone of voice and physical gestures may be interpreted as a threat, leading the suspect, in turn, to overt noncompliance. Thus, the assault-prone officer may produce noncompliance in an otherwise compliant suspect. The suspect's noncompliance is a *real* stimulus, to which the officer may justifiably respond by using physical force, e.g., push the suspect over the hood of the car. This further exacerbates the situation, leading to a scuffle, clubbing, or shooting. Similar progressions characterized both officers and inmates with records of assault.

In either case, the individual in our culture has learned that when things get out of control, a rapid escalation in violence may provide a solution to the situation. In this manner, over time and encounters, *NR* shapes the individual to become increasingly violent. It may also be the case that an increasing spectrum of cues become signals for threatening situations. Both Toch (1969) and Berkowitz (1978) emphasize that for violent people it is their *perception* of a situation as being threatening that is most often the antecedent for an assault.

Berkowitz (1978) interviewed 65 white males with long histories of violence. The great majority (83%) had prior convictions for crimes; two-thirds of these convictions were for violent behavior. The attacks were most likely to occur on weekends, at night, and 85% were related to drinking. The incident was most likely to start with an argument or a perceived insult by another person. When provoked, the goal for most in-

Figure 7.3
Two Components of Escalation

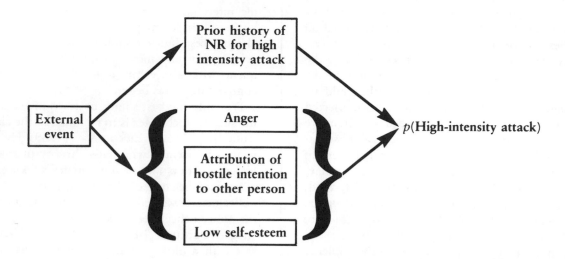

mates was to hurt the other person. This is in keeping with the findings from laboratory studies of victim pain reactions as a positive reinforcer for the angry, extremely antisocial person (see Chapter 5).

In both of these clinical studies, the first stage was generated by an insult or an argument. If this is the first step in a sequence, then it may be possible to disrupt the ensuing steps by defusing the situation. That possibility was investigated by Sykes and Brent (1978). In a situation where an officer's request was met by the suspect's noncompliance, the officers were trained to simply repeat the request in a civil manner. Their field study showed that this simple expedient increased the likelihood of compliance and reduced violence.

The clinical studies by Berkowitz and Toch suggest that at some point early in the interchange, the violent person is more likely to attribute a malevolent intent to the behavior of the other person. This attribution is accompanied by autonomic arousal and an otherwise simple argument becomes a potential battleground. These people all *believed that they were provoked.* As shown in Figure 7.3, the variables of negative attribution and anger seem to be likely candidates as determinants or concomitants of assaults. There is, then, a need to investigate these two variables empirically. But how is it one can obtain measures of anger and attribution *in situ*? My colleague, J.B. Reid, is exploring the possibility of using participants' reports of critical incidents occurring during the pri-

or 24 hours, i.e., a variant of Parent Daily Report. During the probe, the informant is asked for information about setting, antecedents, and outcomes. This approach could easily be expanded to include information about anger and attribution.

Straus (1973) has gone on to provide what he believes is a quantifiable model for describing escalating family processes. He particularly emphasizes positive-feedback loops supporting the upward spiral in violence. He also emphasizes violence as a systems by-product. In one analysis, families were classified according to the power of the wife and the husband. This score was based on information about who made decisions such as which car to buy, how to spend family income, where to vacation, which house to buy, how the children were disciplined and whether or not the wife worked. In families where the wife was more powerful than the husband, the mean violence directed by wives to husbands was highest. The wives' violence score was lowest in families where the husbands' power was highest. Husbands, on the other hand, tended to be more violent to their wives under either extreme of power differential; i.e., either the wife or husband was much more powerful than the spouse.

Some Formulations about Escalation

The foregoing clinical studies and our own experience with over 200 treated cases emphasizes two interrelated components for the escalation process. It is assumed that the first increase in intensity comes about during an extended aversive interchange. This is the first component. I think these extended chains may also be accompanied by increasing anger and hostile attribution. The second component concerns the relation between NR and intensity changes. Given a successful outcome for an increase in amplitude, NR increases the likelihood of a high-intensity response with future presentations of that same stimulus.

In a normal family, if the parent escalates and spanks the child, the child is likely to submit. Neither the parent nor the child are likely to escalate during this trial or during the one which follows. However, if the parent of the socially aggressive child tries to spank, he or she is likely to be met with anything *but* submission. The child may respond in a synchronous fashion by hitting back. The reaction may be a temper tantrum, loud yelling, or whatever, but it is very likely that the child will respond in some high-amplitude coercive fashion. The formulation by Straus (1973) about power differentials can also be applied to this situation. One can certainly think of the socially aggressive child as being "powerful." I think the powerful person is more likely to counteraggress; he or she is also more likely to provide a synchronous increase in amplitude. A pilot analysis by J. Reid of TAB scores for mother and child supported this hypothesis. In a related study, Reid demonstrated that in Normal and Stealer samples 80% to 90% of the mothers tended to have higher TAB scores than did their target children! However, a larger proportion of dyads in the Social Aggressor sample showed the child to be higher than the mothers. This asymmetry, noted by Reid, may be extremely important because a more recent study by Loeber and Reid (in preparation) showed that this variable related to the child's later becoming an *assaultive adolescent*. In that retrospective study, those families studied at OSLC whose children later showed up in police files as assaultive, Stealers, or "clean" were examined for variables which might differentiate among them. The pattern for the 12-year-old who was later identified as assaultive was to have the highest TAB score among family members. Relative to other family members, these children occupy a powerful role.

A recent study by Reid, Patterson, and Loeber (1981) showed that families in which the members perform coercive behavior at high rates (TAB scores) are more at risk for hitting. The hypothesis was that the frequency of coercion covaries with intensity. The analysis showed correlations in the range of .4 to .7 between TAB and Hitting scores. The correlations were consistent across family members and samples. This suggests that interactions which are frequently coercive place the dyad at greater risk for NR based increases in amplitude. The question is how does this relation between frequency and intensity come about?

The beaten wife or child has probably been a participant in prior escalating interchanges. Both the wife and child have probably increased the amplitude of their attacks and counterattacks prior to the first beating. The first beating was one additional step in a process which had been going on for some time.[7] If both members of a dyad are disposed to react in an irritable fashion (see Chapter 8), then the dyad is at greater risk for escalation. Given a system where escalation is an accepted means for problem solving, then physical violence is a predictable by-product. Incidentally, our recent work in treating child abusive families convinces me that there may be *several* progressions leading to violence in families, in addition to the escalation model. There seem to be some families in which the child and wife use very little coercion but *still* are beaten by the father.

It is also assumed that once a high-amplitude response is well established in the repertoire, it may be evoked under an increasing range of situations; i.e., the individual is likely to "explode" at school, as well as at home. I would expect that some of the violent inmates and policemen studied by Toch and Berkowitz also beat their wives and children. Why do some individuals develop a general disposition to quickly escalate to violence in many situations while others are violent in only one or two settings? The studies reviewed in Chapter 4 established the correlation between anger, arousal, negative attribution, and the likelihood of attack. What is now required are studies demonstrating that these variables relate to high-amplitude attacks and the disposition to generalize across many settings.

The Toch-Berkowitz formulation also stresses the contribution of low self-esteem to this process. From their viewpoint, it is the person with low self-esteem that is most likely to be caught up in the anger/negative-attribution cycle. This seems like a sensible idea that is difficult, but not impossible, to test. It is included here because it fits what many of the OSLC families have described.

While speculating about ideas that have (as yet) little empirical support, there is one further note that may be of use. Is it possible that a short fuse, or anger related arousal itself, are subject to reinforcement? Attack reactions that are accompanied by high levels of arousal are probably more likely to be successful. The recent work in biofeedback provides an interesting method for testing this possibility. If this formulation is true, then the arousal

Figure 7.4
Escalations in Intensity During Extended Chains

(adapted from Patterson, 1980, pp. 31-33)

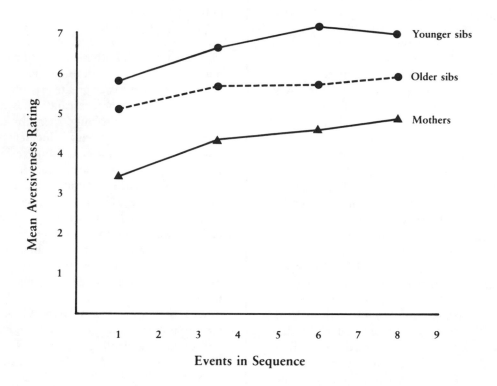

itself may have been shaped by the same contingencies which shape the assaultive responses. Anger may then be a concomitant rather than a determinant for assault. Are low boiling points and assaults shaped by similar *NR* contingencies?

Trained Fighters Escalate More Quickly

The early researchers who studied animal aggression in laboratory settings had commented on how rapidly trained fighting mice escalated in intensity (Lagerspetz, 1964). Ulrich, Johnston, Richardson, and Wolff (1963) also made this observation in their studies of pain-elicited aggression (*PEA*). If both the aggressor and the victim had been previously trained, then the fighting quickly escalated to high-intensity attacks. The reaction of the victim may also contribute to the escalation process. The reviews by Knutson (1973) and by Cairns and Scholz (1973) showed that the intensity of victim reaction to the attack correlated with the likelihood of escalation to yet higher intensities during future attacks. At the other extreme, when the victim was nonreactive or

drugged, the attacks were not likely to occur in *PEA* procedures.

These studies are of great interest because they relate to the irritability hypothesis described in Chapter 8. As shown there, it is the general disposition of both members to react in an irritable fashion that determines the child's performance level. I think that this disposition *also* relates to escalation. Cairns and Nakelski (1971) carried out a classic series of studies which relate to this issue. The first study established that isolated mice were more vigorous in their explorations when later introduced to cage mates in their home cage. The vigor of their greeting was reciprocated by equally intense reactions for the normally-reared mice. These vigorous interchanges were associated with frequent escalations to physical violence. Cairns reasoned that the likelihood of such escalation from vigorous greeting to fighting would be greatest if both members had previously been isolated, less if one member had been isolated, and least of all if neither had been. For the three groups, the data showed the incidence of fighting to be .33,

Table 7.10
Escalation in Intensity of Coercive Sequences as a Function of Prior Pay Off

Likelihood that reaction of mother to prior chain extension was:

Subject	Base-rate p third event longer than second event	Nonaversive	Mother "backed off" from aversive to nonaversive	Mother "backed off" from high to lower aversive	Mother remained the same aversive	Mother increased aversive	Reinforcement effect
Summer	.49 (.43)†	.51	.17	.05	.03	.24	.55‡
Autumn	.30 (.24)	.74	.22	.00	.04	.00	.50

†Corrected base rate.

‡Probability that the child's coercive Event 3 was longer than the child's Event 2, given that Mother "backed off."

.18, and .00 respectively. It may be that the isolated mice ignore cues from the other mice which would normally dampen an escalation process. They may also fail to provide such cues. I'm not sure that "vigor" is directly analogous to "irritability," but the Cairns studies describe a process which quickly gets out of control that bears more than a metaphorical relation to escalation in families.

In the context of family interaction, Patterson (1980a) hypothesized that the problem child was a more highly trained aggressor than the mother. If this is the case, one would expect problem children to escalate the intensity of their coercive behaviors more quickly than mothers. Fifty-nine extended coercive chains consisting of four or more events in sequence served as the data base (Patterson, 1980a). Mothers were involved in two-thirds of these chains. The aversiveness for each component was rated in each extended chain. The mean ratings for younger and older siblings and mothers as they tried to cope with the problem child are shown in Figure 7.4.

The initial reaction of the problem child (not shown in Figure 7.4) was to immediately escalate to almost maximum intensity (between 7 and 8) and remain there. The writer assumes such rapid escalation is characteristic of well-trained aggressors in general and problem children in particular. The rapid escalation of the younger and older siblings is due to the relatively sophisticated training to which they have been subjected. The ANOVA for repeated measures showed an F value of 11.17 ($p < .001$) for groups and an F value of 5.13 ($p < .003$) for trials. The question that is yet to be answered is why did the mothers escalate so slowly?

Experimental Tests of NR and Escalation

The key assumption is that NR arrangements can produce across-trial increases in the intensity of attack behavior. Thus far, there are only two single-subject studies which directly test this hypothesis. For these studies, it was assumed that a NR arrangement would increase the likelihood that the child's next coercive event in the sequence would be of higher intensity or of longer duration.[8] The duration of the coercive response served as the major dependent variable (increases in rated intensity for an event were a less frequent form of escalation in intensity).

Four to six hours of baseline data were scored for two preschool children, Autumn and Summer. The protocols were scored twice. First, intensity ratings were assigned to each coercive event in the interactions of these preschoolers with their mothers. The intensity ratings were based on the mean ratings of the code categories provided by mothers of normal children (Jones, Reid, & Patterson, 1975). Then, each coercive chain for the child was scored for duration and/or intensity changes by six-second units. If the child escalated in intensity during the second coercive event in a sequence, what was the impact on the mother? The data in Table 7.10 describe the outcomes for the various stages of the interchange. First it is necessary to know what the base-rate likelihood would be that the third coercive event would be longer than the second. In general, how likely were the children to escalate in intensity? The p values were .43 for Summer and .24 for Autumn. The mother's most likely reaction to such increases was to remain nonaversive (.51 for Summer's mother and .74 for Autumn's).

Given that the mother had been abrasive and the child increased the duration of his counterattack, how likely was it that the mother would back off? If the mother backed off, the child, in effect, had "won." If negative reinforcement functions as it should, then winning should be associated with an increased likelihood that ensuing events could be of greater intensity. This next event is number three in the sequence. As can be seen in the last column in Table 7.10, for Autumn the conditional probability was .50; this compared favorably to the corrected base rate of .24.

At a microsocial level, the effect of the NR arrangement was to increase the likelihood that the next trial would be of greater intensity. Escalation not only "worked" on a short-term basis, but, in addition, it altered the p values for ensuing events. Note, however, the long-term impact of "escalation → win" was not strongly reflected in the data for Summer. The conditional p value was only .55, as compared to the corrected base rate of .43.

Two single case studies do not constitute a confirmation of the hypothesis, especially when one of them (Summer) gave only marginal support. As they stand, the analyses illustrate the fact that family interaction data *can* be used to test such hypotheses. A heavy reliance upon the use of duration as a dependent measure for intensity change does not seem satisfactory until studies demonstrate that duration changes are equivalent to intensity changes. The new OSLC coding system provides measures of changes in intensity. This improved technology should make it possible to construct a more conclusive test of the NR escalation hypothesis.

What are some of the parameters which increase the likelihood of escalation? The best source of data and ideas on this topic are to be found in the programmatic work by Cairns and his colleagues (Cairns, 1979a,b). One of the parameters which they have identified was discussed earlier. They found that mice being reared in isolation were more vigorous in their explorations of new cage mates and also reacted more vigorously to their explorations. He also cites the study by Hall (1973) which demonstrated that it is possible to manipulate the likelihood that one member of the dyad will use high-amplitude aggression. This, in turn, alters the likelihood for the other member. Dyad interchanges can be manipulated by preprogramming the behavior of one member—a simple idea, but a powerful means for exploring the escalation hypothesis. In the Hall (1973) study, one child was exposed to a film portraying high-amplitude aggression. When he later joined another child to play with an inflated Bobo doll, the pair quickly escalated the amplitude of their attacks on the doll. One can turn this idea around as Cairns had done with mice and immobilize the other member of a dyad in a situation which might otherwise elicit attacks. Given a nonreactive victim, there was not only no escalation, there were fewer attacks. This same effect was obtained in the studies by J. Knutson described earlier.

What are the other variables which might preprogram one member of a dyad in such a way as to alter the likelihood of escalation? Medication for the mother or child might produce a decrease in the risk of escalation, but it is, at best, a short-term solution. In the long run, the family would be better served by procedures which would permanently change the system. For example, the observation study by Minton, Kagan, and Levine (1971) showed that mothers were most likely to escalate the amplitude of their punishment, given that the first punishment was ineffective. This makes sense; if the first punishment doesn't work, they try harder! This suggests that when the child engages in punishment acceleration, the parent may escalate in amplitude. In fact, a study of abused children showed that they were more likely to accelerate when punished than were other antisocial children or normals. It also suggests that training mothers to use a punishment (such as time out) that *works* the *first time* will reduce the likelihood of escalation.

Implications

When the victim complies, the attack is terminated. The price for submission is that there is an increase in the likelihood of future attacks. If, however, the victim counterattacks, then the interchange may escalate in intensity. What is one to do? The data from laboratory studies suggest if one person *lowers* the rate of attacks, then the other person is likely to follow suit (Dengerink, 1976). Lindskold (1978) reviews the evidence suggesting that in game-theory settings, conciliatory efforts and declaration of cooperative intent reduces conflict. However, findings reviewed in this chapter suggest that while backing down or submission on the part of one person reduces conflict over the *short* term, it also *increases* the likelihood of *future attacks*. If backing down is followed by an increase in amplitude, then the future may well bring more high-amplitude attacks. A permissive, accepting stance by the victim does not work; neither does nattering or half-hearted counterattacks.

If the coercive process is well under way, there are several things that must be done. First, the situations producing the conflict should be changed. If the exchanges are between equals, as perhaps in marital conflicts, then the differences must be negotiated, as detailed in the social learning approaches to marital conflict, e.g., Jacobson and Margolin (1979). In the case of parents and children, much of the conflict may be about ambiguities in the definitions of what is and what is not acceptable behavior. For them, it may be necessary to begin by clearly spelling out the rules. However, given an antisocial child, it is more the case that he or she does not accept the fact that the parent has *the right* to control the child's behavior. If the child dominates the situation, then *NR* arrangements are given full play.

Second, the parents must learn to stay out of coercive interchanges, to ignore them as much as possible. When they do get involved, they must use (nonviolent) punishment, and they must win each time they do so. As outlined in Chapter 6, the punishment "should" be nonviolent in nature, e.g., time out, work details, or loss of privileges. The point is that high-rate, intense aggression is *not amenable* to warm, accepting treatment. As the studies in Chapter 11 demonstrate, coercive child behavior does not change as a result of extinction arrangements (withdrawing social attention), nor is it reduced by successful efforts to shape prosocial behaviors. *Extremely antisocial behavior must be punished to be changed.* The alternative is to live in a family system in which *NR* plays a dominant role in determining the quality of interaction among family members.

The implication is that for families of antisocial children *fighting is bad.* For them, fighting is a process which often gets out of control. It becomes a system run by *NR* arrangements rather than by the participants. This position on fighting is in marked contrast to the current emphasis on "letting it all hang out." Prestigious publications, such as Bach and Wyden (1968) emphasize fighting as a necessity for a couple's survival; e.g., couples who fight together are couples who stay together, provided that they know how to fight properly. It may be that there are some deeply inhibited people who cannot say that they need some facet of their relationship changed. Perhaps fighting is a means for such a person to change a situation in which he or she is miserable. However, even there, one wonders at how often fighting leads to physical violence. Out of 47 million married couples, 3.3 million wives and .25 million husbands experience severe beatings from their spouses (Margolin, 1979). These are appalling statistics; it means that married couples constitute a population at risk for violence. Straus (1978) and his colleagues present equally impressive statistics for the occurrence of violence in families. He, too, shares a concern

about the wisdom of encouraging couples to fight as a means of changing relationships. I think that we should teach families how to *control* conflicts and at the same time teach them humane ways of changing each other's behavior.

At an even more speculative level, I would like to consider the role of *NR* as it relates to guilt induction, and socialization. There is one pattern which I have observed in middle- and upper-middle-class homes. They use a category of aversives not listed in the OSLC code—guilt. These guilt inductions are swiftly done and are so subtle that often they can only be tracked by the family members themselves. For example, an implicit assumption is that if Family Member A performed more perfectly, then Family Member B could relinquish responsibility for making Family Member A feel guilty. When this is accomplished with a smile or a joke, the visitor is hardly aware that it has taken place. Aversives of this kind must be extremely difficult for a child to learn to cope with. I think that they may relate to cerain neurotic patterns. In any case, guilt induction would be a fascinating variant of *NR* to study. What does the child learn to do in order to terminate that kind of discomfort?

One of the things which has always intrigued me is the apparent "sameness" of people after they pass through adolescence. Over long periods of time their clothing changes, hair color changes, and they have new job titles. However, their social behaviors remain surprisingly constant. The long-term follow-up studies of adults seem to corroborate this impression. I think that as adults we only change in reaction to massive intrusions, usually crises of some kind. However, even here some persons react to crises by escape and avoidance rather than by learning new skills. By running away these people fail to learn new skills and new perspectives. *NR* strengthens the avoidance behavior of those who run away. It can also strengthen the development of new coping skills for those who stay to confront the situation. It is our clinical impression that many of the families of antisocial children use escape-avoidance techniques: "If it's unpleasant, stay away from it; pretend it doesn't exist, and it will go away." The alternative is to solve the problem and come up with a means of reducing the likelihood of future crises of the same kind. But problem solving and looking toward the future are perspectives which seem difficult for these distressed families to assimilate. Why is this?

I believe that, in general, the role of *NR* (and punishment) has been underestimated in most modern social learning theories. For example, it is possible that children's prosocial behaviors are acquired as much as a means of avoiding/escaping parental scolding than as a result of positive reinforcement for success. Field studies of the acquisition of prosocial behaviors may very well demonstrate that NR plays an equal role in socialization with positive reinforcement. My own impression is that adults provide rich sources of modelling and positive reinforcement for infants and preschool children but that, by school age, positive reinforcement schedules become very lean. That is not to say they are insufficient; that remains to be determined. Until these much needed studies begin, I think we should stay open to the possibility that, for the socialization of older children, pain-control techniques play a role equal in importance to positive reinforcement.

Acknowledgment

The writer gratefully acknowledges the careful critique of this chapter by John Knutson. His incisive comments led to numerous changes in the earlier version. As it now stands, there remain some areas in which John would accuse me of being "soft"; but this was as close as I could come to his hard-headed, Iowa position.

Footnotes

1. Hineline (1977) discusses some of the reasons for choosing this term rather than using one drawn from the more familiar escape/avoidance paradigm. The Skinnerian psychologists have a general tendency to define terms in such a way as to clearly differentiate themselves from investigators working within alternative frameworks. In the long run, these distinctions may not be useful. For example, the perspective taken by Hineline and others is to focus on the impact of NR on the response as an operant. The dependent variable is the rate of responding. This de-emphasis on the S-R aspect of avoidance learning differentiates the operant from the Pavlovian approach. As stated earlier, the present writer believes that, in the long run, we must understand the details of the process by which stimuli acquire control over responses. For this purpose, $p(R_j|A_i)$ seems to be a more appropriate dependent variable.

2. In the first study, the analyses were based on six-second units; i.e., the code system sampled an event and a reaction to the event every six seconds. The effect of this decision was to split some continuous events, such as Cry, into six-second episodes. This decision undoubtedly distorts some functional relations. In Table 7.2, some events tabulated (such as $\overline{A}_i$ occurring during an extended coercive chain) would be thought of as antecedents for the next component in a coercive chain. It is not known if an $\overline{A}_i$ occurring prior to the first coercive event in a sequence can be thought of as being similar to an $\overline{A}_i$ that is an antecedent for an event occurring midway in the chain.

One way of clarifying this problem would be to analyze only those $\overline{A}_i$ occurring prior to the first coercive event in a sequence. Data were prepared in such a format for the Patterson and Cobb (1973) study. These data were tabulated to generate the probability of $\overline{A}_i|$Coercive Initiation. The probability value for the distressed sample was .38 and for the nondistressed sample was .28 (Patterson, 1976). Those values were based on populations of events; the findings summarized in Table 7.2 were based on samples of subjects.

3. Note the conditional probability for counterattack is $p(\overline{R}_j|\overline{A}_i)$. This, in turn, is functionally related to the likelihood of an aversive A_i, given that a coercive response has occurred—$p(\overline{A}_i|\overline{R}_j)$. To derive the latter from the former, all that is required is knowledge of $p(\overline{A}_i)$ and $p(\overline{R}_j)$. For example, regarding the data in Table 7.5, application of Bayes' theorem would show .20 of the antecedents for the child's Hit were someone else's Hit (Phillips, 1973). In effect, knowledge of his particular antecedent accounts for a good deal of what it is we need to understand about the problem child's hitting. (See Chapters 8 and 9 for a more extensive discussion.)

4. During baseline phases, if the child did whine, the mother was instructed to wait until he stopped for 12 seconds and then hang up. In so doing, Woo avoided the danger of strengthening Whine but exposed himself to the alternate problem of strengthening a competing behavior. In retrospect, it would have been better to commit the error leading to the most conservative interpretation of the data; e.g., have the mother hang up the phone if the child whined at baseline.

5. The nature of these studies was explained to the mother, including the fact that she could be asked to do something that would for a short time make her child more obnoxious. At the completion of the studies, a careful debriefing was carried out, including a discussion of the data itself if the parents were interested.

Many parents volunteered for these studies, less for the considerable amounts of money involved than for the possibility of receiving treatment. Five of the six families in the extended baseline series went on to receive treatment at OSLC. Interestingly enough, the therapists often remarked upon how quickly these families responded to intervention. There was a good deal of speculation about whether being a subject in these sample experiments would be an effective preparatory procedure; i.e., it teaches the parent that her behavior has an immediate and powerful impact.

6. There are two options to the investigator choosing to work with intensity changes. On the one hand, he can ask victims or participants to rate the intensity of these events. This is the simpler approach and the one adopted in these preliminary analyses (see Chapter 4). A second and more difficult approach is training the observers to scale events for their intensity. J. Knutson (personal communication) carried out pilot studies in 1979 demonstrating the feasibility of this approach. The new code being developed at OSLC will also attempt to measure intensity.

7. There must, of course, be several paths by which an individual moves to high-amplitude aggression. One of the more interesting alternatives

has been described by Megargee (1967) in his studies of "overcontrolled aggression." He believes that for some violent people the antecedent is not a gradual escalation in amplitude; rather, it is a process of rumination and isolation. This produces a disruption of inhibitions against killing, i.e., a cognitive rather than dyadic escalation process.

8. In the present discussion, an intensity increase referred to *either* the amplitude of the event itself (volume of yelling, intensity of the blow, or increase in general aversiveness), or it consisted of extending the duration of the event; e.g., 30 seconds of crying is considered a more intense reaction than 10 seconds of crying. A response followed by the termination of a long chain should be strengthened more (due to NR) than a response followed by the termination of shorter chains. Similarly, termination of a high-intensity $\overline{A}_i$ should be a more effective NR arrangement than termination of a low intensity $\overline{A}_i$.

Perspective on Chapter 7

by Dr. John F. Knutson

In analyses of both human and nonhuman behavior, a pattern of increasingly intense interactions characterizing extended aversive exchanges is commonly reported. Described as escalation by several authors, it seems crucial for any theory of aggressive behavior to provide an explanation for this pattern. The present chapter develops the thesis that negative reinforcement provides a suitable account of the escalation that occurs during extended aversive dyadic exchanges, and as the chapter documents, there are many reasons that make a negative reinforcement analysis of escalation very appealing. However, from my perspective, negative reinforcement provides an incomplete analysis of escalation.

One of my primary concerns regarding the viability of a negative reinforcement analysis of escalated coercive exchanges is that whenever a reciprocated coercive exchange occurs, negative reinforcement *has* to occur. That is, when one member of a dyad provides an aversive event to the other member of a dyad, and the second member reciprocates with an aversive, as soon as the exchange terminates or shifts to nonaversive interac-

tions the conditions for negative reinforcement exist for both members of the dyad. Since escalated and nonescalated aggressive exchanges do not continue indefinitely, both members of the coercive dyad are exposed to negative reinforcement regardless of whether escalation occurs. In nonreciprocated coercive exchanges, only one member of a dyad would be negatively reinforced (the victim) and the other member might be positively reinforced. Given an arrangement in which some negative reinforcement is always occurring in coercive exchanges, to invoke negative reinforcement as a causal factor in escalation it is necessary to show that there is some differential effect of negative reinforcement on some persons (escalators) or on some coercive responses. The assessment of different utility functions for the various counterattacks described in this chapter is consistent with the possibility that some counterattacks (reciprocal responses) have greater utility than others, and that they could be differentially reinforceable and differentially affected in escalated exchanges. However, one of the complexities that concerns me is the implicit assumption in the utility analysis that social stimuli are relatively stable or transsituationally consistent with respect to their positive or negative valence. Since basic laboratory research with nonhuman subjects documents that stimuli are not transsituationally effective as reinforcers or punishers, it is my position that social stimuli are also not likely to be transsituationally equally reinforcing or equally aversive. Thus, it seems that the relationship between negative reinforcement and the escalation hypothesis will need further research regarding the utility functions of particular reciprocated attacks given specific antecedents. Obviously, such analyses will require enormous amounts of data to assess sequential patterns in altered conditional probabilities. I believe such data will have both theoretical and practical significance as intervention strategies and further research on aggression are considered.

My second concern regarding the present negative reinforcement analysis of escalation is that there is the implication that it can account for the development of escalated patterns when it is actually a model that accounts for the maintenance of escalated behavior. To provide a complete analysis of escalation, the negative reinforcement model should be expanded to consider factors that cause the emergence of escalated exchanges that are then negatively reinforced. One area of research that might be conducted is an assessment of the number of behavioral units (reciprocated dyadic exchanges) that must occur before a dyad displays an escalated pattern. I also believe that there needs to be some consideration of individual differences in reactivity to social exchanges. That is, it seems plausible that the number of presentations of social aversives required to push a deviant child over the threshold for engaging in more intense exchanges would be less than the number of aversives required for a nondeviant child. While negative reinforcement can account for an escalated pattern on succeeding interactions, it suggests a trial and error or random process account of escalation on initial interactions. I would also like to see a consideration of the possibility that some individuals are more reactive to the negative aspects of social exchanges, and therefore are more likely to be negatively reinforced by shifts to nonaversive interactions or the termination of exchanges. Work in my laboratory with nonhuman subjects suggests that the density of noxious stimulation in a finite period preceding an aggressive sequence is a factor that relates to evoking an escalated response. Thus, an analysis of the length of a dyadic exchange (time or number of behaviors) and some weighted mean or weighted moving average of the aversiveness of preceding antecedents might be included within a negative reinforcement model of escalation.

One of my primary concerns about the negative reinforcement analysis of escalation is the position that negative reinforcement of coercive behaviors contributes to intraindividual differences among responses to stimuli but is not a major factor in individual differences in the likelihood of responding with escalated coercive behaviors. I agree that negative reinforcement can contribute to intraindividual differences in responses to stimuli; however, the contribution of negative reinforcement to individual differences in coercive patterns is also important. Research in my laboratory (again with nonhuman subjects) has demonstrated that negative reinforcement can result in differences among groups in aggressive responding under standardized aggression test settings. It seems to me that the analysis presented in this chapter could be expanded to include negative reinforcement of escalation contributing to differences between deviant and nondeviant groups. Since Patterson and his colleagues have demonstrated that the ambient level of noxious exchanges is greater in socially aggressive families, the probability that negative reinforcement will occur is greater and the possibility of reciprocating effects of negative reinforcement leading to an increase in group differences seems obvious.

In summary, I would like to see the negative reinforcement analysis include a greater consideration of the development of individual differences as well as an expansion of the analysis to consider the role of the antecedent events contributing to the escalated pattern that is then negatively reinforced.

Chapter 8
Abstract

As described here, interactional psychology consists of two components: structure and process. Structure is defined by the functional relations between events adjacent in time. One form of structure, the *intra*subject, is defined by the functional relation between a subject's own behavior at one point in time and his subsequent behavior. Intrasubject structure describes patterns or series of the individual's reactions that tend to repeat themselves. The second form of structure is *inter*subject. Here the functional relation is between one person's behavior and the other person's reaction to it.

Process refers to changes in structure. It is assumed that there are mechanisms within interaction that can alter either inter- or intrasubject structure. A molecular focus upon structure and process defines what is meant by a microsocial analysis. It is assumed that such an analysis provides an alternative means for understanding some forms of deviant behavior.

It is also assumed that some aspects of microsocial process are altered by events that impinge from outside the dyad. In effect, some microsocial variables may be altered by macrosocial variables, such as crises or stress.

Findings from observation data and from experimental studies are reviewed as they relate to these issues.

Chapter 8

A Microsocial Analysis of Structure and Process

". . . physics does not endeavor to explain nature. In fact, the great success of physics is due to a restriction of its objectives: it only endeavors to explain the regularities in the behavior of objects. This renunciation of the broader aim, and the specification of the domain for which an explanation can be sought, now appear to us an obvious necessity. In fact, the specification of the explainable may have been the greatest discovery of physics so far." (Wigner, 1964, p. 995, cited by Fiske, 1974, p. 10).

If one closely examines the minutiae describing the interchange between two persons, it becomes apparent that certain sequences of events tend to be repeated. For present purposes, the focus will be upon events that are immediately adjacent in time. A tabulation of event sequences will identify some events that are reliably associated with other events. In the discussions that follow I will use the terms functional relations, covariation, and pattern to describe this probabilistic relation between one event and another. These patterns define what I mean by *structure* in social interaction. The assumption underlying this approach to studying family interaction is that an empirical analysis of these structures will contribute to our understanding of aggression.

The analysis of only two or three adjacent events might seem too limited a base from which to build an understanding of something as complex as family interaction. However, at this stage in the development of social-interactional psychology, it seems wise to begin with simple two-event or three-event patterns. How can variance in performance levels be accounted for by measures of these simple patterns? Once we know this, we can proceed to more complex patterns and determine empirically how much additional information is needed. Another consideration is the fact that the more complex the pattern, the larger the data set required to establish it.

Functional relations are not immutable; they change over time. If data are collected repeatedly in the same setting, then it is possible to describe these changes precisely. This makes it possible to know when a change has occurred and to begin the search for the variables that produced the change. In this sense, a microsocial analysis is also concerned with process.

There are two major components of interactional structure. One is the *intra*subject and the other the *inter*subject component. Intrasubject refers to the disposition of the individual to continue what he is doing. Given that he is talking, there is a better-than-chance likelihood that this same behavior will reappear in the sequences that follow. As we shall see, this is a significant feature for members of families of antisocial children. Once they react in an irritable fashion, they are likely to continue.

The intersubject component refers to the fact that some aspects of the individual's behavior are correlated with the behavior of the other member of the dyad. In this type of dyadic exchange the other person consistently reacts with B whenever the subject does A (i.e., the pattern of B given A, $(B|A)$ recurs). Again, there are certain intersubject components that are of particular interest. For example, in his study of normal and aggressive preadolescents, Raush (1965) concluded that the variable that differentiated them was the disposition to start a conflict. Given that the other child was behaving in a prosocial manner, the aggressive child was more likely than his normal counterpart to start a conflict.

Normally the probability values describing a functional relation fluctuate about a mean value. The likelihood of $B|A$ may increase in one session and decrease in another. However, for many functional relations, the mean value based upon three or four sessions in one week will correlate well with a mean value based upon three or four sessions during the following week; i.e., the mean is stable. I think that many of the day-by-day fluctuations about this mean are determined. The question is, what causes the functional relation between event A and event B to shift from one day to another? Under what conditions will the mean value itself shift from a zero slope and begin to reflect long-term increases or decreases?

As a general case there are two sets of variables that I believe are associated with stable changes in structure. One set has to do with stressors that impinge upon the individual from outside the family. Chronic family crises, for example, increase the likelihood of irritable reactions by the mother (see Chapters 4 and 10). The second (and more likely) source of change is to be found in long-term shifts in outcomes for interchanges with the other person.

Predicting Behavioral Events

The entire set of assumptions underlying the analysis of structure and process rests upon the idea that behavior is governed by immediately impinging events. If this is true, then careful observations of external events should allow us to understand and predict some types of behavioral events.

Our training in motivational and cognitive psychology led us to approach this assumption with a good deal of trepidation. We thought initially that it would be true for some limited behaviors of very young children. In retrospect, it should not have been so difficult for us to give credence to the idea that much of ongoing social behavior is controlled or determined by the observable behavior of other persons. The general stance had been described in hortatory volumes by Kantor (1959) and others. Furthermore, investigators in ethology were already *doing* these kinds of studies (Hinde, 1974). They had laid down an impressive empirical foundation for this assumption, at least as it applied to primates, birds, and fish (Tinbergen, 1951). For example, Altmann (1965) observed the social interactions of rhesus monkeys. His code sampled the entire repertoire of their social interactions. The uncertainty of prediction, given just the information for the number of code categories in the system, was 6.91 bits. The term bits is a logarithmic expression of uncertainty which, in turn, relates to the number of alternatives and their likelihoods of occurrence. As shown in Figure 8.1, given data for the base-rate values for the categories (approximation 1), there was a reduction in uncertainty of 2.09 bits. Further information about immediate antecedent events produced a comparable reduction in uncertainty. Information about two immediately prior antecedents produced an additional reduction of about the same magnitude. The more information available, the greater the ability to predict. In fact, the increase in predictability seems linear as one moves from just information about base rates to first and second antecedents. We were further heartened by Raush's (1965) work. He collected data for disturbed boys and showed that the immediately prior social behavior accounted for 30% of the variance in the performance of ongoing social behavior.

How many prior events must be included for a proper understanding of coercive behavior? Karpowitz (1972) showed that roughly half of the social events of significance in controlling the child's behavior were to be found in the immediately preceding event. The other half were to be found in patterns of the second and third antecedent events. Each cumulative step back along interactional sequences requires large increases in data. At some point one simply must decide that the increment in prediction from adding information about prior behaviors of the dyad is not worth the cost. What happens when we begin with information about target subject base-rate values and then add information about the prior behavior of the other member of the dyad (intersubject component) plus the prior behavior of the target subject (intrasubject component)? The Karpowitz (1972) and Raush (1965) studies reassure us that much is to be gained by considering the immediately prior behavior of the other person; but what are the increments if we proceed further back through the antecedents?

Loeber (in preparation) studied ten mother-

Relation Between the Order of Approximation
and the Conditional Uncertainty of any Behavioral Event

(from Altmann, 1965, p. 510)

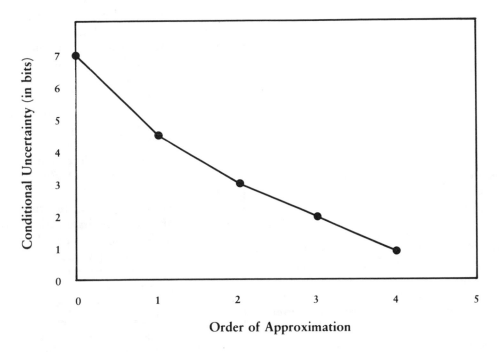

Order of Approximation

Reprinted with permission from "Sociobiology of the rhesus monkey. II. Stochastics of social communication," *Journal of Theoretical Biology,* 1965, *8.* Copyright by Academic Press Inc. (London) Ltd.

child dyads plus siblings to determine the answer to that question. Five of the families were normal and five were referred because of an antisocial child. The interactions among members of families in the clinical sample were consistently less predictable at all junctures than were the interactions of members of the normal families. Summing across the two samples, the behavior of the target children was, on the average, 15% predictable if based only upon knowledge of base-rate values for code categories. The comparable figure from Altmann's (1965) study of rhesus monkeys was 30%. Information about the immediately prior antecedent gave an average predictability of .19, an average of .23 for two antecedents, and .28 for three antecedents. The findings for mother-child interaction are similar to those from the Altmann study.

These studies by Raush (1965), Altmann (1965), Karpowitz (1972), and Loeber (in preparation) emphasize the importance of using immediately prior antecedents as a predictive base for ongoing behavior. Do these prior events "control" ongoing behavior, or are these events merely correlated with events that follow? How do we demonstrate which prior behaviors are important and which are not? These questions will be considered in the sections that follow.

The Search for Structure

The search begins with the investigation identifying a target event. For convenience, these events are labeled R_j's. The first target event in a sequence is R_1. The next target event by the same subject is labeled R_2 and so on. Events that precede target events are antecedents (A_i). Those events that follow a target response are labeled consequences (C_i). The first event in a sequence occurs at time t, the second at $t+1$, the third at $t+2$, and so on. The antecedent immediately prior to a target event occurs at $t-1$; $t-2$ describes the antecedent before that, and so on.

Any given event in the dyad sequence serves a dual role. Its label depends upon which member of a dyad is the "target subject." When he or she is identified and an entry point is arbitrarily selected, then the first event, R_1, is assumed to be a *reaction* to the prior behavior of the other person. However, if we suddenly shift the focus to the other member of the dyad, then this same target event would serve as a C_i for the prior R_j of the other person.

In our own analyses the target events have almost always been the 14 categories from the FICS that define coercive behaviors. The subject has usually been a problem child. During the first decade, our work focused primarily upon the functional relations that were defined by the event that immediately preceded or followed the child's coercive target response. These studies revealed two interwoven themes that describe (at a behavioral level) what is meant by social interaction. One of these themes is the intersubject component, and the other is the intrasubject component.

The Intersubject Component for Coercion

". . . like other forms of social conduct, performance of injurious actions is extensively regulated by environmental cues (Bandura & Walters, 1959). A theory of aggression must therefore explain not only how aggressive patterns are developed, but also how it is that some are elicitors of aggression while others are not. . . ." (Bandura, 1973, p. 115)

The study of intersubject components constitutes a search for those behaviors of the other person that control the occurrence of aggressive behaviors. The first question is, how do you identify these controlling events in ongoing social interaction? The second question is, how do you prove that they *control* attacks? The identification of a functional relation (or correlation) is the first step in analyzing structure. Proof of a causal connection is the second, *necessary* step.

To find a functional relation, one begins with the data for the base-rate value for the target event. For example, let's give Whine the high base rate of .023. This means that the child spends 2.3% of his interactions whining. This base-rate value is important because it serves as a reference point for comparing the conditional p values for this or that functional relation. To be of interest, the conditional value must be significantly different from the base-rate value. According to Sackett (1976), if the base-rate value falls below 1%, then one cannot effectively employ the binomial Z statistical analyses in making formal comparisons between the conditional and the base-rate values.

Let's assume that the child engaged in 640 inter-

actions with his mother. Of these, 15 involved the child's whining. This gives a base-rate value of .023. Is there anything that the mother does that is associated with an altered probability for child-Whine? Does scolding increase the likelihood? Will a hug be associated with a decrease or an increase? The next step is to tabulate all of the mother behaviors that immediately preceded the child's 15 Whines. In tabulating these antecedents, any one of the 29 code categories might occur. By way of illustration, assume that in the mother's 640 reactions to the child she yelled 18 times. Four of her Yells (*YE*) were followed by the child's Whine (*WH*) behavior. The p(Child Whine|Mother Yell) is 4/18 or .222. The next question concerns the significance of this tenfold increase in predictability of child-Whine. The binomial-Z value for this comparison was 5.57. It is reasonable to conclude that mother-Yell and child-Whine are functionally related.

The binomial-Z statistic provides a useful means for comparing base-rate and conditional p values given the qualifiers noted by writers such as Gottman (1979) and Gottman and Bakeman (1979). They recommend *not* presenting the confidence values for the statistic because it might lend an aura of unwarranted precision to the discussion. Gardner, Mitchell, and Hartmann (1979) note that there are two kinds of dependence tested in the 2×2 chi-square table employed by most of us. One is the serial dependency for within-subject behavior; the other is the functional relation between the behavior of one person and another. As they point out, if the level of within-subject (across time) serial dependency exceeds a correlation of .50, it seriously biases a test of independence. Even lower levels of serial dependency produce large increases in Type I errors. As they note, this problem applies both to chi square and to the use of binomial Z. The reader is advised to consult the paper by Gardner et al. (1979) for a careful review of the problems in this type of analysis.

At this point, however, there is a problem to consider. Even a simple event, such as Whine, reflects *both inter-* and *intra*subject control. The likelihood of child-Whine may be related to the mother's behavior at $t - 1$; it may also be related to what the child was doing at $t - 2$. While this point has been made by Thomas and Martin (1976), it has, unfortunately, been largely ignored. As they point out, one can control for this duality by using either a multiple-regression or a conditional-probability format. The paper by Martin, Maccoby, Baron, and Jacklin (1980) compared the two techniques in their analyses of infant and mother interactions and found the results to be comparable.

When I encountered this problem a decade ago, I was not aware of these more elegant solutions. Examination of the interaction protocols suggested that when the child was coercively engaged, there was an increased likelihood at $t+1$ for the occurrence of all 14 coercive behaviors. To control for this "thematic effect," I selected only those target events in which the target event was the first event in a coercive sequence, or a single, isolated coercive event, i.e., only those Whines *not* embedded in a prior coercive matrix. The procedure followed for the study by Patterson and Cobb (1973) was to take only those target events preceded by 18 seconds of interaction in which the target child's prior behaviors were prosocial. The analysis was based upon the pooled observation data from 32 families of antisocial children referred to OSLC and data from 26 matched normal families. These were essentially working-class families; about 30% were father-absent homes. Each of the families was observed for a minimum of six to 12 sessions. Target events were *initiations*. An initiation of a coercive behavior was defined as an isolated or initial event in a coercive sequence; by definition, an initiation of a prosocial behavior meant that it was preceded by 18 seconds in which neither member of a dyad had interacted with the other.[1] Only those events in which the other member served as agent for both the antecedent and the consequence were included. There were 10,626 initiations (prosocial and coercive); of these, 2,041 were coercive (.192). The comparable value for a sample of nondistressed boys was .142.

The analysis was carried out in order to examine intersubject components that would be relatively free of thematic effects from the child's ongoing coercive behavior. Given that the child *initiates* a Whine, what is the likelihood that it was preceded by mother-Disapproval, etc.? As Don Hartmann (personal communication) points out, a more balanced view would include the results of a comparable analysis based upon the excluded data from coercive chains.

The functional relations for ten coercive behaviors are summarized in Table 8.1. The first column lists 24 categories that might have served as antecedents for the target child's coercive behaviors. The conditional p values in the next two columns describe the likelihood that a variable served as an A_i for the total body of initiations; e.g., for the deviant boys, only .004 of all their initiations were preceded by Approval; for Normals the value was .010. The values that head each column are the base rates for initiations. For example, Disapproval made up only 6.1% of all initiations for

boys in the clinical sample and 4.7% for boys in the normal sample. Only those conditional values that were appreciably different from the base rates are listed; the decision rules for identifying these controlling antecedents are presented in Patterson and Cobb (1973) and Patterson (1977a).

The interpretation of these values is straightforward. For example, in the clinical sample, given the target child's Disapprove, then the likelihood of the other family member's Whine in the prior 6-second interval was .160. This conditional p value was several times larger than the base rate of .061 for Disapproval. This suggests that Whine and Disapprove were functionally related, i.e., correlated. Note, too, that a similar relation holds for the normal sample. The reader should note that the p values were calculated from populations of events; some families probably contributed disproportionately to these relations.

There are several features about Table 8.1 that are worth noting. First, it is apparent that some variables were much better defined, or accounted for, by an A_i controlling stimulus than were others. The low-rate events, such as Destructive, High-Rate, and Humiliate, remain poorly understood; Dependency, Cry, and Command Negative occurred at such low rates that they were not analyzable. It was possible to provide a clear delineation only for the higher rate events. That, of course, is a sensible outcome; it should be easier to identify significant functional relations for target events that occur at high rates.

Each target response had one or more antecedent events that seemed correlated with its occurrence. This set of empirical relations for a target response defines what is meant by the term network. Notice that the sizes of the networks vary considerably even among target responses of comparable base rates. For example, Tease has about twice as many correlated A_i's as Yell. This variation in the size of networks could represent omissions built into the original code. We may not have been sampling the appropriate behaviors, at least not the ones that relate to Yell. On the other hand, some responses may be more predictable than others. For example, some responses may be less correlated with immediately impinging environmental events.

The second feature of the data presented in Table 8.1 has to do with the *kind* of antecedents that most powerfully "elicit" the target response. For six out of the ten target events, the most powerful elicitor was an antecedent of the same code category as the target response. For the clinical sample, for example, the likelihood of Physical Negative as an antecedent, given Physical Negative,

Table 8.1
Antecedents Relating to Changes in the Likelihood of Initiating Coercive Responses

Given an initiation of $\bar{R}_j$, then the likelihood of A_i was

Antecedents	$p(A_i)$ Dev.	$p(A_i)$ Nor.	Destructive .002† Dev.	Nor.	Disapproval .061 Dev.	.047 Nor.	High Rate .008 Dev.	.002 Nor.	Humiliate .004 Dev.	.002 Nor.	Ignore .007 Dev.	.002 Nor.	Negativism .026 Dev.	.019 Nor.	Physical Negative .010 Dev.	.003 Nor.	Tease .011 Dev.	.007 Nor.	Whine .011 Dev.	.012 Nor.	Yell .011 Dev.	.007 Nor.
(no. of initiations)			18‡	0	646	159	88	6	38	5	72	7	278	64	106	11	117	25	120	39	116	22
Approve	.004	.010									.046											
Attend	.146	.138			.025	.028	.004				.003		.006						.006			
Command	.085	.104			.028	.020					.001								.001		.001	
Command Neg.	.010	.007			.010																	
Comply	.006	.006			.132	.158			.053				.074		.044							
Cry	.002	.002													.087							
Dependency	.001																					
Disapproval	.055	.055			.200	.217					.017		.041	.044					.022	.032	.044	
Destructive	.001	.000	.125																			
High Rate	.004	.000					.614															
Humiliate	.004	.002			.270				.162		.167											
Ignore	.004	.001															.111					
Laugh	.009	.019			.115										.042		.042	.048			.032	
Noncomply	.006	.004														.167						
Negativism	.007	.006				.158			.026				.218	.316	.051		.051					
Normative	.117	.063			.008	.014							.005		.005		.002					
Play	.141	.173			.048		.021						.009						.006	.003	.015	
Physical Negative	.007	.004			.141	.200								.133	.296	.200					.070	
Physical Positive	.005	.005											.080									
Talk	.367	.389			.074	.040	.003	.003	.005		.012		.037	.024	.006	.001	.008	.002	.019			
Tease	.006	.004			.209						.045				.060		.149	.357			.060	
Receive	.003	.002													.059	.200	.088					
Whine	.002	.003			.160	.222					.111						.160					
Yell	.004	.001									.077						.077				.128	

†Values in the row are base rates for *initiations* of target event by target child.

‡Number of initiations.

---

was .30; Tease as an antecedent, given Tease, was .15; and Yell as an antecedent, given Yell, was .13. While all of these conditional probabilities far exceed their respective base-rate values, it is clear that when we speak of "connections" or "bonds," the reference is probabilistic. There is nothing even in the comparatively large value of .30 that implies the mechanistic, wired-in connections usually ascribed to theories about stimulus-response bonds.

The third characteristic of these data that stands out is the similarity in patterns of functionally related stimuli for the two samples. Generally speaking, a stimulus that controls a response for the normal sample will also control the same response for the clinical sample. There are some interesting exceptions to this but enough overlap to lead one to suspect that the basic structure for the two samples may be very similar. In future investigations it would be wise to calculate these values separately for individuals so that appropriate statistical comparisons could be made.

In passing, it should be noted that there are some difficulties in locating stimuli that are associated with *reduced* likelihood of occurrence. One simply looks for $p(R_j|A_i)$ values that are appreciably *lower* than the base rate for the target event, i.e., CN as an A_i for Disapprove. However, given a clinical event that has a base rate of .010 or less, then even when the conditional p is .000, there is the difficulty that most statistical comparisons are not appropriate. This approach is not an effective means for studying controlling stimuli when the target events are low-frequency events. For this reason, very few of our publications have dealt with the problem of antecedent events associated with a decreased likelihood of occurrence for the target event.

The Utility of Functional Relations

What do networks tell us about target events? This section outlines a series of steps for determin-

Figure 8.2
The Utility of Functional Relations

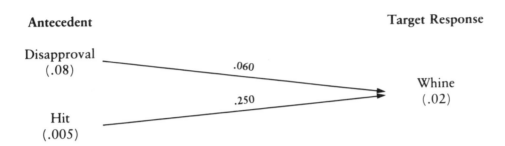

The figures in parentheses are base-rate values for the antecedents and the target response.
The figures not in parentheses are the conditional probabilities describing the functional relation $p(R_j|A_i)$.

ing how much a single functional relation, or an entire network, tells us about a target event. For present purposes, I am equating the terms usefulness or utility with information about target events. The more complete the information about which antecedents are significantly related to child-Hit, the more useful it is to me as a therapist. The two key pieces of information are the magnitude of the probability value for the functional relation and the frequency with which the antecedent occurs.

The information about networks of controlling antecedents is a useful beginning to our understanding of children's aggressive behavior, but it is conceivable that such a network, or a single functional relation, might be of little predictive value. By way of illustration, assume that both Disapproval and Hit are significant controlling antecedents for Whine. Given Disapproval as an antecedent, then the likelihood of Whine was about once in 16 trials. Given Hit as an antecedent, then the odds of a Whine were one in four. Both of these antecedents serve significant functions as controlling stimuli for Whine. Both sets of functional relations could also be of interest from the standpoint of theory construction.

If we raise the question of which antecedent has the greater impact, then clearly Hit has the higher conditional p value. However, note that in the illustration the base-rate value for Hit is extremely low. Given that our task is to understand or to manage Whine, then this particular antecedent adds little to what it is that we must know. Clearly, from the standpoint of management or predictability, it is necessary to take into account the base rate for the controlling antecedent stimulus.

There are a number of ways in which this can be done. The joint contribution of the base rate for the antecedent and its impact upon the target event could be expressed in terms of reduction in uncertainty (Attneave, 1959); or, as Suomi (1979) suggests, it could be described by the ratio:

$$\frac{p(R_j|A_i).}{p(R_j)}$$

The magnitude of this ratio is an index of one's ability to predict R_j given a knowledge of the functional relation $R_j|A_i$. But, as can be seen, it leaves out information about how frequently the antecedent occurs. The approach by Patterson and Cobb (1973) provides a means for including $p(A_i)$ as follows:

$$p(A_i) \; \frac{p(R_j|A_i)}{p(R_j)} = \text{power}$$

Taking the data in Figure 8.2, each conditional p value is multiplied by the base rate for the antecedent. Then dividing this figure by the p(Whine) value of .02 gives the estimate of the "power" of that antecedent. Twenty-four percent of the occurrences of Whine were related to Disapproval; only about 6% were related to Hit as the antecedent. Actually, neither one of these variables meets the arbitrary criterion of $> 40\%$ used by Patterson and Cobb (1973) when constructing functionally defined response classes. Don Hartmann (personal communication) suggests that this p value could also be expressed in correlational terms. This would describe power in terms of variance accounted for. If these findings regarding child-Whine were available to the therapist, it would

Table 8.2
Power Indices for Coercive Responses
(adapted from Patterson & Cobb, 1973, p. 180)

Coercive Response	Problem Family		Nonproblem Family	
	$p(\bar{R}_j)$	Power Index for $\bar{R}_j$	$p(\bar{R}_j)$	Power Index for $\bar{R}_j$
Command Negative	.002	.472	†	
Disapproval	.061	.780	.047	.798
Destructiveness	.002	.053	†	
High Rate	.008	.850	†	
Humiliate	.004	.734	†	
Ignore	.007	.956	†	
Noncomply‡	.038	.997	.038	.999
Negativism	.026	.743	.019	.796
Physical Negative	.010	.673	.003	.631
Tease	.011	.584	.007	.596
Whine	.011	.939	.012	.256
Yell	.011	.326	.007	.091

†Only R_j with 10 or more events included.

‡By definition (in the code), the A_i *must* be Command.

suggest that he could most easily reduce child-Whine by training family members to cease their use of Disapproval. In so doing, child-Whine would be reduced by about one-fourth.

In the above example, information about only these two variables would provide a poor basis for designing an experiment in which one proposes to manipulate Whine. There are simply too many possible *alternative* antecedents that might exert more powerful control than either Disapprove or Hit. The equation that we developed to describe power is simply a restatement of Bayes' theorem. Given information from both antecedents, the $p(R_j|A_i)$ is only .30. This, in turn, means that there is much about Whine that is left unexplained by these analyses. We shall return in a later section to the implication of such findings for the design of experiments.

It should be noted in passing that a lower base-rate value for the target event covaries with a lower p value for power. The Patterson and Cobb (1973) study showed a correlation of .49 ($p < .10$) between the frequency with which a coercion variable occurred and the power index. This makes sense in that only significant functional relations enter into calculations for the power index. It is simply more difficult to find significant relations for low base-rate events.

Suppose that it is important that one understand *Whine* as a target event, and the analysis shows that the antecedents account for only 30% of the occurrences of Whine. There are several steps one might take. First the problem may be that the code is defective. Perhaps the more powerful antecedents for Whine were not sampled. Given this situation, I would begin by carefully observing some high-rate Whiners to see what I had missed when constructing the first code. Second, the antecedents for Whine may not be consistent across families; therefore, a series of single case studies might result in greater precision. Third, given a sample of dedicated, high-rate Whiners, I would systematically *sample settings* for each child. I assume, then, there would be some settings associated with higher p(Whine) than others. By concentrating upon those subsets, the base-rate values for both the target response *and* the antecedents would likely be more manageable (higher). In this fashion, one uses whatever data are at hand to design a more powerful approach to the question.

The data in Table 8.2 were based upon the study of initiations from samples of clinical and normal families (Patterson & Cobb, 1973). For *both* samples the controlling antecedents accounted for 70% to 80% of the occurrence of Disapproval and Negativism. In both samples the networks account for 50% to 60% of the occurrences of Tease and Physical Negative. Presumably, if the networks were extended backwards to include the child's own prior behavior (as in the Loeber [in preparation] study), we might account for more variance. However, even a reliance upon immediately prior antecedents tells us much of what we need to know about ten of the 14 responses. While the information from the two samples is generally similar, note the interesting discrepancy in the case of Whine as a target event. Here the controlling variables sampled by the code provided a very high power index for the clinical sample but much less for Normals.

It should be clear that social interaction is an incredibly flexible structure. The p values that describe the functional relations between adjacent events are of low magnitude, and they shift over time. Even the key concept, "base rate," is not a static quantity. It may vary across time and as a function of which settings are sampled.[2] It may also be the case that the boundaries that define the antecedent event may be changed. For example, other events whose meaning is similar to the originally conditioned antecedent may elicit the same response. Studies by Berkowitz (1973a) and Staats and Staats (1958) suggest that this might be the case. For example, stimuli that are contiguously paired with the eliciting event may temporarily produce the "same" reaction (Staats, Staats, & Crawford, 1962).

If not reinforced, the antecedent → response connection may eventually weaken and be replaced by still others, that, in turn, may prove to be transitory examples of controlling events. In any case, change is the rule. This requires a certain amount of flexibility in how one defines an event and flexibility in how one thinks about connections between events. The structure of human interaction is in many ways analogous to that of the Eskimo umiak. This ocean-going craft is beautiful in design and function. It *shifts* and *adjusts itself* as it moves over waves but, at the same time, retains its essential design and purpose.

Causal Status

Sequential data collected in the field represent only the first stage in constructing a performance theory about social interaction. Significant correlations do not prove causality. To test for causal relations experimental manipulations are required. Since most of our work in the early 1970's was focused upon identifying which antecedents were significant and which were not, we decided to study the causal implications of the significant functional relations first. However, our initial findings did not seem in keeping with the conventional wisdom about what determined children's coercive behavior. For example, when questioned, most mothers "explained" coercive child behavior as being caused by the child's being in a bad mood, being tired, or being upset. The mothers' explanations reflected the current theories, i.e., deviant behaviors were caused by underlying *motives, drives,* or *affective* states. Certainly it is reasonable to think of fatigue or depressed mood as a partial elicitor for coercive reactions. However, as outlined in Chapter 4, it is not a requirement that all elicitors be accompanied by arousal. Some controlling events (for example, prosocial ones) seem to control behavior without any noticeable change in autonomic state. This being the case, we reasoned that perhaps some coercive reactions could be under fairly tight stimulus control. It seemed that a single subject ABAB reversal design might best demonstrate this control. If the controlling events were presented during the manipulation at B_1, there should be a corresponding increase in the target behavior, as compared to the rate during either the first or second baseline periods. Then a presentation of the controlling event at B_2 should replicate the effect. If the outcome provided a tight fit to our experimental expectations, it would demonstrate the causal status of the antecedent event. It would, however, leave open questions concerning its concomitants; it would not necessarily rule out autonomic arousal.

The next problem was to decide what and how to "manipulate." To learn how to carry out such studies, we began in the laboratory where some modicum of control was possible. It was hoped that what we learned there could be used to design experiments that could then be carried out in field settings.

A number of pilot tests led us to believe that the phenomenon, "mother-on-the-phone," might be a powerful event that controlled many coercive behaviors of preschool children. The first study used an ABAB design in which the mother freely interacted with the child during both baseline (A) phases (Atkinson, 1971). During the experimental (B) phases, the mother was totally involved in a task that required making visual discriminations while listening to a telephone, *and* she was placed behind a barricade so the child could see her but not touch her. In retrospect, the procedure was a good example of overkill; the controlling event was much more powerful than it needed to be. However, at that time we simply did not know what would be necessary in order to achieve experimental control.

Each of the 14 coercive code categories were analyzed separately to determine the magnitude of behavior changes across the four conditions. As

Table 8.3
Experimental Manipulation of Coercive Child Behaviors

(adapted from Atkinson, 1971, p. 14)

Coercive Child Behaviors	Mean Rate per Minute				
	Baseline 1	Experimental 1	Baseline 2	Experimental 2	F Values
Command	0.014	0.029	0.007	0.021	1.22
Cry	0.003	0.211	0.030	0.183	7.98***
Destructiveness	0.014	0.125	0.002	0.069	19.53***
High rate noise	0.004	0.022	0.001	0.017	1.03
Negativism	0.000	0.011	0.009	0.028	1.32
Whine	0.007	0.049	0.038	0.043	3.22*
Yell	0.003	0.074	0.001	0.074	4.11*
Mean	.006	.074	.013	.062	

*$p < .05$

***$p < .001$

shown in Table 8.3, the ANOVA for repeated measures produced significant F values for four of the comparisons (Cry, Whine, Yell, and Destructive). The mean rates for the target responses were significantly higher during the manipulation than during the baseline periods. The data from this sample offered firm support for the idea that some coercive child behaviors were under tight stimulus control. Using a similar procedure in the course of his work on negative reinforcement, Devine (1971) replicated this general effect.

The finding that some mother behaviors reliably produced child-Yell, child-Whine, child-Cry, and child-Destructive was not very surprising. However, the fact that *removing* the controlling stimulus produced *abrupt* cessation of the target behaviors did surprise both the experimenters and the mothers. These results encouraged us to go on and design studies that would be closer to what could be seen taking place in the home.

The search began for an event that could be manipulated in the matrix of ongoing social interaction. We decided to focus upon a target response that occurred often when normal preschool children and their mothers visited the OSLC laboratory. In that situation, the child's Whine was more to be expected than his "hello." The setting for the next several studies was still the laboratory. The mother-child pair was observed during semistructured interaction, and the data were analyzed to identify the behavior of the mother that reliably preceded child-Whine. The dyad returned several days later to participate in an ABA procedure;

each phase lasted for ten minutes. During the experimental period, the previously identified significant antecedent was repeatedly presented. For the ten preschoolers, the mean likelihood of Whine during the three phases was .007, .317, and .043 respectively. The differences among the means were highly significant (Patterson, 1977b). It is of some interest to note that the likelihood of child-Whine, given the mother's antecedent, was quite stable; the correlation for the conditional p values across sessions, separated by several days, was .67 ($p < .05$).

The three studies showed that the general idea of testing for stimulus control was feasible. It was possible to observe mother-child interaction in the laboratory and identify an event that controlled child-Whine. When the controlling event was presented in the second session, it increased the likelihood of child-Whine. When the mother stopped presenting it, the child stopped whining. However, the studies left some key questions unanswered.

First, could one simply go into a home, observe for three or four hours, and identify stimuli that controlled behavior? We were not quite ready to believe that such a level of precision would be possible for data from field settings. We knew that field data produced significant correlations, but would these functional relations stand up under experimental manipulations? It had already required two years of devoted effort by a team of assistants to come this far. However, for all that effort, we really had only studied *one* target response. In the last study (which most closely approximated field conditions) the majority of the preschoolers' Whines were controlled by the same antecedent (mother-Tease). It was not at all clear that we would be successful *in situ,* where the latitude open to the mother and child seemed practically infinite.

It was with some trepidation that the first field study was designed by the writer, Kate Whalen and Hal Dengerink. The experimental design now

---

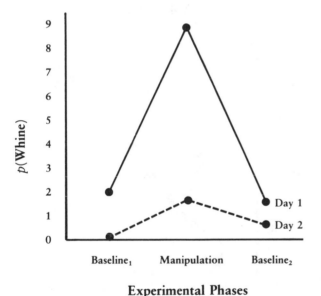

Figure 8.3
Experimental Manipulation
of Child-Whine

(from Patterson, 1979b, p. 151))

---

included two stages: first, to observe in the home and identify an antecedent that controlled a target-child behavior; then to design an ABA experiment that would demonstrate that the antecedent really controlled the behavior. Then we wanted to replicate the experiment on the following day. Several baseline sessions in the home of a 3-year-old child showed that mother-Ignore reliably elicited child-Whine. For two baseline sessions, the conditional probability values were .83 and .43; the base rates for Whine on those two days were .23 and .07 respectively. Following the baseline study, an ABA reversal design was employed on two consecutive days. During each of the five-minute baseline periods, the mother was instructed to interact normal-

ly with her son. During the five-minute B phase, the mother was told to ignore every initiation made by the child to communicate with her. If, during that time, his whining/crying got out of hand, she was instructed to interact briefly with him and then return to the mother-Ignore condition. Following this, the baseline condition was reintroduced (A_2). Identical ABA procedures were followed on the second day. Figure 8.3 summarizes the findings testing the status of the controlling stimulus identified during the baseline sessions. The data offered strong support for the hypothesis that mother-Ignore was an event that reliably controlled the child's whining behavior. There was at least a twofold increase in p(Whine) when this controlling event was introduced. When removed, the behavior returned to its baseline level on Day 1 and partially returned to its baseline level on Day 2. These replicated findings gave modest support to the idea that for *this* child a functional analysis of family interactions was indeed an effective means for identifying a stimulus that reliably controlled his whining behavior.

As we pursued this problem further, we soon produced two or three studies that either failed or, at best, produced inconclusive outcomes.[3] The problem lay in our confusing the concept of significant functional relation ($p[R_j|A_i]$) with the term "control." As noted earlier, it is possible to have a significant correlation between an antecedent and an R_j, but it may provide little information about the target response. The antecedent may occur infrequently, and/or it may be only *one of many* "controlling" antecedents. That being the case, it would be difficult to design a study that could control for these unknown variables. During an experimental phase in a laboratory study, these other antecedent events are left free to vary. This, in turn, means that in some studies the data for rate of target responses will not demonstrate tight experimental control.

One can think of a significant functional relation as denoting "control" in a statistical sense, but the prediction of experimental or *treatment* manipulations requires that we specify *how much* control. In earlier analyses of functionally defined response classes, we used the concept of a power index to decide which functional relations belonged to a class of responses. It was decided to apply this concept to the problem of predicting the outcomes of experimental manipulations. Again, the information from the base rate for R_j, the base rate for A_i, and $p(R_j|A_i)$ are used to calculate the power index. If the antecedent variable accounted for more than 40% of the occurrence of the target event, then it seemed reasonable to bet that an experimental manipulation would be successful. A more conservative approach would be to identify the two or three antecedents that control most of the occurrences for R_j, and then design an experiment that controls for all but one antecedent.

Three stages were involved in the design of each study. First, we observed in the home and identified the functional relations for several high-rate coercive child behaviors. Then we calculated the power scores for each and selected the relation in which the antecedent accounted for more than 40% of the occurrences of R_j. Then, to establish the reliability of the data, we replicated the manipulation for one or two sessions. We also began to role-play the experimental procedures with the mother *prior* to actually running the study. For example, if she was to give a command when cued, then an experimenter would role-play several practice runs with her while another staff member removed the child to another room. As these studies progressed and the procedures became increasingly intricate, the number of training trials were increased accordingly.

The studies also involved an improved version of the FICS. Marion Forgatch took over the complex task of coordinating the observers and data tabulators (we had no funds for computers). She organized the data in such a way that we could retrieve the conditional p values from field data in a day or two, and thus design the experiment for the following session. This reorganization was necessary for the new series of studies. The first study in this new series took place in the home of a mother and her preschool child. Several days of observation identified a functional relation that was of particular interest because it described a target response (Argue) that had not previously been studied. The base rate for Argue was .031. Given mother-Argue as an antecedent, then the conditional p for child-Argue was .531. That seemed encouraging. The next question was about power. Did mother-Argue exert enough control to serve as a proper base for an experiment? The base rate for mother-Argue was .024; the compound probability (.024 × .531) was .013. The power for this antecedent was obtained by dividing this figure by the base rate for child-Argue (.031); 42% of the target events were accounted for by this single controlling event. Our best guess, then, would be that an experiment employing this controlling event should be successful.

Several further improvements were made in the experimental procedures and design. First, each of the three phases (ABA) in a session was increased to 20 minutes. This was more in agreement with our stability estimates (Chapter 3) that showed

this amount of data was an absolute minimum for estimating $p(R_j)$. The trade-off for increased stability was that both mother and experimenter were under greater stress. It is this stress that sets an upper limit on the amount of time that can be used in field-study manipulations. Less than 20 minutes per phase means a less stable estimate of the experimental effect. However, more than 20 minutes of manipulation is difficult to tolerate. The second increase in precision involved more careful training of the mother *prior* to the study. One of the experimenters played the role of the child and, when cued, the mother began to argue.

Figure 8.4 summarizes the results of the two days during which an ABA design was followed.

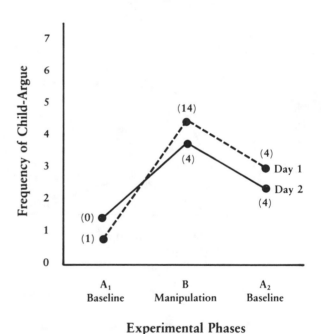

Figure 8.4
Experimental Manipulation of Child-Argue

The figures in parentheses refer to the frequency of Mother-Argue.

The data demonstrate the controlling status of mother-Argue. When the mother increased the rate with which she presented these elicitors during the B phases, there were commensurate increases in child-Argue. Mother-Argue determines child-Argue; so the prediction was confirmed. But note the failure of the target event to return altogether to the first baseline (A_1) levels. This reflects the problem of controlling the behavior of the *mother.* As shown in Figure 8.4, during A_2 the mother initiated *many more* Argues than she had in A_1. This happened on both days. Controlling the controller is obviously a complicated affair.[4]

The next study is included as an illustration of what happens when the impact of antecedents upon R_j was significant but *not* powerful. This could come about because the antecedent occurs infrequently and/or because the magnitude of $p(R_j|A_i)$ is low. Very low power values mean that there are variables other than those being manipulated that control the target event. During any phase of the study, increases in rate of the target event may occur as the result of these "uncontrolled" controlling events. Summer was a moderately well-behaved preschool child with a likelihood of .069 of ignoring her mother. This was even more likely to occur following mother-Command (conditional p of .208). The binomial-Z value was 2.69; so the functional relation is noteworthy; however, the power for mother-Command was a very low 15.9%. This meant that there were many events other than mother-Command that controlled Summer-Ignore. Each of four sessions involved an ABA design. On each day during A_1, the mother made zero Commands. During the B phase she was cued to make 20 Commands. During A_2 she was cued to make five Commands. Increasing mother-Commands produced the expected increase in Summer-Ignore. However, even though mother reduced her commands during A_2, Summer continued to ignore. Variables other than those we manipulated were obviously controlling the target event. A low power score means a sloppy experiment.

These studies are an illustration of what remains to be done. They are not sufficient for testing the hypothesis that statistically defined functional relations denote a causal status for the antecedent event. The studies completed thus far do support this assumption. In passing, it should be noted that the mothers who participated in these studies learned much from their experience. To them, it came as a surprise to find how much *their* behavior controlled the reactions of their children. Those who later went into parent training made very rapid progress in learning child management skills.

An Analysis of Settings

The next hypothesis tested was that the networks controlling a particular coercive behavior vary from one setting to another. Each setting requires its own discriminations as to when, who, what, and how one can maximize payoffs for coercion. Settings are specific with regard to the an-

tecedent networks controlling a behavior. As a pilot study, two 6-year-old boys were observed in the home and in the classroom. In both settings antecedents were identified that correlated with the boys' most frequently occurring coercive responses. There was *very little overlap* in the stimuli for the two settings in the events controlling the same responses. The Fisher exact chi square was used to test for the overlap in networks controlling coercive behaviors. The chi square ($p < .02$) showed a significant association. Given a controlling stimulus for a target event in one setting, then there was an excellent chance that the same antecedent *would not* control the same target event in the other setting. Obviously, with an N of only two cases, one cannot generalize from these findings, but they do suggest the importance of carrying out microsocial analyses in different settings.

In the same study there was one antecedent and target event connection that was built into the code, so it was found in both settings (child-Noncomply|adult-Command). It was decided to alter the $A_i \rightarrow R_j$ bond in the home and determine whether the effects generalized to the school. To alter the connection found in the home, both mothers were trained to use time out in the home whenever the children noncomplied following mother-Command. Following the manipulation, both boys showed a significant increase in p(Comply|mother-Command). The effects did *not* generalize to teacher-Command and child-Noncomply in the school. For Ben, the conditional baseline p in school was .20; the post-manipulation p value was .20. For Bobby, the comparable values were .30 and .23 respectively. Altering $A_i \rightarrow R_j$ connections in one setting may not generalize to the same stimulus and response in a new setting. I think this is especially the case when the stimulus is provided by different agents; this is in keeping with an earlier analysis in which we found that agent and agent behavior had very different implications for control of behavior (Patterson & Cobb, 1971).

In his 1968 publication, Mischel made a compelling case for the necessity of studying the impact of settings upon behavior. The pilot studies outlined here illustrate how such studies might proceed. For example, the studies reviewed in Chapter 2 showed that response hierarchies for the performance of aggressive behaviors are highly predictable from one setting to another. However, it also seems that the specific antecedents (and perhaps consequences) that control them vary from one setting to another. I think future studies will show that the networks that control the responses will vary from one setting to another. What are the implications of such an idea? One implication is concerned with the problem of generalization of treatment. If one alters the antecedent → response structure in one setting, then it would have little or no effect on the antecedent → response structures in the other. This is certainly in accord with reviews of the clinical literature on treatment outcomes. Hill Walker's classic studies on generalization from token-culture classroom to regular classroom are a good example. His studies showed little generalization unless steps were taken to involve the teachers and peers in the regular classroom (Walker, Hops, & Johnson, 1975). These studies and our own clinical experience are in agreement—to obtain "generalization" for treatment, the microsocial structure must be altered in *both* settings. Even if the same stimulus-response bond is found in two settings, the bond is provided by *different* agents. The stimulus compound (agent + agent behavior) is different from one setting to another.

These speculations are based upon a very small set of analyses. Again, the studies presented were intended to be more illustrative of a microsocial approach than confirmatory. Are all the $A_i \rightarrow R_j$ connections this setting specific? We don't know. Under what conditions *will* a child generalize experiences across settings? It *must* be the case that such generalizations *do* occur, but what are the parameters that facilitate or inhibit this most important process? If the controlling networks differ, how can it be that the response hierarchies are stable across settings? These are questions for the next generation of studies.

Functionally Defined Classes of R_j's

At a microsocial level it is possible that each child has a *unique* network of functional relations. Significant functional relations that are found for one child could be specific to that child alone. What is understood about one child may not generalize to other children. If that is so, then interactional psychology would stand immobilized in a small cloud of disparate facts. The writer believes that this is not the case. Instead, it is assumed that structural units exist that generalize across subjects; these units are sufficient in their complexity to challenge the most avid seeker. The implicit assumption is that members of our culture share certain beliefs about how to react to this or that stimulus. If this is true, then similar functional relations will be found across families. For example, most adults do not expect perfect obedience from their children, so there is, then, a functional relation between mother-Command and child-Noncomply that holds across families. It also assumed that certain target responses share similar networks of significant antecedents, *and* that these networks generalize across families.

Antecedent behaviors provided by family members were examined to determine which, if any, covaried with the initiation of each of the 14 coercive responses (see Table 8.1). These functional relations were, in turn, examined to determine whether the same networks controlled several coercive responses. In effect, this second step would identify a functionally defined class of coercive responses. Patterson (1977a) reanalyzed these controlling antecedent networks, described in the Patterson and Cobb (1973) study, utilizing a more rigorous set of decision rules that slightly altered the constituents of the functional relations. The revised classes are presented in Figures 8.5 and 8.6.

The first one was labeled *Social Aggression*. As shown in Figure 8.5, there are five controlling events that share in common the fact that each is associated with an increased likelihood for the *initiation* of Tease and Physical Negative. For example, given Noncomply as an antecedent, the conditional p was .088 that the problem child would tease and .059 that he would hit (Physical Negative). Hitting and teasing are functionally related in that both are controlled by similar networks of antecedents.

Do target responses that "share" networks of significant antecedents also share networks of functionally related reactions (consequences)? To answer this question, the data were analyzed from a sample of antisocial children (Patterson, 1977a). The analysis showed that the Social Aggressor response class primarily involved siblings. The findings for consequences, summarized in Figure 8.5, were from the reactions of male siblings to coercive behaviors of problem children. There were three consequences *shared* by the target events that defined this response class. These were Physical Negative, Tease, and Yell. In each instance the $p(C_i | R_j)$ value was greater than the $p(C_i)$. The latter are the figures in parentheses. It may be that these shared networks occur only if the target subject is a problem child. To test the generalizability of these findings, the siblings were used as target subjects, and the reactions of the problem child were examined. Sibling-Tease and Physical Negative were significantly correlated with the following reactions from the problem child: Physical Negative, Tease, Yell, Disapproval, and Whine.

The target events that comprise the response class, Social Aggression, are functionally related to their antecedents. The responses that make up this class share in common a network of five antecedent stimuli. They also share in common a set of

Figure 8.5
Functionally Defined Response Class Social Aggression

(adapted from Patterson, 1977a)

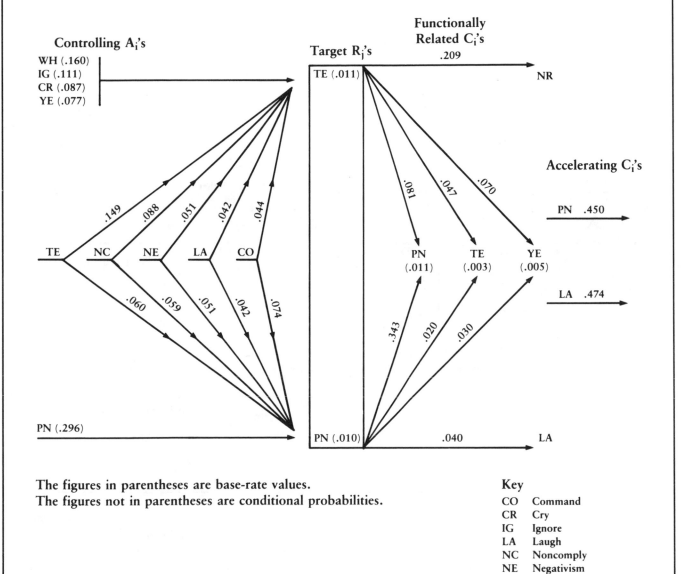

The figures in parentheses are base-rate values.
The figures not in parentheses are conditional probabilities.

Key

CO	Command
CR	Cry
IG	Ignore
LA	Laugh
NC	Noncomply
NE	Negativism
NR	No Response
PN	Physical Negative
TE	Tease
WH	Whine
YE	Yell

three consequences. These consequences are functionally related to these target events; the responses reliably *produce* the consequences.

Given that a consequence is functionally related to a target response, it may have a dual impact

upon future behavior. It may function as a reinforcer or a punisher and have a long-term effect in altering the connection between the antecedent and target event. The C_i may also have an immediate impact in terms of accelerating or decelerating

183

Figure 8.6
The Functionally Defined Response Class Hostile

(adapted from Patterson, 1977a)

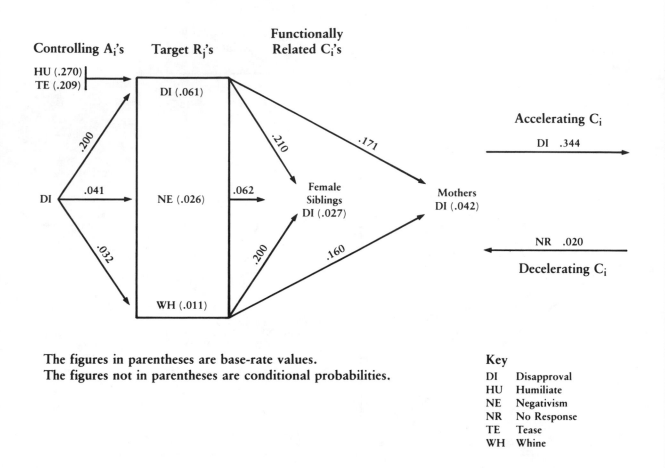

The figures in parentheses are base-rate values.
The figures not in parentheses are conditional probabilities.

Key
DI   Disapproval
HU Humiliate
NE Negativism
NR No Response
TE Tease
WH Whine

the likelihood of an *immediate* recurrence for the target response. The data used to test this hypothesis involved the reactions of *all* family members (Patterson, 1977a). Given a socially aggressive response as a target event and a Physical Negative as a consequence, the likelihood of a *recurrence* of the socially aggressive response was .450. This value was compared to the base rate for recurrence of socially aggressive responses and was found to be significant. As consequences, both Physical Negative and Laugh serve to *accelerate* the ongoing occurrence of members of this response class.

Figure 8.6 summarizes the findings for the second functionally defined response class. The data were obtained from the study on initiation by the problem child by Patterson and Cobb (1973). The search for shared networks produced three re-

sponses for a class labeled Hostile. The antecedent controlling the initiation of each of the three target responses was Disapproval. The family members most involved in providing these antecedents were the mother and female siblings (Patterson, 1977a). *Hostile* behaviors are the problem child's means of coping with verbal assaults by female members of the family. Note, too, that the counterattacks to these intrusions were also *verbal*.

As shown in Figure 8.6, his hostile reactions were a reliable means for producing yet further Disapproval reactions from both mothers and female siblings. This second analysis was based upon the interactions of 37 socially aggressive problem children. The figures in parentheses give the base-rate values for these consequences separately for female siblings and for mothers. As can

184

be seen there, the problem child's hostile reactions were associated with increased likelihoods of Disapproval as a consequence for both mothers and female siblings.

The third stage of the analysis searched for consequences that would decelerate or accelerate the likelihood of recurrence of the child's hostile behavior. In that study (Patterson, 1977a), the base rate for the comparison was the likelihood for immediate recurrence of hostile behavior based upon interactions with all family members. The results of the analyses are also shown in Figure 8.6. The consequence, Disapproval (by family members), produces an accelerating impact, as shown by the p value of .344 for immediate recurrence of Hostile. If, however, family members acted as if nothing had transpired (No Response), the effect was to decelerate Hostile.

What is the utility of generating functionally defined classes of this kind? I think it is useful to know that male siblings are more likely to produce socially aggressive reactions from the problem child, while mothers and female siblings are more likely to produce hostile reactions. As noted in Chapter 5, parental "nattering" differentially affects the two functionally defined classes. Hartup (1979) introduced the felicitous phrase, "functional equivalence," to describe functionally defined response classes. In Figure 8.6 the findings show that child reactions, such as Whine, Negativism, and Disapproval, have very different topographies but produce similar *reactions* from the female adults against whom they are directed. They are also functionally equivalent in the sense that each is elicited by Disapproval. As we shall see in Chapter 11, these responses also tend to covary when subjected to an across-subject correlational study. The findings raise an interesting question about what a functionally defined response class means. For example, if the connection between an antecedent and one target response were altered would it generalize to all other members of that functionally defined class?

Thus far, one study has been completed that relates to this issue. In this study, negative reinforcement was used to strengthen the $A_i \rightarrow R_j$ connection for one member of a functionally defined class but not for the other. What was of interest was the alteration in the nonmanipulated $A_i \rightarrow R_j$ connection. The details of the procedures are presented in Appendix 8.1. The analysis of baseline data showed that Pumpkin's Ignore and Provoke were controlled by the same antecedent, mother-Command. On three consecutive days the mother was cued to issue four commands during each baseline period and 16 during the experimental condi-

tion. During this phase, whenever Pumpkin provoked, the mother was to terminate the aversive condition and talk nicely to Pumpkin. As expected, the negative reinforcement arrangement strengthened the $A_i \rightarrow R_j$ bond over the baseline levels on each of the three days. Strengthening mother-Command $\rightarrow$ child-Provoke *did not* alter the connection between mother-Command $\rightarrow$ child-Ignore. The mean conditional p value for the other $A_i \rightarrow R_j$ connection remained at its baseline value. Even though both connections share the same antecedent event, they seem to be autonomous. More studies of this kind must be carried out before we decide this crucial issue. At this juncture, we should think of responses as being functionally equivalent but also autonomous.

Manipulations of classes. There is an interesting sense in which one can manipulate members of a functionally defined class. If one increases the density with which functionally significant antecedent events are presented, then this should increase the frequency for all target responses within that class. However, the impact of this manipulation will not be the same for all members of the response class. It will vary as a function of how much control is exerted over each target response by the antecedent event. The power index should be of some assistance in predicting which members will be affected by manipulating the antecedent and which will not. The one study reported in Patterson (1979b) identified five coercive child behaviors as members of a functionally defined response class. All members were controlled by mother-Command. During the ABA manipulation, mother commands were increased during the B phase. It was predicted that during the experimental phase there would be increases in frequency for each of the five target responses beyond what was obtained during the two baseline periods. The manipulation showed the predicted effect for one response for which the power score was .51 and for a second for which the power score was only .27. Two responses for which the power score was less than .10 showed no significant effects for the manipulation. One response for which the power score was only .04 showed an increase during the manipulation and then a return to baseline.

This manipulation has been replicated several times; it has some interesting implications for treatment. Given a baseline study for a clinical case, a functional analysis would likely show that certain mother behaviors reliably control some class of functionally related coercive child behaviors. By having her carefully track and reduce the frequency with which she presents the controlling event, there would be a predictable drop in all child responses with power scores over .40. This would not only give the mother some small respite but also teach her about the impact of her behavior upon that of the child. (We haven't tried this yet).

Variance Accounted For

The stated function of a coercion performance theory is to account for variance in observed behavior. Identifying the controlling events provided by the behavior of the other person is a step toward accomplishing this goal. As shown in this chapter and in the more general case by Loeber (in preparation), the conditional p for $(R_j|A_i)$ compared to the $p(R_j)$ describes the increment in predictability for both intersubject and intrasubject components; $p(R_j|A_i)$ defines a small part of the events that determine extended coercive chains. However, by itself, information about the density of controlling antecedents would account for only very small portions of the variance for the child's overall level of coercive performance. As we shall see in the next section, it is the variables that determine extended chains that also account for the major portion of performance variance. There are some interpersonal components that do contribute to the likelihood of chain extension. These components will be discussed later in this chapter. The variance accounted for in the child's performance level will be presented in Chapters 11 and 12.

One would expect that effective treatment would result in several *kinds* of changes in the stimuli that control the behavior of the problem child. The connections between antecedents and the child's coercive target behaviors should become weaker. Abrasive antecedents presented by family members should decrease in number. The network of antecedents controlling prosocial behaviors may increase. In one study, 94.7 hours of therapist time produced only modest changes in an extremely difficult family; the comparison of baseline to intervention showed a reduction of 50% in overall deviancy for the problem child (Patterson, 1973). A functional analysis showed that of the 35 antecedents controlling the child's 14 coercive R_j's, only a few continued to do so at termination. Eighty-five percent of the controlling stimuli showed some reduction in their power scores at termination. While many of these reductions in power score were minor, the trends were in keeping with the general notion that effective treatment alters the *structure* of family interaction. When the family moved to a job in a different city, the therapy was far from complete. The residual *high* rates of deviant behavior and the fact that at termination nine *new* controlling events appeared had ominous implications. A telephone call a year later indicated that the child had been institutionalized.

In summary, then, some aspects of the behavior of family members show orderly relations among events adjacent in interactional sequences. The behavior of one person elicits, in a probabilistic sense, certain reactions from other members of the family. There are certain networks of antecedent events that reliably control several responses. These functionally defined response classes occur across families. The experimental studies carried out thus far suggest that antecedent events that are correlated with target events may also be thought of as "controlling events"; i.e., increases or decreases in the frequency with which the antecedent events are presented produce corresponding changes in the target events.

Intrasubject Component

In social interaction sequences our immediate reactions reflect, in part, an extension of what we were doing a moment ago. In that sense, the individual's ongoing social behavior has its own intrasubject structure. Most of us have a sense about this; at a phenomenological level there is an awareness of continuity in our own ongoing behavior. While our next reaction may surprise others, it is seldom a surprise to us. This sense of orderliness or predictability about our own behavior agrees with the findings from a large number of studies by such investigators as Sackett (1977), Bartlett (1951), Raush (1965), and Gottman (1979). The findings also emphasize the fact that much of what we call social behavior comes in "chunks." Once an event begins, it is likely to continue.

This, in turn, leads us to reconsider in what form we should express our dependent variables for microsocial analyses. As pointed out by Hartup (1979), frequency and rate measures necessarily distort this most important characteristic of social behavior. Behavioral events must be described by both their *duration and frequency*. The dependent variable for future interactional studies at OSLC will almost certainly be duration measures.

This perspective has several implications. For one thing, the concept of duration introduces the necessity of considering boundaries for an event. These were also questions considered in the 1960's by R. Barker and his colleagues (Barker, 1963). When does an event begin, and when does it end? When the contingency is embedded in the continuous flow of social interaction, *what* is the unit of behavior being reinforced? What is strengthened; is it the event that preceded the reinforcer? Or is it the structure in which the target response is embedded? Must structure be taken into account when defining the boundaries?

This problem of units, boundaries, and relevant contingencies has always been with us, *even* in the more tightly controlled laboratory setting. I became intimately aware of the relation between reinforcement effects and response structure while studying children's preference in a two-choice preference task involving a continuous series of trials (Patterson & Hinsey, 1964). Following one study, the event recorder tapes from the performance of 24 subjects during baseline and "conditioning" were festooned across the walls. By walking and looking, it became apparent that during *baseline* the response sequence for many subjects was *highly structured*. They simply alternated ABABA, etc. Was the reinforcer contingent upon the child's preference for A, or the pattern ABAB in which it was embedded? Most of the children whose baseline preference scores for A and B were close to 50/50 splits employed the alternation strategy. The proportion of responses involved in such alternation patterns was highly stable ($r = .88$), as shown in comparing the p values for the first and second 100 trials in an extended baseline study. Only 49% of these "alternation" children showed a shift in preference during conditioning. This was in contrast to the 80% for those with infrequent alternation and 63% for those with moderate alternation.

Other investigators working with more complex manipulations involving the operant shaping of speech noted similar problems. Salzinger, Portnoy, Zlotogura, and Keisner (1963) found that when attempting to reinforce pronouns, they often produced side effects, such as changes in *rate* of speech, or in certain subgroups of words.

Thomas and Martin (1976), Thomas and Malone (1979), and Martin, Maccoby, Baron, and Jacklin (1980) raise one further implication. They note that a covariation between A_i and R_j reflects *two* sets of determinants. One is the eliciting status of the controlling antecedent event; the other is the subject's own prior behavior. For example, the target subject's first response may elicit two outcomes. One is the reaction of the other person, which increases the likelihood of R_2; but R_1 may also directly elicit R_2. For example, one study of 18-month-old infants interacting with their mothers showed that *both* members were more influenced by their *own* prior behavior than by the antecedent reaction of the other person (Martin et al., 1980). This paper underscores the importance of the *intra*subject component as a determinant for ongoing behavior.

Serial Dependencies

There are two techniques in general use that identify intraindividual serial dependencies, i.e., the relation between the target person's behavior at t and at $t + 1$. One procedure is correlational and the other is conditional probability analyses (Martin et al., 1980; Gottman, 1979; Sackett, 1977). Both provide essentially the same information. Both can be lagged for the subject's own immediately prior behavior at $t - 1$ or prior behavior at $t - 2$, etc. For the moment, it seems that the one that is used depends upon which computer programs are available and whose paper most recently influenced the investigator.

Regardless of which statistic is employed, there are certain questions about the interconnection of the individual's own behavior that must be answered. Unfortunately, these necessary studies have hardly begun. For example, it would be useful to know the correlations between adjacent segments (Lag 1) for prosocial and for coercive behaviors separately for each family member. It would also be useful to have some estimate for the duration of such thematic effects. Given that the problem child has engaged in a coercive behavior, how many subsequent behaviors are characterized by an increased probability for yet further coercive behaviors? Sackett (1977) has analyzed such sequences for primates, as has Gottman (1979) for married couples, but no comparable studies for families have been made. Are the coercive child's own behaviors interconnected if we examine adjacent ten- or 20-minute time blocks? Are the behavior frequencies correlated if based upon observations made over a series of days? To understand how the problem child's behavior is structured, we must first have the answers to these questions.

In our own analyses, we began by asking whether some problem-child behaviors were more likely to persist (have longer durations) than others. The analysis focused upon the likelihood of a second response given the first $(p[R_{t + 1}|R_t])$. Patterson (1976) analyzed the data for a mixed sample of 27 antisocial and 27 matched nonproblem boys. The six to ten baseline sessions for each child were combined to form a population of *response* events. The p values for the continuance or recurrence of each of the 14 coercive responses are given in Table 8.4. Given the first Physical Negative, there was a very good chance that behavior would continue to the next six seconds for both the clinical (.23) and nonclinical samples (.17). Notice that for Cry the probability for continuance was very high for both samples. Nine of the 14 coercive responses showed greater likelihoods of con-

Table 8.4
Likelihood of Recurrence/Persistence
of a Coercive Response

(adapted from Patterson, 1976, p. 272)

Code Category	Nonproblem Boys, N = 27 $p(\bar{R}_t \mid \bar{R}_{t-1})$	Antisocial Boys, N = 27 $p(\bar{R}_t \mid \bar{R}_{t-1})$
Command Negative	.000	.144
Cry	.658	.594
Disapproval	.114	.203
Dependency	.231	.225
Destructive	.182	.610
High Rate	.281	.492
Humiliate	.000	.203
Ignore	.231	.100
Noncomply	.158	.187
Negativism	.177	.284
Physical Negative	.167	.225
Tease	.159	.255
Whine	.379	.253
Yell	.254	.206
Social Aggression (PN & TE)	.171	.263
Hostility (DI, NE, HU, IG, WH)	.270	.334
Total Deviant Behavior (all 14 $\bar{R}_j$'s)	.302	.388

tinuance for the clinical than for the nonproblem sample.

The data reviewed earlier showed that for the clinical sample there is a higher likelihood of a coercive behavior being initiated (.19 versus .14 for Normals). The data in Table 8.4 showed that there was a greater likelihood of continuance for the clinical than for the normal sample (.39 versus .30 for Normals). In examining more recent data relating to the likelihood of continuance for Normals, I was surprised to see *p* values of 0.0 for about half of the sample! These children *always* emitted a single coercive behavior and then *stopped*. There was only one child in the Social Aggressor sample for whom the *p* value was 0.0.

The 1976 study was based upon a mixed sample of antisocial boys, some referred because of stealing and others for social aggression. There was, in addition, the already noted complication that results from sampling events rather than subjects; i.e., the contribution of a few individuals *may*

badly skew the resulting *p* values. The next analysis was based upon the samples of 30 socially aggressive boys and 20 matched normal boys described in Appendix 5.1. The analyses were carried out separately by age and by the quality of the antecedent. Each prior behavior of the other person was categorized as positive, neutral, or aversive.

The data in Table 8.5 summarize two different ways of describing coercive sequences. The first was simply counting the number of events in each coercive sequence. This was tabulated separately for each child; i.e., the sample was children, not events. As shown there, the coercive sequences for socially aggressive boys were significantly longer (mean 1.50 events) than were those for nonproblem boys (mean 1.16 events).

Another way of expressing this is to calculate the conditional *p* of a second coercive event (or a repetition) given a first event. As expected, the boys in the clinical sample were significantly more likely than Normals to continue their coercive chains. Across contexts (antecedents) the values were .28 and .13 respectively.[5] The likelihood of chain extension was significantly greater for the clinical sample when the antecedents were either positive or aversive. It can also be seen for both samples that chain extension was most likely to occur when the antecedent was *positive*. This finding was counterintuitive. One would have thought chain extensions were more likely to occur during the attack and counterattack responses that characterize episodes with aversive antecedents.

These lag, conditional, or correlational analyses hardly scratch the surface of possible response dependencies. What about the patterns involving more than a single category, e.g., episodes such as Yell → Whine → Hit? Thus far at OSLC we have considered only those possibilities that involve homogeneous sequences. When one considers the permutations and combinations generated by 29 alternatives, the prospect is overwhelming. Furthermore, the intrasubject thematic effect does not necessarily have to appear as a patterned sequence. Given a coercive event, there may be an increased likelihood for further coercive events at any one or all of the next dozen subject reactions. Sackett's (1977) sequential analysis is a means for identifying such an effect (Gottman, 1979; Gottman & Bakeman, 1979).[6] The procedure requires that one begin with a criterion behavior, such as a coercive behavior, and then search at each lag that follows for a recurrence of coercive behaviors. The likelihood of a coercive event is calculated for each lag; Sackett carries this out to 16 lags in his analysis of primate interactions. I think this is potentially a powerful tool for the analysis of family

Table 8.5
Comparisons for Duration of Coercive Sequences

Antecedent	Normals		Social Aggressors		F values for		
	Younger (N = 10)	Older (N = 10)	Younger (N = 15)	Older (N = 15)	Samples	Age	Interaction
Mean Number of Events in Sequence							
General	1.15	1.16 (9)	1.54	1.46	30.21***	0.31	0.60
Mean Likelihood Event Extension $p(\overline{R}_t|\overline{R}_{t-1})$							
General	.13	.13	.30	.25	28.79***	0.85	0.60
Aversive	.06 (9)†	.16 (7)	.31	.30	11.68**	0.61	1.04
Neutral	.35 (8)	.16 (9)	.22 (14)	.14	1.24	3.98*	0.64
Positive	.14 (9)	.14 (9)	.32	.35	13.46***	0.07	0.06

*$p < .05$
**$p < .01$
***$p < .001$

†Numbers in parentheses refer to analyses that are based on a subgroup of the entire sample.

interactions. For example, is the duration of these ripple-like effects greater for some family members than for others? Are the likelihoods for the recurrence of a coercive behavior greater at Lag 6 or Lag 16 for members of clinical than for members of nonclinical samples? If so, it means the possibility for extended conflicts and/or the restarting of conflicts is higher for members of the clinical samples.

Inter- and Intrasubject Components Together

For ease of discussion, the inter- and intrasubject components of structure have been viewed separately. In actuality, the labels, inter- and intrasubject components, are a kind of convenient fiction. The separate labels imply an independence that does not exist. For example, given an A_i that controls R_2, the subject's prior behavior, R_1, is also functionally related to R_2. It is my assumption that the subject's R_1 and the other person's A_i are *also* functionally related. *Each* juncture in the sequence is functionally related to what follows. The relative contribution of one or the other must vary as a function of type of target response and who the reactive agent is. As yet there are few comparative studies, although the few that have been done note the larger contribution of the subject's own prior behavior (Martin et al., 1980; Thomas & Malone, 1979).

The most convenient metaphor for the overall structure would be a giant probability tree. Given massive amounts of data, we could empirically trace out the multiple paths or outcomes that are possible from a single initiating event. As an example of this, Figure 8.7 follows the course for a single target event and the consequences that controlled its recurrence. A prior analysis for a single subject identified a functionally defined class (Hostile) of behaviors, all controlled by the same network of antecedents (Patterson, 1974c). The base rate for hostile initiations was .120. The data from the 50 observation sessions also showed a common set of consequences that increased the likelihood for recurrence of events in this class.

Given the target event, then the likelihood that the parents would supply an accelerating consequence was .285. This type of consequence had been identified as the intersubject component most likely to contribute to the child's continuing to perform the target event. As can been seen in the figure, the occurrence of the accelerating consequence at this juncture was correlated with a dramatic increase in the likelihood of a recurrence for the target event (.519). Notice, however, that the intrasubject component is very much in evidence (.481). This means that *regardless* of parent reactions, the child is likely to perform two target events in sequence. It *cannot* be said, then, that at this juncture the intersubject component contributes very much.

Now there are shifts in structure that emphasize the nonstationary and dependent status of the con-

Figure 8.7
Inter- and Intrasubject Components
(adapted from Patterson, 1974c, p. 908)

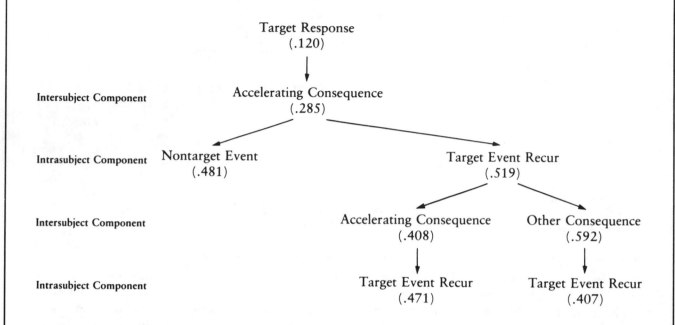

Numbers in parentheses refer to the likelihood of occurrence.

sequences for this family; i.e., the events are not independent of trials and sequences (Coombs, Dawes, & Tversky, 1970). First, given two target events in sequence, the parents become *increasingly* likely to provide the reaction (.408) that is most likely to accelerate the child's coercive behavior! The more extended the child's chain, the more likely he was to receive the accelerating consequence. However, recent studies of such sequences by E. Thomas (in preparation) suggest that these increases may be expected because of probability summation and do not necessarily demonstrate that longer chains have some unexpected functional utility.

Note in the original study the *intra*subject component remains in evidence. Given that the parents reacted by providing first an accelerating consequence and then a nonaccelerating consequence in sequence, the likelihood of a third target event remained a very high .407. This is in contrast to the likelihood of .471 when the intersubject components had been supportive of his prior two target events. This, incidentally, was a very deviant child. The extreme persistence of his intrasubject

coercive component is an indication of this.

The simplest assumption that one can make about interaction sequences is that they can be categorized by a limited number of states (e.g., positive, negative, and neutral), and that the state at any given time is a function of the immediately prior state (Coombs et al., 1970). These are the assumptions underlying the Markov chain. Does family interaction meet the requirements for a Markov chain? I don't think so, but we are just beginning to examine this question. The findings from the probability tree data suggest that some sequences are associated with marked increases in the likelihood of coercive child behavior. Could not such a sequence be considered an "event"? I have a sense that this very important dialogue is just beginning. For example, Raush (1965) also noted that for antisocial children the likelihood of unfriendly acts did not seem to follow a simple Markov process. What is required are studies that formally compare predictions from Markov analyses to the empirical findings.

Patterson and Moore (1979) studied a mother-child dyad that was illustrative of the functional

Figure 8.8
Inter- and Intrasubject Components for Tina and Mother

(from Patterson & Moore, 1979, p. 92)

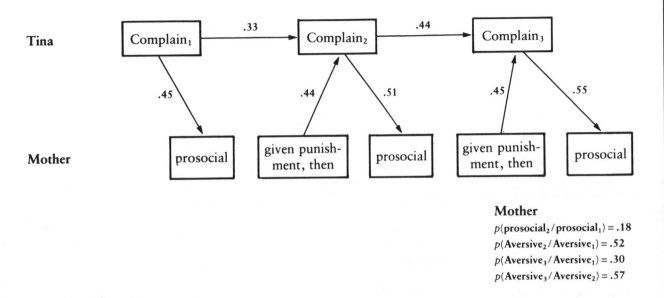

Patterson & Moore, Interactive patterns as units of behavior. In S. Suomi, M. Lamb, and G. Stephenson, editors, *Social Interaction Analysis: Methodological Issues* (Madison: The University of Wisconsin Press; ©1979 by the Board of Regents of the University of Wisconsin System). Reprinted with permission.

relation between the inter- and intrasubject components. The study was based upon 60 sessions in the home of 6-year-old Tina and her mother. Tina-Complain served as a dependent variable for a series of analyses. As a general case, the intrasubject analysis showed that Tina's mother was disposed to continue her irritable reactions once she initiated them to the child (.52). However, given that the mother's reaction was prosocial, the likelihood was only .18 that she would continue into a second interval. As shown in Figure 8.8, once Tina began to complain, the likelihood of a second Complain was .33; the likelihood of a third Complain, given a second, was .44. The intrasubject components for coercives were of high magnitude for both the mother and the daughter. Note that at each point in the sequence, Tina-Complain, there was a strong likelihood of the mother's being prosocial! These probability values constitute a reliable increase over the base-rate likelihood for a prosocial reaction from the mother.

Given that the mother punished Tina's first Complain, then the likelihood of a second Complain was .44. The intersubject component (mother-Punish) seemed to increase the probability of recurrence. Notice, however, that the intersubject component added nothing to the prediction of the third target event.

As a next step, we analyzed the outcomes for patterns. For example, an aggregate of two child-Complains was accompanied by a likelihood of .75 that the mother's reaction to the first and had been noxious. Given an aggregate of three Complains in sequence, then the likelihood of at least one of the mother's intervening behaviors having been noxious was .88. The claim was made that these findings support the idea that extended chains may have a unique function; i.e., the child persisted *until* the mother terminated her aversiveness and/or shifted to prosocial behavior. Was the mother significantly more likely to react in a prosocial manner to the third Complain than to the first? If so, then the sequence is not independent of phase. Does a sequence of three Complains constitute an event whose function is demonstrably dif-

191

ferent from that served by a single Complain? A series of discussions with Ewart Thomas convinced me otherwise. By using base-rate information and probability summation, he was able to provide a reasonably close fit to our empirical findings for likelihoods of the mother's intervening noxious and prosocial responses as a function of the number of Complains. I find his argument persuasive and stand neutral on the issue of whether social interaction does or does not fit a Markov model.

A more convincing demonstration of how social interaction departs from a Markov chain has been presented by Raush (1965). The reader should note, however, that the format was completely bilateral in that it assumed that the behavior of Subject A was always followed by a reaction from Subject B; i.e., Subject A's second behavior never directly followed his first behavior. (See Thomas and Martin [1976] and Thomas and Malone [1979] for examples of more flexible models.) In the Raush study, six hyperaggressive boys were observed prior to, during, and following treatment. Their behaviors were classified as either friendly (F) or unfriendly (Un). Early in treatment, the base rates for these behaviors were $p(F)$ of .70 and $p(Un)$ of .30. The conditional p's of most relevance were $p(F_2|Un)$ of .25 and $p(F_2|F_1)$ of .55. These conditional p values plus the base-rate values can be used to describe the p that the process will be in state F or Un at any given trial. A straightforward application of Baysean theory would show the likelihood of the dyad being in an unfriendly state at time 2, time 3, time 4, and so on. As shown in Figure 8.9, for the data collected prior to treatment, these boys were increasingly likely to become engaged in unfriendly acts as the sequence proceeded. Their observed behavior suggested an even greater likelihood than predicted by the Markov chain analysis. The contributing factor lay in their great likelihood of launching "unprovoked" attacks; the conditional was .08 for Normals and .45 for the clinical sample. After two years of treatment, the conditional dropped to .19; this also means a lower p for Un in general.

The Raush study is undoubtedly one of the most important studies published in interactional psychology. It served as a prelude to the analyses and extensions by Cairns (1979), Suomi, Lamb, and Stephenson (1979), and Gottman (1979). For example, here he presents a means by which the reader can test for the question of whether social interaction follows a Markov chain or not. Does social interaction function as if neither party has a memory? Is the state in the next trial completely described by the state of the dyad at $t-1$? Does the model hold for some interactions but not oth-

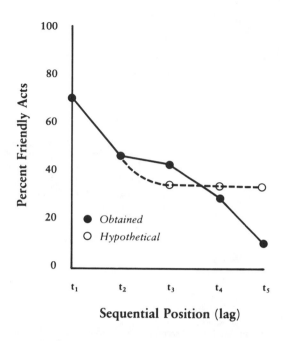

Figure 8.9
Interaction Sequences of Hyperaggressive Boys

(from Raush, 1965, p. 495)

Sequential Position (lag)

ers? Just how generalizable is it? These are interesting questions for which available code systems and computer software offer a technology sufficient to provide some answers.

There are many questions yet to be answered concerning the relative contributions of inter- and intrapersonal components and whether their position in a sequence makes any particular difference. However, given our present incomplete understanding of these matters, can these concepts be applied to the task of constructing a performance theory? The section that follows employs inter- and intrasubject components to construct variables that account for differences in the problem child's coercive performance level.

Irritable Exchanges

Earlier in this volume it was noted that socially aggressive children live in aggressive families. At a microsocial level, what is meant is that members of these families are disposed to react irritably with each other, particularly in their interactions with the problem child. There are four measures of irritability: crossover, counterattack, punishment acceleration, and continuance. Inter- and intrasubject components that measure these dispositions provide the empirical basis for examining this process. The general idea is that problem families are more likely to start conflicts. Given that a conflict is started, the other members are likely to react in such a way as to keep the conflict going. This formulation is similar to the one presented by Gottman (1979). His laboratory study showed that when a distressed spouse initiated an aversive, the other was likely to respond in kind. His sequential lag analyses of the husband and wife reactions that followed the initiation were characterized by an alternation. The couple seemed to "take turns" being aversive. The net effect was to extend the conflict. He labeled this process "negative-affect cycle."

The first hypothesis is that members of families of antisocial children are more likely than members of normal families to "start" conflicts. Given that the other family member is behaving in a neutral or prosocial manner, there is a significantly greater likelihood that members of distressed families will initiate an attack; this is labeled "crossover." A comparison of the likelihoods for samples of Normals, Stealers, and Social Aggressors (Table 7.4) showed significant differences for all family members. The mothers, fathers, and siblings in the clinical samples were about twice as likely as Normals to start a conflict with the target child. When examining the likelihood for the problem child initiating a conflict, the differences among samples were significant only for his interactions with the mother (Table 7.4). In fact, the problem child's favorite target for starting fights was the mother by a factor of two to one.

The importance of the crossover phenomenon was first noted by Raush (1965). He found this to be the intersubject variable that most significantly differentiated between the interactions of aggressive and normal children. Given a friendly reaction, the clinical sample was more likely to make an unfriendly response. The crossover variable will be examined in Chapters 11 and 12 to determine the significance of its contribution to problem child performance level. Presumably families whose members are characterized by greater dispositions for starting fights would have problem children with higher TAB scores.

The next variable is also an intersubject component. Given that either member starts a conflict, what is the likelihood that the other will counterattack? If a fight starts but no one reacts, then the fight is likely to stop right there. If, however, the other family member reacts by nattering, then it is likely that the conflict will be extended. This reaction has been labeled counterattack. The hypothesis is that members of families of antisocial children will be characterized by a greater likelihood of counterattacks. The comparisons among normal and clinical samples (Table 7.6) showed that all of the trends were in keeping with the hypothesis. The disposition to counterattack was significant for some dyads but not for others.

In the clinical samples the mother and the father were significantly more likely than parents of normal families to react irritably to coercive initiations by the target child. The problem child was significantly more likely than normal children to react irritably to coercive initiations by the mother. It is important to note that at this second point in the sequence it is the irritable reactions of the *parents* and the *problem child* that were significant. This suggests that to understand the aggressive child it may be necessary to study the parent-child interchanges with even greater care than sibling-child interchanges. This hypothesis is examined in detail in Chapter 12. Chapter 11 summarizes the covariations between measures of child antisocial behavior and the dispositions of family members to react irritably to coercive initiations.

Given an initiation by a family member and a counterattack, what is the likelihood that the aversive exchange will continue? This next conditional p value describes the punishment-acceleration index encountered in Chapter 6. In their interactions with the target child, the mother, father, and siblings from families in the clinical samples showed nonsignificant trends for a greater likelihood of chain extension than did members of normal families (Table 6.8). However, the problem child showed significantly greater punishment-acceleration indices than did normal children in his interactions with mother, father, and siblings.

The next measure describes the disposition to persevere in one's irritable reactions regardless of the reaction of the other family member. Table 8.6 summarizes the findings for the six comparisons involving the target child and other family members. The data were based upon samples of Normals, Social Aggressors, and Stealers described in Appendix 6.2. As can be seen in the table, this intrasubject component significantly differentiated normal from clinical samples for five out of the six dyads. Members of distressed families were more likely to persist in their irritable reactions regardless of how the other person reacted. The findings summarized in Chapters 11 and 12 show this particular variable to be a key to understanding children's socially aggressive behavior. The mothers'

Table 8.6
Probability of Irritable Continuance for Dyads Involving the Target Child

Continuance of Irritable Reactions by:	Mean Probability for Samples			F Value
	Normals (N = 38)	Social Aggressors (N = 37)	Stealers (N = 38)	
Mother interacting with Target Child	.122	.266	.217	15.00***
Target Child interacting with Mother	.125	.321	.238	13.86***
Sibling interacting with Target Child	.208	.279	.259	1.50
Target Child interacting with Sibling	.142	.302	.273	8.29***
Father interacting with Target Child	.111	.262	.203	9.04***
Target Child Interacting with Father	.049	.283	.202	9.70***

***$p < .001$

Figure 8.10
Likelihood of Irritable Reactions at Different Junctures for Mother-Child Dyads

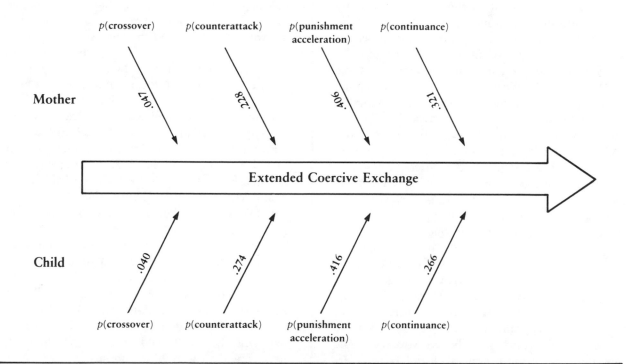

and, to a lesser extent, the fathers' disposition to continue their irritable reactions account for the largest portion of the variance in the performance of antisocial child behavior. In another study, the mothers' irritable reactions during family problem solving correlated with poor problem resolution (Forgatch & Patterson, in preparation).

The material discussed in Chapters 11 and 12 emphasizes the role of the problem child's interac-

tion with the *mother* as a key to understanding what produces the problem. Figure 8.10 presents the data for the Social Aggressor sample that describe the disposition of one or the other to react in an irritable fashion. Given that they are interacting with each other in a neutral or prosocial fashion, the likelihood is .09 that one or the other will initiate an attack. Given ten exchanges per minute, the odds are very high that in a ten-minute

Table 8.7
Intercorrelations Among Irritability Values for Mother-Child Dyad

Child-Mother Variables:	Mother-Child Variables:			
	Crossover	Punishment	Continuance	Punishment Acceleration
	Intercorrelations for Mothers			
Crossover	.31	.49	.50	.26
Punishment	.74	.33	.56	.54
Continuance	.57	.67	.58	.63
Punishment Acceleration	.11	.57	.81	.44
	Intercorrelations for Children			

Note: Any correlation over .20 is significant at $p < .05$.

period a conflict will start. Once a conflict begins, both the child and the mother tend to persist in their irritable reactions, and there is about one chance in four of an *extended* interchange. For such a dyad, finding a peaceful interlude must be a precarious business.

I think the four irritability measures (crossover, counterattack, punishment acceleration, and continuance) can be thought of as facets of a trait. The assumption would be that the disposition to react in an irritable fashion would be stable across time and across settings. For both the mother and the child (and other family members as well) it is a style of interacting with people and a means of coping with problems. As a first step in testing such a hypothesis, it would be assumed that all four measures of irritability would intercorrelate. Table 8.7 summarizes the intercorrelations for values that describe mother-child interchanges for a sample of 112 families. The figures above the diagonal describe the relations among the measures for mothers' behavior. Those below the diagonal describe the relations among measures for the child. The figures in the diagonal are the correlations between trait scores for mother and child.

There seem to be larger correlations among the measures for the child than for the mother. For example, the correlation between the likelihood of child crossover and child punishment was .74. The comparable value for mothers was .46. In either case the irritability values tend to covary. In that sense, it can be said that the four measures form a kind of trait cluster for the mother and the child.

The child trait for aggression can be viewed in several ways. On the one hand, it is a stable disposition to react to family members in an irritable fashion. The studies reviewed in Chapter 3 showed that the child's TAB score was stable from one week to the next and even from one year to the next. We have come to think of this as a trait measure for social aggression. It is also the case that the child's irritability p values define what is meant by the TAB score, i.e., its component parts. As shown in Chapter 11, each of the p values correlates heavily with the TAB score. However, I believe it is also the case that the child's disposition to react irritably reflects the fact that others are reacting to him in a similar manner. Social aggression, as measured by TAB scores, irritability scores, or Parent Daily Report, is a *bilateral trait*. It reflects the disposition of the child to react irritably; the magnitude also reflects the disposition of family members to respond in kind. Note in Table 8.7, for example, that with the exception of crossover, the trait scores for mother and child *intercorrelate*. Children with very high probability of continuance scores are interacting with mothers who are similarly disposed.

A bilateral definition implies that if an individual performs socially aggressive behaviors at high rates, then the members of his social environment are the major determinants. The child's aggressive behavior can be changed by *either* altering his disposition to initiate and react aversively and/or by altering these same dispositions for his family members.

Some Implications of Bilateral Emphasis

The focus upon inter- and intrasubject components emphasizes the fact that much of each member's ongoing behavior is *jointly* determined. A given event partially reflects the prior behavior of the other person, as well as his own immediately prior behavior. An extended coercive interchange may then be said to be the outcome of a *bilateral exchange*. As the interchange unfolds, both members of the dyad alter each other's reactions. Such a bilateral point of view of parent-child interaction has, of late, become fashionable (Bell, 1968; Bell & Harper, 1977). This viewpoint is in marked contrast to the earlier child psychologists who, with some notable exceptions such as R. Barker (1963), viewed the child as a passive-reactive organism. Parental attitudes and child-rearing practices had impact upon the child. Child behavior was thought to mirror the interplay between the forces of genetic endowment and environmental exigencies.

In the past decade the field of psychology has matured sufficiently to provide a more complex alternative. From that perspective the child is viewed as an active participant. He actively selects, stores, and organizes information; i.e., he is both a reactor and a selector. As noted by Baltes and Reese (1977) there are a number of philosophical problems raised by the bilateral perspective. Is the effect to be thought of as quantifiable and made up of component parts or as a qualitative emergence which can only be defined as a "whole"? I have made a case for the idea that these are mutual actions that are additive and unidirectional. As I perceive it, the child is an active participant whose behavior is a reaction to the behavior of the other family members and also constitutes a stimulus for their behaviors. A behavioral event is an effect and a cause; in fact, one could describe several interchanges as a linear series of cause-and-effect relations. These and the related questions of fixity and independence of events in interactional sequences will be the focus for the next generation of studies about structure and process.

Acknowledgments

The writer is deeply grateful for the extensive efforts of Katie Whalen and Marion Forgatch, who served as research assistants for the experiments reported here. Their patience and innovative response to challenge made this phase of our explorations a very productive one.

I also wish to thank Alice Harris and Rolf Loeber for their critique of the earliest drafts of this chapter. John Reid provided his usual thorough critique for a later version. Finally, there is the kindly Dr. Hartmann, who sacrificed countless evenings of his social life to generate 18 pages of critique for what I had previously thought of as a flawless manuscript. My riposte required three weeks of writing time; the resulting chapter is, I believe, considerably improved. And to you, Don Hartmann, I say:

"John zegt dat je je moeder eens moet schrijven en doe haar de groeten van hem."

Footnotes

1. We conducted a computer analysis to determine how much data would be lost by decision rules requiring up to 30 seconds of prosocial antecedents. Informal analyses suggested that extending the interval beyond 18 seconds resulted in the loss of too much data. Less than 18 seconds would mean a lack of certainty about whether the thematic component had been disrupted. This analysis should be repeated with larger samples and presented with statistical analyses describing the outcome for the various decisions.

2. The term base rate does not refer to a fixed number. It is always relative to the setting(s) in which the data were collected. By definition, sampling across the population of (all) settings would give lower base-rate values for all behavior. Eventually, the study of interactional psychology must delineate base-rate values separately by setting.

3. The magnitude of the conditional p values obtained in these studies in no way matched the precision noted by Hinde (1974) in his review of the findings from ethology, e.g., for agonistic displays in birds. For the ethologist, knowing whether the wings are raised or the nape is erect during body-horizontal conditions provides considerable predictive power. The event mother-Ignore is, by comparison, a much less powerful event.

4. The parents' ability to make fine discriminations about their own or their child's behavior definitely sets a ceiling on the complexity of behaviors that can be studied in these studies. If the mother's definitions differ from those of the experimenter, then the study will not be successful. A case in point involved our efforts to study *reinforcement* effects with Spring as the subject. It was assumed that if the sequence mother-Argue → Spring-Argue was followed by mother terminate her Argue

and interact in a prosocial manner, this would *negatively reinforce* Spring's Argue. During baseline, the p(Spring-Argue|mother-Argue) was .52; the mean duration of Spring-Argue was 8.83 seconds.

During the four days of experimental manipulation, it became obvious that the mother could not differentiate Spring-Argue from Spring-Complain, -Disapprove, or -Whine. Not being able to clearly discriminate that event meant that she was not successful in reinforcing Argue *contingently*. As a result, four days of effort produced no real changes in the $A_i \rightarrow R_j$ bond. The mean conditional p value for mother-Argue given Spring-Argue was .56.

5. Note that our original estimates for response sequences $R_2|R_1$ (chain extension) in the 1976 study were considerably higher. I do not understand the discrepancy between early and late samplings for Normals except to note that the late additions were less deviant. Snyder (1977) found *no* differences between normal and clinical samples in the likelihood of chain extension (p values of .30 and .29 respectively). The findings for his clinical sample exactly match those for the OSLC sample, but there was a major discrepancy in findings between his normal sample and those for OSLC.

6. Computer programs for conducting sequential data analyses are available from Roger Bakeman, Department of Psychology, Georgia State University, Atlanta, Georgia 30303 (see also Sackett, 1977).

Chapter 9
Abstract

Turn-taking is presented as a primitive building component for synchronous interactions. Synchronicity refers to the functional relation between the behavior of one person and the immediate reaction of another. It has particular relevance to extended episodes. The data indicate that the use of approval by family members is not consistently synchronous; however, aversive events produce both matched and nonmatched synchronous reactions.

Both positive events and aversive events produce "ripple effects," i.e., increased probabilities for a general continuance of the behavior. Distressed family members are thought to be characterized by a greater general disposition to be aversive with each other and nondistressed family members by a greater disposition to be positive with each other.

The concepts of reciprocity and exchange seem highly relevant to family distress and breakdown. However, a review of the social learning studies to date suggests that analyses of social interaction have not yet provided a suitable means for testing hypotheses relating to reciprocity.

Chapter 9

Turn-Taking, Synchronicity, and Reciprocity

The functional relation between the behavior of one person and another is embedded in larger structures. The nature of these larger structures varies a good deal. In some instances they are conventions built into the culturally defined programs which govern large segments of our behavior. In fact, one might think of them as "rules" that stipulate what is appropriate and what is not. One of the most interesting examples of this would be "turn-taking" during talking. This basic social interaction skill is taught during infancy. Gradually, turn-taking becomes so much a part of our repertoire that its presence is not noted. However, turn-taking does generate much of the structure identified in sequential data, and marked disruptions in turn-taking may evoke the use of such labels as "monologist" or "eccentric." The research literature relating to these topics will be considered in more detail in a later section of this chapter.

Turn-taking tells us only that we should expect to find alternation when we study social interaction. It is a background theme against which interactional melodies are played. It means that the content of what one person does is often reflected in the behavior of the other person. For example, two elderly checkers players sitting at their table in the park engage in only two or three categories of behavior, but they *alternate* both in their verbal reactions and in many of their motor movements. Their behavior is functionally related. The pat-

terned sequence persists for a very long period of time. Cairns labeled such extended structures as *synchronous:* the term "refers to a property of interactions which obtains when one person's acts are coordinated with and supportive of the ongoing activity of another individual" (Cairns, 1979a, p. 298). As I use the term, it refers to any kind of functional relation between the behavior of one person and another, including extended interchanges. These interchanges are often characterized by a shared content. Cairns notes that one of the properties of punishment is that it disrupts these ongoing themes. Incidentally, it is interesting to consider punishment in this role of establishing the "setting" for an event. One of the functions of punishment may be that it redefines the setting; i.e., it signals that this is the end of one theme and the beginning of another.

To understand extended structures (or synchronous interactions as Cairns puts it) we need to develop a means of cataloging episodes. Interactional psychology must eventually return to the task set for us by Roger Barker (1963) and his colleagues. They introduced the study of behavioral "episodes." They carried out a series of methodological studies which demonstrated that judges could agree at a modest level in identifying the boundaries where one episode ended and another began. Given a catalog for episodes, we could begin the search for determinants. Much of the information about these antecedents must be built into the setting itself. At high noon it is appropriate for elderly men to play checkers in the park, but in the evening young people gather in the same setting to hold hands.

The microsocial data presented earlier showed that given either the A_i or the R_j, we can make some reasonably good guesses about which other events might have occurred in the same sequence. A catalog of episodes and a search for their antecedents could take us to the more interesting task of predicting without relying upon information about the prior or the following event. Such analyses would require a whole new generation of code systems. The codes which now exist limit the questions to much more mundane considerations. What do we know about turn-taking? Does synchronicity hold for the immediate exchange of positives and aversives?

Turn-Taking

In the short run, there is for most of us a comfortable sense of continuity about ongoing interactions in which we are involved. There is a vague sense of predictability about it all. Most interactions do *not* contain many surprises. A novel twist, a sudden humorous shift is the exception, not the rule. Those who are capable of producing such effects are highly valued (and well paid). A vaguely sensed comfort (almost boredom) is the rule for most normal family interaction sequences. Much of the sense of continuity comes from two structural components which are built into the infant's repertoire even prior to the acquisition of language skills. These consist of an early disposition to match the behavior of the other person with regard to both the content and duration of the response. As noted by Shields (1976, p. 315) ". . . reciprocal activities between the child and its caretaker in which each monitors and responds to the behavior of the other are well established before the first identifiable words appear." Lieven's (1976) tape recordings of 17- to 18-month-old infants interacting with their mothers also showed symmetry for their interaction. Given an infant vocalization, the likelihood that the mother would vocalize was .76 for one mother, .51 for another, and .29 for a third. Given that the mother vocalized, the likelihood that the infant would vocalize was only in the .20's. As the study progressed, two of the three infants became increasingly likely to synchronize their vocalizations with those of the mother. Although no data were presented regarding the mother's description of these interchanges, it sounded as if the infant would vocalize *and then stop* as if expecting the mother to vocalize and then respond in kind. As Lieven viewed it, this was a basic communication skill.

One might think of this as a kind of modeling effect made up of *two* components. First, there is a matching of the other person's behavior for *content;* e.g., smiles produce smiles; vocalizing evokes vocalizing. Second, there is a rough matching for *duration* of the behavior. In effect, the infant learns very early to take turns. Shields (1976) sees this communication skill as essential for the acquisition of language. The child must learn to take into account turn-taking plus a reflection and/or extension of the meaning of what is being said.

Turn-taking is so commonplace that we no longer note its occurrence. With maturation, the skill is elaborated by special cuing systems which signal the end of an utterance and invite turn-taking from the other person. In social interaction the pause between turn-taking is the point of maximum uncertainty. From the viewpoint of the speaker, his *own* behavior is *highly predictable;* i.e., during this time there is a reduction in uncertainty. Much of his "sense" of continuity comes from the fact that the connection between his consecutive responses is eminently logical and predictable. What is surprising from his standpoint is how others *react* to this logical sequence. Some persons, for example, might perceive a perfectly straightforward, supportive comment as being an attack! In this vein, Gottman (1979) found significantly greater discrepancy for distressed than nondistressed couples between the sending of a positive communication and having it received as such by the other. Even without such distortion, awaiting the response of the other is the point of greatest uncertainty. Which response will he make? Will he shift topics, or will he leave to talk to someone else? From the perspective of an individual, turn-taking in social interaction is experienced as a sequence of regular pulsations from greater to lesser uncertainty. As a dyad, they take turns in being uncertain. In long-standing relationships the uncertainty should be of a lesser magnitude than it is for newly formed relationships.

The monologist chooses not to take any risk; he is absolutely certain of who will be talking five minutes from now. Very likely, he also knows what *he* will be talking about. Gottman (1979, p. 48) notes a pattern for distressed families in which turn-taking is replaced by monologue. Here, each person talks *to* the others; but he or she does not react to what the others have said! It is not the rapid alternation which implies, "Yes, I understood. Now here is how I react to it. What is your reaction?" This disruption of turn-taking may be an interesting but, as yet, largely neglected feature of familial conflict. One might think of distressed families as having ritualized patterns of fighting which are highly predictable in both their linkage and outcome. In that regard, Gottman makes the following fascinating observations:

"These findings are reminiscent of the second law of thermodynamics that relates greater energy in a physical system with greater degree of disorder. The second law of thermodynamics also associates high energy (and hence, less order and patterning) with the capacity of a system to undergo spontaneous change. In other words, systems that are highly patterned are more difficult to change than more randomly patterned ones." (Gottman, 1979, p. 48)

Signaling Turn-Taking

Turn-taking could be a deadly bore. For example, imagine if it were completely set by time constraints. Then one could engage in conversations that alternate speakers every two minutes, or perhaps engage in 7.5-minute parallel monologuing. The fact that social interaction is more flexible than that suggests the presence of subtle cuing mechanisms.

There have been a series of programmatic studies by Exline at Delaware, then by Kendon, Argyle, and Cook at Oxford which have added greatly to our understanding of this cuing process. This work consists of a series of elegant studies on gaze as it is coordinated with speech and social interaction. Much of the results from a decade's work are summarized in Argyle and Cook's *Gaze and Mutual Gaze* (1976). The combination of field and laboratory findings implicate gaze as an important source of information, particularly for the onset and offset of social discourse. For example, mutual gaze is an important prelude to initiating a social contact. Avoidance of mutual gaze by the spouse, a colleague, or the committee chairman signals, "No, not now!" Typically, when listening, we look at the person who is speaking; the person talking also tends to meet our gaze. At the end of an utterance, Person A gives a prolonged gaze to Person B. Person B then looks away and begins his utterance (see pp. 98-124 for a fascinating account of these findings in Argyle and Cook, 1976). Gestural and other nonverbal cues also provide signals which relate to turn-taking. For example, a hand in mid-gesture at the end of an utterance means, "Wait, more is coming!" Other investigators have noted shifts in body posture just prior to initiating an utterance.

Turn-taking etiquette is often violated. The tactics of the "conversation nibbler" are a good illustration of this. This extremely high-rate person can also be a borderline monologist. He speaks rapidly, then when it's *your* turn, does he quietly gaze and listen? No. No indeed! In your mid-sentence, he begins rapidly nodding his head, interjecting a "Yes, hmm, yes, yes." All of this makes you feel as if you are moving much too slowly, and when you awkwardly pause trying to catch your verbal balance, he charges in. He gets half your turn. Etiquette prevents your saying anything. Besides, there is no label for what he has just done to you.

Obviously dyads do not continue their synchronous turn-taking indefinitely. What determines when a conversation will shift to a new topic or stop altogether? It should be noted that empirical work on this question has a very short history. Therefore, much of what we wish to know has not yet been examined. However, it seems that cues which signal and support ongoing interchanges have both verbal and nonverbal components. For example, Argyle and Cook (1976, p. 63) review a series of studies in which visual cues were absent during telephone conversations. Here, one finds less synchronicity, i.e., more pauses and shorter utterances. Verbal cues, such as "hmm" and "ah" occur more often.

During social interchange the speaker uses gaze to indicate the boundary of one utterance and as a prelude to his next statement. At this point the other person may signal his interest with head nods and hmms. The content of what is being discussed may eventually become of less interest to one or both participants. If they become satiated, one or both persons may avert their gaze, and the topic shifts through a rapid sequence until listening, gaze, and turn-taking are resumed. This sequence of rapid satiation and quick channel shifting is in full bloom in such settings as the airplane or long bus trip. If both persons engage in it, then the shifts can cover entire life histories in very short order. The cocktail party is, of course, the classic example. Not only does channel shifting occur by topics but, in addition, every several minutes one must shift partners. Careful attention to turn-taking and its accompanying verbal and nonverbal signal systems seems most evident during formal occasions. Greetings, introductions, and goodbyes seem to be carefully monitored exchanges. Even here, however, the rules vary somewhat as a function of social class and, of course, by culture (Argyle & Cook, 1976).

If much of social interaction is indeed characterized by turn-taking, then the data should take certain forms. First, there should be a matching of category content. If Person A talks then Person B

Table 9.1
Synchronicity and Symmetry for Positive Events
(adapted from Margolin, 1977, pp. 18-22)

Behaviors	Husband $p(X_H|X_W)$	$p(X_H)$	Wife $p(X_W|X_H)$	$p(X_W)$	r_{XY}
Possible Reinforcers					
Approve	.000	(.002)	.000	(.004)	.27
Smile	.022	(.006)	.067*	(.012)	.22
Turn-Taking					
Attention	.331*	(.151)	.307*	(.145)	.27
Talk	.196*	(.058)	.205*	(.051)	.95**

*Comparison of conditional to base rate, z-score significant at $p < .05$.

**Comparison of conditional to base rate, z-score significant at $p < .01$.

talks and they continue to take turns, this should be reflected in the conditional p value, $p(A$ Talk| B Talk). Either this value or its converse should be greater than the base rate for Talk by either person. In other words, knowing what one person is doing should provide a basis for "predicting" what the other member of a dyad is doing. The concepts of synchronicity and turn-taking lead us to expect people to alternate roles of speaker and listener. The *content* of their behavior will also be functionally related. The content may be similar, matched, or the behavior of one may complement the other, e.g., Tease-Laugh. Synchronicity refers only to the fact that the content is functionally related. Notice, however, that it is possible to obtain high across-subject correlations from *nonsynchronous* interchanges. Two children engaging in parallel play would *not* generate significant conditional p values, but both would have high scores on Play. This lack of symmetry for the two modes of analysis poses a special problem. We will return to this problem later.

At this point it would be useful to design field studies to collect data on the synchronicity of positive and aversive interactions for children of different ages and sex in several settings. To my knowledge these studies have yet to be carried out. There is, however, a subset of findings which relate to this issue and which are also of interest because of their relevance to coercion theory. It concerns the synchronicity of rewards and punishment in family interactions. Does synchronicity extend to include a *matching* for the reinforcing or punishing behavior of the other person?

Synchronous Matching for Reward and Punishment

Reinforcement

There is nothing in the reinforcement theory literature which would lead one to expect a *matching* of positive events on a moment-by-moment basis. Conventions of social intercourse dictate that it is *unacceptable* to match positive events except in very special circumstances. "I like your new hairdo," followed immediately by the reply, "Thank you, I like your new dress," is acceptable behavior only for very young children or the most superficial level of adult discourse (e.g., *pro forma* greeting behavior, cocktail party discourse). Intimates have very special rules about this: touch may elicit touch; kiss may elicit kiss. But ordinarily adults do not seem to be synchronous in their use of positive events such as approval and praise.

At one level, almost any behavior could be thought of as a *potential* reinforcer. However, to provide a test for the matching hypothesis, I searched for data relating to a single event which most investigators would agree, a priori, is a reinforcer. Approval seemed to be a good example of such an event. There are two sets of findings which provide data relevant to the concept of synchronous matching for positive events.

The data in Table 9.1 summarize the findings from the Margolin (1977) study of married couples. The reactions were tabulated for 27 couples as they interacted in a 20-minute videotaped problem-solving situation. The base-rate values are

Table 9.2
Reactions to Target Child Behaviors by Male Siblings

Reactions by Male Siblings

Target Child Behaviors	Approve		Command		Disapprove		Negativism		Physical Negative		Tease		Whine		Yell		Base Rates		TAB		Total Frequency of Target Behavior	
	Dev.	Nor.	Dev.	Nor.	Dev.	Nor.	Dev.	Nor.	Dev.	Nor.	Dev.	Nor.	Dev.	Nor.	Dev.	Nor.	Dev.	Nor.	Dev.	Nor.	Dev.	Nor.
Approve	.000	.087	.000	.000	.059	.000	.000	.000	.000	.000	.000	.000	.000	.000	.000	.000	.002	.003	.059	.000	17	23
Command	.000	.000	.000	.000	.045	.000	.000	.000	.011	.000	.011	.020	.000	.000	.011	.000	.011	.007	.489	.360	88	50
Disapprove	.000	.000	.010	.000	.198	.116	.010	.000	.046	.000	.010	.014	.005	.000	.005	.000	.026	.010	.360	.217	197	69
Negativism	.000	.000	.018	.000	.109	.100	.027	.100	.009	.100	.000	.000	.000	.000	.009	.000	.014	.001	.236	.400	110	10
Physical Negative	.000	.000	.000	.000	.051	.375	.000	.000	.343	.125	.020	.000	.040	.000	.030	.000	.013	.001	.576	.500	99	8
Tease	.000	.000	.035	.000	.221	.235	.012	.000	.081	.000	.047	.059	.012	.000	.070	.000	.011	.003	.558	.412	86	17
Whine	.000	.000	.000	.333	.000	.000	.000	.000	.143	.000	.071	.000	.000	.000	.000	.000	.002	.000	.214	.333	14	3
Yell	.000	.000	.000	.000	.155	.000	.000	.000	.048	.000	.012	.000	.000	.000	.012	.167	.011	.001	.369	.167	84	6
Base Rates	.000	.001	.005	.003	.024	.008	.002	.002	.010	.001	.003	.002	.002	.001	.005	.002						
TAB	.000	.000	.011	.005	.111	.082	.007	.010	.071	.015	.012	.015	.008	.000	.016	.005			.427	.303		

presented in parentheses. The figures of greatest interest were the conditional p values describing the immediate reaction of the spouse given that the other spouse had approved. The average likelihood of the husband's approval, given an immediately prior approval by the wife, was .000. The comparable conditional for wives was also .000. Spouses in that situation were not synchronous in their use of this "reinforcer." In fact, there was a trend for the conditionals to be *less* than the base rate (i.e., approval by one person was related to an inhibition for the use of approval by the other).

In my experience, a laugh or a smile seems to elicit a like reaction in others. Bales (1953), in fact, found very high conditional p values for such behaviors in his observation studies of group process. Notice in Table 9.1 the sizeable increase in the conditional probability for Smile given Smile by the other spouse. Given that one would list Smile as a potential reinforcer (and I do) it seems that synchronous matching may apply to some reinforcers (Smile) but not others (Approve).

Also included are two examples of turn-taking behavior—Attention and Talk. As expected, the conditional values were very high for both spouses. Given that a spouse attended, it was very likely that it would be matched by an attending reaction by the spouse; i.e., A talks and B attends, then B talks and A attends.

The second set of data were drawn from a sample of 36 families of normal children and 37 families of socially aggressive children. The data presented in Table 9.2 describe a sample of events rather than subjects. The sample size is listed on the right side of the table. Given that the target child approved, the various reactions of his male siblings are listed by columns. For the clinical sample, the likelihood of an approval reaction by siblings was .00 and it was .087 for the normal sample. For normals the conditional p value differed significantly from its base-rate value. It seems that synchronous matching of approval may hold for normal siblings; it did not hold for siblings from distressed families. An examination of comparable data for mothers' and fathers' reactions to target children revealed an interesting pattern. For normal samples, given child-Approve the likelihood of a synchronous reaction by fathers was .160 and for mothers .077. In both cases the p values far exceeded base-rate expectations. However, for the clinical sample the likelihood of a comparable synchronous reaction for fathers was .00 and for mothers it was .069. The latter probability represented a tenfold increase over the expected value for mother-Approve. It seems then that synchronicity for Approve may hold for reactions to target children in normal families. For distressed families the reactions of mothers to target children may be synchronous but the reactions of fathers and male siblings are not.

Aversives

Conventional wisdom suggests that an attack evokes an attack. Raush (1965) was one of the first to provide field data which demonstrated this effect. His observations of normal and antisocial preadolescents in a residential setting showed a similar disposition across the samples. Given an unfriendly initiation, the antisocial boy reacted in an unfriendly manner .80 of the time; for normals, the comparable value was .77. While accepting the general principle, one would wish to know more about the magnitude of this effect for family members as well.

The study by Margolin (1977) of married couples in a laboratory setting also showed significant synchronous matching for aversives. Given a criticism by the wife, then the likelihood the husband would criticize was .034 (this in contrast to his base-rate value of .007). Given that the husband disagreed, the likelihood that the wife would disagree was .159 (her base rate for Disagree was .049). Synchronous relations were also found for Interrupt (Husband and Wife), Complain (Husband), Not Tracking (Wife), and Put Down (Husband and Wife). In this problem-solving situation, it was not only the case that an aversive elicited an aversive, but it was likely to elicit the same kind of aversive.

An analysis of sibling interactions showed a threefold to fourfold increase over base-rate values in the likelihood of a counterattack given an aversive antecedent (Patterson, 1980b). These increases in conditional p values were particularly dramatic for male siblings in families of Social Aggressor children when attacked by another male sibling (.49) or by a female sibling (.38). In that study, mothers and fathers were generally less likely to counterattack than were siblings.

The data in Table 9.2 tell a similar tale. Given that the problem child is coercive (high TAB score), then the likelihood of a counterattack by the male sibling was .43. Given a normal family, this likelihood was .30. It is interesting to note that these values were considerably lower than the figures obtained by Raush (1965) in the residential treatment setting. The remainder of the information in Table 9.2 suggests a significant matching effect comparable to the data from the Margolin (1977) study of distressed couples. For male siblings, Disapproval was matched by a synchronous Disapproval, Physical Negative by Physical Negative and so on.

There seems to be synchronicity for the exchange of aversives among family members. This general effect has been obtained by many investigators (Snyder, 1977; Wahler, in preparation). As a general case there is a twofold to fourfold increase in the likelihood of an attack, given an abrasive intrusion by another family member. Furthermore, there is a tendency to match the type of counterattack to the type of intrusion.

Ripple Effects

As noted earlier, synchronicity does *not* refer *only* to functional relations between adjacent events. It is just that it is sensible to begin our analysis by looking at these moment-by-moment co-variations. However, our understanding of social interaction will be advanced much further as we focus upon questions concerning more extended episodes. For some time now we have believed that to understand the overall level of aggression in family members, we must understand what it is that determines extended coercive chains. By the same token, an understanding of extended prosocial behavior would tell us much about affection.

What produces extended interchanges? The simplest notion is that each event may have a "ripple effect" (Rue Cromwell suggested this idea to me a decade ago). The occurrence of a single coercive event might be accompanied by a slight increase in the likelihood of other coercive events over the next few moments. Similarly, a single hug, approval, or smile may increase the likelihood for prosocial behaviors over a series of interactions. Gottman (1979) was one of the first to examine this effect. Figure 9.1 summarizes interactions across a series of laboratory tasks for distressed and nondistressed couples. Given that a spouse responded positively at Trial One, then the lag-sequential analysis showed that the other spouse was significantly more likely to respond positively at Trial Two. This, in turn, was followed by a trend for the initiator *also* to be more likely to respond with a positive in later trials. In fact, a positive event seemed to produce Cromwell's "ripple" of positive effects, which endured for at least seven trials.

A study of mothers and their 18-month-old infants showed that such effects were not limited to married couples in laboratory situations (Martin, Maccoby, Baron, & Jacklin, 1980). Given a Mother-Positive (Talk, Touch, Hold, Smile, Attend, Comply), then the likelihood was .20 that the child would initiate a positive in the next 5-second interval, .16 at Trial Two, .13 at Trial Three, and .11 at Trial Four. The comparable initiations by mother, given a prior positive by the child, were .21, .18, .16, and .16 respectively. Only those sequences were included where the reactor had not been engaged in the behavior just prior to the criterion event; i.e., the reactor truly initiated a prosocial behavior. This enhancing effect was traced out to 35 seconds (7 trials) in the Martin et al. (1980) study.

I believe that the ripple effect for positive events will be shown to be of greater magnitude and

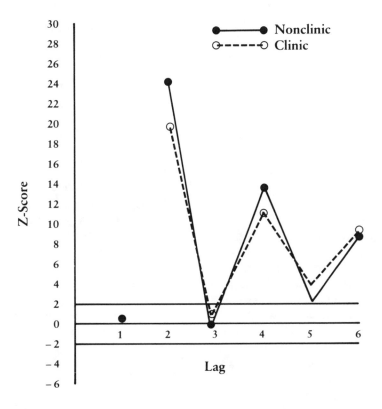

longer duration for normal families than for clinical families. The ripple effect for aversive events should tend to be of a greater magnitude and longer duration for families in the clinical sample. Gottman (1979) found a significantly greater magnitude of effects in his auto-lag comparison of distressed and nondistressed couples when testing for negative events. He did not find that the magnitude of positive effects significantly differentiated the two samples. Gottman's finding of an aversive ripple effect for distressed couples led me to look for a similar phenomenon among the families of antisocial children (see Chapter 8).

These ripple effects underscore the potential importance of intradyad components. In fact, a ripple effect suggests an extended impact upon intradyad components. Gottman (1979) found significant cross-lag (intradyad) relations in his analyses. This meant that, given that one spouse reacted in a generally positive manner, then it was likely that the other would respond in kind. Patterson and Moore (1979) used sequential-lag analysis to identify an event which produced a significant negative effect and then identified the intradyad components which contributed to it. Given a positive reaction by the mother, child-Complain was likely to stop. Given mother-Aversive, then child-Complain was likely to continue. The longer the episode, the more likely the final outcome was to be a positive consequence.

Ripple effects imply structural underpinnings; but exactly what are they? The findings suggest that one of the key differences between normal and clinical families lies in their relative disposition to be positive or negative in their reactions with each other. Members of families with antisocial children seem to declare a moratorium on etiquette and, placing malevolent interpretations on positive, neutral, and negative behaviors alike, they constantly make ready for battle. Once they begin, their battles are longer.

Shopping and Mutuality

There is yet another sense in which the behavior of dyad members can be said to covary. However, these relations do *not* imply that the behavior of Person A is currently functionally related to that of Person B. Two persons may have similar dispositions because each of them shopped for, and found, a person with similar values, interests, and preferences for play. They also display similar dispositions because, over time, each has modeled and supported the development of this disposition in the other. Shopping and reinforcement-for-matching are thought to be two variables which determine the similarity of behaviors found among friends and family members.

Shopping

It is assumed as a general case that each of us shops among settings, persons, and activities in such a way as to maximize reinforcement. The person most likely to respond to your behaviors in a supportive manner is the person whose response hierarchy (of skills) is most like your own (Patterson & Reid, 1970).[1] Even in a nursery school the "jocks" tend to affiliate with jocks, the popular with the popular, the scholars with the scholars, and so forth. By a process of elimination, those children with the lowest status in the peer group affiliate with each other. In effect, "likes" interact with "likes." Rankings for the frequency with which two friends engage in various trait behaviors will tend to be similar. As a pair, they select the same settings and often share the experience together. They would also show higher intradyad *trait correlations*. Child A and Child B both engage in a good deal of rough-and-tumble play. Notice that while the two friends both select rough-and-tumble play, their behavior in that setting does not have to be synchronous. On occasion, each of them may enter that setting independently and engage in a form of parallel play. Similarly, a husband and wife may have selected each other because each required few social contacts. Both spend hours each day watching TV, but their behaviors may or may not be functionally related.

Friends shop for and find similar settings. On those occasions when their behaviors in those settings *are* synchronous, then they tend to reinforce each other for engaging in behaviors that are appropriate for that setting. Friends should become more similar over time, at least along the dimensions for which they selected each other. Similarly,

normal family members should demonstrate a loosely organized cluster of values, recreational interests, and personality traits as a result of sharing the same settings. The intercorrelations among the shared traits may not be high, but they should be more similar to each other than they are to strangers. Some settings within family life are associated with high likelihoods for certain kinds of reactions. For example, playing Monopoly or cards together would increase the likelihood of synchronous Laugh or Smile. Reading to a child would raise the level of mutual Touch and synchronous Talk and Attend. It is thought that there are significant variations among family members in their likelihoods of selecting such settings.

To understand the similarity between the aversive behaviors of members of a dyad it is necessary to examine *three* factors: the relative frequency for aversives may reflect the fact that the members of the dyad selected each other because they were similar; they may also have shaped each other to be more (or less) aversive; finally, many aversive events might be synchronous with aversives provided by the other member of the dyad.

The problem of multiple determinants intrudes when we attempt to analyze the relation between what a person does *to* others and what he receives *from* others. Suppose that we study ten children in a nursery school setting. These children are very different with respect to the general trait extraversion. Some are very outgoing and initiate many contacts with others. They also tend to be very reinforcing to peers. According to the shopping hypothesis, these gregarious children will tend to select others who are similarly disposed. Leiter (1977) studied free-play situations in a nursery school setting. He found that children who made frequent initiations to others received significantly more initiations from others. Charlesworth and Hartup (1967) studied children in four nursery school classes. They found a correlation of .79 ($p < .01$) between the total number of reinforcers given and the total number received. Those who gave the most received the most; they also tended to give to the greatest number of people. There was a correlation of .62 ($p < .01$) between the number of reinforcements given and the number of persons to whom they were given. Similarly, the correlation between the number of reinforcers received and the number of persons from whom they were received was .70 ($p < .01$).

I think the Charlesworth and Hartup (1967) correlations might reflect differences in the rate of social interaction. Children who interact more give and receive higher frequencies of social reinforcers. For example, Reid's (1967) study of 24 in-

Table 9.3
Mutuality Among Family Members for Positive Consequences

	Pearson Product Moment Correlations					
Target	Problem Child	Father	Mother	Male Sibling	Female Sibling	Median Correlation
Problem Child		.44	.60**	.45*	.43*	.44
		(02) (02)	†(03) (02)	(02) (02)	(02) (02)	
Father			.09	.60*	.41	.43
			(02) (02)	(02) (03)	(01) (01)	
Mother				.29	.83**	.44
				(01) (03)	(03) (03)	
Male Sibling					.51*	.48
					(03) (02)	
Female Sibling						.47

*$p < .05$

**$p < .01$

†In 3% of interactions with the mother, the problem child *received* these consequences. In 2% of the interactions, he gave the mother these consequences.

---

dividuals from five families showed a correlation of .56 ($p < .01$) between rate of social interaction and the number of initiations made by family members to the target child.

Mutuality

Mutuality refers to the overall degree of similarity between members of a dyad in their disposition to engage in a particular behavior "X." It does not necessarily refer to a disposition to react in a synchronous fashion (i.e., person A does X so person B responds immediately in kind). Rather, it is the case that over an extended period of time person A engages in X about as frequently as does person B; mutuality refers to a common level over time. This could, for example, describe the dispositions to reinforce other people. Mutuality would imply that you get what you give. Children who give the most reinforcers receive the most. Family members who initiate the most coercive behaviors receive the most. For example, Patterson and Reid (1970) obtained high covariations in rankings (in the .50 to .60 range) for giving and receiving both rewards and punishments among family members. At that time we labeled the relations as "reciprocity correlations." Similar correlations were noted for husbands and wives (Patterson, Weiss, & Hops, 1976). In retrospect, I think it was a mistake to apply the concept of equity, balance, or equality to either inter- or intradyad correlations. Gottman

(1979) has sounded a similar note of caution. Correlations of this kind are of interest, but any single inference drawn from them is confounded by the equally likely contribution of other determinants (e.g., shopping, shaping similar behaviors, and shared settings).

We are beginning to suspect that there may be a characteristic "family constant" for positive and aversive consequences. Relative to other families, Family A tends to react positively about .50 of the time regardless of content or person, while the level for Family B is about .30. We would also assume that there is greater similarity among family members than among individuals of the same age and sex from several different families.

As an example of this mutuality among family members, Table 9.3 summarizes the data from the first 22 families referred to OSLC. The positive consequences, Approve, Physical Positive, and Laugh, were tabulated as outcomes of interactions among dyads for each family. The frequency with which a given agent provided these consequences was divided by the total number of interactions for that agent (within that dyad). This provided a control for differential selection among family members. It did not, of course, control for the fact that the dyad might mutually select preferred activities. The data for the six to ten baseline sessions in the home provided the data base. The data strongly suggest a mutuality in the level of ex-

Table 9.4
Intradyad Covariations for Synchronous and Nonsynchronous Events

Family	Number of Sessions	Nonsynchronous Exchanges			Synchronous Exchanges			
		Approval	Comply	Volunteer	Play	Talk	Work	Physical Positive
Tofu	20	−.05	−.07	−.25	.40	.72***	−.01	.57**
Pumpkin	21	.08	.18	.41	.12	.51*	.39	.51*
Spring	20	.03	−.07	.35	.45*	.54*	−.15	.63**
Summer	15	.36	.62*	.00	.57*	.76***	.67**	.68**
Pluto	20	−.01	.07	.00	.21	.70***	.35	.59**
Eclipse	20	.24	.07	−.18	.36	.58**	.34	.40

*$p < .05$
**$p < .01$
***$p < .001$

change for these three positive consequences.[2] A later analysis will demonstrate an even higher order of mutuality for the exchange of aversives.

What do these mutuality correlations mean? Do they reaffirm the fact that family members share a common level, or do they describe more than that; i.e., the members actually maintain a kind of equity or equality in the giving and receiving of reinforcers, as suggested by Patterson and Reid (1970), Conger and Smith (1981), and others? An expedient means for determining which is a more reasonable alternative would be to test for covariations *across time* for a dyad.[3] It would rule out the differences in familial level, which I think is the prime determinant for the intradyad correlations. However, even such an intradyad correlation would not control for shared selections of settings nor synchronous matching, which would build in covariations.

In the study by Wills (1971) the husbands and wives specified what it was about the behavior of the other person that functioned as a Please (*P*) and what was for them a Displease (*D*). They were called at the end of each day for 14 days and asked, item by item, whether each of their preselected *P* or *D* behaviors had occurred. Each spouse was interviewed separately. The Pleases (reinforcers) were analyzed separately as to whether they were instrumental acts (take out garbage, run an errand) or affectional (give a hug). First he searched for serial dependencies. There was an average Lag₁ (1 day) correlation for affectional Pleases of .30; the average intradyad correlation was .29. For instrumental *P*'s it was .25. This was

not a convincing set of findings for the across-spouse covariation required for support of the 1970 reciprocity-in-exchange hypothesis.

The next study examined the same alternative hypothesis using the data from six mother-child dyads. They were observed in their homes for a baseline of 15 to 21 sessions. The intradyad day-by-day covariations were calculated for four variables thought to be positive reinforcers and for three turn-taking variables. The *PPM* correlations are summarized on Table 9.4. The findings support the relation between synchronous behaviors and high positive values for intradyad correlations. Turn-taking behaviors, such as touching and talking, produce high values for *intra*dyad covariations. The three events thought to be nonsynchronous but reinforcing did *not* produce significant *intra*dyad correlations. It seems that the mutuality hypothesis is the most conservative position to take in viewing the usual correlations one obtains when analyzing the data from dyads across families.

In the case of the *inter*dyad correlations for aversive events, there are two major determinants. As noted earlier, aversive interchanges tend to be synchronous. I think that families are also characterized by differences in the *level* for aversive events, and that families are more homogeneous than a random assortment of individuals matched for age, sex, or familial role. Taken together, this would suggest that when studying aversives, both the inter- and intradyad correlations will be high and positive.

Margolin (1977) studied a sample of videotapes

Table 9.5
Mutuality for Coerciveness Among Family Members

Family Member	Problem Child	Father	Mother	Male Sibling	Female Sibling	Median
Problem Child		.81**	.24	.61**	.63**	.62
Father			.32	.86**	.74**	.78
Mother				.48*	.62**	.40
Male Sibling					.76**	.69
Female Sibling						.70

*p < .05
**p < .01

of mildly distressed couples attempting to solve some of their own marital conflicts. The tapes were coded separately for the husband and the wife. The interdyad correlations were very high for aversive categories such as Complain, .74; Criticize, .81; Disagree, .89; Deny Responsibility, .75; Excuse, .65; Interrupt, .79; and Put Down, .74. These dyad correlations strongly emphasized the trait of mutuality for aversive events for husband and wife.

The data in Table 9.5 summarize familial mutuality for interchanges between dyad members. For each member, the total interaction with the other member served as the denominator; the frequency with which each was coercive to the other served as the numerator. The same sample of 22 cases, analyzed in Table 9.3, provided the data for this study. It can be seen there that, with one interesting exception (mothers), there is a very high order of mutuality. About twice as much variance is accounted for by these correlations than the correlations for positive consequences (Table 9.3). The intradyad data from mother-child pairs presented in Table 10.1 suggest a similar theme. On days when the child was particularly coercive, the mother responded in kind. The median intradyad correlation for TAB scores was a substantial .49 (range .41 to .61). Dyads are synchronous for aversive events. Given this, then it follows that mutuality will hold when analyzing data for aversive events *across* dyads.

Reciprocity

In 1970 we introduced the concepts of exchange and reciprocity as two pivotal concepts necessary for understanding families of antisocial children (Patterson & Reid, 1970). Exchange simply meant that some behaviors of one person served as

a reward for the behavior of the other; i.e., partners have *reciprocal* effects upon each other. We certainly were not the first to see its relevance to family interaction (Burgess & Bushnell, 1969); however, it seemed to be an idea whose time had come for it quickly made its appearance in the fields of marital therapy (Stuart, 1975; Azrin, Naster, & Jones, 1973) and in intervention with families of delinquents (Alexander & Parsons, 1973).

The derivations from these premises seem to have important applications to family life. Marital satisfaction, the duration of marital relations, and love itself were said to relate to the exchange of reinforcers (Hatfield, Utne, & Traupman, 1979). In some important sense intimates *are* interdependent; each relies upon the other as an important source of reinforcement. Each has discovered the other to be a unique source of rewards (Huston & Burgess, 1979).

Originally, the concepts were taken from the fields of sociology and anthropology, where they had a long history. The latter recognized the crucial role played by barter with the exquisitely balanced rules for equity among primitives. Among sociologists the idea of economic exchange theory had been applied to governments, groups, and families by theorists such as Homans (1961).[4] Nord (1969) defined the value of a social reward in terms of its availability (market demand or scarcity). Schaffer (1977) wrote, "The basic characteristic of all interpersonal behavior is reciprocity" (p. 172). Gouldner (1960) suggested that a norm of reciprocity may be universal and related to the stability of some social systems and the contingent exchange of gratifications. He went so far as to suggest that members of a dyad are reciprocal *because* each member has a moral norm binding him to reciprocity. Others, such as Homans (1961) and Huston and Burgess (1979), assume that self-interest is best served by reciprocal exchanges. Each person learns that he will receive valued reinforcers only if he reciprocates by giving them in equal measure. The early theorists were followed by enthusiastic translations of economic exchange theories to social interaction.

In that tradition, many writers note the relation between an imbalance in the exchange of rewards and a disruption in a relationship (Blau, 1964; Emerson, 1972; Huston & Burgess, 1979). We found this to be an attractive idea and applied it directly to the families of antisocial children. It was assumed that the deviant behavior of the child was *produced* in general by a low level of rewards within the family *and* an imbalance in exchange. The same formulation was applied to distressed couples (Patterson, Weiss, & Hops, 1976).

The problem with our early attempts to use exchange theory lay in the means by which we proposed to test it. Our approach was to apply microsocial techniques to a problem which simply does not lend itself to such a simplistic analysis. First of all, the analyses were not focused upon the *kinds* of rewards central to exchange theory. In Levinger's (1979) discussion, he lists the following: money, goods, information, status, services, and love. While one can think of Approve or Physical Positive, as measured by the FICS, as a *subset* for love, it is, at best, a minuscule component of the broader concept(s) which were important to exchange theory. Even if one accepts the belief that the code category, Approve, *is* a relevant component, the measure leaves out the crucial dimension played by the cognitions of the receiver. "According to equity theory, people become more committed to relationships when they perceive that the value of each participant's outcomes are proportional to the relative value of each individual's investments" (Huston & Burgess, 1979, p. 11).

Equity, then, is less in the eye of the observer than it is in the mind of the receiver. Equity is a relative term that requires some measure of the cognitions of the participants. The final judgment is a function of an intricate balancing of "goods" given "costs" and what is available *outside* of the relationship (Huston & Burgess, 1979). As a result, the appropriate means of study must include some self-report information about costs, values, and satisfactions. Such broad-gauge measures relate to satisfaction, duration of relationships, and conflicts in the manner predicted by exchange theory (Hatfield et al., 1979).

As noted earlier, the study of equity or equality poses some unique problems when applied to microsocial data. We have already seen that the correlations of, say, mother-child dyads across families simply did not mean what we thought they meant. The covariation of dyad scores across sessions controlled for some of the confounds. Approval as a potential reinforcer did *not* survive these analyses. Even if it had, the more recent formulation by Huston and Burgess (1979) points to one further complex issue. R. Burgess (personal communication) presents four different definitions to test for balance in social exchange. The first is *direct exchange*. A reinforces, and B responds *in kind*. Reciprocity implies that in the exchange there is an equivalence in *kind and amount*. In his next two measures of balance, Burgess raises the consideration of individual differences in experience. From this relative frame of reference, a *matching exchange* requires calculation of the frequency with which A reinforces B, divided by the frequency with which A reinforces all other persons. Relatively speaking, how much does A reinforce B? A match requires that the two relative p's for A and B be the same. His fourth measure, *equity*, stipulates that the ratio of $p_1|p_2$ should equal $p_2|p_1$. With this in mind, the best that can be said is that the research literature based upon microsocial analyses is simply not relevant to the main tenets of exchange theory. The key lies in our ability to specify *what* it is that is reinforcing for each member *and* to be able to design a method of measurement that will adequately describe "amounts" given and received. This, in turn, requires that the individuals' cognitions be taken into account.

What is needed is a means of having family members specify which aspects of their interactions with others are reinforcing. An experimental manipulation in which one family member increased the frequency of these "perceived reinforcers" should be accompanied by a reciprocal increase in the frequency with which the other person supplies events perceived as reinforcers by the other. Both persons must be well aware of what is perceived as a reinforcer by the other. One such experiment has been carried out in a field setting.

The study by Wills et al. (1974) involved seven married couples. Over the 12-day baseline, both spouses were called each day for a listing of how many "Pleases" they had received from their spouses during the previous 12 hours. The wives reported receiving an average of 1.56 Pleases per hour during the preceding five days of baseline (Days 7-12). The husband was then told by phone what rate of Pleases he had been giving his wife and was instructed to double that figure for the next two days. As shown in Table 9.6, for that pe-

Table 9.6
Analysis of Changes in Affectional Behavior During Reciprocity Manipulation

(from Wills et al., 1974, p. 806)

Reported by:	Average rate/hour for Baseline	Average rate/hour for Manipulation	t for correlated means (df = 6)
Pleasurable Behavior			
Husbands	1.45	1.64	.64
Wives	1.56	2.38	2.01*
Displeasurable Behavior			
Husbands	.63	.40	−1.39
Wives	.66	.56	− .91

*$p < .05$, one-tailed.

Reprinted with permission from "A behavioral analysis of the determinants of marital satisfaction," *Journal of Clinical and Consulting Psychology,* 1974, *42*(6). Copyright by the American Psychological Association.

riod (Days 13 and 14) the wives reported a substantial increase in Pleases received. Reciprocity would have it that over such an extended interval, the *wife* would have ample opportunity to provide an *increase* in Pleases (reinforcers) which she gave to her husband. Because of the manner in which the study was designed, she would be well aware of what constituted a Please for her spouse.

As shown in Table 9.6, there *was* a nonsignificant trend for the husbands to report an increase in Pleases. There was also a nonsignificant *decrease* in the magnitude of Displeases reported by both spouses. Incidentally, many of the wives spontaneously reported that the increase in Pleases received made them feel as if they were on a second honeymoon.[5]

This miniature study is a prototype of the kind of field study which could provide useful information about exchange and balance in family structures. As things now stand, there is a very large gap between the microsocial analyses of structure and the complexity involved in questions concerning the exchange of rewards. What is needed are studies of these issues that do not rely solely upon either self-report data or upon manipulations in a laboratory setting.

The controlled studies described in Jacobson and Margolin (1979) attest to the relevance of exchange theory to the newly developing techniques for resolving many severe marital conflicts. The sense of injustice characterizing spouses about to separate is very keen. Their descriptions of what is wrong are seldom stated in the language of exchange theory, but the fit for the ideas is often very close. There is also a sense of this in the families of

antisocial children, a feeling that the individuals are not "getting their fair share."

My hunches about the concept of exchange and balance remain pretty much what they were in the early 1970's. These are important ideas that have great relevance for the treatment of distressed families. While committed to the relevance of the ideas, I remain unconvinced that any of our current microsocial data apply to them. My hunch is that it is here that some of our most interesting contributions will be made in the next generation of research on interactional issues.

Acknowledgements

The writer wishes to acknowledge the contribution made by Robert Burgess to this chapter. The current text was written in response to his critique of an earlier draft of this chapter. Many of the ideas expressed in this revision were the outcome of a two-day seminar presented by Bob to the OSLC staff. Certainly he cannot be held responsible for the author's current position. It was, however, his clearly enunciated position which led to improvements in this chapter.

Footnotes

1. D. Byrne's early work suggested a correspondence between attraction and similarity in attitudes (Byrne & Rhamey, 1965). His later work on liking and similarity extended these findings to demonstrate a relation between liking and rein-

forcement. The general formulation is in general agreement with Hartup's (1978) analysis of children's friendship patterns. Friends are more similar along a number of traits, such as sociability, physical attractiveness, perceived kindness, and friendliness. Children who are effective social reinforcers are also more likely to be selected as friends.

2. As can be seen, the mean levels tend to balance reasonably well for all dyads such that no one family agent stands out clearly as a victim. Dyads in each family were then examined to determine the proportion characterized by inequitable exchanges. For seven normal families there was an average of one dyad in ten showing an inequity in which one person gave (at least) twice as much as he or she received. In the distressed families, the percent of inequitable dyads ranged from .20 to 1.00; the mean was .56. For the distressed families, the correlations between percent inequity and mean baseline TAB score (for the family) was $-.19$ (n.s.)

3. Another means of parceling out the family-level confound would be to calculate the correlation separately for each family. Several investigators have, in fact, calculated such correlations (Reid, 1967; Conger & Smith, 1981). I also carried out endless hours of such calculations and "found some" for both distressed and normal samples. However, by their very nature, correlations define a relation *sans* differences in *mean* level for variable X and Y. I then began examining the raw data to calculate the different measures of equity suggested by Burgess. These new calculations did not differentiate distressed from nondistressed samples. Others may well follow that same path, but I, for one, could not find my way through the thicket of problems which surround it.

4. The writer believes that the models for economic exchange do not really fit social interaction in the home setting. This metaphor and those from game theory were both rejected because the laws of cost, supply, and demand did not seem to provide a close fit to what could be observed in the home. If the mother gave ten hugs to one child, it in no way limited the number that she could give to a second child. It didn't seem that a zero-sum game described the exchanges which took place.

Nemeth (1970) reviewed studies which showed that in social interchanges characterized as zero-sum games, one seldom gets either cooperation or reciprocity. Given a limited supply of rewards, then each person attempts to maximize his own gain. In such a world, one would attempt to work out rules for an equitable exchange, but only as a temporary expedient. In the long run, each person attempts to win at the other's expense.

5. The across-couple trait correlation for the Wills et al. (1974) sample was .97. In a comparable study by Birchler, Weiss, and Vincent (1975), the correlation for 12 distressed couples was .74 and for 12 nondistressed couples it was .97.

Chapter 10
Abstract

Four family management (*FM*) variables are described that are thought to determine individual differences among children in their rates of antisocial behaviors. These include: (1) house rules, (2) monitoring, (3) contingencies, and (4) problem solving, negotiation, and crisis management. It is thought that parents differ in the effectiveness with which they practice these skills. Furthermore, their implementation varies as a function of crises and stressors that impinge upon the parents. Data are presented that demonstrate a covariation between the mother's TAB score and daily crises and community supportive contacts. These four variables are thought to mediate the covariation between antisocial child behavior and traditional variables such as broken homes, divorce, psychiatric condition of parent, marital discord, and lower social status.

It is assumed that the effect of disruptions in these *FM* variables is an increase in the rate of coercive child behavior. Furthermore, measures of *FM* variables are thought to correlate with differences in performance level for family members.

Chapter 10

The Management and Disruption of Families

Microsocial analyses provide a description of family structure that, in turn, reflects a history of interaction. The hypothesis (untested as yet) is that many of the coercion-related structures arise as a function of disruptions in parental family management skills.

Family management (*FM*) variables are thought to account for a significant amount of the variance associated with differences among children in rates of performance of antisocial behaviors. This is being tested in a large-scale longitudinal planning study. It is assumed that measures of *FM* skills will also demonstrate low-order positive correlations with the traditional measures of child-rearing practices; i.e., variables such as laissez-faire, authoritative, warm, and punitive should correlate with our measures of *FM* practices.

Measures of *FM* practices are designed to give a molar perspective on *what* the parent is doing that relates to the maintenance of the family system. I assume that effective family management requires a high order of skill, *and* that parents of antisocial children are lacking in their performance of one or more of these skills.

An interactional stance does not prescribe which variables should be studied at either the macro- or microsocial levels. That selection is up to the investigator's intuitive hunches and his theoretical biases. Probably more than anything else, it is a function of that which can be adequately measured. At OSLC our hunches about *FM* variables grew out of our clinical contacts with families. Most of the process of variable selection was just common sense. Our first sessions in the home convinced us that many of these parents did not punish effectively (i.e., their punishment didn't work). Many of them lacked house rules that were clearly specified. These ideas are eminently testable; both hypotheses point to behaviors that can be counted. The list of variables we selected will seem quite ordinary to the reader. Each has a familiar, common-sense ring to it. This is reflected in the title the OSLC group has selected for a new book about family intervention, *Systematic Common Sense* (in preparation). All of these *FM* variables would have had an immediate appeal to my Norwegian grandmother. I can imagine her reading the list and saying, "Ja, but vy do you haff to *teach dis* to people?"

As a matter of fact, it is *not* clear why, in this day and age, such simple skills must be taught. Clinical experience suggests that many of the parents of antisocial children did not have good parental models for the practice of family management skills. Other parents "know" in a general sense what the skills are but have decided for one reason or another to put them into practice selectively. Others are overwhelmed by crises and cannot implement those skills that they do have. My general sense of it is that an increasing number of young parents have had very poor modeling and even less supervision and support for the practice of these crucial skills.

Disruptions in the implementation of family management skills are thought to be the *major* mediating variable for antisocial behaviors in children. These disruptions accelerate the rate at which the child engages in out-of-control behavior. If these disruptions continue, the process will involve siblings and parents, and eventually the entire family will be disrupted.

The extreme conditions experienced in a ghetto place the child at risk for the development of a variety of psychopathologies. Having one or more parents who are psychotic also places the child at risk. However, as Garmezy and Nuechterlein (1972) point out, the *majority* of children survive these conditions with few signs of adult pathology. In a longitudinal study (Rutter, 1979), given the extremes of deprived neighborhood, *plus* parent criminality, *plus* bad child rearing, poverty, low intelligence, and large family, over one-fourth of the children showed *no* evidence of any kind of delinquency or antisocial behavior. Given that both parents are psychotic, three of five children will show no major sign of pathology (Garmezy & Streitman, 1974).

It is hypothesized that for children at risk, the practice of family management skills constitutes a set of moderating variables that will account for many of these false-positive predictions. It is the psychotic parent who does not have family management skills that will most likely produce an antisocial and/or schizophrenic child. The child living in extreme poverty, with low intelligence, will survive the experience *if* the parents practice effective family management. Effective family management practices include the following: clearly stated house rules, monitoring, providing consequences contingently, and problem solving.

Crisis Disruption of FM Practices

There are individual differences among parents in the skill with which they practice family management. While their relative rankings would show positive correlations over time intervals of a few weeks or months, the effective implementation of these skills may be disrupted under conditions of extreme parental stress, e.g., severe illness, unemployment, divorce, severe depression, or a psychotic breakdown. As a corollary of this hypothesis, it is thought that these skills may also be disrupted by the cumulative impact of *minor* crises or "hassles" that impinge upon all families. Given that these hassles occur frequently and/or persist for a period of days, then there will be an erosion of family management skills. These disruptions will, in turn, be accompanied by increases in antisocial child behavior.

The impact of major crises on effective family management is summarized in Figure 10.1. In a path-analytic sense, the causal arrows move from a crisis (such as divorce) *to* a disruption in family management *to* an increase in antisocial child behavior. In each instance these two correlations are expected to be higher than would be the case for the covariation of crises with antisocial behavior. As an alternative, it is conceivable that having an antisocial child could produce marital conflict, drinking, or psychiatric problems in parents.

Not all parents going through a divorce will demonstrate a disruption in family management practices, but those who do are likely to experience an increase in antisocial child behavior. In effect, information on crises tells us when to expect an increased likelihood for disrupted family management and a commensurate increase in the likelihood of antisocial child behavior. The one exception (that we know about) to this two-step progression is the bilateral relation between mother depression and child social aggression (see Chapter 12). It is thought that the child's extremely aversive interactions contribute to the mother's depression. Given that an acute depression may also disrupt family management, the relation is thought to be bilateral.

There is another empirical linkage for the functional relations presented in Figure 10.1. That is the relation between parental crises and deviant child behavior. Rutter and his colleagues analyzed the data from the Isle of Wight and inner-city London studies of 10-year-old children. They identified six variables that were reliably associated with child psychiatric disorders, including antisocial problems. These variables were: (1) severe marital discord, (2) low socioeconomic status, (3) large family size, (4) father criminal history, (5) maternal psychiatric problems, and (6) admission to care by local authorities (Quinton & Rutter, 1976, cited in Rutter, 1979). Figure 10.2 summarizes the findings when the families were categorized into those with none of these risk factors, one of them, two, three, and four or more. Note that a *single* crisis did not place the child at significantly greater risk than was the case for peers who were living in a similar (but nonstressed) environment. However, there was an exponential increase in the likelihood of a child psychiatric problem as the risk factors increased from one to three and three to four.

It is only in the past decade that systematic empirical studies have been carried out to study the

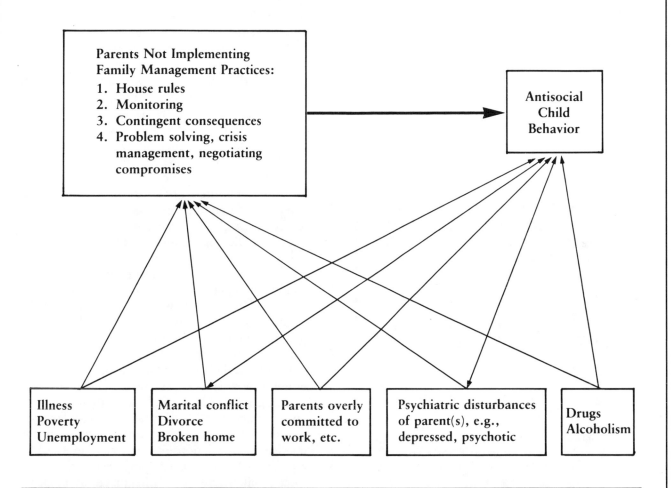

Figure 10.1
The Relation Among Family Management Practices, Crises,
and Antisocial Child Behavior

Parents Not Implementing
Family Management Practices:
1. House rules
2. Monitoring
3. Contingent consequences
4. Problem solving, crisis
   management, negotiating
   compromises

Antisocial
Child
Behavior

Illness
Poverty
Unemployment

Marital conflict
Divorce
Broken home

Parents overly
committed to
work, etc.

Psychiatric disturbances
of parent(s), e.g.,
depressed, psychotic

Drugs
Alcoholism

effect of stress upon human behavior. Much of the contemporary work on these problems is based upon the work of Selye (1976) and Holmes and Masuda (1974). The latter researchers found a convincing correlation for a variety of samples between simple checklist measures of environmental stress and the incidence of psychosomatic disorders. In Chapter 4 it was demonstrated that their concept of crises as "stress" can readily be applied to family interaction. Daily mood shifts for three of the mothers were shown to covary with daily fluctuations in conflicts and crises from outside and from within the family. Systematic studies of families in divorce showed a similar covariation for an across-subject design. The self-esteem of mothers and fathers became more negative following separation. The divorce crisis was also followed by increases in oppositional child behavior

(Hetherington, Cox, & Cox, 1976).

The idea that stress, crises, and familial conflicts may have a cumulative effect upon both the mood of the caretaker *and* the quality of family interaction is certainly in keeping with the general perspective presented in sociology and anthropology. As mentioned earlier, the excellent description by Lewis (1968) in *La Vida* documents the steady attrition of spirit and gradual sense of helplessness that accompanies extreme poverty. Tonge et al. (1975) obtained descriptions of a comparable environment during systematic interviews with multiproblem families from large metropolitan areas.

Familial stressors that alter the caretaker's mood may *also* produce a disruption in his or her implementation of family management practices. The prediction is that day-by-day fluctuations in minor hassles will produce day-by-day fluctuations in the caretaker's mood and/or family management practices. These, in turn, will covary with changes in coercive child behaviors. To test this, the data collected in the homes of the five

Figure 10.2
Multiplicity of Risk Factors
and Child Psychiatric Disorder

(from Rutter, 1979, p. 52)

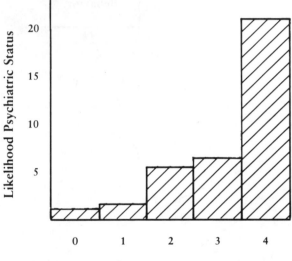

Number of Stressor Variables

Reprinted from *Social Competence in Children*, edited by Martha Whalen Kent and Jon E. Rolf, by permission of University Press of New England. Copyright 1979 by the Vermont Conference on the Primary Prevention of Psychopathology.

mother-child dyads (presented in Chapter 4) were reanalyzed. Each involved a mother and preschool child and occasionally a young sibling. Each family was observed in the home for a minimum of 20 sessions; each session lasted about an hour. The variations in the mothers' TAB scores served as the criterion variable. In a previous study the uncorrected test-retest reliability for the child's score was .78 ($p < .01$) for an interval of one week and .74 ($p < .05$) for 12 months. On each day the mother filled out three questionnaires: one of three versions of the Lubin Checklist (as a measure of mood), the Crisis Checklist, and a version of R. Wahler's Insularity Checklist. The Insularity Checklist generated one score each day for the frequency of contacts from the community, an estimate of the number of minutes these contacts lasted, and an estimate of what proportion were

positive (supportive). The daily crises score merely summed across the number of items checked; no effort was made to weight those that seemed obviously more severe.

The hypothesis was that measures derived from observations of the coerciveness of the mother interacting with her child would correlate with each of the following: the aversiveness of the child with whom she dealt, the daily hassles with which she had to cope, the daily contacts from her support system, and her general mood. It should be noted that *all* of these components are likely to be interactional; e.g., her mood and abrasive manner will elicit coercive reactions from the child. The interactional data for these mothers were analyzed to determine the magnitude of the covariation of these variables with the mothers' TAB scores.

It can be seen in Table 10.1 that for three subjects the composite set of six or more variables accounted for a good proportion of the variance in the scores measuring the mothers' coerciveness. For all families the measure of the child's coerciveness was the *main* contributor. The child's behavior would be the variable most involved in eliciting and maintaining the mother's coercive behaviors. However, in terms of what accounts for the remainder of the variance there are clearly different patterns of relations for different mothers. For example, for the mother of Eclipse it was her general mood for the day and the number of crises that determined how abrasive she was.

As a general case, it can be seen that what goes on at a microsocial level reflects, in part, the impact of macro variables that impinge from outside the dyad. The relationships between the variables are outlined in Figure 10.3. As shown there, for some families crises may disrupt family management practices; this produces an increase in stealing and/or socially aggressive behavior in the problem child (and siblings as well). For others, the crises may also increase the negativity of their reactions to the child; e.g., they are slightly more likely to be irritable and increase their punitiveness or launch "unprovoked attacks." This, in turn, accelerates coercive child behavior. At this point, both parent and child are likely to escalate the intensity of their aversiveness.

For the moment we can only speculate that these relations exist. Currently we are carrying out a study of children at risk for delinquency which will provide data to test these relationships. The across-subject design provides measures of crises, mood, irritability p values for all dyads, and multiple measures of each of the four *FM* variables. Multivariate analyses will tell us which of these variables are crucial and what the unique contri-

Figure 10.3
Factors Contributing to Antisocial Child Behavior

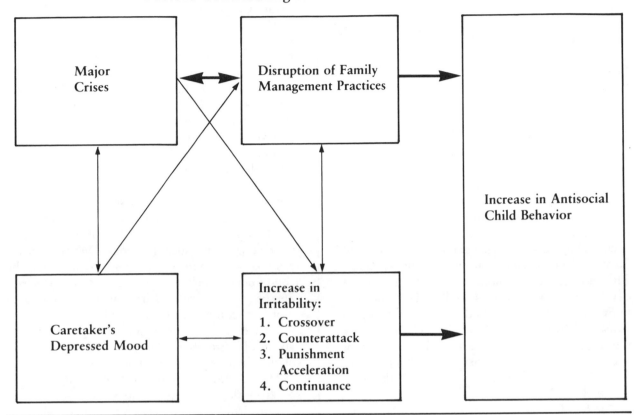

Table 10.1
Variables Which Covary with Mother's Day-by-Day Fluctuations in Coerciveness

	Correlations with Mother's TAB Score						
Family	Minutes of Community Contact[1]	Frequency of Contacts[2]	Positive Contacts[3]	Child's TAB Score[4]	Mother's Lubin Score[5]	Frequency of Crisis[6]	Mult R†
Tofu	−.01	.02	−.11	.49*	.26	−.23	.59
Pluto	.32	.42	.30	.41	.26	.43	.76‡
Eclipse	−.05	.12	.08	.58**	.60**	.40	.82‡
Spring	.43	.01	.26	.61**	.22	.09	.74
Pumpkin	−.14	−.16	.44*	.42	−.14	.07	.61‡

Independent Variables

1. $\bar{x}$ number of minutes contact with community per day
2. $\bar{x}$ number of interactions with people in community
3. $\bar{x}$ number of positive interactions
4. $\bar{x}$ total aversive behavior (TAB) observed for child
5. Mother's $\bar{x}$ Lubin score
6. $\bar{x}$ number of crises

*$p < .05$

**$p < .01$

†The value includes the contribution of the six independent variables listed in this table.

‡The value includes the contribution of the sibling's TAB score in addition to the six independent variables listed in this table.

butions are for each of them.

Most theories about family life assume that family management skills are a given condition. From that perspective, only neurotic conflict between the parents can interfere with the successful implementation of family management skills. As a result, therapy techniques that are based on these theories focus upon resolving these neurotic conflicts with the expectation that success here will be followed by changes in deviant child behavior. Perhaps antisocial children drawn from samples of middle-class families might be described by such a process. These parents may "know" family management skills but are too busy fighting with each other to apply them. However, when this formulation is applied to the OSLC sample of working-class and single-parent families, it is grossly inaccurate. Most of these parents do *not* have the skills to avoid crises or to contain them when they do occur. They have *not* learned the conflict containment skills practiced by most middle-class parents. They do not seem to model or monitor the child's development of prosocial skills. They do *not* know how to manage a child. The model that provides the best fit to the OSLC clinical sample is one that emphasizes impaired learning of family management skills plus stressors that further disrupt the application of the fragments of skill that they do possess.

The family as a unit obviously has *many* functions. Of primary interest here is its function as a vehicle for teaching the child basic survival skills and controlling the child's use of antisocial behavior. It is the function of the family to model and support the child's learning how to relate to others, how to work, and how to survive in the academic world. The school, the peer group, and society at large have much to do with the teaching of these survival skills, but unless the family prepares and then supports the child in polishing these skills, he will not be in a position to profit from what these socializing agents have to teach him. For example, parents must first teach the child the rudiments of work skills at home. This teaching takes place under the guise of doing simple chores and "giving" to others as part of the child's role in the family. The child is also trained there to accept criticism. Hopefully such correction is presented in a reasonable manner. The child learns to match what he *does* to what he *says* he will do, i.e., to keep his word. The child learns the rudiments of how to form close relationships with others by relating to parents and to siblings. The child must learn how to be close enough to maintain a sense of self-worth and yet be neither possessed nor distant. The family also teaches rudimentary work

skills that are necessary for survival in school. The classroom studies reviewed earlier showed that antisocial children lacked the simple, work-oriented skills that are a prerequisite for survival in the first grade (Cobb, 1972; Cobb & Hops, 1973; Hops & Cobb, 1974). These rudimentary skills *must* be polished and altered by peers, teachers, and agents from outside the family. If the initial phase of training in the home has been omitted, it is very unlikely that the child will profit much from later stages of experience involving teachers and peers. If his primary mode of interacting with peers is explosive and immature, then they will not teach him the subtleties of how one goes about interacting with equals.

It must be said at this point that this book is not focused upon the prosocial aspects of family life. We simply have not studied the process of teaching children prosocial skills, and few of our measures were designed for such questions. Our primary focus has been upon the process of controlling the child's deviant behavior. All of the four *FM* variables listed in Figure 10.1 have as their prime function the containment of familial crises. Later, when we bring the development of prosocial survival skills into focus, the list of *FM* variables will obviously have to be expanded.

The general assumption is that children do not outgrow their early proclivities for antisocial behavior. Unless taught otherwise, they will continue to take what they want, and they will use pain control when it suits their immediate purpose. Parents must teach their children prosocial alternatives to these coercive techniques, *and* they must *also* punish their children when these coercive techniques are employed. The data are far from complete, but our best guess is that both parental functions are necessary. Training children to use prosocial skills is necessary but not sufficient; the parent must also monitor and punish, in a reasonable fashion, those coercive behaviors that are "naturally" employed by all toddlers.

Only a parent loves the child enough to go through the hundreds of trials in which the child learns when he can, or cannot, use pain control techniques. Later, his wife or his psychoanalyst may give him love and support equal to that given by his mother, but they cannot teach him at a molecular level those subtle skills that he should have learned prior to age 6 or 7. Parental power, relative to a preschool child, is simply overwhelming. Social workers, friends, or therapists do not possess an equivalent means for punishing adolescent and adult deviant behavior. They may help the adolescent feel better about his antisocial behavior, but usually they cannot *stop* the behavior in the sense that a parent can. In my more cynical moments, I feel that *only* a parent (or a surrogate parent) who lives with the antisocial child can teach him to change.

Changing the antisocial behavior of a child requires the application of *FM* skills. The supervision and support for the application of these skills is the focus of the treatment program for these families (Patterson, Reid, Jones, & Conger, 1975). As noted earlier, each of these skills simply restates the common sense practices which are employed by most of us in raising children.

Rule Setting

The setting of house rules by parents was so taken for granted that it took years of clinical contact before we even labeled this as a problem for families of antisocial children. Harbin and Madden (1979) noted the disorganized, chaotic lifestyle that characterized violent families. I think that an absence of rules is likely to be found in families in which physical violence is used. Like the other three *FM* components, the effective employment of household rules is thought of as necessary, but not sufficient, for producing change in antisocial behavior. While the setting of house rules should be negotiated with the child, in the last analysis it is the responsibility of the *parent;* parents and children are *not* equal. As J. Haley (1978) points out in *Problem Solving Therapy,* the question of *who* it is that *sets rules* lies at the very core of problems confronting many families. In antisocial families, the problem child does *not* grant the premise that parents (or therapists) have the right to set household rules.

Household rules (some implicit and others explicit) state the scheduling of time and effort among family members. More importantly, they spell out what is, and what is not, acceptable behavior. It came as a shock to find that in many of the homes we have studied at OSLC, such rules did *not* exist! For these families, for example, there was no set time for eating; it could occur at any time between 4:00 p.m. and midnight. What was eaten, who ate it, and where it was to be eaten changed from one day to the next. Sometimes it was a can of beans, opened and left on the table with several spoons stuck in the can. At other times, one of the children would attempt to cook some meat but would find his meal picked clean by family members walking through on their way to the street. For many children, even though supper was cooked by a parent, there was no way of predicting the quality of the food or who would be there to share it. These impressions are in accord with the findings that show a relation between an-

tisocial child behavior and parental negligence (Robins & Ratcliff, 1978).

Most families have a schedule for cleaning, repairing equipment, buying groceries, paying bills, and for doing chores. They have agreed upon times for getting up in the morning and for going to bed. Time is set aside for exchanging information about the day's activities. There are times for doing things together; there are shared interests and activities. For members of middle-class families, these agreements hardly need to be stated. In the study by Wadsworth (1979), the home visitor found the homes of delinquent children to be poorly managed.

Families also set specific limits upon each other's behavior. For some families yelling is acceptable, but hitting is not; borrowing a comb is okay, but taking money from someone's dresser is not. In many of the homes studied, there were no rules about bouncing and playing on the furniture (so long as the child didn't step on a parent).

Whatever the rules are, they establish limits that determine the point at which a particular behavior will be monitored and punished. Some rules about aggression exist in almost *all* families; i.e., there is some point at which the parent will try to stop the interchange. However, families differ on how clearly the rules are stated; they also differ in the threshold at which the implied limit is exceeded. As we shall see, they also differ in terms of the likelihood of an effective punishment being applied for transgression.

One of the first steps in treating these families is to help the entire family outline one or two household rules (others will be added). When the smoke settles, it becomes apparent that the children emphatically disagree as to the right of the parent to institute household rules. The efforts of these young tyrants are amazing to behold. When chores were being discussed, one young preadolescent rose to the challenge, "I ain't gonna do it; I ain't no nigger." He assumed it was perfectly equitable for his mother to go on making his bed and putting away his clothes! A 12-year-old broke into tears at the suggestion that she must be home by 2:00 a.m., "All my friends are there . . . they'll laugh . . . you bitch!" The nature of the counterattack varies, but it is characteristic of antisocial children that they know how to strike the parental Achilles' heel. For some parents it is guilt; for others it is a basic uncertainty about what is fair and what is not.

The field studies concerned with the application of reinforcement theory suggest that changes are brought about more rapidly by rule statement plus contingencies rather than by manipulating reinforcing contingencies alone. As a treatment device, setting up household rules is *not* sufficient, in and of itself, to produce change. A well-controlled laboratory study by Hobbs and Forehand (1978) demonstrated that rule setting, per se, was not sufficient. Mothers of preschool children outlined their expectations that requests would be met with child compliance. Each noncompliance was met with, "You did not do what I told you to." This was a relatively ineffective method for producing compliance. Sixty seconds of time out for noncompliance was significantly better. This replicates the effect obtained by Becker et al. (1967) for the classroom. There, too, the teacher's statement of rules about disruptive behavior produced no effect *until contingencies* for noncompliance were introduced. It is not the absence of rules, per se, that produces the problem. It is the absence of rules *plus* the absence of contingent punishment that generate the problem.

For some parents, the lack of rules is no accident; it is their means for avoiding a confrontation. When the child stays out all night, if there is no rule to the contrary, then it is *unclear* that the parent must punish. When these parents try to punish or impose sanctions, they must be prepared for a confrontation. Most of these parents wish to avoid this at all cost. They may natter and scold, but they do not confront—no rules, no confrontation. For others, their use of punishment is as unplanned as is their chaotic, unscheduled existence. They have several jobs and there is little time for thinking of house rules or punishment.

The hypothesis is that households that are disorganized and/or characterized by poorly defined rules are more likely to have antisocial children. In the longitudinal planning study currently under way, we have interviewed over a hundred children and mothers and fathers of children from grades four, seven, and ten. A subset have also been observed in their homes. For each of the three grades, those items that seemed, a priori, to relate to the house rules concept were correlated with three criterion measures of antisocial behavior. The findings support the hypothesis that disorganized households with few rules are associated with more antisocial children. At the time of this writing the multivariate analyses have not been completed. These analyses will tell us how much of the variance in each measure of antisocial behavior is accounted for by a composite measure of household rules.

Parental Monitoring

At a basic level, monitoring implies a general awareness of the child's whereabouts. It is really a set of expectations held by the parent as to when the child returns from school, whom he is with in the evening, and when he can be expected to return. If the child does not appear at the expected time, then the parent becomes concerned. He or she may call friends or go out and search for the child. Most parents of out-of-control children are unlikely to do either of these. Monitoring means taking the five minutes necessary to see that he did his chores and that they were done properly; e.g., check to see if the tools were put away. This is also the time to reinforce the child for a task well done. At another level, it means noticing that he is tearing the stuffing out of the chair. It means attending to the rough-and-tumble play of siblings before it gets out of hand.

There is another aspect of monitoring that is much more subtle. In normal families there is a regular time for sharing information. It includes *all* family members; it is *not* an interview by a parent who acts like a disapproving policeman, nor does it have the overtones of a cross-examination. It is, rather, a genuine expression of interest in the activities and well-being of other family members. It begins with an expression of this interest; e.g., "How was your day?" When the question is given, the parent *listens* to the answer. Some parents complain that their children never tell them what they are doing. Closer inspection shows that they do not listen when the child responds; worse yet, they criticize many aspects of what the child *does* report.

These information exchanges are sharing experiences that make a significant contribution to building emotional attachments among family members. When used by skilled parents (such as the parents we studied in the summer of 1979), it is clear that these exchanges are a *major* socializing mechanism. The parents use examples from the interchanges to teach their children about important values and skills. These interchanges *do not become lectures*. Rather, they are brief and done with good humor; e.g., "Yes, he is clumsy, but he had polio when he was a baby, so he can't help it. He is a good person in spite of how he walks." The laughter, exclamations, and intense interest of the entire group is repeatedly made contingent upon certain kinds of prosocial behavior. It is this focus, this warmth and involvement with each other, that makes a group of people into a family.

Parents of antisocial children may wish to engage in such interchanges, but when they attempt to initiate these interchanges they quickly deteriorate into abrasive, sarcastic attacks. They do not, therefore, know in a general sense what their children are doing nor whom they are with. In addition, they do not monitor the child's work chores or homework study times. Most of these parents have given up asking the problem child and/or siblings to do anything. "It is easier to do it myself." Indeed, it *is* easier.

At no other time of life will the individual find anyone who cares enough to monitor him 16 hours a day and who has the power to give him feedback about what he is doing. If the parents do not perform this act of love and commitment, who will? What agency worker has that kind of time? If he/she had the time, what contingencies would be required in order to get the child to respond to the feedback? *No monitoring means no punishment.* No punishment means that the child slips even further out on the deviancy dimension.

Finally, the community and/or family forcibly calls parental attention to extreme events, such as assault, firesetting, and stealing. In effect, the parent must be aware of it; the events are so salient that the parent must respond in *some* way. However, the parent who is uninvolved and/or fearful of a confrontation with the child has one final resource. He or she can deny that the event really was an example of something to be punished. As Reid and Patterson (1976) note, many parents of young stealers simply refused to label a given event as "stealing"; e.g., "I didn't see him do it. That teacher is always after him; the kid said he didn't do it, so what can I do? He said that a kid gave him that radio." Effective treatment required a subtle *relabeling* of events so that the parent could then (reluctantly) agree to take action.

Detection and Labeling

Other investigators have noted that parents of antisocial children were less likely to monitor their child's activities. For example, Wadsworth (1979) found that parents of delinquents were less likely to check on their child's school progress. All parents monitor and set sanctions for *some* deviant child behaviors, e.g., attack with a weapon upon family members, setting fire to the house. Harbin and Madden (1979) report exceptions even here. They describe instances of brutal assault in which the parent was a passive spectator. However, it is generally the case that all parents identify and label some behaviors as deviant. Even though an act is categorized as deviant, it doesn't necessarily mean that the parent then implements effective sanctions. However, an absence of such a classification would mean an absence of negative sanctions. Classification as a deviant act would, at best, place the child *at risk* for a negative sanction.

For the moment, let's assume that there is a gen-eral consensus among parents as to which child behaviors are normal and which are deviant. For each distribution (normal and deviant), the events are ordered from most to least preferred. The ordinates describe the expected frequency of occurrence for the event in a population of children. As shown in Figure 11.2, there is an area of ambiguity represented by the overlap between the distribution of deviant and prosocial behaviors. There are some prosocial behaviors, such as Cry or Whine, where it is not clear whether the behavior is an undesirable prosocial act or a very mild deviant event. There are other behaviors, such as attack with a knife, that most adults would identify as deviant. Given that the deviant behaviors fall along a dimension of acts directed against persons, then the assumption is that the parent of the problem child operates on a very strict criterion value. He or she reacts in an *irritable* fashion to many "minor" events that parents of normals would ignore (this is detailed in Chapter 8). The laboratory findings by Lorber (1981) are in keeping with this formulation. He compared the reactions of parents of normal and antisocial children to videotaped interactions of various families. They were to press one button when they viewed an antisocial act and another for a prosocial act. Parents of problem children were significantly more *over*inclusive in their categorization of socially aggressive acts and *under*inclusive when classifying prosocial behaviors.[1]

I think that parental criteria vary as a function of the *kind of deviancy*. My hunch is that Robins' and Ratcliff's (1978) negligent parent, or the unmotivated parents of stealers, would tend to set their threshold value to *minimize their response cost*. Therefore, when categorizing acts against property (vandalism, firesetting, stealing), they would probably classify as deviant *only* those events that are *extreme*, e.g., setting fire to the parents' home. On the other hand, being accused by the teacher of stealing would not necessarily be classed as deviant. Parents of stealers are thought to be characterized as having a lax criterion for acts against property (see Figure 11.2). As yet this hypothesis has not been tested. For these parents one important function of treatment is to help them readjust their criteria further to the left so that they will accurately classify as deviant more of the child's behaviors that are directed against the property of others.

In the last decade a number of investigators have recognized the importance of the manner in which the parent categorizes behavioral events as deviant or normal. These studies provide a preliminary base for understanding the accuracy of parental tracking. For example, one can understand why parents generally tend to *underestimate* frequencies for almost any test event they are asked to track. In contrast to a professional observer, a mother is tracking a *multitude* of events, many of which occur simultaneously; it stands to reason that she would "miss" many. In the pilot study by Peine (1970), three mothers and their preschool children were observed in a laboratory setting. The mothers and trained observers collected data over a series of trials on a number of target events for many behaviors. The across-trial correlations were in the .80's for mothers and observers. However, on the average, the mothers underestimated the level of deviancy by 183%! The mothers simply saw less of it than the trained observer. Incidentally, if these findings were confirmed by additional studies, it would raise questions about the efficacy of survey data in estimating base-rate values for deviant child behavior. These data may seriously underestimate *rates* of deviant child behavior.

The Peine study needs to be replicated and extended. The author carried out one such study with a group of Stanford undergraduates as observers (and co-investigators). The data showed the expected Peine Effect; i.e., the mothers underestimated the actual frequency of most behavioral events as compared to the rates recorded by observers. However, when mothers served as observers for interactions of other mother-child dyads, their rates were much closer to the rates recorded by the observers. Underestimation was primarily a function of being a participant in the ongoing process.

However, such a variable would not differentiate mothers of problem and nonproblem children. What is the impact of repeated exposure to high rates of deviant behavior? Does the mother habituate to deviancy? A study by Lorber (1978) provided a direct test of the habituation-exposure hypothesis. He used college students to observe videotapes of parent-child interaction. His findings demonstrated that prior exposure to high rates of coercive child behavior was followed by significant decreases in the *accuracy* of tracking deviant child behavior. The findings are in keeping with the habituation-exposure hypothesis. Does the same process also relate to the parental disposition for overinclusiveness of socially aggressive acts?

Finally, there are a series of studies that have investigated the relation between tracking and labeling. If the mother of the problem child were trained (as she is in OSLC treatment programs) to more accurately track the minutiae of deviant behavior, would she see her child in a more, or a less,

favorable light? In the study by Erickson (1973), one group of observers tracked deviant child behaviors, and a third group simply observed carefully. Those tracking deviant behaviors formed a less favorable general impression than the observers in the other two groups. Observers who tracked prosocial events formed more favorable impressions. The latter finding was replicated in the study by Hines (1974), while the former was not.

Before leaving this topic, there is one further question that needs to be emphasized. It seems conceivable that future studies will demonstrate that parents of problem children are *highly selective* in their errors of classification. They might correctly classify all deviant child behaviors as deviant *except* stealing, lying, and firesetting. Are there patterns in what it is that parents classify as deviant? *How* does this selectivity develop?

Currently, the monitoring-labeling FM skill is being measured in a variety of ways (Patterson, Stouthamer-Loeber, & Loeber, in preparation). There are items from the Observer Impression Inventory that provide a rating of parental monitoring. Did the parents talk with the child about his day or not? The Parent Daily Telephone Interview provides a daily check on whether the parent tracked the child's whereabouts over the preceding 16 hours. These various measures were used to generate three clusters of variables that measured parental monitoring. All of these composites contributed to a multiple-regression analysis using four different measures of antisocial behavior. The multiple correlation with peer nomination scores for antisocial child behavior was .26 ($F = 2.85$, $p < .05$); with delinquency life-style (self-report) the correlation was .46 ($F = 10.73$, $p < .0001$); and for Total Aversive Behavior (observation) the correlation was .30 ($F = 1.90$, n.s.). The discriminant function analysis produced a percent correct classification of 82.7% between children with and without court records. These findings suggest that monitoring may contribute more to our understanding of stealing and delinquency than to our understanding of social aggression.

Parental Sanctions

"One of the striking features of most studies of multi-problem families is the chaotic state of their patterns of supervision and discipline. Moreover, poor supervision has been one of the common antecedents of delinquency in most investigations. . . . Good supervision and *well-balanced discipline* can serve to protect children from a high-risk background . . . in conditions of chronic stress and poverty, strict parental supervision of the child's activities was more effective in preventing delinquency than was a happy family atmosphere. . . ." (Rutter, 1979, p. 64)

From the standpoint of coercion theory, parents of antisocial children are more likely to be *noncontingent* in their reactions to both prosocial and deviant child behaviors. Their inept use of punishment is a major determinant for antisocial child behavior. Their inept use of positive reinforcement is a major determinant for many of the child's skill deficits. These statements go far beyond the presently existing data base. They constitute a set of working hypotheses that guide many of our ongoing investigations at OSLC. These hypotheses were generated primarily from our clinical contacts with these families.

In keeping with Lorber's (1981) laboratory findings, these parents tend to "overlook" prosocial behavior. They *forget* to *reinforce.* Many of the reinforcers that *are* given tend to be presented contingent upon no particular response; i.e., they are *noncontingent.* When disciplining is necessary, they tend to nag, scold, lecture, and natter, but *they do not confront.* They do not say, "No." They do not say, "Stop that behavior here and now." In that they do not back up many of their threats, their *punishment* is *noncontingent.* When they do confront the child, it tends to be in a weakened form that all parties know will not stand for long. They often use "grounding"; e.g., "You stay in this house and in this yard for the next month." For emphasis, the father stomps out of the house in self-righteous indignation. Three days later the child slips away for an hour and presents what seems to be a reasonable excuse, "My bike tire was flat." Within a few days he is back on the street again, and the incident is forgotten.

As a general case, we might assume that parental consequences are forthcoming when the parents' expectations are exceeded. That seems relatively straightforward in that it suggests that parents differ in the points at which they set their criterion thresholds for reward and punishment. Given this, it should be possible to assess these thresholds and correlate them with the behaviors that the parents are observed to provide consequences for. As yet there are no studies that directly test this hypothesis. In thinking about these criterion thresholds, there are several hypotheses that come to mind. The first is that parents of antisocial children react consistently to maximize their *immediate comfort* and *satisfaction.* In the short run, it is aversive to be distracted from one's own affairs in order to track child behavior and set consequences. I also think that many of these parents

believe that it is impossible to change behavior by the use of reinforcement. The effect of a contingency becomes apparent only after many trials. Behavior change is a mystery. Because parents do not understand the determinants of their child's behavior, they tend to have poorly articulated future goals for their children. If you believe that events are generally outside the control of the individual, then there is little reason for a commitment to long-term goals for child rearing. This is in keeping with the general time frame for these parents, which is the immediate present. I think that the emphasis upon immediate comfort and the relative lack of long-term goals may relate to a lax criterion-threshold score for both reinforcement and punishment confrontations; this may also covary with the lack of attachment of parents to the caretaking role, which seems to characterize parents of stealers in particular. For others, it may relate to the fact that they are terribly angry with the child and feel it is inconsistent to reinforce a child who does such awful things to them. For these parents, reinforcing the child is hypocritical; "Why should I reward him for doing what he should do!"

The criterion threshold for punishment may be equally complex. I suspect that for many families the determining variable is *fear.* It is an avoidance of the pain that results from confrontation. A well-practiced antisocial child is a formidable adversary in such a confrontation. For others, the threshold may be set at a lower level because the spouse interferes with attempts to punish behaviors that are not extreme. Other parents seem to believe that their particular child deserves special consideration. For example, both parents work and feel guilty about its effect on the child, or the child had a severe illness that warrants special treatment.

At a very speculative level, these parents seem to operate on an *affect basis.* They reward and punish on the basis of how they "feel" rather than on the basis of some set of clear-cut criteria. They natter because they are irritated. They physically assault because they are angry. They reward when they are *very* pleased, i.e., excited. This affective change occurs *only* when the child has done something truly outstanding. Rewards are, therefore, low base-rate events in the lives of these people. Ordinary prosocial behaviors are taken for granted. Small improvements in behavior are "expected" and, therefore, are not rewarded. Praise is reserved for Olympian levels of performance and, even then, may be accompanied by criticism. This, in turn, works against the concept of "shaping" behavior by providing positive reinforcement for small increments of improvement. The natural outcome of reinforcement-for-excellence is a large set of skill deficits.[2] The implication of the affect base for punishment was detailed in Chapter 6. It was suggested there that nattering related to extended coercive chains and to increments in intensity.

There is one further implication the affect-base concept has when applied to rewards. As noted by Kahneman and Tversky (1973), the strategy of rewarding only for excellence is likely to result in a loss of belief in the efficacy of rewards. It is almost always the case that the next response will be *inferior* to the exceptional one; i.e., to the observer, the effect of reward is to *weaken* performance! There is yet another aspect of social reinforcement that leads many of these parents to doubt its efficacy. Most of the so-called reinforcing events are probably not, in and of themselves, automatically activating. They are low-key and, therefore, not as readily noted as are aversive events. As Solomon and Corbit (1974) point out in their two-stage theory, both the anticipation and aftermath of aversive events are characterized by powerful autonomic reactions. However, in the case of most positive social reinforcers, the affective reaction occurs primarily during *deprivation*. At an affect level, the child understands about the familial support system when he visits a friend's house for the first time and discovers that he is homesick! The young couple that has grown accustomed to intense mutual sharing and support feel intense love when the spouse is *absent* for a few days. The writer believes that this delay of affect that is evident during deprivation rather than when the reinforcement occurs leads many parents to steadfastly refuse to believe in the power of positive reinforcement. In that sense, pain is obvious, and support (reinforcement) is not.

Positive Reinforcement

The hypothesis is that parents of antisocial children are less effective than parents of normal children in their use of positive reinforcement to shape prosocial behavior. This breaks down into three hypotheses. First, the parents of antisocial children tend to use *fewer* reinforcers for prosocial behaviors, e.g., approval. Second, they are less likely to use social reinforcers *contingently*. The third hypothesis describes the outcome for these oversights. Variables that measure these aspects of parental skill would be expected to show low-order correlations with various measures of the child's prosocial survival skills.[3] The more inept the parent is as a reinforcer, the more unskilled the child.

What is it that adults reinforce children for?

There are data suggesting that the sex and *personality* of the nursery school teacher significantly determine the reinforcing contingencies provided for boys and girls in that setting. The observation study by Fagot and Patterson (1969) showed that female nursery school teachers reinforced *both boys and girls* for feminine behavior. On the other hand, they were *unlikely* to provide positive consequences for behaviors that were considered to be masculine. Male peers *did* reinforce masculine behaviors. Robinson (1976) compared 20 male caregivers (nursery school teachers), 20 female caregivers (teachers), and 20 male engineers. Judges from all three groups *thought* that boys should be reinforced for masculine behaviors and girls for *both* masculine and feminine behaviors. However, actual observations of their interactions in a nursery school showed that both male and female caregivers reinforced boys and girls more for feminine behaviors than for masculine behaviors! They also punished masculine behaviors more than feminine behaviors. Questionnaire data showed that the male and female caregivers were more feminine in their personality scores than were the male engineers (i.e., less oriented toward endurance and achievement and more oriented towards sympathy, affection, and emotional support).

In effect, well-trained nursery school teachers reinforce differentially as a function of their own *personal values* rather than what they believe the child needs; i.e., all teachers reinforce males for feminine behavior even though they agreed that boys needed to be supported for being masculine! Fagot (1978a & b), in her review of the rather extensive literature that was based upon her first publication, concluded that the general effect was reliable across investigators.

In an analogous fashion, does the personality of the parent correlate with the likelihood that he or she will contingently reward the child? Does it covary with his or her perspective on internal-external control, or his or her emphasis upon the immediate present versus long-term strategies? We know very little about the variables that determine the nature of parental reinforcement. We do know that in normal families events that seem to function as reinforcers occur with some regularity. Physical Positive (touches) by mothers occurred at a rate of .06 per minute and Approval at the rate of .10 (Reid, 1978). The rate of occurrence for these reinforcers was significantly lower for mothers of antisocial children (Patterson, 1980a). A comparison of rates for mothers giving approval to the target child showed a mean of .009 for a sample of Normals, .007 for Social Aggressors, and .005 for Stealers. The samples of mothers also varied in terms of what they approved of. For example, given child-Comply, the likelihoods for mother-Approve were .028, .018, and .006 respectively. The conditional probabilities, given child-Play, were .010, .005, and .001 respectively. These findings are in keeping with the hypothesis that the parents of antisocial children provide less positive reinforcement for the maintenance of prosocial behaviors.

There is one further dimension along which parents differ in their use of positive reinforcement. This difference did not become apparent to us until the summer of 1979. As a basis for constructing the new code system (MOSAIC), we were spending a good deal of time in the homes of "super normal" families. These families *often* engaged in something we had almost *never* seen in families of antisocial children. The phenomenon might be characterized as an intensive "How-was-your-day" exchange. At this time, information was shared about the day's activities. These exchanges provided a rich basis for explicit "That's good" statements. In addition, it was a time during which the children received undivided and *noncritical* parental *attention* and *interest*. The child's report elicited both sustained interest and a discussion with the parents. I suspect that these periods of shared information are a powerful mechanism for shaping the child's values and interests. Given that this was a frequent occurrence, one would expect that the members of normal families would be more homogeneous than distressed families in values, interests, and recreational activities.

These considerations are an important feature of the treatment procedures for distressed families. In the beginning stages of treatment there is an emphasis upon parental tracking of *prosocial* behaviors and an emphasis upon the use of both social and nonsocial (money, points, privileges) rewards for these behaviors (Patterson, Reid, Jones, & Conger, 1975). The prosocial behaviors typically include doing chores, being cooperative, playing well with siblings, doing homework, or bringing home a positive report from the teacher.

Punishment

Parents of antisocial children punish *more often* than do parents of normal children. This is true regardless of what type of punishment is considered. Their children may engage in three or four times more deviant behaviors, and these parents respond by engaging in considerably more scolding, threatening, and hitting. I'm not sure whether these parents use deprivation of privileges, withholding allowance, or work as punishment more frequently than parents of normal children. However, in spite of all this punishment-like activity, children with conduct problems perceived their parents as being unable to set limits (Goldin, 1969). Even when limits were set, the children perceived their parents as being unable to enforce them. Why is this? The observation data discussed earlier showed that parents of socially aggressive and abused-child families were significantly more likely than parents of normals to respond aversively to deviant child behavior. They punish more *frequently, and* they are more *likely* to punish. If this is so, then why are their children more antisocial? In spite of all of this "activity," these parents are unskilled in their use of punishment. There are three components to this lack of skill.

The first problem is that their criterion threshold value for *confrontation* is *too low* (see Figure 11.2). They threaten and scold *very* often, but they seldom follow through. As used here, confrontation means that the parent responds in such a way as to both stop the immediate deviant event *and* to reduce the likelihood of its future recurrence. Effective confrontation means both the immediate *suppression* of ongoing behavior and weakening the connection between the event and its controlling antecedent. My hypothesis is that the problem child often wins in such an out-and-out confrontation; therefore, these parents natter, but they do not confront. In their study of severely disrupted families from inner-city London, Quinton (1980) noted that parents of antisocial children (more often than parents of the control sample) did not bring punishment to some firm conclusion.

When the parents of problem children do confront, they often respond with anger rather than with some other more appropriate response. The result can be a severe beating. Reid, Taplin, and Lorber (1981) found that roughly 30% of the OSLC clinical sample was comprised of abused children who had been referred for treatment because they were out of control. If an angry parent punishes extremes of deviant behavior, then in terms of the Kahneman and Tversky (1973) formulation, this would have several interesting implications. As applied to antisocial children, it is unlikely that a series of two coercive episodes would *both* be characterized as extreme; i.e., the second should tend to be less extreme than the first. Therefore, given that the extreme behavior was punished, and that the second was less extreme, then the logical conclusion is that physical violence works! The same syllogism that convinces the parents of antisocial children that reward does not work may also provide support for the idea that physical punishment accompanied by anger does. In addition, the beating would also have short-term effects that are reinforcing to the parent, i.e., the child behaves.

However, the child's extremely deviant acts are embedded in a pattern of related acts that occur at high rates. The child who sets fires also steals, lies, and spends a great deal of time unsupervised (see Chapter 11). An occasional beating for a particular theft does not change the problem. The child continues to come in at all hours of the night, he lies, his chores are not done, and he is failing in school. The parent cannot beat him for each occurrence of these high-rate acts. None of these are extreme enough to exceed the criterion threshold value; they are, therefore, neither labeled as deviant nor punished. While the parents are irritated by these recurring problems, they do not necessarily perceive that these child behaviors need to be changed (confronted). As noted in earlier discussions, their nattering elicits further coercive interactions and is associated with extended coercive interchanges. As shown in the Loeber (1980) analysis, such extended chains were correlated with hitting.

Nattering makes things worse. Members of antisocial families are more likely to natter than their normal counterparts. This second skill deficit seems to relate to the parents setting their criterion threshold value *too strictly*. Almost anything the child does can irritate the parent and elicit nattering. Sallows' (1972) function analysis showed that not responding was the most effective way of reducing the likelihood of extended coercive sequences. If the parent behaved as if the coercive response never existed, it was unlikely to continue. Our observations in normal homes gives support to this theme. Effective parents often "overlooked" a coercive child behavior and simply *deflected* the behavior. They might use humor or they might respond verbally in such a way as to alter the meaning of the entire interchange. When they did choose to punish. it was not accomplished by a casual threat, scolding, or sarcasm (nattering). They stopped whatever else they were doing and persisted in their punishment *until* the behavior stopped. The OSLC treatment program teaches parents of problem children either to deflect the sequence or to punish it effectively (Patterson, Reid, Jones, & Conger, 1975). They are also taught to use *nonphysical* forms of punishment, which can be applied to *each* occurrence of deviant behavior. Effective parent training would require pairing stop commands with an appropriate back-up punishment. This should increase the effectiveness of parental punishment. This was, in fact, demonstrated and replicated in the outcome studies reviewed in Patterson and Fleischman (1979).

The third type of parental deficit lies in a frequent use of commands, many of which are poorly stated. This may be thought of as a form of nattering, but it has some special properties that lead me to think that it should be considered separately. A parental command can start up the coercion process in an otherwise quiet interval. The fact that the children have been poorly trained means the parent must issue *more* commands. The data from the Observer Impression Inventory showed a trend for parents of Social Aggressors and Stealers to be more likely to issue commands that were unclear (.30 and .26) than were parents of Normals (.11). The F value was .66 ($df = 2:41$, $p < .20$).

Given that the parent is irritable, a request can quickly become a command. Many of the commands are accompanied by overtones of things that happened in the past, a litany of yesterday's sins and omissions. These negative accompaniments increase the likelihood of noncompliance (this hypothesis is untested). A command is qualitatively different from a request; it is the difference between the drill sergeant's "Get in here!" and "Could you come here for a minute, please?" The parent of the problem child is not only more likely to command but, in addition, to tack on further aversive baggage, "Damn it, you never do what I tell you to; now get in here!" For many parents of problem children, one cannot be certain of just what it is that they wish done; what *is* communicated is anger and impatience. On the other hand, the skilled parent is more likely to express even a request in nonabrasive terms, "I think your toy will get broken if you leave it there; what do you think?"

The observation study by Halverson and Waldrop (1970) showed that some mothers tend to have a consistently abrasive style whether they are coping with their own children or other children. The correlations were .52 and .48 between likelihood of negative statements delivered by the mother to her own children and other male and female children respectively. They also found that boys who were rated as impulsive elicited more commands from their mothers. This relation between rates of deviant child behavior and mother commands is also a consistent finding. Delfini et al. (1976) compared homes of aggressive children to homes of nonaggressive children. Parents of problem children not only gave significantly more commands, but for the clinical sample, child deviancy and mother commands correlated .63 ($p < .01$). The Lobitz and Johnson (1975) studies provided further confirmation for these findings. They also demonstrated the causal relation between increases in parental commands (for both normal and deviant behaviors) and deviant child behavior.

The assumption is that measures of these three skill deficits will covary. Parents of antisocial children should be less likely than parents of normals to *confront* their children for serious deviant behavior. They should also be more likely to natter about minor deviations they might better ignore. Finally, they should issue *more* commands and commands of poorer quality. These hypotheses will be tested by the assessment measures constructed for the study of children at risk for delinquency. That study includes a structured interview that contains nine items relating to these questions, a revised Observer Impression Inventory with 11 items that are relevant, and a daily Parent Telephone Interview that contains yet more items relevant to punishment and disciplinary practices (Patterson & Stouthamer-Loeber, in preparation). The analyses produced two rather different sets of composite scores. The first set, which we labeled Obedience, consisted of four composite scores based upon interview and questionnaire data. The multiple regression analysis showed a correlation of .36 ($F = 5.07$, $p < .001$) with delinquent lifestyle (self-report), .47 ($F = 9.42$, $p < .0001$) with peer nominations for antisocial behavior, and .21 ($F = 0.61$, n.s.) with TAB scores. The discriminant function analysis showed a correct classification of 69.9%, differentiating children with court offenses from those without. The second set of items was based upon observers' *global* ratings following each observation in the home. This set of four variables, labeled Discipline, correlated .56 ($p < .001$) with TAB scores for fourth grade children but were nonsignificant for measures relating to stealing and delinquency.

Problem Solving

It is assumed that parents of antisocial children are less skilled in solving family problems than parents of normal children. This skill deficit is thought to covary both with rates of antisocial behavior and with the number of crises that impinge upon the family.

Effective family management requires a resolution of the crises that constantly impinge upon families. Some crises arise from within the family, such as an unresolved conflict between two family members. Some crises arise from outside the family, such as debts, unemployment, and conflict at work. Ideally, it is the shared responsibility of the husband and wife to anticipate many of these crises before they arise and to resolve those which do occur. Most of us have some crises that tend to re-

cur. For example, Hicks and Platt (1970) showed that in normal families the *kind* of problems encountered did not change over time. However, I think that in distressed families these unresolved crises accumulate. For example, 50 normal and 50 distressed couples were compared in the study by Birchler and Webb (1977). Their response to an area-of-change questionnaire showed an average of 28.5 areas thought to require change by distressed couples. This is in contrast to 6.9 areas for nondistressed couples. Presumably, families of conduct-problem children would demonstrate a similar accumulation of unsolved problems. In the Birchler and Webb study, the distressed couples reported a mean of 3.4 conflicts per week; this was in dramatic contrast to the mean of 1.0 for nondistressed couples. Quinton (1980) noted that distressed families had twice as many unresolved conflicts and crises as did matched controls from the same area of inner-city London.

The accumulation of unsolved conflicts and crises relates in part to the fact that little time is given to problem solving, and even when time is given, members of distressed couples demonstrate a lack of the skills that are necessary to put the time to good use. Videotapes of their problem-solving sessions showed that during problem-solving situations distressed couples engaged in significantly more coercive behavior than did nondistressed couples (Birchler, Weiss, & Vincent, 1975). A similar phenomenon was observed in a comparison of families of normal and antisocial children (Forgatch & Patterson, in preparation). As one observes these interchanges, the desperation of the people involved can be seen very clearly. A discussion about an area of change has the quality of having been repeated many times before; the thrust and repartee have a well-practiced quality. The outcome is anticipated, and the forthcoming impasse is viewed with mounting frustration. As the impasse is reached, the language becomes increasingly sharp and argumentative.

These problem-solving tasks may take place in a laboratory setting, but the interchanges are far from sterile. The most salient features are the coerciveness of the participants. The comparison study showed that the mother's rate of aversive behavior during familial problem solving correlated negatively with observers' ratings for the quality of the solution reached by the family.

Families of conduct-problem children have a long history of failure in solving problems. Their efforts to solve crises and conflicts are not followed by perceivable changes in anyone's behavior. Even if a discussion results in some type of an agreement, the changes are either temporary, or simply never occur. Talking and negotiating were probably never very popular modes for producing behavior change with these people. Failure makes these activities even less attractive. Discussion and requests quickly degenerate to demands. Demands are accompanied by negative verbal statements, "You are a drunk just like your old man. Every payday you take off and drink up half of your paycheck." Here, the wife does communicate in a general way the area that needs to be changed; i.e., the husband should *first* bring his paycheck home (and *then* go off with the boys). However, he is more likely to respond to one of the two insults than to the issue itself. In fact, he is most likely to counterattack by emphasizing some aspect of the spouse's perceived failures. "You are such a bitch; you drive me to it." First one, then the other, becomes angry. When the discussion ends, the problem solving has been effectively *sidetracked*. It is added to the accumulation of unsolved crises, which will probably be rerun on the next payday. This contributes to the attrition in esteem for both self and others. It is further proof that things will never change. Similar disruptions in communication and inept technique have been identified in other clinical samples as well. For example, R. Liberman and his colleagues at Camarillo work with family members of schizophrenic patients (Liberman, et al., 1979). Their training in problem-solving skills for patient and family members heavily emphasizes the concepts of receiving skills, processing skills, and sending skills. Their approach draws heavily from the work of Spivack, Platt, and Shure (1976).

The treatment program for family members of antisocial children emphasizes the following skills: (1) stating the problem in neutral terms; (2) specifying clearly what changes are desired; (3) accompanying such requests with a positive statement about some other aspect of the person that is appreciated (this communicates to the other that he/she is a good person, but there is this one specific behavior that is a problem); (4) training the recipient to paraphrase the request (it is amazing how many of these family members have learned to effectively "tune out" requests for change. It is interesting to note that this also is a key portion of the Liberman et al. (1979) social skills training for schizophrenics and their family members); (5) brainstorming alternative solutions; and (6) consequences are also set because it is expected that the agreement will occasionally be broken. Typically, these agreements are written down and involve two or more persons stipulating areas of change.

Clinically, this training process is extremely delicate; it is, in fact, at the very core of the OSLC treatment program for families of antisocial children. This brief description is not intended to fully describe the process but only to illustrate something that normal families do with little fanfare. Probably the best description of the clinical process is to be found in the recent publication by Jacobson and Margolin (1979). Problem solving becomes most evident when it is absent. It is only when the debris of unsolved problems is everywhere that this omitted mechanism comes into focus (see Illustration #3).

It is a sad commentary that even in normal families there is often sufficient disruption in the processes of problem solving that family members engage in higher rates of coercion than should be necessary. Bales (1953) noted that the most abrasive small groups encountered in his laboratories were *families!* Halverson and Waldrop (1970) noted a similar lack of tolerance in dealing with one's own family members. In that study, mothers of preschool children were observed to be five times more abrasive in interactions with their *own child* than they were in interactions with other children in the same setting! In many instances it is not so much the case that family members do not know how to cope with each other in a pleasant fashion, but they do not try to do so. It is not learning, but performance, that is the issue. The study by Vincent, et al. (1979) was a classic in this regard. They arranged for distressed and nondistressed couples to solve problems in a laboratory situation. On counterbalanced trials, each spouse engaged in problem solving with a spouse and a nonspouse of the same sex. Problem-solving processes were significantly disrupted when distressed spouses interacted. These disruptions were not observed when the same individuals interacted with nonspouse adults of the same sex! It can be inferred that problem-solving skills were available to the distressed spouses. It was as if family members, particularly those in distressed relations, declared a moratorium on etiquette and rational attempts to *change* a problem situation. They engaged, instead, in something that seemed analogous to nattering. They express irritation and annoyance, but this does not produce change in each other's behavior.

Typically, what is missing for the caretaker is a support system for problem solving. As noted in an earlier discussion, it is not the presence of more external crises that determines the psychiatric status for an individual; it is, in addition, a function of the availability of a support system. Is there a friend, a relative, or a husband who can provide daily assistance in dealing with unsolved problems? In family sessions, is there one other adult

Illustration #3: The Rising Tide of Unsolved Problems

who will join a coalition on the crucial issues? Is there one other member in family meetings who can be counted upon to join in brainstorming for a new alternative to solving an old problem? Is there another adult present who can stay calm when the caretaker commits some unspeakable breach of problem-solving etiquette? Wahler (1979) noted lower rates of aversive behavior on those days when the mother received positive support from outside the family. The modest correlations in Table 10.1 showed a similar covariation for four of five mothers. Were problems being "solved" during these contacts, or was it the emotional support that was involved? At this point, we don't know.

There is a related issue that also requires further investigation. It is assumed that extreme stress can temporarily disrupt the performance of normal problem-solving skills. For example, Forgatch and Patterson (in preparation) found a significant correlation between frequency of crises and mothers' negative verbal behavior during familial problem solving. One can think of the dissolution of a marriage as being a time when there is a severe stress,

and the support systems are severely disrupted. The studies of families in the process of getting a divorce showed a rising tide of antisocial behavior for the children (Hetherington, Cox, & Cox, 1978; Wallerstein & Kelly, 1976, 1980). I think that such severe stress disrupts problem solving and other family management practices as well.

There are several other studies that suggest that when parents are in severe conflict, the children are more likely to be out of control. It is not clear whether the relation is due to the parents interfering with each other's child management attempts, or whether the parents are just not making the effort. To what extent is disrupted problem solving implicated as well; e.g., crises, internal or external, accumulate that, in turn, reduce the efforts of the caretaker to manage the children? The Johnson and Lobitz (1974a) study found a correlation of $-.48$ ($p < .01$) between parental reports of marital satisfaction (on the Locke-Wallis) and the child's observed rate of coercive behavior in the home. Similarly, Oltmanns, Broderick, and O'Leary (1977) found correlations in the $-.3$ to

−.4 range using parent self-reports as criterion data. They also cite several other studies with similar findings. They note the general tendency for parents of children referred for treatment to report less satisfaction with their marriage. Reid, Taplin, and Lorber (1981), in their study of child-abusive families, noted a significant tendency for these parents to display high rates of coercive behavior when interacting with each other. These studies reiterate the idea that FM variables may serve as mediators between antisocial child behavior, on the one hand, and those variables identified in the research literature that often show low-level correlations with it, e.g., marital discord, broken homes, large family, low income, and criminality of parents. Presumably it is the interaction of one or more of these at-risk variables accompanied by a disruption in family management practices that would increase the predictive efficiency. Not *all* children who live in the ghetto become delinquent. Not all homes in which there is severe marital discord produce an antisocial child. Given that family management skills are practiced by either parent, then the at-risk child may make a perfectly normal adjustment.

Measurements of family problem-solving skills are obtained from four different modes of assessment. A structured intake interview contains 25 items relevant to this issue; the Observer Impression Checklist has four; and the daily telephone call may provide additional information. The assessment procedure of key importance is thought to be a videotape of efforts during family interactions. Here the members are asked to solve one of their own previously identified problems. In the second episode, they are asked to plan a family outing. The interaction is coded by a complex system, PANIC (Forgatch & Wieder, in preparation), which contains 40 content codes, 13 measures of nonverbal behavior, and ten qualifier categories. The studies of children at risk for antisocial behavior have demonstrated that several of the composite scores from the PANIC correlated significantly with the child's TAB score, as well as his status as delinquent or nondelinquent. In the preliminary analyses of the data for 85 families, the construct measuring mother irritability during problem solving correlated .32 ($p<.01$) with the child TAB score and .31 ($p<.01$) with peer nominations for antisocial behavior. The covariation with court reported delinquency and with a self-report of delinquent life-style score were nonsignificant (Forgatch & Weider, in preparation).

The Family is Disrupted

A single-minded focus upon the management of aversive events leaves out those aspects of family that are of greatest interest to most of us. Where is the sense of shared purpose, values, interests, and recreational activities? Where is the sense of belonging and caring? As suggested in Figure 10.4, these are the aspects that become the casualties of a disorganized family. If crises and conflicts are not properly managed, then there will be lowered rates of shared activities, lowered responsiveness, and an increased sense of powerlessness and isolation.

The ratio of positive to aversive components in the interaction might index the family's progression toward disruption in functioning. In Lennard and Revenstein's (1969) review of the Bales studies, the ratio of positive to negative events during small-group tasks was 0.77:1.00 for the least satisfied group and 6.20:1.00 for the most satisfied group. Normal control families had scores of 1.05:1.00, and families with a schizophrenic member had scores of 0.61:1.00. Birchler et al. (1975) found a significant difference between distressed and nondistressed couples using a similar measure. In disrupted families there were fewer positive events and considerably more aversive events.[4] It should be noted that at OSLC no systematic work has been done in exploring the use of such a ratio; it might, for instance, differentiate Stealer and Social Aggressor families from Normal families. It may also describe families who have moved further along a dimension of disorganization and anarchy.

As the process of disorganization continues, most of the family members avoid/escape each other's presence. It is simply unpleasant to be around other members of the family. As a result, the rates of social interaction are reduced, as are shared activities. The comparison of distressed to nondistressed couples by Birchler et al. (1975) showed lower rates of interaction for the clinical sample. For them, unsolved arguments suddenly emerge in the context of an otherwise pleasant Sunday drive. This phenomenon is so prevalent that marital therapists advocate a "problem-solving time and place" by appointment; distressed couples are "not allowed" to bring up conflict topics at any other time. One logical solution is to reduce the amount of social interaction. This probably also happens to families of socially aggressive children. Picnics, visits with relatives, vacations, camping trips, and Thanksgiving dinners all become battle grounds. In these families, coercive processes *cannot* even *be turned off* when relatives or observers are present in the home. The classic studies by Johnson and Lobitz (1974, 1975) reviewed in Chapter 3 showed that families of coer-

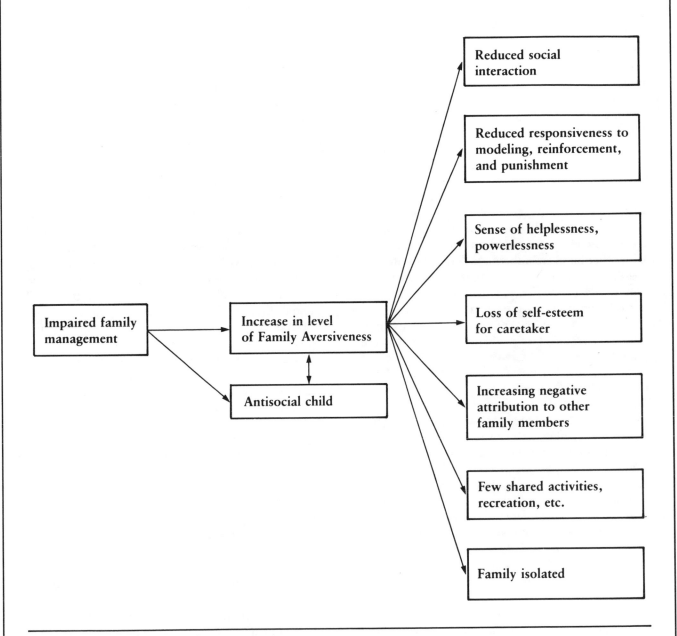

Figure 10.4
Outcomes for Disrupted Family Management Practices

cive children could not "fake good" even when asked to do so!

Many of the parents in the clinical families had to give up trying to go out without the children—baby-sitters simply refused to tolerate the chaos. The parents simply stay home, turn up the TV, and escape as best they can. Interactions are unpleasant, and one way of handling this is the simple expedient of no longer making plans for sharing activities. For most of these families it also means not doing anything for recreation. Our

work with distressed and nondistressed married couples also supported this concept (Patterson, Weiss, & Hops, 1976). Birchler and Webb (1977) showed that significantly more happy couples (56%) engaged in shared activities than did unhappy couples (46%). This agrees with earlier findings that suggested that marital satisfaction correlated positively with the amount of shared recreation-leisure time (Birchler et al., 1975; Barnett & Nietzel, 1979). Blood and Wolfe (1960) and Tonge, James, and Hillam (1975) found fewer shared activities in their casework study of multiple-problem families. The Fagan et al. (1977) longitudinal design showed parents of younger delinquent-prone boys were characterized by lower rates of shared leisure and recreational activities. Again, one cannot isolate cause and effect from such covariations. These findings do *not* offer direct support for the writer's hypothesis that high rates of coercive family behavior *cause* reduced rates of shared recreational activities.

The imbalanced ratio, reductions in social interaction, and the reduction in shared activities are accompanied by more subtle shifts that, themselves, carry ominous implications for the family. The hypothesis is that members of such families become less responsive to each other's reinforcement and become more likely to make negative attributions. The latter produces an increased likelihood for unprovoked attacks; this, in turn, increases the general sense of uncertainty in dealing with other family members. As detailed in Chapter 12, the net effect of these changes is reflected most graphically in the decrease in self-esteem for the person who occupies the role of caretaker.

The battles over ancient issues and the accumulation of new unsolved problems continue, and the increasing level of aversive interchanges and decreasing positive experiences demand an explanation. Each member must explain to himself how this could be; each can see that he has *tried* to relate to the others. Certainly the individual's good intentions are obvious to everyone, particularly to the individual. Why *others* would behave so badly is the matter of concern. Each family member becomes adept at reading the malevolent intentions of the others. These negative evaluations, in turn, feed the process of disruption. This important facet of the coercion process is poorly understood. In an extended baseline observation of a preschool child, there was a correlation of .64 ($df = 18$, $p < .01$) between the child's rate of aversive behavior (TAB score) in the home and the mother's ratings on a scale that included, "He is being naughty just to get my goat." On days when he was more aversive, she increasingly attributed malevolent intentions to his behaviors. It is assumed that the attributional process is generalized to include all family members. Each tends to perceive him- or herself as essentially powerless to do anything about what is going on in the family.

As noted earlier, the studies by Dodge (1980) showed that in otherwise neutral situations, the antisocial child was significantly more likely to attribute hostile intentions to the other and to attack. Similarly, if the other person had been experienced as aggressive, this also increased the like-

lihood of attack. These two hypotheses from Dodge's work may well relate to a phenomenon identified by David Littman as "crossover" (Littman & Patterson, 1980). In a normal household there are occasional unprovoked attacks upon other persons. These attacks are crossovers in that the attacker shifts the interactional state from a prosocial to a coercive one. In fact, as noted earlier, this characterizes about two-thirds of a normal child's coercive behavior; i.e., the antecedents are prosocial or neutral. The data in Chapter 7 showed that families of antisocial children were more likely to engage in crossover. It seems reasonable to suppose that such behaviors would produce negative attributions.

These shifts in the level of coercive interchanges, reduced interactions and shared leisure time, reduced responsiveness, and increasing hostile attributions take their toll at the interactional level. There also seem to be accompanying shifts at a molar level. The family itself is, or becomes, isolated from the support systems provided by the community. Wahler, Leske, and Roberts (1977) noted that mothers of antisocial children who lived in the ghetto area had an average of less than 2.6 social contacts per day; most were initiated by people outside the family who were *not* friends, e.g., agency workers. By contrast, the mothers of antisocial children from *non*ghetto areas had an average of 9.5 daily social contacts, most of them from friends. Other investigators have also noted the insular quality of distressed married couples (Birchler et al., 1975) and for families of delinquents (Fagan et al., 1977).

The isolated quality of these families is of interest. It suggests that those families most in need of community support systems are least likely to make use of the opportunities that are offered. These families seem to function like an island of poorly organized and slightly xenophobic inhabitants. For example, there are a number of survey studies that note the tendency for parents of aggressive children to be noncooperative when asked to fill out questionnaires or to participate in studies (Eron, Walder, & Lefkowitz, 1971, Rutter, Tizard, & Whitmore, 1970; West & Farrington, 1973). Longitudinal studies, such as the one by Eron et al. (1971) also note that these same families tend to be highly mobile. D. Elliott (personal communication) believes that most of their moves are within a limited area; that is, they move from one place to another within the city in order to escape from crises that build up as a result of their futile efforts to cope with an assortment of irate neighbors, bill collectors, and agency personnel. West and Farrington (1973) made a similar observation.

Caretakers occupy center stage for this process of family disruption. Confrontation with failure is their daily fare. They can perceive the rising tide of coercive interchanges, the failure of family members to form positive attachments, and the failure of their children in academic and peer-related activities. Many of them are also in the position of negotiating with agency personnel in order to satisfy day-by-day needs. As noted in Chapter 4, these experiences take their toll by generating a sense of helplessness and reduced self-esteem. The correlation between mothers' depression and general negative self-evaluation with antisocial child behavior will be examined in detail in Chapter 12.

My clinical experience suggests that the disorganized family moves in a steady progression toward increasing anarchy (see Chapter 12). In this progression, children come increasingly to occupy elements of the parental role. Pain control more often escalates to high-intensity techniques, including physical violence.

Implications

Disrupted families can change. During the past decade we have become convinced that to treat antisocial children one must change the social environment in which they live (Patterson, Reid, Jones, & Conger, 1975). The family, school, and peer group constitute the major components of the child's environment. The key concept is that it is the *parent who must change the problem child*. To do so, he or she must learn *how* to be an effective parent. If one can be taught to improve in his or her application of family management skills, then this dismal process of disruption, avoidance, and lowered self-esteem can be stopped. The role of the therapist is that of teacher and facilitator for such change. It is his/her role to help the parent alter values and norms concerning deviant child behavior and to overcome the fear or hesitation in confronting the child on these issues.

The family management variables outlined here are the core of the treatment program. They are, in fact, an outgrowth of the therapy process itself. Each of these *FM* skills must be carefully role-played and supervised. Simple as they are conceptually, they prove extremely difficult in their application. The problem is, how does one provide an empirical base for our sense of deep commitment to these *FM* variables? The success rates in teaching them to parents have been gratifying; the outcome studies are briefly reviewed in Chapter 13. However, a successful application of the *FM* variables does not, of course, establish the causal status that we ascribe to them. Their contribution to

individual differences in stealing, social aggression, assault, and child abuse is the focus of the current children-at-risk study. Those family management variables that survive these multivariate analyses will be incorporated into a longitudinal study planned for 1982. I think only a longitudinal design can answer the questions that must be raised about the OSLC analyses of *FM* variables. Even though the analyses demonstrate that this or that pattern of *FM* variables differentiates Social Aggressors from Stealers, or from abused children, we will not know what is the cause and what is the *outcome* of a process. Is it the disruption in practice of a particular *FM* variable that, early on, initiates a process that eventually *produces* a Stealer? I assume that there are such differentiating patterns and that *FM* variables will be shown to play a key causal role for antisocial child behavior.

Footnotes

1. These results should be accepted with caution in that they are in sharp disagreement with the findings by Bogaard (1976), who carried out the first study in this series. Both the larger sample size and automated procedures in the Lorber (1981) study lead me to give greater credence to the findings from this study. Finally, a replication and extension by P. Holloran (in preparation) provide data that are in close accord with those in the Lorber study.

2. Many parents seem to use such contingencies very skillfully to produce children who are high achievers. However, I believe that a careful study would show that they carefully track and reinforce intensively at the early stages of learning. Only later do they seem to shift to the extreme, "I'll be pleased only if you get straight A's." The parents of antisocial children leave out the initial block of training trials.

Even if the parent is successful in reinforcing high achievement behaviors, he may end up with a child who detests the whole academic enterprise. The parent has been reinforcing contingent upon the child's being "better-than," i.e., for successful competition. The programmatic work by Lepper and Dafoe (1980) and others showed very convincingly that, even when successful, the child prefers not to engage in such activities.

3. Some parents may be able to effectively use aversives to shape prosocial skills in the child, e.g., negative reinforcement for skilled performance and punishment for inept performance. An adequate prediction of child skill level would require the inclusion of measures of parental skill in

using such pain control techniques.

4. What I have in mind here are families of antisocial children. Although I have never studied them systematically, I wonder if families of "neurotic" children would not display a comparable imbalance. The problem there would be that of knowing *when* an aversive had occurred. It is my impression that in these families the aversives are very subtle and, perhaps, idiosyncratic to each family.

Chapter 11
Abstract

The hypothesis that there is a continuity between early and later forms of antisocial behavior is examined. The corollary for the continuity hypothesis is that deviant-child behavior covaries with disruptions in family management practices. Antisocial children are said to have the following in common: a tendency to be extremely noncompliant, a tendency to maximize short-term gains, relative nonresponsiveness to social reinforcers and punishments, attentional deficits, arrested socialization, poor survival skills, and poor prognosis for adjustment as adults.

Antisocial behavior is defined by two subsets, Stealer and Social Aggressor. By definition, the subsets are characterized by different symptoms ascribed to them by parents at intake. The discriminant-function analyses for samples of Normals, Stealers, and Social Aggressors show that mothers and, to a lesser extent, fathers of Stealers are more distant and unfriendly. Parents of Social Aggressors, particularly the mothers, are more coercive.

The covariation of microsocial measures of irritability with performance level for Social Aggression is examined. In a multiple-regression analysis, the likelihood of Continuance for mothers and fathers and the likelihood of Crossover for siblings accounted for significant amounts of variance for differences in performance level, as measured by TAB and PDR scores. These findings support a bilateral definition of aggression; i.e., the reactions of family members are a major determinant for differences in the target child's performance level.

Multimethod assessments for family management variables are correlated with four criterion measures of Social Aggression. For two samples, the scores for parental Discipline and Obedience correlate significantly with the criterion measures. The family management variables, Monitor, Obedience, and Problem Solve, covary significantly with four different measures of protodelinquent and delinquent behavior. Stealers and Social Aggressors seem to be characterized by disruptions in different aspects of the family management process.

Chapter 11

Similarities and Differences Between Social Aggressors and Stealers

One function of this chapter is to pull together the diverse themes and scattered findings that have been presented in preceding sections. The findings from both the microsocial and the family management variables will be summarized in terms of the amount of variance accounted for in measures of antisocial performance. The other goal of the chapter is to pursue the topic of similarities and differences between Stealers and Social Aggressors. As presented thus far, children with these problems are said to belong to a larger class, antisocial; the implication is that they share some characteristics that differentiate them from normal children. The first section of this chapter outlines the elements that they have in common. When we began treating these families, it gradually became apparent that families of Stealers and Social Aggressors differed in some important respects; the family processes that produced Stealers differed from those that produced Social Aggressors. Both processes seemed to differ from what was observed in normal families. The second and third sections of this chapter will focus upon family-process variables that differentiate among Social Aggressor, Stealer, and Normal samples

Characteristics Shared by Antisocial Children

The most salient element shared by the Stealer and Social Aggressor is noncompliance. As noted earlier, most of the antisocial children referred for treatment were said by their parents to be disobedient. These disobedient children are unpleasant to be around. They take, they are abrasive, and they give little in return. Secondly, each subset of antisocial children is thought to be an example of arrested socialization. Each child, in his own way, maximizes his immediate gains/pleasures at someone else's expense. The third characteristic shared by antisocial children is a reduced responsiveness to social stimuli. They are less responsive to ordinary social reinforcers and to threats and scolding. They are characterized by attentional deficits that, in turn, may relate to an insensitivity to some aspects of the behavior of other persons. The fourth characteristic thought to be shared by antisocial children is skill deficits in the crucial areas of work, peer relations, and academic achievement. In the following section, each of these shared characteristics will be discussed in detail.

Noncompliance

The one thing shared by all antisocial children referred for treatment is noncompliance. During the intake interview, when asked to describe the difficulties they have with their child, 89% of the parents say, "This child does not mind." This, of course, is also noted as a problem even for parents of "normal" children. Rutter, Tizard, and Whitmore (1970) found that 31.5% of the parents of

239

normal, preadolescent children perceived disobedience as a problem in their own families.

During the preschool years, noncompliance is the first indication of a lack of effective parenting skills. Teaching compliance becomes an issue generally at about 2 to 3 years of age. In this training, the parent can positively reinforce the child when he complies with a request, and/or the parent can firmly punish noncompliance. For some reason, parents of antisocial children are not successful in teaching compliance. It may be that they forget to reinforce compliance, that they neglect to firmly punish noncompliance, and/or their children are simply of a more difficult temperament. For whatever reason, the data generally show antisocial children to be about half as compliant as are normal children of the same age.

In addition to the inept use of contingencies, it may be that the mother of the problem child lacks skill in her use of commands and requests. Forehand, Wells, and Sturgis (1978) observed 18 mother-child dyads, both in the home and in the laboratory. The children had been referred for treatment of noncompliance. The likelihood of the noncompliance observed in the home served as the criterion variable in a multiple-regression analysis. The key variable accounting for most of the variance for the multiple-regression coefficient of .74 was a measure of the mother's tendency to give vague commands. Stephen Johnson and his group were among the first to differentiate among the various kinds of parent commands (Johnson, Wahl, Martin & Johansson, 1973). He introduced two dimensions. He noted first that some commands were "stop" commands, e.g., "Stop teasing your sister." Others were initiating commands, e.g., "Please clean up your room." The other dimension had to do with the clarity of the communications to the child. He noted that mothers of distressed families tended to give vague commands for which compliance might be difficult even if the child were determined to be obedient.

I think that high rates of parent-command and accompanying child-noncompliance are the first step in a progression that produces an antisocial child. It can mean two things. First, the parent has been unsuccessful in teaching many prosocial, self-management skills. Given this deficit, the parent substitutes many commands: "Clean up your room," "Hang up your coat," "Take out the garbage." Second, it could mean that the child's rate of coercion is very high, and the high rate of stop-commands is the parent's reaction to this situation.

As expected, mothers of antisocial children use more commands than do mothers of nonproblem children. The observed rates per minute for mothers of Normals, Stealers, and Social Aggressors were .280, .423, and .413 respectively. The F value was 4.95 ($p < .01$). (See Appendix 6.2 for details about the samples.) In addition, parents of problem children often accompany commands with expressions of irritation and/or threats. This disposition is assessed by the FICS category Command Negative; these are commands accompanied by sarcasm or threats. For normal mothers, the mean rate was .002; for mothers of Stealers it was .020; and for mothers of Social Aggressors it was .013. The F value was 6.33 ($p < .001$).

Parent commands have several functions in relation to child deviant behavior. On one hand, maternal commands may initiate a conflict; i.e., they may serve as crossovers. On the other hand, many parent stop-commands are probably a reaction to coercive initiations by the child; i.e., they are a type of counterattack. Because of this dual role, it would be expected that rates of parent commands would covary with rates of child deviancy, e.g., as reported in Johnson and Lobitz (1974a) and Lobitz and Johnson (1975).

Noncompliance to parent requests is a kind of rule breaking that occurs in the presence of the parent. It is assumed that the level of noncompliance covaries with more general measures of child deviancy. In keeping with this hypothesis, Griest, Wells, and Forehand (1979) found that the correlation between observed rates of noncompliance and observed rates of deviant child behavior was .50 ($p < .05$). A study based on OSLC samples produced comparable results. In the comparison involving 34 Social Aggressors, 36 Normals, and 32 Stealers, the mean rates of noncompliance for the target children were .148, .033, and .084 respectively. The F value of 19.11 ($p < .001$) showed that these differences were significant. Note that while the Stealers were more noncompliant than Normals, they were less so than Social Aggressors. The finding that antisocial children were significantly less compliant than Normals has been replicated by a number of investigators (Johnson & Lobitz, 1974a; Forehand, King, Peed, & Yoder, 1975).

The level of compliance varies as a function of age and sex of child and sex of parent. Of course, many parents feel that children mind their fathers better than their mothers. Data have been reported confirming this impression. Children showed significantly more compliance to fathers' (mean .56) than to mothers' (mean .49) positive commands (Hetherington, Cox, & Cox, 1976). Similarly, girls were significantly more compliant (mean .57) than boys (mean .47).

240

For a given age range, the research findings show a rather surprising consistency across settings in the likelihood of compliance. The likelihood of compliance or p(Child-Comply|Parent-Command) for normal 3- and 4-year-olds was .72, as reported by Johnson et al. (1973) for interactions in the home, .60 in the Johnson & Lobitz (1974a) laboratory study, .69 for structured laboratory interactions in the study by Terdal, Jackson, and Garner (1976), and .62 in a free-play situation in the Forehand et al. (1975) study. The latter found no difference for social class. It seems, then, that the normal range of compliance for 3-and 4-year-olds is 60% to 70%. This range holds fairly consistently across settings.

At a very speculative level, I think even in the preschool years that parents of Stealers and Social Aggressors may differ in the kind of difficulties they have with child disobedience. Parents may be highly selective as to what kind of disobedience they will tolerate. For example, the parent of a Stealer may tolerate rule violations concerning vandalism and stealing, but will not tolerate noncompliance to a direct request. In other words, children who steal are involved in a different type of noncompliance. They disobey all rules when there is no adult to enforce them, i.e, rules about other people's property, rules about when to come home, rules about which friends to play with, and rules about stealing. These children are perceived as disobedient by their parents. On the other hand, parents of Social Aggressors will tolerate noncompliance to direct commands, but will not tolerate violations of rules about property damage or theft. Social Aggressors are also perceived by their parents as disobedient.

We will return to parent selectivity about deviancy in a later section. The hypothesis presented here is that the kind and magnitude of disobedience permitted during the preschool years has a great deal to do with the form of antisocial behavior expressed during school-aged years.

Arrested Socialization

It was implied in earlier discussions that the antisocial child functions somewhat like an overgrown infant (see Chapter 2). He shares the infant's philosophical position, i.e., to maximize short-term payoffs and ignore the long-term costs. Like the infant, he makes frequent use of coercive means to get what he wants and to avoid doing anything displeasing. Like the infant, he has not yet been taught to comply to the majority of requests made by adults. Like the infant, his prosocial skills are, at best, rudimentary. It is this configuration of characteristics that defines what is meant by *arrested socialization*.

In addition to skill deficits, he may even engage in the whining, clinging, dependent behavior of the immature child when interacting with adults. In a very real sense, the antisocial child may be thought of as immature. However, I think the antisocial child has in his repertoire a wider range of pain-control techniques that are applied to a wider range of people. The antisocial child coerces siblings, peers, teachers, and parents.

Infants, Stealers, and Social Aggressors maximize short-term payoffs. By definition, they do not delay gratification, and it goes without saying that these immediate payoffs are usually obtained at the expense of other persons. This is part of normal development; it is what normal infants do. If they want a toy, they take it. If they do not like the food being offered, they throw it on the floor. If their mother refuses to give them candy at the supermarket, they have a temper tantrum. Infants and antisocial children are the original "here and now" people.

An antisocial child takes what he wants and avoids that which is unpleasant or boring. Rather than learn the socially reinforcing skills leading to cooperation and acceptance, he uses pain control to produce compliance. Rather than join in, he disrupts. Rather than learn to anticipate crises, he avoids them as long as he can and then explodes. The antisocial child can be thought of as someone who has never quite grown up. However, unlike Peter Pan, he is not a child's delight. There is also a price for continuing to employ these infant-like techniques. The metaphor that nicely describes the position in which the antisocial child finds himself has been drawn by the economist Hardin (1968) and is further elaborated by Platt (1973). The Hardin essay, "The Tragedy of the Commons," points out a basic dilemma posed as the outcome for a competitive strategy. In his essay each shepherd increases the size of his flock to maximize his short-term gains. But as his competitors increase the size of their herds, the outcome is the inevitable destruction of the village commons. The shared grasslands that had once supported them all are lost.

In a similar vein, social interactions have both short-term and long-term payoffs. The problem child who utilizes coercive events with skill produces increased likelihoods for certain kinds of payoffs by family members. However, in so doing, he fails to note that there is an increase in the likelihood of the family members' punitive reactions and their future surprise attacks upon him. For example, the correlation between the child's overall coercive performance (TAB scores) and the mother's likelihood of a counterattack in coping with him was .72. His TAB score correlated .82 with the mother's likelihood of Crossover. In other words, the higher the rate with which the child (Normals, Stealers, and Social Aggressors) employed pain-control techniques, the more likely, in the long run, that the mother would react to him punitively. She also becomes more likely to launch unprovoked attacks upon him. This is a nicely coordinated dance in which a price is exacted for maximizing immediate gratification. Other family members respond in a similar fashion to the child. The comparable correlations for fathers between child TAB and paternal punitiveness and Crossover were .68 and .79 respectively. For siblings the correlations were .44 and .58.

In effect, the problem child acts impulsively, often producing immediate compliance or attention but, in so doing, increases the likelihood of future unpleasant and unpredictable experiences. This, in turn, contributes to his sense of outrage; it also provides a justification (if, indeed, he requires any) for initiating future attacks of his own. It seems as though these children have unwittingly invented a perpetual motion machine. Rather than levers, belts, and cogs, they substitute rage, immediate gratification, and a lack of awareness of long-range consequences. In retrospect, it is easy to see why various treatments for aggression have focused on draining off rage or teaching self-control and delay of gratification. These characteristics of the aggressive child are obvious to even the most casual spectator. The question is, however, are these causes or concomitants for the processes producing antisocial behavior?

The antisocial child is a person caught up in the immediate moment. In samples of younger out-of-control children, it has been deemed of sufficient importance for a number of experienced researchers to focus on teaching children techniques designed to give greater internal control over impulses (Meichenbaum, 1979; Spivack & Shure, 1974). This rush for immediate gratification is also characteristic of older delinquents, as noted in the literature reviewed by Quay (1965). There is also an empirical base for this hypothesis. For example, Riddle and Roberts (1977) reviewed the literature on scores from the Porteus Maze Test. The findings provided consistent support for the concept that delinquents are significantly more impulsive, have less foresight, and are less able to delay gratification in solving mazes. The careful study by Weintraub (1973) not only provided additional support for these inferences, but compared several direct measures of delay of gratification as well. The Porteus Maze Test, The Kagan Matching Fa-

miliar Figures (MFF) Test, and DePree's Delay of Gratification task were administered to two clinical samples and a normal sample. He correlated the five dependent variables that measure impulsiveness for the total sample. The median correlation among variables was .53; this provided strong support for a general trait of impulsiveness. On all of these variables, the antisocial clinical samples showed significant differences in their scores when compared to Normals or problem children who were "internalizing." The antisocial children showed less of a tendency to delay gratification and a greater likelihood for impulsive behavior.

Responsiveness to Social Stimuli

I think there are disruptions in the development of several interrelated mechanisms that further accelerate the drift toward both increasing deviancy and greater deficits in prosocial skills. The first is concerned with learning to respond to social stimuli. It is during the preschool years that much of the training for responsiveness to social stimuli takes place. Just as the antisocial child is significantly retarded in his learning of obedience, he is also retarded in his development of learned responsiveness to social stimuli. This reduced responsiveness applies to social reinforcers *and* to threats and scolding. As a result, the antisocial child may fail to make subtle discriminations regarding the behavior of the people with whom he is interacting. It is important to emphasize that the issue is relative nonresponsiveness. Being somewhat less attentive will, I think, lead to the slower development of some key social skills. This, in turn, has a profound impact upon the eventual adjustment of the antisocial child. For example, given reduced responsiveness, it might take him longer to learn how to form close relationships. Given that he is also coercive, then he may never learn.

A child is involved in literally thousands of interchanges each day. Parents, siblings, peers, and teachers present him with cues to which he reacts. In these interchanges he must learn to make subtle discriminations between this or that social cue, and then react in an appropriate fashion. What if the subject finds the reactions of other persons to be relatively neutral in regard to their reinforcing value? Worse yet, as in the case of Gottman's (1979) distressed couples, what if the other person's positive reactions were experienced as neutral or as punishing? It is likely that these fumbling, inept approaches would be experienced by others as aversive and lead them to label the child as socially handicapped. Being perceived by peers as "different" or "deviant" could, in turn, initiate a new process having unfortunate implications for the child.

What is the evidence for antisocial children making faulty discriminations in situations involving social reinforcers? In the last decade, there have been a series of well-executed laboratory studies relating to this issue. Prominent among these is the series of doctoral dissertations at the University of Minnesota directed by N. Garmezy. Phipps-Yonas (1979) compared antisocial delinquent children, normal, and hyperactive children to children of normal, schizophrenic, and (nonpsychotic) psychiatrically disordered mothers. The procedures were designed to test for selectivity in attention and for the ability to shift focus; reaction time served as the dependent variable. The Antisocials differed from all the other groups in that their reaction times were significantly slower and more variable than the other groups. The next study in the series was by Driscoll (1979), who worked with the same four samples on a set of procedures measuring the amount of incidental learning occurring during two different discrimination tasks. The antisocial samples were shown to have learned significantly less than the other groups on both the required and the incidental learning tasks. The results from these first two studies are supported by findings from other investigators. For example, the Camp (1977) and Camp, Zimet, Doomineck, and Dahlm (1977) series of studies compared younger aggressive and normal boys on a variety of laboratory and academic tasks. The findings showed a general impairment for antisocial boys on those tasks, reflecting an impulsive style of responding.

For me, the key study was the first of the Minnesota group's investigations of attentional deficits. Marcus (1972) tested 240 children in a simple reaction-time procedure, using an auditory signal involving both regular and irregular preparatory intervals (1, 2, 4, 7, and 15 seconds). Two conditions were used. In the cognitive-facilitation procedure, the children were informed about the length of preparatory intervals to be used in the next trial. In the motivational-facilitation condition, the children were told that a short reaction time could win a desired toy. Each of the four clinical groups was matched with a group of normal children. Based on the work of Achenbach (1966), referred children were classified as Internalizers or Externalizers. Children labeled as Externalizers were said by their parents to lie, steal, fight, and so on. The two other clinical groups were children of schizophrenic mothers and children of depressed mothers. The Internalizer sample was not significantly different from Normals under any of the four experimental conditions. The finding most relevant to the present discussion was that the Externalizers and the children of schizophrenic mothers were less effective than Normals under the cognitive-facilitation conditions. However, when the antisocial sample was provided an external reinforcer, they were no different from Normals! The author concluded that for the antisocial group the problem of attention was instead a problem in motivation. A similar effect was obtained in the instrumental conditioning studies by Johnston (1976) and Levin and Simmons (1962a, b). They found that antisocial children learned as well as Normals when nonsocial reinforcers were introduced.

These consistent findings raise some interesting questions. Does a monetary reinforcer enhance the saliency of the cues, produce a higher state of arousal, or actually strengthen $A_i \rightarrow R_j$ connections more effectively than social reinforcers? However one may conceptualize the difference between monetary and social reinforcers, the assumption is that both Stealers and Social Aggressors would display comparable deficits on almost any set of learning tasks involving social reinforcers or social punishment as consequences. When applied to the learning of subtle discriminations inherent in social interaction, then even a slight reduction in responsiveness could have a profound effect. The question is, just how solid is the evidence for such an assumption? While there is over a decade's work relating to this issue from laboratory and field studies, it must be said that the quality of the studies leaves much to be desired. For this reason, I entertain the hyporesponsiveness hypothesis with great interest but with an equal measure of skepticism.

In the early 1960's, during the first blush of enthusiasm for verbal conditioning studies, Johns and Quay (1962) demonstrated that antisocial adults did not condition as well as neurotic adults. The general effect was replicated by Quay and Hunt (1965). Ruenster (1970), cited in Sallows (1972), used a simple discrimination task with reaction time as the dependent variable and obtained a reliable difference between delinquents and normal children. Zylstra (1966) also obtained a significant effect for institutionalized delinquents compared to Normals; he employed the Taffel conditioning procedure. Johnston (1976) demonstrated diminished responsiveness for delinquents on both a Taffel and an autokinetic procedure. For both procedures, the institutionalized delinquents were less responsive than Normals to both peer and adult reinforcing agents. They were also less responsive to disapproval. What was of particular interest was the fact that when money was used as a reinforcer, the delinquents were slightly *more* responsive than were Normals. A similar finding was demonstrated for the marble-box apparatus by Levin and Simmons (1962a, b). Fifteen hyperactive-aggressive boys showed minimal change when reinforced by an adult for shifting their preferences on a two-hole apparatus. However, in a subsequent study, they showed significant changes in preferences when food was served as a reinforcer. There have also been a number of studies employing similar procedures providing inconclusive results. Sarbin, Allen, and Rutherford (1965), Hedlund (1971), Orzech (1962), Bryan and Kapche (1967), and Bernard and Eisenman (1967) all failed to find differences between antisocial and normal children.

The difficulty with this series of studies lies in the nature of the procedures. This entire genre of studies was flawed by their failure to deal adequately with the problem of subject awareness. As noted in Chapter 5, the reviews by Parton and Ross (1965), Dulany (1962), Spielberger (1962), and Patterson and Hinsey (1964) concurred in identifying "methods" as making greater contributions to scores measuring reinforcement effects than did reinforcement contingencies. However, given these possible confounds, the studies did serve the function of forcibly introducing the responsiveness hypothesis. They also introduced the idea of selective responsiveness.

A decade later, the results from behavior modification studies carried out in the home and the classroom extended these earlier findings. A large number of studies showed that, for extreme cases, extinction procedures were not effective for managing oppositional children's coercive behavior (Corte, Wolf, & Lecke, 1971; Laivgueur, Peterson, Sheese, & Peterson, 1973; Herbert, et al., 1973; Budd, Green, & Baer, 1976; Walker & Buckley, 1973). Of even greater relevance for the present discussion was the finding that for oppositional children, even in well supervised situations, adult attention and approval were not effective in increasing such prosocial behavior in the home (Herbert et al., 1973) or in the classroom (Hops, Walker, & Greenwood, 1977). In fact, in both studies the contingencies produced a reduction in task-oriented behavior.[1] This corresponded with our clinical experience in treating these families. We began by training parents to use only social reinforcers, such as approval or attention, to shape competing prosocial behaviors (Patterson & Gullion, 1968). However, within a few months, those of us working with extreme cases found ourselves teaching parents to use time out as a punishment and to include nonsocial back-up reinforcers such as money, treats, and special privileges (Wahler, 1968). Each of us found it clinically expedient to introduce these back-up reinforcers and punishment as well. If we did not use them, we produced little change in behavior.

The studies reviewed in Chapter 6 suggested that antisocial children may be less responsive to control by parental nattering or disapproval. The studies reviewed here suggest that these children may also be less responsive to social reinforcers. There is much yet to be done before either set of evidence is entirely convincing. For the present, the main support for the hyporesponsiveness hypothesis is from clinical experience rather than from definitive experimental studies. Given these qualifiers, it would be useful to speculate briefly about the possible determinants for this condition. Two general possibilities come to mind: temperament and the ratio of contingent to noncontingent reinforcement.[2] Each will be briefly considered below.

It is conceivable that some children, early on, are characterized by a hyporesponsiveness to positive and aversive social stimuli. For example, Mednick and Christiansen (1977) and others hypothesize a genetic predisposition for hyporesponsiveness to aversive stimuli (see Chapter 6). The loosely organized study of temperament by Thomas, Chess, Birch, and Hertzog (1960) is also in keeping with such speculations. The difficult children they studied could have achieved that status because they were hyporesponsive to social stimuli. For the moment, the Thomas et al. (1960) explanation is not appealing because of the difficulties in measuring what is meant by *temperament*. For example, does the fact that the 2-year-old child is difficult to manage reflect a constitutional difference and/or differences in the reaction of the parent to the child?

The contingency hypothesis has been presented by Cairns (Paris & Cairns, 1972; Warren & Cairns, 1972) and by J.S. Watson (1979). They have discussed it particularly as it relates to the problem of hyporesponsiveness to positive reinforcement. Simply stated, the idea is as follows: to the extent that social reinforcers are initially supplied in a noncontingent fashion then they will be less effective in shaping behavior when used in later trials. Two functional relations define what is meant by this statement. The first includes the likelihood of a positive consequence given a target behavior ($p[C^+|R_j]$). The second is the likelihood of the same consequence given all nontarget behavior ($p[C^+|nonR_j]$). Given that parental approval or attention is forthcoming for deviant behavior as well as for task-oriented behavior, then attempts to use these same events in a contingent fashion will have little impact. For example, if a great deal of positive regard is provided by the well-intentioned nursery school teacher (no matter what the child does), then when she attempts to use these reinforcers contingently, they will provide little control. I think this process may also describe mothers of antisocial children, where positive reactions to coercive child behavior and positive reactions for prosocial behavior have similar probabilities of occurrence.

Cairns and his colleagues have carried out programmatic studies demonstrating such an effect. In the first of a series of studies, they demonstrated in six classrooms of educationally retarded children that an average of 38% of the teachers' positive evaluations occurred independently of any discrete response made by a child. In fact, only 28% of such teacher behaviors were clearly contingent (Paris & Cairns, 1972). Then, on a discrimination task, children from similar classrooms were shown to be relatively nonresponsive to praise. They were, however, responsive to a stimulus signifying "correct." In a third study, 56 children from educationally-retarded classrooms participated in a discrimination learning task. One group received praise when correct; others were told when they were wrong (i.e., they were punished). The punished group showed a significant change in their behavior, while the rewarded group showed only a weak effect. The fourth study (Warren & Cairns, 1972) established the relation between prior exposure to noncontingent social reinforcers and reduced responsiveness on a subsequent task. The experiment provided the necessary controls by comparing the effects of prior contingent social reinforcement and prior noncontingent social reinforcement. The experiment also provided for various levels of exposure to these prior conditions. Those children exposed to high levels of noncontingent reinforcement showed less behavior change on the subsequent task. Those with prior exposure to high levels of contingent social reinforcement showed a facilitation effect; i.e., they were more responsive.

Antisocial children receive significantly fewer positive social reinforcers, such as Approval (Patterson, 1979b). Their assumed hyporesponsiveness to positive reinforcers, such as Talk or Attend, may relate to the fact that the likelihoods for these consequences are similar for both deviant and prosocial behavior. Presumably, in normal families the likelihood of a positive reaction is higher for prosocial than for deviant behaviors.

Skill Deficits

During preschool years, normal children come under the control of social reinforcement. They also learn to delay gratification and to acquire the rudiments of basic social survival skills. Even at the preschool level, the normal child has acquired a complex set of skills relating to self-help, work, and to initiating and maintaining social interaction. These skills serve as substitutes for the child's earlier coerciveness. The basic training for these skills takes place in the home prior to the child's entrance into public school. It is here he learns to sit still and listen, comply with reasonable requests, and carry out simple assignments on a regular schedule. It is also here that he learns to be attentive to other people's behavior, know when he has hurt their feelings, when he is boring them, or when he has pleased them.

As noted in Chapter 2, when predicting adult adjustment, the level of the child's social skills is thought to function as a moderating variable. Young children who are socially aggressive but socially skilled have a better prognosis for adjustment than young problem children lacking in social skills. It is assumed that the antisocial child who is also unskilled is most at risk for chronic delinquency.

In middle-class families, training the child to work begins in the preschool years. The child is given a series of tasks analogous to adult work situations, e.g., cleaning up his room, simple chores that are carried out while an adult is present, then chores that are not continuously supervised, and finally part-time jobs for neighbors. In these situations, the child is told clearly what is expected and what the rules are. He is given feedback if the task is not properly carried out (i.e., he is monitored) He is also expected to carry them out on a consistent basis. Later on, he may receive his allowance contingent upon successful completion of his chores. Presumably, these work skills will also generalize to other settings such as school.

The studies reviewed in Chapter 2 suggested that antisocial children were less likely to be expected to do chores at home or to hold weekend or summer jobs. There are some fascinating observation data available from the Whiting and Whiting (1975) study of six cultures, suggesting that the more simple the culture, the more likely its members are to assign chores to young children. The mean number of chores varied from 2.4 per day for a more simple culture to a low of 1.0 for the most complex culture (a small community in New England). In the simpler agrarian cultures, the mothers assigned more tasks and were also more likely to emphasize obedience.[3]

The studies reviewed in Chapter 2 also showed that peers consistently rejected antisocial children. Rutter et al. (1976) underscored the magnitude of the problem with data that showed fully *half* of the antisocial boys were not liked by peers! The recent investigations of the determinants for peer rejection agree in identifying coerciveness as the major variable (Gottman, 1977; Hartup, 1977). For samples of younger children, rejection covaried with child aversiveness. On the other hand, the use of positive reinforcement covaried with acceptance by peers.

My clinical experience with these children leads me to believe that the antisocial child also lacks an awareness and appreciation for how others feel. The work by Feshbach and Feshbach (1969) and Radke-Yarrow and Waxler (1976, 1979) suggests that during the preschool years the normal middle-class child learns to empathize with other persons' feelings. Antisocial children behave as if the pain they inflict on others is of little consequence. They seem to portray the general attitude outlined by Ryan's *Blaming the Victim* (1976). He examined aggression in different cultures and found that, generally, the victim was denigrated and placed in the position of readily deserving that which he received. My clinical experience with antisocial children suggests that they, too, perceive their victims with a kind of self-righteous contempt. The children they attack deserved the assault because: "They are always after me; I just get 'em first. Every day they say this stuff to me, so I just slug 'em." Ryan (1976) also notes that the penchant for blaming the victim characterizes society in general.

Only a few studies compare normal and antisocial samples for social skills. Achenbach and Edelbrock (1978) found that children categorized as delinquent scored lower on a measure of social skills than did Normals. Children classed as Social Aggressors scored lower on social skills than did those categorized as delinquent. Cox, Gunn, and Cox (1976) also found that behavior-problem children were significantly less skilled than were Normals.

In light of the earlier discussion, antisocial children may not find ordinary social behaviors to be very reinforcing or very punishing. This could mean that the child is less motivated to learn the subtle discriminations required of the adolescent and adult. Given that this process continues, then these children may function like social sleepwalkers. What they do in social interaction is often "not quite right." This reduced motivation, accompanied by the fact that their parents are nei-ther effective models nor skilled at tracking prosocial skills, result in the child's skill deficits becoming increasingly obvious. If one assumes that antisocial children have attentional deficits, then the lack of social skills becomes more understandable. Maintaining an extended interchange with a peer, particularly an older one, requires good timing and careful attention to subtle variances. If, for example, the child is talking in a monologue, he may ignore the shift in gaze signaling that the peer is ready to take his turn. By plunging in and monopolizing the peer's attending behavior, he may then miss the extended, averted gaze signaling boredom. On the occasion of his next meeting he may encounter a slightly cool reception; repeated trials may produce more obvious distancing. An effective interaction must provide support to both members. This means taking turns; one person talks, the other listens. At intervals the roles are reversed. These shifts require the ability to make very precise discriminations. These discriminations are the basic processes underlying social interaction. The writer believes that it is in this sense that the antisocial child is flawed.

What is the long-term outcome of a child's failure to notice that he just hurt his best friend's feelings? If he missed classifying the hurt expression even one-third of the time, what would that mean? How will peers label such a child, especially if he also has a tendency to fly off the handle easily? What is the likelihood that such a child will be a skillful competitor in sports? At a speculative level, it is, I think, the antisocial child's lack of basic social survival skills that contributes as much to his marginal adjustment as an adult as does the antisocial behavior itself. These are very unskilled people.

The Differences Between Social Aggressors and Stealers

While antisocial children may share some traits in common, it is hypothesized that Stealers and Social Aggressors differ from each other in two important respects. First, they are thought to differ in the kinds of parenting practices associated with them. A general formulation will be presented that delineates these different processes. A later section presents the empirical findings that relate to these assumptions. By definition, Stealers and Social Aggressors differ in the kind of problems or referral symptoms described by parents. However, it is assumed that these referral symptoms may also reflect different underlying progressions. In these progressions, the performance of one problem behavior is related to the performance

Figure 11.1
Parental Processes Relating to Three Kinds of Antisocial Behavior

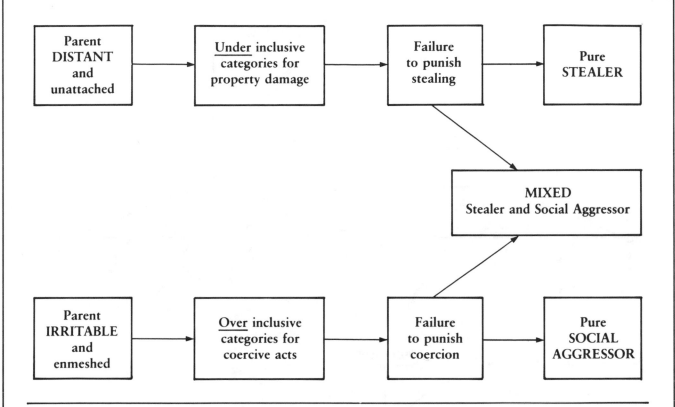

of yet more "extreme" but lower rate problem behaviors. The evidence for such progressions is briefly reviewed in this section.

Parenting Practices

Two aspects of the parents' behavior comprise the key mechanisms thought to differentiate Stealers and Social Aggressors from each other and from Normals. It is assumed that parents differ in what it is that they classify as deviant (e.g., some parents believe temper tantrums are normal but that stealing is deviant). The deviancy-categorizing process, in turn, determines which child behaviors will be monitored and which will be punished. Parental monitoring and punishment practices directly determine the rate at which antisocial behavior will be performed.

As shown in Figure 11.1, parents of Stealers are thought to be relatively uninvolved in the role of caretaker. They are not motivated to extend themselves in the service of the child. They are sufficiently skilled in child management so that they do not permit face-to-face coercive behavior from ei-

ther the target child or from his siblings. I suspect that they are motivated only enough to teach the child a bare minimum of survival skills. For example, they are probably not motivated enough to monitor his school work and support high-level achievement.

The second outstanding feature of these parents lies in their lack of concern for property violations. They tend to ignore minor violations that occur in the home; e.g., taking money from Mother's purse is not categorized as stealing, nor is taking an item that belongs to a sibling. Given that the child can explain why he took it, then no punishment is forthcoming for these protodelinquent behaviors. A similar pattern characterizes what happens when neighbors, storekeepers, and police officers accuse him of theft. He "explains it," and consequently the event is not categorized as a deviant act, and, of course, no punishment occurs.

It is hypothesized that parents punish what they believe to be "deviant." The parents of "pure" Stealers tend to be overly *exclusive* in their classification of property violations that are thought to

Figure 11.2
Applications of Signal Detection Model
to Parent Classification of Deviant Child Behavior

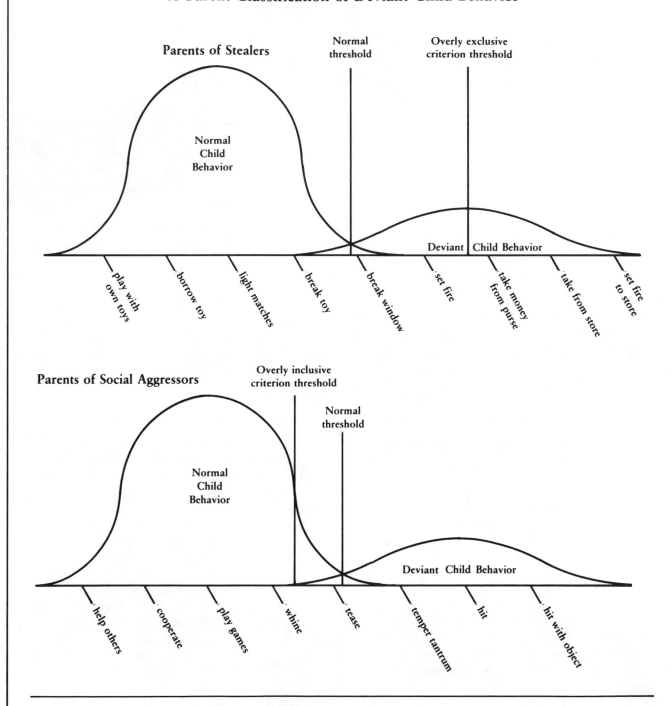

be deviant. As shown in Figure 11.2, they classify as deviant only the most extreme acts directed against property. These same parents may classify encopresis, hitting, or wetting the bed as deviant. Almost *all* families train their children *not* to light fires indiscriminantly. The idea of applying a signal detection model to this problem was suggested by D. Littman and P. Holleran. Both have completed laboratory studies to test the possibility of applying it to parent deviancy classification. As yet, however, there are no studies that test the hypothesis that parents of Stealers are overly exclusive;

248

i.e., compared to parents of Normals, they classify many acts against property as normal. For the present, the hypothesis is based upon clinical experience.

Given that the hypothesis is true, it is not at all clear how such misclassification might come about. Do these expectations about what is normal and what is deviant precede the problem child, or do they arise as an outcome of the parents' interactions with him? These questions are the crucial ones for the next phase in the development of a coercion theory. I suspect that in the case of parents of Stealers, their expectations precede the problem child. These expectations may relate to prior criminal and quasi delinquent histories of the parent. However, for the moment this is sheer speculation. The data reviewed in a later section of this chapter will address the issue of the breakdown in parental monitoring and punishment as it relates to stealing and delinquent behavior.

As shown in Figure 11.1, the parent characteristics that relate to producing Social Aggressor symptoms are thought to be quite different from those that produce Stealer problems. Rather than being distant and unattached, the parent of the Social Aggressor tends to be overly enmeshed and *very irritable*. It is hypothesized that when differentiating between coercive and normal acts, these parents will tend to be overly *inclusive;* i.e., they tend to classify many behaviors as deviant that parents of Normals would classify as borderline acceptable. Normal parents let a good deal go by; they ignore borderline events. The mother of the Social Aggressor becomes an impassioned participant, scolding and threatening at the slightest provocation. Even though she becomes readily involved, she fails to confront the child and punish effectively. As noted earlier, the irritable reactions make the situation worse.

Neither type of parent directly confronts the child. Parents of Stealers and Social Aggressors are similar in their failure to punish the relevant antisocial behavior. One parent misclassifies stealing and avoids the necessity of punishing it. The other parent substitutes nattering for punishment.

Our analysis of referral problems suggests that a substantial number of children are socially aggressive, *and* they steal. In Figure 11.1, these cases are labeled "Mixed." They are thought to be produced in homes that are characterized by the worst features of both processes. These parents are poorly motivated to do anything for the child, *and* they are irritable in their face-to-face contacts with him. These parents have a faulty mode for categorizing both acts directed against property and acts directed against persons. As illustrated in Figure 11.2, they would tend to be very reluctant to classify most acts of stealing or vandalism as being deviant. However, if the child's behavior is unpleasant for the parent, *then* the reaction is likely to be irritable. These parents are generally unskilled in their use of punishment. They are completely committed to here and now. If the child steals from a neighbor, let the neighbor take care of it himself, but *do not bother* the parent. If the child is making noise, yell at him until he stops.

These children steal, and they are socially aggressive; they are also at very high risk for being physically abused. In a retrospective study, Reid et al. (1981) showed that OSLC cases who were physically abused had very high TAB scores. This would classify them as Social Aggressors. In a more recent analysis, Reid found that almost all of these abused children were also Stealers! This suggests that a mixed sample that both steals and is socially aggressive must have very unusual parents. I suspect that they are not only at grave risk for abuse but for a variety of adult adjustment difficulties as well. I also suspect that the mixed cases are most at risk for becoming delinquent adolescents. If this is true, then the child known to the juvenile court as delinquent will be inadequately monitored and punished for rule breaking by his parents. He will also reside in a household comprised of distant and irritable people.

Symptom Progressions

There are two assumptions about the problems for which antisocial children are referred. First, it is assumed that Stealers and Social Aggressors differ in terms of the kinds of symptoms that are of concern to the parent. Second, it is assumed that the symptom patterns describing these two samples also define some underlying progressions. In these progressions, there is an orderly sequence from higher rate to lower rate symptoms. In the present context, it was thought that the progressions would also move from less extreme to more extreme forms of deviancy. As used here, the term progression implies transitivity; children who exhibit the more extreme low base-rate symptoms will also have performed all of the preceding problem behaviors in the sequence.

To examine these questions, we must obviously begin by asking the adults who interact with the child to describe the kinds of problem behaviors that he presents. The literature reviewed in Chapter 3 showed that parent reports about child deviant behavior should be accepted with a good deal of caution. Two studies showed agreement of only 36% between *independent* reports of mothers and

Table 11.1
A Symptom Structure for Stealers

Variables	Parent-Reported Symptoms:			
	Disobedient (.89)	Lie (.68)	Steal (.56)	Firesetting (.23)
Likelihood of p_1 progression	$p(\text{Lie}|\text{Disobey})$ .72	$p(\text{Steal}|\text{Lie})$ .70*		$p(\text{Fireset}|\text{Steal})$ .32*
Likelihood of p_2 alternate path	$p(\text{path other than Disobey}|\text{Lie})$ .06	$p(\text{path other than Lie}|\text{Steal})$ .14		$p(\text{path other than Steal}|\text{Fireset})$ .22

The figures in parentheses refer to base-rate values.

*Significantly greater than its base-rate value.

fathers as to the nature of the child's symptoms (Dreger, et al., 1964; Lapouse & Monk, 1958). The latter study also showed poor agreement between parent and child reports about deviant behaviors. Reid and Patterson (1976) studied a sample of children referred at the request of community agencies because the boys were known for some time to have been high-rate Stealers. A 30- to 60-day baseline study showed that each child actually stole *at least* twice a month. However, during the intake interview, 21% of these parents *failed to even mention stealing* as a problem. The sample of 38 Stealers described in Appendix 6.2 showed a similar pattern. Each child in this carefully selected sample was known by the court and/or family to be a high-rate thief. At the intake interview, 15% of the parents failed to mention stealing as a problem when going over the symptom checklist. It seems reasonable to conclude that the false-negative error for parent reports of stealing at intake is somewhere around 15% to 20%; i.e., the child steals often, but the *parents do not label it as a problem.*

Clearly one must entertain many reservations about data based upon parent reports of symptoms. However, as noted in Table 2.9, our own studies of symptom clusters by Chamberlain (1980), and the earlier work by Jenkins and Hewitt (1944), and Achenbach (1978) reported in Table 2.8, clearly identified differences in symptoms for Stealers and Social Aggressors. It occurred to me that it might be useful to know if these two clusters of symptoms were really made up of transitive progressions; i.e., all children who set fires also steal and lie, but not all liars set fires. If such progressions could be shown, then one option for treatment might be to alter high-rate symptoms occurring early in the sequence and thus have an

impact on low base-rate events found later in the progression. Such progressions would also be of interest in that they might identify the sequence children follow in performing deviant behaviors. Given such a sequence, then a longitudinal study might show that, first, children become high-rate liars, *then* some of these will begin to steal, and *then* a certain proportion of them may begin to set fires.

I began by following the procedures described by Guttman (1944) and identified scalogram progressions for both Social Aggressor and Stealer symptoms. For both progressions it was possible to obtain reproducibility coefficients around .90 and to replicate the effect. However, a conversation with John Robinson and a careful reading of his critique of scalograms (Robinson, 1973) led to a decision to reconsider this means of analyzing the data.[4]

The parent-reported symptoms for the scalogram progression were reanalyzed using a conditional-probabilities format. For this, there are two pieces of information needed at each juncture. What is the likelihood if the subject performs A (a high-rate symptom), that he will also perform B (a lower rate symptom) or ($p[B|A]$)? Secondly, given that he performs Symptom B, what is the likelihood that the structural "path" was through A ($p[A|B]$)? A comparison of each conditional to its appropriate base rate ($p[B]$ and $p[A]$ respectively) can provide a basis for testing the significance of each conditional p value. A significant p value would mean that the adjacent symptoms are a part of the *same structure.* A series of such values describes a "path" that leads to such infrequent events as firesetting. This is of particular interest to the student of low base-rate events.

In Table 11.1 there are three sets of information.

First, there is the base rate for each symptom. The data were based upon intake information from the 114 cases referred to OSLC. The symptoms are ordered by base-rate values. As shown there, the likelihood of occurrence in that sample for Disobey was .89, for Lie it was .68, and so on. In passing, it should be noted that the analysis would be facilitated if these values did not exceed .50 for any of the symptoms. This could be accomplished by calculating these values based upon a general population of cases referred to child guidance clinics rather than just a population of antisocial children referred to OSLC.

The second row of figures contains the conditional p value for the lower rate symptom given the presence of the higher incidence symptom; e.g., given Disobey, what is the likelihood of Lie? It can be seen that 72% of disobedient children were also said by their parents to lie, and 32% of all Stealers were also said to set fires. The appropriate next step was to compare each conditional to its appropriate base-rate value. The linkages Steal given Lie and Firesetting given Steal were significant. The findings imply that a study of the higher incidence problems, such as Lie and Steal, may tell us much about the low-rate problem, Firesetting. One might, for example, study the stimuli that control these higher rate symptoms as a means for understanding firesetting. By definition, low base-rate events are almost impossible to study. However, the analysis of progressions of this kind may make the study of low base-rate events feasible. One might also study which family management or microsocial variables determine whether the child will move from A to B, or from B to C. Why do some children lie but *not* steal?

The third row in Table 11.1 provides a rather different kind of information. Functionally, the p_2 value is independent of either the base-rate value or p_1. The metaphor I apply here is that of "alternative paths." Conceivably a child could move to Firesetting by a number of alternative paths, only one of which is Disobedient $\rightarrow$ Lie $\rightarrow$ Steal. In keeping with the metaphor, p_2 describes the likelihood of an *alternative* path. Only 14% of children accused of stealing were not accused of lying. Only 22% of Firesetters arrived at this juncture by a path other than Steal. These p values describing the likelihood of alternative paths suggest that if we understood the determinants for Lie and/or Steal, we would know much of what we need to know about Firesetting.[5]

The Guttman Scalogram had identified the symptom, Wander, as part of this progression. However, the probability analyses showed both the p_1 and p_2 values were nonsignificant. Yule's Y-statistic also showed that it did not correlate well with the other symptoms (Robinson, 1973). The Guttman coefficient of reproducibility was recalculated for the four symptoms. The CR was a very acceptable .95.

The next task was to search for a similar progression for social aggression. The symptom clusters identified in Tables 2.8 and 2.9 were analyzed in an attempt to form Guttman Scalograms for Social Aggressors. The most promising candidate was the sequence: Noncomply $\rightarrow$ Quarrel with Siblings $\rightarrow$ Hit $\rightarrow$ Tease $\rightarrow$ Temper Tantrums. The CR values were a borderline .84 for one sample and the same for a replication sample. However, the probability analyses showed *no significant linkages* at any juncture in the progression.

What does it mean when one cluster of symptoms forms a transitive progression and the other does not? My notion is that there *is* such a progression for social aggression that describes a drift towards *increasingly high-amplitude* behaviors. What is necessary is to change the intake checklist to focus upon symptoms that would tap into such a progression, e.g., kicks others, hits with object, attacks with sharp object, and threatens to kill others.

There is a very appealing implication of these findings that should also be noted. The hypothesis is that parent *perception* of child problem behavior is not correlated so much with the *onset* of the problem as with the frequency of its occurrence. If the problem has been occurring at a high rate for an extended period of time the parent will eventually perceive it as a problem. The data for the Stealer progression suggest that first the child begins to lie at noticeably high rates. Then, at a *later* point in time, the parent may become aware of stealing events that occur in the home and/or the neighborhood. At a still later point, the parent may come to perceive firesetting as a problem.

Interactional Variables

It is hypothesized that when using social interaction variables, Social Aggressors will be differentiated from Normals and from Stealers by the higher levels of coerciveness for all family members. It is also expected that the family interaction patterns for children who steal will not be significantly more irritable than those for families of normal children.[6] However, the pilot study by Reid and Hendricks (1973) suggests that parents of Stealers may be differentiated from parents of Normals by variables measuring distance and involvement in social interaction. Data will be presented that address this issue.

251

The general formulation presented earlier suggested that the key differentiating variables lie in the parents' tracking and punishment of antisocial acts that occur within the family and outside the home. It is expected that measures of parent monitoring and child-obedience will covary significantly with measures of protodelinquent behavior (stealing, firesetting) and, for older children, with measures of delinquency. On the other hand, family management variables most characteristic of social aggression are thought to be measured by house rules, discipline, and problem-solving skills. The relevant correlational findings will be presented in later sections of this chapter. However, a related set of hypotheses concerns the effect of these disruptions in management upon social interaction patterns. It is assumed that irritable, hostile interactions are correlated with disruptions in family management. The distant, uninvolved interactions supposedly found in families of Stealers are assumed to correlate with inept parental monitoring and punishment. The latter is measured by the family management variable, Obedience.

The first step was to determine whether families of Social Aggressors were significantly different in interaction patterns from families of Normals and families of Stealers. The analyses proceeded in a sequence of two steps. First, three samples were selected from OSLC files (see Appendix 6.2 for details). Each case met several criteria in order to be selected. For the normal sample, the parents claimed that the child was normal, the juvenile court records showed no police offenses, and the TAB score was in the normal range. Stealers were identified by parent complaint and/or court records of police offenses. In addition, the PDR records showed three or more stealing events at some point during the study at OSLC. The Social Aggressors were described as antisocial during the intake interview, and parent complaints did *not* include stealing. In addition, their baseline TAB score was equal to, or greater than, .45.

The goal was to use "ideal" samples as a basis for constructing the first phase in testing for observed differences in family interactions. The manner in which the samples were selected insured significant differences in the TAB scores for normal and Social Aggressor target children, but the question was whether the TAB scores for Stealers would be intermediate between the scores for Normals and Social Aggressors, as found in the Reid and Hendricks (1973) study. In the current study, the mean TAB score for Normals was .17, for Stealers .65, and for Social Aggressors .98. The differences were highly significant ($F = 25.12$, $p < .0001$). The Duncan Multiple Range Test

showed that Stealers were significantly more coercive than Normals but significantly less coercive than Social Aggressors. This was almost an exact replication of the Reid and Hendricks (1973) pilot study.

The next question is, how well can the three samples be differentiated by the observed behavior of the target child? The samples were first compared for each of the 29 FICS categories. The results of the ANOVA summarized in Appendix 11.1 showed that 15 of the comparisons were significant. These variables were then used in a discriminant-function analysis that generated two functions. The canonical coefficient for the first function was .608. It was defined by a large coefficient (.88) for Noncomply and .73 for Disapproval. The canonical correlation for the second function was only .286, defined primarily by a negative coefficient for Command Negative. Taken together, the two functions accurately classified 61.5% of the cases from the three samples. The F value for the Wilks'-Lambda was 10.95 ($p < .001$).

The two clinical samples were nicely separated from the Normals by the first function, which was labeled "Negativistic." The F values were significant in showing the clinical cases to be more negativistic. The second function, labeled "Threat" or "Put-down," differentiated between the Stealers and Social Aggressors, as shown by an F value of 7.87 ($df = 3:104$, $p < .001$). The Stealers were more likely to employ Command Negative than were the Social Aggressors. Together, the two functions accurately classified 94.6% of the Normals and 60.7% of the Social Aggressors. However, Stealers were classified only at the chance level; 45% of the Stealers were misclassified as normal. It seems, then, that at an interactional level the Stealer child may be indistinguishable from Normals, but Social Aggressors may differ from both. However, a plot of the clinical-case TAB scores employed in the preceding analyses showed a very interesting pattern. The TAB scores for one-half of the Stealers were an almost exact match for the distribution of scores for Social Aggressors. Half of the Stealers were "pure," and the other half were mixed cases. This means that for referrals to the OSLC clinic (as a rough approximation) 25% should be pure Stealers, 33% pure Social Aggressors, and 42% mixed cases. It seemed that there were not two, but *three,* subsets for antisocial children: "pure" Stealers, "pure" Social Aggressors, and "mixed" Stealers and Social Aggressors.

The proper basis for investigating the problem would be comparisons from samples of pure Stealers (who are not Social Aggressors), pure Social

Table 11.2
Variables Differentiating Among Samples of Antisocial Children

Code Categories	Mean for Samples			F Values
	Stealer (N = 10)	Social Aggressor (N = 17)	Mixed (N = 16)	
Child Behavior				
Command Negative	.00	.01	.04	4.93*
Disapproval	.04	.16	.21	2.72
TAB Score	.20	.91	.97	5.43**
Father Behavior				
Command Negative	.01	.02	.06	6.87**
No Response	.11	.08	.16	3.81*
TAB Score	.28	.62	.72	4.09*
Mother Behavior				
Disapproval	.18	.26	.34	2.71
No Response	.13	.09	.18	3.55*
TAB Score	.55	.78	1.06	6.10**

*$p < .05$
**$p < .01$

Aggressors (who are not Stealers), and mixed cases of children who are both Stealers and Social Aggressors. Simard (1981) made such a set of comparisons based upon 18 families of pure Stealers, 12 families of pure Social Aggressors, and 13 families of boys who represented both sets of problems. The samples were subsets of the clinical samples described in Appendix 6.2. The ANOVA comparing mothers, then fathers, with target children on all code categories produced eight significant variables. The general pattern was for family members in the mixed group to be slightly *more* coercive than members of Social Aggressor families and a great deal more so than members of Stealer families. The family members of mixed cases also tended to engage in more No Response than did families from either of the other samples. In effect, families of Stealers behaved more like Normals, while families of mixed cases seemed slightly more distant and more coercive than did families of Social Aggressors.

The eight variables identified by Simard were then used in a discriminant-function analysis. The means and F values for a slightly different subset of samples than Simard's are presented in Table 11.2. Two functions were derived that correctly classified 81.4% of the clinical cases. The F value

for the Wilks'-Lambda was 6.91 ($p < .01$). The canonical correlation for the first function was .76. A very high TAB Score placed most Social Aggressors at one extreme for this function, while high use of threatening commands (Command Negative) placed the mixed cases at the other extreme. The canonical correlation for the second function was .63. The distant father (No Response), who made few threatening commands (Command Negative), placed the pure Stealers in the upper range for this function.

The large number of variables, the number of analyses, and the small samples involved hardly provide grounds for confidence in these findings. However, the data required for replication have already been collected as part of the longitudinal planning study. The new analyses have yet to be done, but it does seem reasonable to summarize the hypotheses generated thus far. The findings from the pilot studies suggest that the parents of pure Stealers are more distant and uninvolved in their interactions with family members than are parents of normal children. They are also more distant than are parents of Social Aggressors. Mothers and siblings of Social Aggressors are significantly more coercive in their interactions with family members than their counterparts in either

Table 11.3
Factor V: Social Aggression

(from Carlson, 1981a, b)

Factor loading	Coded behavior	Definition
.536	NE	NEGATIVISM: A statement in which the verbal message is neutral, but which is delivered in a tone of voice that conveys an attitude of, "Don't bug me; don't bother me."
.423	NO	NORMATIVE: A person is behaving in an appropriate fashion and no other code is applicable.
−.633	PL	PLAY: A person is playing, either alone or with other persons.
.459	PN	PHYSICAL NEGATIVE: A subject physically attacks or attempts to attack another person with sufficient intensity to potentially inflict pain.
.487	TE	TEASE: Teasing another person in such a way that the other person is likely to show displeasure and disapproval or when the person being teased is trying to do some other behavior but is unable to because of the teasing.

	HA	SA	NOR
	.064	.907	−1.142

families of Normals or Stealers. It is also hypothesized that families of mixed cases will be more *coercive* and the *parents* more *distant* than either of the other two clinical samples. My hunch is that it is this pattern that will be found to characterize most of the families of delinquent adolescents.

It is also assumed that these microsocial variables will covary with disruptions in family management practices. Presumably, some family management practices will be shown to covary with distance and others with irritability in family interaction. The sections that follow detail the available findings that contribute to our further understanding of Social Aggressor and Stealer differences.

Social Aggressors

Essentially, the Social Aggressor is a child who directs his attacks against people rather than against property. The symptoms identified by the factor-analytic studies that relate to this class are summarized in Tables 2.8 and 2.9. Some of these symptoms were demands attention, screams loudly, fights, argues, disobeys, is destructive, yells, runs around, whines, and is hyperactive. The clinical labels that Social Aggressors might receive would vary from conduct problems, to immature, to hyperactive. However, the Social Aggressors of particular interest in the present context are those who fight, hit, and have temper tantrums. The first question examined concerned the possibility

of homogeneous classes of responses occurring during their interactions with family members. If such classes were to be found, it would imply a common process. The remainder of the section summarizes the findings relating to a performance theory for Social Aggression. How much of the variance can be accounted for by microsocial variables measuring the irritable reactions of family members? How much variance can be accounted for by measures of family management variables?

Classes of Observed Responses

Three different techniques of constructing response classes have been followed. Factor analysis, scalogram analysis, and functional analytic procedures have been used to identify the covariations in observed behavior that might characterize Social Aggressors.

Carlson (1981a, b) carried out a factor analysis for a combined sample of normal and clinical cases observed at OSLC. The analysis for the 29 code categories produced six factors. The one labeled Social Aggression is summarized in Table 11.3. As the second step in his analysis, he used the factor scores to differentiate a subset of Social Aggressors from a group diagnosed as Hyperactive. The two samples were significantly differentiated from each other (as well as from Normals) by their score on this factor.[7] Children who met the OSLC requirements for the label, Social Aggressors, were observed to Hit, Tease, and to be more

Negativistic than were antisocial children who had previously been diagnosed as also being Hyperactive.

The Social Aggression factor identified by Carlson was similar to one obtained by a scalogram analysis of code categories. A Guttman Scalogram analysis of the 14 coercive code categories (Patterson & Dawes, 1975) produced a progression for six behaviors. Rank ordered by base rates, the progression was: Noncomply, Negativism, Tease, Physical Negative, Negative Command, and Humiliate. For the clinical sample, the coefficient for reproducibility was .92; for a sample of Normals, it was also .92. Note that both the factor-analytic and scalogram techniques identified Noncomply, Tease, and Hit as members of the same response class.

Two of these responses were described in Chapter 8 as defining a class of functionally related responses (Patterson & Cobb, 1973; Patterson, 1977a). The initiation of Tease and Physical Negative was produced by a shared network of controlling antecedents. This class was also shown to share a common set of accelerating consequences (Patterson, 1977a). The latter study also showed that the family members most involved in eliciting Physical Negative and Tease were *siblings*. Siblings also provided the consequences most likely to accelerate the responses.

It is interesting that children characterized by such a broad spectrum of antisocial problem behaviors demonstrate such consistent interaction patterns that the same pattern of responses have emerged from three different analytic techniques. At a more speculative level, I think that all of these problem behaviors share a common coercive function. The way in which it is manifested varies somewhat as a function of what the parents will accept. Why is it that if parents permit Tease and Noncomply, they also permit Physical Negative?

Microsocial Analyses for a Performance Theory

The concept of a bilateral trait implies that the child's performance of coercive behavior is the outcome of two dispositions. Each member of the dyad brings his own disposition to react irritably; the performance level for the dyad is a function of the product of these two dispositions. It was hypothesized that measures of the irritable reactions of other family members would account for significant amounts of variance in measures of the child's aggressive performance. It was also assumed that measures of the child's irritable reactions would account for significant amounts of variance in the parent's daily reports measuring his deviancy level.

First, it was of some interest to examine the relation between the child's performance level and his own irritable reactions. This study could be thought of as a kind of component analysis of TAB scores. Each of four irritable reactions (Crossover, Counterattack, Punishment Acceleration, and Continuance) was correlated with the child's own TAB score. The data are from the combined sample of Stealers, Social Aggressors, and Normals described in Appendix 6.2. These heterogeneous samples could produce a spurious inflation in magnitude for these correlations, so they should be interpreted with caution. Each of the child's four irritability scores was calculated separately for interactions with his mother, father, and siblings. As shown in Table 11.4, all four measures of his interactions with each of the family members correlated with his TAB score. Generally speaking, his disposition to start up conflicts and counter the attacks by others seemed to be the major components.

The first test of the bilateral hypothesis requires that the child's irritable reactions to others account for some of the variance in a measure of his performance level. In this context, the use of his own TAB score as the dependent variable would generate a hopelessly confounded state of affairs. However, the use of TIRO (Telephone Interview Report Observation) as a measure of deviancy would not present such a problem. The correlations between the child's irritable reactions and the TIRO scores are also summarized in Table 11.4. As shown there, it was the child's disposition to react irritably to his mother that correlated with parent-reported levels of child deviancy. The multiple regression for the measures of child reactions to the mother and her TIRO reports produced a correlation of .502. The F value was 5.30 ($p < .001$). The findings offer strong support for the first part of the bilateral hypothesis.

It seems, then, that the problem child's irritable exchanges with his mother may function as a prime determinant for her daily reports of his level of deviancy. However, the bilateral perspective requires that one must also analyze the *reactions* of family members to the child. Measures of the mother's irritable reactions to the child accounted for over 40% of the variance available in the child's TAB score as a measure of his coercive performance (see Tables 12.3 and 12.5). Similarly, the measures of father and sibling irritable reactions to target children also accounted for significant variance. Combining the key measures from the analyses for mothers with those from fathers and siblings provided a multiple regression of

Table 11.4
Covariation of Child's Performance Level and Child's Irritability p Values

When child is interacting with:	N	PPM Correlations of Irritability Variables							
		Crossover		Counterattack		Punishment Acceleration		Continuance	
		TAB	TIRO	TAB	TIRO	TAB	TIRO	TAB	TIRO
Mother	112 (69)	.83***	.43***	.72***	.40***	.47***	.37**	.60***	.29*
Father	68 (38)	.79***	.09	.68***	.04	.46**	.13	.51***	.15
Sibling	104 (62)	.58***	−.08	.44***	.05	.31*	.21	.48***	.17

The figures in parentheses are the N's for TIRO data.

$*p < .05$

$**p < .01$

$***p < .001$

Table 11.5
Coercion Levels by Family Members

Family Members	Mean TAB Score by Samples			F Value	Duncan
	Social Aggressor	Stealer	Normal		
Target Child	.98 (34)	.65 (37)	.17 (36)	25.12***	SA > ST > N
Mother	.87 (34)	.89 (37)	.45 (37)	11.51***	SA & ST > N
Father	.68 (14)	.50 (25)	.34 (26)	4.51**	SA > N
Siblings	.66 (31)	.53 (33)	.31	5.00**	SA > N

The figures in parentheses are N's.

$**p < .01$

$***p < .001$

.581. The F value was 5.90 ($p < .001$) (Patterson, 1981b).

These findings support the idea that the problem child's performance level is related in some fashion to the manner in which other persons react to him. It follows, then, that most aggressive children must live in families of aggressive people; i.e., in part, the child's aggression is a *reaction to* their noxious intrusions. If this is true, it would follow that if the problem child is more coercive than the normal child, then the mean level of coerciveness must be higher than normal for some (or all) members of his family.

To study the first question, the TAB scores were calculated for each family member in the samples of Normals, Stealers, and Social Aggressors from Appendix 6.2. Between-sample comparisons were made separately for each family agent, including problem child, mother, father, and the mean for siblings. As shown in Table 11.5, Social Aggressors were five times more coercive than were Normals, and Stealers were performing at about three times the level of Normals. The mothers, fathers, and siblings of Social Aggressors were significantly

Table 11.6
Enmeshment with Target-Child Coercive Episodes

| Antecedent | Normal | | Social Aggressor | | F value by: | | |
	Younger	Older	Younger	Older	Group	Age	Interaction
Parents							
Overall	.79	.79	.89	.82	2.00	0.74	0.59
Aversive	.66	.69	.94	.85	7.54**	0.13	0.63
Neutral	.81	.90	.96	.84	0.42	0.05	2.09
Positive	.84	.73	.78	.76	0.05	0.75	0.36
Siblings							
Overall	.64	.62	.57	.58	0.81	0.02	0.06
Aversive	.54	.38	.45	.47	0.00	0.68	1.14
Neutral	.90	.89	.81	.79	1.76	0.04	0.00
Positive	.66	.70	.52	.48	5.33*	0.00	0.34

*$p < .05$
**$p < .01$

more coercive than were those of Normals. Mothers of Stealers were also significantly higher than were mothers of Normals. These TAB scores for family members summarize each person's coercive initiations plus coercive reactions to the coercive behaviors of all other family members. However, these scores do not tell us which family members are actually involved in the interactions with the identified problem child. How often are parents or siblings a part of his coercive episodes?

The data in Table 11.6 summarize the findings from two separate analyses of the samples of 30 Social Aggressors and 20 Normals described in Appendix 5.1. In the first analysis, if either or both the mother and father were involved at *any point* in the problem child's coercive chain, it was tabulated as "involved." For example, the problem child and a sibling might have been fighting; if the mother intervened, it would be counted as "involved." It can be seen that for normal and clinical families alike, roughly *80% of the time parents were involved* in target-child episodes. There was a nonsignificant trend for parents in distressed families to be generally more involved than parents of Normals. Given that the problem child was counterattacking (aversive antecedent), there was a .90 likelihood that a parent was involved at *some point!* For normal families, this likelihood was significantly less. Clearly, parents are involved in a surprising proportion of all coercive episodes involving the problem child. To change the problem child requires that one change the parents.

Comparable analyses of problem-child interactions with siblings showed that they were involved in roughly 60% of the interchanges with problem children (Patterson, 1979a). This suggests an *enormous overlap* between siblings and parents. Both must have been involved in the *same interchanges* about 40% of the time! Note, too, the curious fact that the overlap seemed to be highest for conflicts that had neutral antecedents. What is there about such an antecedent that defines it as a kind of vortex drawing several family members into a confrontation with the problem child?

Obviously, much coercion in normal and distressed families is a *group enterprise.* Any given coercive episode is very likely to involve *three* (or more) *persons!* This bears an interesting relation to a finding from studies of assaultive behavior (Loeber & Janda, in preparation). They found that in the normal sample, hitting tended to occur during altercations between siblings. However, for the families in the clinical sample, hitting was more likely to occur when the mother became involved in conflicts among children.

The findings support the hypothesis that Social Aggressors live in aggressive families. As a general case, many of the conflicts seem to involve more than two persons. However, it is entirely possible that the parents and siblings in these families are coercive *only* when they interact with the *identified problem child.* A study by Patterson (1979a) compared parents and siblings from normal and clinical samples under two conditions. One comparison examined the interactions among family

Table 11.7
Correlations Among Family Management Variables and Child Aggression

Lack of Family Management Skills	Correlation with Child (MOSAIC) TAB Score	Parent Report of Physical Aggression	Peer Rating of Physical Aggression
Monitor	.49*	.35**	.06
Obedience	.27	.68***	.28*
Discipline	.47†	.37†	.40*
Problem Solving	.28	.06	.12

*p < .05
**p < .01
***p < .001
†p < .10

members including the problem child, and the other excluded interactions with him. The analysis revealed the curious fact that (with one exception) when the parents interacted with siblings, or with each other, their behavior fell within the *normal range* of coerciveness. The exception involved father and male sibling interactions. The parents of Social Aggressors seem to allow *all* children to be coercive in their interactions with *each other*. Even in the absence of the problem child, the siblings were two to five times more coercive than were normal siblings! Apparently, siblings in families of Social Aggressors are generally disposed to be irritable in their dealings with one another. However, for these parents, the identified problem child becomes a kind of *storm center*. It is in the presence of the problem child that the parents become maximally coercive. The Social Aggressor occupies a very special niche within the family; his deviancy status is tied directly to his ability to elicit coercive reactions from his parents, particularly the mother.

Family Management Variables

From 1979-1981 an effort was made in the longitudinal planning study to translate the family management variables into assessment procedures. A sample of over 200 normal children from grades 4, 7, and 10 were measured by a battery of over 18 assessment procedures. The children and their families participated in home observation sessions using the new code system (MOSAIC by Toobert, Patterson, & Moore, 1981), and videotaped problem solving (PANIC by Forgatch & Wieder, 1981). Laboratory measures of parent perception of child deviancy (Holleran, in preparation) were also employed. The children and their parents were interviewed separately, filled

out numerous questionnaires, and also responded to brief daily telephone interviews. Only small subsets participated in some of the more costly procedures.

Separate studies were made for each of the four family management constructs. In each case, several dozen variables were identified from the various assessment batteries that seemed (a priori) to relate to the construct. Following this, each item was intercorrelated with all other items, as well as with each of the four criterion measures of antisocial behavior. These correlation matrices were constructed separately for each of the three grades. Composites or clusters of variables were identified that intercorrelated significantly *at each grade level* and correlated with one or more criterion measures of antisocial behavior at two or more grade levels. A given family management construct might be defined by one to four such composite scores. At the time of this writing, the analyses have been completed for Monitor, Discipline, Obedience, and Problem Solve. The construct, House Rules, is still being analyzed.

Table 11.7 summarizes the findings for the relation between the family management scores and three criterion measures of aggression (Loeber, Patterson, & Dishion, in preparation). Only the findings for the youngest sample (the 4th graders) are presented here. The criterion measures consisted of a TAB score based upon data from the MOSAIC code, a composite from several items from a parent-report questionnaire that measured the child's physical aggression, and items from peer nomination that also measured physical aggression. All three criterion measures intercorrelate (range .41 to .46).

It can be seen that the pattern of correlations

varies somewhat as a function of which criterion measure serves as the focal point. This can most easily be put in perspective by comparing the findings to the patterns obtained for the sample of 7th graders. In general, it is the disruption in Obedience and Discipline that relates most closely to the widest range of criterion measures in the two grade levels. The two variables are indirect measures of the parents' use of punishment for deviant behavior (Patterson & Stouthamer-Loeber, in preparation). The Obedience score was based upon four composite scores that describe parent and child perceptions about the extensiveness of the child's rule breaking. The data sample questionnaire data from fathers and mothers, as well as interview material from the mother and child. The Discipline score was based upon *global* ratings made by observers following each visit to the home. The composite describes how effectively the parents use punishment in coping with the ongoing coercive behavior of the child.

The assumption is that patterns of family management variables will differentiate pure Stealers from pure Social Aggressors. As yet, no formal test has been made for this hypothesis. However, the set of findings summarized in Loeber, Patterson, & Dishion (in preparation) suggest that the Obedience and Discipline scores account for the larger share of variance in measures of Social Aggression. The analysis by Patterson, Stouthamer-Loeber, and Loeber (in preparation) suggests that it is the Monitoring, Problem Solving, and Obedience scores that account for variance in measures of attacks against property.

While the findings in Table 11.7 are based upon very small samples, they are strongly supportive of the hypothesized relation between family management practices and socially aggressive behavior. In this normal sample, the disruption of family management procedures covaried with increases in antisocial child behavior. We plan to replicate the findings using a longitudinal design, where it will be possible to demonstrate the predictive power of the family management variables. We also assume that pre- and post-measures for these variables would show significant improvement in family management practices following treatment. The third set of studies will search for the covariation between disruptions in management processes and changes in microsocial variables such as Crossover and Continuance.

Prognosis for Adjustment as Adults

The findings reviewed in Chapter 2 showed consistent support for the stability of antisocial behavior across long periods of time. Findings from both retrospective (Robins, 1966) and longitudinal designs (Shea, 1972) showed early antisocial patterns put the individual at greater risk for criminal behavior, institutionalizaton, and general marginal adjustment as an adult. Indeed, a reading of the preliminary findings suggests the hypothesis that extremely antisocial children may be at greater risk for later adult pathology than are children who have one parent diagnosed as schizophrenic (Garmezy & Devine, 1982).

Our current speculations would have it that young Social Aggressors, who are also socially unskilled, will grow up to be marginally adjusted adults. We are beginning to suspect that it is the mixed case (the young Social Aggressor who steals) who is most at risk for adolescent delinquency and status as a career offender. However, this is all very speculative. The purpose of the discussion that follows is to review the findings relating to the long-term implications of symptoms that would be categorized as Social Aggressive.

The findings from the West and Farrington (1973) study showed that boys rated by teachers as aggressive at age 9 had a .14 chance of being later identified as *violent adolescent* delinquents. In fact, 70% of the violent adolescent delinquents had been rated as aggressive at age 13 years; 48% had been so rated at age 9. McCord's (1977) well known follow-up study of the Cambridge-Sommerville sample collected teachers' ratings of boys when they were about 7 years of age. Official records were then obtained for the men who were now in their forties. The teachers' ratings showed a cluster of relations among temper tantrums, bullying, and getting into fights. Of these, only temper tantrums were related to later criminality.

A retrospective study by Loeber, Janda, and Reid (in preparation) identified adolescents with assault experience, who had been studied earlier at OSLC. Their analyses showed significant differences in family processes for the sample later identified as Assaulters. The children studied earlier, who were at risk for later assault, had a higher TAB score than did all other family members. Relatively speaking, children at risk for later assault were the most coercive members of their own families. In the majority of families from normal and clinical samples, it is the mother who has the highest ranking TAB score.

Stealers and Delinquents

There are two assumptions that are central to this section. The first is the continuity hypothesis. Robins (1966) emphasized the continuity between early forms of antisocial child behavior and later antisocial behavior. In the present context, we emphasize the continuity between early protodelinquent behaviors such as lying, stealing, firesetting, vandalism, and adolescent delinquency. The second assumption is that there is a related continuity in family process, from the young child engaged in protodelinquent activities, to the older adolescent chronic offender. Specifically, it is assumed that both early and later forms of antisocial behavior are accompanied by disruptions in parent monitoring and a failure to punish attacks against property. Given that a child remains antisocial over a long period of time, then the family processes that support these behaviors must also remain stable over time. These key assumptions can only be tested in longitudinal designs. The literature relating to the continuity for protodelinquent and delinquent behavior will be reviewed in a later section. As yet, there are no data testing the related hypothesis about continuity in family process. Lacking such data, we can only proceed with a more indirect test and use a cross-sectional design. Here, the assumption is that the pattern of family management variables relating to protodelinquent measures for a younger sample will be similar to that which covaries with measures of delinquent behavior for an older sample. Those findings will be summarized in a later section.

Normal Stealing

Almost everyone has stolen. In the study of self-report data by Hood and Sparks (1970), many normal adults reported stealing regularly. During the toddler and preschool ages, it is perfectly respectable to "steal"; however, it is not labeled as such. It becomes a "symptom" only if the child *persists* in doing it at high rates when he is of school age. If it persists through age 7 or 8, then the community is likely to become concerned.

I assume that it is entirely "natural" for an infant to reach for, and take, objects that are of interest to him. Early on, however, the parent quickly intervenes when he reaches for objects that represent a potential danger, e.g., scissors, lighted cigarettes, a heavy lamp. At some later point (probably *much* later) the child is trained to "respect the property rights of others." That this early training is, for a time, rather tenuous is witnessed by Hartup's (1974) observation of nursery school children. He found that 78% of their quarrels were altercations about "possession." It may also be the case that many early disputes among siblings concern possession of objects and/or territory. By the age of 3 or 4, children are generally trained to understand what belongs to whom and which objects are jointly shared by family members. The parent may begin this training by teaching the child

which things belong to which other people. Then he may be taught to ask permission before using things that belong to someone else.

The data in Figure 11.3 attest to the eventual success achieved by most parents. This longitudinal study of an essentially middle- and upper-class sample showed that with girls the vast majority of parents were successful by the time their daughters reached the age of 5 or 6; i.e., they did not steal often enough for it to be a concern of the parent (MacFarlane, Allen, & Honzik, 1954). Parents of boys reported more concern about stealing than did parents of girls. From ages 3 to 10 there was a steady decline in concern.

The Isle of Wight survey by Rutter, Tizard, and Whitmore (1970) showed that 5.7% of parents were concerned about their sons stealing at ages 10 to 13, and 2.6% expressed similar concerns about their daughters. The comparable percentages reported by teachers were 3.4 and 1.6 respectively. Based upon a psychiatric interview, 30.2% of the boys identified as Stealers were diagnosed as "disturbed." The comparable percentage for female Stealers was 13.5. For those samples the base rates for psychiatric disturbance were 4.4% and 2.4%. Sometime between the ages of 5 and 10, taking things is no longer perceived as normal and acceptable behavior. At that time, the episode will be relabeled as stealing and is associated by adults with "emotional disturbances."

The data from cross-cultural, self-report studies reviewed by Hood and Sparks (1970) strongly emphasized the fact that many persons *do not stop stealing* at the age of 4 or 5; they simply reduce their rates of stealing and are discreet enough about it to reduce the likelihood of being apprehended. For example, adolescents' self-report data covering a three-year period showed a mean incidence of 1.1 events of petty thefts ($2.00 or less) (Elliott & Voss, 1974). The mean for major theft ($2.00 to $5.00 value) was 3.4 events. The self-report rates for females were roughly 30% less than the comparable figures for males.

If the young child regularly steals from family, neighbors, and peers at school, he is likely to be caught eventually, or at least be suspected of being a Stealer. This is my "frequency labeling" hypothesis. The children most at risk for being labeled are those engaged in the higher rates of deviant episodes. For our purposes, a Stealer is a child between the ages of 6 and 12 who is "caught" stealing about once every three or four months. The hypothesis is that, if permitted, the young Stealer will *persist* in maximizing short-term gains. If the family permits a 5-year-old to steal, the chances are very good that they will be equally permissive

Figure 11.3
Parents' Reports of Stealing as a Problem Behavior
(adapted from MacFarlane, Allen, & Honzik, 1962, pp. 66-67)

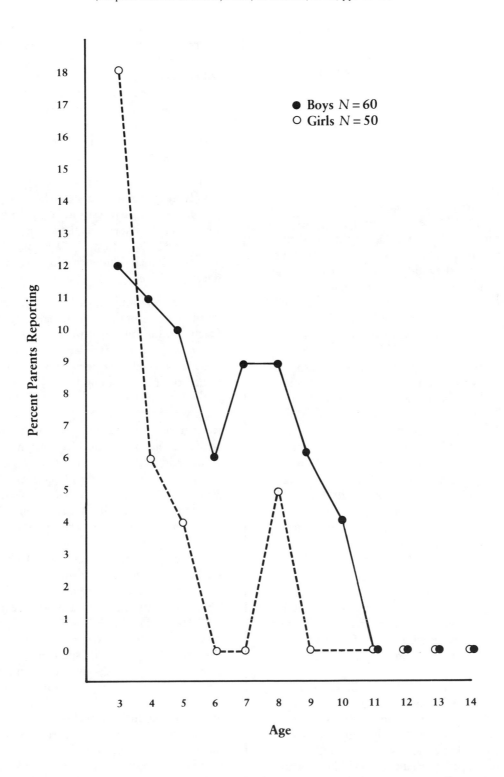

● Boys N = 60
○ Girls N = 50

Percent Parents Reporting

Age

about stealing when the child is 10 or 12. Given a continued lack of monitoring and punishment for stealing, then the child may drift into the pattern of a career offender. The hypothesis is that any time up to about age 15, the parent can bring this problem behavior under control. Beyond that age, it may be that other forces, such as the peer group or work place, may have a greater impact than the parent upon the youth's behavior.

Speculations about the Families of Chronic Offenders

The parents of young children at risk for becoming chronic offenders have some special characteristics that were noted in earlier sections. Many of the parents of Stealers were *not attached* to their children (Reid & Patterson, 1976). They did not seem to care what happened to their children; an apt label for this subset would be "unmotivated parent." There was another group that seemed attached to the child but could not identify with the role of *parent*. They cared for the child; they fed him; but they did not want to be responsible for training him. They particularly did not wish to monitor and confront the child's antisocial activities going on outside the home. The parents of Stealers shared a distaste for using the term "steal" (Reid & Patterson, 1976) when describing their children. It seemed that *any* and all "explanations" given by the child were accepted if they contributed to the parents' belief that their child did not steal. In fact, it took us months to figure out a procedure to get around the fact that many of these parents could not believe that the problem even *existed!* To them, the term "steal" meant something analogous to proven in a court of law. Often they would not accept the word of a neighbor, a teacher, or a storekeeper as "proof."

I suspect that part of the difficulty these parents had in labeling stealing related to the fact that many had delinquent careers of their own. Parents with criminal histories would be less likely to monitor and punish antisocial behavior, such as stealing. The correlation between antisocial behavior of the child and criminality of the father has been supported in studies by McCord (1980), Robins (1966), and Mednick and Christiansen (1977).

There is, of course, an extensive literature about the *child's role* in acquiring or rejecting cultural norms. The child's internalization of cultural norms has been a major concern for theorists in sociology, developmental psychology, and personality. Generally, it is assumed that children and adults alike know what society's rules and expectations are and, secondly, that they desire to conform to these rules; i.e., the rules are "internalized." The cultural-strain theorists assume that the knowledge is present, but the original bonding of the individual to cultural norms has been disrupted by factors such as extreme deprivation or frustration. Deviant acts occur as a result of the disruption. The culture-deviance theorists, on the other hand, would assume the rules that have been internalized reflect cultural values that are, themselves, "deviant." From this perspective, the individual is conforming, but to a deviant subculture.

Control theory represents yet another perspective on this problem. The most coherent statement of control theory, together with a description of its empirical underpinnings, has been provided by Hirschi (1969):

"In the end then, control theory remains what it has always been, a theory in which deviation is not problematic. The question, 'Why do they do it?' is simply not the question the theory is designed to answer. The question is, 'Why won't we do it?' There is much evidence that we would if we dared." (Hirschi, 1969, p. 34)

As I understand control theory, attachment or bonding is assumed to be a necessary (but not sufficient) condition for conformity. The accompanying commitments, involvement, and belief systems are also thought to be necessary (but not sufficient) conditions for conformity to cultural norms. I would tend to agree with Hirschi (1969) that there is not much of a bond between the child who steals and his parent(s), or between the child who steals and his peer group for that matter. To this I would add that many of the parents of Stealers are not attached to the role of parent. Their lack of motivation has been a major problem during our efforts to specialize in the treatment of Stealers. It was almost impossible to get parents of Stealers to come in for treatment (Reid & Patterson, 1976). After being referred, they tended to drop out of the baseline study at alarming rates. A recent analysis of the factors determining early dropout from treatment showed that almost invariably these were Stealer families. Those that did participate in treatment seldom carried out their assignments. The problem was of such magnitude that it prompted us to design and carry out a study to determine the impact of providing "parenting salaries." The publication by Fleischman (1979b) demonstrated a significant increment in parent participation in the training program if salaries were made contingent upon their carrying out their assignments. From the perspective of coercion theory, neither parental motivation nor parental skills are thought to be a given condition.

The assumption presented here is that most chronic adolescent offenders begin their careers very early; i.e., by the time the child reaches the age of 6 or 7 a discerning observer would note the pattern. However, our clinical experience suggests that some chronic offenders begin their careers in early adolescence. We don't know what the relative occurrence of early and late starting processes might be. In our experience, there is a ratio of about 2 to 1 (early to late) for our sample of chronic offenders. My hunch is that the late starters are the product of a breakup in family structure, e.g., divorce, severe illness, or unemployment. We also have no data on the relation between early and late starting and the risk for career adult offenses. However, the research literature consistently relates early starting of police offenses with risk for adult offenses, so I will pursue the formulation about early starters a bit further.

Recent discussions with R. Loeber led to a formulation about early starters that is viewed as a kind of transitive progression beginning with the disruption or absence of parental monitoring of the child's protodelinquent attacks against property. The 5-, 6-, and 7-year-old steals with increasing frequency from family, neighbors, and stores. He is also engaged in frequent acts of vandalism. On both counts, he quickly learns to lie as a means of covering up his activities. In fact, it is his lies that may be noted first by parents and other adults. The third step in this progression would be that he receives much more unsupervised street time than normal children of this age would be given. Fourth, during his wanderings, he will very likely encounter older and more experienced antisocial children. This peer support base may emerge slowly, but we see it as an important step in the child's increasing commitment to an antisocial career. The current OSLC study involves a sample of 109 chronic delinquent offenders. Half of their police offenses occurred in the company of peers or siblings. About one youth in five committed at least one offense in the presence of a sibling (usually an older sibling).

It is assumed that the early starter is engaged in frequent acts of theft and vandalism; these occur at a steady rate throughout his school years. The high density of offenses eventually leads to his being labeled as antisocial. This high density also places the child at risk for increasingly "serious" crimes, such as arson, assault, burglary, and so on. The hypothesis is that density covaries with labeling and with the seriousness of the crime. It is also assumed that the early starter is most at risk for becoming an adult offender.

Family Processes Relating to the Continuity Hypothesis

Regardless of when the antisocial behavior of the child begins, it is produced by a disruption in parental monitoring and punishment for antisocial attacks. For the adolescent, this disruption could occur during a time of severe marital conflict between the parents, a major illness, a move to a new neighborhood or unemployment for the parents. It is also assumed that if the antisocial behavior continues over time, parental monitoring and punishment remain disrupted. If the preadolescent terminates his antisocial career, this would likely be produced by the parents reinstating control of their child.

The first study of the relation of family management variables to the continuity hypothesis used a cross-sectional design for two age groups. One sample consisted of 60 families of 4th grade children, and the other combined a sample of 100 families of 7th and 10th grade children. For each sample, parent-report data identified children thought to lie and steal (Patterson & Loeber, 1981). For the older sample, these two criteria plus police-offense data were used as dependent variables.

As can be seen in Table 11.8, for the older sample it is the Monitor score and, to a lesser extent, Obedience and Discipline scores that correlate heavily with measures of delinquency based upon official records. The adolescent child with police offenses is characterized by parents who tend not to track him closely. The child is disobedient both at home and at school. Even when the child is disruptive in the presence of his parents, their discipline techniques are erratic and ineffective.

The next hypothesis was that (for the older sample) parent reports of *proto*delinquent behaviors, such as lying and stealing, would covary with court records of police offenses. As shown in the study by Patterson and Loeber (1981), the correlation between lying and police offenses was .31 ($p < .001$), and for stealing and police offenses it was .46 ($p < .001$). It was assumed that the same family management variables that covaried with police-offense data correlate with the measures of protodelinquency. As shown in Table 11.8, the pattern of the correlations was quite similar. The measures for Monitor, Obedience, and Discipline all correlated with parent reports of Lie and Steal. These findings offer strong support for the hypothesized continuity from measures of protodelinquency to measures of police offenses and also for the assumption that they share a common familial process.

Table 11.8
Covariations of Family Management Variables
with Measures of Protodelinquent and Delinquent Behaviors

(from Patterson & Loeber, 1981)

Lack of Family Management Skills	4th Grade Sample		7th and 10th Grade Samples		
	Lie	Steal	Lie	Steal	Police Offense
Monitor	.48***	.22	.48***	.44***	.58***
	(59)	(60)	(92)	(89)	(100)
Obedience	.39**	.16	.54***	.35***	.31**
	(46)	(48)	(87)	(81)	(90)
Discipline	.45**	.39*	.34*	.37*	.36*
	(10)	(18)	(35)	(33)	(36)
Problem Solve	.35	—†	—	—	—
	(22)				

The figures in parentheses are N's.

†These correlations have not been calculated. More tapes are being scored to increase the N's.

*$p < .05$
**$p < .01$
***$p < .001$

The next feature of the continuity hypothesis to be tested was that the same pattern of family management variables would *also* correlate with measures of protodelinquent behavior for the younger age group. As shown in Table 11.8, the measures for Monitor, Obedience, and Discipline all covaried significantly with parent reports of Lie. However, the findings for Steal only partially supported the hypothesis. Only the covariation between Steal and Discipline was significant. The findings provide general support for the continuity in family process patterns that maintain earlier and later protodelinquent behaviors.

The Continuity of a Delinquent Career

The hypothesis is that young children who steal are at risk for adolescent delinquency and for adult adjustment problems as well. The magnitude of the adjustment problems is thought to relate to the level of work and relationship skills possessed. Presumably, children characterized as high-rate Stealers, who are also lacking in social skills, are at greater risk for becoming career offenders. Both the deviancy status and the lack of social survival skills are thought to relate to parental skills in family management. The career offender is more likely to be an early starter. Presumably, it is the high density of his attacks against property that leads to his eventually being labeled as antisocial. It was also assumed that the more frequent his attacks, the more likely they would be to eventually escalate to more serious episodes. Wolfgang, Figlio, and Sellin's (1972) extensive Markov analyses showed that the movement from one type of crime to another seemed random. There was no systematic progression or path toward any particular crime. The child did not first steal cars, then progress to burglary, and finally become assaultive. The systematic analysis of self-reported delinquency from the National Probability sample by Elliott and Huizinga (1980) also failed to find evidence for either a progression or the concept of specialization. The most that can be said is that the high-rate offender was more likely to engage in all forms of serious crime. The career delinquent self-reports higher frequencies of status (less serious) offenses, as well as crimes *against persons* (theft and property damage). This relation is not, however, symmetric; i.e., not all children who report frequent status offenses go on to more serious crimes. I interpret these studies to mean that we should be concerned primarily about the *frequency* with which a child engages in *status* and *nonstatus* offenses. For the young child, this could mean a general focus upon rule-breaking behavior at home, in the school, and in the community.

There are no studies that test the assumed covariation between amount of unsupervised time and lack of punishment with increases in depredations against property. Nor are there tests for the assumed relation between density and labeling. As they now stand, these assumptions are based primarily upon our clinical experience in working with these families. If a young child has a great deal of unsupervised, on-the-street time, he responds to targets of opportunity. The unguarded bicycle is appropriated, then discarded. A building site is vandalized; tires are slashed. The teacher's purse left on the floor by her desk is examined. Most of the depredations are unplanned. The chance that his activities will be detected is slight. However, if his rate is high enough, then eventually he will be caught. When caught, the first, second, third, or even tenth instances are usually of little moment. "He is just a little wild; did you hear what he. . . ?" Over time, the offenses become more serious, and/or the sheer weight of an accumulation of these events eventually leads some adults to take a rule violation as being serious. At that point, he may be referred to the court and labeled as delinquent. *The label did not cause the behavior.* His frequent escapades increased the odds of his eventually being caught, and his persistence led to his being labeled as deviant. Even though he is labeled as delinquent, this child probably does not perceive himself as deviant, criminal, or delinquent. As noted in the review by Elliott, Ageton, and Canter (1979), there is substantial empirical evidence that many embezzlers, auto thieves, check forgers, and persons involved in assaults or rape *do not* view themselves as criminal or delinquent! In their study, delinquent children who were caught and labeled suffered no loss in self-esteem. Interestingly enough, those who were caught, labeled, *and* counseled did show a more negative evaluation of self.

Most investigators are convinced that the peer group plays a critical role in the development of the career offender. While we share this conviction, it is also the case that the necessary data are lacking for a test of the process described earlier. If the young child has a great deal of unsupervised time, does this relate directly to a high density of antisocial acts, or is it mediated by his finding an antisocial peer group? Survey studies have consistently shown that rural and small-city delinquents tend not to be gang members (Call, 1965; Lentz, 1956). For example, Lentz (1956) reported that only 22% of rural delinquents were members of gangs, as compared to a rate of 87% for metropolitan delinquents. In his study, the majority of rural delinquents were "loners." This also characterizes most of our clientele; however, it is evident in working with chronic delinquents and Stealers alike that many of these children know each other. Occasionally, they "work" together. More often than not, they meet casually on the street.

The young, high-rate Stealers treated at OSLC do not seem to have close ties to family members. Contrary to popular press, he is not an angry shark cruising in a dedicated search for prey. Rather, he is an aimless wanderer. He drifts through school and across the community. In his wake he leaves a trail of petty, and sometimes not-so-petty, crimes. He drifts through relationships in the same meaningless fashion. He does not think of himself as good or bad. Above all, it is not he who is responsible for what happens; he is only sometimes lucky and sometimes not. Unless helped, he becomes a piece of psychological flotsam, drifting on a current of offenses that gradually increase in frequency and seriousness. When his drift has achieved chronic status (five or more offenses), his prospects for adult adjustment are not good. While still a juvenile, he may proceed to adult crimes. In his follow-up study of Philadelphia delinquents, Wolfgang found that 76% of the chronic juvenile delinquents later became adult criminals (Wolfgang, 1977). Wolfgang's follow-up study of Philadelphia delinquents takes a provocative stance on the criminal career: ". . . at *whatever* age the chronic offender begins his fourth or fifth offense he will commit further offenses with very high probability . . . the probability that an offender after his fourth offense will recidivate is about .8" (p. 17). As Wolfgang points out, given such continuity, the juvenile/adult statutory dichotomy makes little sense. It is *not the age* of the offender that should be of concern to us but, rather, the *number of offenses.* As the number of offenses increases, so does the likelihood for commission of yet another offense (Wolfgang et al., 1972).

I find myself in accord with Wolfgang's position but would urge that the continuity is apparent at a much earlier age. I believe that by the age of 7 or 8, high-rate stealing places a child at great risk for chronic delinquency as an adolescent. Gersten et al. (1976) factor analyzed the data from a large-scale survey of Manhattan children. Over a five-year interval, the stability for the delinquency dimension was .44. The authors believe that these delinquent behaviors stabilize after the age of 10, while antisocial behaviors, such as fighting and conflict with parents, may stabilize as early as 6 years of age. The most relevant study testing the continuity between juvenile and adolescent stealing was carried out by Moore, Chamberlain, and Mukai (1979). They examined the court records for 60 antisocial children studied earlier at OSLC. At the time of this follow-up study, all were 14 years of age or older. During their initial contact, the 21 Social Aggressors were, on the average, 8.4 years of age; the 25 Stealers were, on the average, 9.8 years of age. Slightly more than half (.57) of these children were *both* Stealers and Social Aggressors. The mean age of the normal sample was 8.8 years. Community records indicated that all of them were in residence in the community during the period studied. The data show that boys with stealing as a complaint were at grave risk for being picked up at least once by the police. The likelihood was .77. In fact, 52% of the young Stealers became *chronic* offenders (four or more offenses). Nonstealer clinical cases ("pure" Social Aggressors) were no different from Normals.

The findings for the Stealer sample were partially confounded due to the fact that at the time of referral 42% of these young Stealers *already* had at least one police contact! This represents a *very early* start indeed. It is of particular interest because in the research literature such early beginnings are often associated with increased likelihoods for later chronic offenses and recidivism following incarceration. In the OSLC study, the follow-up records showed that even if those with prior police contacts were excluded, the likelihoods were .56 for Stealers, .13 for Nonstealers, and .15 for Normals. It seems reasonable to conclude that young boys *referred* for stealing were at great risk for at least one police contact by the age of 14.

Given that many of the families who moved from the community may have contained children at risk, and that the peak years for delinquent activity are not 14, but 15 through 16, then it seems reasonable to conclude that the Moore et al. figures are probably underestimates. By age 18, probably a much larger proportion of young Stealers become chronic offenders. Given that crimes against persons are more likely to peak at about that age, then it seems too soon to conclude that (nonstealing) Social Aggressors are not at risk for delinquency. Would *nonreferred,* high-rate Stealers be at risk for chronic delinquency? That is the topic for a longitudinal study that is currently being prepared.

Acknowledgments

The writer wishes to thank Alice Harris, Tom Dishion, and Rolf Loeber for their careful critiques of earlier versions of this chapter.

Footnotes

1. Before leaving these studies, it might be noted that the introduction of punishment (such as time out) did bring the deviant behaviors under control in the studies by Corte et al. (1971), Laivgueur et al. (1973), Budd et al. (1976), Wahler (1968), and Walker and Buckley (1973).

2. Probably the simplest idea would be that prolonged exposure to aversive interaction produces a reduced responsiveness to either positive or aversive reactions. One could also imagine prolonged aversive interactions being correlated with the likelihood of a negative set, but there are no studies that relate to either of these ideas.

3. The data from the Whiting's study also showed the amount of infant caretaking correlated significantly with the child's observed nurturant-responsibility behavior. It may be that more "advanced" cultures do the child a double disservice by not expecting him to be responsible in some fashion to other family members, i.e., to *give* as well as to *take*. In addition to making the child relatively "functionless," modern society has deprived the child of that which he can learn from being responsible for the well being of another. This, as noted by many modern writers (such as A. Adler), seems to be something lacking in our modern culture.

4. The *concept* of transitive progression is certainly a useful one. However, the adequacy of the Guttman coefficient as a means for describing it has, from the beginning, been open to serious questions (Festinger, 1947, cited by Robinson, 1973). As Menzel (1953) and others have pointed out, the value for *CR* is affected both by the item marginals and the number of items. The efforts by Menzel (1953), Schooler (1968), and others to correct these limitations still leave unanswered the problems detailed in the Robinson critique (Robinson, 1973). I found Robinson's arguments sufficiently compelling to lead me to search for a different way of summarizing information about progressions.

5. R. Vreeland (in preparation) carefully rechecked all of the OSLC records for *any* mention of firesetting and identified 36 children referred to OSLC. Ninety-three percent of this more loosely defined group of Firesetters were also Stealers. This in contrast to the comparable figure of 78% from Table 11.1.

In passing, the interview study by Nielsen and Gerber (1979) has just a hint of data suggesting that we should look for vandalism (at school) and cruelty to animals as lower base-rate symptoms that are part of this same progression.

6. Based upon the Reid and Hendricks (1973) study, there is a hypothesis that families of Stealers are more distant and/or uninvolved than either families of Normals or families of Social Aggressors. The measures of these concepts (based upon the FICS) were not thought to be effective translations of either distance or parent involvement. The newer measures from the MOSAIC and PANIC codes may prove to be more useful in this regard. At the time of this writing, the appropriate analyses have yet to be completed.

7. Carlson (1981a) showed that roughly one-fifth of the antisocial children referred to OSLC had been previously diagnosed by a physician as hyperkinetic and were medicated for that problem. In his factor-analytic study, Carlson (1981b) showed that Noncomply and Disapproval (and other items like them) loaded on a factor that he labeled *Verbal Assertion*. High scores on this factor significantly differentiated the Hyperactive from both Social Aggressor and the Normal samples. Both the Hyperactive and Social Aggressor children performed at about the same coercive levels, at least as shown by their TAB scores. They differed, however, in the kinds of deviancy that made up the high levels of performance. The Hyperactive child tended to be more *verbally* coercive, and the Social Aggressor more oppositional (including physical) in his interactions.

Chapter 12
Abstract

The requirements of the caretaker role are reviewed. Particular emphasis is given to training the caretaker to use effective family management skills and noncoercive reactions to irritable child behaviors. The effect of disruptions in family management is compared to the effect of permissive, laissez-faire child rearing.

The father is cast as a key member of the mother's support system, with adjunct functions in child management. Fathers' and mothers' irritable reactions to problem children are compared in terms of variance accounted for in the criterion measure of child performance. The analyses emphasize the key role played by the mothers' irritable reactions. A comparison of mothers and fathers from intact families further emphasizes the differences in parental role. A comparison of mothers' and fathers' self-report data from clinical and normal families reiterates the fact that family pressures and/or lack of adequate support produces depressed mothers. As compared to Normals, mothers of antisocial families show significant elevations on almost all of the clinical scales for the MMPI. Fathers of normal and antisocial families show no significant differences on their MMPI scores. It is hypothesized that the caretaker bears the brunt of crises that impinge from outside the family and the conflicts occurring within the family itself.

Chapter 12

Mothers: Everyone Loves Them, But . . .

"In the United States today, *parents rather than the state have primary responsibility for socializing their young.* Socialization is an adult-initiated process by which the younger person through education, training, and imitation acquires his culture as well as the habits and values congruent with adaptation to that culture. There is no way in which parents can evade having a determining effect upon their children's personality, character, and competence. Children are not the originators of their own actions in the sense that their parents are or should be." (Baumrind, 1978, p. 129)

While some children may, by temperament, be more difficult to control than others, in any given setting it is the adult who is the major determinant of how much aggression will occur there. The parent, the teacher, and the playground supervisor determine mean coercive performance level for the peer group. In well-engineered, token-culture classrooms, even groups of *extremely* aggressive children perform at almost zero levels of aggression (Walker & Buckley, 1972). If they choose to do so, adults *can* set the level at which aggression will occur for young children. In actual practice, the mean performance for a setting is determined by some interaction of the adult's child management skills in relation to aggression and the general disposition to be coercive that is brought to the setting by the children. In conjunction with ex-

tremely coercive children a very permissive and/or unskilled teacher would preside over chaos. It is conceivable that a child could be trained to high levels of coercive performance at school or within the neighborhood by peers operating in unsupervised settings. Once trained, the child might generalize his "disposition to be aggressive" to the home; but, again, it is the parent who determines at what level he will be allowed to perform his new-found skill. As a general case, I believe the primary training for extremely coercive children takes place in the home; it is generalized from there to other settings.

If our society has antisocial children, it is the adults who are responsible. The mother and the father (if he is present) allow these behaviors to occur. It may be that they have good reasons for their omissions in child management practices, e.g., overwhelming crises, ignorance, misguided expectations, or an extremely difficult child. Regardless of the reason for the omission, it is a *parent* who must be taught, supervised, and supported to undertake the responsibility of socializing the child. Training the parent in child management skills is a necessary component for producing long-term changes in extremely antisocial children. The emphasis upon parental responsibility is a means of keeping our attention upon the *locus* of the problem. The explanation for both the existence and the solution of the problem may be found *in the parent(s)*.

The purpose of this chapter is threefold: first, to speculate briefly about the caretaker role; second, to examine the differential contributions of the mother and father to the deviancy process; and third, to look at the evidence for the assumption that the caretaker is at risk for psychological problems.

The Role of Caretaker

The contemporary view is that the infant does not require the continuous monitoring of a single adult caretaker. Rather, his needs may be well served by several adults who perform this function. However, regardless of who fulfills the role of caretaker, there are certain components that must be present for effective child management. The infant and preschool child provide the caretaker with a very high density of aversive events. It is important that the caretaker be trained *not* to react in a consistently irritable fashion, or it seems likely that the child will be at risk for increasing antisocial behavior and physical abuse. The caretaker also needs the skills necessary to model prosocial behavior and to employ the painfully slow process of positive reinforcement to teach prosocial skills. Over a period of months and thousands of trials, the child is trained to ask for what he wants rather than to scream or cry. Later, he learns to wait and to ask at an appropriate time. If the caretaker is disposed to react irritably to infant-dispensed coercive behavior, then this crucial beginning of the socialization process may be delayed. I think that training in prosocial skills and reducing infant coerciveness are two separate parenting skills, but when one is absent, the other may also be deficient.

It is my impression that most cultures are fully cognizant of the necessity for the caretaker to react to infant coerciveness in a nonirritable fashion. Most cultures are also aware of the necessity for the parent or some surrogate to spend thousands of hours modeling or reinforcing the child for his slow acquisition of social skills. I think that this awareness is reflected in the cultural insistence that the future caretaker be trained very early to function in a nonaggressive fashion. Even during preschool years, the future caretaker is encouraged to relate to other children in a nonaggressive mode. Their play activities focus upon the details of infant care and housekeeping activities.

The emphasis placed upon warmth and the accompanying prohibitions upon counteraggression are necessary because of the client populations served by caretakers. These clients (the very young, the very ill, the handicapped, and the very old) are demanding, complaining, and aversive. Infants produce what may be the highest density of aversive events of any role in our culture. Persons hospitalized for illness are expected to complain and criticize; the nurse in the role of caretaker is trained to accept such querulous behavior as part of the job. Similarly, some theories emphasize the necessity for the nursery school teacher, the play therapist, and the social worker to be unconditionally open, accepting, and warm. Unconditional positive regard is viewed as a necessary (and, by some, a sufficient) means for helping the child move beyond his or her vicious attacks to more pleasant modes of interaction. The mother and these other professionals have one thing in common: all are participants in inequitable exchanges. They are expected to receive a great number of aversive events but to give none in return. Few of their clients give positive reinforcement directly to the caretaker. The caretaker must then rely upon a support base that can redress the imbalance of positive to aversive experiences.

In most cultures, the training for the caretaker role begins early and is, I think, directly associated with sex role development. Two cross-cultural studies employing observation procedures have shown that after the age of 2 or 3, preschool girls are less aggressive than boys (Omark, Omark, & Edelman, 1973, cited by Maccoby & Jacklin, 1974; Whiting & Whiting, 1975). Maccoby and Jacklin (1974) point to the possibility of a biological basis underlying the general sex differences in rates of aggression. Nurturance and warmth are also an expected facet of the female sex role. The cross-cultural study by Whiting and Whiting (1975) showed that, in general, girls offered help and support more often than boys. These differences, however, were not significant until ages 6 or 7 but were then maintained at ages 8 through 11 years. Across all cultures there was a tendency for older girls to reflect more nurturance. The correlation between age and nurturance for girls was .51; the covariation also held within each of the six cultures. The authors stressed the fact that observed nurturant behaviors covaried with *experience* as a caretaker. Typically, it was the young girl who was assigned the task of caring for a young infant. Incidentally, boys who were assigned such tasks tended to be more nurturant and less aggressive. The review by Maccoby and Jacklin (1974) showed that in free-play situations with preschool children, there were no consistent differences favoring girls as being more nurturant than boys. However, as they point out, an appropriate test of the caretaker role would require data collected in settings in which a child younger than the target was available.

During socialization, both the family and the peer group teach the individual to substitute pro-social skills for the coercive techniques employed by young children. Given that a mother had *not* participated in such a process, then her first infant would be at risk for neglect and abuse. The series of primate studies reviewed in Ruppenthal et al. (1976) showed an appalling lack of skill for mothers who had been reared in isolation. Observation data showed 100% effective maternal care (for first-borns) for feral-reared monkeys, 95% for laboratory-reared monkeys, and 24% for monkeys reared in isolation or with surrogate (cloth or wire) mothers. It was interesting to note that the latter were more adequate if their first offspring was female (39%) rather than male (13%). Those monkeys reared with peers and isolated from adults were observed to be 75% adequate as mothers. As the isolated mothers reared their second and third infants, they improved significantly in their caretaking skills. At the level of primates, then, it seems that the culture must at least arrange for the future caretaker to have the normal socializing experiences.

I believe that this situation is somewhat analogous to the unskilled mothers of antisocial children. It is not that the young mother has been reared in isolation; rather, it seems likely that the mother of the Social Aggressor may have been only partially socialized and displays a general proclivity to react in an irritable fashion in a wide variety of settings. Coerciveness serves as a substitute for the mother's prosocial skills.

I think that the training for caretakers begins early and is rather subtle in its form. The programmatic studies by Beverly Fagot and her colleagues demonstrate clearly defined sex differences in the reinforcement contingencies supplied by adults in the nursery school and the home (Fagot, 1973, 1974, 1978a, b). Fagot (1978a) first empirically demonstrated the differences in play preference of boys and girls in the nursery school setting. A series of studies carried out by Fagot and other investigators showed that nursery school teachers tended to reinforce *both* sexes for *feminine-preferred* behavior about 80% of the time. Male peers tended to reinforce for masculine-preferred behaviors. She then began a series of studies investigating differential reinforcement for sex role behaviors in the home. In the first study, she established six sex-typed behaviors based upon ratings of 38 traits in children as to their perceived masculinity and femininity; e.g., aggression and rough-housing were perceived as masculine behavior in toddlers (Fagot, 1973). In the follow-up study, six

boys and six girls were observed in their (middle-class) homes. There were 46 categories of child behavior; six differentiated between boys and girls. Girls engaged in more doll play, dress-up, and asked more frequently for help; boys were more likely to play alone and/or with blocks (Fagot, 1974). In the next study of toddlers and their parents, Fagot (1978b) again found that both parents were more likely to reinforce *and* criticize girls than boys. The parents were observed to be more likely to provide boys with praise for play with blocks; girls were more likely to be punished for this behavior. Girls, on the other hand, were more likely to receive positive consequences for playing with dolls and other kinds of soft toys; boys were more likely to be punished for engaging in this kind of play.

In summary, the Fagot studies support the idea that preschool boys and girls are differentially reinforced for caretaking-related behaviors. That is not to say that a well socialized young father could not serve effectively in the caretaker role, but I suspect that he would require some training. The most important among these acquired skills would be a disposition to react in a nonpunitive fashion to coercive toddler behavior. Like the young mother, he would also require a support system. The function of the support system is detailed in a later section of this chapter. Suffice it to say here that the absence of such a support system places the caretaker at risk for depression and perhaps other psychological problems as well.

Lacking the necessary longitudinal data, we know very little about the first stages in the development of the coercive process. My best guess would be that it is characterized by one or both of two variables. There is some likelihood that the young caretaker is coping with a difficult infant (see Chapters 4 and 6). However, most "difficult" infants do not become antisocial children. In keeping with the findings from the longitudinal study by Werner and Smith (1977), I think the deciding variable lies in the prior level of socialization of the caretaker. Their findings showed that, given a difficult infant and an unskilled mother, then the child is indeed at risk for later antisocial behavior. The amount of external stress/crises would function as a mediator here. The greater the number of life crises and the less the skill of the caretaker, the greater the risk for the child. However, the key variable is the presence of a well socialized caretaker. Either parent may serve, but they must be functioning at a coercive level that is normal for adults. Their level of socialization must also include a commitment to societal norms about theft, vandalism, and violence, together with a commitment to the caretaker role. My guess is that most parents of antisocial children would not measure up to these criteria. Prior to forming a family, many would be classified as unskilled, disposed to react irritably, and only partially committed to societal norms regarding criminal acts.

Parental Neglect and Permissiveness

It is the parent who is chiefly responsible for the first stage of child socialization. If, for some reason, this responsibility is not met, then the normalizing efforts of other socializing agents, such as peers and teachers, will be hampered. I think it is important, particularly when the child is young, for the parents to be in charge. They make the major decisions and set the standards for conduct. From my own personal bias, the parents would strengthen their role by using more positive reinforcement than punishment. When punishment is used, it should be firm but nonphysical. What concerns us in this section is what happens when the parents relinquish the responsibilities of their role. This rejection may be manifested as parental neglect and/or permissiveness. The literature in developmental psychology will be briefly examined for findings relating various types of antisocial child behavior to parental neglect and permissiveness.

Neglect

In our clinical contacts we often encounter adults who have children but who *do not wish to be parents*. As noted in Chapter 11, children who were high-rate Stealers tended to have parents who were unmotivated. Some of them also neglected the child's physical needs, e.g., meals were sporadic, and laundry and cleaning were haphazard. Others have also commented upon such families. For example, Rothchild and Wolf (1976), cited by Segal and Yahraes (1978) detailed in a dramatic fashion the lack of commitment to the role of parent on the part of parents in counterculture communes.

". . . what they found were communities in which virtually all children were neglected and abused, victims of treatment that would be judged cruel and inhuman by most parents. The authors were struck by the boredom, apathy, and melancholy of the children . . . the parents seemed bent on keeping the children out of their way, even if it meant denying them everything. Themselves still children, they continued to seek gratification without sacrifice, as if it were actually possible to deal with the young without fully accepting their presence in our lives. . . . Nowhere in this new utopia could one find a sense of commitment to the children." (Segal & Yahraes, 1978, p. 101)

This, of course, is an example of extreme neglect. The formulation presented thus far would suggest that these neglected children are at risk for Stealer and/or Social Aggressor problems. The amount of risk depends upon whether the parental neglect is accompanied by an effort to monitor and punish theft and/or a disposition to respond irritably to child coercive behaviors. The field observation studies by Burgess (1978) found that child-neglect families were significantly more coercive in their interactions than families of Normals. It seems, then, that neglected children are at greater risk for social aggression. The correlation between neglect and stealing has yet to be tested.

Permissive Parenting

One can selectively fulfill the requirements of the caretaker role by accepting some responsibilities but rejecting others. One can, for instance, satisfactorily discharge responsibilities regarding food and shelter, but leave matters of conduct, achievement, and leisure time more or less up to the child. As a general case, the extent to which the young child is in control of his social environment places him at risk for antisocial behavior. Permissive child rearing places the burden of control upon the child too early. As a general thesis, the control of antisocial behavior is learned as an outcome of the parent providing firm, consistent, negative sanctions for such behavior. Typically, such punishment is not a part of permissive, laissez-faire child rearing.

Sears, Maccoby, and Levin (1957) interviewed mothers to determine *both* the aggressiveness of the child and the parental recollection of the child rearing practices that brought it about. While the covariations with child aggressiveness were slight, a pattern of relations emerged that is very similar to a pattern that is suggested by coercion theory. They found that mothers of aggressive children were more likely to be *permissive* about aggressiveness, to use physical punishment, and tended to be lacking in warmth. These findings were supported by the observations made by Diana Baumrind at Berkeley. In her first study she compared three small groups of *normal,* middle-class nursery school children. She found that the assertive, self-reliant children had firm, controlling, and loving parents (Baumrind, 1966; Baumrind & Black, 1967). The discontented, withdrawn children had relatively controlling (but detached) parents, and the children lacking in self-control had relatively permissive parents. In her second study (Baumrind, 1971), 95 preschoolers and their parents were studied. Again, she found that firm discipline was associated with *competence* in the child; permissiveness related to a *lack* of self-control. In a longitudinal design, she and her colleagues are studying 134 white and 16 black preschool children from middle-class families.

Schuck (1974) and Olweus (1981) have updated the work on the relationship between parental permissiveness and aggressiveness in the child. Both have analyzed the correlational findings by using causal models; both find low-level support for the covariation. Olweus (1981) used peer nominations for aggressiveness by 6th- and 9th-grade peers as criterion measures. He used a structured interview, similar in format to that designed by Sears et al. (1957), to evaluate child rearing practices. In each sample he particularly focused upon four main variables: the child's temperament, the mother's negativity, the mother's permissiveness for aggression, and the tendency for the mother and father to use power-assertive tactics in coping with the children. In the first sample the causal analyses showed the mother's permissiveness for aggression, the mother's negativism, and the child's temperament all contributed directly to the criterion measure of aggressiveness. The *PPM* correlations of these three variables with peer-nomination scores for aggression were in the range of .30 to .45. The multiple *R* testing for the causal model was .579. A similar pattern of relations was also found for the second, older sample. Here the range of *PPM* correlations was from .23 to .34, and the multiple *R* was .460.

The studies by Olweus (1981) have done much both to correct the difficulties with the earlier studies and to extend the pattern of findings. The difficult child in conjunction with an overly permissive, highly irritable mother is a familiar theme indeed. Note also that these three variables account for a substantial 20% to 30% of the variance in the children's aggressiveness. I believe that the coercion formulation overlaps to a considerable extent with the Olweus temperament-permissiveness-negativity triad. The OSLC definition of the family management variables may simply be a powerful extension of the last two variables in the Olweus triad. However, I think that the differences involve more than that.

The studies by Schuck (1974) and Olweus (1981) have been based upon samples of *normal, middle-class* children. However, the antisocial child (who is the topic of the present volume) is at or beyond the 90th percentile on measures of aggression. Using that standard, Olweus may have had three or four antisocial children in his first sample, and one or two in his second sample. Antisocial children and their families may be further out on a dimension of deviancy than the four samples studied by Schuck (1974) and Olweus (1981). I call this hypothetical dimension *Anarchy;* we will discuss this dimension in detail in a later section of this chapter. For the moment, suffice it to say that its definition includes several variables not explicitly referred to by the Olweus triad.

In addition, there are two tenets central to coercion theory that are *not* included in the Olweus triad. First, I assume that the parents of antisocial children are, generally speaking, unskilled people. As reviewed in Chapter 10, the studies showed that antisocial children viewed their parents as being less skilled; interviewers also perceive the parents of deviant children as less skilled (e.g., Sherman & Farina, 1974). They lack specific skills for punishing deviant behavior and supporting prosocial behavior. Secondly, I assume that the parents of Antisocials differ from those of Normals in their threshold values for categorizing behaviors as deviant (see Figure 11.2). Are these parental views about child deviancy *shaped* by the process of living with these children, or are they the determinants for it? I don't know. However, I *do* know that these views about *what* is deviant and what is not hamper clinical efforts to alter the course of the process once it has begun. Changing these parental perceptions is one of the most difficult aspects of the treatment process.

Ultimately, I think there comes a point when the parent begins to see the child as being *different* and to experience strong negative feelings about him (if he is a Social Aggressor, but perhaps not if he is a Stealer). Is it parental negative attribution and anger that make it so difficult to reverse these processes during treatment? Again, we do not know. There are miniature examples of this that also merit study. It's my impression that, following hospitalization for severe, nonpsychotic illness, many children return to their homes and are permitted to become highly coercive by well-intentioned parents. The parents explain the increase in coerciveness as an emotional upset caused by the child's separation from his family. But some children do *not* return to their prehospital baseline. Sigal (1974) followed previously hospitalized children for five years. Both the target child and his nonhospitalized siblings were ages 7 to 12 years at the time of the follow-up. The former patients were rated as significantly higher on the Petersen-Quay conduct problem scale. Why is this? I think one possibility is that as the coercive performance level climbs, the increasing skill and commitment of the child to this process means that it will be more *painful* to the adult who tries to change the child's behavior. Most parents of antisocial children avoid confrontations with their children. To a lesser degree this may also be what happens with the previously hospitalized child. In addition, the illness itself may give the child a "special" status to parents who feel that he has already suffered enough (see Chapter 13).

The coercive process may begin because the parent has a neglectful, laissez-faire attitude toward child rearing. However, the extremely antisocial child probably has a parent who is also relatively unskilled in teaching prosocial skills. An extended participation in the coercion process also implies that the parent has (or soon acquires) a selectivity about which child behaviors are categorized as deviant and which are not. These cognitions, in turn, relate to parental hesitation to punish antisocial behavior. If the coercive process is permitted to run its course, then it is no longer the caretaker who is in charge of family interactions. The reigning monarch is the socially aggressive child; he and his entourage maintain their hegemony by their skillful use of pain-control techniques.

Anarchy

Given a rejection of the caretaker role, there are several outcomes that may result. The material in Chapter 10 detailed the reduction in social interaction, shared leisure time, and increasingly negative perception of other family members that occur when the caretaker fails to use effective family management practices and the family becomes disrupted. There is also a collapse of the support and problem-solving functions of the family. Given that these disruptions have occurred, there is an accompanying process that is of clinical concern. I have dramatized this process by labeling it *Anarchy*. It represents a transitive sequence. Families at an advanced stage of Anarchy fulfill all of the requirements for the earlier stages. Each stage describes an increasing likelihood for the use of high-amplitude pain control, e.g., beatings and physical assault.

The Anarchy progression rests upon the assumption that the density of coercive interchanges covaries with intensity (Reid, Patterson, & Loeber, 1981). The analyses that support this assumption indicate that family members with high TAB scores are more likely to Hit. Higher TAB scores are also characterized by increasing proportions of extremely aversive behaviors. Given that one family member increases his or her coerciveness beyond the normal range, then the other members become increasingly at risk for being hit. A model for violence among family members is presented in

Figure 12.1. The normal coercion level for a family member is indicated by a blank square; as the coercion level rises, the square is darkened.

The second hypothesis is that as more dyads within the family become more coercive than normal, the risk for physical assault increases commensurately. The connecting lines in Fugure 12.1 indicate that the dyad is characterized by higher-than-normal rates of coercion. The data for the figure were taken from several published studies (Patterson, 1981b; Reid et al., 1981; Reid, 1978). One begins on the left side with normal amounts of coercion. The TAB scores for the normal sample showed a mean value of .21 for fathers, .26 for mothers, and .24 for siblings over the age of 7 (Reid, 1978).

Unfortunately, even among normal families there is some risk for physical assault. In a national probability survey the odds for a physical attack upon a wife were .038 (Straus, 1978). The odds for a child being hit with a fist or an object are probably somewhat higher. For the sample of "normal neighbors" interviewed by Gelles (1972), the odds that an assault had ever occurred in their families were a very high figure of .077. He sampled families from lower socioeconomic levels; I assume that the odds for an entirely normal sample would be considerably less than this. The point is that for a sample of "normal" families during any given year, there is a non-zero likelihood for physical violence. As a conservative estimate, about one family in 20 will include one or more persons who have been beaten.

The data show that for families from the Stealer sample, three of the four roles are noticeably more coercive than normal. The increases are most marked for the deviant child and the mother. The connecting lines show that the mother → target child and mother → sibling interchanges are significantly deviant. As noted in an earlier discussion, there is a strong likelihood that the mixed cases (Stealer plus Social Aggressor) are particularly at risk for child abuse. I assume that these families would also show a high percentage of dyads enmeshed in coercive interchanges.

To illustrate what the next step in the disorganization would look like, data are presented that describe a sample of families of Social Aggressor children. The increase in anarchy is portrayed by the fact that *all* four familial roles are implicated, and the level of coercion is now three to four times greater than that for Normals. The family is largely (but not completely) controlled by the children. The disorganization is not complete in that the role of father is only minimally in conflict with siblings and with the mother. However, even a casual

Figure 12.1
A Progression for Violence

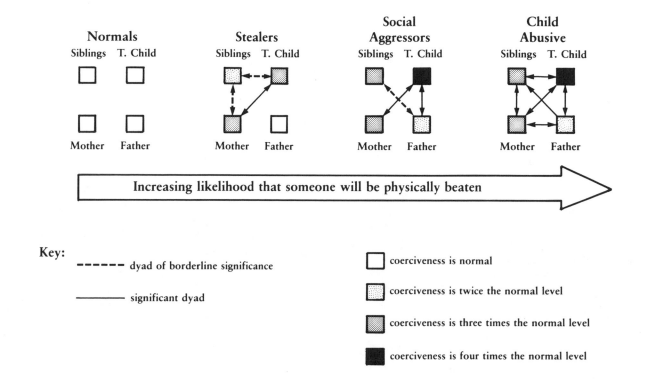

Increasing likelihood that someone will be physically beaten

Key:

- - - - - dyad of borderline significance

————— significant dyad

☐ coerciveness is normal

▫ coerciveness is twice the normal level

▪ coerciveness is three times the normal level

■ coerciveness is four times the normal level

observer would be struck by the fact that in these homes something is wrong. These are families in disarray. I assume that during any given year, one or more family members are at risk for being beaten. As yet there are no data that directly test this hypothesis.

The next step toward anarchy is exemplified by the abused-child sample studied in Reid et al. (1981).[1] As shown in Figure 12.1, *all dyads* are now committed to coercive conflicts. The Reid analysis showed that even the mother and father are significantly engaged in open warfare. The parents in these families were *observed to hit two to four times more often* than were parents of Normals. By definition, at least one child in each family was being beaten. No data are given for the number of beaten wives in this sample, but, clinically, it seems that it would be a sizeable number.

Even in these families anarchy is not complete. I think in most of the families, if the father were present, he would not permit the children to physically injure the mother, nor would the mother be an idle spectator to attacks upon the father. However, there are now appearing in the literature reports of attacks in which the father sits idly by

while the children physically disable the mother. It is hard to conceive of such a group; it is even more difficult to think of it as a "family." Here, anarchy reigns and coercion is king.

The Anarchy progression dramatizes what we see clinically. It may be that these structural changes are indeed accompanied by increasing risk for physical assault. That remains to be seen. The question is why do adults allow this to happen to them?

Mothers as a Storm Center

As noted earlier, young children are totally committed to maximizing short-term payoffs. If left to their own devices, a cluster of siblings would quickly shape each other to very high levels of coerciveness. The effectiveness with which the caretaker practices child management skills determines the level at which antisocial behaviors will be performed. The caretaker's selectivity in categorizing behaviors as deviant determines *which* antisocial behaviors will be permitted and which will be punished. As noted in Chapter 11, there seem to be several paths to antisocial behavior. One involved the adult (unattached to the caretaker role) who

Table 12.1
Comparisons of Mothers from Three Samples

	Mean rate per minute for mothers of:				
Code Categories	Stealers (N = 37)	Social Aggressors (N = 34)	Normals (N = 36)	F Values	Duncan Planned Comparisons
Approve	.055	.068	.097	2.65	
Attend	.709	.670	.786	.64	
Command	.413	.423	.280	4.95**	ST & SA > N
Command Negative	.059	.044	.011	4.07**	ST & SA > N
Comply	.028	.028	.010	5.79**	ST & SA > N
Disapprove	.298	.313	.131	12.12***	ST & SA > N
Laugh	.096	.108	.185	8.20***	N > ST & SA
Noncomply	.019	.012	.007	3.72*	ST > N
Negativism	.007	.008	.002	.77	
Normative	1.718	1.409	1.320	1.29	
No Response	.157	.087	.075	8.88***	ST > SA & N
Physical Negative	.015	.029	.004	2.90	
Physical Postive	.070	.065	.090	.33	
Talk	2.793	3.046	3.586	4.09*	N > ST
Tease	.011	.001	.003	1.15	
Touch	.011	.022	.019	.64	
Work	3.518	3.213	3.490	.31	
Yell	.023	.006	.001	4.14*	ST > SA & N

*$p < .05$
**$p < .01$
***$p < .001$

selectively categorizes coercion within the family as deviant but not acts committed outside of the caretaker's presence. As John Reid put it, "Out of sight, out of mind." These parents punished coercion within the family but permitted stealing, fire-setting, and vandalism as long as it did not occur in their presence. It is the second path that will be of concern for most of the following discussion.

On the second path, the irritable, unskilled caretaker (usually the mother) could simply function as a spectator to sibling-initiated chaos, but, typically, this is not the case. It is much more likely that the mother becomes deeply enmeshed in this process. She and/or the father are directly involved in 70% to 80% of all episodes involving the *target child* (see Table 11.6). The percentages were in the 90's for episodes involving a younger problem child reacting to aversive and/or neutral antecedents.[2]

It would follow, then, that mothers of problem children should differ in their general interaction style from mothers of Normals. The details of these differences are presented in Table 12.1. Generally, the mothers of problem children were more coercive (more Command, Command Negative, Disapprove, and Noncomply) and distant (more No Response, less Talk and Laugh) than were mothers of Normals.

At this point we encounter a mystery. It has to do with the fact that the parents of Social Aggressors are highly selective about *which child* the coercive involvement is focused upon! In one analysis, the contribution of the problem child was removed from the TAB scores for mothers and also for fathers and siblings (Patterson, 1981a). When this was done, there was little real difference between parents of normal children and parents of Social Aggressors. For mothers, the mean likelihood of coercive behavior was .050 and .051 respectively. The comparable values for fathers were .030 and .042. Given that the contribution of the problem child was included, then the means for mothers were .049 for Normals and .065 for Social Aggressors. This increase over the prior value

Table 12.2
Mean Irritability Scores for Three Samples of Mothers

Irritability Variables	Samples			
	Normals (N = 37)	Social Aggressors (N = 37)	Stealers (N = 38)	F Values
Mother's Reaction to Target Child				
Crossover	.021	.047	.041	11.00***
Counterattack	.150	.228	.164	4.12*
Punishment Acceleration	.288	.406	.299	2.45
Continuance	.122	.266	.217	15.00***
Target Child's Reaction to Mother				
Crossover	.007	.040	.027	8.00***
Counterattack	.093	.274	.156	20.82****
Punishment Acceleration	.148	.416	.337	11.64***
Continuance	.125	.321	.238	13.86***

*$p < .05$
***$p < .001$
****$p < .0001$

was significant at $p < .001$. The comparable means for fathers were .033 and .068 respectively. The increase for fathers of Social Aggressors was also significant at $p < .001$. It was true that, with or without the contribution of the problem child, the siblings in socially aggressive families were significantly more coercive than were siblings of Normals.

It seems, then, that there is something "special" about the identified problem child. Why is it that the parents look deviant primarily as a function of their inept handling of *this* child? They seem to be able to control the coercive initiations directed at them by siblings; why don't they cope equally well with the problem child? The parents permit siblings to be coercive with each other but not with them. The point is that parents of Social Aggressors are highly selective about their areas of incompetence. Why is this? In his review of the developmental literature, Bell (1968) noted very low correlations (in the .20's) between sibling reports of their home environment. He also emphasized the *lack* of maternal consistency in affectional behaviors across children. To these trends we would add that there may also be considerable imbalances in the irritability of parents toward children, particularly in distressed families. Do these parents have different deviancy criterion thresholds for the problem child than for the other children? Does the likelihood for parental irritable reactions

differ from one child to the next? These are crucial questions to be answered by the next round of research on coercion processes. They relate to the more general issue of how it is that one member of what is essentially a deviant system receives the label "deviant," while the others do not.

Caretaker Irritability

The hypothesis is that mother-Irritability is a key variable for the understanding of children's social aggression. Mothers provide the reactions that are crucial to the maintenance of high levels of coercive performance. The data that served as the base to test this hypothesis were drawn from samples of Normals, Social Aggressors, and Stealers (see Appendix 6.2 for details). The mean values for each irritability variable are summarized in Table 12.2. The data for mother-Crossover (given an interaction with the problem child) showed significantly higher values for the clinical samples than for the normal sample. Comparing values for mothers to those for fathers and siblings (Table 7.4) showed that in all samples there was a trend for parents to initiate more conflict with the problem child than did siblings. Examination of the child's disposition to start up conflicts with the mother showed a significantly greater effect for the clinical samples than for the normal sample. In the clinical samples the child was more likely to start fights with the mother than with any other

Table 12.3
Irritable Reactions as Covariants for Child Coercive Performance Level (TAB)

Member of dyad	N	Irritable Reactions to Problem Child								Multiple R	F Values
		Crossover		Counterattack		Punishment Acceleration		Continuance			
		r_{XY}	B†	r_{XY}	B	r_{XY}	B	r_{XY}	B		
Mother	93	.41***	.18	.21	−.13	.17	−.22	.46***	.58***	.506	7.41***
Father	68	.17	−.12	.14	−.27	.22	−.02	.42**	.63***	.471	3.41*

†These values are standard partial-regression coefficients. The asterisks describe the level of significance for the tests of significance for the beta.

*$p < .05$

**$p < .01$

***$p < .001$

family member.

The mothers of antisocial children were significantly more likely than those of Normals to punish coercive child behavior (counterattack). The Duncan Multiple Range Test showed that this effect was primarily due to the contribution of mothers of Social Aggressors. There did not seem to be major differences among family members in their disposition to counterattack when coping with the problem child (Table 7.6).

It is of particular interest to note that two laboratory studies have now demonstrated a relation between the mothers' likelihood of counterattack in the home and their system of categorizing child deviancy (Lorber, 1981; Littman, Freund, & Schmaling, in preparation). In comparing 24 mothers of Normals to 24 mothers of antisocial children, Lorber (1981) found the latter were more inclusive in differentiating negative from positive behavior; acts classed as normal by normal mothers were perceived as deviant by mothers in the clinical sample. Measures of the laboratory tracking variables were also shown to correlate significantly with the home observation data measuring the likelihood of mother-Punish given coercive child behavior. Mothers who tended to be overinclusive in categorizing were also more likely to punish. The second study employed a different series of videotaped family interaction for a sample of 27 mothers of Normals and 27 mothers of problem children. These parents were first asked to categorize the child behavior; on their second task they were asked to indicate when they would punish child behaviors (Littman et al., in preparation). The findings agreed with those from the Lorber (1981) study. As compared to Normals,

mothers of antisocial children were overly inclusive in labeling deviant child behavior. On the laboratory task they were significantly lower in their threshold for confronting and punishing the child. Their criterion threshold measure for Punish correlated .42 ($p < .05$) with their likelihood of punishing deviant child behavior in the home. These are important findings. While we are just beginning to explore what they mean, they do suggest a relation between mothers' cognition about deviancy and punishment and their observed behavior.

As shown in Table 12.2, mothers of antisocial children were not significantly different from Normals in their disposition to accelerate when punished by their child. Similar comparisons for siblings and fathers (Table 6.8) also showed nonsignificant differences. However, the problem child *was* significantly more likely than the normal child to accelerate when punished by his mother.[3] As shown in Table 6.8, he was no more likely to accelerate in his interactions with mothers than with fathers and siblings.

The mother's disposition to continue in her irritable reactions regardless of the child's reaction was significantly greater for the antisocial samples than for the normal sample. The comparable disposition for the child was also significantly greater for the clinical samples than for the normal sample. The Duncan Multiple Range Test showed each sample to be significantly different from the other two. It comes as little surprise to find that this disposition to continue is highly correlated for the mother and the problem child. As shown in Table 8.7, the correlation was .58 ($df = 91$, $p < .001$). As shown in Table 12.3, mother-Continuance (given her interaction with the problem

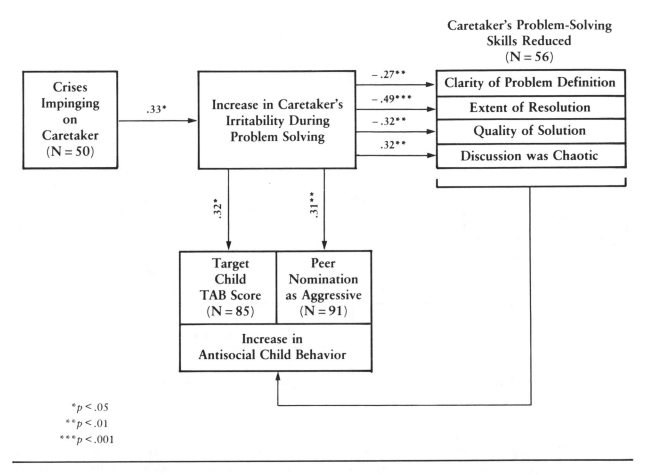

Figure 12.2
Caretaker's Irritability, Problem-Solving Skills, and Antisocial Child Behavior

*p < .05
**p < .01
***p < .001

child) accounted for a major portion of the variance in the child's baseline TAB score. The father's disposition for continuance was also the major variable correlating with the child's performance level. Interestingly enough, this was not the key variable for siblings; irritable reactions by siblings accounted for only half as much variance in problem child performance level as irritable reactions by parents (Patterson, 1981a). The fact that parent-Continuance also served as a major variable in accounting for variance in Parent Daily Report measures of child deviancy further emphasizes the importance of this particular measure of irritability (Patterson, 1981b).

The mother's disposition to react irritably is viewed as an alternative to problem solving. She reacts in such a way as to make the pain stop immediately; as noted in Chapter 7, she is the victim of a reinforcement trap of her own making. Rather than train the child, she scolds. Rather than confront the child and change his deviant behav-

ior, she natters and threatens. I believe that, in part, families train caretakers to be irritable. Irritability becomes a mode for dealing with children and others as well. I suspect that for some mothers irritability is generalized to persons outside the family; but, for present purposes, the key idea concerns the extent to which it generalizes across settings *within* the home. Again, I suspect that for mothers of antisocial children (Social Aggressors and Mixed), irritability becomes highly generalized. Thus far we have only two tests for the hypothesis.

Reid et al. (1981) found that in families of abused children the observed conflict between parents was several times higher than that for Normals. Forgatch and Wieder (1981) constructed a code system to categorize videotaped familial problem solving in a laboratory setting. The construct, mother-Irritability, was shown to correlate with an impressive array of criteria. As shown in Figure 12.2, irritable mothers reported themselves

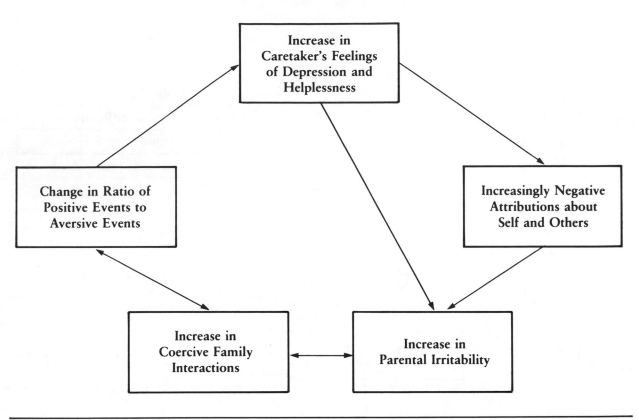

Figure 12.3
A Feedback Loop for Caretaker Depression

Increase in Caretaker's Feelings of Depression and Helplessness

Change in Ratio of Positive Events to Aversive Events

Increasingly Negative Attributions about Self and Others

Increase in Coercive Family Interactions

Increase in Parental Irritability

to have high frequencies of daily hassles. The observers' global ratings showed that families with irritable mothers tended to be less effective in solving their problems. Finally, the coded measure of mother-Irritability correlated with two different criterion measures of antisocial child behavior.

This study demonstrates that the maternal disposition to react irritably interferes, not only with her child management efforts, but also with familial problem solving. It does seem to be a generalized coping response that may serve some short-term purpose, but, in the long run, I think it increases the likelihood that more serious child management problems will occur. The unsolved crises will be added to the accumulation of past failures. I think, too, that this irritability reflects the presence of internal processes. The irritable mother sees herself differently than do other mothers. She feels angry about her family and the uncontrollable situation in which she finds herself. The following section explores these hypotheses.

Erosion of the Caretaker's Mood

Parental personality traits, such as the disposi-

tion to be irritable or to be delinquent, place the child at risk for antisocial problems. In keeping with our interactional stance, we also suspect that some parental dispositions are associated with their membership in a coercive system. The hypothesis is that prolonged immersion in coercive interchange places the individual at risk for depression. Constant conflict plus the lean schedules of positive reinforcement provided for mothers in these families place them at grave risk for depression. For parents of antisocial children, the ratio of positive to aversive events is very low. In part, it is a lack of parental skill that determines this ratio of positive to aversive experience. However, once the imbalance (with its concomitant feelings of depression) occurs, there are two additional outcomes. First, it is thought that there are increases in the likelihood of parental irritable reactions accompanied by an increase in negative attributions about other family members. As shown in Figure 12.3, both increases feed back into family processes to produce further increases in levels of aversive events. In effect, depressed reactions are viewed as the outcome of a process. Here, the depressed reaction feeds the process to further exacerbate an already bad situation.

Impact of Crises upon Mood

As a general case, it is assumed that caretaker skills *partially* determine the intensity and frequency of crises occurring within the family, e.g., conflicts among children or conflicts between parents. The data from a recently completed OSLC study showed that in normal families the mean frequency of crises reported by the parents covaried with the child's level of coerciveness. The greater the number of crises, the higher the child's TAB score. For the combined sample, the correlation was .31 ($df = 84$, $p < .01$). The correlations were higher for 4th graders (.42) than for 7th graders (.34). The family's problem-solving skills correlate with their ability to anticipate crises and to contain the impact of those crises that do arise. The general level of social skills also determines the amount of positive reinforcement from leisure activities, friends, and so forth. In this formulation, then, social-competency variables play a key role.

The literature reviewed in Chapter 4 detailed the frequency with which aversive events occur in normal family life and the higher rates that were obtained for families of antisocial children. The question is, do these aversive events covary with mood shifts? The data from the extended baseline studies presented in Table 4.3 showed such a covariation for three of the five mothers. Days characterized by many crises were also days in which the mother described herself as more depressed. The Hetherington, Cox, and Cox (1980) study of families getting a divorce also provided data that relate to this point. During the early stages of the separation, the mothers reported in an interview that they felt overwhelmed and disorganized by the demands placed upon them as a result of the separation. The interviewer ratings of economic stress correlated significantly with the mothers' reports on the Rotter I-E scale of increased sense of helplessness, i.e., things being out of their control. The stress ratings also correlated with a depression score obtained from ratings of mothers' diaries during this same interval.

The hypothesis presented earlier emphasized the imbalanced ratio of aversive to positive events for caretakers in families of antisocial children. If this is true, then one might expect these mothers to be more depressed than mothers of Normals. OSLC self-report data (MMPI) showed that mothers of antisocial children were elevated about one standard deviation above the mean normal level on the depression scale. There are also a series of studies by Rex Forehand relating to these issues. He, too,

found that maternal measures of depression were significantly higher for families referred for treatment, as compared to nonclinical families (Griest, Wells, & Forehand, 1979). In that study, maternal depression correlated with measures of child deviancy; mothers of deviant children were more likely to describe themselves as depressed.

Which variable was the cause, and which was the outcome? Does mother depression cause antisocial child behavior, or are both variables an outcome of the same process? There is only one study that relates to this issue, a short-term longitudinal study of families during separation and divorce (Hetherington et al., 1980). During the separation, both parent ratings and observation data agreed in identifying increasing out-of-control behavior for the children, particularly for boys. The aggression peaked at one year after separation and then dropped. Ratings of mood from the mothers' diaries showed significant correlations with ratings of child aggression (from that same source) and mothers' checklisting of child aggression. Of most interest were the cross-lag correlations that showed that child aggression early on correlated with the later measures of the mothers' mood. The findings suggested that early disruptions in child behaviors were *causally* related to mothers' later depressed reaction. However, these correlations lend themselves equally well to some alternative explanations, so these findings are not compelling. Even so, it seems reasonable to assume that maternal depression may be produced by child antisocial behavior.

Traditionally, it has been assumed that disturbed children have disturbed parents. For example, Rutter (1966) found that about one child in five with a behavior problem had parents with psychiatric problems. This was significantly greater than the comparable percentage obtained from a matched control group. On the MMPI clinical scales, however, parents of children seen at child guidance clinics did not score as high as parents who were actually psychiatric patients (McAdoo & Connally, 1975). Goodstein and Rowley (1961) compared MMPI profiles from parents of Normals to small groups of parents who had children referred for treatment with four different types of problems. The mothers of antisocial children tended to score significantly higher on depression, hysteria, and psychopathic deviate scales than did mothers of children with personality trait and/or neurotic problems. Wolking, Dunteman, and Bailey (1967) compared MMPI profiles for parents of six different groups of problem children referred for treatment. The mothers of antisocial children scored higher than mothers in the other

Table 12.4
MMPI Data for Several Samples of Mothers

	OSLC Samples					Samples from Other Settings		
MMPI Scale[1]	Social Aggressors (N = 25)	Stealers (N = 34)	Normals (N = 20)	F Tests[2] (df = 2, 78)	Duncan	Normals[3] (N = 50)	Normals[4]	Social Aggressors[5] (N = 29)
L	51.35	48.57	50.15	1.03		—	—	50
F	57.00	56.57	50.60	2.20		—	—	50
K	54.34	49.20	57.05	5.33*	SA & N > ST	—	—	59
Hs	55.35	54.83	47.10	8.47***	SA & ST > N	53	52	52
D	57.54	58.83	51.75	3.27*	ST > N	51	52	57
Hy	59.73	58.54	58.90	1.10		56	56	59
Pd	63.92	61.49	55.85	3.94*	SA & ST > N	54	53	56
Mf	45.04	45.49	43.20	.84		49	49	47
Pa	62.73	56.43	52.45	5.36**	SA > ST & N	52	54	56
Pt	57.50	56.54	50.90	5.98***	SA & ST > N	57	51	55
Sc	59.31	56.69	52.10	3.46*	SA & ST > N	54	52	54
Ma	56.08	56.23	49.10	3.84*	SA & ST > N	49	48	45
Si	57.23	59.71	51.90	3.11		—	—	51

[1]All scales are K corrected.

[2]The F Tests were based upon data for raw scores.

[3]Based upon 50 nonproblem families matched with families referred to the Child Psychiatry Service at Iowa Psychopathic Hospital (Goodstein & Rowley, 1961).

[4]Based upon a sample of nonproblem families matched with a sample referred to a child outpatient clinic for treatment (Liverant, 1959).

[5]Data from 29 families referred for treatment because of an aggressive child (Anderson, 1969).

*$p < .05$

**$p < .01$

***$p < .001$

groups on hysteria and psychopathic deviate scales and lower on the masculinity-femininity scale. The study by Anderson (1969) compared mothers of normal and neurotic children to mothers of antisocial children. The mothers of antisocial children had significantly lower scores on the masculinity-femininity scale.

The data in Table 12.4 summarize the findings for OSLC samples of mothers of 26 Social Aggressors, 35 Stealers, and 20 Normals (see Appendix 6.2 for description of samples). The results are consistent with the earlier analyses (Patterson, 1976, 1980a). Mothers in the clinical samples (as compared to mothers of normal children) showed consistent elevations on almost all of the clinical scales, including depression.

The findings that the clinical samples scored significantly higher on the psychopathic deviate scale replicates the finding from both the Goodstein and Rowley (1961) and the Wolking et al. (1967) stud-

ies. In fact, if one converts the raw scores on the scales to T-scores (with K corrected), it is apparent that this is the peak score on the MMPI profiles for mothers in the OSLC sample. The implication is that these are essentially angry, nonconforming women. That is extremely interesting because of the key role the mother's general irritability plays in determining the child's level of coercive performance. The next step will be to determine if this scale and the depression scores covary with measures of mother irritability.

It was of some interest to compare the MMPI scores for mothers of Stealers to the scores for mothers of Social Aggressors. Mothers of Stealers scored significantly lower on the K and Pa scales, but other than this, the differences between mothers in the two clinical samples were slight. The fact that the two groups scored equally high on the depression scale did not confirm an earlier finding for treated samples (Patterson, 1980a).

Mood, Attribution, and Family Management

The assumption is that the depressed mood of the caretaker may serve as a determinant for three components that further contribute to the disruption of the family. First, there is an increased likelihood of negative attributions about other family members, particularly the problem child. The mother begins to perceive her child as more deviant than he really is. Second (and this may be related to the first), she becomes increasingly more likely to be irritable in her reactions to others. Again, this is particularly true for her interactions with the problem child. Finally, she is likely to become increasingly disrupted in her practice of family management skills, which in turn relates to a commensurate increase in the child's antisocial behavior. The material to be reviewed in this section relates directly or indirectly to these three hypotheses.

It is assumed that depression is accompanied by increased negative attributions, not only about self, but about others as well. At this point, the caretaker begins to see other family members as "not caring." She might even perceive her problem child as intending to make her feel bad. These clinical impressions are supported by the interview data from the Weissman and Paykel (1974) study. Depressed women reported themselves to be generally more hostile to others than nondepressed women. The Novaco (1975) studies also showed a covariation between low self-esteem and the likelihood of attack and negative attributions about the victim. In the Forehand, Wells, and Griest (1980) study of oppositional preschool children, the mother's self-report score on depression correlated much better with her perceptions of child deviancy than it did with *observed* child deviancy. This is in keeping with Chamberlain's analysis of OSLC data (in preparation). In a replicated design, she demonstrated that more depressed mothers reported higher frequencies of deviant child behavior (Parent Daily Report).

The second hypothesis is that increases in the mother's dysphoric moods are associated with increases in her irritable reactions to the child. Thus far, this hypothesis has been tested in only one pilot study in which the covariation held for some dyads but not for others. The findings (Table 10.1 and Patterson, 1981b) are suggestive but hardly compelling.

Incidentally, mothers who are more depressed are not necessarily more coercive with their children. The correlation of mother-depression scores and her observed rates of coerciveness were not significant when tested in three different *across-subject analyses* (Johnson & Lobitz, 1974b; Patterson, 1981a; Forehand et al., 1980). It seems that the intradyad format, with its extended baseline design, may be a more appropriate design when investigating the impact of caretaker mood, crises, and so on upon child management practices (Patterson, 1981b).

There are no studies directly showing that on days when the mother is more depressed she is also less effective in her practice of family management skills. If that mood was shown to covary with coercive child behavior (Table 10.1), one might *assume* that family management practices were disrupted, but that, too, remains to be demonstrated.

Increased Family Management Skills Produce Change in Depression

It is assumed that the inept practice of family management skills produces increases in both crises and family conflicts, and that these, in turn, produce an increase in caretaker depression. If this is true, then successfully training the caretaker in the application of family management skills should reduce family conflicts, crises, *and* the caretaker's depression. The treatment program at OSLC is focused upon the task of teaching parenting skills to members of families of antisocial children (Patterson, Reid, Jones, & Conger, 1975). The treatment outcome data reviewed in Chapter 13 demonstrate that the parents have been successful in applying these skills; i.e., the deviancy levels are significantly reduced for almost all family members. I assume that the dramatic reduction in familial coercion, per se, is sufficient to produce a significant reduction in caretaker depression. I think the frequency of crises is also reduced, but as yet there has been no test of this idea.

To test this hypothesis, the MMPI questionnaire was administered at baseline and again at termination for a small sample of mothers of Stealers and mothers of Social Aggressors (Patterson, 1980b). The comparison showed a significant F value for trials for the decrease in the F scale ($F = 10.53$, $p < .003$) and for the increase in the K scale ($F = 7.98$, $p < .009$). On the clinical scales the decrease in depression ($F = 3.41$, $p < .076$) was of borderline significance, with a highly significant reduction in social introversion ($F = 13.40$, $p < .001$). For both of the latter the bulk of the decrease was contributed by mothers in the Social Aggressor sample. My confidence in these findings was considerably bolstered by the Forehand et al. (1980) replication. Fifteen mothers of oppositional preschool children were trained by student therapists to bring the child's noncompliance within normal range. This was accompanied by a significant reduction in the mothers' depression scores. The parents' perception of the children also became significantly more positive. A more positive perception of the problem child has also been a consistent outcome of social learning approaches to parent training (Patterson & Fleischman, 1979).

The findings from these studies point to an interesting difference between coercion theory and traditional formulations. Most clinicians writing about child guidance clinic populations have noted the high incidence of anxiety, depression, and somatic complaints reported by mothers of problem children. They assumed that these maternal traits were the *cause* of the child's problems and advocated therapy for the mother's neurosis as a means of helping the child. For the mothers of antisocial boys, we can see that these maternal problems may be the result of, rather than the cause for, the process. This being the case, it makes sense to teach her how to manage a difficult child as one means of reducing her depression.

Mothers of Social Aggressors are unskilled, irritable, and mildly depressed people. The irritability and lack of skill seem to be highly generalized, at least within family settings. However, she is often not the only adult present in these families. What, then, is the role of the father in this process?

The Father's Role in the Support System

For a preschool child, there is a need for the continuous involvement of a caretaker. As noted in Chapter 4, children of this age require a command or request from the parent at least once every three minutes. Given that the caretaker does more than just tell a child to stop doing something, or to do something he has not done, then the demands upon caretaker time increase commensurately. For example, teaching simple self-help skills requires hundreds of training trials. Deviant child behavior can and does increase very quickly in rate. These increases (trial runs) must be monitored and dealt with. The child must be monitored in terms of his chores, self-help skills, academic progress, and relationship skills with peers and family. If neither parent functions as a caretaker, then the child begins his drift toward both deficits in prosocial behavior and increases in antisocial behavior.

In some families the caretaker task is shared; in most instances the role is occupied by the mother.

"In the case of the single mother, whatever helps her to be *agentic* as well as *nurturant* will facilitate her ability to rear competent boys and girls. The function of social support systems for the single parent should be to help her or him to perform well both instrument and expressive functions. . . ." (Baumrind, 1979, p. 15)

Baumrind, in her lucid style, then goes on to emphasize the importance of what she labels as "symmetric" or shared child care. Chodorow (1978) also calls for "equal parenting." Both of these writers speak from a feminist position; however, neither would disagree that at least one person should be *committed* to the role of caretaker. There seems to be a general consensus in the literature that the commitment does not have to be made by the *biological mother* (as was once thought to be the case). Rather, it may be a shared role. It may also be assumed by professional caretakers, as demonstrated in the Israeli Kibbutz system. There a trained adult cared for a small group of infants and children, who were then returned to their working parents late each afternoon. These children received warmth and affection from teachers, peers, and parents alike. They also received skills training and supervision from both parents and supervisors. The studies of these experiments have consistently shown no ill effects resulting from sharing the caretaker role among a group of committed adults.

However, whether or not the caretaker role is shared, those who serve in this capacity do so only at a very high cost to themselves. The details of this cost have been presented in Chapter 4 and at other points throughout this volume. Even with a normal infant or preschool child, the cost to the caretaker is high. Given a difficult child plus a difficult marital and/or economic situation, then the cost may be overwhelming. By itself, there is little about the caretaker role, per se, that generates *positive* reinforcers. It is, rather, the function of the support system to provide positive experiences that will keep the ratio of aversive to positive experiences in balance. I believe that the father makes his primary contribution to family management by providing a support system. The caretaker (usually the mother) is primarily responsible for the child and family management. The father provides the back up (or support) necessary to maintain the skillful implementation of these management practices.

The caretaker support system can be put together in a number of ways. It may include a spouse, friends, relatives, or neighbors. However it is constructed, these are the people who provide outside contact, almost on a daily basis. It is these people who support the caretaker in their daily telephone calls, the coffee session, and in the quiet talk after dinner. I think the spouse can play a key role here, partly because he usually has more time to invest than friends and relatives (or agency workers)! At this point, I am not referring only to his reinforcing the caretaker for child management skills. I am referring to his role in bringing friends over, and in arranging pleasant weekend activities. This indirect support serves the important function of redressing the imbalanced ratio brought about by the presence of children and daily crises. Who is it that plans the pleasant activities for single-parent families living in isolation from relatives?

The second function that can be served by the father is that he can take *direct* responsibility for some aspects of child management. When he is home, and a sibling conflict arises, he can monitor, set consequences, and solve problems. He can also question the adolescent as to his/her whereabouts and negotiate the appropriate time for a return in the evening. Most fathers can and do carry out some adjunct child management activities, but the actual amount of time probably varies with the age of the child, social class, and employment status of the father. It is probably the case that even the most committed father actually handles only a small fraction of the daily round of child management problems. For example, the Fagot (1974) study of normal, middle-class toddlers showed that roughly 70% of child care was carried out by mothers and only 30% by fathers. It is my impression that in distressed families the fathers are even less involved than this. In a later section of this chapter we will examine the research findings relating to differences in interactive style between mothers and fathers.

The third function served by the spouse, or other members of the support system, is to provide a reserve force when the caretaker confronts the children on some crucial issue. If the caretaker sets up a house rule or negotiates an agreement, then it should be the case that the spouse supports and, if possible, monitors and enforces it. In this fashion the parents present a *united front*. Their cohesive stance communicates the message that in this household the parents are in control.

Most children (rightly or wrongly) *perceive* their fathers to be the more powerful parental figure. For example, a survey study by Kagan (1956) showed that 70% of elementary-school-aged girls and 83% of boys said they were more afraid of their fathers than their mothers. Roughly 60% reported that if they were bad, they were most likely to be punished by their fathers. Kolb and Straus (1974) obtained ratings from the children as to their parents' marital happiness. Then the families

participated in laboratory tasks measuring the relative dominance of the mother, father, and child. Regardless of social class, *child dominance* of either parent was associated with *less* perceived marital happiness. The negative correlations were higher for middle- than for lower-class families and were also higher when the mother was dominated by the child than when the father was dominated. I think that in most normal families the children perceive the alliance between the caretaker and the father as being more powerful than any coalition of children within the family. Sibling coalitions generally become effective only when the alliance between parents is disrupted. When the parents are in conflict, sibling-based coalitions have an increased likelihood of controlling the family.

Aside from the psychological effect of having the father present and in agreement, he is often an important contributor as a strategist in handling crises, as well as child management problems. Most young parents find it necessary to spend hours checking strategies with other parents, relatives, and friends. "What do you do when. . . ." The popularity of how-to manuals suggests the necessity for this kind of brainstorming of alternative ways to manage children. Who brainstorms alternative coping strategies with the adolescent single parent living in isolation?

Disruptions in Parental Alliance

The hypothesis is that disruptions in the caretaker's support system are likely to produce two outcomes. First, the impact of crises will be enhanced and perhaps lead to depression. Second, the caretaker is placed at risk for a disruption in her skillful performance of family management practices; this, in turn, produces an increase in antisocial child behavior.

A study by the anthropologists Goody and Groothues (1979) provides data in keeping with the first hypothesis. Field notes were collected on 20 West African couples working in London as to the frequency and intensity of crises. The couples were also categorized as to whether the spouses jointly shared in caretaking responsibilities or whether their roles were segregated in relation to domestic chores, finances, leisure, parental roles, and future planning. The analysis showed that if the couples retained their traditional segregated roles, they were more likely to be rated as under high stress. A jointly shared role structure, on the other hand, was related to lower stress. These findings are in keeping with the study of families involved in divorce (Hetherington et al., 1976, 1980). The separation produced a marked increase in stress reported by both husbands and wives. Each reported difficulty in coping with the functions and duties previously fulfilled by the other person. Incidentally, in the 1980 report, Hetherington showed that for both intact and divorced families there was less deviant child behavior when the parents agreed upon child discipline than when they disagreed; i.e., when the alliance regarding child management was still intact.

If there is severe marital conflict, the support system is likely to be disrupted. This does not happen for all couples in conflict; there are undoubtedly some who continue to cope with crises and family management problems even though they are in severe conflict over some aspect of their relationship. However, I think that for most parents the effects of their conflict generalize and reduce their efficiency in the performance of child and family management practices. As yet there is no study that directly shows a breakdown in family management skills during marital conflict, but Rutter et al. (1976) cites several studies showing a relation between marital discord and children's conduct problems. Similarly, the review by Oltmanns, Broderick, and O'Leary (1977) showed that, in general, parents of children referred for treatment were less satisfied with their marriages. In their study of cases referred for treatment, they found negative correlations in the $-.3$ to $-.4$ range between parental ratings of child deviancy and marital satisfaction. Johnson and Lobitz (1974b) took the analysis one step further by providing independent measures of the two variables. The mothers and fathers of 36 young, antisocial children referred for treatment filled out the Locke-Wallace measure of marital satisfaction. These scores were correlated with the referred child's observed rate of deviant behavior. The correlations showed that marital disruptions covaried with increases in child deviancy.

Burgess and Conger (1976) observed family interaction in the homes of normal and abused families. Among other things, they found that mothers from the abuse sample complied with *spouse* requests only 20% of the time, as compared to 64% compliance for women in the control families. One suspects marital conflict, but it was not directly measured in that study. In their comparison of Abused Child, Social Aggressor, and normal families, Reid et al. (1981) found that in families of abused children, the rates of parental coercive interchanges were shown to be 18 times higher than those found for either of the other samples! These findings provide only indirect support for the assumed relation between the disruption of family management practices and marital discord.

They do, however, run contrary to some ideas that are currently popular, e.g., marital fighting is inevitable, necessary, and desirable (Charny, 1969). On the contrary, severe and repetitive marital discord is indicative of a disintegrating family structure. The fights *may* serve a short-term cathartic function for the spouses, but in the long run it means a disruption in the support system required by the caretaker and commensurate increases in child deviancy.

Empirical Definitions of the Father's Role

It was stated earlier that fathers served a dual role in maintaining the family as a system. One role is direct and the other is indirect. When the father is present, it would be expected that he would carry out some child management responsibilities, as well as support the caretaker in her efforts. Are the observed behaviors of fathers discernibly different from those of mothers? Are the interactions of fathers in clinical families different from those of fathers in normal families?

The data in Table 12.5 summarize the comparisons for two samples that would tend to show maximum differences in parental behaviors. Mothers and fathers were compared for samples of *intact* Social Aggressor and intact normal families (see Appendix 6.2 for details). The 2×2 analysis of variance was done separately for each code category. Six of the 29 comparisons were significant. Fathers in both samples performed the following behaviors more often than did mothers: Attend, Normative, and Tease. They were significantly less involved than mothers in the use of Command, Touch, and Work. As a pattern, these findings suggest the role of a somewhat playful spectator. When the observers were present, the fathers tended to spend more time than mothers engaging in No Response (NR), or they quietly watched (AT) what was going on. Fathers also Tease and Play more often; there was a borderline trend for lower TAB scores. It may be stretching things a bit to label the father as a resident "good guy," but he does leave the major child management category (Command) up to the mother. It is also the mother who engages in the necessary housework, while the father Attends, or sits and reads. The teasing may represent a kind of verbal playing analogous to findings for fathers in infant and toddler research. Both Lamb (1976) and Clarke-Stewart (1978) observed fathers to be significantly more playful than mothers. It is interesting to note that in the latter study the fathers' involvement in play and the duration of his interactions with the toddler correlated with measures of infant IQ at the age of 3.

Table 12.5
A Comparison of Parents from Normal and Clinical Samples

| Code Categories | Mean Rate for Samples | | | | F Values by: | |
| | Social Aggressors | | Normals | | | |
	Mother (N = 16)	Father (N = 16)	Mother (N = 26)	Father (N = 26)	Sample	Parent
Approve	.085	.041	.111	.085	3.21	3.08
Attend	.845	1.072	.737	1.029	.30	4.07*
Command	.433	.264	.289	.190	6.95**	9.70**
Command Negative	.027	.020	.012	.017	1.14	.02
Comply	.024	.020	.011	.018	2.32	.33
Disapprove	.274	.251	.122	.107	18.21***	.28
Dependency	.000	.000	.000	.001	1.65	1.02
Humiliate	.007	.009	.002	.001	4.94*	.00
Ignore	.027	.030	.010	.003	2.02	.83
Laugh	.132	.102	.193	.003	2.92	2.97
Noncomply	.007	.014	.007	.005	1.05	.07
Negativism	.002	.004	.003	.004	.04	.39
Normative	1.333	3.352	1.243	2.645	2.18	38.98***
No Response	.095	.087	.067	.076	1.61	.03
Play	.587	1.190	.982	1.122	.31	1.25
Physical Negative	.007	.006	.004	.001	3.72	1.49
Physical Postive	.086	.107	.104	.047	.31	.77
Receive	.008	.012	.007	.014	.06	2.16
Self Stimulation	.008	.033	.003	.008	3.40	2.38
Talk	3.299	2.819	3.462	3.265	1.54	1.63
Tease	.008	.032	.004	.013	2.24	4.23*
Touch	.063	.011	.026	.011	1.66	3.99*
Work	3.310	.716	3.667	1.573	2.84	42.75***
Yell	.006	.007	.001	.000	5.46*	.08
TAB	.800	.637	.452	.342	18.02***	3.16

*$p < .05$
**$p < .01$
***$p < .001$

The data in Table 12.6 summarize the mean rates of occurrence for each of the FICS categories for three samples of fathers of Stealers, Social Aggressors, and Normals (see Appendix 6.2). While there were only a few significant findings, the pattern was similar to that which was obtained for a similar comparison for mothers. Fathers in the clinical samples tended to be more distant (NR), less talkative (TA), more aversive (DI), and less approving (AP) than were fathers of Normals. It should be emphasized that the findings defining this pattern are few in number. This reduced set of variables did successfully discriminate among the groups in the discriminant-function analysis that appeared in Chapter 11. The significant functions were a weak reflection of those that were obtained for mothers. Fathers of Stealers were more distant in contrast to the other two samples. Fathers of Social Aggressors and Stealers were more coercive than were fathers of Normals.

Fathers' Irritability

The data summarized in Table 12.7 suggest that there are differences in the fathers' irritability as they react to the target child for samples of both normal and distressed families. The fathers in the clinical samples were signficantly more likely than fathers of Normals to crossover and to continue. Note, too, that the fathers were more likely than the problem child to start up a conflict.

Table 12.6
Comparisons of Fathers from Three Samples

Code Categories	Mean rate per minute for fathers of			F Values	Duncan
	Stealers (N = 25)	Social Aggressors (N = 14)	Normals (N = 26)		
Approve	.047	.039	.085	5.00**	N > ST & SA
Attend	.927	1.040	1.030	.19	
Command	.221	.291	.190	1.80	
Command Negative	.037	.021	.017	1.47	
Comply	.020	.020	.018	.04	
Disapprove	.165	.272	.107	4.94**	SA > ST & N
Laugh	.090	.100	.136	1.31	
Noncomply	.012	.015	.005	1.13	
Negativism	.005	.004	.004	.09	
Normative	3.325	3.309	2.645	1.34	
No Response	.136	.092	.077	3.35*	ST > N
Physical Negative	.008	.007	.001	2.23	
Physical Positive	.039	.113	.047	2.46	
Talk	2.373	2.852	3.265	3.31*	N > ST
Tease	.010	.036	.014	2.18	
Touch	.006	.009	.011	.34	
Work	1.585	.686	1.573	1.64	
Yell	.004	.007	.000	1.56	

*$p < .05$
**$p < .01$

Table 12.7
Mean Irritability Scores for Three Samples of Fathers

Irritability Variables	Samples			F Values
	Normals (N = 26)	Social Aggressors (N = 14)	Stealers (N = 25)	
Father's Reaction to Target Child				
Crossover	.013	.038	.022	6.91**
Counterattack	.078	.143	.103	2.33
Punishment Acceleration	.251	.496	.308	3.11
Continuance	.111	.262	.203	9.04***
Target Child's Reaction to Father				
Crossover	.004	.019	.016	1.58
Counterattack	.079	.184	.131	4.67*
Punishment Acceleration	.038	.414	.244	13.59***
Continuance	.049	.283	.202	9.70***

*$p < .05$
**$p < .01$
***$p < .001$

The multivariate analysis (Table 12.3) showed that the fathers' irritable reactions were significantly correlated with the child's coercive performance level. The multiple correlation between the fathers' p values for irritability and the children's TAB scores was .471. The F value was 3.41 ($p < .05$). While Father's irritability adds something to our understanding of the child's performance level, it can be seen from Table 12.3 that the measures of fathers' behavior account for less variance than the comparable measures of mothers' behavior. A further analysis showed that when the measures of p(Continuance) for fathers and mothers were combined, the measure of mother irritability accounted for all of the unique variance (Patterson, 1981b).

In terms of understanding the families of antisocial children, my general sense is that the information about fathers' interaction is only a weak reflection of what we already know from analyses of the mothers' data. This reiterates the theme that the burden of the caretaker role falls primarily upon the mother. What the father does in the way of child management is similar, but he does less of it. His interactions with the children determine less of their behavior. The question that continually presents itself is, why don't the fathers in clinical families perceive that the caretakers' child management procedures are not working and introduce new procedures? Why does he imitate the techniques used by the mother when they are ineffective?

Fathers' Self-Report

As noted earlier, when the family is severely stressed by conflicts from within or crises from without, it is the caretaker who bears the brunt. The accompanying hypothesis is that fathers are usually only slightly affected by such stressors. The feelings of anxiety, depression, anger, confusion, and isolation that characterize caretakers in distressed families are *not* a part of the self-perceptions of fathers. I think this is partially related to the fact that they do not see family management as being a significant feature of their responsibility. Earlier pilot studies showed that their self-perceptions were like those of fathers in nondistressed families (Patterson, 1976, 1980a).

The study by Tavormina, Boll, Dunn, Luscomb, and Taylor (1975) was very revealing. The sample involved physically handicapped children whose very presence engenders extreme stress for parents. However, in this case the child's problem was unlikely to have been produced directly by any psychopathology in the parents. Their careful study of physically handicapped children showed that fathers perceived fewer problems than did mothers. On self-report questionnaires the fathers were also less depressed, anxious, irritable, and unstable than were the mothers. The mothers, on the other hand, described themselves as being severely stressed; in fact, their self-statements produced profiles that were similar to those for mothers of antisocial children. The findings are in keeping with the hypotheses being presented here. The caretaker seems to be the one who bears the full brunt of familial stress. The father is only secondarily involved. In addition, I suspect that the positive experiences from his work are sufficient to keep his ratio of aversive to positive experiences in fairly good balance.

Do fathers of antisocial children describe themselves differently than fathers of nonproblem children? Earlier studies suggested few differences in MMPI scores for two small samples (Patterson, 1976, 1980a). Table 12.8 summarizes the findings from OSLC samples of Social Aggressors and Stealers (Appendix 6.2). At this point, we have data for a sample of only eight normal fathers; these data were not included here. For this reason, the OSLC clinical samples must be compared with the Goodstein and Rowley (1961) and Liverant (1959) samples from fathers of nonproblem children. The OSLC samples were of modest size, but, even so, none of the differences exceed .5 SD between the sample of fathers of children referred as Aggressors from the Anderson (1969) study, or the two OSLC clinical samples.

The most noteworthy finding was that none of the clinical samples differed markedly from either sample of fathers of normal children. Unlike the mothers of antisocial children, fathers of antisocial children did not report themselves as being more angry and depressed than normal parents. The fathers of antisocial children, like the fathers of handicapped children, seem to have some kind of acquired immunity that protects them from familial stressors. Given that the family is disrupted, how does the father protect himself from the stress?

Single-Parent Families

As already noted, in most families the function of the father is to carry out *some* child management practices and to provide a back up and support system when needed. To this I would like to add one further function. I think in normal families the father also serves as a corrective factor for the caretaker when she begins to drift into inept or deviancy-producing management techniques. I think that in the normal course of events most of us drift toward the use of techniques that maxi-

Table 12.8
MMPI Data for Several Samples of Fathers

| MMPI Scale | Mean T scores for OSLC Samples[1] | | Mean T scores from Other Samples | | |
	Aggressors (N = 12)	Stealers (N = 21)	Aggressors Anderson (1969)	Normals Goodstein & Rowley (1961)	Normals Liverant (1959)
L	51.00	49.81	46	—	—
F	53.08	53.43	53	—	—
K	56.69	54.33	53	—	—
Hs	54.46	53.19	54	53	52
D	56.62	54.62	56	51	53
Hy	59.77	57.43	56	56	56
Pd	60.54	60.00	64	55	56
Mf	59.00	58.88	54	58	57
Pa	57.00	52.05	53	52	52
Pt	58.62	52.05	54	52	52
Sc	57.92	53.90	55	51	52
Ma	55.69	57.48	55	51	53
Si	48.50	54.29	52	—	—

[1]These scores were K corrected.

mize short-term payoffs, i.e., we become more coercive. It is the corrective impact of feedback from a spouse, friends, and relatives that keeps this drift in check. If the relation is disrupted, and/or the spouse neglects this corrective function, then I think the caretaker becomes increasingly at risk to drift into irritable reactions and to be inconsistent in tracking and punishing antisocial behavior. By definition, single parents would be more at risk for such a drift.

There are several aspects of our contemporary culture that contribute to disruptions in caretaker performance. The population is highly mobile, as shown by the estimate that about one family in seven moves each year (Coates, 1978). Even if the move were only to another residence within the same community, it would still mean a disruption in the support system normally provided by neighbors. A shift to another city would mean an even larger disruption in the support network of friends and relatives. The trend for increases in the number of single-parent families is even more alarming. As noted by Coates (1978), approximately 45% of children born in 1976 will live with a single parent for some period of time. Earlier, the hypothesis was presented that a severe crisis such as separation or divorce is itself associated with prolonged disruptions in family management and is

expected to be accompanied by increases in out-of-control behavior.

The clinical literature has emphasized the relation between broken homes, delinquency, and antisocial behavior (see Chapter 2). For example, Rutter et al. (1970) found that 25% of the antisocial children studied resided in father-absent homes, as compared to a figure of 14.6% for matched controls. M. Hetherington engaged in a series of studies that further elucidate the process. In her first study, she compared intact, father-absent-due-to-death, and father-absent-due-to-divorce homes (Hetherington, 1972). Relatively large samples were compared using an impressive variety of assessment procedures. The findings suggest that for girls, father-absent-due-to-divorce was associated with greater loss of self-esteem, more heterosexual activity, and more conflict with mothers. Many of these effects were exacerbated if the separation had occurred earlier rather than later in the girl's development. In her next studies she compared samples of normal families with families in the process of separation and divorce (Hetherington, Cox, & Cox, 1980). The observation data from both the home and the laboratory concurred in demonstrating an increase in child deviancy for the divorced group. For example, during the first year following separation, there was a significant increase in child noncompliance for boys and girls. The Wallerstein and Kelly (1980) clinical studies of children from families getting a divorce showed a similar outcome. The parents reported that their lives were disrupted for two or three years during the process. Again, there was a general increase in aggression (including stealing) for the children involved. Her case studies give some fascinating details on the difficulties encountered by some of the mothers in effectively managing their children.

Single-parent families do indeed seem to be at greater risk in terms of the likelihood of producing an out-of-control child. It would be useful to know what proportion of single-parent families do, in fact, have antisocial children. I believe that it is also the case that in these families, when the child is out of control, there is a greater likelihood that his performance will be *more extreme,* i.e., his rates are higher than those found for out-of-control boys from intact families. Oltmanns, Broderick, and O'Leary (1977) noted a trend of this kind in their analysis of 62 cases referred for treatment. At OSLC we have noted that single-parent families seemed to produce problem children who coerced and/or stole at extremely high levels (they also seemed difficult to treat). Horne (1980) corroborated this with his analysis of the first few dozen cases referred to OSLC. He compared intact and father-absent families for both normal and out-of-control samples (see Chapter 2). For the normal sample, father presence or absence did not significantly relate to increased coercive behaviors for any family members. However, given a sample of out-of-control families, those with absent fathers tended to have coercive rates twice as high as those for intact families. For the problem child the mean TAB scores were .98 and .41, for mothers .68 and .36, and for older sisters .99 and .13 respectively.

In intact families there is at least a possibility that if one parent is inept in the practice of one or more family management skills, the other may have these skills. If, under temporary stress, things get out of control, they can combine forces to halt the increase in rates of coercive behavior. However, in the single-parent family, the person who ends up as caretaker may be the more unskilled parent. What M. Hetherington calls the "buffering effect" is no longer in operation. The corrective feedback, the back-up punisher, the sympathetic colleague, and fellow negotiator is no longer available. The single parent reacts in an irritable, non-problem-solving manner and loses battle after battle as the coercion levels increase in frequency and amplitude. Here we understand the contribution of the father by observing what happens when he is no longer present.

Footnotes

1. John B. Reid pointed out a fundamental oversimplification in the Anarchy progression. Many of the child-abuse cases now being treated at OSLC consist of parents who have "won." Their children are relatively low-level coercers who are definitely controllable by normal means. The parent, however, when irritated (which is often), expresses it, not by nattering, but by brutal attacks. It seems likely, then, that there may be several paths or progressions that move to assault. The Anarchy progression is only one.

2. The reader should keep in mind that during a session each family member, in turn, served as the target for observation. If two different dyads were in conflict simultaneously, then the observer would record only the behavior that involved the target subject. Given that this occurred seldom (and I think this is the case), then the percent of mother involvement used here is a slight overestimate of the true state of affairs.

3. The reader should recall that this index is somewhat confounded in that it reflects the disposition to extend coercive chains *and* the disposition to extend when punished.

Chapter 13
Abstract

This chapter is a more phenomenological approach to the antisocial child and his family. An effort is made to describe different types of families who are referred for treatment because one or more children are antisocial.

There is also a brief review of the OSLC studies evaluating the outcome of family intervention. This includes replication, follow-up, and the four comparison studies completed thus far.

Chapter 13

Clinical Contacts and Treatment Outcomes

Over the last decade and a half the staff at OSLC has treated and studied over 250 families of antisocial children. The children in these families (both boys and girls) ranged from 3 to 15 years of age. The referral problems for these children included stealing, firesetting, chronic delinquency, conduct problems, and child abuse. At a clinical level, we know more about these families than we have been able to express within the empirical framework of coercion theory. There is a sense of repeating patterns that suggest we should consider constructing a typology for these families. As a staff, we have discussed this possibility but have not yet been able to find the time to initiate the appropriate studies. Nevertheless, I think it is useful to include the outlines of what the clinical staff perceives as a typology. It may prove useful in designing different treatment strategies for different families. Better yet, it may motivate other investigators to systematically study the problem.

It doesn't seem appropriate that the reader could complete a volume about antisocial children without being exposed to what it is like to interact with such children. The classic series of articles and books by Redl and Wineman (1951, 1957) provide a literate and, I think, accurate description of the behavior of socially aggressive children. Their viewpoint is that of therapists deeply involved in trying to help the child adjust to a residential treatment setting. Their graphic account

reiterates a dual theme of anger and unpredictable explosions. The following captures the flavor of such interactions:

". . . abstractedly he undressed himself and began to soap and wash himself, still retaining the kind of somnambulistic facial expression that had first attracted my attention. Suddenly, in a savage outpouring of verbalization, he began to curse with the most primitive swear words at nothing at all. When I asked what was wrong, he shifted to his mother, saying she was a no good bitch, a fucker, was never any good, he hated her, his goddam brother was mean and wouldn't help his father who was going to die and he, Bill, had to go home and help out." Entry: Paul Deutschberger) (Redl & Wineman, 1957, p. 105)

Other investigators showed that the treatment program designed by Redl and Wineman produced significant changes in the behavior of these boys *in the residential setting* (Raush, 1965). However, when the boys were returned first to foster homes and, within a few months, to their own homes, these gains were quickly lost.

". . . thus our 'children who hate' went back into limbo of 'the children that nobody wants.' The spectacle of their retraumatization of strengths that had been so painfully, if incompletely, implanted in their personalities being literally wasted in a battle with a hostile environment, is one that fades slowly, if at all, from our minds.

"And we are still having trouble in recovering from our amazement that . . . it would remain impossible to create adequate treatment channels to rescue these five lives." (Redl & Wineman, 1957, pp. 556-557)

During the 1950's and 1960's, others of us who attempted to work with such children experienced a similar sense of bewilderment and frustration. The fact that some of our best psychotherapists working with a *small* number of clients in *well designed* residential treatment settings could not produce *lasting* change underlined the necessity for coming up with an alternative formulation. We needed a new treatment for aggression. Redl and Wineman's program was the best of its kind, but it conceptualized the problem as being *within the child*. This is in stark contrast to current perspectives (including our own) that view the problem as being *in the family*. This means that effective treatment must make provision for altering the reactions of family members *to* the child and his reactions to them as well. One cannot just place the child in a residential setting, change his behavior, then return him to his family and expect the treatment effects to persist. The family members' well established patterns of interactions, expectations, and feelings will quickly reinstate the child's old, familiar habits. Halfway houses and residential centers give a welcome respite to the community, but they do not produce lasting changes in behavior (cf. review by Patterson, 1980b).

Regardless of one's persuasion about this or that form of treatment, most of us experience the antisocial child in the same way. The following case is introduced to give a sense of what the clinical "experience" is like.

When I met him, he was 6½ years of age. There was nothing about his appearance that identified him as the boy who had set the OSLC project record—his baseline TAB score was an Olympic caliber 3.7 coercive responses per minute! A trim four-footer, he had a sleazy look about him, like a postcard carried too long in a hip pocket. He sat in the reception room, slouched down in the chair and cooly looked me over as I approached. While his mother hardly looked up at my approach, his father seemed friendly enough and said he was glad the treatment was finally about to begin.

We then walked down the hall, renewing the relationship that was begun at the initial interview but was disrupted by the two weeks of baseline study. From the beginning the parents thought it might be necessary to institutionalize their son.

The violence of his temper outbursts was frightening and seemed to be triggered by relatively minor provocations. At school, a simple request to turn in his homework, a mild rebuke, or a suggestion that he had erred in his work could lead to shouted obscenities, overturned desks, or attacks on other children with a pencil held as a dagger. The observers commented that in the home he ruled whatever territory he occupied.

At home, the behaviors coded showed extended bursts made up of Whines and Yells, interspersed with shouted Disapprovals, Noncomplies, and physical attacks upon family members and furniture. During the intervals when he was absent from home, telephone calls would often mark his progress through the neighborhood, e.g., he left school two hours early, stole candy from a store, and appropriated a toy from a neighborhood child.

No baby-sitter would brave this storm center, so the parents had long ago given up the idea of a private life, movies, or weekends together. Both parents worked. The mother (not yet 30 and physically attractive) looked as if she was in the throes of a severe illness. The family physician provided medication for her chronic depression and accompanying fatigue. Work was a reprieve from her morning and afternoon bouts with her son, Don. Our treatment regime provided two therapists in attendance in the home whenever Don was present. Typically, her day began at 7:00 a.m., rousing him from his wet sheets (which *she* changed), then scolding until he went sullenly to his tub. Once there, she washed and dried him as if he were an infant or visiting royalty.

He often dawdled while dressing, which produced a stream of prompts and commands from his mother. Suggested items of clothing were refused; this led to bitter exchanges with the now thoroughly exasperated mother. He emphasized their disagreements by kicking the door and throwing things around the room. Through all of this the mother hovered about, helping to get him dressed. She alternately cajoled and scolded, wheedled and glared.

She stood in attendance while he dined. Not only did she serve, but she finally fed him whenever he deigned to open his mouth. Through it all ran a steady cacophony of yells, cries, and arguments about whether his mother had any right to force these unreasonable requests upon him. The mother alternated between patient and antagonistic answers to his arguments and threats. At one point, she brought a stick from behind the refrigerator door. Her menacing demeanor left little doubt that she regularly employed this weapon. In the face of this ultimate threat, Don showed temporary compliance and moved forward in his glacial progress toward leaving for school.

In the afternoons Don returned from school to pick up the morning refrain. His 4-year-old brother was also available as a partner. The latter (a Machiavellian of considerable stature) knew when to probe, when to attack, and when to withdraw with tearful protestations to the protection afforded by his parents. For example, as Don sat eating his ice cream (with his fingers), the younger brother surreptitiously slipped a more efficient spoon into the mess and ran triumphantly down the hall to hide behind the door in his bedroom. Don ran shrieking after him, grabbed the door, and repeatedly slammed it into his younger brother. The screams brought both parents to the scene. The father listened for a moment to their shouted claims and counterclaims. After a brief pause, he simply began to slap both children. With that, the mother turned, walked quietly back into the kitchen and sat staring out the window.

Later the family was to go for a ride in the car. Both parents began shouting commands. In the rush of the moment, they often overlapped in their targets; e.g., the mother said, "Don, wash your face right now," while the father ordered, "Put on your jacket, Don. Hurry up now." A steady stream of commands was given as they moved toward the car. The children moved at their own pace, largely ignoring both parents.

During the day, the observers noted periods where the interactions seemed warm and positive. For example, on numerous occasions one parent would read to the children, who would often sit for long periods of time entranced with the story. At these times they seemed to be the prototypical loving family unit.

During treatment, the mother expressed considerable doubt that Don could be changed by their efforts. The father, on the other hand, seemed more sanguine. It soon became apparent that the mother was incapable of participating in a program that required her to punish either of her children. The children had perfected a simple means of controlling their mother. It also worked reasonably well on their father. If a parent tried to use time out, their efforts were met with howls of outrage and an inevitable retreat by the parent. When encouraged by the therapist to persist, the mother would often break into tears and disappear into her bedroom. The cost of confrontation was simply too high.

Not all of the children we treat are so unremitting in their coercive efforts. Not all parents are so thoroughly defeated by their children. However,

the theme of coercion (and variations on this theme) is recognizable. The anger of the child and the deference with which he is attended raise the question of why these parents allow themselves to be defeated in this way? Experience with these families suggests that there is no single answer to this question. There are a number of paths to this same outcome. What follows is a series of descriptions of the different family types that produce antisocial children. The accounts are based partially upon what the parents have reported and, in part, reflect our reconstruction of how the process might have begun. Even though the resulting typology is purely descriptive, it might serve several useful functions. For one thing, it offers a set of hypotheses that might be tested in longitudinal studies that attempt to predict which families will produce problem children. Secondly, we believe that the family types might covary with the amount and/or kinds of resistance generated by the therapists' attempts to help these families change themselves (Patterson, Reid, & Chamberlain, in preparation). In either case, it seems appropriate to present these untested hypotheses as a first step in constructing a typology of problem families.

Speculations about Family Typology

It should be kept in mind at the outset that the vast majority of the cases studied have been from welfare, blue-collar, and working-class families. I am sure that what these families have to teach us is different from what might be learned from studying middle-class families with older adolescents. For this reason, the typology to be presented (and many aspects of coercion theory) may not fit what a private practitioner experiences in working with families of antisocial children.

At one point we tried to conceptualize the main dimensions that could account for why families produce antisocial children, and then use them to construct a typology. The resulting structure simply did not adequately reflect the full range of family types. We then set about simply listing them and ignored the fact that they do not fall along any particular set of dimensions. Some of the types reflect particular roles played by one or more parents. Others refer to variables that had something to do with starting the process and/or maintaining it.

We believe that these types relate to different experiences in therapy. Most families who receive training in child management do *not* proceed in a textbook fashion through the various components. For many of them (particularly for families with abused children and chronic delinquents), there are major difficulties. The child *and the parents* may be extremely resistive to doing what they have agreed to do. They may also resist coming to an agreement. In some of these families, up to 30% or 40% of their behavior has been coded as resistive (Patterson, Reid, & Chamberlain, in preparation). The hypothesis is that the family typology may tell us something about the amount and kind of resistance that is encountered.

The Parent-Sibling

When you enter the room for your first meeting with this single-parent family all of the family members are dressed in Levi's, and all are slouched down in their chairs. It is not at all apparent which one is the parent (see Illustration #4). Clinically speaking, there is no parent here. This is a typical single-parent family, where the mother has given up the unpleasant features accompanying the role of caretaker. In fact, this becomes a central issue in the treatment of these families. The *Parent-Sibling* pattern characterizes perhaps one in ten of the families of preadolescent, antisocial children referred for treatment. It was one of the first family types that we noted (Patterson, Cobb, & Ray, 1973).

As much as possible, the mother functions as an equal, a friend. Sometimes the position is based on a misinterpretation of a laissez-faire, egalitarian philosophy. Many of these mothers seem cut off from other adults; the children are their primary source of support. There are few house rules, few schedules, few assigned roles, and no single person punishes antisocial behavior. Each family member defends his or her own territory. Sometimes a temporary vigilante committee may be set up to redress a wrong. Sometimes an older sibling will occupy a very tentative role as housekeeper, but usually this does not include rule setting. In doing away with the disciplinarian features of the parent role, the mother buys friendship from her children. This can often become a major problem in treatment. If she now attempts to set rules and enforce them, the mother fears the children may reject her. The mother's concern about such a rejection is overwhelming.

If some *Parent-Siblings* also hold delinquent values, then the therapists may find themselves in the interesting position of trying to convince the children *and* the mother that stealing is a reprehensible act. The *Parent-Sibling* and the children may form a xenophobic enclave that serves to protect its members from outsiders. In counterculture families we sometimes find both parents adopting this role. They assume little or no responsibility for any aspect of the child's behavior. The child simply fends for himself and, in some extreme cases, comes home only to sleep. The parents assume that if the child is left free to express his own wishes and desires, that gradually inner controls will emerge (a modern expression of the Rousseau thesis and familial analogue to the Summerhill philosophy).

In their clinical studies of families in divorce, Wallerstein and Kelly (1980) noted a very similar pattern. Some of the women in that study had functioned well as caretakers when their marriages were intact. The husbands were the rule setters and disciplinarians. With the dissolution of the marriage, these women found themselves unprepared to serve in the role of disciplinarian, and, in that study, their children tended to become increasingly antisocial. The authors also described many of these mothers as being afraid to set limits for fear of losing their children's affection.

At OSLC, treatment of these families was often difficult. The *Parent-Sibling* was usually overwhelmed by outside crises. Many of them were isolated from other adults and depended upon reinforcers provided by their children. Treatment often included assisting the parent to form satisfactory relationships outside the family. Gradually they learn that needing to be loved all the time by their children makes them terribly vulnerable to manipulation. Although hesitant and terribly disorganized, they eventually learn that all is not lost when rules are set and punishment is employed. Their move to establish the parent role is difficult but satisfying, as they learn that the children actually become more warm and loving when structure is imposed.

The Unattached Parent

There is another type of adult who has also discarded the role of parent. They, too, impose few limits or structure, but they do *not* wish to be a friend or colleague of their children. This group has been noted and labeled "Disengaged" by other investigators (Minuchin, Montalvo, Guerney, Rosman, & Schumer, 1967). These parents occupy no philosophical position; they simply do not care to be parents. These parents are difficult to engage in treatment because they are only vaguely motivated. If their children are socially aggressive, then a cessation of pain is a possible motivator. If, however, the children steal or set fires outside of the household, then the parents are unlikely to be motivated to retrain their children.

Control theory seems to reflect the biases of its middle-class investigators, who emphasize the importance of the attachment or *bonding of the child to the parent* as a necessary condition for sociali-

Illustration #4: The Parent-Sibling

zation (Hirschi, 1969). However, the theory overlooks the possibility that *some parents are not attached to their children.* They are not committed to the role of caretaker. In fact, it was these families that led us to introduce the idea of a "parenting salary" (Patterson, Cobb, & Ray, 1973). The motivator for the parent to participate in treatment could be money, points toward an appointment at the hairdresser, driving lessons, and so on. The experiment by Fleischman (1979b) showed that the contingent use of as little as $10.00 per week significantly increased parental cooperation in the training program.

When we began studying high-rate Stealers, increasing numbers of *unattached parents* were encountered. They presented two problems to the therapy team. First, it was almost impossible to get them to come for treatment; they were not really motivated to change their child. The use of a parenting salary helped to bring them into the clinic, but once they arrived, they provided us with a new problem. They were not only noncooperative, but very resistive. Some of these parents were very critical and/or irritable in their face-to-face interactions with the therapist and their children. Like rebellious adolescents, they actively refused to cooperate and disagreed at very high rates during the treatment sessions. Others wanted to control the situation at all costs and were adept at keeping the discussion away from topics relating to intervention. They tended to miss appointments, come late, and failed to carry out their agreed-upon tasks.

These are difficult parents to have as clients. Their lack of concern for their children is an affront to my more middle-class values. The fact that many of them also have delinquent values further exacerbates the situation. It seems, at times, that there is no common meeting ground. I do not believe that we know how to completely alter this condition. If we had the means for accurately classifying the *unattached* parent, I think it would correlate with recidivism during follow-up.

This Child Is Special

These families present another kind of paradox. They know what to do for their children, but they choose not to do it! It seems a frequent pattern, especially among families with younger problem children.

Some of these parents had previously demonstrated skill in raising children who functioned well. For some reason, these demonstrated skills were held in abeyance when dealing with the problem child. For him, certain house rules were set aside, tracking was very selective, and sanctions were seldom imposed. The reasons for this selectivity were varied. Sometimes it was the case that the child had been diagnosed as *special,* e.g., an early diagnosis of retardation or minimal brain damage, or an extended hospitalization for illness. The parents were told that structure and limits should not be imposed upon their child because it would exacerbate his condition. Whatever the crisis was, the parents seemed to try to make it up to him by removing the constraints that still applied to his siblings. His resulting hyperkinetic and antisocial behavior was then attributed to the prior illness and constituted proof of the necessity for yet further reductions in constraints.

This special status, however, does not serve the child well. In spite of the parents' wish to be more loving to this special child, they cannot help but feel angry and puzzled in the face of his onslaughts. This further adds to the guilt engendered by the original crisis. Many of these parents resort to a "refrigerator" stance, in which their icy demeanor communicates neither anger, guilt, nor love. They minimize their contacts with the child in order to neutralize as much hurt as possible. To a therapist, it may seem reasonable to assume that the icy demeanor *caused* the aggressive behavior.

In our clinical experience, it represents an attempt by trapped parents to deal with an impossible situation. Effective training in child management will often help the parent and the child to risk being intimate with each other and to express affection again. A sizable majority of the parents thus trained report feeling more affection for their child. They generally like being parents. One does get a definite sense of family here. The therapist's problem is how to convince the parent that the normal rules and sanctions should apply to the special child. This must be done in such a way that the parent does not lose face. It should be noted that some of these families are easier to work with in this regard than others.

Overwhelmed

This pattern is another example of parents who know about child management but do not implement it effectively. The parent is simply overwhelmed by circumstances, e.g., a single parent working and raising a family, both parents working, a very large family reared in poverty, a prolonged illness, or extended crises. If both parents are working, neither of them really has the energy to sit down and quietly talk with their child each day. There are long blocks of time when neither parent is home and the child is left with large amounts of unsupervised time. For most children, this in and of itself is a sufficient condition for the child to drift into stealing and vandalism. It also sets the stage for the child to seek out a set of unsavory and probably similarly unsupervised comrades.

The problem here is not a neurotic conflict between spouses. It is not an authoritarian parent, nor even a parent wishing to be loved too much. It is simply that the caretaker is preoccupied. Many of these parents genuinely care about their children. When they are at home they may even be said to have good relationships with them. However, they are more deeply committed to activities that are unrelated to the caretaker role. In some cases, there may be crushing debts to be paid, or the father may be a long-haul truck driver, and the mother may be preoccupied with family crises.

Many of these parents can eventually give up some of their outside commitments, or arrange them in a more balanced fashion, so that one caretaker is always "on duty." There are, however, some parents who must remain absentee caretakers and arrange for after-school care, or monitor the child by telephone. There is a smaller group of these parents who cannot even arrange this much. These people communicate all the right feelings, attitudes, and motivations in treatment. The problem is, they do not totally cooperate in carrying them out. The therapist is often temporarily left in the position of arranging for a surrogate caretaker (including him- or herself).

There is another sense in which parents may be overwhelmed. Some families seem to live in a perpetual state of crisis. We encounter them particularly in samples of families of chronic delinquents and, to a lesser extent, in the abused-child samples. The effect of the stressors they experience is to badly disrupt the already precarious balance of their family management practices. The parents are simply too preoccupied with the problem of reality to conscientiously practice their parenting skills. As a therapist, one has the definite impression that these people could be good parents if only . . . I have the feeling of being slightly out of breath when working with these people. In their attempts to manage their child, one can observe them using punishment, rule setting, ignoring deviancy, and so on. However, these things are tried in quick succession, with no effort to pursue a procedure to its conclusion. The behavior of these parents is as chaotic and disorganized as is their lifestyle.

Sadomasochistic Arabesque

From the problem child's perspective, another label for this family type would be *Divide and Conquer* (see Illustration #5). This ballet requires the committed participation of three partners. The parents never dance together, but each dances separately with the child. When this happens, the abandoned partner tries to stop the music. The reactions of each parent to the child are delicately balanced. Each tracks the behavior of both the child *and* the other parent. One parent occupies the role of the harsh, punitive martinet. When the martinet is present, the behavior of the child is in moderate control. The other parent attempts to balance the perceived severity of the other by being noncontingently warm and *permissive*. As a result, when the despot is not present, the child's behavior is out of control. Deviant behaviors occurring in the despot's presence are punished, sometimes brutally. The despairing despot summarizes the situation: "But he acts okay when I'm home. She is just too easy on him, that's all." Other investigators, such as McCord and McCord (1961), have noted a similar pattern for families of antisocial children.

There are apparently a large number of variations on this theme. In one instance, it was the resident grandparent who functioned as the secret agent, actively sabotaging the efforts of the parents to set limits upon their child. When they attempted to set rules or punish deviant behavior, the grandparent served as the child's advocate and was sufficiently adept to cause confusion in the ranks of the parents' forces. The grandmother served as baby-sitter for more than a decade and, during that time, effectively prevented the parents from setting consequences for stealing, even when the child stole from her!

There is a more frequently occurring variation of this theme; it is the *My-Child* and *Your-Child* pattern. This is often found where a new step-parent joins the family. The wife is not allowed to punish her *husband's* child; he, on the other hand, is not allowed to punish *her* child. The children are, of course, eager participants in this game and feed mildly distorted reports of yesterday's battles to each parent. In one blended family of five children, when the stepfather objected to his wife's children using obscenity in his presence, the children simply repeated his objection to the mother. She launched into a vituperative attack upon him for attempting to punish *her* children. He, in turn, assiduously defended *his* children from her efforts to set limits. Both parents wanted the option of being overly permissive with their own brood. As a result, all five children were out of control and were in frequent contact with the local police. Later, when these parents separated, it was possible for them to effectively apply child management procedures to their own children.

In our treatment of multiple-offending, adolescent delinquents, we encounter this pattern much more frequently than we do with younger antisocial children. For either age group, it causes problems for the therapist. No matter where treatment begins, at least one parent will temporarily feel alienated from the process. The child is an active participant in the arabesque and knows just how to exploit the rift between the parents. Julius Caesar had some knowledge of how to play one tribe of Gauls against another; these children have updated his technique and know how to use it effectively.

It is difficult to do justice to the feelings of the participants. These are interchanges in which people are likely to get physically injured. The rage of the punisher and rule setter is frightening to the child, spouse, and therapist alike. In the punisher's world, there is order, there are rules, and there are sanctions. Warmth and affection are mistrusted, though, in private, the despot will sometimes admit to a terrible loneliness. When the rule setter is home, the child behaves most of the time. There are sporadic beatings, presumably to remind the child who is boss. As the child matures, the beatings merge into physical battles, and the injuries

Illustration #5: Divide and Conquer

increase commensurately. After each confrontation, the other spouse withdraws psychologically, and this increases the despot's resentment toward the child: "If that kid weren't here we would get along fine." When the despot leaves the house, the rules are changed. The other parent is warm and giving (particularly after a major battle) and will cover for the child. This is the time for the child to ask for money, the use of the family car, or an extended weekend with friends. The rule setter suspects the entire sequence, and his or her rage is boundless when later confronted by a police report of the child's most recent escapade. Both parents have suffered defeat. The rule setter has failed, and the "good" parent's efforts to be warm have failed. The child wins the battles but often loses the war because many of these children are eventually removed from their homes.

Treatment of these families is difficult. *Both* the mother and father are resistant. Even if progress is made in getting one to shift positions, the other remains mistrustful. Neither is willing to change unless the other does so first. Any alliance achieved is shaky at best and is easily disrupted by the renewed acting out of the child, producing an "it didn't work" reaction from both parents and perhaps a beating by the martinet. In one family, the author managed to simultaneously shift the behavior of both parents (the result of endless negotiations and monumental compromises). Neither parent trusted the other, nor did they have much confidence in this first therapeutic step. At this point, the father discovered the boy had stolen and sold his father's family jewels (literally). Treatment ended here, and the boy was sent to an institution.

Perfect Parents

Two variations are encountered on this same theme, the most notable being *Mommy and Daddy,* with *Gotcha* as a minor variation. The pattern emerged primarily in the context of our efforts to work with the families of chronic delinquents. It may have characterized some families of younger Social Aggressors and Stealers, but we failed to note this. The general picture presented is of a *perfect* middle-class family. It is as if one were observing a TV show; their lines are carefully chosen, the voices and feelings are carefully modulated. The parents speak of love and responsibility. The children are neatly dressed and are usually well behaved during the sessions.

The parents have usually read a number of books on the subject of child psychology or parent training. At first sight, the therapist may be enchanted, thinking: "Here, at last, are parents interested in our theory; this will be fun." If the therapist has a middle-class orientation, he or she may feel they can identify with this family. Some of the parents were subjected to brutal conditions in their own childhood experience, and they want to make sure that this does not happen to their children. After assiduous study, they set out to do what they believe middle-class parents do. They want to be *Perfect Parents* and raise perfect children.

A salient variation on this theme is that of *Mommy and Daddy.*[1] Some of these parents tend to drop the first person pronouns and substitute Mommy and Daddy. In talking to the child about transgressions of house rules, they do not say, "You took my car without asking, and that makes me mad." Such confrontations are avoided at all cost. The direct expression of anger is also avoided as long as possible. The communication comes out more like, "Mommy and Daddy feel there is still some misunderstanding about the car. As you know, you are still under age, and according to the law. . . ." They lecture their child, *but they do not confront him.* Sweet reason prevails. The child sits with downcast eyes, awaiting the lecture's end. If the child appears to listen, and if he claims to feel sorrow and repentance, then the parents are satisfied. The parents believe in reason, information-giving, and in the redeeming virtues of guilt. The child's weeping is accepted as a sign of guilt. The point is, *at no time* do the parents punish him for his behavior; instead, they lecture. During their discourse, one or both parents bring to bear much of their store of understanding about why children do what they do. They read, then reread, the child's intentions. When they are finished, not a blemish in the child's character remains unvarnished.

These are people who are trying to be rational. They don't usually hit their child, but sometimes their facade crumbles, and a beating ensues, or the child is ejected from the house. A major battle produces profound guilt reactions in the parents. This, in turn, is deftly utilized by the child to obtain even more freedom from parental control.

The parent who must be thought well of by the child at all times is vulnerable to a variation on the general theme. This subtheme is called *Gotcha.* For such parents, being accused of being unfair or illogical is painful enough to halt their attempts to punish a wrongdoing. The child may also interject guilt as an even more powerful means of neutralizing the parental role. Guilt induction may involve accusations that the child is unloved, e.g., because the mother works, or because the child is adopted. The possibilities are endless. For example, after much urging by the therapist, a mother told her son that coming in late at night would cost him part of his allowance. On the videotape, one can see the trepidation with which she made this perfectly reasonable statement. Amid the acclaim and applause by the two therapists present, the son murmured very quietly, "Yeah, like I always knew." "What?" asked the mother. "That money means more to you than I do," hissed her delinquent son. The mother looked as if she had been struck in the face. Needless to say, she did not enforce the rule.

Guilt induction is the main mechanism employed by children who are playing *Gotcha.* It can be done with threats; e.g., "Okay, I'm going to run away. I know you want me to anyway." A successful manipulation has had a prior history of years of trial-and-error training. The child keeps trying new combinations until he or she *finds one that works*. The parents' mistake is in *allowing* it to work. In our clinical experience, families of this type are surprisingly difficult to treat. The problem in each case is to get them to *stop lecturing* and openly confront their child and to be consistent in confronting even the less deviant prototypes of extreme behaviors.

Misattribution

This type of parent emerged during our recent study of abused children. At one level, they seem terribly misinformed about what a 2- or a 5-year-old can do or needs to do. The behavior of the child is evaluated against standards that are more appropriate for an older child. For example, one mother explained that she had to beat her child because he refused to do what she asked him to do. She would make a request, then repeat it. The child she was beating was 13 months of age!

Another aspect of the problem is that the discrepancy between the child's behavior and the parent's expectations is viewed as a reflection of the child's *malevolent intentions*. The parent can become so preoccupied with negative attributions about the child that even his most innocent behavior is viewed as hostile. For example, when asked why she persisted in slapping her child's face, one mother explained that when her 18-month-old pursed his lips and blew, it meant that he was insulting her. She slapped him to teach him to be more respectful.

While many abused children have been observed to be highly coercive, some of them interact well within normal limits. Even within this subset of abused children, the parents seem to function with a kind of thought disorder analogous to projection. They take many aspects of their child's behavior very personally. This, combined with a profound ignorance of the intellectual and motor abilities for children of different ages, sets the stage for repeated misunderstandings. It is our clinical impression that many of these families can be helped.

Miscellany

In our clinical experience, we have encountered another repeated pattern that does not necessarily fit a particular type of family. We call it *Last Stop*. These parents seem to be trying to carry out their assignments, but, for some mysterious reason, nothing works. Failure follows failure in quick succession, and the child's antisocial behavior increases dramatically. At the peak of the experience, the parents quietly announce that they have arranged to place the child outside of the home. A moment's reflection brings to mind the fact that they had raised this possibility early in treatment. The therapy experience was a means of proving to themselves that their child was impossible to cope with.

There is another family type I have heard about but have not yet encountered. The protagonists are two parents who agree on punishment and house rules and have a clear grasp of what is deviant, protodeviant, and normal. However, these parents are extremely authoritarian and oppressive when dealing with their child. To keep from being crushed, the child must engage in a kind of neurotic acting out.

The problem with typologies is that it is very difficult to find a "pure" type of anything. The same is probably true here. As a staff, we have agreed on the importance of classifying families, but, as yet, we have not begun to do so. I suspect that when we do begin, we will find that most families fit into *several* categories. It may also be the case that one parent fits one category, and the other would best be described by a different pattern. However that may be, the time has come to begin the construction of an empirical base for a typology of families.

Some Speculations

It is an interesting exercise to use a few simple concepts from coercion theory to construct a taxonomy of families. The earlier analyses suggest that there are two general dimensions of parent behavior that are of particular interest. The first one describes the extent to which the parent is either distant or irritably enmeshed. As this dimension is presented in Figure 13.1, it is somewhat distorted, for it suggests that a parent is either distant or enmeshed. As indicated earlier, we suspect that some parents of delinquents may be *both*. Keeping that possibility in mind, for the moment let's view it as a type of bipolar dimension. As such, it is analogous to the bipolar factor for parent behavior that was so carefully delineated by E. Schaefer (1971). His bipolar factors were labeled Psychological Autonomy (detachment, emancipation, indifference) at one end and Psychological Control (intrusive, intolerant) at the other. These bear more than a passing resemblance to my a priori dimension of Distance and Enmeshment. Notice that in Figure 13.1 normal parents do not fall within either extreme of this dimension (i.e., they are neither Distant nor Enmeshed).

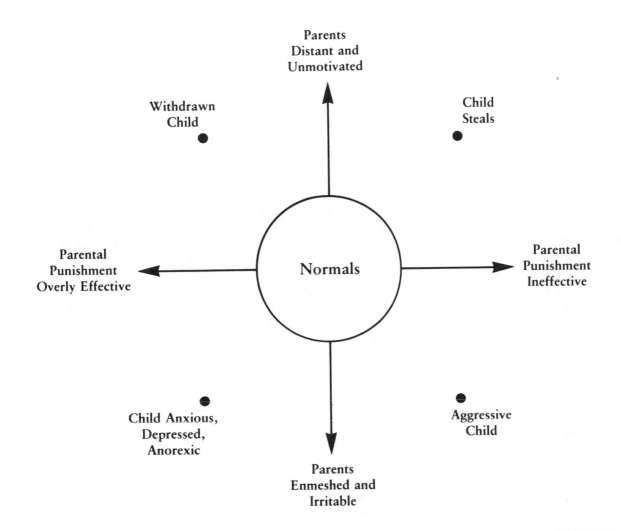

Figure 13.1
Hypothetical Relationship Between Parent Behavior and Child Pathology

Parents
Distant and
Unmotivated

Withdrawn
Child

Child
Steals

Parental
Punishment
Overly Effective

Normals

Parental
Punishment
Ineffective

Child Anxious,
Depressed,
Anorexic

Aggressive
Child

Parents
Enmeshed and
Irritable

As used here, distant parents would be characterized by lower rates of observed prosocial interaction with children (i.e., less talking, laughing, and playing). These parents would also score significantly higher on categories such as No Response. In addition, these parents probably share less leisure time with their children than parents of Normals.

The enmeshed, irritable parents tend to interact at high rates with their children. The factor that differentiates them from Normals is that a disproportionate share of their interactions are negative. In some families, this would mean very high values for the irritability measures (crossover, counterattack, punishment acceleration, and continuance). In other families, this might be expressed by criti-

cisms too subtle for the FICS to measure. The displeasure and dissatisfactions of the parents do not, however, go by unattended by the child.

The second a priori dimension concerns the ability of the parents to use punishment *to change behavior*. Assuming, for the moment, that we do *not* have an effective measure of punishment effectiveness, it may be premature to introduce such a concept. Nevertheless, I think it is a key concept for understanding several very different types of child pathology. The a priori dimension of punishment effectiveness is similar to the bipolar factor of lax and firm control identified by Schaefer (1971). My dimension differs in that it emphasizes punishment as *the* method of control.

As shown in Figure 13.1, some parents are *less*

effective than Normals in their use of punishment, while others are significantly *more* effective. In the latter homes, the parents "win" almost every confrontation. Furthermore, if they are also enmeshed, they tend to be assiduous trackers of child behavior. No transgression is insignificant, and almost everything the child does arouses the anger of the parent. Even *successful* child performances are not quite good enough. As suggested in Figure 13.1, I am guessing that the neurotic child is the outcome of these parenting practices.

The enmeshed, irritable parent who is ineffective in the use of punishment produces the Social Aggressor. The relation was detailed in Chapter 11. It is also supported by the Olweus (1981) causal modelling analysis of parent and child behavior.

The child who steals is depicted as a member of a household in which the parents are distant and inept in the use of punishment. These are parents who do not track rule breaking that occurs outside the home (see Chapter 11). Transgressions that are brought to their attention go unpunished.

The last quadrant in Figure 13.1 describes a highly speculative guess. The parents are distant but extremely effective in the use of punishment to control children. It is suggested that the child's withdrawn behavior is a coping device for avoiding parental criticism, a kind of last-ditch defense by a child who has already lost most of the battles with the parent. The only data even remotely bearing upon this hypothesis has been collected by H. Hops (personal communication). His analyses were based upon observation in homes of normal and withdrawn children. The findings showed that the fathers of withdrawn children were significantly more likely than fathers of Normals to react punitively to neutral and prosocial behaviors! Hops' findings do not test the hypotheses that these fathers were more distant or more effective in their use of punishment. I am assuming, however, that both hypotheses apply to these fathers.

In constructing the four quadrants of Figure 13.1, I have used only two concepts to classify most of the functional disorders of childhood. Obviously this cannot be. However, the discussion does serve the useful purpose of illustrating the potential of these two simple concepts. I do think that the Distance-Enmeshment and Punishment Effectiveness dimensions relate to more than just antisocial child problems. The extent to which they covary with other child problems such as withdrawal, anxiety, or depression is a matter for further empirical analyses.

Treatment Outcomes

At this point, we have treated over 200 families of extremely antisocial children. One of the most heartening features of our work relates to the fact that these parents have been able to change the problem child's behavior as well as their own. The focus in this treatment has been to reprogram the social environment in which the child lives. The most efficient means for bringing this about was to train all of the family members, particularly the parents. The focus of training was upon the skills these people seemed to lack (Patterson, Reid, Jones, & Conger, 1975). As noted earlier, it was during these clinical contacts that we gradually identified the four areas of family management detailed in Chapter 10.

It is assumed that family management skills are "teachable." If the parents of antisocial children can learn to perform these skills, then they should be able to significantly reduce the problem child's deviant behavior. In fact, the coercion levels for the entire family should be reduced. If the outcome evaluation data reflected such changes, it would give indirect support for the central status of family management variables as they relate to antisocial behavior; i.e., changing family management variables produced changes in antisocial behavior.[2]

In the OSLC treatment program, the teaching and supervision of effective family management skills is viewed as a *necessary* (but not sufficient) component. There is a second component that is also thought to be necessary (but not sufficient). The therapist must be skilled in coping with the resistance to change that characterizes the majority of the families referred for treatment. Ordinarily, this level of clinical skill requires several years of supervised clinical experience. In fact, the measurement and analysis of this second component (clinical skill) is the focus of our current research on treatment.

By the mid 1960's, I believed that the new family intervention technology was sufficient to change families of antisocial children. Moreoever, I thought it might be possible simply to give the parents a book to read that would tell them how to accomplish these changes (*Living with Children*, 1968). We quickly learned that treatment for these families was much more complex than we had anticipated. At that time, there were five other centers developing social learning procedures for antisocial children. All of these groups collected observation data prior to, during, and following treatment. After a decade of work, the data showed *no significant* behavior change (as measured by TAB scores) for three of the six groups! It is my impression that the successful and unsuccessful groups differed in two respects. The unsuccessful efforts used time-limited treatment procedures and were carried out by graduate student therapists.

By the early 1970's, we were beginning to believe that perhaps there was more to treatment than just the technology described in our treatment manual (Patterson, Reid, Jones, & Conger, 1975). A systematic study by Fleishman (1979a) convinced us that clinical skills must be added as a second, necessary component. In his study, half the line staff from three community agencies were trained and supervised in the application of social learning components. They were carefully monitored to see that they applied social learning techniques. In fact, the analysis of therapy tapes showed the trainees to be "on task" much of the time. The tapes were then rated on such global measures of clinical skill as warmth, humor, and smoothness of flow. Compared to the OSLC staff, the trainees were found to be *cold, mechanical,* and *nonfluent.* When that study was done, clinical skills were not thought to be particularly important, so the majority of the on-site monitors were not even trained as family therapists. Their focus while on site was not on the intricacies of working through resistance but, rather, on the minutiae of applying social learning technology. The dropout rate for treated families was very high. Observation data were collected for 12 families of socially aggressive children that were treated by the agency staff. The mean baseline TAB score of the children treated was 1.00; at termination, the score was .96 (Fleischman, 1979a). The Fleishman study and the experiences at other parent training centers treating similar families emphasized the need to study the second component (clinical skill).

Our research strategy has focused upon a sequence of five questions: (1) Using consecutive, treated cases, can a significant reduction in observed rates of coercive behavior be demonstrated for the child and for other family members? (2) Can this effect be replicated by the *same* therapists using more or less the same procedures; i.e., is the effect a reliable one? (3) Do the treatment effects persist over a 12-month period? (4) Is it possible to train other therapists to produce the same effects? (5) Are the effects specific to the treatment? The following is a brief review of the studies that relate to these issues.

The general format for the OSLC studies has been to employ professional therapists trained at the center and supervised during weekly staff meetings in which videotaped treatment sessions are viewed. Treatment continues for as long as is thought necessary. The families are assessed at baseline, termination, and for 12 months after treatment. In addition to parent global ratings, the parents provide daily telephone reports for selected symptoms (PDR). Home observations provide TAB scores for each family member at baseline, termination, and follow-up. The first studies demonstrated significant reductions in both PDR and TAB scores from baseline to termination (Patterson, Cobb, & Ray, 1973). This effect was replicated using essentially the same therapy staff (Patterson & Reid, 1973). A series of detailed analyses followed that included the combined samples from these earlier pilot studies (Patterson, 1974a, b).

The next question concerned the stability of these treatment effects. Patterson & Fleischman (1979) studied 106 families of antisocial children treated at OSLC. Eighteen percent of them dropped out during the baseline assessment, a figure in keeping with the 24% to 30% dropout rates for traditional child therapies. Of the 86 families who received four or more weeks of treatment, 33% refused to participate in the 12-month follow-up. The 50 families who participated both in treatment and in follow-up were observed in the home and contacted by phone (PDR) each month during follow-up. Figure 13.2 shows that, at termination, 76% of the problem children had TAB scores within the normal range. At the end of the follow-up phase, the comparable value was 84%. The ANOVA for repeated measures showed significant reductions from baseline to follow-up for both the TAB and PDR scores. Findings were also summarized demonstrating significant reductions in TAB scores for siblings and for mothers. Parent perceptions of the problem child also showed significant improvement.

If training families in family management skills effectively produced a reduction in the coercion levels for these families, then one might expect the treatment effects to persist (Patterson & Fleischman, 1979). When crises and conflicts arise after treatment, if the parents reinstate the family management procedures, they should "work" for them again. In effect, each success is an example of negative reinforcement, increasing the likelihood that in the future they will apply family management procedures. In a sense, the mechanism for persistence is "built in." It should be noted, however, that this same mechanism does not seem to hold for families of Stealers. Reid and Patterson (1976) described the *unmotivated* parents of high-rate Stealers. Apparently, these parents did not find stealing to be particularly aversive. The majority of the Stealers studied were not coercive in their

Figure 13.2
Follow-up Data for Treated Children

(from Patterson & Fleischman, 1979, p. 179)

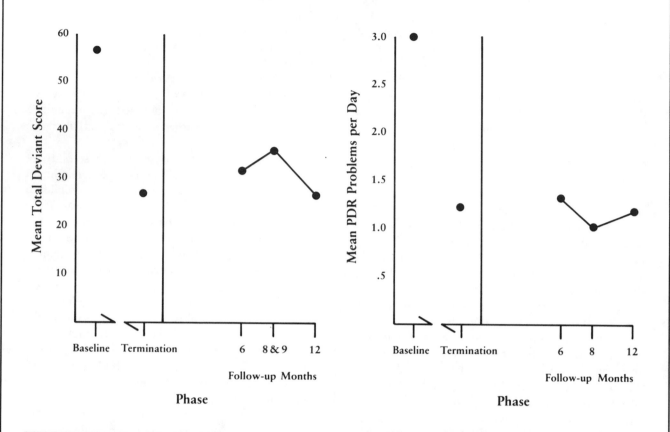

interactions with their parents. While they could be trained to significantly modify the child's stealing in the family and the neighborhood (Reid, Hinojosa-Rivero, & Lorber, 1980), in the long run these parents did not continue to apply family management practices. The community follow-up study showed that by the time the Stealers were 14 years of age, 84% had committed at least one police offense (Moore, Chamberlain, & Mukai, 1979). In fact, 64% were chronic offenders! For the parents, the problem (stealing) was not a problem. I assume that for the parents of Stealers, after invervention there was nothing analogous to a negative reinforcement mechanism that could come into play and maintain the family management practices.

Our current work with the chronic adolescent delinquents presents a similar problem. Many of the parents are unmotivated and/or extremely resistant to changing their behavior. For these cases, when they have brought the stealing and truancy under partial control, the interval between con-

tacts is lengthened. Termination does *not occur*. The data for the first 36 delinquent cases shows that the effects persist over a three-year period (Patterson, Reid, & Chamberlain, in preparation). The reduction in police offense rates was greater for the treatment group than for a randomly assigned control group. At present, the OSLC staff is treating a second sample of young Stealers using the modified techniques that have been developed in the last three years. Long-term follow-up of these cases will determine whether these modifications are sufficient for the task.

The next question concerned the possibility of teaching the OSLC treatment procedures to other therapists. Three new therapists were trained at OSLC over a period of a year or more; each served as a co-therapist with the OSLC staff and participated in the weekly (intensive) videotape feedback sessions. The replication team worked in their own treatment setting; it had its own staff of trained observers, secretaries, and receptionists. Weinrott, Bauske, and Patterson (1979) compared

Table 13.1
Outcome Data for the Treatment of Social Aggressors

(from Weinrott, Bauske, & Patterson, 1979, p. 343)

	Terminated families without follow-up			Terminated families with follow-up data (minimum 4 months)			
	N	Baseline	Termination	N	Baseline	Termination	Follow-up
Original sample	16 $\bar{x}$	1.128	.475	12 $\bar{x}$	.842	.461	.453
(Patterson, 1974a)	SD	.924	.283	SD	.618	.319	.454
Replication sample	18 $\bar{x}$	.826	.361	14 $\bar{x}$	.900	.307	.232
	SD	.458	.383	SD	.493	.349	.193

Reprinted with permission from "Systematic replication of a social learning approach." In P.O. Sjoden, S. Bates, and W.S. Dockens, editors, *Trends in Behavior Therapy.* Copyright 1979 by Academic Press, Inc.

the outcome data for the 16 socially aggressive children treated in the original study to the 18 Social Aggressors treated in the replication study. As can be seen in Table 13.1, both the original and the replication sample showed significant reductions in TAB scores for the identified problem child. The time-series analyses for each case's PDR data showed significant reductions for the majority of problem boys. Fleischman (1981) analyzed the data for the entire set of Social Aggressors and Stealers and demonstrated that the outcomes for the replication sample were similar to those that were obtained in the earlier studies. The findings showed that whatever it was that the OSLC therapy staff did in working with families, it could be taught to others.

Are these changes specific to the treatment? An adequate answer to this question requires a comparison design and random assignment. The first pilot study of this type was designed to control for the passage of time. Six consecutive referrals were placed for two weeks in a waiting-list control group (Wiltz & Patterson, 1974). The next six referrals received the "standard" parent training. At the end of the 5-week period, the experimental group showed a significant decrease in the observation codes measuring those child behaviors that were targeted during treatment. There was no change in comparable scores for the control group. However, this study did not use random assignment; it was also flawed in that there were marked differences in the baseline measures for the criterion variables.

The next pilot study partially corrected both of these defects (Walter & Gilmore, 1973). Twelve consecutive referrals were randomly assigned in

blocks of three to experimental and placebo groups. The analysis showed the samples to be matched for the number of children in the family, occupational status of parent, and age of problem child. There were no significant differences between the groups on baseline TAB and PDR measures. After four weeks, families in both groups were observed in their homes. As shown in Figure 13.3, deviant behaviors that were targeted in treatment were significantly reduced for the experimental group. Comparable scores for the placebo group showed nonsignificant increases for the same time period. The PDR data showed comparable effects, with a significant reduction for the experimental group and no change for the placebo group. These investigators introduced the interesting feature of adding a measure of expectancy for improvement at each "treatment" session for members in both groups. Their analyses showed no significant differences between groups or across trials. Both groups maintained high expectations for a successful outcome.

An adequate comparison study would involve longer time periods that are more representative of the typical duration of OSLC treatment. On the average, families receive from three months to one year of treatment and 20 to 30 hours of therapy time. In the study by Patterson, Reid, and Chamberlain (in preparation), 21 socially aggressive families were randomly assigned to an experimental group or a comparison group. The comparison group was told that they were on a waiting list to receive treatment and were given the option of being referred for treatment to alternative community agencies or to alternative therapists. All but one family in the comparison group chose to exercise

Figure 13.3
Changes in Targeted Deviant Behaviors
for Two Groups

(from Walter & Gilmore, 1973, p. 371)

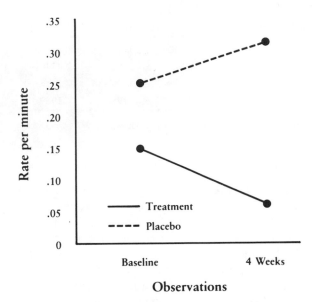

the option. The OSLC staff then arranged for the transfer and also arranged to pay the fee if one was required. When an OSLC family was terminated, their matched control family was also contacted and arrangements made for home observations and daily telephone calls for PDR data.

The mean TAB scores for the treated group at baseline were .92 and at termination were .32. The comparable values for the comparison group were .89 and .74. As predicted, the ANOVA for repeated measured produced an F value for interaction of 4.63 ($df = 1:17$) that was significant at $p < .05$. It showed the changes to be significantly greater for the experimental group than for the comparison group. The study showed that the outcome effects were specific to the treatment itself.

This long series of studies brings us to the most interesting questions of all. Why does the treatment work? What is it that some parents do that makes teaching them parenting skills so difficult? Which clinical skills are most relevant for neutralizing their resistance? These are reasonable questions; they will occupy center stage for our next five years of research.

Acknowledgments

The content of this chapter was drastically altered several times following staff meetings in which the family typology was discussed. My thanks to John Reid, Patti Chamberlain, Marion Forgatch, and Kate Kavanagh. In many respects, this chapter is a summary of *their* clinical contacts with these families. I also wish to thank Marion Forgatch for her careful editing of this chapter.

Footnotes

1. The *Mommy and Daddy* family type arose from the intensive discussion among the research team headed by Marion Forgatch, Deborah Toobert, and Gary Wieder. It emerged as they were studying the videotapes of family problem solving.

2. Given that the data show a significant reduction in deviant behavior, then it will also be necessary to study the problem child's acquisition of prosocial skills relating to work, peer relations, and academic survival. Such studies have yet to be done. Another key area will be the demonstration that treatment changes family management practices. It was only in 1980 that assessment devices were introduced that tap into these variables. Therefore, it will be another year or two before we have data relevant to these questions.

Appendices

Appendix 1.1
The Evolution of Social Learning Theories: Some Significant Contributors

(from Cairns, 1979a, p. 334)

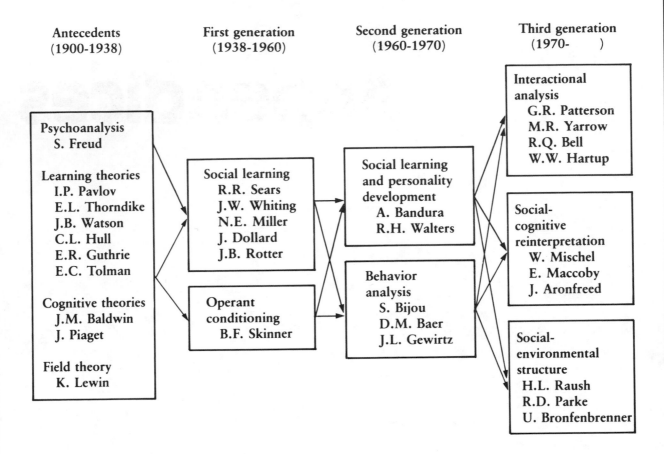

Antecedents (1900-1938)

Psychoanalysis
  S. Freud

Learning theories
  I.P. Pavlov
  E.L. Thorndike
  J.B. Watson
  C.L. Hull
  E.R. Guthrie
  E.C. Tolman

Cognitive theories
  J.M. Baldwin
  J. Piaget

Field theory
  K. Lewin

First generation (1938-1960)

Social learning
  R.R. Sears
  J.W. Whiting
  N.E. Miller
  J. Dollard
  J.B. Rotter

Operant conditioning
  B.F. Skinner

Second generation (1960-1970)

Social learning and personality development
  A. Bandura
  R.H. Walters

Behavior analysis
  S. Bijou
  D.M. Baer
  J.L. Gewirtz

Third generation (1970-   )

Interactional analysis
  G.R. Patterson
  M.R. Yarrow
  R.Q. Bell
  W.W. Hartup

Social-cognitive reinterpretation
  W. Mischel
  E. Maccoby
  J. Aronfreed

Social-environmental structure
  H.L. Raush
  R.D. Parke
  U. Bronfenbrenner

Appendix 3.1
Definitions for the 29 FICS Code Categories
(from Reid, 1978)

AP	Approval	HU	Humiliate	PP	Physical Positive
AT	Attention	IG	Ignore	RC	Receive
CM	Command	IN	Indulgence	SS	Self-stimulation
CN	Command Negative	LA	Laugh	TA	Talk
CO	Compliance	NC	Non-compliance	TE	Tease
CR	Cry	NE	Negativism	TH	Touch
DI	Disapproval	NO	Normative	WH	Whine
DP	Dependency	NR	No Response	WK	Work
DS	Destructiveness	PL	Play	YE	Yell
HR	High Rate	PN	Physical Negative		

AP (APPROVAL): Approval is a clear indication of positive interest or involvement. It is more reinforcing than Attend (AT). AT is a neutral or non-directive response whereas AP has reinforcing characteristics. Approval can be gestural or verbal in nature and need not be elaborate or lengthy, but should be used to indicate even the smallest positive gesture. Approval is directed at behavior, appearance, or personal characteristics of an individual. It *does not* include the granting of permission to carry out an activity. That is coded TA.

AT (ATTENTION): This category is to be used when one person listens to or looks at another person. Attending behavior may either be initiated by a person or may be in response to another person's behavior. Sometimes, when listening is used as a reason for coding AT, it may be difficult to tell if the person is, in fact, listening. In general, unless eye contact or some form of verbal recognition is offered by persons supposedly listening to another person, the behavior of the respondent would be coded NR. Some form of non-verbal recognition is necessary before a person's behavior would be coded AT. A brief glance should not be coded AT when it is an initiation.

CM (COMMAND): This category is used when a direct, reasonable, and clearly stated request or command is made to another person. The verbal statement must clearly specify the behavior which is expected from the person to whom the command is directed. The code system requires that either compliance or non-compliance be coded within 12 seconds. If the command requires compliance in the future, code TA.

CN (COMMAND NEGATIVE): A negative command differs from the *reasonable* command in the manner in which it is delivered. This kind of command must be characterized by *at least one* of the following: (1) immediate compliance is demanded; (2) aversive consequences are *implicitly* or actually threatened if compliance is not immediate; (3) sarcasm or humiliation is directed toward the receiver. Implicit use of aversive consequences is indicated by the tone of voice as well as the statement.

CO (COMPLIANCE): Use this category when a person does what is asked or indicates verbally or behaviorally that he will. Compliance need not follow the CM, CN, or DP immediately; other behavioral sequences can intervene. However, the indication of compliance *must occur within 12 seconds of a behavior coded as CM or CN*. Delay of compliance beyond 12 seconds is NC. Commands which require compliance *after a period of 12 seconds* would not be coded CM or CN, nor would the agreement to comply be coded CO. Both the request and response indicating compliance would be coded TA or possibly DI. These are examples of what might be called future commands.

CR (CRY): Use this category whenever a person sobs or cries tears. Actual tears do not have to be present.

DI (DISAPPROVAL): Use this category whenever a person gives a verbal or gestural criticism of another person's behavior or characteristics. In verbal statements, it is essential that the content of

311

the statement *explicitly* states criticism or disapproval of the subject's behaviors or attributes, looks, clothes, possessions, etc. DI can be coded simultaneously with CM but never with CN, as CN always implies disapproval. Code DI only when verbal disapproval (i.e., "I do not like you doing that") or gestural disapproval is implied by facial expression, vigor of the gesture, or the critical tone of voice. In addition, a DI can only be coded if either the subject or the person interacting with the subject directs the DI at the other member of the dyad. Disapproval of a third person would be coded TA.

DP (DEPENDENCY): Behavior is coded DP when a person is requesting assistance in doing a task that he is obviously capable of doing himself. Everyday requests should not be coded DP—for example, requests made at dinner would be coded TA unless the statement falls under the rules for coding CM. To code a behavior DP, it must meet two criteria: the person is capable of doing the act himself, and it is an imposition on the other person to fulfill the request.

DS (DESTRUCTIVENESS): This category applies to behavior in which a person *destroys, damages, or attempts to damage anything* other than a person; attacks on *persons* are coded PN. The damages need not actually occur, but the *potential* for damage must exist, e.g., grabbing another's breakable materials. The value of the object is of no consideration, nor is the actual amount of damage done.

HR (HIGH RATE): This code is used for any very physically active, repetitive behavior not covered by other categories that, if carried on for a sufficient period of time, would become aversive. If the behavior can be coded by other categories, i.e., YE, PN, DS, then HR is not to be used. HR may be intermittently coded with other specific deviant behaviors. The prime goal in coding HR is to represent symbolically the observed behavior as occurring excessively as measured by its frequency and/or intensity. High rate behavior is the culmination of a series of behaviors which have accelerated until they have reached an intolerable level as judged by the observer.

HU (HUMILIATE): This category is used when a person makes fun of, shames, or embarrasses another person. *The tone of voice* (in terms of nastiness or derisiveness), as well as the language used, is of prime importance in meeting the criteria for coding HU. Derisive or inappropriate laughter can

also be humiliating. Playful verbal statements or nicknames are not humiliations. Some people call each other "stupid" more in terms of endearment than in humiliation.

IG (IGNORE): Ignore is an intentional and deliberate non-response to an initiated behavior. There is no doubt that the subject has heard but has chosen not to respond.

IN (INDULGENCE): Behavior is coded IN when, *without being asked*, a person stops what he is doing in order to do some behavior for another person which that person is fully capable of doing for himself. Common kindness, i.e., pouring a cup of coffee for another while also pouring one's own, handing a nearby dictionary to someone who has asked how to spell a word, are not to be coded IN. The helping person *must stop his own ongoing chain of behavior* and perform an *unnecessary* service for a capable person. Generally, the consequence of IN is RC. Care must be taken to distinguish this category from DP and WK.

LA (LAUGH): Whenever a person laughs aloud pleasantly and in an agreeable manner, code LA. Simultaneous talking and laughing, code only LA.

NC (NON-COMPLIANCE): This code is used when a person does not do what is requested of him in response to a CM, CN or DP within 12 seconds of the request being made. Non-compliance can be verbal or non-verbal in nature. Care must be taken to distinguish DI from NC.

NE (NEGATIVISM): This category is used only when a person makes a statement in which the verbal message is neutral, but which is delivered in a tone of voice that conveys an *attitude* of "don't bug me," or "don't bother me." Also included are defeatist, "I-give-up" statements. This code is never to be used if the *verbal* meaning of the statement is interpreted as disapproving (DI) or humiliating (HU).

NO (NORMATIVE): The normative code is used for routine behavior when no other code is applicable.

NR (NO RESPONSE): Use this code when a behavior does not require a response, or when a behavior is directed at another person but the person to whom the behavior is directed fails to perceive the behavior.

PL (PLAY): This category is used when a person

is amusing himself, either alone or with other people. Play need not be restricted to games in which clear rules are defined, i.e., monopoly, scrabble, or card games, but is applicable to many activities such as amusing oneself alone, with a pet, or playing with toys. Play can be verbal or non-verbal.

PN (PHYSICAL NEGATIVE): Use whenever a subject physically attacks or attempts to attack another person. The attack must be of sufficient intensity to *potentially inflict* pain, i.e., biting, kicking, slapping, hitting, spanking, or taking an object roughly from another person. The circumstances surrounding the act need not concern the observer, only the potential of inflicting pain.

PP (PHYSICAL POSITIVE): This code is used when a person caresses or communicates with touch to another person in a friendly or affectionate manner.

RC (RECEIVE): Use this category when a person receives an object from another person or is touched physically by a person and is passively showing no response to the contact. If the person touched responds in some way, then the specific response should be coded rather than RC.

SS (SELF-STIMULATION): Use of this code is for a narrow class of behaviors which the individual does to or for himself and cannot be coded by any other codes.

TA (TALK): This code covers the exchange of conversation between family members. It is used if *none* of the other verbal codes are applicable. Do not use TA in cases when Talk is part of the ongo-ing activity required in PL or WK. Thus, in a game where one person says, "It's your turn," that is not coded TA, but simply as PL. Likewise, in a work situation when one member of a dishwashing team says, "Here are some more dishes," the proper code is WK and not TA.

TE (TEASE): Teasing is defined as the act of annoying, pestering, mocking, or making fun of another person. Teasing behavior is directed in such a manner that the other person is likely to show displeasure and disapproval. This behavior is potentially provocative and disruptive to the other person.

TH (TOUCH): Use of this behavior code indicates non-verbal passing of objects or neutral non-verbal physical contact.

WH (WHINE): When a person uses a slurring, nasal, or high-pitched voice, use this category. The content of the statement can be of an approving, disapproving, or neutral quality; the main element is the voice quality.

WK (WORK): Work is a behavior necessary to maintain the smooth functioning of a household; it is necessary for a child to perform work in order to learn behaviors that will help him to assume an adult role. A definite service performed for another person is also coded as WK.

YE (YELL): This category is to be used whenever a person shouts, yells, or talks loudly. The sound must be *intense enough* that it is unpleasant or potentially aversive if carried on for a sufficient length of time.

Appendix 4.1
OSLC Family Crisis List

Date _____

Case Name _____

Case Number _____

Therapist _____

When you fill this out, just circle whichever of these crises came up in the last seven days. We will ask you to do this once a month.

Family

1. Someone moved in with the family for a day or more.
2. Someone that was living with the family for a month or more left (not a parent).
3. One of the parents left town temporarily (more than one day).
4. One of the children left town overnight or longer.
5. Someone returned from a long trip (over a day).
6. Argument with spouse.
7. Argument with child.
8. Adult came home from work very upset.
9. Child came home from play, work, school, etc., very upset.
10. Conflict with ex-spouse.
11. Conflict with local relative.
12. Conflict with out-of-town relative.
13. Pleasant long-distance call from relative.
14. Received bad news about a family member.
15. Physical fighting with family member.
16. Wife is pregnant.
17. Pregnancy suspected.
18. Birth of a child.
19. Other _____.

Household and Transportation

1. Paid the bills.
2. Didn't have enough money to pay the bills.
3. A major repair was necessary for household or household item.
4. Check bounced.
5. Got a new babysitter.
6. Babysitter quit.
7. Didn't have any clean clothes.
8. Meal burned or ruined.
9. Got evicted.
10. Moved.

11. Pet picked up by dogcatcher.
12. Pet injured—requires veterinarian.
13. Sentimental, useful, or valuable item lost.
14. Automobile accident, no one injured.
15. Automobile accident, someone injured.
16. The car needs repairs.
17. The car broke down or wouldn't start.
18. Caught in a traffic jam.
19. Ran out of gas.
20. Other _____.

Economic

1. Lost some money.
2. Received unexpected bill.
3. Went to apply for welfare or unemployment funds.
4. Welfare or unemployment payments began.
5. Welfare or unemployment stopped payment.
6. Something stolen from the house.
7. Something stolen from family member.
8. Other _____.

Health

1. Family member had a routine visit to doctor or dentist.
2. Family member saw psychiatrist, psychologist, counselor or other (list _____
   _____
3. Someone in the family is ill.
4. Sickness lasted more than three days.
5. More than one person in the family is ill.
6. Severe injury to a family member, e.g., broken leg, pneumonia.
7. Someone in the family learned they have a chronic illness, e.g., cancer, TB, muscular dystrophy, etc.
8. Someone in the family, a relative, died.
9. Other _____.

School

1. Child started new school.
2. School called to complain about child's behavior.
3. Child was sent home from school for behavior.
4. Child was suspended from school.
5. Child skipped school.
6. School complained about child's academic progress (doing poorly).
7. School called to say child may fail one or more subjects.
8. School called to say child may have to repeat grade.
9. Child's report card came out today.
10. Other _____.

Social interchange

1. Adults had a serious disagreement with a neighbor or friend.
2. Child had a serious disagreement with a neighbor or friend.
3. Friend of a family member is having serious problems—called or came by to talk.
4. Family member had an argument with repair man, business person, government official, etc.
5. Other _____.

Legal

1. Someone in the family went to see a lawyer.
2. Someone in the family had a traffic violation and got a ticket.
3. Family member was arrested.
4. Policeman came to the door.
5. Somebody accused a family member of a crime.
6. Family member appeared in court.
7. Other _____.

Appendix 5.1
Samples for Comparison Studies

The samples were drawn from a population of problem and nonproblem families studied at the Oregon Social Learning Center (OSLC) since 1968. Only those cases were selected falling into the age group 3 through 8.5 years or 8.6 through 13.5 years. For the clinical sample, only those cases were included that satisfied the dual requirements for both age and diagnostic label *socially aggressive*. This is the group for which coercion theory was designed. It consisted of boys referred by parents and/or community agents because of high rates of coercive behaviors directed toward other people, e.g., tease, whine, yell, does not mind, and fight. Of those referred for such problems, cases were selected for the sample when the observation data collected in the home indicated that their rates of coercive behavior exceeded .45 responses per minute.

The normal sample was obtained by advertising in the newspaper for families to be observed having nonproblem children. A nonproblem family was operationally defined as one in which the child had not received psychiatric or counseling treatment during the previous year. The families were paid for participation in the study.

There were 30 children in the clinical sample, and 20 in the nonproblem sample. The following table summarizes the demographic data for the four samples including father absence, number of siblings, age of the target child, and occupational level. The findings showed the samples to be comparable on all variables.

Demographic Data for Two Samples

Samples	Age	Mean Number of Siblings	Mean Occupational Level[1]	Percent of Father-Present Families
Socially aggressive (N = 30)	8.3 (2.8-13.5)†	2.2 (0-5)	4.9 (1-7)	68%
Nonproblem (N = 20)	8.7 (4.9-13.5)	2.0 (1-4)	4.1 (1-7)	65%

[1]Parent occupations were classified using Hollingshead and Redlich (1958), where level one was unskilled labor and levels four and five were clerical and skilled labor, respectively.

†Ranges are shown in parentheses.

Appendix 6.1
The Mean Likelihood the Target Child Will Stop After a Single Coercive Response
Given that the Consequence was Neutral or Positive
(Corrected Base Rate)

| Sample | Agent with Whom Child Interacts | | | |
	Mother	Father	Brother	Sister
Abused	$\bar{x}$ 0.76	$\bar{x}$ 0.73	†	$\bar{x}$ 0.81
	SD 0.17	SD 0.21		SD 0.17
	N 19	N 13		N 15
Normal	$\bar{x}$ 0.74	$\bar{x}$ 0.76	$\bar{x}$ 0.79	$\bar{x}$ 0.79
	SD 0.32	SD 0.37	SD 0.28	SD 0.29
	N 35	N 26	N 23	N 26
Social Aggressor	$\bar{x}$ 0.67	$\bar{x}$ 0.72	$\bar{x}$ 0.70	$\bar{x}$ 0.82
	SD 0.20	SD 0.26	SD 0.25	SD 0.15
	N 43	N 23	N 23	N 30

†There were less than 10 subjects in this cell.

Appendix 6.2

Three samples were drawn from the total set of all available families studied at OSLC. The groups were Stealers, Social Aggressors, and Normals. To be included in any of these groups the target child had to be a male between the ages of 5 and 13, and the family participated in a minimum of three baseline home observations.

The demographic characteristics of the subjects in the three samples are described below:

Demographic Information

		Social Aggressors N = 37	Stealers N = 38	Normals N = 38
Target child's age at intake				
	$\overline{x}$	8.25	9.45	8.90
	SD	1.81	2.13	1.98
	range	5.75 → 12.58	5.08 → 12.75	5.25 → 12.08
Family size				
	$\overline{x}$	4.4	5.2	4.5
	SD	1.41	1.72	1.27
	range	2 → 8	2 → 9	2 → 7
Father absent in family				
		51%	32%	26%
Occupational status†				
	$\overline{x}$	4.81	5.1	4.1
	SD	1.91	1.55	1.86
	range	1 → 7	3 → 7	1 → 7

†As measured by the Hollingshead index.

The criteria for inclusion in one of the three groups were defined as follows:

Stealers

The target child had to be stealing at a high rate. High-rate stealing was defined by three or more events. Three methods of recording stealing were used: parent report at intake, Parent Daily Report (PDR), and court records. At intake, parents were asked whether or not stealing was a problem behavior for their child. Eighty-two percent of the parents of the boys in this sample responded affirmatively. During Parent Daily Report telephone calls, 100% of the parents reported the target child to be stealing. Fifty percent of the boys in this sample also had court records for stealing. Ninety-two percent of the boys in this sample had stealing records for two of the three stealing measures.

There were 38 subject families with a target boy who met the criteria to be included in the Stealer sample.

Social Aggressors

Thirty-seven families were identified in which there was a target boy who was identified as a Social Aggressor. The home observation data for these boys showed them to be emitting aversive behaviors at ≥.45 per minute. The parental complaints at intake identified the child as a severe conduct problem. However, stealing was not identified as a major problem. Criteria for stealing (described above) were used, and the following decision rules were applied. If stealing was mentioned by parents at intake, it was required not to have occurred more than once (or be defined as a problem) for a subject to be included in the Social Aggressor sample. If stealing was reported during the PDR calls, it could not occur more than once. If there was a court record of stealing, the event could not have occurred during the baseline or treatment periods. No subject was included in this sample for whom there was a record of stealing on more than one measure.

Normals

Thirty-eight subject families were found who satisfied the criteria to be included in this sample. The home observation data for these boys showed them to be emitting aversive behaviors at $\leq .45$ per minute. Stealing was not a problem for these youngsters. Three subjects were reported to have stolen once during PDR calls. None of these subjects had a court record for stealing.

Appendix 8.1
The Pumpkin Experiment
(prepared by M. Forgatch)

This study was designed to test for the effect of negative reinforcement upon two categories of child behavior. On each of three days the mother and child participated in an ABA reversal design. The study took place in the home.

Methods

Sample

The subject family consisted of a Mother, a Father, and a 3½-year-old boy, who was the target child, and a 2½-year-old sibling. At intake, the mother described the child as being an extremely difficult child to manage. On the problem behaviors checklist she indicated that 20 of the possible 26 were problems. For the first baseline observation probe, the target child's TAB score was .54. There were 21 baseline observation hours. The father was present for seven baseline observations.

The family lived in a pleasant house in a middle-class residential neighborhood in Eugene.

Observation Procedures

The data was collected by two professional observers who had experience and demonstrated reliability in using the FICS. As in the earlier study, observer agreement was checked for 20% of the observations. Weekly retraining sessions were held. The observers were uninformed of the hypotheses and manipulations. Most of the sessions were in the late afternoon. The family was paid $5.00 per observation hour during baseline and $7.50 per hour for experimental manipulations.

The manipulations for this study were carried out with the father absent.

Apparatus

A cuing device was developed to provide immediate feedback to the mother during the manipulation. The apparatus consisted of a transmitter small enough to fit in the experimenter's hand and a receiver worn on the mother's waist, with a tiny hearing device in her ear. This enabled the experimenter to speak directly, yet privately, to the mother. This improved communication between the experimenter and the mother during the manipulation.

Manipulation

The sequence of behaviors selected to be manipulated was: mother-Command → child-Provoke → mother-Positive or -Neutral. These behaviors were easy for the mother to distinguish and to perform. She did, however, emit many more commands than requested.

The mother learned the code definitions for the behavior relevant to the manipulation. She then wrote her commands to Pumpkin for one day. Then the mother and experimenter practiced the sequence of behaviors.

Following each day's manipulation, the experimenter provided the mother with corrective feedback. On the first day of the experiment, during

Effects of Manipulating Negative Reinforcement for Pumpkin's Provoking Behavior

Days	p(Pumpkin-Provoke|Mother-Command)			Frequency Negative Reinforcement		
	A_1	B	A_2	A_1	B	A_2
One	.10	.20	.00	0	5	0
Two	.16	.40	.00	3	5	0
Three	.17	.27	.11	1	5	0
Mean:	.14	.29	.04	Sum: 4	15	0

As shown there, the mean baseline (A_1) was .14. The three sessions of providing negative reinforcement increased the strength of the connection to .29.

The right side of the table showed that the procedures were largely effective in controlling the reinforcing behavior of the mother.

the manipulation (B) phase, the child became extremely out of control. During each of the following three days, the instructions were changed so that, in addition to the negative reinforcement arrangement, the mother was to engage in a structured interaction with Pumpkin, such as play or work together.

Design

The basic design was an A_1, B, A_2 sequence on each of four days in the home. During the daily baseline periods, which lasted 20 minutes each, the mother was instructed to give Pumpkin approximately four commands. This was her base rate for commands.

During the 20-minute daily experimental phase, the mother was instructed to increase her commands fourfold. Whenever Pumpkin responded to the command with a Provoke, the mother was instructed to talk nicely to him, or to play with him, or to begin doing something else. She was instructed not to be aversive following a Provoke in this sequence.

Results

The base rate for mother-Command was .08, for Pumpkin-Ignore .01, and for Pumpkin-Provoke .04. Both of these child target events were functionally related to mother-Command. For child-Ignore, given mother-Command, the conditional p value was .10; the comparable value for child-Provoke, given mother-Command, was .09. These two behaviors constitute a functionally defined response class.

The table summarizes the relation between Child-Provoke and mother-Command during the three conditions for each of the three days.

Appendix 11.1
Sample Comparison by Code Categories for Target Children

Variable	Stealers (N = 37)	Social Aggressors (N = 34)	Normals (N = 36)	$F(2, 99)$	Duncan
AP	.02	.02	.04	5.14**	N > ST&SA
AT	.84	.71	1.07	4.83**	N > SA
CM	.08	.07	.03	9.70***	ST&SA > N
CN	.02	.01	.00	6.33***	ST&SA > N
DI	.13	.20	.05	17.46***	ST ≠ SA ≠ N
DS	.04	.04	.00	3.27*	ST&SA > N
HU	.01	.03	.00	4.14*	SA > N
IG	.01	.01	.00	4.65**	ST&SA > N
NC	.08	.15	.03	19.11***	ST ≠ SA ≠ N
NE	.02	.10	.01	4.31*	SA > N&ST
NR	.09	.08	.04	7.19***	ST&SA > N
PN	.03	.04	.01	5.44**	ST&SA > N
TE	.04	.07	.01	9.87***	SA > ST&N
WH	.04	.11	.01	9.93***	SA > ST&N
YE	.05	.06	.01	5.62***	ST&SA > N

Only those categories for which the differences were significant are listed.

*$p < .05$

**$p < .01$

***$p < .001$

About the Author

Gerald R. Patterson is a research scientist at the Oregon Social Learning Center. His work has been in the areas of aggression, family intervention in the homes of antisocial and delinquent boys, field observation procedures, and marital conflict. Dr. Patterson is the author of *Families* and *Living with Children,* and is co-author of *A Social Learning Approach to Family Intervention,* Volume 1: *Families with Aggressive Children.* He has written many articles for professional journals and has been a consulting editor for *Child Development.*

Dr. Patterson is a past president of the Association for the Advancement of Behavior Therapy and has received a Career Development Award from the National Institute of Mental Health. Much of the present volume was written while he was a fellow in residence at the Center for Advanced Studies in the Behavioral Sciences at Stanford University. In 1979 he was one of the recipients of an award for Outstanding Research on Aggression from the International Society for Research on Aggression. In 1982 he has been selected to receive the Distinguished Scientist Award from the American Psychological Association, Division of Clinical Psychology, Section III.

When Dr. Patterson is not working on research problems he can be found fly fishing for trout and steelhead, and in the Winter searching for powder snow in the trees on the other side of the mountains.

References

Achenbach, T.M. The classification of children's psychiatric symptoms: A factor analytic study. *Psychological Monographs*, 1966, *80* (7, Whole No. 615).

Achenbach, T.M. The child behavior profile, I: Boys aged 6 through 11. *Journal of Consulting and Clinical Psychology*, 1978, *46*(3). 478-488.

Achenbach, T.M., & Edelbrock, C.S. *The classification of child psychopathology: A review and analysis of empirical efforts toward consulting and clinical psychology*, 1978, in press.

Ackerson, L. *Children's behavior problems* (Vol. 1). University of Chicago Press, 1931.

Adler, A. *The practice and theory of individual psychology.* London: Routledge & Kegan Paul Ltd., 1929.

Alexander, J.F., & Parsons, B.V. Short term behavioral intervention with delinquent families: Impact on family process and recidivism. *Journal of Abnormal Psychology*, 1973, *81*, 219-225.

Altmann, S. Sociobiology of the rhesus monkey. II. Stochastics of social communication. *Journal of Theoretical Biology*, 1965, *8*, 490-522.

Anderson, L.M. Personality characteristics of parents of neurotic, aggressive, and normal preadolescent boys. *Journal of Consulting and Clinical Psychology*, 1969, *33*(5), 575-581.

Antonovsky, H.F. A contribution to research in area of mother/child relationships. *Child Development*, 1959, *30*, 37-51.

Argyle, M., & Cook, M. *Gaze and mutual gaze.* London: Cambridge University Press, 1976.

Arnold, J., Levine, A., & Patterson, G.R. Changes in sibling behavior following family intervention. *Journal of Consulting and Clinical Psychology*, 1975, *43*, 683-688.

Atkinson, J.A. *Nonavailability of mother attention as an antecedent event for coercive demands in the preschool child.* Unpublished master's thesis, University of Oregon, 1971.

Attneave, F. *Applications of information theory to psychology: A summary of basic concepts, methods, and results.* New York: Holt-Dryden, 1959.

Averill, J.R. Personal control over aversive stimuli and its relationship to stress. *Psychological Bulletin*, 1973, *80*, 286-303.

Azrin, N.H., Holtz, W. Ulrich, R., & Goldiamond, I. The control of conversation through reinforcement. *Journal of Experimental Analysis of Behavior*, 1961, *4*, 25-30.

Azrin, N.H., Naster, B.J., & Jones, R. Reciprocity counseling: A rapid learning based procedure for marital counseling. *Behavior Research and Therapy*, 1973, *11*, 1-18.

Bach, G.R., & Wyden, P. *The intimate enemy.* New York: Avon Books, 1968.

Bales, R.F. *Interaction process and analysis.* Cambridge, Massachusetts: Addison-Wesley, 1950.

Bales, R.F. The equilibrium problem in small groups. In T. Parsons, R. Bales, & E. Shilo (Eds.), *Working papers in the theory of action.* New York: Free Press, 1953.

Baltes, M., & Reese, H.W. Operant research in violation of the operant paradigm. In B.C. Etzel, J.M. LeBlanc, & D.M. Baer (Eds.), *Contributions to behavioral research.* Hillsdale, New Jersey: Lawrence Erlbaum Assoc., 1977.

Bandura, A. *Aggression: A social learning analysis.* Englewood Cliffs, New Jersey: Prentice-Hall, 1973.

Bandura, A. Behavior theory and the models of man: Presidential address for the American Psychological Association. *American Psychological Association Monitor,* 1974, *5*(11).

Bandura, A. *Social learning theory.* New York: General Learning Press, 1977.

Bandura, A., & Walters, R.H. *Adolescent aggression.* New York: Ronald Press Co., 1959.

Bandura, A., & Walters, R.H. *Social learning and personality development.* New York: Holt, Rinehart & Winston, 1963.

Barber, T.X. Toward a theory of pain: Relief of chronic pain by pre-frontal leucotomy, opiates, placebos, and hypnosis. *Psychological Bulletin,* 1959, *56,* 430-460.

Barker, R.G. *One boy's day.* New York: Harper and Row, 1951.

Barker, R.G. The stream of behavior as an empirical problem. In R.G. Barker (Ed.), *The stream of behavior.* New York: Appleton-Century-Crofts, 1963.

Barker, R.G. *Ecological psychology.* Stanford, California: Stanford University Press, 1968.

Barker, R.G., Gump, P.V., Campbell, W.J., Barker, L.S., Willems, E., Friesen, W., Le Compte, W., & Mikesell, E.H. *Big school-small school.* (University cooperative project #594). Kansas: Midwest Psychological Field Station, 1962.

Barker, R.G., & Wright, H.F. *Midwest and its children.* Evanston, Illinois: Row Peterson, 1954.

Barnett, L., & Nietzel, M. Relationship of instrumental and affectional behavior and self esteem to marital satisfaction in distressed and nondistressed couples. *Journal of Consulting and Clinical Psychology,* 1979. *47,* 946-957.

Baron, R.A. Social reinforcement effects as a function of social reinforcement history. *Psychological Review,* 1966, *73,* 527-540.

Baron, R.A. Aggression as a function of magnitude of victim's pain cues, level of prior anger arousal, and aggressor-victim similarity. *Journal of Personality and Social Psychology,* 1971a, *18,* 48-54.

Baron, R.A. Magnitude of victim's pain cues and level of prior anger arousal as determinants of adult aggressive behavior. *Journal of Personality and Social Psychology,* 1971b, *17*(3), 236-243.

Barrett, D.E., & Radke-Yarrow, M. Prosocial behavior, social inferential ability, and assertiveness in children. *Child Development,* 1977, *48,* 475-481.

Bartlett, M.S. The frequency goodness of fit test for probability chains. *Proceedings of the Cambridge Philosophical Society,* 1951, *47,* 86-95.

Baumrind, D. Effects of authoritative parental control on child behavior. *Child Development,* 1966, *37*(4), 887-907.

Baumrind, D. Current patterns of parental authority. *Developmental Psychology,* 1971, *4*(1), 12.

Baumrind, D. Parental disciplinary patterns and social competence in children. *Youth and Society,* 1978, *9*(3), 239-272.

Baumrind, D. *New directions in socialization research.* Paper presented at the Society of Research in Child Development, San Francisco, 1979.

Baumrind, D., & Black, A. Socialization practices associated with dimensions of competence in preschool boys and girls. *Child Development,* 1967, *38,* 291-307.

Bechtel, R.B. The study of man: Human movement and architecture. *Transaction,* May 1967, 53-56.

Becker, W.C. The relationship of factors in parental ratings of self and each other to the behavior of kindergarten children as rated by mothers, fathers, and teachers. *Journal of Consulting Psychology,* 1960, *24,* 507-527.

Becker, W.C., Madsen, C.H., Arnold, C.R., & Thomas, D.R. The contingent use of teacher attention and praise in reducing classroom behavior problems. *Journal of Special Education,* 1967, *1,* 287-307.

Bell, R.Q. A reinterpretation of the direction of effects in studies of socialization. *Psychological Review*, 1968, *75*, 81-95.

Bell, R.Q., & Harper, L.V. *Child effects on adults.* Hillsdale, New Jersey: Laurence Erlbaum Associates, 1977.

Bem, D. Self perception: An alternative interpretation of cognitive dissonance phenomenon. *Psychological Review*, 1967, *74*, 183-200.

Benning, J.J., Feldhusen, J.F., & Thurston, J.R. *Delinquency prone youth: Longitudinal and preventive research.* (Eau Claire County Youth Study, Phase III). Wisconsin State Department of Health and Social Services, 1968.

Berkowitz, L. The contagion of violence: An S-R mediational analysis of some effects of observed aggression. In W.J. Arnold & M.M. Page (Eds.), *Nebraska Symposium on Motivation.* Lincoln: University of Nebraska Press, 1970.

Berkowitz, L. Control of aggression. In B.M. Caldwell & R. Riecute (Eds.), *Review of child development research.* University of Chicago Press, 1973a.

Berkowitz, L. Words and symbols as stimuli to aggressive responses. In J. Knutson (Ed.), *The control of aggression: Implications from basic research.* Chicago: Aldine Press, 1973b.

Berkowitz, L. Some determinants of impulsive aggression: Role of mediated association with reinforcement for aggression. *Psychological Review*, March 1974, 165-176.

Berkowitz, L. Is criminal violence normative behavior? *Journal of Research in Crime and Delinquency*, 1978, *15*(2), 148-161.

Berlyne, D.E. Arousal and reinforcement. In D. Levine (Ed.), *Nebraska Symposium on Motivation.* Lincoln: University of Nebraska Press, 1967.

Bernal, M.E., Delfini, L.F., North, J.A., & Kreutzer, S.L. Comparison of boys' behavior in homes and classrooms. In E. Mash, L. Handy, & L. Hamerlynck (Eds.), *Behavior modification and families.* New York: Brunner/Mazell, 1976.

Bernal, M.E., Gibson, D.M., Williams, D.E., & Pesses, D.I. A device for recording automatic audio tape recording. *Journal of Applied Behavior Analysis*, 1971, *4*, 151-156.

Bernard, J.L., & Eisenman, R. Verbal conditioning in sociopaths with social and monetary reinforcement. *Journal of Personality and Social Psychology*, 1967, *6*(2), 203-206.

Bing, E. Effect of child-rearing practices on development of differential cognitive abilities. *Child Development*, 1963, *34*, 631-648.

Birchler, G.R., & Webb, L.F. Discriminating interaction patterns in happy and unhappy marriages. *Journal of Consulting and Clinical Psychology*, 1977, *45*(3), 494-495.

Birchler, G.R., Weiss, R.L., & Vincent, J.P. Multi-method analysis of social reinforcement exchange between maritally distressed and nondistressed spouse and stranger dyads. *Journal of Personality and Social Psychology*, 1975, *31*(2), 349-360.

Black, R.W. Shifts in magnitude of reward and contrast effects in instrument and selective learning. *Psychological Review*, 1968, *75*, 114-126.

Blau, P.M. *Exchange and power in social life.* New York: John Wiley and Sons, 1964.

Blood, R.O., & Wolfe, D.M. *Husbands and wives: The dynamics of married living.* New York: The Free Press, 1960.

Blumberg, M. When parents hit out. In S.K. Steinmetz & M.A. Straus (Eds.), *Violence in the family.* New York: Dodd, Mead & Company, 1974.

Blumenthal, M., Kohn, R.L., Andrews, F.M., & Head, K.B. *Justifying violence: Attitudes of American men.* Institute of Juvenile Research, University of Michigan, 1972.

Blurton-Jones, N.G. Some aspects of the social behavior of children in nursery school. In D. Morris (Ed.), *Primate ethology.* London: Weidenfeld & Nicholson, 1966.

Bobbitt, R., Gourevitch, V., Miller, L., & Jensen, G. Dynamics of social interaction behavior: A computerized procedure for analyzing trends, patterns, and sequences. *Psychological Bulletin*, 1969, *71*, 110-112.

Bogaard, L. *Relationship between aggressive behavior in children and parent perception of child behavior.* Unpublished doctoral dissertation, University of Oregon, 1976.

Brackbill, Y., & O'Hara, J. The relative effectiveness of reward and punishment for discrimination learning in children. *Journal of Comparative and Physiological Psychology*, 1958, *51*, 747-751.

Bradburn, N.M., & Caplovitz, D. *Reports on Happiness.* Chicago: Aldine Publishing Co., 1965.

Brady, J.V., Porter, R.W., Conrad, D.G., & Mason, J.W. Avoidance behavior and the development of gastroduodenal ulcers. *Journal of the Experimental Analysis of Behavior,* 1958, *1,* 69-72.

Bronfenbrenner, U. Socialization and social class through time and space. In E.E. Maccoby, M. Newcomb, & E.L. Hartley (Eds.), *Readings in social psychology.* New York: Holt, Rinehart & Winston, 1958.

Bronfenbrenner, U. Towards an experimental ecology of human development. *American Psychologist,* 1977, 513.

Brown, G.W., Bhrolchain, M.N., & Harris, T. Social class and psychiatric disturbance among women in an urban population. *Sociology,* 1976, *9,* 226-259.

Brown, G.W., Birley, J.L., & Wing, J.K. Influence of family life on the course of schizophrenic disorders: A replication. *British Journal of Psychology,* 1972, *121,* 241-258.

Brown, G.W., & Rutter, M. The measurement of family activities and relationships: A methodological study. *Human Relations,* 1966, *19,* 241-263.

Bryan, J.H., & Kapche, R. Psychopathy and verbal conditioning. *Journal of Abnormal Psychology,* 1967, *72,* 71.

Budd, K.S., Green, D.K., & Baer, D.N. An analysis of multi misplaced parental social contingencies. *Journal of Applied Behavior Analysis,* 1976, *9,* 459-470.

Buehler, R.E., Patterson, G.R., & Furniss, J.M. The reinforcement of behavior in institutional settings. *Behavior Research and Therapy,* 1966, *4,* 157-167.

Burgess, J.M., Kimball, W.H., & Burgess, R.L. *Family interaction as a function of family size.* Paper presented at the Southeastern Conference on Human Development, 1978.

Burgess, R.L. Child abuse: A behavioral analysis. In B.B. Lahey & A.E. Kazdin (Eds.), *Advances in child clinical psychology.* New York: Plenum, 1978.

Burgess, R.L., & Bushnell, D. *Behavioral sociology: Experimental analysis of social process.* New York: Columbia University Press, 1969.

Burgess, R.L., & Conger, R.D. *Family interaction patterns related to child abuse and neglect: Some preliminary findings.* Paper presented at the International Congress on Child Abuse and Neglect, Geneva, Switzerland, September 20, 1976.

Burgess, R.L., & Huston, T.L. (Eds.). *Social exchange in developing relationships.* New York: Academic Press, 1979.

Burton, R.V. Validity of retrospective reports assessed by the multitrait-multimethod analysis, *Developmental Psychology Monographs,* 1970, *3*(3), 2.

Buss, A.H. *The psychology of aggression.* New York: John Wiley & Sons, 1961.

Buss, A.H. Instrumentality of aggression feedback and frustration as determinants of physical aggression. *Journal of Personality and Social Psychology,* 1966a, *3,* 153-162.

Buss, A.H. The effect of harm on subsequent aggression. *Journal of Experimental Research in Personality,* 1966b, *1,* 249-255.

Buss, A.H. Aggression pays. In J.L. Singer (Ed.), *The control of aggression and violence.* New York: Academic Press, 1971.

Byrne, D., & Rhamey, R. Magnitude of positive and negative reinforcements as a determinant of attraction. *Journal of Personality and Social Psychology,* 1965, *2,* 884-889.

Cairns, R.B. Fighting and punishment from a developmental perspective. *Nebraska Symposium on Motivation.* Lincoln: University of Nebraska Press, 1972.

Cairns, R.B. (Ed.). *The analysis of social interaction: Methods, issues, and illustrations.* Hillsdale, New Jersey: Lawrence Erlbaum Associates, 1979a.

Cairns, R.B. *Social development: The origins and plasticity of interchanges.* San Francisco: W.H. Freeman and Company, 1979b.

Cairns, R.B., & Green, J.A. How to assess personality and social patterns: Observations or ratings? In R.B. Cairns (Ed.), *The analysis of social interaction: Methods, issues, and illustrations.* Hillsdale, New Jersey: Lawrence Erlbaum Associates, 1979.

Cairns, R.B., & Nakelski, J.S. On fighting mice: Ontogenetic and experimental determinants. *Comparative and Physiological Psychology,* 1971, *74,* 354-364.

Cairns, R.B., & Scholz, S. Fighting mice: Dyadic escalation and what is learned. *Comparative and Physiological Psychology,* 1973, *85,* 540-550.

Caldwell, B.M. A new "approach" to behavioral ecology. In J.P. Hill (Ed.), *Minnesota Symposia on Child Psychology* (Vol. 2). Minneapolis: University of Minnesota Press, 1968.

Caldwell, B.M. A new approach to behavioral ecology. In J.P. Hill (Ed.), *Minnesota Symposia on Child Psychology* (Vol. 5). Minneapolis: University of Minnesota Press, 1971.

Call, D.J. *Delinquency, frustration, and noncommitment.* Unpublished doctoral dissertation, University of Oregon, 1965.

Camp, B.W. Verbal mediation in young aggressive boys. *Journal of Abnormal Psychology,* 1977, *86,* 145-153.

Camp, B.W. Zimet, S., Doomineck, W., & Dahlm, N. Verbal abilities in young aggressive boys. *Journal of Educational Psychology,* 1977, *69,* 129-135.

Campbell, A. The American way of mating. *Psychology Today,* 1975, *8,* 37-43.

Campbell, B.A., & Church, R.M. (Eds.). *Punishment and aversive behavior.* New York: Appleton-Century-Crofts, 1969.

Carlson, W. *Hyperactive, socially aggressive, and normal children observed in their natural home environment.* Unpublished manuscript, 1979. (Available from Humboldt State University, Arcata, California 95521.)

Carlson, W. *Factor generated response class scaling.* Unpublished manuscript, 1981a. (Available from Humboldt State University, Arcata, California 95521.)

Carlson, W. *Hyperactive, conduct disordered, and normal children observed in their natural home environments.* Unpublished manuscript, 1981b. (Available from Humboldt State University, Arcata, California 95521.)

Casey, I.G. *A comparison of the effectiveness of approval and disapproval in modifying children's behavior.* Unpublished doctoral dissertation, University of Wisconsin, 1967.

Chamberlain, P. *Standardization of a parent report measure.* Unpublished doctoral dissertation, University of Oregon, 1980.

Chamberlain, P. *Parent report data: Methodological considerations.* OSLC manuscript in preparation.

Charlesworth, R., & Hartup, W.W. An observation study of positive social reinforcement in the nursery school peer group. *Child Development,* 1967, *38,* 993-1002.

Charny, I.W. The origins of violence between spouses and siblings. *Family Process,* 1969, *8,* 1-24.

Chodorow, N. *The reproduction of mothering, psychoanalysis, and the sociology of gender.* Berkeley, California: University of California Press, 1978.

Christensen, A. *Cost effectiveness in behavior family therapy.* Unpublished doctoral dissertation, University of Oregon, 1976.

Christiansen, K.O. The genesis of aggressive criminality: Implications of a study of crime in a Danish twin study. In J. DeWit & W.W. Hartup (Eds.), *Determinants and origins of aggressive behavior.* The Hague, Paris: Mouton, 1974.

Church, R.M. The varied effects of punishment on behavior. *Psychological Review,* 1963, *70,* 369-402.

Church, R.M. Response suppression. In B.A. Campbell & R.M. Church (Eds.), *Punishment and aversive behavior.* New York: Appleton-Century-Crofts, 1969.

Church, R.M. & Getty, D.J. Some consequences of the reaction to an aversive event. *Psychological Bulletin,* 1972, *78,* 21-27.

Cicirelli, V.G. Mother-child and sibling-sitting interactions on a problem solving task. *Child Development,* 1976, *47,* 588-596.

Clarke-Stewart, K. Interactions between mothers and their young children: Characteristics and consequences. *Monographs of the Society for Research in Child Development,* 1973, *38*(6-7, Serial No. 153).

Clarke-Stewart, K.A. And daddy makes three: The father's impact on mother and young child. *Child Development,* 1978, *49,* 466-478.

Clement, P.W., & Milne, D.C. Group play therapy and tangible reinforcers used to modify the behavior of eight-year-old boys. *Behavior Research and Therapy,* 1967, *5,* 301-312.

Coates, J.M. Population and education: How demographic trends will shape the U.S. *Futurist,* February 1978, 35-42.

Cobb, J.A. *Survival skills and first grade academic achievement.* Unpublished manuscript, Center of Research and Demonstration in the Early Education of Handicapped Children, University of Oregon, December 1970.

Cobb, J.A. The relationship of discrete classroom behaviors to fourth-grade academic achievement. *Journal of Educational Psychology,* 1972, *63*(1), 74-80.

Cobb, J.A. & Hops, H. Effects of academic survival skill training on low achieving first graders. *Journal of Educational Research,* 1973.

Cohen, J.A. Coefficient of agreement for nominal scales. *Educational and Psychological Measurement,* 1960, *20*(1), 37-46.

Collins, R.C. *The treatment of disruptive behavior problems by employment of a partial-milieu consistency program.* Unpublished doctoral dissertation, University of Oregon, 1966.

Conger, J.J. & Miller, W.C. *Personality, social class, and delinquency.* New York: John Wiley & Sons, 1966.

Conger, R.D., & Burgess, R. *Reciprocity: Equity system stability.* Unpublished manuscript, 1978. (Available from the University of Georgia, Athens, Georgia.)

Conger, R.D., & Smith, S.S. Examining equity in dyadic and family interactions: Is there any justice? In E. Filsinger & R. Lewis (Eds.), *Marital observation and behavioral assessment: Recent developments and techniques.* Beverly Hills, California: Sage Press, 1981, in press.

Connolly, K., & Smith, P.K. Reactions of preschool children to a strange observer. In N. Blurton-Jones (Ed.), *Ethological studies of child behavior.* Cambridge: Cambridge University Press, 1972.

Coombs, C., Dawes, R., & Tversky, A. *Mathematical psychology: An elementary introduction.* Englewood Cliffs, New Jersey: Prentice-Hall, Inc., 1970.

Coopersmith, S. *The antecedents of self-esteem.* San Francisco: W.H. Freeman & Co., 1967.

Corah, N.L., & Boffa, J. Perceived control, self-observation, and response to an aversive stimulation. *Journal of Personality and Social Psychology,* 1970, *16,* 1-4.

Corte, H.E., Wolf, M.M., & Lecke, B.J. A comparison of procedures for eliminating self injurious behavior of retarded adolescents. *Journal of Applied Behavioral Analysis,* 1971, *4,* 201-213.

Cox, R.D., Gunn, W.B., & Cox, M.J. *A film assessment and comparison of the social skillfulness of behavior problem and nonproblem male children.* Paper presented at the Association for the Advancement of Behavior Therapy, New York, December 3-5, 1976.

Cronbach, L.J., Gleser, G.C., Nanda, H., & Rajaratnam, N. *The dependability of behavioral measurements: Theory of generalizability of scores and profiles.* New York: John Wiley & Sons, 1972.

Cureton, L. *Early identification of behavior prob-*

lems (Final Report, Vol. 1). American Institute for Research, Silver Springs, Maryland, 1970.

Dawe, H.C. An analysis of two hundred quarrels of preschool children. *Child Development,* 1934, *5,* 139-157.

Dawes, R.M. *Jackknifing Guttman scales and unfolded scales.* Unpublished manuscript, 1978.

Delfini, L.F., Bernal, M.E., & Rosen, P.M. Comparison of deviant and normal boys in home settings. In E.J. Mash, L.A. Hamerlynck, & L.C. Handy (Eds.), *Behavior modification and families.* New York: Brunner/Mazel, 1976.

de Madariaga, S. *Hernan Cortes: Conqueror of of Mexico.* New York: Doubleday, 1967.

De Master, B., Reid, J.B., & Twentyman, C. The effects of different amounts of feedback on observers' reliability. *Behavior Therapy,* 1976, *8,* 317-329.

Denenberg, V.H. Developmental factors in aggression. In J.F. Knutson (Ed.), *The control of aggression.* Aldine Publishing Co., 1973.

Dengerink, H.A. Personality variables as mediators of attack instigated aggression. In R. Geen & E. O'Neal (Eds.), *Perspectives in aggression.* New York: Academic Press, 1976, in press.

Dengerink, H.A., Schnedler, R.S., & Covey, M.K. The role of avoidance in aggressive responses to attack and no attack. *Journal of Personality and Social Psychology,* 1978, *36,* 1044-1053.

Deur, J.L., & Parke, R.D. Effects of inconsistent punishment on aggression in children. *Developmental Psychology,* 1970, *2,* 403-411.

Devereaux, E. The role of peer group experience in moral development. In J. Hill (Ed.), *Minnesota Symposia on Child Psychology.* University of Minnesota Press, 1970.

Devine, V.T. *The coercion process: A laboratory analogue.* Unpublished doctoral dissertation, State University of New York at Stony Brook, 1971.

Dodge, K. Social cognition and children's aggressive behavior. *Child Development,* 1980, *51,* 162-170.

Dohrenwend, B.S., & Dohrenwend, B.P. (Eds.). *Stressful life events: Their nature and effects.* New York: John Wiley & Sons, 1974.

Dollard, J., Doob, L.W., Miller, N.E., Mowrer, O.H., & Sears, R.R. *Frustration and aggression.* New Haven, Connecticut: Yale University Press, 1939.

Douglas, J.W. The school progress of nervous and troublesome children. *British Journal of Psychiatry,* 1966, *112,* 1115-1116.

Douglas, J.W., Lawson, A., Cooper, J.E., Cooper, E. Family interaction and the activities of young children. *Journal of Child Psychology and Psychiatry,* 1968, *9,* 157-171.

Dreger, R.M., Lewis, P.M., Rich, T.A., Miller, K.S., Reid, M.P., Overlade, D., Taffel, C., & Flemming, E. Behavioral classification project. *Journal of Consulting Psychology,* 1964, *28,* 1-13.

Driscoll, R. *Incidental and intentional learning and social competence in high risk children.* Paper presented at the 87th Annual Convention of the American Psychological Association, New York, September 1979.

Dulany, D.E. The place of hypotheses and intentions: An analysis of verbal control in verbal conditioning. In C. Eriksen (Ed.), *Behavior and awareness: A symposium of research and interpretation.* Duke University Press, 1962.

Eibl-Eibesfeldt, I. Phylogenetic adaptation as determinants of aggressive behavior in man. In J. DeWit & W.W. Hartup (Eds.), *Determinants and origins of aggressive behavior.* The Hague, Paris: Mouton, 1974.

Elliott, D.S. *Experimental study of the labelling hypothesis.* Paper presented at the Annual Conference of the American Society on Criminology, Philadelphia, November 1979.

Elliott, D.S., Ageton, S.S., & Canter, R.J. An integrated theoretical perspective on delinquent behaviors. *Journal of Research in Crime and Delinquency,* January 1979, 3-27.

Elliott, D.S., & Huizinga, D. *Defining patterned delinquency: A conceptual typology of delinquency offenders.* Paper presented at the 32nd Annual Conference of the American Society on Criminology, San Francisco, November 1980.

Elliott, D.S., & Voss, N.L. *Delinquency and dropout.* Lexington, Massachusetts: D.C. Heath & Co., 1974.

Emerson, R. Exchange theory (Part I): A psychological basis for social exchange. In J. Berger, M. Zelditch Jr., & B. Anderson (Eds.), *Sociological theories in progress.* New York: Houghton-Mifflin Co., 1972.

Erickson, M.R. *Effects of initial information and observational set upon social perception.* Unpublished doctoral dissertation, University of Oregon, 1973.

Eriksen, C.W. (Ed.). *Behavior and awareness: A symposium of research and interpretation.* Durham, North Carolina: Duke University Press, 1962.

Erlanger, H.S. Social class and corporal punishment in child rearing: A reassessment. *American Sociological Review,* 1974, *39,* 68-85.

Eron, L.D., Walder, L.O., Huesmann, L.R., & Lefkowitz, M.M. The convergence of laboratory and field studies of the development of aggression. In J. DeWit & W.W. Hartup (Eds.), *Determinants and origins of aggressive behavior.* The Hague, Paris: Mouton, 1974.

Eron, L.D., Walder, L.O., & Lefkowitz, M.M. *Learning of aggression in children.* Boston: Little Brown & Co., 1971.

Estes, W.K. An experimental study of punishment. *Psychological Monographs,* 1944, *57*(3, Whole No. 263).

Estes, W.K. Reward in human learning: Theoretical issues and strategic choice points. In R. Glaser (Ed.), *The nature of reinforcement.* New York: Academic Press, 1971.

Fagan, O.S., Langner, T.S., Gersten, J.C., & Eisenberg, J. *Violent and antisocial behavior: A longitudinal study of urban youth. Interim report.* New York: Division of Epidemiology, Columbia University School of Public Health, 1977.

Fagot, B. Sex related stereotyping of toddlers' behaviors. *Developmental Psychology,* 1973, *9,* 429.

Fagot, B. Sex differences in toddlers' behavior and parental reaction. *Developmental Psychology,* 1974, *10*(4), 554-558.

Fagot, B. Reinforcing contingencies for sex role behavior: Effect of experience with children. *Child Development,* 1978a, *49,* 30-36.

Fagot, B. The influence of sex of child and parental reactions to toddler children. *Child Development,* 1978b, *49,* 459.

Fagot, B., & Patterson, G.R. An in vivo analysis of reinforcing contingencies for sex-role behaviors in the preschool child. *Developmental Psychology,* 1969, *1*(5), 563-568.

Fawl, C.L. Disturbances experienced by children in their natural habitats. In R. Barker (Ed.), *The stream of behavior.* New York: Appleton-Century-Crofts, 1963.

Ferguson, L., Partzka, L., & Lester, B. Patterns of parent perception differentiating clinic from nonclinic children. *Journal of Abnormal Child Psychology,* 1974, *2,* 169-182.

Feshbach, N., & Feshbach, S. The relationship between empathy and aggression in two age groups. *Developmental Psychology,* 1969, *1,* 102-107.

Feshbach, S. Aggression. In P.H. Mussen (Ed.), *Carmichael's manual of child psychology* (Vol. 2). New York: John Wiley & Sons, 1970.

Festinger, L. The treatment of qualitative data by scale analysis. *Psychological Bulletin,* 1947, *44,* 149-161.

Field, M.H., & Field, H.F. Marital violence and the criminal process: Neither justice nor peace. *Social Service Review,* 1973, *47(2),* 221-240.

Fiske, D.W. The limits for the conventional science of personality. *Journal of Personality,* 1974, *42(1),* 1-11.

Fleischman, M.J. *Training and evaluation of aggressive children.* Proposal submitted to NIMH Crime and Delinquency section, April 1979a.

Fleischman, M.J. Using parenting salaries to control attrition and cooperation in therapy. *Behavior Therapy,* 1979b, *10,* 111-116.

Fleischman, M.J. A replication of Patterson's intervention for boys with conduct problems. *Journal of Consulting and Clinical Psychology,* 1981, *49,* 342-354.

Fleischman, M.J., & Szykula, S.A. A community setting repliction of a social learning treatment for aggressive children. *Behavior Therapy,* 1981, *12(1),* 115-122.

Follick, M.J., & Knutson, J.F. Punishment of irritable aggression. *Aggressive Behavior,* 1977, *4,* 1-17.

Forehand, R., King, H., Peed, S., & Yoder, P. Mother-child interaction: Comparison of a noncompliant clinic group and a nonclinic group. *Behavior Research and Therapy,* 1975, *13,* 79-84.

Forehand, R., Wells, K., & Griest, D. An examination of the social validity of a parent training program. *Behavior Therapy,* 1980, *11,* 488-502.

Forehand, R., Wells, K., & Sturgis, E. Predictors of child noncompliant behavior in the home. *Journal of Consulting and Clinical Psychology,* 1978, *46,* 179.

Forgatch, M., & Wieder, G. *The parent adolescent naturalistic interaction code (PANIC).* Unpublished manuscript, 1981. (Available from the Oregon Social Learning Center, 207 E. 5th, Suite 202, Eugene, Oregon 97401.)

Forster, A. Violence of the fanatical left and right. *Annals of American Academy of Political and Social Science,* 1966, *364,* 141-148.

Fowles, D.C. The three arousal model: Implications of Gray's two factor learning theory for heart rate, electrodermal activity, and psychopathy. *Psychophysiology,* 1980, *17(2),* 87-104.

Freud, S. *Beyond the pleasure principle.* London: Psychoanalytic Press, 1922.

Friedrich, L.K., & Stein, A.H. Aggressive and prosocial television programs and the natural behavior of preschool children. *Monographs of the Society for Research in Child Development,* 1973, *38(4).*

Furman, W., & Masters, J. *A Bayesian approach to convergent discriminant validation: illustrated by validationals between social learning constructs of reinforcement and punishment and their affective consequences.* Unpublished manuscript, 1978. (Available from the University of Minnesota Institute of Child Welfare.)

Gardner, W.P., Mitchell, C., & Hartmann, D.P. *Some problems in the analysis of sequential data.* Paper presented at the annual meeting of the Association for the Advancement of Behavior Therapy, San Francisco, December 1979.

Garmezy, N. The experimental study of children vulnerable to psychopathology. In A. Davids (Ed.), *Child personality and psychopathology* (Vol. 2). New York: John Wiley & Sons, 1976.

Garmezy, N., & Devine, V.T. Project competence: The Minnosota studies of children vulnerable to psychopathology. In N. Watt, J. Rolf, & E.J. Anthony (Eds.), *Children at risk for schizophrenia.* New York: Cambridge University Press, 1982, in press.

Garmezy, N., & Nuechterlein, K. *Invulnerable children: Fact and fiction of competence and disadvantage.* Paper presented at the meeting of the American Orthopsychology Association, Detroit, April 1972.

Garmezy, N., & Streitman, S. Children at risk: The search for the antecedents of schizophrenia. Part 1. Conceptual models and research methods. *Schizophrenia Bulletin,* Spring 1974, No. 8.

Gelfand, D.M., Gelfand, S., & Dobson, W.R. Program reinforcement of patient behavior in a mental hospital. *Behavior Research and Therapy,* 1967, *5,* 201-207.

Gelles, R.J. *The violent home: A study of physical aggression between husbands and wives.* Beverly Hills, California: Sage Publications, 1972.

Gelles, R.J. *An exploratory study of intrafamily violence.* Unpublished doctoral dissertation, University of New Hampshire, 1973.

Gelles, R.J. *Violence towards children in the United States.* Paper presented at the meeting of the American Association for the Advancement of Science, 1977.

Gersten, J.C., Langner, T.S., Eisenberg, J.G., Simcha-Fagan, O., & McCarthy, E.D. Stability in change in types of behavioral disturbance of children and adolescents. *Journal of Abnormal Child Psychology,* 1976, 4, 111-127.

Gewirtz, J. Deprivation and satiation of social stimuli as determinants of their efficacy. In J.P. Hill (Ed.), *Minnesota Symposia on Child Psychology* (Vol. 1). Minneapolis: University of Minnesota Press, 1967.

Gewirtz, J. & Boyd, E. Experiments on mother-infant interaction underlying mutual attachment acquisition: The infant conditions the mother. In T. Alloway, P. Pliner, & L. Krames (Eds.), *Attachment behavior.* New York: Plenum Publishing Corp., 1977.

Glairn, J.P., & Annesley, F.R. Reading and arithmetic correlates of conduct and problems and withdrawn children. *Journal of Special Education,* 1971, 5, 213-218.

Glenn, N. Psychological well being in the post parental stage: Some evidence from national surveys. *Journal of Marriage and Family,* 1975, 37, 105-110.

Glueck, S., & Glueck, E. *Delinquents and nondelinquents in perspective.* Cambridge: Harvard University Press, 1968.

Goldin, P.C. A review of children's reports of parent behaviors. *Psychological Bulletin,* 1969, 71, 222-236.

Golding, W. *Lord of the Flies,* New York: Coward-McCann Inc., 1962.

Goldstein, M.J., and Judd, L., Rodnick, E.H., Alkire, A., & Gould, E.A. A method for studying social influence and coping patterns with families of disturbed adolescents. *Journal of Nervous and Mental Diseases,* 1968, 147(3), 233-251.

Goodenough, F.L. Inter-relationships in the behavior of young children. *Child Development,* 1930, 1, 29-47.

Goodenough, F.L. *Anger in young children.* Minneapolis: University of Minnesota Press, 1931.

Goodstein, L.D., & Rowley, V.N. A further study of MMPI differences between parents of disturbed and nondisturbed children. *Journal of Consulting Psychology,* 1961, 25(5), 460-464.

Goody, E., & Groothues, C.M. Stress in marriage: West African couples in London. In V.S. Khan (Ed.), *Minority families in Britain.* MacMillan, 1979.

Gottman, J.M. Toward a definition of social isolation in children. *Child Development,* 1977, 48, 513-517.

Gottman, J.M. *Marital interaction: Experimental investigations.* New York: Academic Press, 1979.

Gottman, J.M., & Bakeman, R. The sequential analysis of observation data. In S. Suomi, M. Lamb, & G. Stephenson (Eds.), *Social interaction analysis: Methodological issues.* Madison: University of Wisconsin Press, 1979.

Gottman, J.M., Gonso, J., & Rasmussen, B. Social interaction, social competence, and friendship in children. *Child Development,* 1975, 46, 709-718.

Gouldner, A.W. The norm of reciprocity: A preliminary statement. *American Sociological Review,* 1960, 25, 161-177.

Grant, M. *The army of the Caesars.* New York: Charles Scribner's Sons, 1974.

Graubard, P.S. The relationship between academic achievement and behavior dimensions. *Exceptional Children,* 1971, 37, 755-757.

Graziano, A.M., & Fink, R.S. Second-order effects in mental health treatments. *Journal of Consulting and Clinical Psychology,* 1973, 40, 356-364.

Green, E.H. Group play and quarreling among preschool children. *Child Development,* 1933, 4, 302-307.

Green, R.G., Stonner, D., & Shope, G.L. The facilitation of aggression by aggression: Evidence against the catharsis hypothesis. *Journal of Personality and Social Psychology,* 1975, 31, 721-726.

Greenwood, C.R., Hops, H., Delquardri, J., & Guild, J. Group contingencies for group consequences in classroom management: A further analysis. *Journal of Applied Behavior Analysis,* 1974, 7, 413-425.

Griest, D., Wells, K., Forehand, R. An examination of predictors of maternal perceptions of maladjustment in clinic referred children. *Journal of Abnormal Psychology*, 1979, 88(3), 277-281.

Griffith, W. *Behavior difficulties of children as perceived and judged by parents, teachers, and children themselves.* Minneapolis: University of Minnesota Press, 1952.

Grimm, J.A., Parsons, J.A., & Bijou, S.W. A technique for minimizing subject-observer looking interactions in a field setting. *Journal of Experimental Child Psychology*, 1972, 14, 500-505.

Gurin, G., Verhoff, J., & Feld, S. *Americans view their mental health: A nationwide survey.* New York: Basic Books, 1960.

Guthrie, E.R. The competing skeletal response hypothesis. In E.E. Boe & R.M. Church (Eds.), *Punishment: Issues and experiments.* New York: Appleton-Century-Crofts, 1978.

Guttman, L.A. A basis for scaling qualitative data. *American Sociological Review*, 1944, 9, 139-150.

Haggard, E. Experimental studies in affective processes: I. Some aspects of cognitive structures and active participation on certain autonomic reactions during and following experimentally induced stress. *Journal of Experimental Psychology*, 1943, 33, 257-284.

Haley, J. *Problem solving therapy.* San Francisco: Jossey-Bass, 1978.

Hall, W.M. *Observational and interactional determinants of aggressive behavior in boys.* Unpublished doctoral dissertation, Indiana University, 1973.

Hall, R.V., Lund, D., & Jackson, D. Effects of teacher attention on study behavior. *Journal of Applied Behavior Analysis*, 1968, 1, 1-12.

Halverson, C.F., & Waldrop, M.F. Maternal behavior toward own and other preschool children: The problem of "ownness." *Child Development*, 1970, 41, 839-845.

Hamburg, D., & vanLawick-Goodall, J. Factors facilitating development of aggressive behavior in chimpanzees and humans. In J. DeWit & W.W. Hartup (Eds.), *Determinants and origins of aggressive behavior.* The Hague, Paris: Mouton, 1974.

Harbin, H.T., & Madden, D.J. Battered parents: A new syndrome. *American Journal of Psychiatry*, 1979, 136(10), 1288-1291.

Hardin, G. The tragedy of the commons. *Science,*

1968, 162, 1243-1248.

Hare, R.D. Psychopathy, autonomic functioning, and the orienting response. *Journal of Abnormal Psychology Monograph Supplement*, 1968, 73(3), 1-24.

Harris, A.M. *Observer effect on family interaction.* Unpublished doctoral dissertation, University of Oregon, 1969.

Harris, A., & Reid, J.B. The consistency of a class of coercive child behaviors across school settings for individual subjects. *Journal of Abnormal Child Psychology*, 1981, in preparation.

Hartmann, D.P. Influence of symbolically modeled instrumental aggression and pain cues on aggressive behavior. *Journal of Personality and Social Psychology*, 1969, 11, 280-288.

Hartmann, D.P. Considerations in the choice of interobserver reliability estimates. *Journal of Applied Behavior Analysis*, 1977, 10, 103-116.

Hartup, W.W. Peer interaction and social organization. In P. Mussen (Ed.), *Carmichael's manual of child psychology.* New York: John Wiley & Sons, 1969.

Hartup, W.W. *Violence in development: The functions of aggression in childhood.* Papers presented at the American Psychological Association, Montreal, Quebec, Canada, 1973.

Hartup, W.W. Aggression in childhood: Developmental perspectives. *American Psychologist*, 1974, 29, 336-339.

Hartup, W.W. Peer interaction and the process of socialization. In M.J. Guralnick (Ed.), *Early intervention and the integration of handicapped and non-handicapped children.* Baltimore: University Park Press, 1977.

Hartup, W.W. Children and their friends. In H. McGurk (Ed.), *Child social development.* London: Methuen, 1978, in press.

Hartup, W.W. Levels of analysis in the study of social interaction: An historical perspective. In M.E. Lamb, S.J. Suomi, & G.R. Stephenson (Eds.), *Social interaction analysis.* Wisconsin: Univeristy of Wisconsin Press, 1979.

Hatfield, E., Utne, M., & Traupman, J. Equity theory and intimate relationships. In R. Burgess & T. Huston (Eds.), *Social exchange in developing relationships.* New York: Academic Press, 1979.

Hedlund, C.S. *Relationship of positive social reinforcement to delinquency and sub types of delinquent behavior: A text of Patterson's etiolog-*

ical model. Unpublished master's thesis, University of West Virginia, 1971.

Hefferline, R.F. Learning theory and clinical psychology: An eventual symbiosis. In A.J. Bachrach (Ed.), *Experimental foundations in clinical psychology.* New York: Basic Books, 1963.

Hefferline, R.F., Keenan, B., & Harford, R.A. Escape and avoidance conditioning in human subjects without their observation of the response. *Science,* 1959, *130,* 1338-1339.

Helfer, R.E., & Kempe, C.H. (Eds.). *The battered child.* Chicago: University of Chicago Press, 1968.

Henry, M.M., & Sharpe, D.F. Some influential factors in the determination of aggressive behavior in preschool children. *Child Development,* 1947, *18,* 11-28.

Herbert, E. *Parent programs—bringing it all back home.* Paper presented at the meeting of the American Psychological Association, Miami, 1970.

Herbert, E.W., Pinkston, E.M., Hayden, M.L., Sajwaj, T.E., Pinkston, S., Cordua, G., & Jackson, C. Adverse effects of differential parental attention. *Journal of Applied Behavior Analysis,* 1973, *6,* 15-30.

Herrnstein, R.J. Relative and absolute strength of response as a function of frequency of reinforcement. *Journal of Experimental Analysis of Behavior,* 1961, *4,* 267-272.

Herrnstein, R.J. Formal properties of the matching law. *Journal of the Experimental Analysis of Behavior,* 1974, *21,* 159-164.

Hetherington, E.M. Effects of father absence on personality development in adolescent daughters. *Developmental Psychology,* 1972, *7(3),* 313-326.

Hetherington, Cox, & Cox, 1976—*see* Hetherington, Cox, & Cox, 1978.

Hetherington, E.M., Cox, M., & Cox, R. Aftermath of divorce. In J.H. Stevens, Jr. & M. Matthews (Eds.), *Mother-child, father-child relations.* Washington, D.C.: National Association for the Education of Young Children, 1978.

Hetherington, E.M., Cox, M., & Cox, R. Family interaction and the social, emotional, and cognitive development of children following divorce. In V. Vaughn & T. Brazelton (Eds.), *The family: Setting priorities.* New York: Science and Medicine, 1979.

Hetherington, E.M., Cox, M., & Cox, R. *Stress and coping in divorce: A focus on women.* Unpublished manuscript, 1980.

Heyns, R.W., & Lippitt, R. Systematic observational techniques. In G. Lindsey (Ed.), *Handbook of social psychology* (Vol. I). Cambridge, Massachusetts: Addison-Wesley, 1954.

Hibbs, D.A. Problems of statistical estimation and causal influence in time-series regression models. In H.C. Costner (Ed.), *Sociological methodology.* San Francisco: Jossey-Bass, 1973-74.

Hicks, M.W., & Platt, M. Marital happiness and stability: A review of the research in the sixties. In C. Broderick (Ed.), *A decade of family research.* National Council on Family Relations, 1970.

Hinde, R.A. The study of aggression: Determinants, consequences, goals, and functions. In J. DeWit & W.W. Hartup (Eds.), *Determinants and origins of aggressive behavior.* The Hague, Paris: Mouton, 1974.

Hineline, P. Negative reinforcement and avoidance. In W. Honig & J.E. Staddon (Eds.), *Handbook of operant behavior.* New Jersey: Prentice-Hall, 1977.

Hines, P.A. *How adults perceive children: The effect of behavior tracking and expected deviance on teachers' impressions of a child.* Unpublished doctoral dissertation, University of Oregon, 1974.

Hirschi, T. *Causes of delinquency.* Berkeley: University of California Press, 1969.

Hobbs, S.A., & Forehand, R. Important parameters in the use of timeout with children: A re-examination. *Journal of Behavioral Therapy and Experimental Psychiatry,* 1977, *8,* 365-370.

Hoffman, W.H. Statistical models for the study of change in the single case. In C. Harris (Ed.), *Problems in measuring change.* Madison Wisconsin: University of Wisconsin Press, 1967.

Hokanson, J.E. Vascular and psychogalvanic effects on experimentally aroused anger. *Journal of Personality,* 1961, *29,* 30-39.

Hokanson, J.E., & Edelman, R. Effects of three social responses on vascular processes. *Journal of Personality and Social Psychology,* 1966, *3,* 442-447.

Hokanson, J.E., Willers, K.R., & Koropsak, E. The modification of autonomic responses during aggressive interchange. *Journal of Personality,* 1968, *36,* 386-404.

Holleran, P.R. *Noise and aggressiveness as determinants of aggressive behavior.* Unpublished doctoral dissertation, University of Notre Dame, 1977.

Holleran, P. *Parent perception and delinquency.* OSLC manuscript in preparation.

Hollingshead, A.B., & Redlich, F.C. *Social class and mental illness.* New York: John Wiley & Sons, 1958.

Holmberg, M.C. *The development of social interchange patterns from 12 to 42 months' cross-sectional and short-term longitudinal analyses.* Unpublished doctoral dissertation, University of North Carolina, 1977.

Holmes, T.H., & Masuda, M. Life changes and illness susceptibility. In B.S. Dohrenwend & B.P. Dohrenwend (Eds.), *Stressful life events: Their nature and effects.* New York: John Wiley & Sons, 1974.

Homans, G.C. *Social behavior: Its elementary forms.* New York: Harcourt, Brace & World, Inc., 1961.

Honig, A.S., Tannenbaum, J., & Caldwell, B. *Maternal behavior in verbal report and in laboratory observations.* Paper presented at the meeting of the American Psychological Association, San Francisco, 1968.

Hood, R., & Sparks, R. *Key issues in criminology.* London, Weidenfeld & Nicholson, 1970.

Hops, H., & Cobb, J. Initial investigations into academic survival-skill training: Direct instruction and first-grade achievement. *Journal of Educational Psychology,* 1974, 66(4), 548-553.

Hops & Cobb, 1977—*see* Hops & Cobb, 1974.

Hops, H., Walker, H., & Greenwood, C.R. Peers—a program for remediating social withdrawal in the school setting: Aspects of a research development process. *CORBEH Report #33,* October 1977.

Horne, A. *Aggressive behavior in referred and nonreferred one- and two-parent families.* Presented as part of a Symposium on Advances in Behavioral Treatment of One-Parent Families. Paper presented at the 88th Annual Convention of the American Psychological Association, Montreal, Canada, Sept., 1980.

Hotchkiss, J.M. *The modification of maladaptive behavior of a class of educationally handicapped children: Operant conditioning techniques.* Unpublished doctoral dissertation, University of Southern California, 1966.

Hull, C.L. *Principles of behavior.* New York: Appleton-Century-Crofts, 1943.

Huston, T.L., & Burgess, R.L. Social exchange in developing relationships: An overview. In R. Burgess & T. Huston (Eds.), *Social exchange in developing relationships.* New York: Academic Press, 1979, in press.

Jacobson, N.S., & Margolin, G. *Marital therapy.* New York: Brunner/Mazel, 1979.

Jenkins, R.L., & Glickman, S. Common syndromes in child psychiatry. *American Journal of Orthopsychiatry,* 1946, 16, 244-253.

Jenkins, R.L., & Hewitt, L. Types of personality structure encountered in child guidance clinics. *American Journal of Orthopsychiatry,* 1944, 14(1), 84-94.

Jennings, H.H. *Leadership and isolation* (2nd Ed.). London: Longmans, Green & Co., 1950.

Johns, J.H., & Quay, H.C. The effect of social reward on verbal conditioning in psychopathic and neurotic military offenders. *Journal of Consulting Psychology,* 1962, 26, 217-220.

Johnson, S.M., & Bolstad, O.D. Methodological issues in naturalistic observations: Some problems and solutions for field research. In L.A. Hamerlynck, L.C. Handy, & E.J. Mash (Eds.), *Behavior change: Methodology, concepts, and practice.* Champaign, Illinois: Research Press, 1973.

Johnson, S.M., & Bolstad, O.D. Reactivity to home observation: A comparison of audio recorded behavior with observers present or absent. *Journal of Applied Behavior Analysis,* 1975, 8, 181-185.

Johnson, S.M., Bolstad, O.D., & Lobitz, G.K. Generalization and contrast phenomena in behavior modification with children. In L.A. Hamerlynck, L.C. Handy, & E.J. Mash (Eds.), *Behavior modification with families. I. Theory and research. II. Applications and developments.* New York: Brunner/Mazel, 1976.

Johnson, S.M., & Christensen, A. Multiple criteria follow-up of behavior modification with families. *Journal of Abnormal Child Psychology,* 1975, 3, 135-154.

Johnson, S.M., & Lobitz, G.K. Parental manipulations of child behavior in home observations. *Journal of Applied Behavior Analysis,* 1974a, 7, 23-31.

Johnson, S.M., & Lotitz, G.K. The personal and marital adjustment of parents as related to observed child deviance and parenting behaviors. *Journal of Abnormal Child Psychology,* 1974b, 2(3), 192-207.

Johnson, S.M., Wahl, G., Martin, S., & Johansson, S. How deviant is the normal child: A behavioral analysis of the preschool child and his family. In R.D. Rubin, J.P. Brady, & J.D. Henderson (Eds.), *Advances in behavior therapy* (Vol. 4). New York: Academic Press, 1973.

Johnston, M. Responsiveness of delinquents and nondelinquents to social reinforcement. *British Journal of Social and Clinical Psychology,* 1976, *15,* 41-49.

Jones, R.R. Behavioral observation and frequency data: Problems in scoring, analysis, and interpretation. In L.A. Hamerlynck, L.C. Handy, & E.J. Mash (Eds.), *Behavior change: Methodology, concepts, and practice.* Champaign, Illinois: Research Press, 1973.

Jones, R.R., Reid, J.B., & Patterson, G.R. Naturalistic observations in clinical assessment. In P. McReynolds (Ed.), *Advances in psychological assessment* (Vol. 3). San Francisco: Jossey-Bass, 1975.

Kaffman, M., & Elizur, E. Infants who become enuretic: A longitudinal study of 161 Kibbutz children. *Monographs,* 1977, *42*(2), 1-61.

Kagan, J. The child's perception of parent punishment. *Journal of Abnormal and Social Psychology,* 1956, *53,* 257-258.

Kagan, J., & Moss, H. *Birth to maturity.* New York: John Wiley & Sons, 1962.

Kahneman, D., & Tversky, A. On the psychology of prediction. *Psychological Review,* 1973, *80*(4), 237-251.

Kanfer, F.H. Self-regulation: Research issues and speculations. In C. Neuringer & J.L. Michael (Eds.), *Behavior modification in clinical psychology.* New York: Appleton-Century-Crofts, 1970.

Kanfer, F.H., Cox, L., Greiner, J., & Karoly, P. Contracts, demand characteristics, and self-control. *Journal of Personality and Social Psychology,* 1974, *30,* 605-619.

Kanfer, F.H., & Phillips, J. *The learning foundations of behavior therapy.* New York: John Wiley & Sons, 1970.

Kanfer, F.H., & Seidner, M. Self-control: Factors enhancing tolerance of noxious stimulus. *Journal of Personality and Social Psychology,* 1973, *25,* 381-389.

Kantor, J.R. *Interbehavioral psychology.* Granville, Ohio: The Principia Press, Inc., 1959.

Kaplan, H.B., Burch, N.R., & Bloom, S. Physiological covariation and sociometric relationships in small groups. In P.H. Leiderman & D. Shapiro (Eds.), *Psychological approaches to social behavior.* Stanford University Press, 1964.

Karpowitz, D. *Stimulus control in family interaction sequences as observed in the naturalistic setting of the home.* Unpublished doctoral dissertation, University of Oregon, 1972.

Kass, R.E., & O'Leary, K.D. *The effects of observer bias in field-experimental settings.* Paper presented at a symposium, "Behavior analysis in education," University of Kansas, Lawrence, Kansas, April 9, 1970.

Kelly, R., & Stephens, M.W. Comparison of different patterns of social reinforcement in children's operant learning. *Journal of Comparative Physiological Psychology,* 1964, *57,* 294-296.

Kendon, A. Some functions of gaze direction in social interactions. *Acta Psychologica,* 1967, *26,* 22-63.

Kent, R.N., O'Leary, K.D., Diament, C., & Dietz, A. Expectation biases in observational evaluation of therapeutic change. *Journal of Consulting and Clinical Psychology,* 1974, *42*(6), 774-780.

Kirkpatrick, R. *Deviant behavior of children in multiple settings.* Unpublished master's thesis, University of Oregon, 1978.

Knutson, J.F. Aggression as manipulable behavior. In J. Knutson (Ed.), *The control of aggression: Implications from basic research.* Chicago: Aldine Publishing Co., 1973.

Knutson, J.F., & Hyman, M. Predatory aggression and irritable aggression: Shock-induced fighting in mouse-killing rats. *Physiology and Behavior,* 1973, *11,* 113-115.

Kohn, M.L. Social class and schizophrenia: A critical review and reformulation. *Schizophrenia Bulletin,* 1973, *7,* 60-79.

Kolb, T.M., & Straus, M.A. Marital power and marital happiness in relation to problem solving ability. *Journal of Marriage and the Family,* 1974, *36,* 756-766.

Kopfstein, D. The effects of accelerating and decelerating consequences on the social behavior of trainable retarded children. *Child Development,* 1972, *43,* 800-809.

Kuenstler, W.H. *Differential effects of positive and negative social reinforcement on juvenile delinquents and Sunday school students.* Unpublished doctoral dissertation, University of Houston, 1970.

Kuo, Z.Y. The genesis of the cat's response to the rat. *Journal of Comparative Psychology,* 1930, *11,* 1-35.

Kuo, Z.Y. Further study on the behavior of the cat toward the rat. *Journal of Comparative Psychology,* 1938, *25,* 1-8.

Lacey, J.I. Somatic response patterning and stress: Some revisions of activation theory. In M. Appley & R. Trumball (Eds.), *Psychological stress: Issues in research.* New York: Appleton-Century-Crofts, 1967.

Lagerspetz, K. *Studies on the aggressiveness in mice.* Helsinki: Suomalainen Tiedeakatemia, 1964.

Lagerspetz, K. Modification of aggressiveness in mice. In S. Feshbach & A. Fraczek (Eds.), *Aggression and behavior change.* New York: Praeger, 1980.

Laivgueur, H., Peterson, R.F., Sheese, J.G., & Peterson, L. Behavioral treatment in the home: Effects on an untreated sibling and long term follow-up. *Behavior Therapy,* 1973, *4,* 431-441.

Lamb, M.E. Fathers: Forgotten contributors to child development. *Human Development,* 1975, *18,* 245-266.

Lamb, M.E. The role of the father: An overview. In M.E. Lamb (Ed.), *The role of the father in child development.* New York: John Wiley & Sons, 1976.

Lambert, W.W. Promise and problems of cross cultural exploration of children's aggressive strategies. In J. DeWit & W.W. Hartup (Eds.), *Determinants and origins of aggressive behavior.* The Hague, Paris: Mouton, 1974.

Lang, P.J. The application of psychophysiological methods to the study of psychotherapy and behavior modification. In A.E. Bergin & S.L. Garfield (Eds.), *Handbook of psychotherapy and behavior change: An empirical analysis.* New York: John Wiley & Sons, 1971.

Lapouse, R., & Monk, M.A. An epidemiologic study of behavior characteristics in children. *American Journal of Public Health,* 1958, *48*(9), 1134-1144.

Lazarus, R.S., & Lanier, R. Stress related transactions between person and environment. In L.A. Pervin & M. Lewis (Eds.), *Perspectives in interactional psychology.* Plenum Publishing Co., 1978.

Lefcourt, H.M. The function of the illusion of control and freedom. *American Psychologist,*

1973, *28,* 417-425.

Leiter, M.P. A study of reciprocity in preschool play groups. *Child Development,* 1977, *48,* 1288-1295.

Lennard, H., & Revenstein, A. *Patterns in human interaction.* San Francisco: Jossey-Bass, 1969.

Lentz, W.P. Rural urban differentials and juvenile delinquency. *Journal of Criminal Law, Criminology, and Police Science,* 1956, *47,* 331-339.

Lepper, M.R., & Dafoe, J.L. Incentives, constraints, and motivation in the classroom: An attributional analysis. In I. Frieze, D. Bar-Tal, & J. Carroll (Eds.), *Attribution theory: Applications to social problems.* San Francisco: Jossey-Bass, 1980, in press.

Levin, G.R., & Simmons, J. Response to praise by emotionally disturbed boys. *Psychological Reports,* 1962a, *11,* 10.

Levin, G.R., & Simmons, J. Response to food and praise by emotionally disturbed boys. *Psychological Reports,* 1962b, *11,* 539-546.

Levinger, G. Sources of marital dissatisfaction among applicants for divorce. *American Journal of Orthopsychiatry,* 1966, *36,* 803-807.

Levinger, G. A social exchange view on the dissolution of pair relationships. In R. Burgess & T. Huston (Eds.), *Social exchange in developing relationships.* New York: Academic Press, 1979.

Levitt, E.E. Research on psychotherapy with children: An evaluation. *Journal of Consulting Psychology,* 1957, *21,* 189-196.

Levitt, E.E. Research on psychotherapy with children. In A.E. Bergin & S.L. Garfield (Eds.), *Handbook of psychotherapy and behavior change.* New York: John Wiley & Sons, 1971.

Lewis, O. *La vida.* Panther Modern Society, Secker, Warbberg, and Panther, 1968.

Liberman, R.P., Wallace, C.J., Vaughn, C.E., Snyder, K.S., & Rust, C. *Social and family factors in the course of schizophrenia: Towards an interpersonal problem-solving therapy for schizophrenics and their families.* Paper presented at the Conference on Psychotherapy of Schizophrenia: Current Status and New Direction, Yale University School of Medicine, New Haven, Connecticut, April 1979.

Lichtenstein, E. How to quit smoking. *Psychology Today,* 1971, *4,* 42-44.

Lieven, E.V.M. Turn-taking and pragmatics: Two issues in early child language. In B.N. Campbell

& P.T. Smith (Eds.), *Recent advances in the psychology of language.* New York: Plenum Press, 1976.

Lindner, R. The jet propelled couch. In R. Lindner, *The fifty-minute hour.* New York: Rhinehart & Co., 1955.

Lindskold, S. Trust development, the GRIT proposal, and the effects of conciliatory acts in conflict and cooperation. *Psychological Bulletin,* 1978, *85,* 772-793.

Littman, D., Freund, R., & Schmaling, K. *Parental categorization of child behaviors.* OSLC manuscript in preparation.

Littman, D., & Patterson, G.R. *Unpredictable aggression: A common dilemma.* OSLC manuscript in preparation, 1980.

Littman, D., Patterson, G.R., & Forgatch, M.S. *Maternal attribution. . . .* OSLC manuscript in preparation, 1980.

Liverant, S. MMPI differences between parents of disturbed and non-disturbed children. *Journal of Clinical Psychology,* 1959, *23,* 256-260.

Lobitz, W.C., & Johnson, S.M. Parental manipulation of the behavior of normal and deviant children. *Child Development,* 1975, *46,* 719-726.

Lobitz, G.K., & Johnson, S.M. Normal versus deviant children: A multi method comparison. *Journal of Abnormal Child Psychology,* 1976, *3*(4), 353-373.

Loeber, R. *Optimal prediction of family interactions on the basis of series of antecedents.* Paper presented at the meeting of the Association for the Advancement of Behavior Therapy, San Francisco, December 1979.

Loeber, R. *Child precursors of assaultive behavior in males.* Research proposal submitted to the National Institute of Mental Health, Crime and Delinquency Section, October 1980.

Loeber, R., & Janda, W. *Mother intervention in sibling conflict.* OSLC manuscript in preparation.

Loeber, R., Janda, W., & Reid, J.B. *Family interactions of assaultive adolescents, stealers, and nondelinquents.* OSLC manuscript in preparation.

Loeber, R., Patterson, G.R., & Dishion, T., *Multiple gating: A multi-stage assessment procedure for identifying youth at risk for delinquency.* OSLC working paper, July 1981.

Lorber, R. *The effects of set induction upon tracking of child behavior.* Unpublished master's thesis, University of Oregon, 1978.

Lorber, R. *Parental tracking of childhood behavior as a function of family stress.* Unpublished doctoral dissertation, University of Oregon, 1981.

Lorenz, K. *On aggression.* New York: Harcourt, Brace & World, Inc., 1966.

Lott, A.J., & Lott, B.E. Group cohesiveness as interpersonal attractions: A review of relationships with antecedent and consequent variables. *Psychological Bulletin,* 1965, *64,* 259-309.

Lovaas, O.I. Effect of exposure to symbolic aggression on aggressive behavior. *Child Development,* 1961a, *32,* 37-44.

Lovaas, O.I. Interaction between verbal and nonverbal behavior. *Child Development,* 1961b, *32,* 329-336.

Lykken, D.J. A study of anxiety in the sociopathic personality. *Journal of Abnormal Psychology,* 1957, *55,* 6-10.

Lytton, H. Observation studies of parent-child interaction: A methodological review. *Child Development,* 1971, *42,* 651-684.

Maccoby, E. (Ed.) *The development of sex differences.* Stanford University Press, 1966.

Maccoby, E., & Jacklin, C. *The psychology of sex differences.* Stanford University Press, 1974.

MacFarlane, J.W., Allen, L., & Honzik, M. *A developmental study of the behavior problems of normal children between 21 months and 14 years.* Berkeley, California: University of California Press, 1962.

Madsen, C., Becker, W., & Thomas, D. Rules, praise, and ignoring: Elements of elementary classroom control. *Journal of Applied Behavior Analysis,* 1968, *1,* 139-150.

Magee, R.D. Correlates of aggressive defiant classroom behavior in elementary school boys: A factor analytic study. *Dissertation Abstracts,* 1964, *25*(2), 1340-1341.

Maier, N.R. *Frustration in the study of behavior without a goal.* Ann Arbor, Michigan: University of Michigan Press, 1961.

Marcus, L.M. *Studies of attention in children vulnerable to psychopathology.* Unpublished doctoral dissertation, University of Minnesota, 1972.

Margolin, G. *A sequential analysis of dyadic com-*

munication. Paper presented at the meeting of the Association for the Advancement of Behavior Therapy, Atlanta, Georgia, December 1977.

Margolin, G. Joint marital therapy to enhance anger management and reduce spouse abuse. *American Journal of Family Therapy,* 1979, in press.

Martens, E.H., & Russ, H. Adjustment of behavior problems of school children: A description and evaluation of the clinical program in Berkeley, California. *U.S. Office of Education Bulletin,* 1932, 78(18).

Martin, B. Reward and punishment associated with the same goal response: A factor in the learning of motives. *Psychological Bulletin,* 1963, 60, 441-451.

Martin, J.A., Maccoby, E.E., Baron, K.W., & Jacklin, C.N. The sequential analysis of mother-child interaction at 18 months: A comparison of micro analytic methods. *Developmental Psychology,* 1980, in press.

Mash, E.J. Behavior modification and methodology: A developmental perspective. *The Journal of Educational Thought,* 1976, 10, 5-21.

Masling, J., & Stern, G. Effect of the observer in the classroom. *Journal of Educational Psychology,* 1969, 60, 351-354.

McAdoo, W., & Connally, F. MMPI's of parents in dysfunctional families. *Journal of Consulting and Clinical Pscyhology,* 1975, 43, 270.

McCaffrey, J., & Cummings, J. *Behavior patterns associated with persistent emotional disturbances of children in regular classes of elementary grades.* Onodaya County, New York: Mental Health Research Unit, New York State Dept. of Mental Hygiene, 1967.

McClearn, G.E., & DeFries, J.C. Genetics and mouse aggression. In J.F. Knutson (Ed.), *The control of aggression: Implications from basic research.* Chicago: Aldine Publishing Co., 1973.

McCord, J. *A life history approach to criminal behavior.* Paper presented at the American Society on Criminology, Atlanta, Georgia, November 1977.

McCord, J. Antecedents and correlates of vulnerability and resistance to psychopathology. In R. Zucker & A. Rabin (Eds.), *Further explorations in personality.* New York: John Wiley & Sons, 1980.

McCord, J., & McCord, W. Cultural stereotypes

and the validity of interviews for research in child development. *Child Development,* 1961, 32, 171-185.

Mednick, S., & Christiansen, K.O. *Biosocial bases of criminal behavior.* New York: Gardner Press, 1977.

Mednick, S.A., & Hutchings, B. Criminality in adoptees and their adoptive and biological parents: A pilot study. In S.A. Mednick & K.O. Christiansen (Eds.), *Biosocial bases of criminal behavior.* New York: Gardner Press, Inc., 1977.

Megargee, E.I. *Matricide, patricide, and the dynamics of aggression.* Paper presented at the Annual Convention of the American Psychological Association, Washington, D.C., 1967.

Meichenbaum, D. Cognitive-behavioral modification: Future directions. In P. Sjoden, S. Bates, & W.S. Dockens (Eds.), *Trends in behavior therapy.* New York: Academic Press, 1979.

Menzel, H. A new coefficient for scalogram analyses. *Public Opinion Quarterly,* Summer 1953, 268-280.

Mercatoris, M., & Craighead, W.E. The effect of nonparticipant observation on teacher and pupil classroom behavior. *Journal of Educational Psychology,* 1973.

Meyer, W.J., & Seidman, S.B. Relative effectiveness of different reinforcement combinations on concept learning of children at two developmental levels. *Child Development,* 1961, 32, 117-127.

Miller, N.E. Theory and experiment relating psychoanalytic displacement to stimulus reponse generalization. *Journal of Abnormal and Social Psychology,* 1948, 43, 155-178.

Miller, N.E., & Dollard, J. *Social learning and imitation.* New Haven, Connecticut: Yale University Press, 1941.

Miller, S.M., & Grant, R. The blunting hypothesis: A view of predictability and human stress. In P. Sjoden, S. Bates, & W.S. Dockens (Eds.), *Trends in behavior therapy.* New York: Academic Press, 1979.

Minton, C., Kagan, J., & Levine, J. Maternal control and obedience in the two-year-old. *Child Development,* 1971, 42, 1873-1894.

Minuchin, S., Montalvo, B., Guerney, B., Rosman, B., & Schumer, F. *Families of the slums.* New York: Basic Books, 1967.

Mischel, W. A social-learning view of sex differences in behavior. In E. Maccoby (Ed.), *The development of sex differences.* Stanford, California: Stanford University Press, 1966.

Mischel, W. *Personality and assessment.* New York: John Wiley & Sons, 1968.

Mischel, W. On the interface of cognition and personality: Beyond the person-situation debate. *American Psychologist,* 1979, 9, 740-755.

Moore, D. *Determinants of deviancy: A behavioral comparison of normal and deviant children in multiple settings.* Unpublished manuscript, University of Tennessee, 1975.

Moore, D., Chamberlain, P., & Mukai, L. Children at risk for delinquency: A follow-up comparison of aggressive children and children who steal. *Journal of Abnormal Child Psychology,* 1979, 7(3), 345-355.

Moore, D., Forgatch, M., Mukai, L., & Toobert, D. *Interactional coding system.* Unpublished manuscript, Oregon Social Learning Center, 1977.

Moore, S. Correlates of peer acceptance in nursery school children. *Young Children,* 1967, 22, 281-297.

Moos, R.H. Behavioral effects of being observed: Reactions to a wireless radio transmitter. *Journal of Consulting and Clinical Psychology,* 1968, 32(4), 383-388.

Moustakas, C.E., Sigel, I., & Schalock, H. An objective method for the measurement and analysis of child/adult interaction. *Child Development,* 1956, 27, 109-134.

Murphy, L.B. *Social behavior and child personality.* New York: Columbia University Press, 1937.

Myers, J., Lindenthal, J., & Pepper, M. Social class, life events, and psychiatric symptoms. In B.S. Dohrenwend & B.P. Dohrenwend (Eds.), *Stressful life events.* New York: John Wiley & Sons, 1974.

Nelson, C., & Knutson, J.F. Sex, strain, and housing: Variables influencing the effects of prior shock exposure on shock-induced aggression. *Aggressive Behavior,* 1978, 4, 237-252.

Nelson, R.O., Lipenski, D.P., & Black, J.L. The relative reactivity of external observations and self monitoring. *Behavior Therapy,* 1976, 7, 314-321.

Nemeth, C. Bargaining and reciprocity. *Psychological Bulletin,* 1970, 74, 297-308.

Nielsen, A., & Gerber, D. Psychosocial aspects of truancy in early adolescence. *Adolescence,* 1979, 14(54), 313-326.

Nisbett, R.E., & Wilson, T.D. Telling more than we can know: Verbal reports on mental processes. *Psychological Review,* 1977, 84(3), 231-259.

Nord, W. B. Social exchange theory: An integrative approach to social conformity. *Psychological Bulletin,* 1969, 71, 174-208.

Novaco, R.W. *Anger control.* Lexington, Massachusetts: Lexington Books/D.C. Heath & Co., 1975.

Novick, J., Rosenfeld, E., Block, D.A. Situational variations in the behavior of children. Paper presented at a lecture, "Research on child development," Minneapolis, Minnesota, 1965.

O'Conner, R.D. Modification of social withdrawl through symbolic modeling. *Journal of Applied Behavior Analysis,* 1969, 2, 15-22.

O'Leary, K.D., Kent, R.N., & Karpowitz, J. Shaping data collection congruent with experimental hypotheses. *Journal of Applied Behavior Analysis,* 1975, 8, 43-51.

Oltmanns, T., Broderick, J., & O'Leary, K. Marital adjustment and the efficacy of behavior therapy with children. *Journal of Consulting and Clinical Psychology,* 1977, 45(5), 724-729.

Olweus, D. Personality factors and aggression with special reference to violence within the peer group. In J. DeWit & W.W. Hartup (Eds.), *Determinants and origins of aggressive behavior.* The Hague, Paris: Mouton Press, 1974.

Olweus, D. Development of multi-faceted aggression inventory for boys. *Reports from the Institute of Psychology,* 1975, 6.

Olweus, D. *Longitudinal studies of aggressive reaction patterns: A review.* Paper presented at the 21st International Congress of Psychology, Paris, July 1976.

Olweus, D. *Aggression in the schools: Bullies and whipping boys.* New York: John Wiley & Sons, 1978.

Olweus, D. Stability of aggressive reaction patterns in males: A review. *Psychological Bulletin,* 1979, 86(4), 852-875.

Olweus, D. Familial determinants of aggressive behavior in adolescent boys: A causal analysis. *Developmental Psychology,* 1981, in press.

Omark, D.R., Omark, M., & Edelman, M. *Dominance hierarchies in young children.* Paper presented at the Congress of Anthropological and

Ethnological Science, Chicago, 1973.

Orzech, M. *The effect of verbal reward and verbal punishment on delinquent and nondelinquent adolescent boys.* Unpublished doctoral dissertation, Wayne State University, 1962.

Paris, S.G., & Cairns, R.B. An experimental and ethological analysis of social reinforcement with retarded children. *Child Development,* 1972, *43,* 717-729.

Parke, R.D. Effectiveness of punishment as an interaction of intensity, timing, agent, nurturance, and cognitive structure. *Child Development,* 1969, *40,* 213-235.

Parke, R.D. The role of punishment in the socialization process. In *Early experiences and the process of socialization.* New York: Academic Press, 1970.

Parke, R.D. Rules, roles, and resistance to deviation: Recent advances in punishment, discipline, and self control. In *Minnesota Symposia on Child Psychology.* Minneapolis, Minnesota: University of Minnesota Press, 1975.

Parke, R.D. Interactional designs. In R.B. Cairns (Ed.), *The analysis of social interaction.* Hillsdale, New Jersey: Lawrence Erlbaum Associates, 1979.

Parke, R.D., Deur, J.L., & Sawin, D.B. The intermittent punishment effect in humans: Conditioning or adaptation? *Psychonomic Science,* 1970, *18*(4), 193-194.

Parke, R.D., & Levy, J.L. Schedule of punishment and inhibition of aggression in children. *Developmental Psychology,* 1972, *7,* 266-269.

Parke, R.D., & Walters, R.H. Some factors determining the efficacy of punishment for inducing response inhibition. *Monographs of the Society for Research in Child Development,* 1967, *32*(109).

Parmillee, A. European neurological studies for the newborn. *Child Development,* 1962, *33,* 169-180.

Parton, D.A., & Ross, A.O. Social reinforcement of children's motor behavior: A review. *Psychological Bulletin,* 1965.

Parton, D.A., & Ross, A.O. A reply to "The use of rate as a measure of response in studies of social reinforcement." *Psychological Bulletin,* 1967, *67,* 323-325.

Patterson, D.S. *Social ecology and social behavior: The development of the differential usage of play materials in preschool children.* Paper presented at the 4th Biennial Meeting of the Southeastern Conference on Human Development, April 1976.

Patterson, G.R. An empirical approach to the classification of disturbed children. *Journal of Clinical Psychology,* 1964, *20,* 326-337.

Patterson, G.R. An application of conditioning techniques to the control of a hyperactive child. In L. Ullmann & L. Krasner (Eds.), *Research in behavior modification.* New York: Holt, Rinehart & Winston, 1965a.

Patterson, G.R. Responsiveness to social stimuli. In L. Ullmann & L. Krashner (Eds.), *Research in behavior modification.* New York: Holt, Rinehart & Winston, 1965b.

Patterson, G.R. Behavioral techniques based upon social learning: An additional base for developing behavior modification technologies. In C. Franks (Ed.), *Behavior therapy: Appraisal and status.* New York: McGraw-Hill, 1969.

Patterson, G.R. Changes in status of family members as controlling stimuli: A basis for describing treatment process. In L.A. Hamerlynck, L.C. Handy, & E.J. Mash (Eds.), *Behavior change: Methodology, concepts, and practice.* Champaign, Illinois: Research Press, 1973.

Patterson, G.R. Interventions for boys with conduct problems: Mutliple settings, treatments, and criteria. *Journal of Consulting and Clinical Psychology,* 1974a, *42*(4), 471-481.

Patterson, G.R. Retraining of aggressive boys by their parents: Review of recent literature and follow-up evaluation. *Canadian Psychiatric Association Journal,* 1974b, *19,* 142-161.

Patterson, G.R. A basis for identifying stimuli which control behavior in natural settings. *Child Development,* 1974c, *45,* 900-911.

Patterson, G.R. Stimulus control in natural settings. In J. DeWit & W.W. Hartup (Eds.), *Determinants and origins of aggressive behavior.* The Hague, Paris: Mouton Press, 1974d.

Patterson, G.R. *Families.* Champaign, Illinois: Research Press, 1975a.

Patterson, G.R. Multiple evaluations of a parent-training program. In T. Thompson & W.S. Dockens (Eds.), *Applications of behavior modification.* New York: Academic Press, 1975b.

Patterson, G.R. The aggressive child: Victim and architect of a coercive system. In L.A. Hamerlynck, L.C. Handy, & E.J. Mash (Eds.), *Behavior modification and families: Theory and research* (Vol. 1). New York: Brunner/Mazel, 1976.

Patterson, G.R. Accelerating stimuli for two classes of coercive behaviors. *Journal of Abnormal Child Psychology,* 1977a, *5*(4), 334-350.

Patterson, G.R. A three-stage functional analysis for children's coercive behaviors: A tactic for developing a performance theory. In D. Baer, B.C. Etzel, & J.M. LeBlanc (Eds.), *New developments in behavioral research: Theories, methods, and applications. In honor of Sidney W. Bijou.* Hillsdale, New Jersey: Lawrence Erlbaum Associaties, 1977b.

Patterson, G.R. Siblings: Fellow travelers in coercive family processes. In R.J. Blanchard (Ed.), *Advances in the study of aggression.* New York: Academic Press, 1979a, in press.

Patterson, G.R. A performance theory for coercive family interaction. In R. Cairns (Ed.), *Social interaction: Methods, analysis, and illustrations.* Hillsdale, New Jersey: Lawrence Erlbaum Associates, 1979b.

Patterson, G.R. Treatment for children with conduct problems: A review of outcome studies. In S. Feshbach & A. Fraczek (Eds.), *Aggression and behavior change: Biological and social processes.* New York: Praeger, 1979c.

Patterson, G.R. Mothers: The unacknowledged victims. *Monographs of the Society for Research in Child Development,* 1980, *45*(5, Serial No. 186), 1-64.

Patterson, 1980a—*see* Patterson, 1980.

Patterson, 1980b—*see* Patterson, 1979c.

Patterson, G.R. Stress: Agent of change for family process. In M. Rutter & N. Garmezy (Eds.), *Coping and stress: A developmental view.* New York: McGraw-Hill, 1981a, in press.

Patterson, G.R. *A bilateral trait for aggression: An interactional analysis of mother-child dyads.* Paper presented at the Conference on Boundary Areas in Psychology: Developmental and Social, Vanderbilt University, Nashville, Tennessee, June 17, 1981b.

Patterson, G.R., & Anderson, D. Peers as social reinforcers. *Child Development,* 1964, *35,* 951-960.

Patterson, G.R., & Cobb, J.A. A dyadic analysis of "aggressive" behaviors. In J.P. Hill (Ed.), *Minnesota Symposia on Child Psychology* (Vol. 5). Minneapolis: University of Minnesota Press, 1971.

Patterson, G.R., & Cobb, J.A. Stimulus control for classes of noxious behaviors. In J.F. Knutson (Ed.), *The control of aggression: Implications from basic research.* Chicago: Aldine Publishing Co., 1973.

Patterson, G.R., Cobb, J.A., & Ray, R.S. Direct intervention in the classroom: A set of procedures for the aggressive child. In F. Clark, D. Evans, & L. Hamerlynck (Eds.), *Implementing behavioral programs for schools and clinics.* Champaign, Illinois: Research Press, 1972.

Patterson, G.R., Cobb, J.A., & Ray, R.S. A social engineering technology for retraining the families of aggressive boys. In H.E. Adams & I.P. Unikel (Eds.), *Issues and trends in behavior therapy.* Springfield, Illinois: C.C. Thomas, 1973.

Patterson, G.R., & Dawes, R.M. A Guttman scale of children's coercive behaviors. *Journal of Clinical and Consulting Psychology,* 1975, *43*(4), 594.

Patterson, G.R., & Fleischman, M.J. Maintenance of treatment effects: Some considerations concerning family systems and follow-up data. *Behavior Therapy,* 1979, *10,* 168-185.

Patterson, G.R., & Gullion, M.E. *Living with children: New methods for parents and teachers.* Champaign, Illinois: Research Press, 1968.

Patterson, G.R., & Hinsey, W. Investigations of some assumptions and characteristics of a procedure for instrumental conditioning in children. *Journal of Experimental Child Psychology,* 1964, *1,* 111-122.

Patterson, G.R., Hops, H., & Weiss, R.L. Interpersonal skills training for couples in early stages of conflict. *Journal of Marriage and the Family,* May 1975, 295-303.

Patterson, G.R., Littman, R.A., & Bricker, W. Assertive behavior in children: A step toward a theory of aggression. *Monographs of the Society for Research in Child Development,* 1967, *32*(5), 1-43.

Patterson, G.R., Littman, R.A., & Hinsey, W.C. Parental effectiveness as reinforcers in the laboratory and its relation to child rearing practices and child adjustment in the classroom. *Journal of Personality,* 1964, *32*(2), 180-199.

Patterson, G.R., & Loeber, R. *Family management skills and delinquency.* Paper presented at the meeting of The International Society for the Study of Behavioral Development, Toronto, August 1981.

Patterson, G.R., McNeal, S.A., Hawkins, N., &

Phelps, R. Reprogramming the social environment. *Journal of Child Psychology and Psychiatry,* 1967, *8,* 181-195.

Patterson, G.R., & Moore, D. Interactive patterns as units of behavior. In S.J. Suomi, M.E. Lamb, & G.R. Stephenson (Eds.), *Social interaction analysis: Methodological issues.* Madison, Wisconsin: University of Wisconsin Press, 1979.

Patterson, G.R., Ray, R.S., & Shaw, D.A. Direct intervention in families of deviant children. *Oregon Research Institute Research Bulletin,* 1968, *8(9).*

Patterson, G.R., Ray, R.S., Shaw, D.A., & Cobb, J.A. *Manual for coding of family interactions.* New York: Microfiche Publications, 1969 (revised).

Patterson, G.R., & Reid, J.B. Reciprocity and coercion: Two facets of social systems. In C. Neuringer & J.L. Michael (Eds.), *Behavior modification in clinical psychology.* New York: Appleton-Century-Crofts, 1970.

Patterson, G.R., & Reid, J.B. Intervention for families of aggressive boys: A replication study. *Behavior Research and Therapy,* 1973, *11,* 383-394.

Patterson, G.R., Reid, J.B., & Chamberlain, P. *Family typology and clinical resistance.* OSLC manuscript in preparation.

Patterson, G.R., Reid, J.B., Jones, R.R., & Conger, R.E. *A social learning approach to family intervention. Vol. 1. Families with aggressive children.* Eugene, Oregon: Castalia Publishing Co., 1975.

Patterson, G.R., Schwartz, R., & Van der Wart, E. The integration of group and individual therapy. *The American Journal of Orthopsychiatry,* 1956, *26(3),* 618-629.

Patterson, G.R., & Stouthamer-Loeber, M. *Parental discipline and children's antisocial behavior.* OSLC manuscript in preparation.

Patterson, G.R., Stouthamer-Loeber, M., & Loeber, R. *Parental monitoring and antisocial child behavior.* OSLC manuscript in preparation.

Patterson, G.R., Weiss, R.L., & Hops, H. Training of marital skills: Some problems and concepts. In H. Leitenberg (Ed.), *Handbook of behavior modification and behavior therapy.* Englewood Cliffs, New Jersey: Prentice-Hall, Inc., 1976.

Paul, G.L., & Lentz, R.J. Psychosocial treatment of chronic mental patients: A review by Sandra Loucks. *Contemporary Psychology,* 1978, *23,* 642-644.

Paul, J.S. *Observer influence on the interactive behavior of a mother and a single child in the home.* Unpublished master's thesis, Oregon State University, 1963.

Paykel, E.S. Life stress and psychiatric disorder. In B.S. Dohrenwend & B.P. Dohrenwend (Eds.), *Stressful life events.* New York: John Wiley & Sons, 1974.

Peine, H. *Behavioral recording by parents and its resultant consequences.* Unpublished master's thesis, University of Utah, 1970.

Perry, D., & Bussey, K. Self reinforcement in high and low aggressive boys following acts of aggression. *Child Development,* 1977, *48,* 653-657.

Perry, D.G., & Perry, L.C. Denial of suffering in the victim as a stimulus to violence in aggressive boys. *Child Development,* 1974, *45,* 55-62.

Petrinovich, L. Probabilistic functionalism: A conception of research method. *American Psychologist,* 1979, *34(5),* 373-390.

Phillips, L.D. *Bayesian statistics for social scientists.* New York: Thomas Y. Crowell Co., 1973.

Phipps-Yonas, S. *Reaction time, peer assessment, and achievement in vulnerable children.* Paper presented at the 87th Convention of the American Psychological Association, New York, September 1979.

Platt, J. Social traps. *American Psychologist,* 1973, *28,* 641-651.

Polk, K. Teenage delinquency in small town America. *Research Report No. 5.* Washington, D.C.: National Institute of Mental Health, 1978.

Pollack, S., Vincent, J., & Williams, B. *Demand characteristics in the classroom observation of hyperactive children: Reactivity to naturalistic observation.* Unpublished manuscript, 1977.

Pritchard, M., & Graham, P. An investigation of a group of patients who have attended both the child and adult departments of the same psychiatric hospital. *British Journal of Psychiatry,* 1966, *112,* 603-613.

Purcell, K., & Brady, K. Adaptation to the invasion of privacy: Monitoring behavior with a miniature radio transmitter. *Merrill Palmer Quarterly of Behavior and Development,* 1966, *12,* 242-254.

Quay, H.C. Personality and delinquency. In H.C. Quay (Ed.), *Juvenile delinquency research and theory*. New York: Van Nostrand Reinhold Co., 1965.

Quay, H.C., & Hunt, W.A. Psychopathy, neuroticism, and verbal conditioning: A replication and extension. *Journal of Consulting Psychology*, 1965, *29*, 283.

Quinsey, V.L. Some applications of adaptation level theory to aversive behavior. *Psychological Bulletin*, 1970, *73*, 441-450.

Quinton, D. Family life in the inner city: Myth and reality. In W. Marland (Ed.), *Education for the inner city*. London: Heineman, 1980.

Quinton, D., & Rutter, M. Early hospital admissions and later disturbances of behavior: An attempted replication of Douglas' findings. *Developmental Medicine and Child Neurology*, 1976, *18*, 447-459.

Rachlin, H., & Herrnstein, R.J. Hedonism revisited: On the negative law of effect. In B.A. Campbell & R.M. Church (Eds.), *Punishment and aversive behavior*. New York: Appleton-Century-Crofts, 1969.

Radke-Yarrow, M., Campbell, J., & Burton, R.V. Reliability of maternal retrospection: A preliminary report. *Family Process*, 1964, *3*, 207-218.

Radke-Yarrow, M., Campbell, J., & Burton, R.V. *Child rearing: An inquiry into research and methods*. San Francisco: Jossey-Bass, 1968.

Radke-Yarrow, M., Campbell, J., & Burton, R.V. Recollections of childhood: A study of the retrospective method. *Monographs of the Society for Research in Child Development*, 1970, *35*(5, Serial No. 138).

Radke-Yarrow, M., & Waxler, C.Z. Dimensions and correlates of prosocial behavior in young children. *Child Development*, 1976, *47*, 118-125.

Radke-Yarrow, M., & Waxler, C.Z. Observing interaction: A confrontation with methodology. In R.B. Cairns (Ed.), *The analysis of social interactions*. Hillsdale, New Jersey: Lawrence Erlbaum Associates, 1979.

Randall, T.M. *An analysis of observer influence on sex and social class differences in mother infant interaction*. Paper presented at the Society for Research in Child Development, Denver, 1975.

Raush, H.L. Interaction sequences. *Journal of Personality and Social Psychology*, 1965, *2*(4), 487-499.

Redl, F., & Wineman, D. *Children who hate*. New York: The Free Press, 1951.

Redl, F., & Wineman, D. *The aggressive child*. New York: The Free Press, 1957.

Reid, J.B. *Reciprocity in family interaction*. Unpublished doctoral dissertation, University of Oregon, 1967.

Reid, J.B. Reliability assessment of observation data: A possible methodological problem. *Child Development*, 1970, *41*, 1143-1150.

Reid, J.B. (Ed.). *A social learning approach to family intervention. Vol. II. Observation in home settings*. Eugene, Oregon: Castalia Publishing Co., 1978.

Reid, J.B., & Chamberlain, P. *Treatment of chronic delinquents: An outcome evaluation*. OSLC manuscript in preparation.

Reid, J.B., & Hendricks, A.F.C.J. A preliminary analysis of the effectiveness of direct home intervention for treatment of predelinquent boys who steal. In L. Hamerlynck, L. Handy, & E. Mash (Eds.), *Behavior therapy: Methodology, concepts, and practice*. Champaign, Illinois: Research Press, 1973.

Reid, J.B., Hinojosa-Rivero, G., & Lorber, R. *A social learning approach to the outpatient treatment of children who steal*. Unpublished manuscript, 1980. (Available from Oregon Social Learning Center, 207 E. 5th, Eugene, Oregon.)

Reid, J.B., & Patterson, G.R. *A social learning approach to family therapy*. 16mm film. Champaign, Illinois: Research Press, 1974.

Reid, J.B., & Patterson, G.R. The modification of aggression and stealing behavior of boys in the home setting. In A. Bandura & E. Ribes (Eds.), *Behavior modification: Experimental analyses of aggression and delinquency*. Hillsdale, New Jersey: Lawrence Erlbaum Associates, 1976.

Reid, J.B., Patterson, G.R., & Loeber, R. *The abused child: Victim, instigator, or innocent bystander?* Paper presented at the Nebraska Symposium on Motivation, Lincoln, Nebraska, March 1981.

Reid, J.B., Taplin, P.S., & Lorber, R. A social interactional approach to the treatment of abusive families. In R. Stuart (Ed.), *Violent behavior: Social learning approaches to prediction, management, and treatment*. New York: Brunner/Mazel, 1981.

Reynolds, G.S., Catania, A.C., & Skinner, B.F.

Conditioned and unconditioned aggression in pigeons. *Journal of the Experimental Analysis of Behavior*, 1963, 6, 73-74.

Reynolds, M.M. Negativism of preschool children: An observational and experimental study. *Contributions to education* (No. 228). Bureau of Publications, New York: Teachers College, Columbia University, 1928.

Ricketts, A.F. *A study of the behavior of young children in anger*. Unpublished master's thesis, University of Iowa, 1931.

Riddle, M., & Roberts, A. Delinquency, delayed gratification, recidivism, and the Porteus image test. *Psychological Bulletin*, 1977, 84(3), 417-425.

Roach, J.L. Some social-psychological characteristics of a child guidance clinic caseload. *Journal of Consulting Psychology*, 1958, 22, 183-186.

Robins, L.N. The accuracy of parental recall of aspects of child development and child-rearing practices. *Journal of Abnormal Social Psychology*, 1963, 55, 261-270.

Robins, L.N. *Deviant children grown up: A sociological and psychiatric study of sociopathic personality*. Baltimore: Williams & Wilkins, 1966.

Robins, L.N., & Ratcliff, K.S. Risk factors in the continuation of childhood antisocial behavior into adulthood. *International Journal of Mental Health*, 1978, 7(3-4), 96-116.

Robinson, B.E. *Sex typed attitudes, sex typed contingency behavior, and personality characteristics of male care givers*. Unpublished doctoral dissertation, University of North Carolina, 1976.

Robinson, J.P. Toward a more appropriate use of Guttman scaling. *The Public Opinion Quarterly*, 1973, 37, 260-267.

Rodnick, E.H., & Garmezy, N. An experimental approach to the study of motivation in schizophrenia. In M.R. Jones (Ed.), *Nebraska Symposium on Motivation*. Lincoln, Nebraska: University of Nebraska Press, 1957.

Roff, M. Childhood social interactions and young adult bad conduct. *Journal of Abnormal and Social Psychology*, 1961, 63, 333-337.

Roff, M. A two factor approach to juvenile delinquency and the later histories of juvenile delinquency. In M. Roff, L.N. Robins, & M. Pollack (Eds.), *Life history research in psychopathy*. (Vol. 2). Minneapolis: University of Minnesota Press, 1972.

Roff, M., Robins, L.N., & Pollack, M. (Eds.). *Life history research in psychopathy* (Vol 2). Minneapolis: University of Minnesota Press, 1972.

Rogers, M.E., Lilienfeld, A.M., and Pasamancek, B. *Prenatal and paranatal factors in the development of child behavior disorders*. Johns Hopkins University Press, Baltimore, 1954.

Rollins, B.C., & Feldman, H. Marital satisfaction over the family life cycle. *Journal of Marriage and the Family*, 1970, 32(1), 20-28.

Romanczyk, R.G., Kent, R.N., Diament, C., & O'Leary, K.D. *Methodological problems in naturalistic observation*. Paper presented at the 2nd Annual Symposium on Behavior Analysis, Lawrence, Kansas, May 1971.

Rosenfeld, H.M., & Baer, D.M. Unnoticed verbal conditioning of an aware experimenter by a more aware subject: The double agent effect. *Psychological Review*, 1969, 76, 425-432.

Rosenthal, R. *Experimental effects in behavioral research*. New York: Appleton-Century-Crofts, 1966.

Rosenthal, R., & Fode, K.L. Three experiments in experimenter bias. *Psychological Reports*, 1963, 12, 491-511.

Rosenthal, R., & Lawson, R. A longitudinal study of the effects of experimenter bias on the operant learning of laboratory rats. *Journal of Psychiatric Research*, 1964, 2, 61-72.

Rothchild, J., & Wolf, S. *The children of the counter culture*. New York: Doubleday, 1976.

Rule, B.G., & Nesdale, A.R. Emotional arousal and aggressive behavior. *Psychological Bulletin*, 1976, 83(5), 851-863.

Ruppenthal, G.C., Arling, G.L., Harlow, H.F., Sackett, G.P., & Suomi, S.J. A ten year perspective of motherless-mother monkey behavior. *Journal of Abnormal Psychology*, 1976, 85(4), 341-349.

Russell, C.S. Transition to parenthood: Problems and gratifications. *Journal of Marriage and the Family*, May 1974, 294-301.

Rutter, M. *Children of sick parents: An environmental and psychiatric study*. London: Oxford Univeristy Press, 1966.

Rutter, M. Epidemiological strategies and psychiatric concepts in research on the vulnerable child. In E. Anthony & C. Koupernick (Eds.), *The child in his family* (Vol. 3). New York: John Wiley & Sons, 1974.

Rutter, M. Protective factors in children's responses to stress and disadvantage. In M. Kent & J.E. Rolf (Eds.), *Primary prevention of psychopathology. Vol. 3. Social competence in children*. Hanover, New Hampshire: University Press of New England, 1979.

Rutter, M., Tizard, J., & Whitmore, R. *Education, health, and behavior*. New York: John Wiley & Sons, 1970.

Ryan, W. *Blaming the victim*. New York: Vintage Books, Inc., 1976.

Sackett, G.P. *A nonparametric lag sequential analysis for studying dependency among responses in observational scoring systems*. Unpublished manuscript, Regional Primate Research Center, University of Washington, 1976.

Sackett, G.P. The lag sequential analysis of contingency and cyclicity in behavioral interaction research. In J. Osofsky (Ed.), *Handbook of infant development*. New York: John Wiley & Sons, 1977.

Sallows, G. *Comparative responsiveness of normal and deviant children to naturally occurring consequences*. Unpublished doctoral dissertation, University of Oregon, 1972.

Salzinger, K., Portnoy, S., Zlotogura, P., & Keisner, R. The effect of reinforcement of continuous speech and on plural nouns in grammatical context. *Journal of Verbal Learning and Verbal Behavior*, 1963, 6(1), 477-485.

Sarbin, T., Allen, V., & Rutherford, E.E. Social reinforcement, socialization, and chronic delinquency. *British Journal of Social and Clinical Psychology*, 1965, 4, 179-184.

Saxe, R.M., & Stollak, G.E. Curiosity and the parent-child relationship. *Child Development*, 1971, 42, 373-384.

Scarpitti, F.R. Can teachers predict delinquency? *The Elementary School Journal*, 1964, 65(3), 130-136.

Scarr, S. The origins of individual differences in adjective checklist scores. *Journal of Consulting Psychology*, 1966, 30, 354-357.

Schachter, S. The interaction of cognitive and physiological determinants of emotional state. In L. Berkowitz (Ed.), *Advances in experimental social psychology* (Vol. 1). New York: Academic Press, 1964.

Schachter, S., & Singer, J.E. Cognitive, social, and physiological determinants of emotional state. *Psychological Review*, 1962, 69, 379-399.

Schaefer, E.S. Development of hierarchical configurant tonal models for parent behavior and child behavior. In J.P. Hill (Ed.), *Minnesota Symposia on Child Psychology* (Vol. 5). Minneapolis, Minnesota: University of Minnesota Press, 1971.

Schaffer, H.R. *The growth of sociability*. Baltimore, Maryland: Penguin Books, Inc., 1977.

Schelle, J. A brief report on invalidity of parent evaluations of behavior change. *Journal of Applied Behavior Analysis*, 1974, 7, 341-343.

Schlesinger, S.E. The prediction of dangerousness in juveniles. *Crime and Delinquency*, January 1978, 40-48.

Schmauk, F.J. Punishment, arousal, and avoidance learning in sociopaths. *Journal of Abnormal Psychology*, 1970, 76, 325-335.

Schoenfeld, W.N. "Reinforcement" in behavior theory. *Pavlovian Journal*, 1978, 13, 135-144.

Schoggen, M., Barker, L., & Barker, R. Structure of the behavior of American and English children. In R.G. Barker (Eds.), *The stream of behavior*. New York: Appleton-Century-Crofts, 1963.

Schoggen, P. Environmental forces in the everyday lives of children. In R.G. Barker (Ed.), *The stream of behavior*. New York: Appleton-Century-Crofts, 1963.

Schoggen, P. Mechanical aids for making specimen records of behavior. *Child Development*, 1964, 35, 985-989.

Schooler, C. A note of extreme caution on the use of Guttman scales. *American Journal of Sociology*, 1968, 74, 296-301.

Schuck, G.R. The use of causal models in aggression research. In J. DeWit & W.W. Hartup (Eds.), *Determinants and origins of aggressive behavior*. The Hague, Paris: Mouton, 1974.

Sears, R.R. Comparison of interviews with questionnaires for measuring mother attitudes toward sex and aggression. *Journal of Personality and Social Psychology*, 1965, 2, 37-44.

Sears, R.R., Maccoby, E., & Levin, H. *Patterns of child rearing*. New York: Harper & Row, 1957.

Sears, R.R., Whiting, J.W., Nowlis, V., & Sears, P.S. Some child rearing antecedents of aggression and dependency in young children. *Genet Psychological Monograph*, 1953, 57, 135-234.

Segal, J., & Yahraes, H. *A child's journey: Forces that shape the lives of our young*. New York:

McGraw-Hill, 1978.

Seligman, M.E. *Helplessness on depression, development, and death.* San Francisco: W.H. Freeman & Co., 1975.

Sells, S.B., & Roff, M. *Peer acceptance-rejection and personal development.* Final Report OE-5-0417 and OE2-10-051, 1967.

Selye, H. *The stress of life.* McGraw-Hill, 1976 (revised).

Shaw, G. *Meat on the hoof: The hidden world of Texas football.* New York: Dell Publishing Co., 1972.

Shea, M.J. *A follow-up study into adulthood of adolescent psychiatric patients in relation to internalizing and externalizing symptoms, MMPI configurations, social competence, and life history variables.* Unpublished doctoral dissertation, University of Minnesota, 1972.

Shelly, M.W. *Isolated and restricted environments.* (Final Report for ONR Contract N 14-68-C-V286 and NR 177-920.) Lawrence, Kansas: University of Kansas, 1970.

Shepherd, M., Oppenheim, A.N., & Mitchell, S. Childhood behavior disorders and the child-guidance clinic: An epidemiological study. *Journal of Child Psychology and Psychiatry,* 1966, *7,* 39-52.

Sherman, H., & Farina, A. Social adequacy of parents and children. *Journal of Abnormal Psychology,* 1974, *83(3),* 327-330.

Shields, M.M. Some communicational skills of young children: A study of dialogue in nursery school. In R.N. Campbell & P.T. Smith (Eds.), *Recent advances in the psychology of language.* New York: Plenum, 1976.

Shirley, M. A behavior syndrome characterizing prematurely born children. *Child Development,* 1939, 115-129.

Siddle, D.A. Electrodernal activity and psychopathy. In S.A. Mednick & K.O. Christiansen (Eds.), *Biosocial bases of criminal behavior.* New York: Gardner Press, 1977.

Sigal, J.J. Enduring disturbances in behavior following acute illness in early childhood: Consistencies in four independent follow-up studies. In E.J. Anthony & C. Koupernik (Eds.), *The child in his family.* New York: John Wiley & Sons, 1974.

Silverman, M.I. The relationship between self esteem and aggression in two social classes. *Dissertation Abstracts,* 1964, *25(4),* 2616.

Simard, K. *From here to delinquency: An investigation of achievement and home-quality characteristics in delinquent and socially aggressive preadolescent males.* Unpublished master's thesis, University of Oregon, 1981.

Singer, D.L. *The control of aggression and violence.* New York: Academic Press, 1971.

Skindrud, K.D. *An evaluation of observer bias in experimental field studies of social interaction.* Unpublished doctoral dissertation, University of Oregon, 1972.

Skindrud, K.D. Field evaluation of observer bias under overt and covert monitoring. In L. Hamerlynck, L. Handy, & E. Mash (Eds.), *Behavior change: Methodology, concepts, and practice.* Champaign, Illinois: Research Press, 1973.

Skinner, B.F. *Walden two.* New York: Macmillan Co., 1948.

Skinner, B.F. *Science and human behavior.* New York: Macmillan Co., 1953.

Skinner, B.F. *Contingencies of reinforcement.* New York: Appleton-Century-Crofts, 1969.

Skinner, B.F. Negative conditioning and periodic reinforcement. In E.E. Boe & R.M. Church (Eds.), *Punishment issues and experiments.* New York: Appleton-Century-Crofts, 1978.

Slovic, P., Fischoff, B., & Lichtenstein, S. Behavioral decision theory. *Annual Review of Psychology,* 1977, *28,* 40.

Smith, H.T. A comparison of interview and observation measures of mother behavior. *Journal of Abnormal Social Psychology,* 1958, *57,* 278-282.

Smith, M. Concerning the magnitude of the behavioral sample for the study of behavioral traits in children. *Journal of Applied Psychology,* 1931, *15,* 480-485.

Smith, P.K., & Green, M. Aggressive behavior in English nurseries and playgroups: Sex differences and response of adults. *Child Development,* 1975, *46,* 211-214.

Snyder, J.J. A reinforcement analysis of interaction in problem and nonproblem families. *Journal of Abnormal Psychology,* 1977, *86(5),* 528-535.

Solomon, R.L. Punishment. *American Psychologist,* 1964, *19,* 239-254.

Solomon, R.L., & Brush, E.S. Experimentally derived concepts of anxiety and aversion. In M.R. Jones (Ed.), *Nebraska Symposium on Motiva-*

tion. Lincoln, Nebraska: University of Nebraska Press, 1956.

Solomon, R.L., & Corbit, J.D. An opponent process theory of motivation: Temporal dynamics of affect (Part 1). *Psychological Review,* 1974, *81,* 119-145.

Solomon, R.L., & Wynne, L.C. Traumatic avoidance learning: The principles of anxiety conservation and partial irreversibility. *Psychological Review,* 1954, *61,* 353-384.

Spielberger, C. The role of awareness in verbal conditioning. In C. Eriksen (Ed.), *Behavior and awareness: A symposium of research and interpretation.* Duke University Press, 1962.

Spivack, G., Platt, J.J., & Shure, M.B. *The problem solving approach to adjustment.* San Francisco: Jossey-Bass, 1976.

Spivack, G., & Shure, M.B. *Social adjustment of young children: A cognitive approach to solving real life problems.* San Francisco: Jossey-Bass, 1974.

Staats, A.W., & Staats, C.K. Attitudes established by classical conditioning. *Journal of Abnormal and Social Psychology,* 1958, *57,* 37-40.

Staats, A.W., Staats, C.K., & Crawford, H.L. First order conditioning of meaning and the parallel conditioning of G.S.R. *Journal of General Psychology,* 1962, *67,* 159-167.

Stark, R., & McEvoy, J. Middle class violence. *Psychology Today,* 1970, *4*(6), 107-112.

Steinmetz, S.K., & Straus, M.A. The family as a cradle of violence. *Society,* 1973, *10*(6), 50-56.

Steinmetz, S.K., & Straus, M.A. (Eds.). *Violence in the family.* New York: Dodd, Mead & Co., 1974.

Stone, L. *The family, sex, and marriage in England 1500-1800.* San Francisco: Harper & Row, 1977.

Straus, M.A. Some social antecedents of physical punishment: A linkage theory interpretation. *Journal of Marriage and the Family,* 1971, *33*(4), 658-663.

Straus, M.A. A general systems theory approach to a theory of violence between family members. *Social Science Information,* 1973, *12*(3), 105-125.

Straus, M.A. Wife beating: How common and why? *Victimology: An International Journal,* 1978, *2*(3-4), 443-458.

Straus, M.A., Gelles, R.J., & Steinmetz, S.K. *Vi-* *olence in the American family.* New York: Doubleday/Anchor, 1979, in press.

Strayer, J. *Social conflict and peer group status.* Paper presented at the Society for Research in Child Development Conference, New Orleans, 1977.

Stuart, R.B. Behavioral remedies for marital ills: A guide to the use of operant interpersonal techniques. In T. Thompson & W. Dockens (Eds.), *Applications of behavior modification.* New York: Academic Press, 1975.

Stunkard, A.J., & Rush, J. A critical review of reports of untoward responses during weight reduction for obesity. *Annual Review of Internal Medicine,* 1974, *81,* 526-533.

Suomi, S.J. Levels of analysis for interaction data collected on workers living in complex social groups. In S. Suomi, M. Lamb, & G. Stephenson (Eds.). *Social interaction analysis: Methodological issues.* Madison: University of Wisconsin Press, 1979.

Suomi, S., Lamb, M., & Stephenson, G. (Eds.), *Social interaction analysis: Methodological issues.* Madison: University of Wisconsin Press, 1979.

Surrott, P.R., Ulrich, R.E., & Hawkins, R.P. An elementary student as a behavioral engineer. *Journal of Applied Behavior Analysis,* 1969, *2,* 85-92.

Swart, C., & Berkowitz, L. The effects of stimulus associated with a victim's pain on later aggression. *Journal of Personality and Social Psychology,* 1976, *33,* 623-631.

Sykes, R.E., & Brent, E.E. Strategies of "taking charge" in police-civilian interaction. In J. Kinton (Ed.), *Police roles in the seventies,* 1978, in press.

Szpiler, J.A., & Epstein, S. Availability of an avoidance response as related to autonomic arousal. *Journal of Abnormal Psychology,* 1976, *85,* 73-82.

Szykula, S. *The Helena Family Center.* Report presented at the Conference of the Association for Advancement in Behavior Therapy, Chicago, November 1979.

Taplin, P.S. *Changes in parental consequation as a function of intervention.* Unpublished doctoral dissertation, University of Wisconsin, 1974.

Taplin, P.S., & Reid, J.B. Effects of instructional set and experimenter influence on observer reliability. *Child Development,* 1973, *44,* 547-554.

Taplin, P.S., & Reid, J.B. Changes in parental consequation as a function of family intervention. *Journal of Consulting and Clinical Psychology,* 1977, *4,* 973-981.

Taquiri, R. Relational analysis: An extension of sociometric methods with emphasis upon social perception. *Sociometry,* 1952, *15,* 91-104.

Tarrier, N., Vaughn, C., Lader, M.H., & Leff, J.P. Bodily reactions to people and events in schizophrenics. *Archives of General Psychiatry,* 1979, *36,* 311-315.

Tavormina, J.B., Boll, T.J., Dunn, N.J., Luscomb, R.L., & Taylor, J.R. *Psychosocial effects of raising a physically handicapped child on parents.* Paper presented at the Annual Convention of the American Psychological Association, San Francisco, 1975.

Terdal, L., Jackson, R.H., Garner, A.M. Mother-child interactions: A comparison between normal and developmentally delayed groups. In L.A. Hamerlynck, L.C. Handy, & E.J. Mash (Eds.), *Behavior modification and families.* New York: Brunner/Mazel, 1976.

Terrell, G., & Kennedy, W. Discrimination learning and transposition in children as a function of the nature of the reward. *Journal of Experimental Psychology,* 1957, *53,* 257-260.

Theorell, T. Life events before and after the onset of a premature myocardial infarction. In B.S. Dohrenwend & B.P. Dohrenwend (Eds.), *Stressful life events: Their nature and effects.* New York: John Wiley & Sons, 1974.

Thomas, A., Becker, W., & Armstrong, M. Production and elimination of disruptive classroom behavior by systematically varying teachers' behavior. *Journal of Applied Behavioral Analysis,* 1968, *1,* 35-45.

Thomas, A., Chess, J., Birch, H., Hertzog, M. A longitudinal study of primary reaction patterns in children. *Comparative Psychiatry,* 1960, *1,* 103-112.

Thomas, D., Loomis, A., & Arrington, R. *Observational studies of social behavior. Vol. 1. Social behavior patterns.* New Haven, Connecticut: Yale University Press, 1933.

Thomas, E.A., & Malone, T.W. On the dynamics of two-person interactions. *Psychological Review,* 1979, *86*(4), 331-360.

Thomas, E.A., & Martin, J.A. Analysis of parent-infant interaction. *Psychological Review,* 1976, *83*(2), 141-156.

Thorndike, E.L. *The fundamentals of learning.* New York: Teachers College, 1932.

Tinbergen, N. *The study of instinct.* New York: Oxford University Press, 1951.

Toch, H. *Violent men.* New York: Aldine Publishing Co., 1969.

Tonge, W.L., James, D.S., & Hillam, S.M. *Families without hope: A controlled study of 33 problem families.* Royal College of Psychiatrists, Ashford, Kent: Headley Bros., Ltd., 1975.

Toobert, D. Nonviolent punishments that work. In G.R. Patterson & J.B. Reid (Eds.), *Systematic common sense,* 1980, in preparation.

Toobert, D., Patterson, G.R., & Moore, D. MOSAIC. In G.R. Patterson & R. Loeber (Eds.), *Assessment of family interaction,* 1981, in preparation.

Tuchman, B. *A distant mirror: The calamitous 14th century.* New York: Alfred A. Knopf, 1978.

Ullmann, L., & Krasner, L. *Case studies in behavior modification.* New York: Holt, Rinehart & Winston, 1965.

Ulrich, R.E., Dulaney, S., Arnett, M., & Mueller, K. An experimental analysis of nonhuman and human aggression. In J. Knutson (Ed.), *The control of aggression: Implications from basic research.* Chicago: Aldine Press, 1973.

Ulrich, R.E., Johnson, M., Richardson, J., & Wolff, P.C. The operant conditioning of fighting behavior in rats. *Psychological Record,* 1963, *13,* 465-470.

Verna, G.B. The effects of four-hour delay of punishment under two conditions of verbal instruction. *Child Development,* 1977, *48,* 621-624.

Vincent, J.P., Friedman, L.C., Nugent, J., Messerly, L. Demand characteristics in observation of marital interaction. *Journal of Consulting and Clinical Psychology,* 1979, in press.

Vreeland, R.G., & Waller, M.B. *Social interactions in families of firesetting children.* Unpublished manuscript, 1980.

Wadsworth, M. *Roots of delinquency: Infancy, adolescence, and crime.* New York: Barnes & Noble, Inc., 1979.

Wahl, G. *Operant analysis of family interactions.* Unpublished doctoral dissertation, University of Oregon, 1971.

Wahler, R.G. *Behavior therapy for oppositional children: Love is not enough.* Paper presented at the Eastern Psychological Association, 1968.

Wahler, R.G. *The insular mother: Her problems in parent child treatment.* Unpublished manuscript, 1979.

Wahler, R.G., Leske, G., & Rogers, E. *The insular family: A deviance support system for oppositional children.* Paper presented at the Banff International Conference on Behavior Modification, 1977.

Wahler, R.G., & Moore, D. *School-home behavior change procedures in a high risk community.* Paper presented to the Association of the Advancement of Behavior Therapy, San Francisco, 1975.

Waksman, S. An empirical investigation of Campbell and Fiske's multistate-multimetrics using social learning measures. *Journal of Abnormal Psychology,* 1977.

Walker, H.M., & Buckley, N.K. Programming generalization and maintenance of treatment effects across time and across settings. *Journal of Applied Behavior Analysis,* 1972, *5,* 209-224.

Walker, H.M., & Buckley, N.K. Teacher attention to appropriate and inappropriate classroom behavior: An individual case study. *Focus on Exceptional Children,* May 1973, *5,* 5-11.

Walker, H.M., Hops, H., & Johnson, S.M. Generalization and maintenance of classroom treatment effects. *Behavior Therapy,* 1975, *6,* 188-200.

Wallerstein, J.S., & Kelly, J.B. The effects of parental divorce: Experiences of the child in later latency. *American Journal of Orthopsychiatry,* 1976, *46*(2), 256-269.

Wallerstein, J.S., & Kelly, J.B. *Surviving the breakup: How children and parents cope with divorce.* New York: Basic Books, 1980.

Walter, H.I., & Gilmore, S.K. Placebo versus social learning effects in parent training procedures designed to alter the behaviors of aggressive boys. *Behavior Therapy,* 1973, *4,* 361-377.

Walters, R.H., & Brown, M. Studies of reinforcement of aggression: III. Transfer of responses to an interpersonal situation. *Child Development,* 1963, *34,* 563-571.

Warden, G.J., & Aylesworth, M. The relative value of reward and punishment in the formulation of a visual discrimination habit in the white rat. *Journal of Comparative Physiological Psychology,* 1927, *7,* 117-127.

Warren, V., & Cairns, R. Social reinforcement satiation: An outcome of frequency or ambiguity? *Journal of Experimental Child Psychology,* 1972, *13,* 249-260.

Watson, J.S. Perception of contingency as a determinant of social responsiveness. In E. Thomas (Ed.), *Origins of the infant's social responsiveness* (Vol. 1). New York: Halsted Press, 1979.

Weick, K.E. Systematic observational methods. In G. Lindsey & A. Aronsen (Eds.), *The handbook of social psychology* (Vol. 2, 2nd Ed.). Reeding, Massachusetts: Addison-Wesley, 1968.

Weinrott, M., Bauske, B., & Patterson, G.R. Systematic replication of a social learning approach. In P.O. Sjoden, S. Bates, & W.S. Dockens (Eds.), *Trends in behavior therapy.* New York: Academic Press, 1979.

Weinrott, M.R., Garrett, B. & Todd, N. *The influence of observer presence on classroom behavior.* Unpublished manuscript, ORI, 1976.

Weintraub, S.A. Self control as a correlate of an internalizing-externalizing symptom dimension. *Journal of Abnormal Child Psychology,* 1973, *1*(3), 292-307.

Weiss, J.M. Effects of coping behavior in different warning signal conditions on stress pathology in rats. *Journal of Comparative and Physiological Psychology,* 1971, *1,* 1-14.

Weiss, R.L. *Marital bittersweets: Conceptual and empirical samples.* Paper presented at the Western Psychologist's Association, San Francisco, 1978.

Weissman, M.M., & Paykel, E.S. *The depressed woman: A study of social relationships.* Chicago Press, 1974.

Welsh, R.S. Severe parental punishment and delinquency: A developmental theory. *Journal of Clinical Child Psychology,* 1976, *5,* 17-21.

Werner, E., & Smith, R. *Kauai's children come of age.* Honolulu: University of Hawaii Press, 1977.

Wessman, A.E., & Ricks, D.F. *Mood and personality.* New York: Holt, Rinehart & Winston, 1966.

West, D.J., & Farrington, D.P. *Who becomes delinquent?* New York: Crane, Russak & Co., 1973.

White, G.D. *The effects of observer presence on family interactions.* Unpublished doctoral dissertation, University of Oregon, 1972.

White, G.D., Nielsen, G., & Johnson, S.M. Time

out duration and the suppression of deviant behavior in children. *Journal of Applied Behavior Analysis,* 1972, *5,* 111-120.

White, M.N. Natural rates of teacher approval and disapproval in the classroom. *Journal of Applied Behavior Analysis,* 1975, *8,* 367-372.

Whiting, B.B., & Whiting, J.M. *Children of six cultures.* Cambridge, Massachusetts: Harvard University Press, 1975.

Wiggins, J.S. (Ed.). *Personality and prediction: Principles of personality assessment.* Reeding, Massachusetts: Addison-Wesley, 1973.

Willems, E.P., & Raush, H.L. *Naturalistic viewpoints in psychological research.* New York: Holt, Rinehart & Winston, 1969.

Willerman, L. Activity level and hyperactivity in twins. *Child Development,* 1973, *44,* 288-293.

Wills, T.A. *The contribution of instrumental and affective events to perceived pleasure and displeasure in marital relationships.* Unpublished master's thesis, University of Oregon, 1971.

Wills, T.A., Weiss, R.L., & Patterson, G.R. A behavioral analysis of the determinannts of marital satisfaction. *Journal of Consulting and Clinical Psychology,* 1974, *42*(6), 802-811.

Wilson, C.C., Robertson, S.J., Herlong, L.H., & Haynes, S.N. Vicarious effects of time out in the modification of aggression in the classroom. *Behavior Modification,* 1979, *3,* 97-111.

Wilson, T.D., & Nisbett, R.E. The accuracy of verbal reports about the effects of stimuli on evaluations and behavior. *Social Psychology,* 1978, *41*(2), 118-131.

Wilson, W. Correlates of avowed happiness. *Psychological Bulletin,* 1967, *67,* 294-306.

Wiltz, N.A., & Patterson, G.R. An evaluation of parent training procedures designed to alter in-

appropriate aggressive behavior of boys. *Behavior Therapy,* 1974, *5,* 215-221.

Wolff, S. Behavioral characteristics of primary school children referred to a psychiatric department. *British Journal of Psychiatry,* 1967, *113,* 885-893.

Wolfgang, M.E. *From boy to man—from delinquency to crime.* Paper presented at the National Symposium on Serious Juvenile Offenders, Department of Corrections, Minneapolis, Minnesota, September 1977.

Wolfgang, M.E., Figlio, R., & Sellin, T. *Delinquency in a birth cohort.* Chicago: University of Chicago Press, 1972.

Wolking, W.D., Dunteman, G.H., & Bailey, J.P. Multivariate analyses of parents' MMPI's based on psychiatric diagnosis of their children. *Journal of Consulting Psychology,* 1967, *31,* 521-524.

Woo, D. *Experimental studies of the reinforcement trap.* Unpublished master's thesis, University of Oregon, 1978.

Wright, H.F. Observational child study. In P. Mussen (Ed.), *Handbook of research methods in child development.* New York: John Wiley & Sons, 1960.

Wright, Q. *A study of war.* Chicago: University of Chicago Press, 1972.

Zajonc, R.B. Family configuration and intelligence. *Science,* 1976, *192,* 227-236.

Zegiob, L., Arnold, S., & Forehand, R. An examination of observer effects in parent-child interaction. *Child Development,* 1975, *46,* 509-512.

Zylstra, J.L. *Assessing delinquent juveniles from their responses to verbal conditioning.* Unpublished doctoral dissertation, University of Washington, 1966.

Author Index

Getty, D.J., 143
Gewirtz, J., 92, 134
Gibson, D.M., 57
Gilmore, S.K., 44, 65, 307, 308
Glairn, J.P., 34
Glenn, N., 81
Gleser, G.C., 51
Glickman, S., 30, 31
Glueck, E., 34
Glueck, S., 34
Goldiamond, I., 2, 52
Goldin, P.C., 227
Golding, W., 68
Goldstein, M.J., 27
Gonso, J., 35
Goodenough, F.L., 17, 21, 42, 47, 115, 127
Goodstein, L.D., 281, 282, 289, 290
Goody, E., 285
Gottman, J.M., 1, 6, 35, 102, 108, 172, 186-188, 192, 193, 200, 201, 204, 205, 207, 242, 246
Gouldner, A.W., 209
Gourevitch, V., 42, 58
Graham, P., 28
Grant, M., 94
Grant, R., 70, 71
Graubard, P.S., 34
Graziano, A.M., 65
Green, D.K., 244, 266
Green, E.H., 16, 38
Green, J.A., 3
Green, M., 20
Green, R.G., 146
Greenwood, C.R., 113, 137, 244
Greiner, J., 72
Griest, D., 32, 81, 240, 281, 283
Griffith, W., 20
Grimm, J.A., 54
Groothues, C.M., 285
Guerney, B., 296
Guild, J., 113
Gullion, M.E., 244, 304
Gump, P.V., 28, 96
Gunn, W.B., 246
Gurin, G., 75
Guthrie, E.R., 2, 6, 116, 143
Guttman, L., 250, 251

H

Hafner, A.J., 27
Haggard, E., 71
Haley, J., 221
Hall, R.V., 108
Hall, W.M., 162

Halverson, C.F., 228, 230
Hamburg, D., 134
Harbin, H.T., 221, 223
Hardin, G., 241
Hare, R.D., 136
Harford, R.A., 91
Harlow, H.F., 271
Harper, L.V., 102, 196
Harris, A., 29, 39, 45, 57-59, 155
Harris, T., 78, 79
Hartmann, D.P., 5, 6, 50, 106, 107, 172
Hartup, W.W., 1, 6, 13, 16, 20, 35, 38, 64, 73, 106, 150, 185, 186, 206, 212, 246, 260
Hatfield, E., 209, 210
Hawkins, N., 45
Hawkins, R.P., 54
Hayden, M.L., 244
Haynes, S.N., 121
Head, K.B., 114
Hebb, D., 134
Hedlund, C.S., 133, 244
Hefferline, R.F., 91
Helfer, R.E., 157
Hendricks, A.F.C.J., 31, 251, 252, 267
Henry, M.M., 16, 20, 21, 35
Herbert, E., 45, 244
Herlong, L.H., 121
Herrnstein, R.J., 101, 116, 117
Hertzog, M., 244
Hetherington, E.M., 24, 25, 73, 112, 217, 231, 240, 281, 285, 286, 290, 291
Hewitt, L., 30, 31, 34, 36, 250
Heyns, R.W., 42
Hibbs, D.A., 82
Hicks, M.W., 229
Hillam, S.M., 78, 80, 217, 233
Hinde, R.A., 107, 134, 170, 196
Hineline, P., 142, 147, 164
Hines, P.A., 224
Hinojosa-Rivero, G., 306
Hinsey, W.C., 118, 187, 244
Hirschi, T., 34, 36, 121, 262, 297
Hobbs, S.A., 222
Hoffman, W.H., 82
Hokanson, J.E., 146
Holleran, P.R., 69, 235, 248, 258
Hollingshead, A.B., 63, 316, 318
Holmberg, M.C., 16, 17, 21
Holmes, T.H., 74, 217
Holtz, W., 52
Homans, G.C., 209, 210
Honig, A.S., 44
Honzik, M., 20, 25, 39, 43, 260, 261
Hood, R., 21, 22, 260
Hops, H., 29, 33-36, 46, 113, 137, 182, 207, 210, 220, 233, 244, 304

O

O'Connor, R.D., 52
O'Hara, J., 118
O'Leary, K.D., 51-53, 231, 286, 291
Oltmanns, T., 231, 286, 291
Olweus, D., 14, 22, 26, 34, 35, 37, 273, 304
Omark, D.R., 270
Omark, M., 270
Oppenheim, A.N., 39
Orzech, M., 133, 244
Overlade, D., 250

P

Paris, S.G., 244, 245
Parke, R.D., 6, 7, 121-125, 133
Parmillee, A., 76
Parsons, B.V., 209
Parsons, J.A., 54
Parton, D.A., 89, 244
Partzka, L., 33
Pasamancek, B., 39
Patterson, D.S., 21
Patterson, G.R., 1, 3, 7, 12, 14, 16, 18, 23, 25,
    28, 29, 31, 34, 38, 42-46, 50, 51, 54, 58-62,
    64, 65, 70-73, 75, 77, 81, 89, 93, 98, 100,
    101, 103-105, 108, 109, 111, 112, 118, 121,
    128-130, 132, 134-137, 139, 141, 144, 145,
    147, 150, 155, 159, 160, 161, 164, 166, 173,
    175, 176, 178, 181-191, 194, 204-212, 221,
    223, 224, 226-228, 229, 231, 233-235, 244,
    250, 255-259, 262-264, 274-276, 279, 282-
    284, 286, 289, 294-297, 304-307
Paul, G.L., 121
Paul, J.S., 53, 54, 57, 59
Pavlov, I.P., 88, 108
Paykel, E.S., 74, 283
Peed, S., 77, 240, 241
Peine, H., 45, 224
Pepper, M., 74
Perry, D., 106, 107
Perry, L.C., 106
Pesses, D.I., 57
Peterson, L., 244, 266
Peterson, R.F., 244, 266
Petrinovitch, L., 7
Phelps, R., 45
Phillips, J., 6, 93
Phillips, L.D., 5, 164
Phipps-Yonas, S., 243
Pinkston, E.M., 244
Pinkston, S., 244
Platt, J., 230, 241
Platt, M., 229
Polk, K., 105

Pollack, M., 28
Pollack, S., 53-55
Porter, R.W., 71
Portnoy, S., 187
Pritchard, M., 28
Purcell, K., 57

Q

Quast, W., 27
Quay, H.C., 31, 242, 243
Quinsey, V.L., 134
Quinton, D., 216, 227, 229

R

Rachlin, H., 116, 117
Radke-Yarrow, M., 3, 35, 43, 58, 107, 122, 246
Rajaratnam, N., 51
Randall, T.M., 54
Rasmussen, B., 35
Ratcliff, K.S., 221, 223
Raush, H.L., 3, 42, 73, 150, 170, 171, 186, 190,
    192, 193, 203, 204, 293
Ray, R.S., 3, 28, 29, 45, 46, 121, 296, 297, 305
Redl, F., 293, 294
Redlich, F.C., 63, 316
Reese, H.W., 196
Reid, J.B., 12, 14, 21, 23, 29, 31, 41-46, 49-52,
    56, 58, 59, 60-62, 64, 65, 67-69, 77, 93, 96,
    112, 118, 130, 131, 137, 139, 147, 155-159,
    161, 206-209, 212, 221, 223, 226-228, 232,
    235, 249-252, 259, 262, 267, 274-276, 279,
    283, 286, 291, 295, 296, 304-307, 311
Reid, M.P., 250
Revenstein, A., 232
Reynolds, G.S., 104
Reynolds, M.M., 76
Rhamey, R., 211
Rich, T.A., 250
Richardson, J., 104, 160
Ricketts, A.F., 16
Ricks, D.F., 75, 78
Riddle, M., 242
Roach, J.L., 39
Roberts, A., 242
Roberts, E., 234
Robertson, S.J., 121
Robins, L.N., 28, 34, 43, 221, 223, 259, 262
Robinson, B.E., 226
Robinson, J.P., 250, 251, 266
Rodnick, E.H., 27
Roff, M., 28, 34-36
Rogers, E., 80
Rogers, M.E., 39
Rollins, B.C., 81

Wing, J.K., 67, 70
Wolf, M.M., 2, 244, 266
Wolf, S., 272
Wolfe, D.M., 233
Wolff, S., 21
Wolff, P.C., 104, 160
Wolfgang, M.E., 157, 264, 265
Wolking, W.D., 281, 282
Woo, D., 145, 153, 154, 164
Wright, H.F., 41, 42, 65
Wright, Q., 94
Wyden, P., 163
Wynne, L.C., 112, 116, 142, 147

Y

Yahraes, H., 272
Yoder, P., 77, 240, 241

Z

Zajonc, R.B., 23
Zegiob, L.E., 54
Zimet, S., 34, 243
Zlotogura, P., 187
Zylstra, J.L., 243

Subject Index

complexity in social interaction, 142 ff.
defined, 89, 141, 143
effectiveness (*vs.* positive reinforcement), 142, 144
effects on $A_i \rightarrow R_j$ connections, 85, 142, 143, 153, 185
and escalation, 95, 141 ff., 155 ff., 161, 162, 165, 166
experimental manipulations *in situ,* 153 ff., 161, 162, 185
and extinction, 147, 148
implications, 162 ff.
likelihood of counterattack and, 150 ff.
long-term *vs.* short-term effects, 142 ff., 162
mixed schedules of negative reinforcement and positive reinforcement, 147, 148, 155
and punishment as members of the same family, 143
reinforcement trap, 144 ff., 279
traditional approaches, 142, 143, 147, 162
utility of, 144, 151 ff.
variance accounted for, 155
Reinforcement, positive
for aggression, 85 ff., 95 ff
and awareness, 90 ff., 145
in the classroom, 96, 202, 226, 245, 271
contingency hypothesis, 102, 107, 108, 244, 245
defined, 86 ff.
effects, learning *vs.* performance, 87, 88
effects on $A_i \rightarrow R_j$ connections, 85, 88 ff., 102 ff.
effectiveness (*vs.* negative reinforcement), 142, 144
effectiveness (*vs.* punishment), 112, 113, 116 ff., 124
mixed schedules of positive reinforcement and negative reinforcement, 147, 148, 155
mixed schedules of punishment and reinforcement, 117, 124
noncontingent ("learned laziness"), 71
pain as a reinforcer, 106, 107, 157, 158, 160
parental rejection of the concept, 113, 164, 225, 226
synchronicity and, 202 ff.
tests for status as, 103 ff.
traditional approaches, 86 ff., 101, 102, 104 ff.
variance accounted for, 89, 101 ff.

Sample characteristics, 18, 62 ff., 97, 249, 252, 253, Appendices 5.1 and 6.2
see also Delinquency and crime, "Mixed," Normals, Social Aggressors, and Stealers
Social Aggressors, 254 ff.
anarchy progression and, 274, 275
differences between Stealers and, 31, 246 ff.

escalation and, 159, 161
family management variables and, 224, 258, 259
microsocial analyses, 255 ff.
parental enmeshment, 247, 249, 257, 303, 304
parents' criterion threshold for classifying deviant behavior, 223 ff., 247 ff.
prognosis for adjustment as adults, 259
response classes, 182 ff., 254, 255
sample criteria, 18, 31, 97, 252, Appendices 5.1 and 6.2
symptom progressions for, 249 ff., 267n.
treatment outcomes, 305 ff.
Social learning theory
development of, 2-8
reinforcement concepts and, 2, 6, 7, 91
see also Performance theory
Stealers, 259 ff.
anarchy progression and, 274, 275
continuity hypothesis, 259 ff.
chronic offenders, families of, 262, 263
drop-out rates for, 262
differences between Social Aggressors and, 31, 246 ff.
frequency labeling hypothesis, 251, 260, 263 ff.
"normal" stealing, 39n., 260 ff.
parents' criterion threshold for classifying stealing behavior, 223, 247 ff.
parents as unattached (distant), 247, 249, 253, 262, 267n., 272, 297, 298, 303 ff.
sample criteria, 18, 31, 252, Appendix 6.2
symptom progression for, 39n., 249 ff., 260, 262, 263
TAB score comparison, 256
treatment outcomes, 305 ff.
Symptom progressions, 249 ff.
Stress
children as stressors, 76 ff.
control of aversive events and, 71, 72, 81
crises as stressors, 78 ff.
disruption of family management practices and, 72, 216 ff.
operational definition, 71
physiological measures of, 70, 71, 81, 146

Thematic effects, 89, 100, 103, 104, 173, 186 ff.
see also Microsocial analyses of structure and process—intersubject and intrasubject components
Treatment outcomes, 304 ff.
and drop-out rates, 65 n., 262, 305
Turn-taking, synchronicity, and reciprocity, 199 ff.
mutuality, 207 ff.
reciprocity, 209 ff.

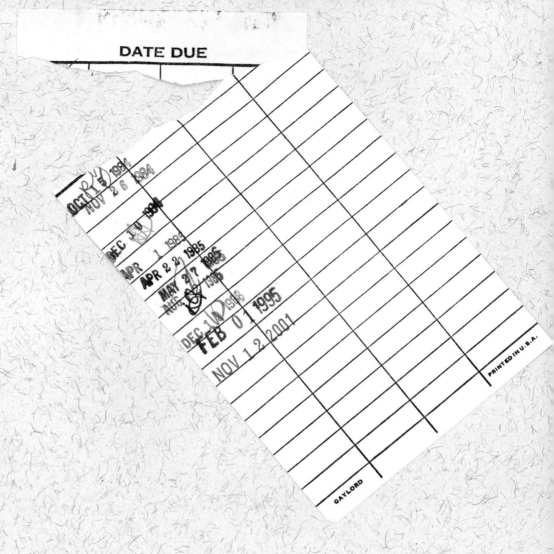